SECRETS OF THE VISUAL BASIC™ 3 MASTERS

Second Edition

Secrets of the Visual Basic™ 3 Masters

Second Edition

Gary Entsminger

A Division of Prentice Hall Computer Publishing
201 West 103rd Street, Indianapolis, Indiana 46290

For Ali and my parents.

SECOND EDITION

International Standard Book Number: 0-672-30437-6

Library of Congress Catalog Card Number: 93-86948

97 96 95 4

Interpretation of the printing code: the rightmost double-digit number is the year of the book's printing; the rightmost single-digit, the number of the book's printing. For example, a printing code of 94-1 shows that the first printing of the book occurred in 1994.

Composed in Goudy and MCPdigital by Prentice Hall Computer Publishing

Printed in the United States of America

Trademarks

Publisher
Richard K. Swadley

Associate Publisher
Jordan Gold

Acquisitions Manager
Stacy Hiquet

Acquisitions Editor
Greg Croy

Development Editor
Phillip W. Paxton

Editorial and Graphics Coordinator
William Whitmer

Editorial Assistants
Sharon Cox
Lynette Quinn

Technical Reviewer
Ricardo Birmele

Marketing Manager
Greg Wiegand

Cover Designer
Jean Bisesi

Director of Production and Manufacturing
Jeff Valler

Imprint Manager
Kelli Widdifield

Manufacturing Coordinator
Barry Pruett

Book Designer
Michele Laseau

Production Analyst
Mary Beth Wakefield

Proofreading/Indexing Coordinator
Joelynn Gifford

Graphics Image Specialists
Sue VandeWalle

Production
Gary Adair
Diana Bigham-Griffin
Katy Bodenmiller
Brad Chinn
Kim Cofer
Meshell Dinn
Terri Edwards
Mark Enochs
Stephanie Gregory
Jenny Kucera
Stephanie J. McComb
Angela M. Pozdel
Beth Rago
Marc Shecter
Greg Simsic

Indexers
Craig Small
Suzanne Snyder

Overview

CONTENTS

Acknowledgments

I would like to thank a number of people who have helped move this book along by reading, editing, and commenting, or by donating code, software, or custom controls to this project: Greg Croy and Ella Davis at Sams, Troy Strain at Microsoft, Don Malin at Crescent Software, Joe Modica at Sheridan Software, Jim Nelch at OutRider Systems, Steve Ward at Ward Systems, Mike Novisoff at MicroHelp, and Alison Brody and Billy Barr at the Rocky Mountain Biological Laboratory.

About the Author

Gary Entsminger was an associate editor of *Micro Cornucopia* for more than five years. He has written and published more than 100 articles in such journals as *Computer Language*, *Dr. Dobb's Journal*, *AI Expert*, *Midnight Engineering*, *Midnight Express*, *Neural Network News*, *AI Week*, and *Turbo Technix*, the Borland technical journal. He is the author of an introductory book on object-oriented programming, *The Tao of Objects* (M&T, 1990), *The Turbo Pascal for Windows Bible* (Sams, 1991), and *Secrets of the Visual Basic for Windows Masters* (Sams, 1992).

INTRODUCTION

To begin simply, Microsoft Windows (or just Windows from now on) is the graphical user interface (GUI) of choice for the vast majority of PC users. There is an explosion of Microsoft Windows users and programmers, and more users will dramatically increase the demand for more applications and more programmers. If you're a PC programmer, you will want to include Windows development skills in your programming repertoire.

Until recently, a developer creating a Microsoft Windows application could expect to learn 600 or more functions at a low level and write applications in either assembly language or C. It was, at best, a difficult, time-consuming task; at worst, it was a scenario restricted to professional or masochistic programmers.

In 1991, Borland International released a version of its world-class compiler, Turbo Pascal, called Turbo Pascal for Windows, which made Microsoft Windows development much easier (it also extended Windows development to include not-necessarily professional programmers). This compiler is the subject of my second book, *Turbo Pascal for Windows Bible* (Sams, 1991).

During 1991, Microsoft also introduced Visual Basic, its Windows application development alternative to C. Visual Basic has most of the power of Turbo Pascal for Windows, but, in addition, it simplifies the Windows development process even more than Turbo Pascal for Windows.

Visual Basic's *visual* and *event-oriented* approach are the keys to simplifying Windows development. In a nutshell, you (the programmer) can develop applications graphically. You point and click, selecting objects, controls, properties, and so on from menus. Programming the interface in Visual Basic is much closer to *user* level than the traditional programming level. You must, of course, add code to the windows (called *forms* in Visual Basic) that you create by pointing to and clicking menu items, but even adding code is simplified by templates, automatic indentation, super-fast syntax checking, and so on.

Visual Basic is a complete programming environment within the Windows environment and it has several advantages:

- Because its core is compatible with previous versions of QuickBASIC (with a few exceptions), only a small learning investment is required by the millions of current QuickBASIC programmers.
- It abstracts many of the 600 Windows application program interface (API) functions to a high level, and therefore enables a programmer to use existing Windows functionality (buttons, dialog windows, menus, and so on) without using the Windows Software Development Toolkit (SDK). Programmers can still call low-level Windows API functions through a dynamic link library (DLL).
- It lets a programmer write, compile, run, and debug applications within the Windows environment, without exiting to DOS. No other popular Windows compiler (including Borland's C++ or Turbo Pascal for Windows) does this as well. The Turbo Pascal for Windows debugger, for example, despite running as a Windows application, awkwardly switches from graphics to text screen during the debugging process.
- It incorporates resource development on-site—that is, within the Visual Basic environment. You don't have to run a resource editor or compiler to add menus, dialogs, controls, and so on to an application.

Theorists, production programmers, and novices are developing intermediate and advanced Windows applications with this smart, event- (and object-) oriented system. This book provides an inside view of Visual Basic aimed at both intermediate and advanced-intermediate developers. I try to use a fresh perspective, utilize advanced techniques, and give you a secret-oriented approach to developing applications with this amazing programming system and language. I describe event- and object-oriented programming, Windows-style, and step you through numerous applications that use the most sophisticated components of Visual Basic—DLLs, dynamic data exchange (DDE), and object linking and embedding (OLE) client control.

If you're a Basic programmer, you can learn Windows programming without giving up a language you already know. You get the best of computing worlds—structured Basic programming and access to Windows. More important, because Visual Basic is general-purpose and fast (as fast as either C++ or Turbo Pascal for Windows in many tests), it's practical for commercial applications.

The addition of Visual Basic to the Basic programming world is having a stunning (and perhaps surprising) effect on the programming market. Basic (in the guise of Visual Basic) is back.

In addition, thanks in part to an interpretive syntax checker, compiling Visual Basic applications is many times faster than both C and C++ compilers for the applications I've tested. Therefore, if you're trying to get a Windows application up and running quickly, or a large application prototyped, Visual Basic is clearly the system of choice. Because Visual Basic applications run as fast, or nearly as fast in most cases, as C or C++, you sacrifice very little by developing in Visual Basic.

The Visual Basic system is also being enhanced at an exceptional pace by way of Microsoft and third-party custom control support. This book goes into considerable depth about the various ways that Visual Basic can be extended with custom controls, DDE, DLL, and OLE client control.

OLE enables a Windows programmer to create applications that can both display data from other applications and edit the data from within the application that created it. OLE, in other words, is DDE with user or application control of the data in other applications.

The use of these sophisticated extensions establishes what Microsoft calls a "document-centered" view of computing. Typically, programmers and users have taken an application-centered view in that a complete task is usually a single application. The document-centered view lets any number of tools work on a document. This is multitasking at a very high level.

For example, your application (created in Visual Basic) might use Microsoft Excel, Quattro Pro for Windows, or another spreadsheet or database to hold and manipulate data; a graphics application or tool to plot the data (such as Paintbrush); a text editor to transpose some aspect of the data; the Windows recorder to run a macro on your data; and your Visual Basic application to filter the data and control operations. This document-centered perspective, which Visual Basic supports, is a giant step forward in the world of multitasking and complex processing.

Although I use Visual Basic examples and applications, this book generally explores Windows and event- and object-oriented programming. I think it will appeal to anyone, not just Visual Basic programmers, wanting to understand application development for Microsoft Windows.

This book is built around examples that explore that tricky interface between real-world problems and ideas and programming techniques. I'll show you how event- and object-oriented programming Visual Basic-style can make such advanced topics as graphics, text and object editors, neural networks, chaos and complexity theory, graphic modeling, the Clipboard, dynamic data exchange between programs, dynamic link libraries, document-centered computing, and so on understandable and manageable.

Because Windows is a graphics environment, it makes sense that a state-of-the-art language such as Visual Basic should be graphically oriented. This book focuses on the display and graphics aspects of applications. In this book, you learn by seeing (illustrations complement explanations) and doing.

In particular, this book shows you:

- How to use the Visual Basic IDE and Windows to best advantage
- How to debug tips and tricks
- How to set up and design complex applications using projects
- How to code shortcuts, optimizations, and efficient memory use
- How to relate to modular scope
- How to organize, code, and test large applications
- How to extend Visual Basic using custom controls, DLLs, DDEs, Windows API, and so on
- How to use OLE
- How to utilize Microsoft and third-party support when you are building large applications
- How to work around or understand the few Visual Basic weaknesses

Examples in the second half of the book use the Windows API and other third-party support to extend Visual Basic. I'm convinced that Windows and Visual Basic (with its many advanced, sophisticated tools and third-party support) together compose *the* cutting-edge system for high-level computing for both commercial and academic developers for the 1990s.

In addition to exploring Windows and Visual Basic in depth, you'll develop several sophisticated applications (a Wizard Project Editor, an OLE Object Editor, and a stock market modeling tool) that you can use as stand-alone applications or as models or starting points for your own Visual Basic applications.

In short, I hope that this book helps you make a little more sense out of the Visual Basic programming system. Writing it certainly helped me better understand Visual Basic and Windows.

ABOUT THE BOOK

Secrets of the Visual Basic 3.0 Masters consists of 15 chapters that explain and demonstrate the power of Visual Basic. In particular, this book focuses on event-driven programming and the utilization of custom controls, DDE, and DLLs to write intermediate to advanced Visual Basic applications. Many examples show you shortcuts and optimization techniques, as well as the limitations of Visual Basic.

The last section of the book consists of reference material, a glossary, and numerous bonus applications based on the custom controls in the Microsoft Professional Toolkit and in third-party custom control packages. Because many vendors have generously contributed custom controls to this book, you can write advanced applications that use these custom controls without buying anything extra. These bonus applications use custom controls to create OLE applications, gauges, keystate indicators, three-dimensional-like applications, applications that use custom dialogs, spin controls, and instant scroll bars.

Although this book was intended to be read straight through, you should feel free to skip around—each chapter (and each chapter's examples) is self-contained.

CONVENTIONS USED IN THIS BOOK

In this book, the monospaced font is used to indicate code, whether in listings or in the text. *Italics* are used for terms introduced for the first time. The code continuation icon, ➥, is used to indicate that a line in Visual Basic is too long to fit on the book page and had to be broken. However, whenever you see this icon *be sure that you type the broken line of code on one line* if you enter it in Visual Basic. Otherwise, Visual Basic will generate an error message.

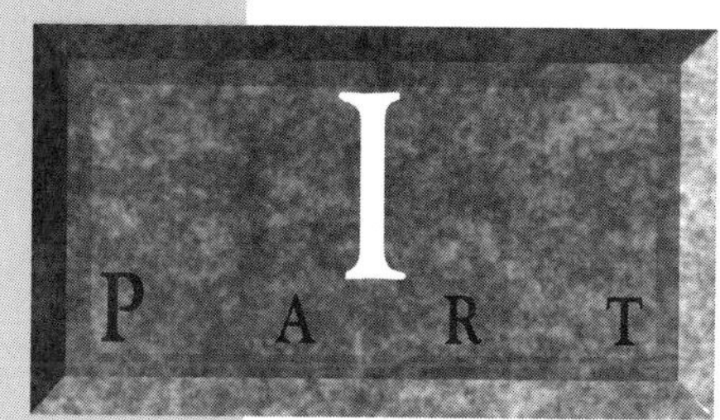

A Review and Overview of Visual Basic 3.0

The Visual Basic System

Objects, Events, and Dynamic Programming

A Brief Tour of Object-Oriented Programming

Object-Oriented Programming, Visual Basic Style

How Event-Oriented Programming Really Works

Using Change Events to Trigger Automatic and Real-Time Updating

Using Focus Events to Automatically Initiate Action

Undoubtedly, the way you think about developing applications is affected as tools and your programming environment change. I think that it's safe to say that during the mid- and late-1980s most programmers thought more about programming algorithms than about the program interface. In other words, programmers concentrated on the procedures that accomplished tasks, not on the way a user interacted with those procedures. If there was time for it, a programmer might have worked on the interface, but not necessarily. You undoubtedly have used many programs that simply come on, do something, and exit or crash. Sometimes, a program doesn't even include a primitive menu, as programmers unfortunately developed these applications as though the user interface was secondary or didn't matter.

When you develop applications within Windows, you acknowledge that the interface is not secondary. This acknowledgment requires a somewhat broader programming view. You must visualize your application existing within a system (or framework or environment) and interacting with the system at large (in this case, Windows) and with other components of the system (other Windows applications).

Programmers not working within a system such as Windows often find it easy to write applications that barely (if that) acknowledge other applications. Quick, clean programming is the ideal that many programmers strive to achieve; quick and dirty programming, however, usually is considered to be good enough. Because DOS doesn't make it easy for applications to interact with each other at a high level, most programmers have ignored other applications; instead writing code for themselves as though nothing else existed except the operating system. Exclude terminate-and-stay-resident (TSR) applications in this scenario.

Windows provides the machinery for various high-level interactions: between applications, between the operating system and applications, and between commonly shared libraries of code and data. To benefit, however, a programmer must "buy in" conceptually to the Windows system. This means simply that you must give the interface its fair share of attention.

Your applications don't have to use menus, controls, and so on, but you must specify some kind of window that contains your application. You must also instruct your application to respond to the *messages* it receives from Windows. You will learn about messages in detail throughout the book, but for now think of them as everything from mouse clicks, double clicks, and keypresses to timer events and input from ports and other applications. This window is your application's connection to the Windows environment. Windows will channel all information intended for your application's procedures through the application window.

In Visual Basic, application windows are called *forms*. These forms can contain *controls* that also can interact with Windows, other forms and controls, and even other applications. All these items (forms, controls, custom controls, printers, and so on) are called *objects* in Visual Basic. Sometimes these objects snap together beautifully and sometimes they don't. The interaction among these objects used to extend Visual Basic is the focus of this book.

An application form, for example, has tremendous flexibility in how much and how well it interacts with Windows. It might use menus, command buttons, DDE links, and so on. This chapter shows you how Windows channels information and how a well-behaved Windows application connects and interacts with Windows. It discusses the object and event programming techniques built into Visual Basic that can help you quickly develop sophisticated applications in Windows. This chapter draws the big picture, a summary of the way in which Windows and Visual Basic work together.

THE ELEMENTS OF APPLICATION DEVELOPMENT

If you have programmed in any language, you undoubtedly have your own ideas about how to develop an application, whether it's for Windows or another operating system. To develop an application for Windows, you have to learn:

- How Windows exchanges information with an application and how to prepare your application to run in a Windows window.
- How to develop your application using events and objects.

These two requirements might sound tough, but the beans and rice of developing a Windows application is still primarily what you are probably accustomed to: writing code to solve problems—code that describes and manipulates information (or data).

The primary difference between developing a DOS application and a Windows application is that with DOS you must create your own user interface (unless you are writing a very primitive application or one that doesn't require an interface). If you are writing a Windows application, you must give your application some kind of interface that connects to the Windows GUI. Giving your application a simple interface, however, is easy because you don't have to build the interface from scratch. You can use the Windows interface and continue to use most of what you already know about programming: variables, procedures, functions, return values, `if-then-else` loops, arrays, program structure, and so on.

To develop a Windows application that solves a problem, you must:

1. Interact with Windows (using the form and control objects that you design with Visual Basic).
2. Get information into the application (the input component).
3. Store information (the data component).
4. Manipulate the information using procedures, functions, or object methods (the operations component).
5. Get the results (the output component).

This information is straightforward and probably familiar to you, except, possibly, for the Windows connection. To connect with Windows, simply use Visual Basic controls and forms.

To get, store, and manipulate information and to obtain the results (see Steps 2 through 5), construct your application along traditional structured programming lines. You can use conditional statements (`if-thens`) and loops (`whiles`, `repeats`, and so on), divide groups of instructions into sections that you can reference by name (procedures, functions, objects), and put task- or object-related procedures, functions, and declarations in modules. This process, again, is programming as you probably already know it (whether you program in Basic or in another similarly structured language such as C or Pascal).

Visual Basic, like most good high-level programming languages such as Turbo Pascal and QuickBASIC, supplies a rich set of data types and built-in operators, controls, procedures, and functions to manipulate information. Visual Basic also enables you to create large applications by dividing any application into pieces (modules and forms) that you can design and test separately.

Visual Basic: An Evolutionary Language

Visual Basic is truly an evolutionary language. It combines procedural and structural programming with two innovative techniques: object-oriented and event-driven programming. In most fundamental ways, Visual Basic is similar to popular languages such as Basic, C, and Pascal. The structure of the Visual Basic language (loops, data types, procedures, operators, input/output, and so on), however, differs somewhat from language implementations such as QuickBASIC, Turbo Pascal, and Turbo C in syntax, but differs primarily in the details. For example, a data type to hold more than one kind of data is called a *record* in Pascal, a *struct* in C, and a *type* in Basic. Any programmer versed in these popular languages will have little trouble understanding Visual Basic. The largest conceptual leap from these languages to Visual Basic is the leap to Windows (not to the language itself) and to a graphical conceptualization of application development rather than a code-oriented conceptualization.

In Visual Basic, for example, you do nothing to create a default application window (called a *form*), and you select a control from the Visual Basic toolbox and position it on a form without writing any code. In Turbo Pascal or C++ you must create the window and the control and position both with code. On the screen in Visual Basic, you drag windows (forms) and controls with the mouse to size and position them.

Visual Basic is an evolutionary language (using both event- and object-oriented programming techniques) and an evolutionary programming system. It is much easier to create Visual Basic applications because you spend less time coding and more time focusing on the problem you want to solve, not on coding the user interface. Ultimately, I want to see the gap between user and programmer narrow, and I believe that Visual Basic is an extraordinary step in the right direction. The ability to create sophisticated applications has never been so available to such a broad group of people. Granted, Visual Basic can't turn every user into a programmer, but it can greatly simplify programming.

A Brief Tour of Object-Oriented Programming

Visual Basic does not implement a complete object-oriented programming (OOP) system, but it does rely on several key concepts of OOP (and in the future, I suspect, it will incorporate more OOP techniques). I'll spend a little time, therefore, telling you how object-oriented programming works and how Visual Basic differs from OOP languages such as C++ and Turbo Pascal for Windows.

Although some writers and programmers de-emphasize the object-oriented nature of Visual Basic, I take the opposite approach. Visual Basic leaves out much of the robustness of OOP, yet retains enough of it to make it an interesting and powerful component of the Visual Basic language and system. Again, you don't need to know everything about OOP to use Visual Basic to great advantage; however, it can be very helpful.

Let's begin your exploration of the secrets of Visual Basic with objects. Our world consists of objects and actions. Objects (the nouns of the grammatical world) have attributes or characteristics. Actions (the verbs of the grammatical world) express behaviors. An aspen sways. Snow falls. She awakens. Her eyes open. The application window sends or receives a message. A user enters text in a dialog box, clicks the mouse, or selects a menu item. Two applications have a DDE conversation. A nifty interface launches a thousand worlds.

From a programmer's perspective, data are the characteristics (or properties) of an object, and procedures (or methods) are its behaviors. You encapsulate an object's characteristics and its behaviors within a single block of source code. Characteristics and behaviors are in one place, physically (in the same block of code) and conceptually (in an object). This is both more convenient and safer than having procedures spread about. Placing data and the operations to manipulate the data together is known as *encapsulation*, a popular term in the object-oriented programming worlds of C++ and Pascal with objects.

In a true object-oriented language (but not in Visual Basic), programmers can create their own object types that the compiler treats just as it treats built-in types. This discussion should sound familiar to you. QuickBASIC, C, and Turbo Pascal programmers have been creating new types all along—by collecting variables into types (in Basic), records (in Pascal), and structs (in C and C++). Objects simply add to the package the functions and procedures to manipulate the data. In the simplest sense, objects are an extension of types, records, and structs in these languages.

Visual Basic contains numerous objects you can use and manipulate. These objects come with properties, methods, and *event procedures*, which make it easier for these objects to interact with other components in the Windows environment. By using these objects, you can significantly simplify your application development. Because responding to events is one of the easiest ways to get things done in Windows, much of this book focuses on working with events. Later in this chapter I'll explain the way in which event-driven programming works.

Generally, you build applications in Visual Basic by creating and adding instances of control and form object types to your application. To create an instance of a Visual Basic control or form (object), either select the control from the toolbox and position it or select Add Form from the Visual Basic menu. In the simplest Visual Basic application, you can simply use the default form (by doing nothing). It is interesting that the default Visual Basic form, which appears on-screen when Visual Basic starts up, will compile as is. If you do nothing but compile the default form, the resulting application runs successfully in Windows. The application consists of a window and a system menu that enables you to exit from the application without crashing. Without doing anything, you can create a complete application. Not even plain DOS is this friendly!

A form, a control, a printer, the Clipboard, and so on are objects. To access a *component* (a property) of an instance of an object type, use the same selection operator you used with Visual Basic types: a period (.). For example, to change the `Height` property of an object (in this case, a command button) type the following line:

```
Command1.Height = Command1.Height + 150
```

Or, to assign a `Text` property to a text box (an object) type the following line:

```
Text1.Text = "This string"
```

Properties such as `Height`, `Text`, `Width`, `Value`, and `LinkTopic` "belong" to objects. Each object has its own selection of properties that you cannot access without going through the object (that is, by specifying first the object you want to work with, then the dot, and then the property of the object).

To use an object, do the following:

1. Specify the object.
2. Indicate the property you want to change or access.
3. Use a normal assignment statement to indicate a new value for the property or the assignment to another variable.

Using object properties is similar to working with Basic types. Objects differ from types in that they can also have procedures, called *methods* in OOP jargon, and event procedures, as well as properties you can access, modify, and send messages to.

MESSAGES DETERMINE THE FLOW OF CONTROL

Conventional programming systems typically view a program as a collection of functions and procedures. These functions and procedures are the active components of the program; data are passive. When you declare data globally, any function or procedure can access the data, which might put it at the mercy of any function or procedure. The likelihood of incorrect data manipulation is high.

If you declare data locally (within a procedure), only the procedure containing the declaration can access the data. Therefore, the data are safer, but a little too restricted in many situations. We need some flexibility—an intermediate solution—if we want data to be accessible by some restricted number of defined functions and procedures. Objects are the solution.

In object-oriented programming, a method (the functions and procedures of an object) "knows" what data it can manipulate, and data "know" which methods can manipulate them. There is no confusion about who controls whom. How do methods and data know these things? Simply, objects contain methods and data; objects take care of (that is, manipulate) themselves. General procedures—the kinds familiar to most structured programmers—cannot access data with an object without using the object's methods, which are designed to manipulate their data.

In a procedural program, the ordering of procedures and control mechanisms, such as `if`, `while`, `select case`, and so on, determine a program's flow of control. This ordering implies that you know how to structure the entire program when you create the program. In programs designed to capture the essence of a dynamic world, this assumption is unrealistic and cumbersome. The world is evolving, and our ideas and models of the world must adapt to survive. A better alternative captures the design flow as the logical relationships among objects.

Object-oriented programming captures these logical relationships in objects, and the messages sent to and received from objects determines the flow of control in an object-oriented application. By sending messages, objects clarify the communication among the components of an application. Objects respond to the messages sent to them and send messages to other objects.

Messages, not data, move through the system. Rather than "invoking a function on some data" (the procedural approach), you can "send a message to an object" (the object-oriented approach). Generally, this is how Windows works — messages move through the systems accomplishing tasks.

To send a message to an object, specify the object and the method (which represents or carries out the message) you want to invoke. Windows handles the details of ensuring that your message gets to the object you specify. If the object exists and the method exists, and if you haven't made an error, Windows routes your message.

For example, to send a message to the Clipboard object's `SetText` method and specify that the Clipboard should get the data selected in a textbook, called `Text1`, type the following line:

```
Clipboard.SetText Text1.SelText
```

This line of code sends the `SetText` message to the Clipboard and tells it to access the `SelText` property of the `Text1` (text box) object. The `SetText` method sets the contents of the Clipboard. In this case, `SetText` sets the contents to the text selected in the text box.

You also can set one object's property by sending a message to another object's method:

```
Text1.SelText = Clipboard.GetText()
```

This line of code sets the text box (`Text1`) object's `SelText` property to the contents of the Clipboard by sending a message to the Clipboard object's `GetText` method.

Much of your programming energy in Visual Basic goes into changing object properties, sending messages to object methods, and writing response code for object events. Although these tasks might sound complicated initially, they simplify Windows programming significantly, as you will discover.

You Can Also Think of an Application as an Object

It's helpful to think of an object as a small program (or *application*, the term I prefer to use). An object has its own data (just as applications do) and an interface for sending and receiving messages. You use applications such as a text editor (an object), which manages its own data (characters and words). Using a keyboard or a mouse, you can send the text editor messages such as "append a specific character," "move back to the previous word," or "search and replace."

In addition, applications consist of objects. Each object of your application handles a task. Each application in an environment handles a task. Therefore, an object-oriented application is really like a multitasking environment. You might use a communication application to send and receive files (data), a database to store data, a spreadsheet to analyze the data, and a desktop publishing system to format and print the data. (A multiprocessing system of this kind that consists of more than one application leads to a document-centered view of computing, which is discussed in Chapter 11, "Into the Heart of OLE," Chapter 12, "DDE, Custom Controls, and DLLs: Intimate Details," and Chapter 15, "Data Awareness and Data Management Applications.")

Theoretically, you can write spreadsheets and database systems yourself, although you don't have to (and may not want to); you can save time and effort by using applications someone else has written. You may want to write applications, however, for tasks your current applications can't accomplish or to connect the applications you have.

An object-oriented application saves time and effort by letting you reuse existing objects (applications or objects within applications). The Visual Basic programming system includes a library of existing objects you can use to get directly into Windows programming. All the objects you need to get started are coded for you. You can use them and, as needed, modify them by changing their properties or re-implementing their event procedures. In addition, you can extend the Visual Basic system by adding custom controls, linking to dynamic link libraries (DLLs), and manipulating and communicating with other applications through dynamic data exchange (DDE) and object linking and embedding (OLE).

Again, you communicate with objects by sending them messages. Therefore, you can generally think of an application as consisting of objects and the messages you send them. (This is not entirely the case in Visual Basic, however, because it also allows general procedures not connected directly to objects.)

This object-oriented view should be consistent with how you think about a Windows application. Each application running in a Windows window is an object that sends and receives messages. To accomplish a task, you send a message to an application window (that is, to an object).

Object-Oriented Programming, Visual Basic-Style

Objects in Visual Basic are predefined. You can define user types (the equivalent of a record in Pascal or a struct in C); but unlike C++ and Turbo Pascal for Windows, you cannot define new objects. In other words, the new types you define in Visual Basic can have only properties or attributes (data fields). They cannot contain behaviors (methods or procedures). You can, of course, create procedures that manipulate those properties, but because the procedures are general and are not encapsulated directly within an object, these "things" you are creating are not objects in OOP lingo. The predefined Visual Basic objects you can manipulate, however, are object-oriented in every sense of the term.

You can use and modify these predefined objects by changing their attributes (called *properties* in Visual Basic) or re-implementing their event procedures. Again, you *cannot* create new objects or add new properties to an existing object. From a sophisticated object-oriented programmer's perspective, this kind of OOP can be limiting. You might want to think of this approach as OOP with a catch: the language contains object-oriented features that it recognizes, which you can use but cannot extend.

Despite this limitation, Visual Basic makes use of objects and object-oriented programming techniques that are very beneficial. Visual Basic also makes it easier to conceptualize a Windows application. Think of it this way: the interface is object-oriented, but the procedural part of an application is not.

Your application interface derives its behavior directly from the existing objects in Visual Basic. You will modify the behavior and attributes of these objects frequently, but you will not have to re-implement unnecessary behavior. This is definitely object-oriented thinking. You will create general procedures, however, in a more structured fashion. If you prefer, you can think of general procedures as objects, and the Visual Basic system will treat them as objects in the sense that they are specific to a form. Visual Basic does not recognize general procedures that are specific to a form outside the form.

General procedures specific to a module, however, are recognized throughout an application, and therefore are object-oriented only in the sense that the application is an object. Although this view of "application equals object" is interesting philosophically, let's stick to a more restricted view in considering the following list as the primary Visual Basic objects:

- Forms
- Controls
- The five system objects:
    1. App
    2. Clipboard
    3. Debug
    4. Printer
    5. Screen

A form can be either a window or a dialog box. In Visual Basic 3.0, a form can include as many as 470 controls (Visual Basic objects such as text boxes, command buttons, and so on). Depending on the type of control you are using, however, the allowable number of controls might be fewer. In addition, Visual Basic 3.0 limits the total number of control names to 254. Thus, to actually reach the 470 control maximum, you must use control arrays. Each control array can contain many controls, yet share a single name.

The maximum number of controls in all open forms in a project is roughly 600, excluding graphical controls and labels. This number corresponds to the Windows 3.1 limit of about 600 open windows. Each non-graphical control (every control except shape, line, image, and label) uses a window.

Visual Basic 3.0 also limits the number of distinct objects (form types, control types, and global objects) in a project to 256 and the number of forms in a project to 230. Visual Basic 3.0 limits the sum of procedures, modules, forms, and DLL declarations to about 5,200. The form, its controls, and its menu (the list of commands at the top of the window) make up the user interface.

Primarily, you use Visual Basic objects by manipulating properties, re-implementing event procedures, and sending messages to object methods.

A property is a characteristic of an object. Each property has a name and a setting. Each setting has a default you can use without changing any code. The setting is equivalent to the value of the property. Depending on the object, the properties differ. For example, a text box (in Visual Basic 3.0) has 40 properties (`CtlName`, `FontSize`, `Height`, `Width`, `Visible`, and so on), a command button has 28 properties, and a combo box has 36 properties. To change a property setting at design time, you use the Properties bar.

To change a property at runtime, use code. For example:

```
TextBox1.Text = "New text"
```

To change the behavior of an object, re-implement the appropriate event procedure. Re-implementing an event procedure is equivalent to writing a procedure except that event procedures are responses to events directed to the application from Windows.

How Event-Oriented Programming Really Works

In Visual Basic, an event is an action recognized by an object. For example, a user clicking a mouse or pressing a key is an event. In addition, the system can generate events (a timer event, for example). One way to make things happen in Visual Basic is to write code that enables the objects in your application to respond to events. You put this event-response code in procedures (subs or functions) called, appropriately, event procedures.

Event procedures are specific to objects and events. For example, if the object is a form and you want to define an action that responds to a user clicking the left mouse button within the form, write an event procedure that responds to the click:

```
FormName_Click
```

Or in general for any object:

```
ObjectName_EventName
```

Note that Windows automatically handles any event (a keypress, a mouse click, and so on) routed to an application in some default manner. You do not have to write event procedures if you are satisfied with the default behavior of an event procedure. A beautiful aspect of Visual Basic is that you write event procedures only for events you want your application to handle in some special way.

When your application loads a form, for example, the form receives a `Load` message, which triggers the `Load` event procedure for the form. The default `Load` event procedure for any form is similar to the following example (the form name is the only difference):

```
Form1_Load ( )
End Sub
```

As you can see, nothing happens in the event procedure. It simply is invoked and ends, and Visual Basic handles the default behavior (that is, loading the form into memory) for you. You can override this default behavior, however. For example, you can initialize some variables every time you load this form:

```
Form1_Load ( )
     A% = 34
     B% = 46
     ...
End Sub
```

The default behavior (loading the form into memory) is still carried out, and now, in addition, two variables are initialized. Knowing when events are triggered and implementing your code within event procedures are vital to writing efficient Visual Basic applications.

The event names for objects are predefined by Visual Basic and include all the event procedures you need to control a mouse pointer, the keyboard, links to other applications, and so on. Each object has its own specific list (or group) of events. The following list shows the event names for a form. (Note that `Activate`, `Deactivate`, and `QueryUnload` are new events in Visual Basic 3.0.) The Visual Basic programming manual (Microsoft Visual Basic Programmers Guide) lists all the events for each Visual Basic object.

```
Activate          LinkError
Click             LinkExecute
DblClick          LinkOpen
Deactivate        LostFocus
```

```
DragDrop            Load
DragOver            MouseDown
GotFocus            MouseMove
KeyDown             MouseUp
KeyPress            Paint
KeyUp               QueryUnload
LinkClose           Resize
                    Unload
```

Whenever an event is recognized by the current object (a form or control), Visual Basic attempts to execute the event procedure (for the object) that corresponds to the event. Figure 1.1 illustrates this process.

At the conclusion of the event procedure, the application returns to an idle state, where, in effect, it waits for the next event.

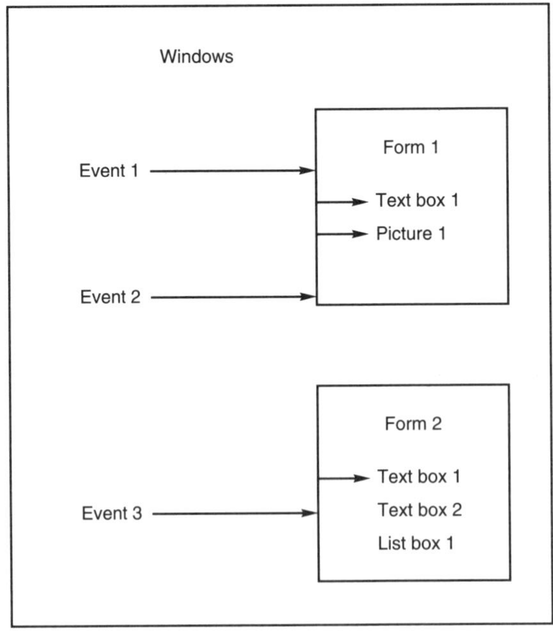

Figure 1.1. Event processing.

The key to writing "smart" applications is to understand how events work, how they trigger other events, and how to build your applications around these events. Because events are being passed through Windows and recognized automatically by Visual Basic forms and controls, you can make your applications simple and efficient by utilizing logical, efficient event processing. To illustrate how events work, I'll focus on two groups of events: `Change` and `Focus`.

Using Change Events to Trigger Automatic and Real-Time Updating

A `Change` event occurs every time the contents of a control change. The triggering of the `Change` event varies with the specific type of control. For example, a text box `Change` event is triggered when the contents of the text box change; a drive list box `Change` event is triggered when a user selects a new drive; and a directory list box `Change` event is triggered when a user double-clicks a new directory or when the `Path` property is changed using code.

In addition, DDE links can modify the data in a control that automatically triggers a `Change` event. When a DDE link updates data in a label, for example, a `Change` event is triggered; when a DDE link updates a picture, a `Change` event is triggered in a picture box.

You can simplify (and dramatically improve) your applications by anticipating `Change` events. More importantly, you can use `Change` events to maintain and stimulate the flow of control in your applications. For example, `Change` events are particularly useful for real-time updating and for automatic updating. Combo boxes, directory list boxes, drive list boxes, scroll bars, labels, picture boxes, and text boxes all respond to `Change` events. These `Change` events indicate that the contents of the control have been altered in some way. Because you can easily determine when a `Change` event will occur (it occurs when the contents of the control change), you can use `Change` events to create dynamic applications that respond automatically to changes in other controls.

For example, you might use a `Change` event in one text box to modify the contents of another text box:

```
Text1_Change()
    Text2.Text = "Change in Text box 1."
End Sub
```

The Change event for any text box control already exists (that is, every text box has a Change event procedure you can modify to suit the needs of your application) simply write the code you want carried out in response to the Change in the text box. You even can have a Change event trigger other Change events:

```
Text1_Change()
     Text2.Text = "Change in Text box 1."
End Sub

Text2_Change()
     Label1.Caption = "Text box 2 changed."
End Sub
```

In this simple example, a change in the contents of a text box called Text1 triggers a change in a text box called Text2 that, in turn, triggers a change in a label called Label1.

Note, however, that using Change events can become complicated and can lead to trouble. For example, if the code went as follows:

```
Text1_Change()
     Text2.Text = "Change in Text box 1."
End Sub

Text2_Change()
     Text1.Text = "Text box 2 changed."
End Sub
```

the Text1_Change event triggers the Text2_Change event, which triggers a Text1_Change event, which triggers a Text2_Change event, ad infinitum. You must be ready for this process, called a *cascading event* (in virtually all cases, you should avoid it). The spreadsheet application in Chapter 3, "Dynamic Events: Controls, Menus, and Dynamic Arrays," makes good use of Change events and demonstrates an easy pitfall into a cascading event through the use of control arrays. (The application also shows you how to avoid cascading events.) The Wizard application in Chapter 6, "Files, Directories, and a Code Wizard," uses PathChange and PatternChange events to make file input and output more user-friendly. The applications in the last few chapters of this book use Change events in conjunction with DDE and OLE links (see Chapter 9, "Extending Visual Basic: Custom Controls and DLLs," Chapter 10, "A Wizard Project Editor and a Wizard Clipboard," Chapter 11, "Into the Heart of OLE," and Chapter 12, "DDE, Custom Controls, and DLLs: Intimate Details" for more information).

Using Focus Events to Automatically Initiate Action

Another useful event group is the Focus events `GotFocus`, `LostFocus`, and `SetFocus`. You can use these events to initiate action automatically when a control or form gets or loses the focus. When a control or form has the focus, user input (from the mouse or keyboard) is channeled (by Windows) to that control or form. For example, if a text box has the focus and a user enters text (using the keyboard), that text appears in the text box. If the text box does not have the focus, the text the user entered appears somewhere else. Therefore, you usually will want to control the focus (or at least know which form or control has the focus) to guarantee that the correct control (or form) is receiving user input.

You can also use Focus events, such as `GotFocus` and `LostFocus`, to indicate action for the control when the control gets the focus (`GotFocus`) or loses it (`LostFocus`). In addition, you can direct user input to a control by giving a control the focus using the `SetFocus` event.

For example, the following simple fragment of code uses the `GotFocus` event to display a message box, which indicates that a particular command button has the focus:

```
Sub Command1_GotFocus()
     Msg$ = " Command1 has the focus now."
     MsgBox Msg$
End Sub
```

You can use a `LostFocus` event to disable a menu item (to make it inaccessible to a user):

```
Sub Text1_LostFocus()
     SearchCom.Enabled = 0   ' false
End Sub
```

Or, you can use the `LostFocus` event to change the background color of a control (a text box, for example) to indicate that the text box is currently not in use:

```
Sub Text1.LostFocus()
     Text1.BackColor = RGB(0,0,255)
End Sub
```

The possibilities are virtually endless, and you will learn how to use Focus events later in this book.

Why Should You Use Event-Oriented Techniques?

Although some programmers who are adept with the DOS text-oriented approach to developing applications might object (no pun intended) to being forced into the Visual Basic event approach, I do not. I don't think that you should, either. I think that this approach is in many ways the best one I've seen or used. It's no secret (pun intended) that the Windows environment is tough for developers. It is easy for users, but tough on developers if you have to build everything from scratch. C programmers, who have to make most of the Windows-application connections themselves, know what I mean. The amount of C code required to get a simple "hello, world" quality application up and running is approximately 100 lines of code. Even a Turbo Pascal for Windows application that uses `ObjectWindows` (the nifty Windows library) requires 20 or so lines because you still must specify objects and controls entirely through code.

Visual Basic takes another approach. It anticipates the objects an application needs and anticipates the events the objects will need to respond to. The objects predefined by Visual Basic include most of the ones you need to design user interfaces that are comparable to state-of-the-art Windows applications such as Microsoft Word and Excel. In addition, these objects already have virtually all the methods, properties, and event-handling capabilities you can imagine. Command buttons, combo boxes, forms, and so on are designed to handle expected events such as mouse clicks and keypresses. In terms of the Windows environment, therefore, you probably can build anything you want from these objects.

An event-driven approach is also important because it gives each application a common way to interact with Windows. If applications interact similarly, they are easier to develop and they work more consistently, particularly if you are using Windows as a multitasking system. An application that understands events can respond as needed and give up control when needed. If you want your application to behave well in the Windows environment, it should learn to think in terms of events. Visual Basic makes this step up to event-oriented development easy because its collection of built-in objects is designed to respond to events.

Visual Basic Objects Already Know How to Recognize Events

Visual Basic objects recognize events. You don't have to anticipate the kinds of events the objects you use need to respond to. They already know which kinds of events they need to know about. For example, both a command button and a file list box can respond to `Click`, `DblClick`, and `KeyPress` events; in addition, a file list box can respond to `PathChange` and `PatternChange` events. A command button has no need to respond to either of these events; therefore, that capability has been left out of the command button (object).

In general, objects recognize the kinds of events that "make sense" for them to respond to. You, in turn, can write event procedures when you want your application to respond specifically to an event. If you don't write specific event procedures for these events, it's no problem. By default, any event without a specific corresponding event is ignored. Therefore, you save development time at several levels because you don't have to create the object and its event-response capability, and you don't have to write event processing code unless you want to override the object's default capability.

Attaching Code to Objects in the Interface

You can create a Visual Basic application at design time, and you can test and debug it during runtime. In Visual Basic, these two times are closely related. (I want to plug the incredibly fast compile times of Visual Basic. One of the reasons I have grown tired of C++ is its pitifully slow compile times—regardless of implementations. If I make bunches of errors, I can correct them much faster in Visual Basic than I can in C++. Don't get me wrong, C++ is a robust, incredible language, but for most of us, Visual Basic delivers applications at a phenomenally faster rate.)

During design time you can create the application's interface from Visual Basic objects. Beginning with a form (or forms), you can add optional controls and menus to the forms. Then you can attach code to these objects. Use the toolbox to add controls, the Properties bar to change the property settings of forms and controls, and the code window to modify the methods for objects or to add general procedures to the application.

Each predefined object in Visual Basic has predefined properties, methods, and event procedures. These properties (like any variable, if you are directly from the old school of structured programming) are typed and have default settings. You can modify these settings, but you can't delete or add new properties. Similarly, you can write code for any of an object's event procedures, but you can't add new event procedures or delete old ones. You can, however, ignore events—which you often will do.

Don't be alarmed, however. You can write general procedures for the application just as you can in QuickBASIC, C, Pascal, and other structured languages. Because these procedures are general, any procedure belonging to a form, control, or menu can call them and pass variables and values to them.

Your application's interface, therefore, will most simply consist of a form. A more complex version can have more forms, controls, and general procedures. If you are a structured programmer, you can think of these general procedures as the code you normally would use to get things accomplished, minus the interface (it has been thought out for you). In general, any application you create will have the look and feel of any other Windows application. The specific behavior and the details of the interface, however—how controls, menus, and forms interact with each other as an application—are up to you. Your applications are still your creative efforts. It's the interface that has been standardized and simplified.

By using Visual Basic's predefined objects for your application interface, you save an enormous amount of time getting an application up and running. You can connect to Windows quickly and easily. Most of your programming time therefore can be spent concentrating on the details of the way in which your application works, not on the way Windows operates or how the Windows connection is made.

In addition, because Visual Basic is graphics-oriented (it's the first programming language I know that has both excellent capability and ease of use), you design your interface by selecting and positioning objects graphically instead of using text (that is, code). For example, in Turbo Pascal for Windows, an excellent Windows programming language, you still must define windows (remember that a window in Visual Basic is a form), controls, and menus using code.

You design your interface in Visual Basic by simply clicking on a toolbox item for the control and then dragging the form with the mouse across a form to place it.

If in Doubt, Design Dynamic Applications

Dynamic variables (the data component of dynamic applications) are useful because you can add any number of instances of them at runtime without knowing the exact number of their instances at compile time.

By delaying system-determining decisions until runtime, you allow code to be disconnected from a type's specific details, and the system becomes more flexible. A working system can be modified, adjusted, and so on, long after it's "finished." Instances of new types can be added easily to the system without disrupting it. (The word *finished* is in quotation marks because I have yet to find a true, finished application. It seems that applications are always changing.)

Visual Basic makes it easy to write dynamic applications through the use of list box controls, dynamic arrays, and control arrays. In addition, Visual Basic 3.0 includes the keyword `New`, which enables you to create new instances of forms at runtime. Each of these dynamic elements is discussed in Chapter 3, "Dynamic Events: Controls, Menus, and Dynamic Arrays," and Chapter 4, "Using Numbers and Forms," and used throughout the book. Creating new instances of forms dynamically is discussed in Chapter 13, "Objects, Instances, and MDI."

A Few Design Guidelines and Notes

Visual Basic offers Windows application developers an exceptionally easy way to create applications that can evolve as users' needs evolve. The Visual Basic secret lies in a combination of traditional ideas (structured and procedural programming) and innovative techniques (event- and object-oriented programming). Any Visual Basic application will use object-oriented techniques, events, and plain structured programming to get the job done. There's even the optional `GoTo`, if you want to abandon structure entirely. I believe that languages such as Visual Basic are the wave of the future, for several reasons:

- They give application developers a high-level path into a complex operating environment (in this case, Windows).
- They significantly simplify interface development. You create instances of forms and controls, but you don't have to create (by way of code) the forms and controls themselves. You simply point, click, and move these *interface elements* around the screen, show and hide them by changing property values, send messages to methods, and so on.

- They provide important development shortcuts. For example, when you double-click a form or control in Visual Basic, a code window opens to that form or control's code, and templates are provided for entering code. In a large application, this simple functionality saves time.
- They speed up overall application development. Because much of the code you need is supplied (forms and controls, for example), you can get a prototype version of an application running quickly.
- They enable developers to think visually and in code. This feature is incredible. After all, Windows is a visual environment, and users interact with the visual components of the application first. Why not let the developer think visually as well?

Although Visual Basic (Versions 1.0, 2.0, and 3.0) isn't entirely object-oriented, it maintains many object-oriented features, and future versions of this amazing programming system undoubtedly will add more OOP capability. The core of the Visual Basic interface already is object-oriented. The next step is to give the user more OOP capability for designing personal object-oriented types.

Designing Your Applications for Change

Object-oriented design anticipates the evolution of real-world systems and applications. When you design an application with Visual Basic, you utilize the consistency of the Windows GUI. The interface remains similar, and the application encapsulates in modifiable objects its response to both the real world and Windows. Because any application of even modest complexity will change, anticipating change is only natural.

In general, change occurs in one of two forms: external to the application or internal, within the application. An external change is a change in the world outside the application (for example, a technological advancement or development) that requires a change in the application's behavior in order for the application to continue to represent the outside world accurately. Simple examples include adding new printers or graphics terminals to enhance an application's communication capabilities, and adding desktop publishing components to a word-processing application. Even without object-oriented programming, structured design techniques can focus easily on these kinds of changes. Note, however, that Windows already specializes in these kinds of application problems—device independence is a central tenet of Windows.

An internal change is a change in the way you (and subsequently, the application) handle a problem. No change in the outside world is required for you to have a better idea about how an application works or handles the problem. This change, which is separate from the problem itself, is between you and the application.

Your reconceptualization of a problem might occur when someone is using the application, during research, or (in a special case) through a stroke of design genius. For example, you might rewrite a sort algorithm to increase its sorting speed when the number of items exceeds a specific threshold, reorganize your code so that it makes more sense to another programmer, or decide that a different design approach is better.

You may discover (by reusing an application in a new situation) that a type created for an application can be improved by redesigning or recomposing it into a different group of objects. Structured techniques (without object-oriented programming) assume implicitly that you have a complete understanding of the application and the world it represents before you begin coding it, and that the programmer or designer will either not make mistakes or learn from those mistakes. In short, structured techniques don't lend themselves well to internal changes.

Object-oriented programming languages (even limited ones such as Visual Basic) attempt to offer the best of both worlds with techniques for creating applications that can adapt easily to external or internal changes. If you are using object-oriented programming for your application design, your ideas easily can grow to keep pace with user needs. You cannot presume to know everything about the application and its "unknown" users before you begin to code. It is nearly impossible to know everything about anything that's the least bit complex. Unfortunately, many application design philosophies have incorporated that assumption.

In Visual Basic, the use of events complements object-oriented programming beautifully by adding another dimension to design flexibility. You can change an object simply by changing the way it responds to events. An object that behaves one way (in response to an event) is certainly not the same object that behaves in another way. Visual Basic makes this aspect of object-oriented programming easy to utilize. In fact, it emphatically encourages it.

Application projects usually don't become disasters during application development—that usually happens afterward, when a user's, designer's, or programmer's understanding of the application changes. Typically, applications don't evolve; they drift toward obsolescence as they become less appropriate for the newer versions of the problems they were designed to solve. If applications are designed well around objects, they have a good chance of survival.

For example, consider how you interact with the world. You begin by collecting the best information you can and creating (in your brain, supposedly) a model of the world based on that information. (This process is happening at brainwave speed, of course, however fast that is.) You then behave based on your model. Although your model undoubtedly is flawed, it is more or less appropriate or good enough for you to survive. (It sounds imperfect and scary, but it's almost assuredly true.) As you proceed through your life, you gain new experience (external factors) and have new thoughts (internal factors) that lead you to change your carefully built, yet flawed, model. You might even develop multiple models to represent the world's various aspects and complexities. You update many of these models regularly in response to new technology and new programming techniques. For example, your perception of how a compiler works, the ways you communicate, and so on, can induce a change in your model. Other models less dependent on new techniques may continue to work well, and you may seldom (if ever) update them.

In this scenario, you might modify some parts of your model or models in response to new external and internal information, and you might not modify other parts. You continually learn from your model and change it accordingly. Typically, if any model stops changing, chances are that it no longer is in step with the world.

An application is an expression of your current understanding of an external problem and your ability to represent it and its solutions. The design and the expression of the design, therefore, are inexorably connected; if the problem changes, your view of the problem changes, and your ability to design and develop an application changes. A good design philosophy (whether or not it's for Windows) must support a view that anticipates change.

Here are a few ideas to keep in mind when you design applications:

- Acknowledge that you can't know everything about a problem or an application before you design it. Accept that you always will learn things about the application that can be learned only after the application is working.
- Try to get some form of the application working as soon as possible, and use each application forerunner to improve your understanding of the problem and application.

Your early versions of the application may be only vague imitators of "more perfect" future versions. Let your applications reflect the evolution of your ideas. Refine and modify as you learn more. Because the object-oriented and event-oriented nature of Visual Basic encourages change, use objects (forms, controls, and event code) to explore new areas.

An additional, and perhaps subtle, aspect of object-oriented design is that it encourages you not to spend too much time creating an application. It encourages you not to try to solve problems that will never happen, not to do everything at once. Also, because object-oriented design tends to isolate the effects of one part of a system from others, changing one part of an application shouldn't disrupt other parts.

- Plan to change the design, not just the application, as you go. This doesn't mean recklessly throwing away parts, but means rather that you should start someplace reasonable and let the design grow as you learn about the problem and the application. In other words, avoid static designs. From the beginning, assume that the application will have to change.
- Expect to make mistakes.

The best way to determine whether you have made a mistake is to use the application. Chances are, your mistakes can be isolated in single objects (forms, controls, and so on) or events, and, therefore, you won't have to throw everything away at one time. Rather, you can modify the application, part by part, to reflect the evolution of your learning about the application and its users.

The Common User Access: A Set of IBM-Sponsored Guidelines

The common user access (CUA) is a set of guidelines designed to help you develop applications consistent with IBM's (and probably Microsoft's) idea of how a Windows application should look and feel. The CUA emphasizes these two primary ideas:

- Users should be comfortable using an application and feel confident in its results.
- Users should control the flow of events.

Looking out for users' comfort and building their confidence comes from making your application consistent with other Windows applications they might have used and also with its own behavior. Each opening of a window should become less mysterious and more familiar. Similar tasks should run in similar-looking windows. If possible, try to use familiar metaphors. A classic example is a card-filing application on a computer that resembles a common card-filing system. Also, avoid limiting users whenever you can. In other words, avoid restricting users' access to certain parts of an application.

Another way of thinking about this is as an event flow. In other words, let users control as much of the flow of the application as possible. This control builds user confidence and alleviates fear of the application and, therefore, the computer.

When you can, use visual cues (icons, shapes, menus, lists, and so on) to help users decide things for themselves. Encourage users to explore the application, and don't make them pay too dearly for mistakes; provide plenty of Undo, Backout, Feedback, and Help commands. An ideal application includes a context- and situation-sensitive Help system, which provides general and specific help.

Each application should have the standard appearance of a main window, a menu, and an event-driven, object-action cycle. Mouse clicks (or double clicks) should do similar things in applications. The same is true with the keyboard. If the applications you already use specify pressing F1 (or Shift-F1 or Ctrl-F1) to call up certain kinds of Help, consider using those keys in your application; make it feel as familiar as possible.

Use windows (that is, forms) efficiently. Don't make a form larger than needed, and remember that the `StartUp` form represents the application. When the application is minimized, for example, it virtually disappears. If possible, note the selection of an object visually. Show the user that an object has been selected or deselected. An excellent example of visual selection and deselection is the icon display used by many drawing applications to represent pens, brushes, and so on. Also, don't restrict the mouse pointer — always leave it free to move from window to window or from application to application. Using the keyboard selection cursor, mark the input focus where input is occurring on the screen.

Make menus conform stylistically to the kinds of menus typically used by applications such as the Program Manager. The Program Manager, by the way, is an excellent example to compare with your applications when you are trying to make them conform to the CUA.

The CUA recommends also using specific menu items for commonly used topics, such as File, Edit, View, Help, and so on. In addition, the CUA recommends specific keyboard accelerators for use with many commonly used topics. (See IBM's CUA specification for more details.)

Use the dialog and file dialog boxes, list boxes, and so on that Visual Basic supplies for you. Using them gives your applications a consistent look and feel. Don't mix too many elements in one application. Remember that you want your application to be as easy to understand and use as possible.

More Design Notes

A form is your window to Windows. Because a form knows how to interact with Windows, you can ignore most of the interfacing details. Write the procedural part of the application, and instruct the application to respond to the events channeled to the application by way of its form.

In general, regardless of the size of the intended application, you should follow similar steps to create it:

1. Create a form for each window in your application.
2. Draw the controls for each form.
3. Design a menu bar for the main form.
4. Set the form and control properties.
5. Write event and general procedures.
6. Test and debug.

During and between each step, save the forms, controls, menu bar, and code as a project. (The first time you save a project, specify names for the form, module, and project files.)

Using a project makes it easier to keep track of the application's components. Use the project to organize both the interface and code. For example, you can create a general procedure file for procedures you use frequently and include them in any project that needs them without rewriting code. When you are satisfied with the application, create an executable file to turn the project into an application.

Each application in this book follows a similar set of steps. In most cases, you can vary the order of these steps. In addition, you can develop and debug pieces of an application without first developing the entire application. For example, you can design the entire menu for an application and test it without writing a line of code. Or, you can code one piece of the application (a form, for example), test it, run it, and so on without worrying about the 10 other forms the application might require. Code what you need and add functionality later.

As a general design guideline, try to keep functionality (the general procedures of an application) and the interface as separate as possible. Develop and modify components separately and add them to the project as they are completed. For example, when a form is good enough temporarily, you can remove it from the Project list to help keep the screen clear. Then, you can return it to the Project list when you want to test it along with another part of the application. Alternatively, you can minimize the forms you're not working on, then restore the forms when you need them.

Developing a Dynamic Style

Remember that Visual Basic encourages the use of dynamic components (control arrays, dynamic menus, and so on). Applications that use dynamic components are more flexible and powerful than static applications, for several reasons:

- They enable users to *feel* in charge of an application because they *see* themselves manipulating the seemingly low-level structure of applications at a very high level. It's exciting, for example, for a user to add and remove items from a menu.
- They enable you, the application developer, to control (and conserve) memory more easily. For example, by using dynamic arrays, an application can allocate memory for the array when it needs it and recover that memory when it doesn't.
- They enable a user to manipulate (or customize) an interface long after you, the developer, have moved on to other projects.

Should You Use One or More Forms?

One design consideration explored early in this book is whether to use one or more forms in an application. You almost always can put all the controls you want on a single form, and then show and hide the controls when you need them. This ability leads to some potential confusion (for you) at design time, however, and ultimately leads to more code. A better design is to use separate forms to maintain separate sets of controls that share functionality. For example, when you are making a dynamic link (as in Chapter 8, "Stretching Your Visual Basic Applications: DDE in Depth"), you should use a separate form to maintain the link.

Because Visual Basic makes it easy to develop multiform applications, when in doubt, add a form, but unload it when you don't need it. Again, as the application gets larger, you will appreciate the separate maintenance of functionality.

ERRORS AND ERROR HANDLING

Trappable errors can occur while an application is running, either within the Visual Basic environment or as a stand-alone executable. Some of these errors can occur during design time or compile time also, and you can correct them temporarily. In general, however, any application you develop should anticipate and prepare for runtime errors.

Chapter 7, "Bulletproof at Runtime: Into the Real World of Errors and Error Handling," develops a general-purpose error handler that can be used as a basis to give error-handling capability to all of your applications. In particular, you will want to give your applications error-handling capability when you are passing them along to other people.

SUMMARY

Although Visual Basic isn't entirely object-oriented and enables you to think as non-object-orientedly as you want, it still makes sense to think in terms of objects. Each form is an object that consists of the controls and the code it needs to handle itself. If a form is intended to carry out a task, therefore, give it the code it needs to handle it. You can think about this another way also: as a one-task, one-form system. Remember, however, that you don't have to. I do this because it makes sense to me and is relevant to my applications.

I'm convinced that Visual Basic is an excellent way to go if you want to get a quick and long-lasting foot in the door of Windows programming. The Visual Basic system makes application development in Windows very easy and requires no major sacrifices. One of Visual Basic's secrets is that it's a graphics development system for developing graphics applications. And, as you will see, it's both fast and flexible. If you've updated to Visual Basic 3.0, it's even faster and more flexible.

The Visual Basic Language: Quirks and Perks

Down and Dirty: Variable Scope and Memory-Allocation Issues

Fixed- and Variable-Length Strings: Why It Makes a Difference Which You Use

User-Defined Types: More Memory Management Issues

Secrets of Recursion

By now, you should have a pretty good idea of how Windows and Visual Basic interact. The Visual Basic system lets you connect your applications to Windows and provides the tools for creating complex, powerful user-interfaces for your applications. In Chapter 1, "The Visual Basic System," you learned about the Visual Basic programming system from the top down. This chapter looks more closely at the Visual Basic programming language, which consists of the commands, functions, and words that let you "talk" to the Visual Basic system and, in turn, to Windows.

This chapter explores the Visual Basic language along some of its more confusing lines: data types, control structures, variable scope, memory allocation, and so on. It looks at the Visual Basic language in general and focuses on quirks, perks, and potential trouble spots.

Visual Basic has much in common with most high-level programming languages and is similar to other dialects of Basic. It's similar to structured languages also, such as

C and Turbo Pascal—a Turbo Pascal or C programmer can come up to speed quickly in Visual Basic because these languages are conceptually alike. Although they use different syntax and have different features, the main difference between them is that Visual Basic forces you to think graphically. However, you can do some things in C and Turbo Pascal (and Turbo Pascal for Windows) that you can't do, or can't do as easily, in Visual Basic. For example, it's easier to manipulate bits in C, and in Turbo Pascal for Windows, you can get higher floating-point precision (extended, with 19 bits of representation, versus a double floating-point with 16 bits of representation).

It's much easier, however, to develop a complex graphical user interface with Visual Basic than with C or Turbo Pascal for Windows. The primary reason is that forms and windows are predefined as objects in Visual Basic and can be added to an application with a simple click—Turbo Pascal for Windows still requires you to think in code when you add windows and controls to an application.

The construction of a Visual Basic application is part code, part form. You don't have to code the form part, but you manipulate it using code. Therefore, at rock bottom, the Visual Basic language—with its structure and syntax—is what you use to get things done.

THE ELEMENTS OF A VISUAL BASIC APPLICATION

Just in case you slept through the Microsoft manuals (or just need a review), let's briefly review the components of a Visual Basic application. An application (Visual Basic-style) consists of a form (or forms) part, its accompanying code part, an optional global module, and optional general-purpose modules.

Visual Basic defines a form as both a "window" and a "file." To avoid confusion, assume that "form" in this book means "window." If I refer to form as a "file," I indicate it as "form file."

A form file is the place to save the visual elements of a form (in the sense of a window) and its accompanying code. The visual elements are the form and any controls put on it. A Visual Basic application can have several kinds of files: forms, modules, custom control, and DLL files; and it must have at least one form (.FRM) file. You create a form file by designing a form and saving it with the File/Save command. If you wish, you can copy the code in a form to a text file, and save it separately by using the File/Save Text command. In fact, because Visual Basic doesn't "clean up" your code files, you occasionally should save your form files as text and reload them into your projects. This action reduces the size of your .EXE (executable) files, particularly when you're going through a long develop/debug cycle.

In Version 1.0, each project can have only one global module. The global module can consist of these elements:

- Global variable declarations
- `Deftype` statements
- Global constant definitions
- User-defined type definitions

A global module cannot include procedures, however. You define global procedures in general-purpose modules (not in the global module), where they can be recognized by the entire application. If you want to create a procedure that is local to a form, attach it to that form using the general procedure object for the form.

Visual Basic 2.0 and 3.0 eliminate the global module and give general-purpose modules all the power of 1.0 global modules. Any module in 2.0 or 3.0 can consist of these elements:

- Global variable declarations
- `Deftype` statements
- Global constant definitions
- User-defined type definitions
- `Private` procedures

`Private` procedures in a module are like procedures in a form. They can only be accessed by the module (or form) they are declared in.

A module (in either version) contains procedures and declarations not necessarily associated with a single (or particular) form. Procedures and declarations in modules are recognized throughout the application. Modules are used to build large and complex applications that contain multiple forms and to create modules of reusable code. For example, you might put all error-handling routines or all file I/O routines in a module.

You cannot declare or implement an event procedure in a module. Event procedures are restricted to forms.

In Version 1.0, the global module is a particular kind of module automatically created for each project. You don't have to use the global module—you can declare all your variables within a form's declaration section or locally (within procedures)—but it's there if you need it. Use the global module when your projects contain more than one form or module and need to recognize the same variable(s). In Versions 2.0 and 3.0, you can define global variables and so on, in any module (you don't need a global module).

Procedures within a module apply to the entire application. Module variable declarations within a module are recognized only within the module. For a pictorial representation of Visual Basic scope, see Figure 2.1.

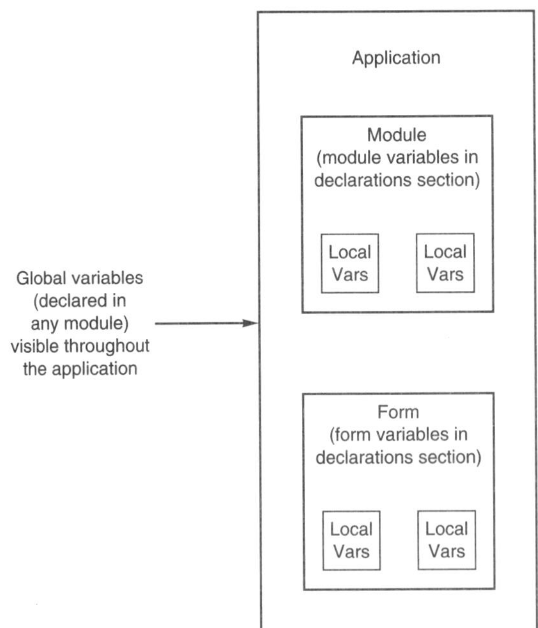

Figure 2.1. Module scope: procedures apply to the entire application, module declarations apply only within a module, and global declarations apply throughout the application.

Down and Dirty: Variable Scope and Memory-Allocation Issues

A variable designates a location for holding data that can change during the execution lifetime (what a strange phrase) of an application. Each variable has a unique name that identifies it in the current scope. "Scope" is a way of saying which part of an application recognizes a variable. You decide where you want a variable to be recognized when you first declare it.

If you need a variable to be recognized throughout the application or by more than one form, declare it in a module using the `Global` keyword. Alternatively, if you're using Version 1.0, you must declare global variables in the global module in the project. Otherwise, in general, declare it in the subroutine that uses it. I say "in general" because Visual Basic handles memory allocation for variables in what can seem to be a confusing way. This issue is reconsidered later in this book, but, for now, consider the following code examples that illustrate Visual Basic memory allocation.

The first example declares a local variable-length string `V$` and uses the `String$` function to create (approximately) a 64K string:

```
Sub Form_Click ()
     Dim V$
     V$ = String$(65000, " ")
End Sub
```

This procedure works, of course (try it). But why does it work? Whenever a variable is allocated within a procedure, it's considered a local variable, and local variables are allocated on the stack. Most languages handle memory allocation for local variables in this way. Unlike some languages that enable you to control the size of the stack, however, the Visual Basic stack is limited to 16K in versions 1.0 and 2.0 and limited to 20K in version 3.0. (This limit is unfortunate, but, as you will see, you can get around it.) In the preceding example, `V$` is declared as a local variable, but it's set to 64K using the `V$ = String$(65000, " ")` statement. So, where is the memory for `V$` being allocated?

Fixed- and Variable-Length Strings: Why It Makes a Difference Which You Use

The interesting quirk here is that variable-length strings aren't allocated in the same way as other local variables. With variable-length strings, the string descriptor is allocated on the stack, but the string itself is allocated in a data segment. Because a data segment can hold 64K of data, a variable-length string (if it's the only variable) can be 64K, the limit for all the variables declared within the general declarations section of a form. Remember, I said that the variable-length string is allocated in a data segment, but I didn't specify which data segment. Each form and each module (including the VB 1.0 global module) has its own data segment. Consider, therefore, the following example, which should help you realize which data segment is being used for the local procedure's variable-length string:

```
' General declaration for the form

Dim V2$

Sub Form_Click ()
     Dim V$

     V$ = String$(65000, " ")
     V2$ = String$(65000, " ")
End Sub
```

This example declares the same local variable-length string, `V$`, and a second variable-length string, `V2$`, in the general declarations section of the form. What happens? (Try it and see.) You get a Visual Basic `Out of string space` message. Now what's happening? You've declared a local variable and a form-level variable. However, the problem you encountered in the first example hasn't changed. Although you're declaring the second string variable at the form level, you're not allocating memory for the variable until you're in the procedure. As noted, a variable-length string declared locally is allocated in a data segment not on the stack. The memory for both strings, therefore, is allocated in the same 64K data segment and will not fit. You need 128K of memory (in data segments) for both variables. (You still don't know which data segment is being used, but let that slide for a minute. For the moment, consider how you can get the required 128K.)

The following code works around this problem by declaring the string variable in the general declaration section for the form and allocating memory for it at the same time. In other words, use a fixed-length string at the form's general declarations level:

```
' General declaration for the form

Dim V2 As String * 65000     ' declare the first string
                             ' and allocate the memory for it

Sub Form_Click ()
```

```
     Dim V$                  ' declare the second string

    V$ = String$(65000, " ") ' allocate memory
                             ' for the second string
    V2 = V$
End Sub
```

In this case, you declare the string `V2` and allocate memory for it at the same time in the `Dim V2 As String * 65000` line. The assignment `V2 = V$` merely verifies that there are two 64K strings. One of them is in the form's data segment. Where is the other one? The following example provides a clue. The global declaration is in any module if you're using Version 2.0 or 3.0, but it must be in the global module if you're using Version 1.0.

```
' Global declaration in a module

Global V2$
' Code in the form
Sub Form_Click ()
     Dim V$

     V$ = String$(65000, " ")
     V2$ = String$(65000, " ")
End Sub
```

In this case, again, declare the first string, `V$`, locally and the second string, `V2$`, in a module. This code generates the familiar Visual Basic `Out of string space` error message. What's happening? Although the declaration level has been changed, it's really a repeat of the earlier example. Although the variable-length string was declared in a module, memory for it isn't allocated until the local procedure is called. Therefore, the purpose again is to allocate two 64K strings in the same data segment. (You still don't know where that data segment is, however.)

The following code works around this problem by declaring the string variable and allocating memory for it at the same time, again using a fixed-length string at the global declarations level:

```
' Global declaration in a module

Global V2 As String * 65000

' Code in the form
Sub Form_Click ()
     Dim V$

     V$ = String$(65000, " ")
     V2 = V$
End Sub
```

The code works, and again you have two 64K strings: one declared and allocated in the module's data segment and one declared in the local procedure and allocated in an unknown data segment. Let's pursue this allocation problem further with an example that uses fixed-length strings at both the declaration and global levels and the variable-length string in the local procedure of a form:

```
' Global declaration in a module

Global V3 As String * 65000


' General declaration for the form

Dim V2 As String * 65000


Sub Form_Click ()
     Dim V$

     V$ = String$(65000, " ")
     V2 = V$
     V3 = V$
End Sub
```

Wonder of wonders, the code works, and produces three 64K strings. (Again, the assignments merely verify string creation.) The fixed-length string `V2` is declared and allocated in the general declaration section for the form. Therefore, it is allocated in the form's data segment. The fixed-length variable `V3` is declared and allocated in the module and, therefore, is allocated in the data segment for the module.

Where is the variable-length string, `V$`, declared within the procedure, allocated? As nearly as I can determine (at this point), variable-length strings must share a 64K data segment because, as the preceding example demonstrates, all the other data segments for the project (this project has no additional modules) have been used. However, because it is not possible to allocate more than one 64K variable-length string anywhere, the total amount of memory available for variable-length strings must be 64K.

The following example also may be helpful. Again, declare two fixed-length strings: one at form level and one at global level. However, rather than declare a variable-length string within the `Click` event procedure as was done previously, declare a third fixed-length string as well:

```
' Global declaration in a module

Global V3 As String * 65000


' General declaration for the form

Dim V2 As String * 65000


Sub Form_Click ()
Dim V As String * 65000
     V2 = V
     V3 = V
End Sub
```

What happens this time? You guessed it—the code doesn't work. As expected, this code generates a Visual Basic `Out of stack space` message. The stack can hold only 16K (20K in Version 3.0) worth of data, and fixed-length strings declared locally are allocated on the stack not in the data segment for the form. The lesson here is to remember that:

- You must distinguish between declaring a variable and allocating memory for the variable. They definitely are not equivalent (as you have just seen).
- You must recognize that Visual Basic handles variable-length strings differently from other variables. Variable-length strings are not treated as simple variables, but as dynamic variables. Memory for the variable-length string itself never is allocated on the stack or in the data segment for the form or global module. The pointer to the string is allocated on the stack. The variable-length string itself is allocated (apparently) in its own data segment.
- You must recognize the relative importance of fixed- and variable-length strings. Although variable-length strings are attractive, they will not always solve the problem if you need several of them. Visual Basic has definite memory allocation limits. As demonstrated, however, a fixed-length string declared locally can be only 16K (20K in Version 3.0) in length (assuming that there are no other variables). A fixed-length string will not always work either. In some cases, the available amount of memory will determine how and where variables are declared. Attention to design therefore becomes very important.

(These problems and other string problems are discussed again in Chapter 4, "Using Numbers and Forms," Chapter 6, "Files, Directories, and a Code Wizard," and Chapter 9, "Extending Visual Basic: Custom Controls and DLLs.")

- In sum, each form and module (and global module in Version 1.0) is given its own data segment (up to 64K) for the allocation of all static data, strings, and simple variables (declared in the general section and in procedures). Each array of any data type also is given its own data segment. Each variable-length string, however, is not given its own data segment, but apparently shares a data segment of 64K. (Note that this discussion of string allocation is entirely relevant to Version 1.0. According to the "Microsoft Visual Basic Programmer's Guide," Versions 2.0 and 3.0 have increased the available memory for strings in some cases. I haven't discovered any of these cases, however. Any string in a `type` in either Version 1.0, 2.0, or 3.0 is limited to 64K. This 64K is the maximum value of a string segment.

DETAILS OF VARIABLE TYPES

The concept of type is essential to programming. A variable's type determines the range of values or states that the variable can assume and the operators you can apply to it. Specific instances of a type have values (or states) that are determined by the operators that manipulate them. Whenever you want to act on something or store a value, you need a variable. And, you have to specify exactly what kind of variable you have in mind. The variable has a type (or data type).

The following fundamental data types are supported by Visual Basic: integer, long integer, single-precision floating point, double-precision floating point, currency (scaled integer), variant, and string. In addition, a type can be user-defined, that is, a composite type made up of any combination of fundamental types.

Table 2.1 shows the amount of memory required to store each of these types, the suffix used to specify a variable type (in a `Deftype` statement), and the range of the type.

Table 2.1. Visual Basic data types.

Suffix	*Data Type*	*Size of Data*	*Range*
%	Integer	2 bytes	–32,768 to 32,767
&	Long integer	4 bytes	–2,147,483,648 to 2,147,483,647
!	Single-precision floating point	4 bytes	–3.402823E38 to –1.401298E-45 for negative values; 1.401298E-45 to 3.402823E38 for positive values
#	Double-precision floating point	8 bytes	–1.797693134862315D308 to –4.94066D-324 for negative values; 4.94066D-324 to 1.797693134862315D308 for positive values
@	Currency (Scaled integer)	8 bytes	–922337203685477.5808 to 922337203685477.5807
$	String	1 byte per	0 to approximately 65,535 bytes or characters (Some storage overhead is required.)
(None)	Variant	Date/time floating point number or string	Date values: Jan.1, 000 to Dec. 31, 1999; numeric values: same range as double; string values: same range as string
None	User-defined	Number of bytes required by elements	

Because memory usually is critical, don't use a larger variable than you need. In a large project, the amount of memory saved by using integers, for example, rather than singles or doubles, can become significant. This is particularly true when you are creating arrays or user-defined types of variables.

Keep in mind the problems discussed earlier in this chapter regarding fixed- and variable-length strings. Variable-length strings are handy when you don't know how large a string will be and when you want to recover the memory used by the string each time you exit a procedure. (Remember also that the memory for a variable-length string always is allocated within the procedure, not when the variable-length string is declared. When fixed-length strings are declared, they immediately use memory that isn't recovered until the application concludes. Fixed-length strings therefore lack versatility and memory efficiency.)

As shown earlier in this chapter, however, you can get more room (or space) for strings in an application by using both fixed- and variable-length strings. This allocation problem likely will recur during your application development career, and it, therefore, is discussed in other chapters of this book.

FUNDAMENTALS OF DECLARING VARIABLES

Before using a variable, you should declare its data type. I say "should" because you can use a Visual Basic variable without declaring it. Any undeclared variable, however, is assumed to be a variant data type that can store numeric, date/time, or string data. In other words, Visual Basic sets aside the amount of space needed for the data. Visual Basic will automatically convert variant types if necessary to make variants compatible. Note, however, that this is less efficient than explicitly declaring a type, if you know the type. As a general practice, I suggest that you always declare variables, except in very simple applications, to make your code more efficient, easier to maintain, and easier for others to follow your code.

There are several ways to declare variables. Depending on what you need, you can use any of the following declarations:

- `Dim` statement (for local declarations)
- `ReDim` statement (for dynamic arrays)
- `Global` statement (for global declarations)
- `Deftype` declarations (for range declarations interpreted automatically)

When you Deftype a variable-range type, Visual Basic automatically interprets a variable within a range as a type based on its spelling. The syntax used in a DefType declaration depends on the type of variable declared.

To declare an integer variable range type, use DefInt:

```
DefInt LetterRange [,LetterRange]...
```

To declare a long integer variable-range type, use DefLng:

```
DefLng LetterRange [,LetterRange]...
```

To declare a single-precision floating-point variable-range type, use DefSng:

```
DefSng LetterRange [,LetterRange]...
```

To declare a double-precision floating-point variable-range type, use DefDbl:

```
DefDbl LetterRange [,LetterRange]...
```

To declare a currency variable-range type, use DefCur:

```
DefCur LetterRange [,LetterRange]...
```

To declare a string variable-range type, use DefStr:

```
DefStr LetterRange [,LetterRange]...
```

Letter1 and Letter2 indicate the range of variables for the default data type. They indicate also the first letter of the variable names and can be any of the upper- or lowercase letters of the alphabet. Case does not matter. A LetterRange of X-Z, for example, sets the default data type for all variables that begin with X, Y, or Z. For example, if you define T-Z as string types, the variable TextMessage automatically is recognized as a string because its name begins with T:

```
Sub SomeProcedure
     DefStr T-Z
     '... other commands here...
     '.........
     TextMessage = "This is a string; first letter is T."
End Sub
```

A Deftype statement affects variables in only the module in which it declares a variable range. For example, a Deftype statement in the module called "Attract" affects only the variables declared in the Attract module. The default data type for other modules is not affected.

When you have specified a range, you can't change any of the variable types within the range using other Deftype statements. If you attempt to redefine a range using a Deftype statement, Visual Basic generates an error message. You can override a `Deftype` statement, however, by using a `Dim` statement or a type-declaration character. For example, if you use `Deftype` to specify a range of integer variables:

```
DefInt A-Z
```

and then override the integer specification in a procedure by explicitly assigning a new data type for a number within the range:

```
FeigenbaumNum# = 4.66920166091
```

the `FeigenbaumNum#` will be treated as a double-precision floating-point number, not as an integer, because a type-declaration character (%, &, !, #, @, or $) has precedence over a `Deftype` statement. One important exception: `Deftype` statements do not affect elements of user-defined types.

USE THE *DIM* STATEMENT TO DECLARE FORM LEVEL AND LOCAL VARIABLES

Typically, you use the `Dim` statement in local procedures to declare local variables and in modules and forms to declare module variables and form variables. Use the `Global` statement in modules to declare global variables. (Note that in Version 1.0 you can only use the `Global` statement in the global module.)

To declare an integer variable using the `Dim` statement:

```
Dim Count As Integer
```

To make multiple declarations on a single line using one `Dim` statement:

```
Dim Index As Integer, BigIndex As Long, Name As String
```

You also can identify a type rather than declaring it using the keyword `As`.

Add a type-declaration character (which determines its type) to the end of the variable name. For example, the following specification indicates an integer variable:

```
Index%
```

a string variable:

```
Song$
```

a single-precision floating-point variable:

```
ScientificNum!
```

Refer back to Table 2.1 for a complete list of type declaration suffixes.

Simple static variables declared with the `Dim` statement are allocated in the form's data segment (if they are declared in the general declarations section of the form) or on the application stack (if they are declared within a procedure). Dynamic variables (such as variable-length strings) are *not* allocated in the form's data segment or on the stack.

USE THE GLOBAL STATEMENT TO DECLARE GLOBAL VARIABLES

Use a `Global` statement in any module in Visual Basic 2.0 and 3.0 (or in the global module in Version 1.0) to declare a global variable. Global variables can be accessed by any component in the project. Note that you cannot declare global variables anywhere in forms (or form modules).

> To make maintaining your applications more efficient, put all your global variable declarations in one location. This will make them easier to find and modify.

For example,

```
Global Salary As Currency
```

declares a global currency variable named `Salary`. The following line:

```
Global Name As String
```

declares a global string variable named `Name`.

Simple static variables declared with the `Global` statement are allocated in the module's data segment. Dynamic variables (such as variable-length strings) and arrays of variables are *not* allocated in the module's data segment.

USE ARRAYS TO GROUP VARIABLES

An *array*—a group of variables sharing a common name—is used as a convenient way of storing and accessing lots of similarly formed data. Each element of an array has a unique index number that identifies it: `Count(1)`, `Count(2)`, `Count(3)`, and so on. You can declare an array locally using the `Dim` statement and globally using the `Global` statement:

```
Dim DGroup (1 To 25) As Integer
Global GGroup (1 To 50) as Integer
```

Visual Basic treats the following statements (which are dimension arrays) as equivalents (as long as there is no `Option Base` statement—an `Option Base` statement declares a default lower bound for array subscripts):

```
Dim X(16,2)

Dim X(0 To 16, 0 To 2)

Dim X(16, 0  To 2)
```

Array subscripts can be negative or positive. The separator `To` can specify any range of subscripts between –32,768 and 32,767. For example:

```
Dim X(-40 To 3200)

Dim Y(-39 To -5, -5 To 0)
```

Any numeric array can hold as many as 65,535 bytes (64K). You can calculate the amount of memory used by a numeric array by multiplying the number of elements in the array by the number of bytes required by the data type of the array. An integer array of 10 elements, for example, requiring 2 bytes per element, uses 20 bytes. A long integer array of 10 elements, using 4 bytes per element, uses 40 bytes. A double-precision floating-point array of 10 elements, using 8 bytes per element, uses 80 bytes. String arrays can be almost 64K bytes (because a small storage overhead, not required for numbers, is required in order to maintain a string array).

If you use a subscript greater than the maximum or less than the minimum subscript specification for the array, Visual Basic generates an error message. Visual Basic also generates an error message if the size of the array exceeds the allowable memory for the type.

How to Use Dynamic Arrays

Dynamic arrays are arrays whose size can change at runtime. Arrays typically declared with `Dim` and `Global` are "fixed-length," and memory is allocated for them when the application starts (if global or declared at form or module level) or when the procedure is run (if local).

To declare dynamic arrays, use the `Dim` statement at either the module or procedure level with empty parentheses; use the `ReDim` statement at the procedure level to define the number of dimensions and elements in the array. For example, first declare the array with an empty dimension:

```
Dim ThisMatrix () As Integer
```

Then, define the number of dimensions with a `ReDim` statement:

```
ReDim ThisMatrix (3, 5)
```

Visual Basic doesn't allocate memory for the array until you use the `ReDim` statement, because the `Dim` statement has declared only the name of the array. The parentheses indicate a dimensionless array. This delayed allocation economizes memory by allocating storage for arrays only when needed.

Alternatively, you can omit the `Dim` statement—simply `ReDim` the array when you allocate the memory for it. The next example omits the `Dim` statement. Each array (regardless of data type) has its own data segment. Thus, the following code works:

```
Sub Form_Click ()
     Dim V$
     Dim V2 As String * 1625
     Size = 65500 / 4
     ReDim Matrix(Size) As String
     V$ = String$(65000, " ")
End Sub
```

Because the variable `V$` is a variable string, it is allocated in a separate data segment. The variable `V2` is a fixed-length string and is allocated on the stack, and therefore is limited to 16K (20K in Version 3.0). The variable `Matrix` is an array and is given its own data segment (up to 64K).

> The `Matrix` doesn't contain 64K elements, but contains (approximately) 64K bytes. Because a string requires 4 bytes per element, it is 64K divided by 4. Note also that 65,501 bytes (one more byte than was used in this example) generates an overflow error on some systems.

The `ReDim` array declaration can be used only within a procedure. When the procedure ends, therefore, the memory allocated for the (dynamic) array is recovered automatically (because the array no longer exists). To see this for yourself, run the following code in single-step mode:

```
Sub Form_Click ()
     Size = 65500 / 4
     ReDim Matrix(Size) As String
     Matrix(1) = "a"
     Matrix(2) = "b"
End Sub
```

First, check the value of `Matrix(1)` before the procedure ends, and then check it after the procedure ends. The first time, you get the value `"a"`. The second time, you get the error message `Reference to undefined function or array`. (See Chapter 4 for another memory allocation and recovery check. In that chapter, a small memory-check application is built to verify when memory is and is not recovered.)

Because the dynamic array effectively disappears when you exit the procedure, however, use a static array or save the array data (to a file, for example) before you exit from the procedure if you need to maintain the data outside the procedure.

You can also redefine the dimensions with `ReDim` using variables:

```
Sub Form_Click()
     X = 3
     Y = 2
     ReDim ThisMatrix(X,Y)
End Sub
```

Dynamic arrays are useful for storing information at runtime when you don't know the size of the information you need to store at compile time. Also, if you use dynamic arrays within procedures, the memory used by the dynamic array is reclaimed by the application when the procedure returns. Dynamic arrays are very useful, and are used in several applications later in this book.

In Version 3.0, you can use the ReDim array declaration in conjunction with the New keyword to dimension an array of instances of a form. For example, the following global declaration (in a code module) declares an array of instances of a textform (named Form1):

```
Global TextForms () As New Form1
```

Then within a procedure, the following ReDim declaration actually creates the array (of three forms) and allocates memory for them:

```
Sub   SomeProcedure()
ReDim TextForms(3)
End   Sub
```

Note that the array of instances of textforms are created and shown automatically in response to the ReDim declaration. This innovative and important use of ReDim with the New keyword is discussed in detail in Chapter 13, "Objects, Instances, and MDI."

BUILD DYNAMIC APPLICATIONS WITH CONTROL ARRAYS

A control array is a group of controls of the same type (for example, a group of list boxes or a group of picture boxes) that share event procedures and a common control name. Each control has a unique index number, and all the controls in a control array must have the same Name property setting.

To create a control array:

1. Use the toolbox to draw the controls for the array.
2. Select a control you want to include in the array (by clicking it).
3. Select Name from the Properties list box.
4. Select the Settings box, and type a name for the control.
5. Select the Enter button.
6. Repeat steps 2 through 5 for each control you want in the array, and type the same name as in Step 4. (When you type the same Name for the second control, Visual Basic displays a dialog box asking you to confirm that you want to create a control array.)
7. Select Yes to create the control array, or No to cancel.

To remove a control from a control array, change the control's `Name` property.

When a control in the control array recognizes an event, Visual Basic calls an event procedure for the group and passes the index as an additional argument, enabling you to determine which control recognizes the event. In Chapter 3, "Dynamic Events: Controls, Menus, and Dynamic Arrays," an interesting mini-spreadsheet is built using a control array of labels and text boxes.

USER-DEFINED TYPES: MORE MEMORY MANAGEMENT ISSUES

A user-defined `Type` in Visual Basic is similar to a C `struct` or a Pascal `record`. It can include any simple data types (integer, double, and so on) or another user-defined type that you previously have defined. It looks like this:

```
Type RecordVar
     Field1 As Integer
     Field2 As Single
     Field3 As Long
     Field4 As Double
     Field5 As String
     Field6 As String * 15
     ...
End Type
```

In Verison 1.0, a user-defined type must be defined in the global module, but you can declare instances of a user-defined type in other modules or procedures (see Figure 2.2). In Versions 2.0 and 3.0, a user-defined type can be defined in any code module in the project.

For example, in the following fragment, declare the variable `Employee` as a user-defined type having two fields:

```
Type Employee
     Name As String * 20
     Salary As Long
End Type
```

Then, declare `CurrentEmployee` as a variable of type `Employee` using the `Global` statement:

```
Global CurrentEmployee As Employee
```

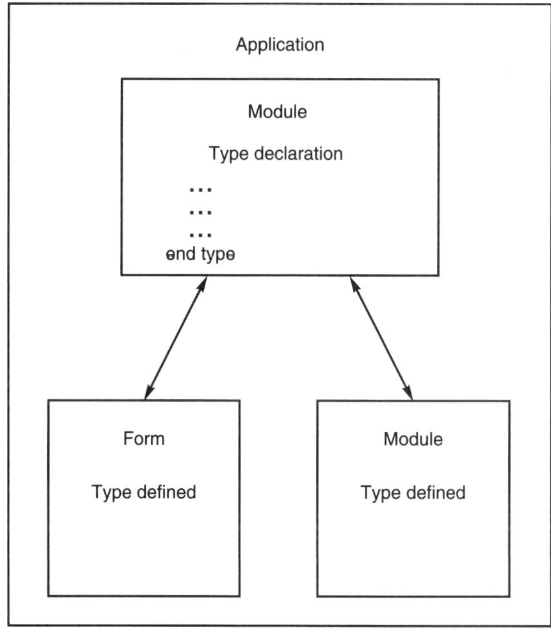

Figure 2.2. The user-defined type is defined in the global module; instances of the user-defined type are declared in other modules or procedures.

You can declare a variable of a user-defined type in a module or procedure using the `Dim` statement also after you define the user-defined type in a module (or the global module in Version 1.0):

```
Dim CurrentEmployee As Employee
```

Because the allocation of memory within a type can become confusing, let's explore a little.

For example, suppose that you declare a type:

```
Type Record
     S1 As String
     S2 As String
End type
```

and then use it in a specific instance:

```
Sub Form_Click ()
    Dim Rec As Record

    Rec.S1 = String$(65000, " ")
    Rec.S2 = Rec.S1
End Sub
```

What happens to this code? It generates a Visual Basic `Out of string space` error message for the same reason discussed earlier. `Rec.S1` is a variable-length string, and it uses all 64K of string space.

Now suppose that you change the record allocation to:

```
Type Record
     S1 As String * 65000
     S2 As String
End type
```

You have changed `S1` from a variable-length to a fixed-length string. What happens in this example? The code generates an `Out of stack space` error message because you have declared the instance of the record type `Rec` in a procedure. Visual Basic therefore allocates memory for `Rec` on the stack.

The solution is to declare `Rec` in the form (or the module's) declarations section:

```
Dim Rec As Record
```

Then the following code works:

```
Sub Form_Click ()
    Rec.S1 = String$(65000, " ")
    Rec.S2 = Rec.S1
End Sub
```

Visual Basic now has allocated memory for `Rec` in the form's data segment, and `Rec` no longer is limited to the stack size 16K (or 20K in Version 3.0).

One last example demonstrates just how many strings you can get from Visual Basic.

Declare the type:

```
Type Record
    S1 As String * 65000
    S2 As String

End Type
```

Then declare an instance of the type in the general declarations section of the form:

```
Dim Rec As Record
```

Then run the following code:

```
Sub Form_Click ()
     Dim S3$
     Rec.S1 = String$(65000, " ")
            Rec.S2 = Rec.S1
     S3$ = String$(65000, " ")

End Sub
```

This code produces three strings of 64K each: a fixed-length string with memory allocated when it's declared in a module (or global module in 1.0) (`Rec.S1`), a variable-length string allocated in the module's data segment (`Rec.S2`), and a variable-length string (`S3$`) allocated in the form's data segment.

You can squeeze approximately another 9K string from Visual Basic by declaring a local string variable:

```
Sub Form_Click ()
     Dim S4 As String * 9000
     Dim S3$
     Rec.S1 = String$(65000, " ")
            Rec.S2 = Rec.S1
     S3$ = String$(65000, " ")
End Sub
```

Memory for `S4` is allocated on the stack, and the 9K (as opposed to the possible 16K stack size, or 20K in Version 3.0) limit is still puzzling at this point.

When to Use Static Variables

A static variable is a local variable (one declared at the procedural level) whose value is preserved after the procedure returns.

In a declaration, use `Static` rather than `Dim` (or `Global`) to indicate a static variable:

```
Static VarA(16,3)

Static VarB(0 To 16, 0 To 3)
```

Use the keyword `Static` in nonstatic procedures to explicitly declare static variables. You must use `Static` to declare a fixed-size array in nonstatic procedures. Within static procedures, you can use either `Static` or `Dim` to declare static variables. You can make a procedure static; that is, you can make all local variables in the procedure static by preceding the keyword `Sub` with `Static`:

```
Static Sub AProcedure (X#, Y#, Z#)
     Dim ALocalVar As Integer
     LocalVar = 1
     ....
End Sub
```

In this fragment, `ALocalVar` is a static variable because it's declared locally in a static procedure.

Static variables are useful when you want to retain the values of a procedure's local variables for subsequent procedure calls. For example, the following static function counts itself each time it's called. It's capable of keeping track because any variable—`Count`, in this case—in a static function (that hasn't been declared previously as a global variable) is automatically static, and therefore retains its value after the function returns:

```
Static Function Count (X#) As Single
     Dim ACount%
     ACount% = ACount% + 1
     Print ACount%
     Count = ACount%
End Function
```

Or, if you declare a static array within a procedure, the static array retains its values between procedure calls. For example:

```
Sub Form_Click ()
    Static Matrix(16000) As String
    Matrix(1) = "a"
End Sub
```

In this case, the character `"a"` is retained in the `Matrix(1)` position between calls. Note, however, that the array is declared within the procedure, and therefore isn't visible outside the procedure.

DETAILS OF CONTROL STRUCTURES

A control structure is a Visual Basic statement or set of statements that controls decisions and loops in code. Visual Basic has several control structures, which are discussed in detail here (and used throughout this book):

- `If...Then` blocks
- `If...Then...Else` blocks
- `Select...Case` statements

- `For` loops
- `Do` loops
- `While` loops

The following guidelines and details can help you decide when to use specific control structures.

The If...Then Statement

Use an `If...Then` statement to execute one or more statements conditionally.

A condition is a Boolean expression—in other words, one that can be either true or false. Usually a condition is a relational test such as `Diameter > 2` or `Y <> X`. Relational tests can use any of the following relational operators:

`<`	Less than
`<=`	Less than or equal to
`>`	Greater than
`>=`	Greater than or equal to
`<>`	Not equal
`=`	Equal

For example:

```
If (X > 1) Then
     Y = 50                    ' set a variable value
     Control1.Visible= -1      ' turn a control on.
End If
```

The If...Then...Else Statement

Use an `If...Then...Else` statement to define several blocks of statements from which Visual Basic selects one block to execute.

For example:

```
If X > 25 Then
     Control1.Visible = -1     ' turn on a control
ElseIf X <=0 Then
     Control2.Visible = -1     ' turn on another control
Else
     Control1.Visible = 0      ' turn off both controls, if on
     Control2.Visible = 0
End If
```

SELECT...CASE STATEMENT

Depending on the value of a specified variable, use a `Select ... Case` statement to initiate actions. Use `Select ... Case` rather than an `If...Then...Else` to repeatedly test a variable.

For example:

```
Select Case X                           ' Test X
     Case 1
          TextBox1.Text = "Case 1"      ' Report X
     Case 2
          TextBox1.Text = "Case 2"
     Case 3
          TextBox1.Text = "Case 3"
     Case 4
          TextBox1.Text = "Case 4"
     Case Else
          TextBox1.Text = " Out of cases"

End Select
```

WHEN TO USE FOR LOOPS

Use a `For` loop to execute a block of statements a set number of times. You can also use the optional `Step` command to create odd (and odder) counters. For example:

```
For Counter = 1 To 30 Step 2        ' For odd Counters
     CounterSqr = Sqr(Counter)      ' Find square root
     Print Counter " " CounterSqr   ' Print results
Next


For Counter = 1 To 30 Step 5        ' For odder Counters
     CounterSqr = Sqr(Counter)      ' Find square root
     Print Counter " " CounterSqr   ' Print results
Next
```

WHEN TO USE DO LOOPS

Use a `Do` loop to repeat a block of statements while a condition is true or until a condition becomes true. For example, the following loop tests the value of X before executing any statements:

```
Do While X < 5
     SqrX= Sqr( X)
     Print SqrX
Loop
```

The following loop executes the statements first and then tests the condition of X before continuing to loop:

```
Do
     SqrX= Sqr( X)
     Print SqrX
Loop While X < 5
```

Is One Loop Faster Than Another?

By nature, I'm curious about how things work and how fast they work. I decided to benchmark the Visual Basic loops, and the following code uses the `Time$` statement to get the time between tests of the various loops. Note the use of the `Exit Do` statement in the final test, which has an embedded `If/Then` statement in a `Do` loop:

```
Sub Form_Click ()
    Print Time$
    X = 1
    While X < 50000       '28  seconds (1.0)
        X = X + 1         ' 5 seconds (2.0); 4 seconds (3.0)
    Wend
    Print "Done Loop1--While"
    Print Time$
    For X = 1 To 50000    '18 seconds (1.0)
    Next X                ' 3 seconds (2.0); 1 second (3.0)
    Print "Done Loop2_For"
    Print Time$
    X = 1
    Do
        X = X + 1         '28 seconds (1.0)
    Loop Until X = 50000 ' 5 seconds (2.0); 3 seconds (3.0)
    Print "Done Loop3--Do"
    Print Time$
    X = 1
    Do
    If X < 50000 Then     '28 seconds (1.0)
        X = X + 1         ' 5 seconds (2.0); 4 seconds (3.0)
    Else
        Print Time$
        Print "Done Loop4--If"
        Exit Do
    End If
    Loop
End Sub
```

As you might expect (or hope to expect), the Visual Basic loops that test a condition all are comparably fast. Loops 1, 2, and 4—`While/Wend`, `Do/Until`, and `Do(If/Then)/Loop` all took exactly 28 seconds to perform 50,000 iterations on my Zeos 386 notebook computer running at 20 MHz using Version 1.0. Using Version 2.0, the times were much faster (5 seconds and 3 seconds). Using Version 3.0, the times were slightly faster than Version 2.0 (4 seconds, 3 seconds, and 1 second). Perhaps the only slight surprise here is that the `If/Then` nested within a `Do/Loop` is just as fast as the straightforward `Do/Until`; that surprise withers, however, when you consider the code. Each of these loops tests a condition, and testing the condition is time consuming.

The `For/Next` loop is by far the fastest loop, requiring only 18 seconds to iterate 50,000 times using Version 1.0, 3 seconds using Version 2.0, and 1 second using Version 3.0. The zippy speed here is attributable to the lack of explicitly testing a condition. Again, this shouldn't be surprising.

My conclusion of this brief, fairly uneventful test, therefore is straightforward: If you want to test a condition, any loop is comparably efficient. How you want to test the condition is the critical factor. If you don't want to test a condition, but just loop a specific number of times, by all means use the `For/Next` loop. If you want an impressive speed improvement, get Version 3.0.

USE PROCEDURES TO SPECIFY A TASK

Procedures can be either of two types: `Sub` (not returning a value) or `Function` (returning a value). All your executable code within your Visual Basic applications must be in `Sub` or `Function` procedures. You can't nest procedures. In other words, you can't declare procedures within other procedures. In general, try to put task-specific code within procedures to make it easier to maintain and reuse code.

Visual Basic procedures can be recursive; that is, they can call themselves (repeatedly) to perform a task. You can declare variables in `Sub` procedures explicitly or not explicitly. Variables that you explicitly declare (using `Dim`) in a procedure are always local to the procedure. Other variables used but not explicitly declared in a procedure still are considered local unless you explicitly declare them at some higher level outside the procedure.

Global variables declared in any code module (but not a form or form module) in Versions 2.0 and 3.0 can be accessed by any procedure within any module in a project. Module variables declared in any module are accessible only to procedures in that module. Variables declared within a procedure are accessible only to the procedure where they're declared.

If a procedure uses a variable not explicitly declared in the procedure and the name of that variable matches the name of a global variable, global constant, control in a form, or function, Visual Basic assumes that the variable refers to that higher-level variable, constant, control, or function. Therefore it's not necessarily a safe practice to use variables without explicitly declaring them. I suggest that, as a general practice, you should always declare variables, except in very small projects.

Note that you can't use `GoSub`, `GoTo`, or `Return` to enter or exit a `Sub` procedure. You must explicitly invoke the procedure, using a procedure call. The following code demonstrates calling a procedure:

```
Sub SomeSub ()
     AnotherSub      ' Procedure, Another Sub, has no parameters.
End Sub
```

Recursive procedures are discussed in detail in the following section, "Secrets of Recursion."

A `Function` procedure is similar to a `Sub` procedure, except that it returns a value. As in `Sub` procedures, you can explicitly declare variables used in `Function` procedures or not explicitly declare them. Variables explicitly declared (using `Dim`) in a procedure are always local to the procedure. Other variables used but not explicitly declared in a procedure also are considered to be local unless you explicitly declare them at some higher level outside the procedure. Note that Visual Basic Version 2.0 does not allow you to explicitly declare a variable at any level using a type declaration character. Variables using type declaration characters must be explicitly declared.

> According to the Microsoft documentation, Visual Basic may rearrange arithmetic expressions to attain greater internal efficiency. I can't verify this, but if this is the case, you should avoid using a `Function` procedure in an arithmetic expression if that function changes the value of variables in the same expression.

SECRETS OF RECURSION

One important programming technique to many of us who pursue artificial intelligence (AI) topics is recursion. Recursion, in a nutshell, occurs when a procedure calls itself. For example, the calculation of the factorial of a number can be handled beautifully by recursion. The famous Quick Sort routine can be implemented elegantly also using recursion. In short, a recursive procedure in Visual Basic might look like the following:

```
Sub SomePro(SomeVal As Integer)
      '....some commands here
      '....probably change the value of SomeVal
      '....call SomePro with new SomeVal
      SomePro SomeVal
End Sub
```

Somewhere within the procedure, usually near the final line, the procedure calls itself. Presumably, there's a test somewhere within the procedure to enable the procedure to stop calling itself repeatedly. Otherwise, the loop continues until the system runs out of memory resources.

Recursion can be a problem for some compilers because of the way the invoking of procedures is generally handled. Each time a procedure is called from another procedure (not necessarily itself), the compiler must keep track of data and the address of the calling procedure. This information is maintained in the application's stack.

When a procedure calls itself, it must keep track of the same information just as though it were calling a different procedure. (Yes, it's strange, but true.) Programming languages such as PROLOG that have been optimized for recursion work around this, but Visual Basic does not. To illustrate recursion's bookkeeping problem, consider the following code:

```
Sub Recurse
      Static Count%
      Count% = Count% + 1
      Text1.Text = Str$(Count%)
      Recurse
End Sub
```

This routine does nothing more than keep track of how many times it calls itself—the result is displayed in a text box. Note that it uses a static count variable rather than passing the variable to itself each iteration. This routine runs exactly 386 times on my computer using Versions 1.0 or 2.0 and 433 times using Version 3.0. Because the stack is 16K in Versions 1.0 and 2.0, 16K/386—or about 45 bytes—are used per procedure call for bookkeeping. In Version 3.0, 20K/433 equals about 47 bytes per procedure. In an intensive recursive project, 386 (or even 433) procedure calls might be woefully inadequate. What should be done? Abandon Visual Basic? Not necessarily. There is a simple, though less elegant, solution: iteration.

Consider the following code:

```
Sub Form_Click()
      LargeNumber% = 1000
      For I% = 1 To LargeNumber%
            Recurse
      Next I%
End Sub

Sub Recurse ()
      Static Count%
      Count% = Count% + 1
      Text1.Text = Str$(Count%)
End Sub
```

In this example, a separate procedure (the `Form_Click` event procedure) calls the `Recurse` procedure repeatedly rather than having `Recurse` call itself. Because Visual Basic no longer must keep track of each call to `Recurse`, the bookkeeping maintained on the stack is minimal. In fact, this procedure runs indefinitely.

In general, any recursion can be recoded as an iterative routine, albeit with what might be counterintuitive logic. However, at least you can use serious recursion in Visual Basic if you need to.

Note, however, that the Visual Basic stack limitation isn't always a problem. You can do "real" recursion in many cases. For example, the following code uses a recursive algorithm (described by Dromey in *How To Solve It By Computer*, Prentice-Hall International series in computer science, 1982) to calculate the greatest common divisor of two numbers. It uses two text boxes to obtain user input (the two numbers) and report the progress of the results:

```
Sub Form_Click ()
  Dim Result As Double
  Dim M As Double
  Dim N As Double
  M = Val(Text1.Text)
  N = Val(Text2.Text)
  Result = GCD(M, N)
End Sub
```

```
Function GCD (N As Double, M As Double) As Double
  Text1.Text = Str$(M)
  Text2.Text = Str$(N)
  If M = 0 Then
     GCD = N
  Else
     GCD = GCD(M, N Mod M)
  End If
End Function
```

Chapter 4 returns to the greatest-common-divisor algorithm, and shows you a glossier nonrecursive version.

OTHER BASICS AND VISUAL BASIC

If you've written code in another version of Basic, you can port it easily to Visual Basic, although you might have to make some changes in order for the code to behave properly. The easiest way to get existing Basic code into the Visual Basic system is to use the `Load Text` command. This command lets you import a text file containing code into the current project, and it lets you use it in your code. To import a text file into the code window:

1. Select `Load Text` from the Files menu (use the Code menu in Version 1.0).
2. Select from the Files menu the ASCII file you want to import.
3. Select Replace to replace all code in the current code window with the imported text, select Merge to add the text at the insertion point, or select New to open a new module and load the text into it.

You probably will have to modify the Basic code to conform to the Visual Basic system. For example, BASICA applications don't use procedures, and Visual Basic requires that all code be in procedures. You therefore will have to at least convert BASICA code into one or more procedures.

In addition, Visual Basic doesn't support the following BASICA keywords:

BLOAD	INP	PMAPWINDOW
BSAVE	IOCTL	POKE
CALL ABSOLUTE	IOCTL$	POS
CALLS	KEY	PRESERVE
CHAIN	LOCATE	PRESET
CLEAR	LPOS	RESTORE
COLOR	LPRINT	RUN

COM	MKD$	SADD
CSRLIN	MKI$	SCREEN
CVD	MKL$	SET MEM
CVDMBF	MKS$	SLEEP
CVI	MKSMBF$	SOUND
CVS	ON COM	STICK
CVSMBF	ON KEY	STRIG
DATA	ON PLAY	SWAP
DEF FN	ON STRIG	TROFF
DEF SEG	ON TIMER	TRON
DRAW	OUT	USING$
ERDEV	PAINT	VARPTR
ERDEV$	PALETTE	VARPTR$
FIELD	PCOPY	VARSEG
FILES	PEEK	VIEW
FRE	PEN	WAIT
INKEY$	PLAY	WIDTH LPRINT

If the Basic code you're porting to Visual Basic uses any of these keywords, they will not be recognized by Visual Basic and will have to be changed. In addition, you will have to modify Basic `Print` and `Input` statements; several other Basic key words such as `Declare`, `DefType`, `Dim`, `ReDim`, `Input$`, `On Error Go To`, `Option Base`, `Return`, and `Width` require minor changes to work correctly in Visual Basic. For more information about porting the various Basic dialects to Visual Basic, refer to the *Visual Basic Programmer's Guide* that came with your Visual Basic software.

Summary

That's about it for this basic look into some of the quirks and perks of the Visual Basic language. I haven't tried to cover every aspect of the language in this chapter, just some of the more confusing ones. As we pursue the secrets of Visual Basic, we will explore different and more subtle aspects of the Visual Basic language.

Secrets of the Visual Basic for Windows Masters is not intended to replace the manuals (the *Programmer's Guide* and *Programmer's Reference*) that accompanied your Visual Basic software, but to supplement them. You should use all of them to explore this fascinating system.

Dynamic Events: Controls, Menus, and Dynamic Arrays

Use Change Events to Automate Spreadsheet Cell Updating

Sort Spreadsheet Cells by Sorting Controls

Use Dynamic Arrays to Conserve Memory

This chapter focuses on the specific application domain and the dynamic nature of controls, menus, and arrays. It spotlights application techniques that enable users to add and delete controls, menu items, and array elements at runtime. Applications using these dynamic components are more flexible and powerful than static applications for several reasons:

- They enable users to *feel* in charge of an application because they *see* themselves manipulating the seemingly low-level structure of applications at a very high level. It's exciting for a user, for example, to add and remove items from a menu.

- They enable you, the application developer, to control (and conserve) memory more easily. For example, by using dynamic arrays, an application can allocate memory for the array when it needs it and recover that memory when it does not.
- They enable a user to manipulate (or customize) an interface long after you, the developer, have moved on to other projects.

In this chapter, you'll develop several applications that explore this dynamic flexibility: DYNAM1, DYNAM1B, DYNAM1C, DYNAM1D, DYNAM1E, DYNAM2, DYNAM3, and DYNAM4 (on the disk). In addition to creating dynamic events and controls, you can create routines to sort controls, add and delete cells from a spreadsheet, and save and reload spreadsheet data. DYNAM1E is a relatively complete mini-spreadsheet that includes automatic updating of summation data for a group of cells and all the other features just mentioned. This chapter has lots of goodies, so let's get to them.

Control Arrays: A Recap

A control array is made up of a group of controls of the same type that share a common control name and common event procedures. For example, a group of list boxes or a group of text boxes can form a control array. Unlike an individual control (that is, one that's not part of a control array), each control in a control array has a unique index number. All the controls in a control array must have the same `Name` setting.

Control arrays are particularly useful in creating spreadsheet-type applications and custom menus; mini-applications of both of these are developed in this chapter.

In general, to create a control array:

1. Draw a control for the array.
2. Enter a name for the control in the `Name Properties` list box.
3. Draw a second control of the same type.
4. Enter the same name for this control in the `Name Properties` list box. A dialog box opens and asks you whether you want to create a control array (see Figure 3.1).

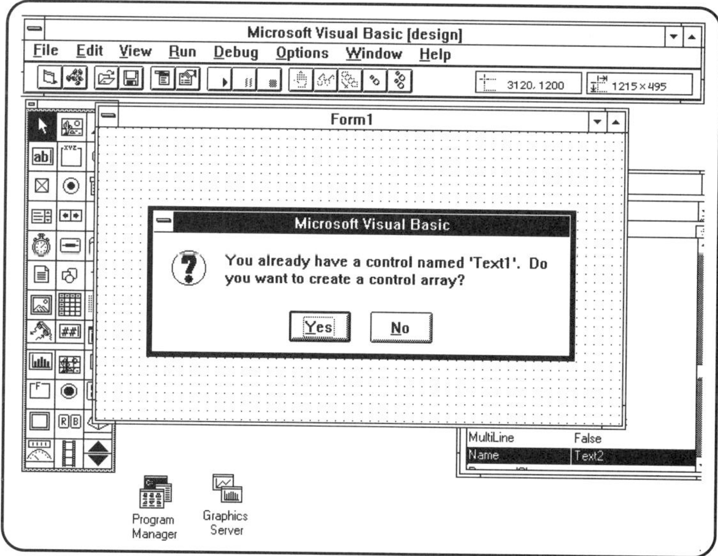

Figure 3.1. The control array dialog box.

5. Select Yes.
6. Continue to draw controls and enter the same name in the `Name` box. The index for the control is updated automatically as the control is added to the array (note the Index setting in the Properties bar in Figure 3.2).

To remove a control from a control array, change the control's `Name` property to something other than the `Name` for the array. Also, make sure the `Index` property of the control you're removing from the array contains `novalue`. The `Index` property of a control has a value (0 to 32,767) if (and only if) the control is part of a control array. When a control in the array recognizes an event, Visual Basic calls an event procedure for the group and passes the index as an additional argument. By examining this index, the application can determine which control recognizes the event. Event procedures for control arrays include the additional Index argument `(Index as Integer)` (see Figure 3.3).

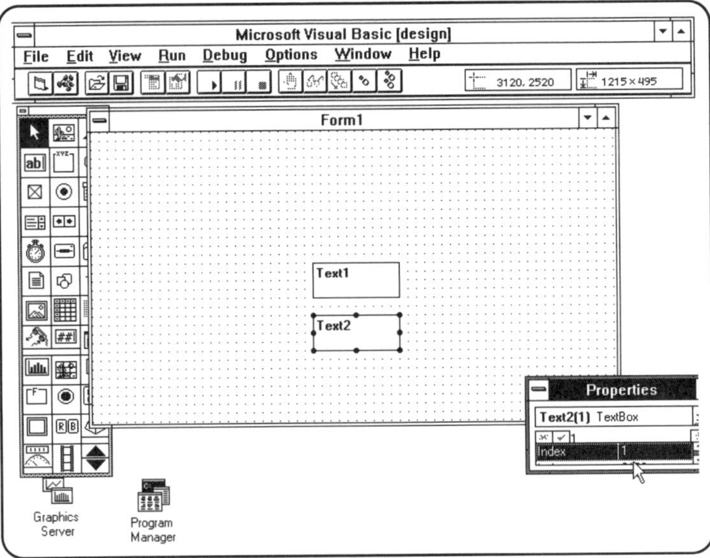

Figure 3.2. The control array index setting.

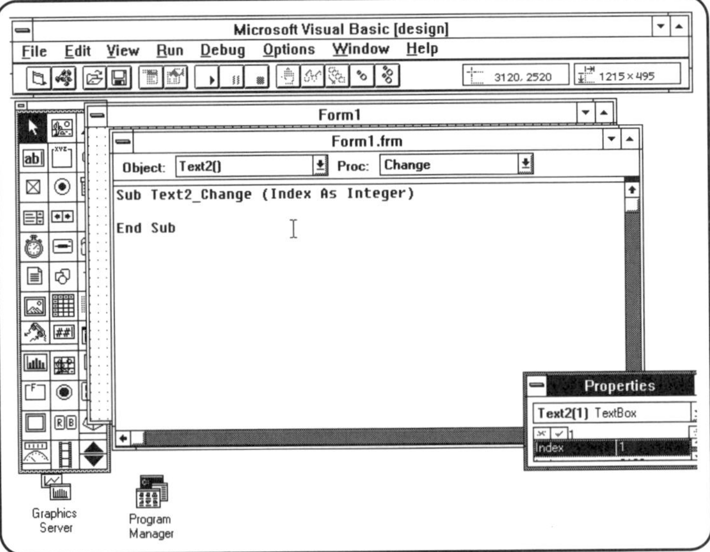

Figure 3.3. The control array (note the index argument).

DEVELOP A DYNAMIC SPREADSHEET USING CONTROL ARRAYS

Application1 (called DYNAM1 on the disk) is a first go at a mini-spreadsheet application. It allows a user to dynamically add and delete cells (made up of text boxes) at runtime. In addition, a user can enter numbers in the cells, and by selecting a command button, sum the numbers in all currently active cells.

Cells are created dynamically using a `Load` statement. They are set and positioned using the text box `SetFocus` method and the `Top` property. They are initialized to 0 using the `Text` property and are shown using the `Visible` property. The following steps show you how to do it:

1. Use the form automatically created by Visual Basic (by default).
2. Add the controls for the application. DYNAM1 uses three command buttons to add and remove controls and to sum values in all active cells. (DYNAM1 uses a control array made up of text boxes to represent the individual cells of the spreadsheet. Figure 3.4 shows these controls on the form in the design mode.)

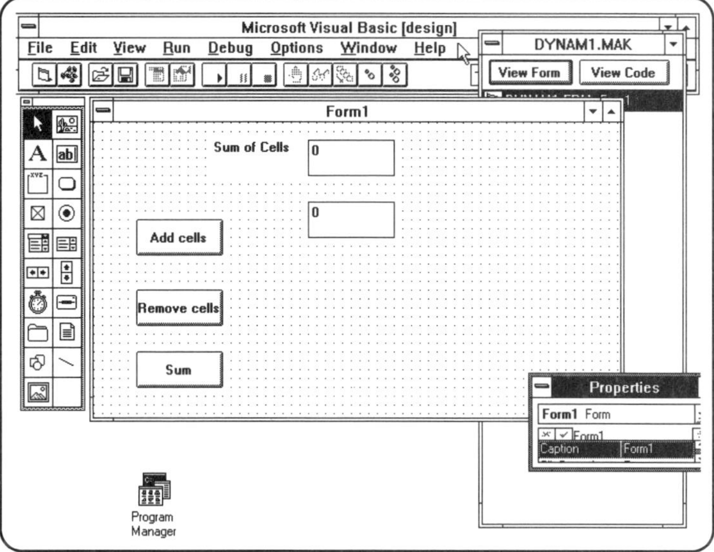

Figure 3.4. The controls for DYNAM1.

3. If you want a menu, create it here. (For now, however, omit the menu in this application and proceed to Step 4).

4. Set the form and control properties.

Set the `Name` property of each text box to the same name as previously described. You should note that I've changed the name of the control array (from the default `text` to `cell`) in my code in this chapter and on the disk. Setting the `Index` properties in this way sets up the control array also. Change the captions of the command buttons to indicate Adding, Removing, and Summing cells (refer to Figure 3.4). Note also that the object property bar (in the code window) indicates a control array with parentheses (see Figure 3.5).

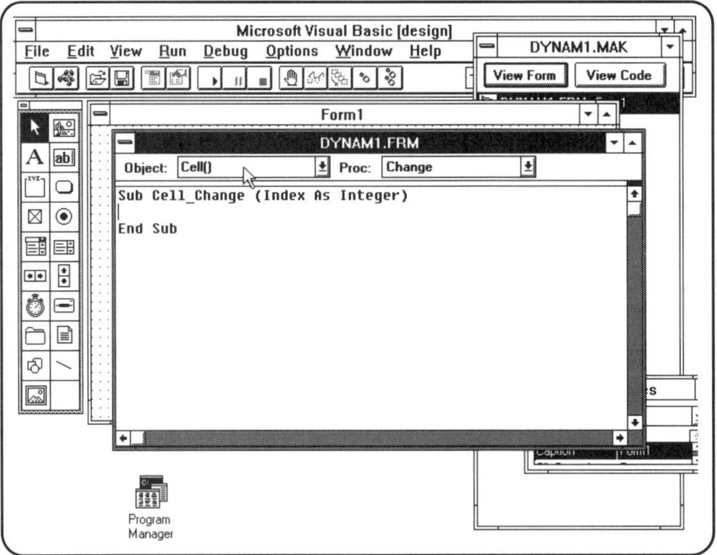

Figure 3.5. The object bar in the code window indicating the control array with parentheses.

5. Declare any nonlocal variables and write the event procedures for the three command buttons and for the `Form_Load` event.

It is convenient to use the form's `Load` event to set any initial values for an application because this event (if it is designated within the start-up form) always is called first when the application starts.

`Form_Load` sets the text box count variable (`MaxId%`) to 1 to indicate that the application will have at least two text boxes (0 and 1) shown by default:

```
Sub Form_Load ()
    MaxId% = 1              ' Set beginning text box (cell) count
End Sub
```

Note that `MaxId%` is a form-level variable. Use the code window to add the command click event procedure (see Figure 3.6).

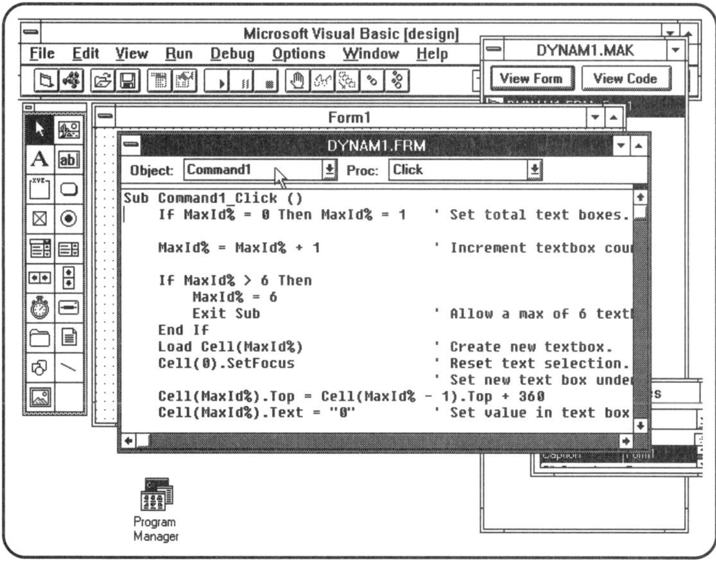

Figure 3.6. `Command1_Click()` *in the code window.*

The `Add` command looks like this:

```
Sub Command1_Click ()

    MaxId% = MaxId% + 1                 ' Increment text box count.

    If MaxId% > 6 Then
        MaxId% = 6
        Exit Sub                        ' Allow a maximum of 6 text boxes
    End If                              ' for this mini-spreadsheet.

    Load Cell(MaxId%)                   ' Create new text box.
    Cell(0).SetFocus                    ' Reset text selection.
                                        ' Cell = control array name
                                        ' Set new text box under
                                        ' previous text box.
```

```
    Cell(MaxId%).Top = Cell(MaxId% - 1).Top + 450

    Cell(MaxId%).Text = "0"            ' Set value in text box to 0.
    Cell(MaxId%).Visible = -1          ' Display new text box.
End Sub
```

The Remove command uses an `Unload` statement to remove text boxes. In addition, it decrements the cell count and resets the focus to the Sum text box at the top:

```
Sub Command2_Click ()
    If MaxId% = 1 Then Exit Sub     ' Keep first two text boxes, no matter what.
    Unload Cell(MaxId%)             ' Delete last text box.

    MaxId% = MaxId% - 1             ' Decrement text box count.

    Cell(0).SetFocus                ' Reset text box selection to focus at the
top
                                    ' i.e. on the Sum text box
End Sub
```

Note that the `SetFocus` method indicates which cell will have the focus (that is, the cursor). Finally, the `Sum` command uses a loop to add the contents of all the existing cells. Again use the code window to add the event procedure (see Figure 3.7).

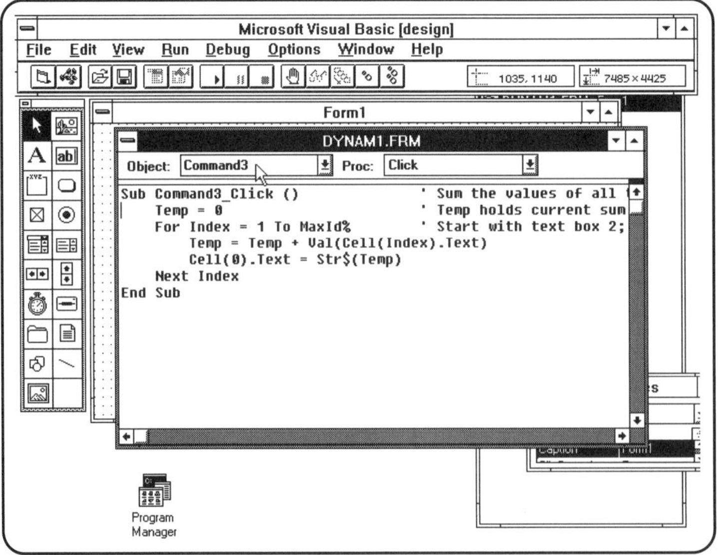

Figure 3.7. `Command3_Click()` *in the code window.*

The Sum command looks like this:

```
Sub Command3_Click ()               ' Sum the values of all text boxes.
    Temp = 0                        ' Temp holds current sum for loop.
    For Index = 1 To MaxId%         ' Start with text box 2; omit sum box.
        Temp = Temp + Val(Cell(Index).Text)
        Cell(0).Text = Str$(Temp)
    Next Index
End Sub
```

The complete code for DYNAM1 is contained in Listing 3.1.

LISTING 3.1. DYNAM1.

```
' general declarations

Dim MaxId%


' command event procedures


Sub Command1_Click ()

    MaxId% = MaxId% + 1  ' Increment text box count.

    If MaxId% > 6 Then
        MaxId% = 6
        Exit Sub    ' Allow a maximum of 6 text boxes.
    End If
    Load Cell(MaxId%)                    ' Create new text box.
    Cell(0).SetFocus                     ' Reset text selection.
              ' Set new text box under previous text box.
    Cell(MaxId%).Top = Cell(MaxId% - 1).Top + 450
    Cell(MaxId%).Text = "0"           ' Set value in text box to 0.
    Cell(MaxId%).Visible = -1         ' Display new text box.
End Sub
Sub Command2_Click ()
    If MaxId% = 1 Then Exit Sub     ' Keep first two text boxes.
    Unload Cell(MaxId%)             ' Delete last text box.

    MaxId% = MaxId% - 1             ' Decrement text box count.

    Cell(0).SetFocus                ' Reset text box selection.

End Sub
Sub Command3_Click ()               ' Sum the values of all text boxes.
    Temp = 0                        ' Temp holds current sum for loop.
```

continues

LISTING 3.1. CONTINUED.

```
    For Index = 1 To MaxId%         ' Start with text box 2; omit sum box.
        Temp = Temp + Val(Cell(Index).Text)
        Cell(0).Text = Str$(Temp)
    Next Index
End Sub


' form event procedures

Sub Form_Load ()
    MaxId% = 1
End Sub
```

Figure 3.8 shows the application running after several cells have been added dynamically.

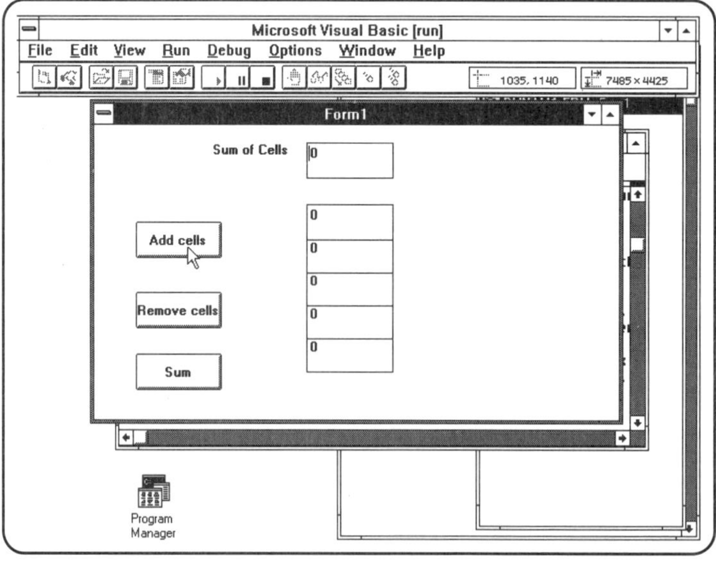

Figure 3.8. DYNAM1: adding cells.

Figure 3.9 shows the application running after several cells have been summed.

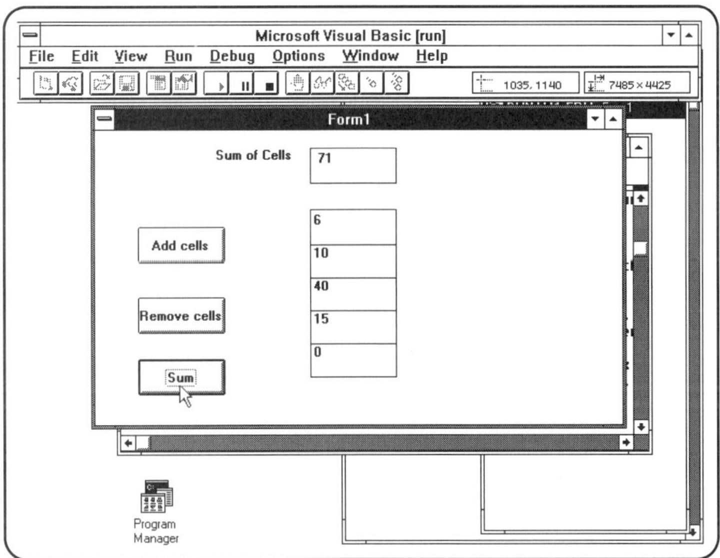

Figure 3.9. DYNAM1: summing cells.

Use Change Events to Automate Spreadsheet Cell Updating

One thing to notice about DYNAM1 is that the SumCell isn't updated to reflect changes to the other cells in the control array. If you want to resum the cells, press the Sum control button. It would be convenient in certain circumstances to have this cell (and perhaps others) updated automatically. For example, if you want to update the SumCell and determine the mean and standard deviation every time a cell value changes or every time a cell is added or removed, use the `Change` event for the cell control array to trigger the sum and mean automatically.

Let's revise the mini-spreadsheet application just developed to:

- Enable automatic updating.
- Add mean and standard deviation cells.

Let's begin with automatic updating. The simplest way to implement an automatic updating scheme is to use the `Change` event for the object that will initiate change. In this case, you want to update the SumCell (`Cell(0)`) every time one of the value cells changes; in other words, resum the cells every time a cell changes. Summing is handled by a `Command3_Click`:

```
Sub Command3_Click ()                ' Sum the values of all text boxes.
    Temp = 0                         ' Temp holds current sum for loop.
    For Index = 1 To MaxId%          ' Start with text box 2; omit sum box.
     Temp = Temp + Val(Cell(Index).Text)
     Cell(0).Text = Str$(Temp)
    Next Index
End Sub
```

Initiate automatic summing by invoking the `Command3_Click` event procedure every time a cell changes:

```
Sub Cell_Change (Index As Integer)
    Command3_CLick
End Sub
```

Simple? Yes, but disastrous.

Cascading Events: A Major No-No

I deliberately coded this version of the application to demonstrate a potential pitfall. Run the revised application (DYNAM1B) to see what happens: an `Out of stack space` message appears. If you step through the code, you can see why. Every time a cell is updated, the SumCell is updated (resummed). Because the SumCell is `Cell(0)`, a member of the control array, it triggers a `Change` event, which in turn resums the cells, causing another `Change` event, and so on. Avoid this *cascading event*, as it is called in Visual Basic lingo. Figure 3.10 illustrates the cascade.

Fortunately, you easily can avoid this scenario by either setting a Watch flag or by redesigning the application to eliminate the cascade. The best solution in this case is to redesign the application by replacing `Cell(0)` in the control array with a SumCell that is not part of the control array. To modify the existing code (DYNAM1), simply delete the 0 from the Index property of the first cell of the control array and change its name to `SumCell`. This makes it a distinct control, not a member of a control array. Now, when a cell value is changed, the cells are resummed, but a cascading event does not ensue. The new `Command3_Click` looks like this:

```
Sub Command3_Click ()                ' Sum the values of all text boxes.
    Temp = 0                         ' Temp holds current sum for loop.
    For Index = 1 To MaxId%          ' Start with text box 2; omit sum box.
        Temp = Temp + Val(Cell(Index).Text)
        SumCell.Text = Str$(Temp)
    Next Index
End Sub
```

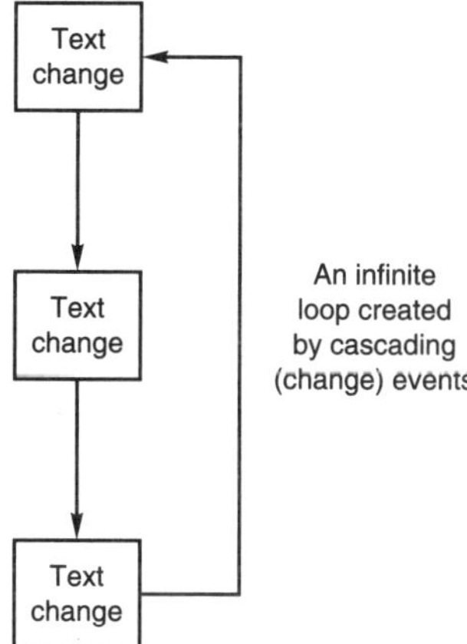

Figure 3.10. Cascading events.

The only change is that `SumCell` (with no index) replaces the `Cell(0)`. Note that you will also have to change all references to `Cell(0)` to `SumCell` (in `Command1_Click`, for example).

The application code, however, still has a problem or two to address. What happens when you remove a cell? The cells have to be resummed; therefore, every time a cell is removed, invoke the `Command3_Click` event procedure:

```
Sub Command2_Click ()
    If MaxId% = 1 Then Exit Sub ' Keep first two text boxes.
    Unload Cell(MaxId%)         ' Delete last text box.

    MaxId% = MaxId% - 1         ' Decrement text box count.
                                ' Previous reference to Cell(0) removed

    Command3_Click
End Sub
```

Add Features: Automatic Mean, Variance, and Standard Deviation

Now that a new mechanism for updating (in general) is in place, you can add controls (and procedures) for finding other values (mean and standard deviation, for example). To automatically update the mean, add a command button for the mean and implement the event. You'll also need a text box to display the mean. I call this text box `MeanCell`. The mean is simply the value of the `SumCell` divided by the number of cells, or, in other words, the mean equals the average:

```
Sub Command4_Click ()
        Temp = Val(SumCell.Text)
        Temp = Temp / MaxId%
        MeanCell.Text = Str$(Temp)
End Sub
```

The standard deviation is a useful way of determining how a group of data points is clustered about the mean. It's a fairly complex-looking equation, where *x* is a data point and *n* is the number of data points (see Figure 3.11).

$$\text{s.d.} = \sqrt{\frac{\Sigma(x-\mu)^2}{N}}$$

Figure 3.11. The standard deviation equation.

The variance (another useful statistic) is the square of the standard deviation (see Figure 3.12):

$$\text{var} = \left[\sqrt{\frac{\Sigma(x-\mu)^2}{N}}\right]^2$$

Figure 3.12. The variance equation.

To find the standard deviation and the variance and to update the text boxes that report the results in Visual Basic, add two command buttons (one for the standard deviation and one for the variance) to the form and implement the following code in response to a standard deviation click:

```
Sub SDev_Click ()
    Dim SD2 As Double
    SumX = 0                             ' Temp holds current sum for loop.
    For Index = 1 To Cell_ID%            ' Start with text box 2; omit sum box.
     SumX = SumX + Val(Cell(Index).Text)
     SumX2 = SumX2 + Val(Cell(Index).Text) * Val(Cell(Index).Text)
    Next Index
    If Cell_ID% <> 1 Then
    SD2 = ((SumX2 - (SumX * SumX) / Cell_ID%)) \ (Cell_ID% - 1)
    SDevi = Sqr(SD2)
    SDCell.Caption = Str$(SDevi)
    VarCell.Caption = Str$(SD2)
    End If
End Sub
```

Note that you also need text boxes to display the standard deviation and variance, called `SDCell` and `VarCell` in the code. Add the `SDev_Click` event to the

`Cell_Change` event procedure so that the standard deviation and the variance also are updated automatically every time a cell changes.

```
Sub Cell_Change (Index As Integer)
    Sum_Click
    Mean_Click
    SDev_Click
End Sub
```

How to Remove Cells Selectively

Let's add two more features: selected cell removal and cell sorting. Previously, users could remove only the "last" cell; it would be much better, however, to allow users to remove a specific cell. First, create a control array of cell labels called `CellLabel` to indicate the name of each corresponding cell. This gives the user the option of labeling each cell. Then you can proceed to handle the selected removal of cells as follows:

- Employ an input box to allow the user to indicate which cell is to be removed. To begin, indicate the cell by indicating its number (as an alternative, use the value of the cell label), and then loop through the cell labels until a match is found.
- If a match is found, the cell count is updated, all the cells are pushed forward, and the last cell (and the cell label) is deleted.
- The cell statistics (mean, standard deviation, and so on) then are automatically triggered and subsequently updated. Previously, you simply used the name `Command2` for the command button that activated a Remove. Let's change this name to `Remove` to make it clearer.

Here's the routine (note that `Cell_Id%` is a general declaration for the form):

```
Sub Remove_Click ()
    If Cell_Id% = 1 Then Exit Sub ' Keep first two text boxes.
    Prompt$ = "Which cell do you want to unload?"
    Response$ = InputBox$(Prompt$, "Remove Cells", "Label")
    Count% = 0
    For Cell_Num% = 2 To Cell_Id%
        If CellLabel(Cell_Num%).Text = Response$ Then
           Count% = Count% + 1
           Index% = Cell_Num% + 1
           For I% = Index% To Cell_Id%
               Cell(I% - 1).Text = Cell(I%).Text
               CellLabel(I% - 1).Text = CellLabel(I%).Text
           Next I%
        End If
```

```
    Next Cell_Num%
    For I% = 1 To (Count%)
        Unload Cell(Cell_Id%)   ' Delete last text box.
        Unload CellLabel(Cell_Id%)
        Cell_Id% = Cell_Id% - 1 ' Decrement text box count.
    Next I%
    Sum_Click
    Mean_Click
    SDev_Click
End Sub
```

Sort Spreadsheet Cells by Sorting Controls

To sort the cells (by label), implement a simple bubble sort. This sort is very efficient in this case because the spreadsheet is limited to a screen full of cells. The bubble sort merely compares adjacent cells and moves (bubbles) the cells toward the beginning if necessary. Note that you must create a temporary cell and a temporary label to hold the values of a cell/label combination intended to bubble down a position. Without the temporary cell/label, you would lose the information in the cell/label being written over during the first stage of the exchange:

```
Sub Sort_Click ()
  Changes% = 0
  If Cell_Id% = 1 Then Exit Sub ' Keep first two text boxes.
  For Num% = 1 To (Cell_Id% - 1)
    For Cell_Num% = 1 To (Cell_Id% - 1)
     S1$ = CellLabel(Cell_Num%).Text
     S2$ = CellLabel(Cell_Num% + 1).Text
     If S1$ > S2$ Then
            TempCell$ = Cell(Cell_Num% + 1).Text
            TempLabel$ = CellLabel(Cell_Num% + 1).Text
            Cell(Cell_Num% + 1).Text = Cell(Cell_Num%).Text
            CellLabel(Cell_Num% + 1).Text = CellLabel(Cell_Num%).Text
            Cell(Cell_Num%).Text = TempCell$
            CellLabel(Cell_Num%).Text = TempLabel$
      End If
    Next Cell_Num%
  Next Num%
  Changes% = -1
End Sub
```

Avoid More Cascading Events

Again, avoid a cascading event. You don't want the cell summation data to be updated every time a cell is bubbled. The `Changes%` variable handles this by acting as a Watch flag. Set `Changes%` to False (0) while the sort is going on. Set `Changes%`

to True (–1) to allow a `Cell_change` event when the sort is done. As the following code demonstrates, a `Cell_Change` event is nullified if the `Changes%` variable isn't True:

```
Sub Cell_Change (Index As Integer)
    If Changes% <> 0 Then      ' Override the change if Changes% is True,
        Sum_Click              ' Otherwise, trigger other events.
        Mean_Click
        SDev_Click
    End If
End Sub
```

Listing 3.2 shows the complete application at this stage:

Listing 3.2. DYNAM1E in progress.

```
' General Declarations
Dim Cell_Id%
Dim Changes%


Sub Form_Load ()
    Cell_Id% = 1
    Changes% = -1
End Sub

Sub Cell_Change (Index As Integer)
    If Changes% <> 0 Then
    Sum_Click
    Mean_Click
    SDev_Click
    End If
End Sub


Sub Add_Click ()                        ' This was Command1_Click in the text.
                                        ' Renamed here for clarity.
    Cell_Id% = Cell_Id% + 1             ' Increment text box count.
    Load Cell(Cell_Id%)                 ' Create new text box.
    Load CellLabel(Cell_Id%)

    Select Case Cell_Id%
    Case Is < 11
     Cell(Cell_Id%).Top = Cell(Cell_Id% - 1).Top + 360
     CellLabel(Cell_Id%).Top = Cell(Cell_Id% - 1).Top + 360
    Case 11
     Cell(Cell_Id%).Top = Cell(1).Top
     Cell(Cell_Id%).Left = Cell(1).Left + 965
```

continues

LISTING 3.2. CONTINUED

```
     CellLabel(Cell_Id%).Top = CellLabel(1).Top
     CellLabel(Cell_Id%).Left = CellLabel(1).Left + 3600
    Case Is > 11
     Cell(Cell_Id%).Left = Cell(1).Left + 965
     Cell(Cell_Id%).Top = Cell(Cell_Id% - 1).Top + 360
     CellLabel(Cell_Id%).Left = CellLabel(1).Left + 3600
     CellLabel(Cell_Id%).Top = CellLabel(Cell_Id% - 1).Top + 360
    End Select

    Cell(Cell_Id%).Visible = -1
    Cell(Cell_Id%).Text = "0"          ' Set value in text box to 0.
    CellLabel(Cell_Id%).Visible = -1
    CellLabel(Cell_Id%).Text = ""      ' Set value in text box to 0.
End Sub


Sub Mean_Click ()
     Temp = Val(SumCell.Caption)       ' This was Command4_Click
     Temp = Temp / Cell_Id%            ' in the text. Renamed here
     MeanCell.Caption = Str$(Temp)     ' for clarity.
                                       ' MeanCell has been changed
                                       ' from a text box to a label
                                       ' to save resources.
End Sub


Sub Remove_Click ()
    If Cell_Id% = 1 Then Exit Sub ' Keep first two text boxes.
    Prompt$ = "Which cell do you want to unload?"
    Response$ = InputBox$(Prompt$, "Remove Cells", "Label")
    Count% = 0
    For Cell_Num% = 2 To Cell_Id%
     If CellLabel(Cell_Num%).Text = Response$ Then
         Count% = Count% + 1
         Index% = Cell_Num% + 1
         For I% = Index% To Cell_Id%
          Cell(I% - 1).Text = Cell(I%).Text
          CellLabel(I% - 1).Text = CellLabel(I%).Text
         Next I%
     End If
    Next Cell_Num%
    For I% = 1 To (Count%)
     Unload Cell(Cell_Id%)     ' Delete last text box.
     Unload CellLabel(Cell_Id%)
     Cell_Id% = Cell_Id% - 1   ' Decrement text box count.
    Next I%
    Sum_Click
    Mean_Click
```

```
    SDev_Click
End Sub


Sub SDev_Click ()
    Dim SD2 As Double
    SumX = 0                          ' Temp holds current sum for loop.
    For Index = 1 To Cell_Id%         ' Start with text box 2; omit sum box.
     SumX = SumX + Val(Cell(Index).Text)
     SumX2 = SumX2 + Val(Cell(Index).Text) * Val(Cell(Index).Text)
    Next Index
    If Cell_Id% <> 1 Then
    SD2 = ((SumX2 - (SumX * SumX) / Cell_Id%)) \ (Cell_Id% - 1)
    SDevi = Sqr(SD2)                  ' SDCell and VarCell have been changed
    SDCell.Caption = Str$(SDevi)      ' from text boxes to labels to save
                                      ' resources.
    VarCell.Caption = Str$(SD2)
    End If
End Sub


Sub Sum_Click ()
    Temp = 0                          ' Temp holds current sum for loop.
    For Index = 1 To Cell_Id%         ' Start with text box 2; omit sum box.
     Temp = Temp + Val(Cell(Index).Text)
     SumCell.Caption = Str$(Temp)
    Next Index

End Sub


Sub Sort_Click ()
    Changes% = 0
    If Cell_Id% = 1 Then Exit Sub ' Keep first two text boxes.
    For Num% = 1 To (Cell_Id% - 1)
       For Cell_Num% = 1 To (Cell_Id% - 1)
     S1$ = CellLabel(Cell_Num%).Text
     S2$ = CellLabel(Cell_Num% + 1).Text
     If S1$ > S2$ Then
          TempCell$ = Cell(Cell_Num% + 1).Text
          TempLabel$ = CellLabel(Cell_Num% + 1).Text
          Cell(Cell_Num% + 1).Text = Cell(Cell_Num%).Text
          CellLabel(Cell_Num% + 1).Text = CellLabel(Cell_Num%).Text
          Cell(Cell_Num%).Text = TempCell$
          CellLabel(Cell_Num%).Text = TempLabel$
     End If
       Next Cell_Num%
    Next Num%
    Changes% = -1
End Sub
```

How to Save and Reload Spreadsheet Data

Finally, complete this application by saving and reloading cell (spreadsheet) databases. A simple sequential I/O routine handles it. For each cell, save the label and the corresponding text for the label:

```
Sub Save_Click ()
    FNum% = FreeFile
    Open "Test.Dbs" For Output As FNum%
    Write #FNum%, Str$(Cell_ID%)
    For I% = 1 To Cell_ID%
        Write #FNum%, Cell(I%).Text
        Write #FNum%, CellLabel(I%).Text
    Next I%
    Close FNum%
End Sub
```

Then reverse the process to retrieve the data:

```
Sub LoadDb_Click ()
    FNum% = FreeFile    ' Determine next file number.
    Open "Test.Dbs" For Input As FNum%
    Input #FNum%, Num$

    Num_Cells% = Val(Num$)
    For I% = 2 To (Num_Cells%)
        Add_Click
    Next I%
    I% = 1
    While Not EOF(FNum%)
        Input #FNum%, StringData$
        Cell(I%).Text = StringData$
        Input #FNum%, StringData$
        CellLabel(I%).Text = StringData$
        I% = I% + 1
    Wend
    Close FNum%
End Sub
```

There you have it, a simple but useful automatic updating modeling spreadsheet system that enables a user to add and selectively delete cells, save and reload databases, and sort the current database. Figures 3.13 and 3.14 show the application running.

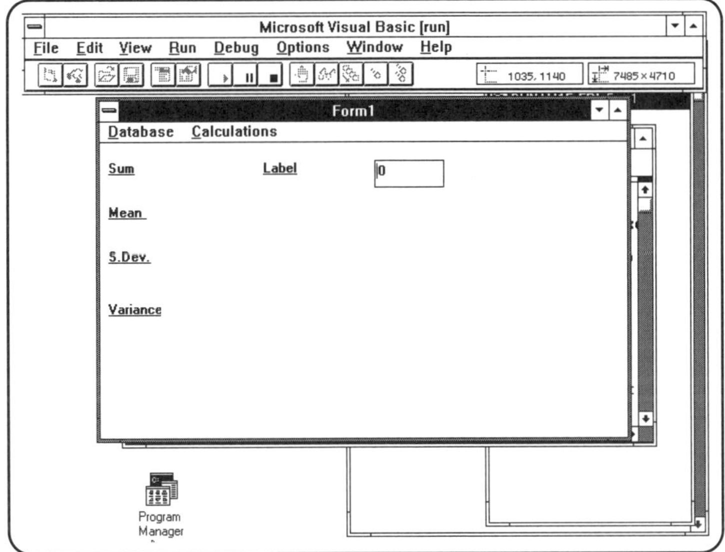

Figure 3.13. DYNAM1E at startup.

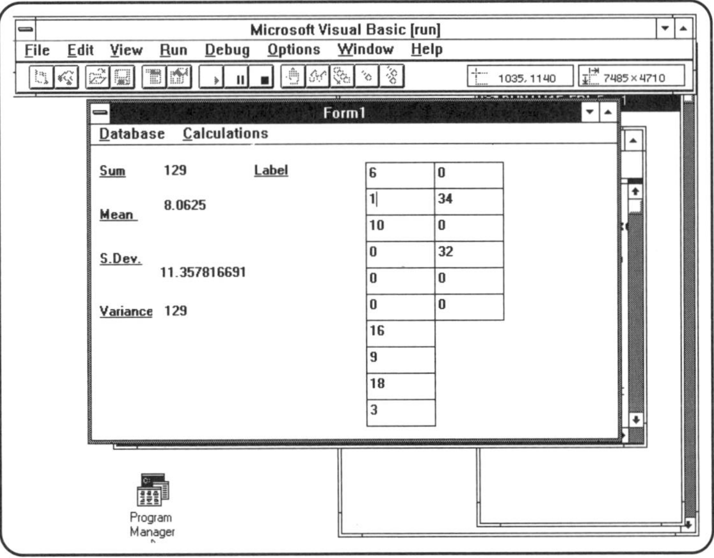

Figure 3.14. DYNAM1E after automatic cell updating.

Listing 3.3 shows the complete application.

LISTING 3.3. DYNAM1E.

```
' Form-level declarations

Dim Cell_ID%
Dim Changes%


' Events


Sub Form_Load ()
    Cell_ID% = 1
    Changes% = -1
End Sub

Sub Cell_Change (Index As Integer)
    If Changes% <> 0 Then
    Sum_Click
    Mean_Click
    SDev_Click
    End If
End Sub


Sub Add_Click ()
    Cell_ID% = Cell_ID% + 1              ' Increment text box count.
    Load Cell(Cell_ID%)                  ' Create new text box.
    Load CellLabel(Cell_ID%)

    Select Case Cell_ID%
    Case Is < 11
     Cell(Cell_ID%).Top = Cell(Cell_ID% - 1).Top + 360
     CellLabel(Cell_ID%).Top = Cell(Cell_ID% - 1).Top + 360
    Case 11
     Cell(Cell_ID%).Top = Cell(1).Top
     Cell(Cell_ID%).Left = Cell(1).Left + 965
     CellLabel(Cell_ID%).Top = CellLabel(1).Top
     CellLabel(Cell_ID%).Left = CellLabel(1).Left + 3600
    Case Is > 11
     Cell(Cell_ID%).Left = Cell(1).Left + 965
     Cell(Cell_ID%).Top = Cell(Cell_ID% - 1).Top + 360
     CellLabel(Cell_ID%).Left = CellLabel(1).Left + 3600
     CellLabel(Cell_ID%).Top = CellLabel(Cell_ID% - 1).Top + 360
    End Select

    Cell(Cell_ID%).Visible = -1
    Cell(Cell_ID%).Text = "0"          ' Set value in text box to 0.
    CellLabel(Cell_ID%).Visible = -1
```

```
    CellLabel(Cell_ID%).Text = ""      ' Set value in text box to 0.
End Sub


' Find the mean of cells

Sub Mean_Click ()
     Temp = Val(SumCell.Caption)
     Temp = Temp / Cell_ID%
     MeanCell.Caption = Str$(Temp)

End Sub


' Selective removal of cells

Sub Remove_Click ()
    If Cell_ID% = 1 Then Exit Sub ' Keep first two text boxes.
    Prompt$ = "Which cell do you want to unload?"
    Response$ = InputBox$(Prompt$, "Remove Cells", "Label")
    Count% = 0
    For Cell_Num% = 2 To Cell_ID%
     If CellLabel(Cell_Num%).Text = Response$ Then
         Count% = Count% + 1
         Index% = Cell_Num% + 1
         For I% = Index% To Cell_ID%
          Cell(I% - 1).Text = Cell(I%).Text
          CellLabel(I% - 1).Text = CellLabel(I%).Text
         Next I%
     End If
    Next Cell_Num%
    For I% = 1 To (Count%)
     Unload Cell(Cell_ID%)    ' Delete last text box.
     Unload CellLabel(Cell_ID%)
     Cell_ID% = Cell_ID% - 1 ' Decrement text box count.
    Next I%
    Sum_Click
    Mean_Click
    SDev_Click
End Sub


' Standard deviation event

Sub SDev_Click ()
    Dim SD2 As Double
    SumX = 0                          ' Temp holds current sum for loop.
    For Index = 1 To Cell_ID%         ' Start with text box 2; omit sum box.
     SumX = SumX + Val(Cell(Index).Text)
```

continues

LISTING 3.3. CONTINUED

```
     SumX2 = SumX2 + Val(Cell(Index).Text) * Val(Cell(Index).Text)
    Next Index
    If Cell_ID% <> 1 Then
    SD2 = ((SumX2 - (SumX * SumX) / Cell_ID%)) \ (Cell_ID% - 1)
    SDevi = Sqr(SD2)
    SDCell.Caption = Str$(SDevi)
    VarCell.Caption = Str$(SD2)
    End If
End Sub


' Sum event

Sub Sum_Click ()
    Temp = 0                           ' Temp holds current sum for loop.
    For Index = 1 To Cell_ID%          ' Start with text box 2; omit sum box.
     Temp = Temp + Val(Cell(Index).Text)
     SumCell.Caption = Str$(Temp)
    Next Index

End Sub


' Sort cells

Sub Sort_Click ()
    Changes% = 0
    If Cell_ID% = 1 Then Exit Sub      ' Keep first two text boxes.
    For Num% = 1 To (Cell_ID% - 1)
       For Cell_Num% = 1 To (Cell_ID% - 1)
     S1$ = CellLabel(Cell_Num%).Text
     S2$ = CellLabel(Cell_Num% + 1).Text
     If S1$ > S2$ Then
          TempCell$ = Cell(Cell_Num% + 1).Text
          TempLabel$ = CellLabel(Cell_Num% + 1).Text
          Cell(Cell_Num% + 1).Text = Cell(Cell_Num%).Text
          CellLabel(Cell_Num% + 1).Text = CellLabel(Cell_Num%).Text
          Cell(Cell_Num%).Text = TempCell$
          CellLabel(Cell_Num%).Text = TempLabel$
     End If
       Next Cell_Num%
    Next Num%
    Changes% = -1
End Sub


' Save a database
```

```
Sub Save_Click ()
    FNum% = FreeFile
    Open "Test.Dbs" For Output As FNum%
    Write #FNum%, Str$(Cell_ID%)
    For I% = 1 To Cell_ID%
     Write #FNum%, Cell(I%).Text
     Write #FNum%, CellLabel(I%).Text
    Next I%
    Close FNum%
End Sub


' Load a database

Sub LoadDb_Click ()
    FNum% = FreeFile    ' Determine next file number.
    Open "Test.Dbs" For Input As FNum%
    Input #FNum%, Num$

    Num_Cells% = Val(Num$)
    For I% = 2 To (Num_Cells%)
     Add_Click
    Next I%
    I% = 1
    While Not EOF(FNum%)
     Input #FNum%, StringData$
     Cell(I%).Text = StringData$
     Input #FNum%, StringData$
     CellLabel(I%).Text = StringData$
     I% = I% + 1
    Wend
    Close FNum%
End Sub
```

In Chapter 14, "Using the Grid Custom Control and the Bonus PRHALL.VBX," you'll develop another approach to creating and using spreadsheets.

How to Control the Tab Order

By default, Visual Basic assigns tab order to controls in the order in which you draw them on a form. Each new control is placed last in the tab order. You can change this order at design time with the Properties bar, or at runtime through code.

To change tab order at design time:

1. Click a control to select it.
2. Select `TabIndex` from the Properties list box. (Visual Basic displays the current tab position in the Settings box.)
3. Enter the number for the tab order position you want the control to have.
4. Click the Enter button.

You can determine the tab order of controls at design time by pressing Tab.

To enable or disable a tab stop at design time:

1. Click a control to select it.
2. Select `TabStop` from the Properties list box. (Visual Basic displays the current Boolean value in the Settings box.)
3. Select True to designate the control as a tab stop, or False to bypass the control.
4. Click the Enter button.

When you change a control's tab order position, Visual Basic automatically renumbers the tab order positions of other controls to reflect insertions and deletions. All controls except menus and timers are included in the tab order. At runtime, invisible or disabled controls and controls that cannot receive the focus (frames and labels) remain in the tab order; they are bypassed, however, when you tab through controls.

A control whose `TabStop` property has been set to False still maintains its position in the actual tab order as set by the `TabIndex` property, even though the control is skipped when you tab through controls (with the Tab key).

If TABINDEX < 0, Visual Basic generates an error.

Make the User's Life Easier: Create Dynamic Menus

Visual Basic also makes it easy to add menu items at runtime—you can create a menu that contains a menu control array. A menu control array consists of one or more menu items that share event procedures and a common name. Every menu item has a unique index number, but all the items have the same `Name` value. You can designate one or more contiguous menu items as a control array. After the control array is set up, users of the application can dynamically add or remove menu items at runtime.

This application (DYNAM2 on the disk) uses a menu control array to add and delete applications from the menu (these applications are named by the user at runtime). This application shows you how to add and remove menu items. Later, Chapter 11, "Into the Heart of OLE," returns to this application and uses its dynamic nature in conjunction with file I/O to create an application shell. See Chapter 11 for more details.

In general, to create a menu control array with only one item:

1. Create the menu item.
2. Enter a number in the Index text box.

To create a menu control array with more than one menu item:

1. Create a menu item.
2. Enter a number in the Index text box. This number determines the menu item's position within the control array.
3. Create another menu item with the same control name.
4. Enter a different number in the Index text box.
5. Repeat Steps 2 through 4 for each additional menu item.

Visual Basic handles the control array as follows: When a control in the array recognizes an event, Visual Basic calls an event procedure for the group and passes the index as an additional argument, enabling the application to determine which control recognizes the event. Let's create the application.

Step 1. Use the default form.

Step 2. Add the controls (because there are no controls this time, however, ignore this step).

Step 3. Add the menu. (Here's where the work starts.)

Open the Menu Design window and create the following menu items with the specifications shown in Table 3.1:

- Applications
- Add Application
- Remove Application

TABLE 3.1. DYNAM2 MENU CONTROLS AND PROPERTY SETTINGS.

Caption	*Name*	*Indented*	*Index*
Applications	`Applica`	No	
Add Application	`AddCom`	Yes (1)	
Remove Application	`RemoveCom`	Yes (1)	
(no caption)*	`AppName`	Yes (1)	0

*Leave the caption box blank.

Also, uncheck the Visible property box on the item with no caption and make the new menu item visible by setting the `Visible` property in code every time a menu item is added. Figure 3.15 shows the menu design window in one stage of development.

Enter a number in the Index text box of `AppName` to indicate a control array (see Figure 3.16).

Step 4. Set the form and control properties.

Change the name of the form caption to read Dynamic Menus (see Figures 3.16 and 3.17).

Step 5. Write event and general procedures.

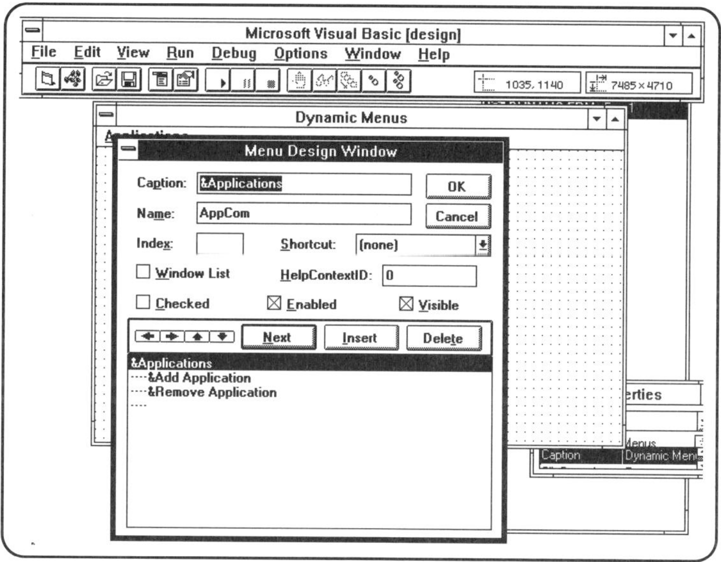

Figure 3.15. The menu design window in one stage of development.

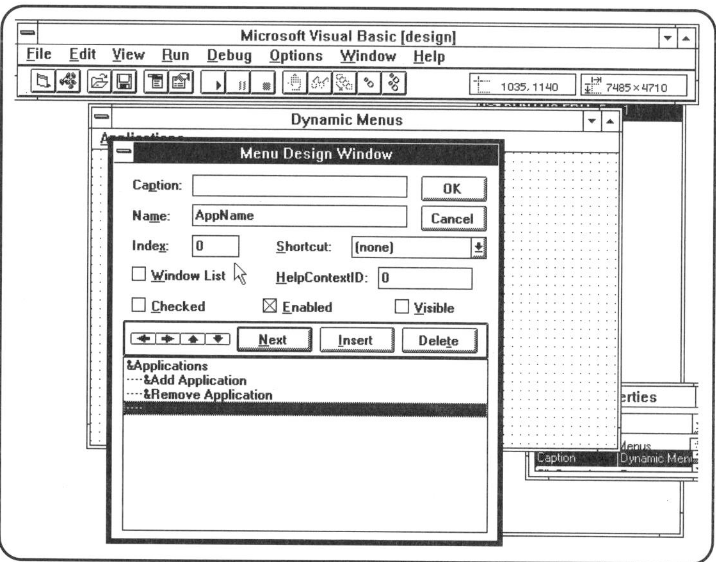

Figure 3.16. Use index to indicate a control array.

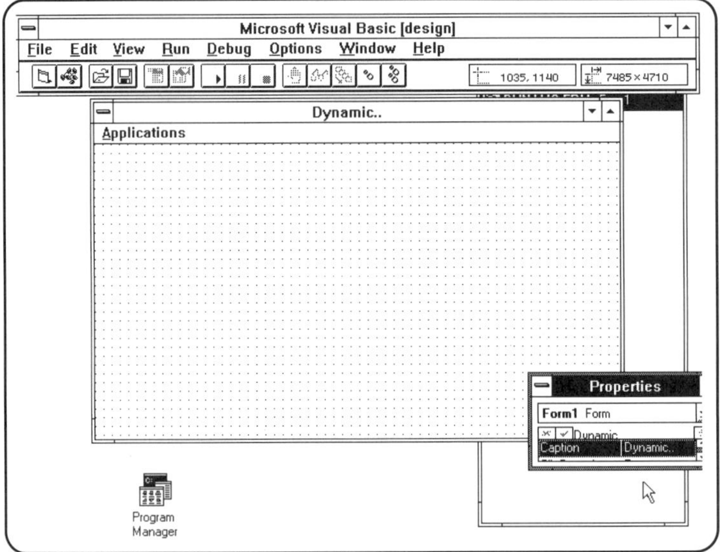

Figure 3.17. The dynamic menus form caption.

Use the `Load` statement to dynamically add a menu item to the menu control array at runtime:

```
Load AppName(MenuNum)   ' MenuNum is the next available index #
```

Use the `Unload` statement to dynamically remove a menu item from the menu control array at runtime:

```
Unload AppName(MenuNum)
```

Note that `AppName` is the `Name` of the menu item for which you set the index earlier. Note also that `MenuNum` must be a nonlocal variable; declare it in the general declarations of the application:

```
Dim MenuNum As Integer   ' if in the global declarations section of the form
```

or in the global module:

```
Global MenuNum As Integer     ' if in the global module
```

To indicate that an item will be added to the menu at runtime, open the code window by first double-clicking the `Add Application` item in the menu (in design mode) (see Figure 3.18).

To indicate that an item is to be added or removed, write the code to add or delete menu items using the `Load` and `Unload` statements (see Figure 3.19).

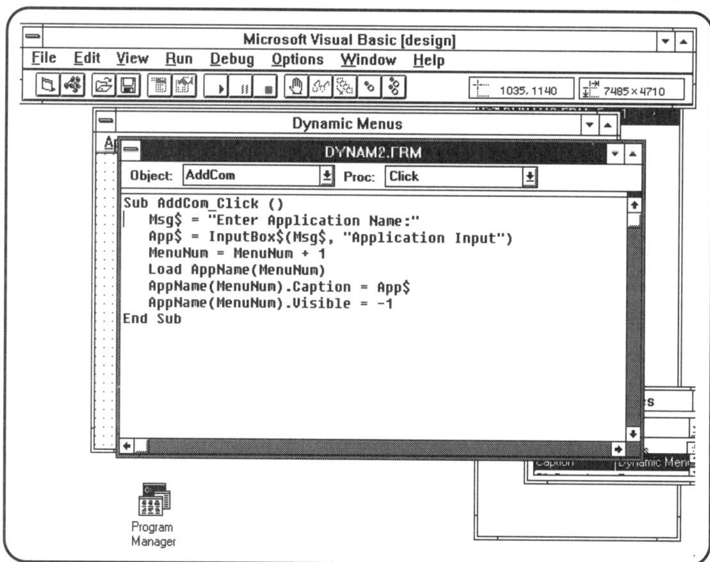

Figure 3.18. The code window view.

To add an item:

```
Sub AddCom_Click ()
   Dim App$
   Msg$ = "Enter Application Name:"
   App$ = InputBox$(Msg$, "Application Input")     ' Use an input box to
   MenuNum = MenuNum + 1                            ' communicate with user.
   Load AppName(MenuNum)                            ' Load the application.
   AppName(MenuNum).Caption = App$                  ' Set its caption.
   AppName(MenuNum).Visible = -1                    ' Make it visible.
End Sub
```

To remove an item:

```
Sub RemoveCom_Click ()
    Msg$ = "Enter the number of the menu item to remove"
    Num% = Val(InputBox$(Msg$))                ' Communicate with user.
    If Num% > MenuNum Or Num% < 1 Then         ' Verify that number is legitimate.
           MsgBox "Number is out of range."
           Exit Sub                            ' If not, bail out.
    End If
```

```
    For I% = Num% To MenuNum - 1              ' Reorder applications.
        AppName(I%).Caption = AppName(I% + 1).Caption
    Next I%
    Unload AppName(MenuNum)                   ' Unload this application.
    MenuNum = MenuNum - 1                     ' Reset number of active applications.
End Sub
```

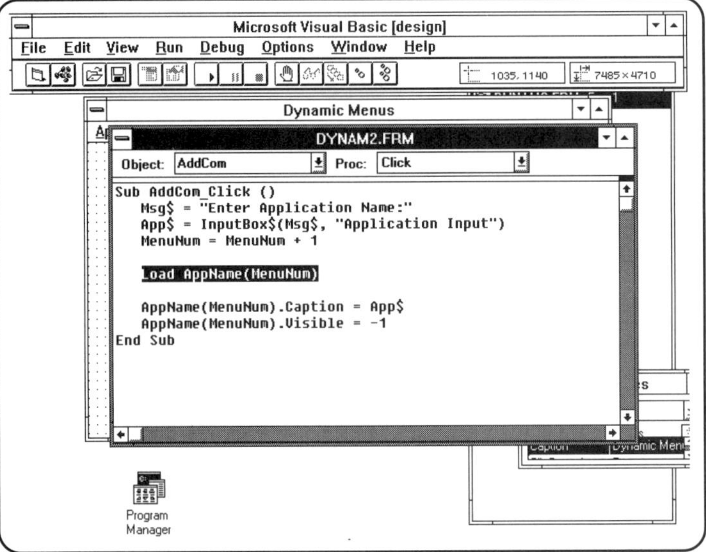

Figure 3.19. Use Load and Unload to add or delete menu items.

Next, write the code to indicate what happens when a user selects a new menu item:

```
Sub AppName_Click (Index As Integer)
    MsgBox (AppName(Index).Caption)     ' Just identify the selected application.
End Sub
```

Modify the `Form Load` event to set any nonlocal variables at start-up:

```
Sub Form_Load ()
    MenuNum= 0
End Sub
```

It's useful to use the start-up form's Load event to initialize nonlocal variables.

The complete code for DYNAM2 is contained in Listing 3.4.

Listing 3.4. DYNAM2.

```
' general declarations

Dim MenuNum As Integer


' AddCom event

Sub AddCom_Click ()
   Msg$ = "Enter Application Name:"
   App$ = InputBox$(Msg$, "Application Input")
   MenuNum = MenuNum + 1 if App$ = " " then exit Sub
   Load AppName(MenuNum)
   AppName(MenuNum).Caption = App$
   AppName(MenuNum).Visible = -1        ' Set to visible because AppName
End Sub                                 ' is set to NOT visible in menu design.


' AppName event

Sub AppName_Click (Index As Integer)  ' Each dynamically added application
    MsgBox (AppName(Index).Caption)   ' will use this event.
End Sub


' RemoveCom event

Sub RemoveCom_Click ()
    Msg$ = "Enter the number of the menu item to delete"
    Num% = Val(InputBox$(Msg$))
    If Num% > MenuNum Or Num% < 1 Then
           MsgBox "Number is out of range."
           Exit Sub
    End If
    For I% = Num% To MenuNum - 1
        AppName(I%).Caption = AppName(I% + 1).Caption
    Next I%
    Unload AppName(MenuNum)
```

continues

LISTING 3.4. CONTINUED

```
    MenuNum = MenuNum - 1
End Sub


' form event

Sub Form_Click ()
    MenuNum = 0
End Sub
```

Note that the `AppName.Visible` property must be set to visible every time a new application is added to the menu. This step is necessary because `AppName.Visible` is set to invisible during menu design. If it is not set to invisible (by unchecking the Visible box during menu design), a blank line appears in the menu. *The Visual Basic Programmer's Guide* (page 117), one of the Visual Basic manuals, suggests that the caption property be set to a hyphen (-) to indicate a separator bar when you add menu items dynamically. However, this action doesn't really create the desired effect because a separator bar appears every time you add a new menu item dynamically. As a test, change the `AppName Caption` property to a hyphen (-) and the `AppName.Visible` property to `Visible` (using the Check box in menu design) and review the results.

Run the application. Figure 3.20 shows the input box displayed after the Add Application menu item is selected. Figure 3.21 shows a message box displayed to indicate that one of the added applications has been selected. Figure 3.22 shows the input box requesting the menu item number to be removed. Figure 3.23 shows the `Out of range` error message.

At runtime, you cannot remove commands created during design time.

SYSTEM COMMANDS: USING SHELL

To get an idea of how powerful a menu control array can be, let's modify this application slightly to use the `Shell` command (a system command) to run an application based on the name (and path) in the array. The following code modification—adding the `Shell` command and removing the message box just used—does the trick:

```
Sub AppName_Click (Index As Integer)
    x = Shell(AppName(Index).Caption, 1)    ' x (the return value) isn't used
here.
End Sub
```

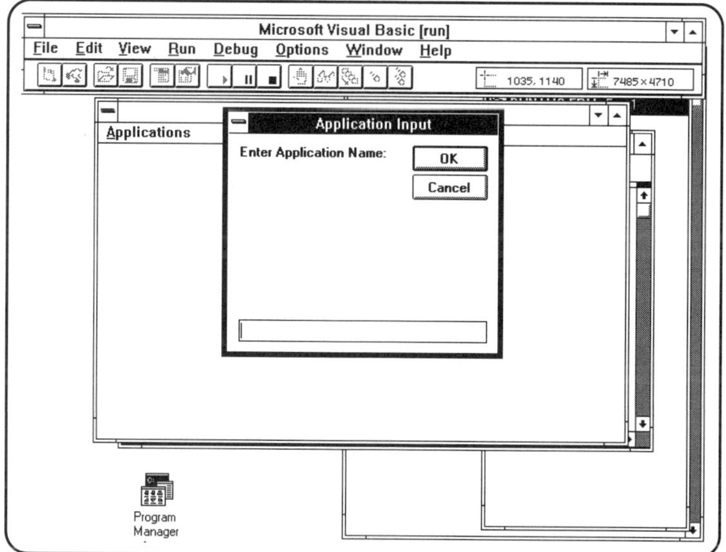

Figure 3.20. The Add Application Input box.

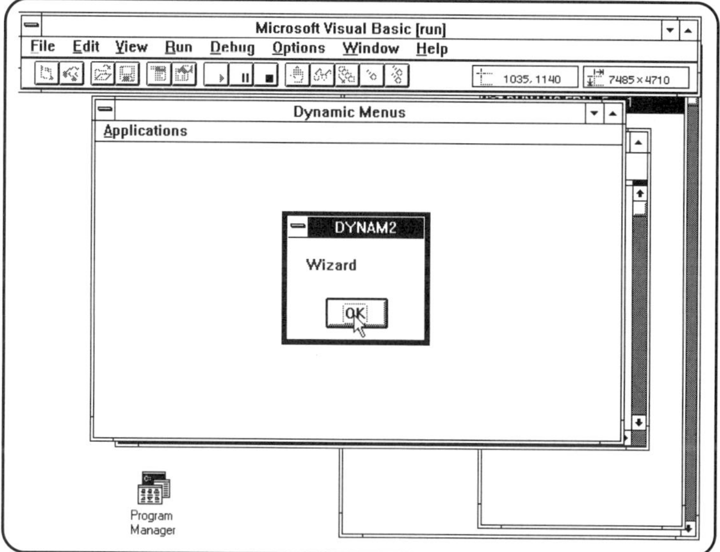

Figure 3.21. A message box is displayed to indicate that one of the added applications has been selected.

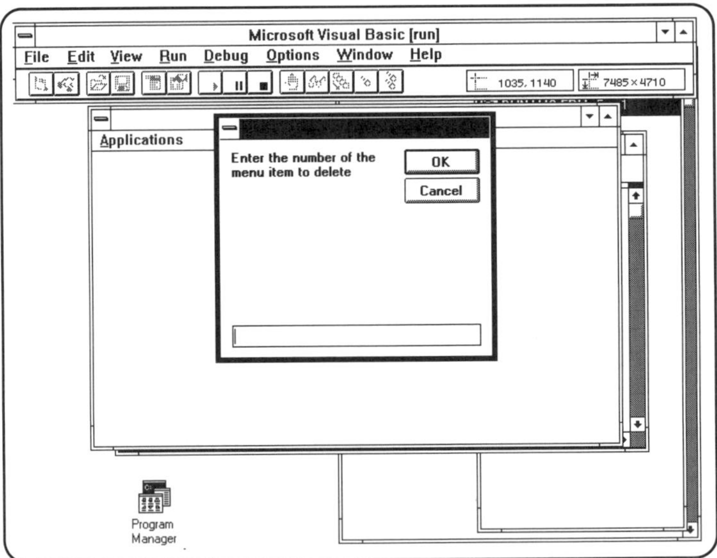

Figure 3.22. The input box requesting the menu item number to be removed.

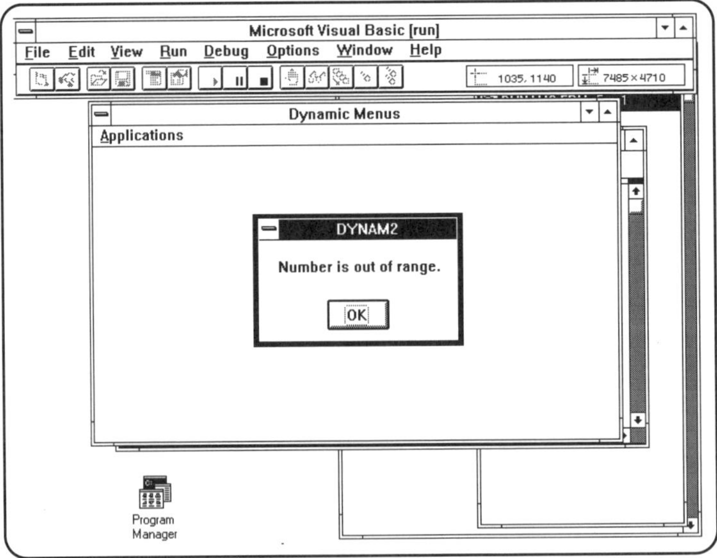

Figure 3.23. The out of range error message.

Now, when a user clicks the application in the menu, the application's `Click` event procedure tries to *shell out* (that is, execute) the application. The `"1"` in the `Shell` command indicates that the application should be run in a normal window, and that the application should get the focus. Alternatively, you can run the application (using `Shell`) in minimized and maximized windows and give the application the focus or not. Figure 3.24 shows a complete pathname for an application entered in the input box.

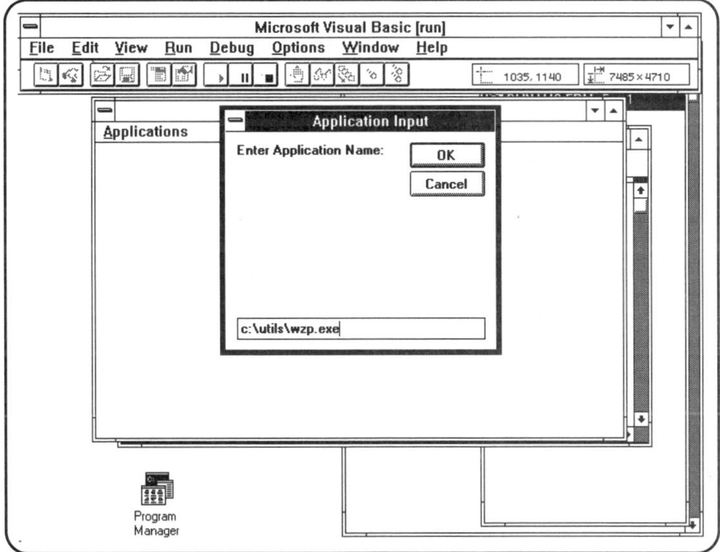

Figure 3.24. A complete pathname for an application entered in the input box.

Figure 3.25 shows the results of executing the `Shell` command after the application is clicked. This application (called `WZP`) is a DOS-based, not a Windows-based, application I wrote in Turbo Pascal (without Windows support). The `Shell` command, therefore, is very flexible; it can run both Windows-specific and non-Windows applications. The complete code for DYNAM3 is contained in Listing 3.5. Note that Figure 3.25 indicates which DOS application is running, but does not show the application itself. In this example, `WZP` is running in the background and Windows is running in the foreground.

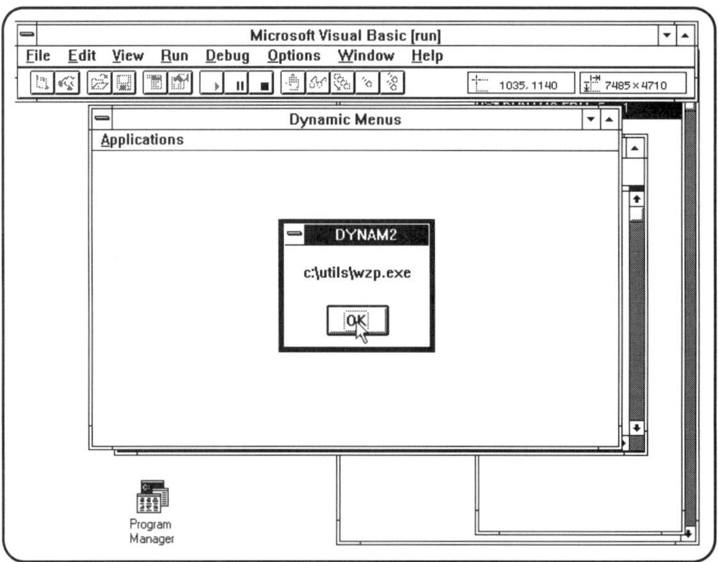

Figure 3.25. A message indicating that a DOS-based application is running in the background.

LISTING 3.5. DYNAM3.

```
' general declarations

Dim MenuNum As Integer



' AddCom event

Sub AddCom_Click ()
   Msg$ = "Enter Application Name:"
   ZApp$ = InputBox$(Msg$, "Application Input")
   MenuNum = MenuNum + 1
   Load AppName(MenuNum)
   AppName(MenuNum).Caption = ZApp$
   AppName(MenuNum).Visible = -1
End Sub


' AppName event

Sub AppName_Click (Index As Integer)
    ' MsgBox (AppName(Index).Caption)
```

```
    x = Shell(AppName(Index).Caption, 1)     ' Run the application.
End Sub


' ReMoveCom event

Sub RemoveCom_Click ()
    Msg$ = "Enter the number of the menu item to remove"
    Num% = Val(InputBox$(Msg$))
    If Num% > MenuNum Or Num% < 1 Then
           MsgBox "Number is out of range."
           Exit Sub
    End If
    For I% = Num% To MenuNum - 1
        AppName(I%).Caption = AppName(I% + 1).Caption
    Next I%
    Unload AppName(MenuNum)
    MenuNum = MenuNum - 1
End Sub


' form event

Sub Form_Load ()
    MenuItem = 0
End Sub
```

You might have noticed that this application (DYNAM3) is still somewhat crude. For example, if a user inputs an incorrect pathname, the application explodes. Not good. Also, if a user enters the same name for the application (in either DYNAM2 or DYNAM3), duplicate application names will exist in the menu. For a better approach to both of these problems, see the improved applications in Chapter 11.

Use Dynamic Arrays to Conserve Memory

Before abandoning dynamic matters of this sort for a chapter or two, I will provide a little more detail about one other important dynamic capability of Visual Basic: the dynamic array.

Dynamic arrays, you will recall, are arrays that can be resized at runtime. Resizing an array at runtime is convenient when:

1. The size of the array you need during design time is unknown.
2. You want to use an array briefly and then discard it in order to reclaim the memory it was using.

To create a dynamic array that is local to a procedure, use the Dim and ReDim statements in conjunction. First, use the Dim statement without dimensions to declare an array; then use the ReDim Statement at the procedure level to actually dimension the array. The ReDim statement, therefore, allocates the storage space for the array. After the procedure returns, the memory allocated by ReDim is returned also to the application.

You can dimension (Dim) a dynamic array this way:

```
Dim TestArray() As Integer     ' Declare dynamic array.
```

Then, ReDim it:

```
Size = 50
ReDim TestArray(Size)       ' ReDim array with Size elements.
```

In Versions 1.0 and 2.0, the size of any numeric array (including dynamic arrays) is limited to 65,535 bytes. In Version 3.0, arrays can be huge—as large as 64M in Windows enhanced mode and 1M in Windows standard mode. Arrays larger than 64K, however, cannot include variable-length strings or arrays of objects (such as forms).

The ReDim statement initializes all elements of numeric arrays to zero and all elements of string arrays to null strings. The fields of record variables are initialized to zero, including fixed-length string elements. The maximum number of dimensions you can specify with ReDim is eight if you first define the array with Dim. If your array requires more than eight dimensions, use the ReDim statement within a Sub or Function procedure to initially declare a local dynamic array variable, and omit Dim altogether. When you declare a local dynamic array variable in this manner, your array can have as many as 60 dimensions.

You can use the ReDim statement repeatedly to change the number of elements in an array. However, you cannot use ReDim to change the number of dimensions in an array. For example, if you declare an array with two dimensions (for example, ReDim A(30,30)), you cannot later use ReDim to change it to an array with three dimensions (for example, ReDim A(15,15,15)). Similarly, you cannot declare an array of integers and later use ReDim to change it to some other data type.

You can use the ReDim statement also to declare or resize an array of user-defined types. For example, you can declare a variable Employee as a user-defined type and then let the ReDim statement allocate space for an array called Staff that consists of 250 employees:

```
' global declarations

    Type Employee
         Name As String
         Salary As Integer
    End Type


' general declarations

    Dim Staff() As Employee


' procedure-level allocation

Sub SomeSub
    ReDim Staff(1 To 250)
    '....do something with Staff here.
End Sub
```

Note that a user-defined type declaration (using the `Type` statement) can occur in only the global module in Version 1.0. A user-defined type declaration can occur in any code module in Version 2.0 or Version 3.0. The `ReDim` statement can be used in only a procedure.

By delaying the actual size allocation of the array in this manner, no memory is allocated needlessly. The type `Staff()` is declared (with `Dim`), but memory for it is never allocated until the `ReDim` statement is used in the procedure `SomeSub`. Also, the memory allocated for `Staff` at the procedure level is recovered after the application exits the procedure if the `Dim` statement occurs with the procedure. If the `Dim` statement is used as a general declaration to declare the array, memory is not recovered after the application exits the procedure. If you need to manipulate the size of the array or conserve memory, dynamic arrays are a great way to go.

One final, small dynamic example for this chapter (in Listing 3.6; called DYNAM4 on the disk) uses `ReDim` to size a dynamic array that previously was declared with a `Dim` statement (in a global declaration). The array size is determined by the size of a file, in this case the AUTOEXEC.BAT file, in the root directory.

File I/O in this example is handled a byte at a time—each byte of the file is stored in a byte of the array. The array then is converted to a string a byte at a time and displayed in a text box. Note that all this conversion from array to string to text box is cumbersome and is used here only for demonstrative purposes. Chapter 6, "Files, Directories, and a Code Wizard," and 9, "Extending Visual Basic: Custom Controls and DLLs," discuss file I/O in detail to discover better ways of handling data and files. I'm using file I/O to demonstrate quickly how you can dynamically allocate an array depending on some variable in the application, in this case, File Size. Figure 3.26 shows the application in motion (it uses a text box control (Text1)) to display results.

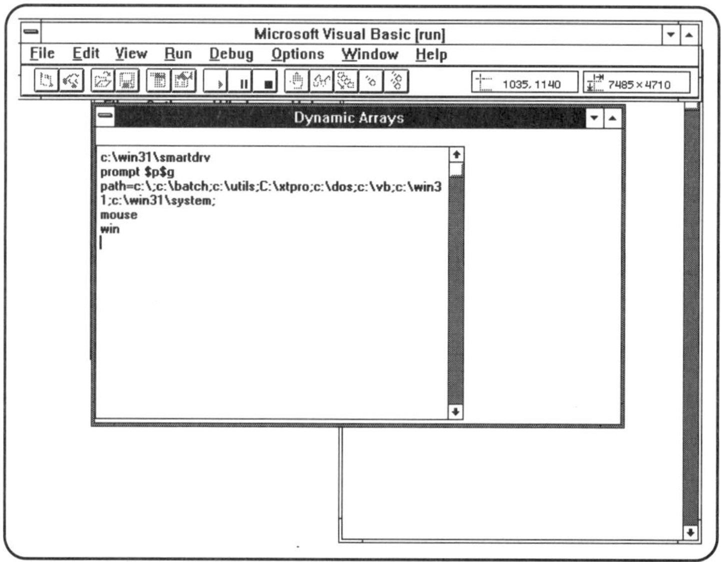

Figure 3.26. The DYNAM4 application in motion.

LISTING 3.6. DYNAM4.

```
' General Declarations
Dim TestArray() As String  ' Declare dynamic array.
Dim Size As Integer        ' Declare integer variable.

Sub Form_Click ()
    DynamicArrayApp
End Sub

Sub DynamicArrayApp ()
    V$ = String$(1, " ")
    FNum% = FreeFile
    Open "c:\autoexec.bat" For Binary As FNum%
    FileLength% = LOF(FNum%)
    ReDim TestArray(FileLength%)
    I% = 0
    While Not EOF(FNum%)
         Get FNum%, , V$
```

```
            TestArray(I%) = V$      ' Put a random number in each array element.
            I% = I% + 1
        Wend
        Close FNum%
        Stri$ = ""
        For I% = 0 To FileLength% - 1
           Stri$ = Stri$ + TestArray(I%)
        Next I%
        Text1.Text = Stri$
End Sub
```

Summary

That's it for this stage of dynamic development. Use the examples in this chapter as models for your own applications that use dynamic controls, menus, and arrays. Dynamic components are some of the most flexible and convenient tools in your Visual Basic bag of tricks. They are so important, in fact, that you will use them repeatedly.

Using Numbers and Forms

A basic aspect of computing is the manipulation of numbers. In this chapter you'll develop several applications that manipulate numbers in a playful (and useful) way. In addition, these applications explore several optional user interfaces you can create with Visual Basic. Because Visual Basic supplies you with so many tools and so many options for using those tools, you can vary these interfaces considerably and still not give up any Windows compatibility. Each application in this chapter illustrates some design variation.

The first application uses a single form to control several functions. The second and third applications use one form per function and a `StartUp` form to kick off the application. As these applications show, it's easy to construct an application of one or many forms. Each form, in turn, can be a complete, self-controlling application, a component of a larger application, or both.

Although this chapter focuses on using controls to display and manipulate numbers, it also discusses some important design issues. For example, when should you extend an application to more than one form? How

Why Use a Nonlocal Variable?

Text Box Formatting Issues

Recap: Tab Order of Controls

Make the User's Life Easier: Use Keyboard Shortcuts

Show and Hide Multiforms: Memory and Access Considerations

Build a Simple Memory Check Application

many controls should be put on a single form? Should a main (`StartUp`) form control the showing and hiding of subsidiary forms, or should that be determined by the individual forms?

The first application in this chapter (called MATH1 on the disk in the back of this book) uses a single form to display and manipulate all the controls needed to support two functions. Because these two functions do not use all of the same controls (which are attached to a single form), MATH1 shows and hides controls each time the user requests a function. The second and third applications (MATH2 and MATH2b) use two forms to control the two functions and a third form to control the application. By using a `StartUp` (or managing) form, you can create powerful multitasking systems, and these applications will show you the way.

This chapter explores the differences in the various designs and code of the applications. Ideally, the material in this chapter shows you how to apply *your* design preferences to *your* applications. Remember that there is no single way to design applications for Windows (or any other environment) that is necessarily best for every situation; it is best to explore, to be creative.

You may find it helpful to load the projects from the *Secrets* disk into Visual Basic and familiarize yourself with the active application while you read the application discussions.

PUT TWO MATH FUNCTIONS ON A SINGLE FORM

Here's the plan. Some of you undoubtedly remember the (good?) old days when you had to calculate such mathematical "entities" as square roots, means, standard deviations, and so on by hand. At the very least, you needed to understand generally how these kinds of calculations worked. (I hope I don't reveal my age here.) I think that you may get a kick out of the kinds of examples explored in this chapter and in the following chapter (the rest of you can apply the design concepts of these examples to your own applications, so don't feel left out).

MATH1 uses a single form and two sets of controls to handle user input and its own output for two functions: calculating the square root of a number and determining the greatest common divisor of two numbers. To help illustrate, the two functions display their output as they calculate.

The square root function is based on an algorithm described by R. G. Dromey in his excellent book, *How To Solve It By Computer* (Prentice-Hall International series on computer science, 1982). The algorithm works as follows:

1. Get two numbers: one used to determine a square root and one used as a termination error value.
2. Set an initial guess (called the current guess) for the square root; a good initial guess is half of the number, but any guess will do.
3. Repeatedly assign the current guess to the last guess and generate a new guess using an averaging formula until the absolute difference between the current and the new guess is less than the termination error.

See the code in Listing 4.1 for more information. (For more nitty-gritty details explaining the rationale for using this algorithm, see Dromey's discussion in *How To Solve It By Computer*.)

The greatest common divisor (GCD) function also is based on an algorithm described by Dromey. It works as follows:

1. Get the two numbers that you want to use to find the greatest common divisor.
2. Repeatedly get the remainder by dividing the larger integer by the smaller; assign this remainder to a new smaller integer, and the previous smaller integer to a new larger integer until the remainder equals 0.

Again, the code in Listing 4.1 shows the mathematical details, and Dromey discusses these algorithms for approximately 20 pages in *How To Solve It By Computer*.

Why Use a Nonlocal Variable?

The way these two functions find the values you want differs enough to require distinct controls for both input and output. You can, of course, display both sets of controls on the form simultaneously, but showing a group of controls that are not needed would be confusing at best. A better approach is to create each function's controls separately and to control them as a set.

MATH1 takes the following approach: every time a user selects a function (using a menu), the following events occur:

- The user's selection is noted in a nonlocal variable called `FType`.

  A nonlocal variable can be a global variable declared in a code module in Version 2.0 or 3.0 (or in the global module in Version 1.0), a module-level variable declared in another module, or a form-level variable declared in the general declarations section of the form's code. A nonlocal variable is used because you will want the variable to retain its value outside any local procedure so that other procedures can read it (and change it).

  Where to declare a variable is always an important design consideration based primarily on either of two considerations:

  1. Which procedures can access (and potentially change) the variable.

  2. Memory management considerations.

  In this example, the focus is on the first consideration because it's the one you usually are concerned with first. Chapter 9, "Extending Visual Basic: Custom Controls and DLLs," addresses Windows and Visual Basic memory management problems in more detail. For now, simply use a nonlocal variable to enable other procedures to see the value of the variable (`FType`) in order to behave correctly based on that value.

- The application notes also what the last function was in another nonlocal variable called `LastFType`. This variable is used to hide the previous function's controls.

- The application calls the `ControlCenter` (a simple procedure used to manipulate controls), which determines the controls it needs to turn on and off, based on the `FType` and `LastFType` settings. The `ControlCenter` shows and hides by changing the `Visible` property of the controls specified in a `Select...Case` statement. The code is discussed later. For now, however, let's design the interface.

  Step 1. Select a form (use the default form for a new project).

  Step 2. Add the controls.

Two sets of controls are needed for this application: one set for each function. Although the pattern used here works for any number of sets, it can get messy (and memory intensive) if several controls are added to a form.

Add Square Root Controls

Several controls have to be drawn for the Square Root form:

- Two text boxes for input: one for the number used to determine the square root and one for a user-defined error.
- Two text boxes for output: one to show progression as the application moves closer to an acceptable square root and one to show the reduction in error as the application progresses.
- A command button to let the user decide when to compute.
- Labels to identify the text boxes.

Figure 4.1 shows these controls on the form. Add them by selecting controls from the toolbox and moving them into position. Figure 4.1 also shows the MATH1 menu bar, created with the Menu Design window.

Add Greatest Common Divisor Controls

Draw the controls for the greatest common divisor function (although several controls are needed, you can reuse some of the square root controls):

- Three text boxes for input: two for the numbers used to find the GCD and one for a user-defined error. (Because the form already has two of these, add one additional text box.)
- Two text boxes for output: one to show progression as the application moves closer to an acceptable GCD; one to show how the remainder is changing and, therefore, to indicate how the function is progressing. (The two text boxes from Square Root will do.)
- A command button to let the user decide when to compute (again, the command button from Square Root will do).
- Labels to identify the text boxes. (Most of these, except the one for Number 1, need to be changed.) Figure 4.2 shows these controls on the form. Add these controls by selecting them from the toolbox and then moving them into position.

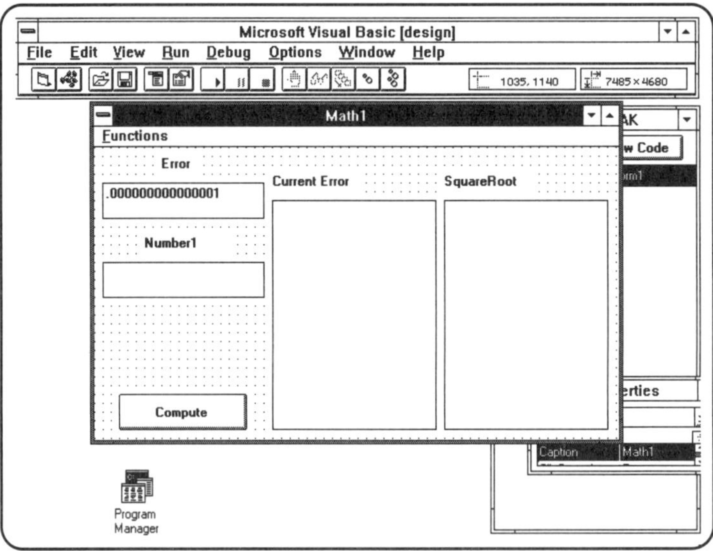

Figure 4.1. The Square Root controls.

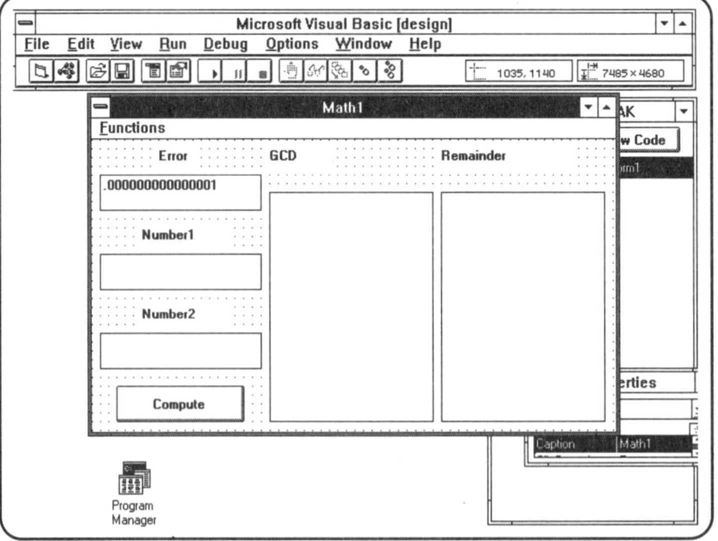

Figure 4.2. The greatest common divisor controls.

Create the Menu for the Application

Use the menu design window to create a Functions menu (see Figure 4.3).

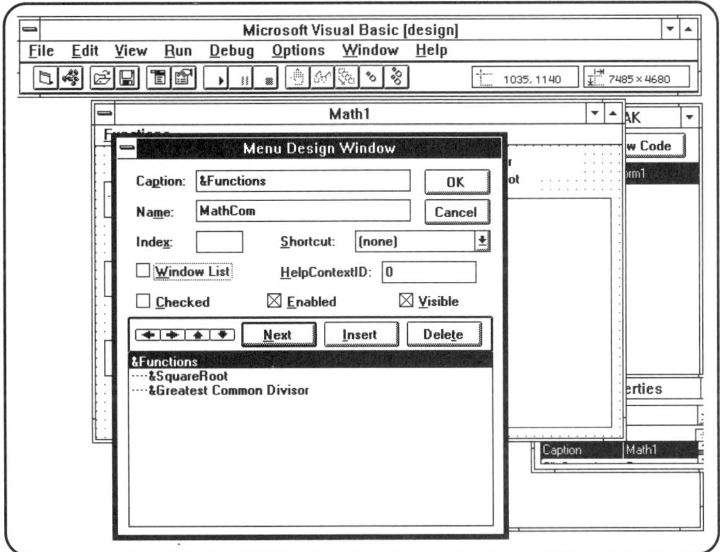

Figure 4.3. Menu design for MATH1.

Set Form and Control Properties

Set the form's `Caption` property to indicate the application's name, MATH1, and set the text boxes to show default values as shown in this section.

For the Square Root form:

- Set a default error of approximately .000001 for the Error text box text property. I called this text box `SRFixedError` (its `Name`); therefore, the property setting is

  ```
  SRFixedError.Text = .000001
  ```

- Set the other text boxes (1 number input and 2 output) to blanks (see Figure 4.4).
- Set the two output text box multiline properties to True. This action enables the text box to show multilines rather than the default single-line display.

- Set other `Names` as you see fit. For example, I've chosen to use an `SR` prefix for controls used on the Square Root form and a `GCD` prefix for controls used on the Greatest Common Divisor form.

Figure 4.4 shows MATH1 in design mode, and, therefore, the controls for both applications are on the form at the same time. Although at this point it may not seem like many controls for the form, imagine that you're designing controls for 15 functions that use many more distinct controls. The form soon becomes too crowded for words (or controls), and much too crowded for you to work with. What is the solution to this potential mess? Multiform applications.

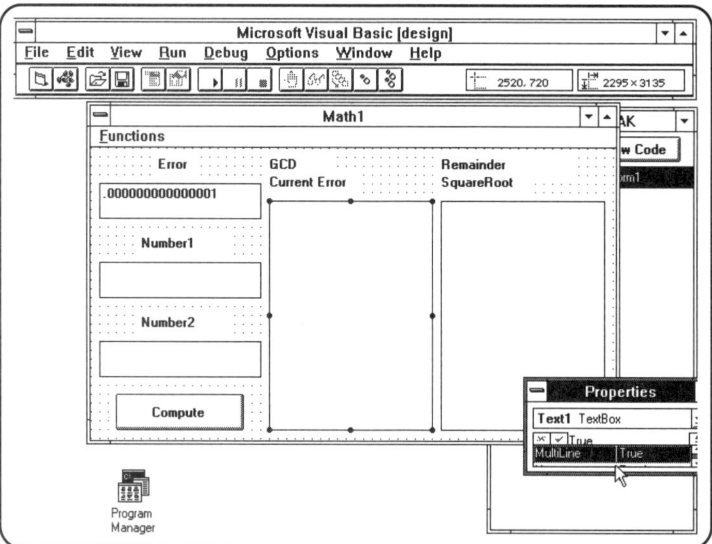

Figure 4.4. The property setting.

For the GCD:

- Set the additional input text box to a blank, and set any additional control names. Now attach the code.
- You need some code to carry out the function. Use general procedures (rather than event procedures).

`SquareRoot` looks like this:

```
Sub SquareRoot ()
Dim g1 As Double
Dim g2 As Double
```

```
Dim num As Double
Dim CurEr As Double

    nl$ = Chr$(13) + Chr$(10) ' carriage return
    Text2.Text = nl$          ' output formatting
    Text1.Text = nl$
    num = Val(InNumber1.Text) ' Get the number to square root.
    g2 = num / 2              ' An initial wild guess.
    Do
        g1 = g2               ' Set initial guess to old guess.
        g2 = (g1 + num / g1) / 2    ' A new guess.
        Text2.Text = Text2.Text + nl$ + Format$(g2)
        CurEr = Abs(g1 - g2)   ' Compare the guesses.
        Text1.Text = Text1.Text + nl$ + Format$(CurEr)
        i = i + 1
    Loop Until CurEr < Val(SRFixedErr.Text) Or i = 15
                                    ' Quit when error is sufficiently low.
End Sub
```

The GCD looks like this:

```
Sub GCD ()
Dim r As Long
Dim n As Long
Dim m As Long

    nl$ = Chr$(13) + Chr$(10) ' carriage return for formatting
    Text2.Text = nl$          ' more formatting setup
    Text1.Text = nl$
    n = Val(InNumber1.Text)   ' Get the numbers to GCD.
    m = Val(InNumber2.Text)
    Do
        r = n Mod m           ' Divide #1 by #2 and get the remainder.
        n = m                 ' #1 = #2
        m = r                 ' #2 = remainder
        Text1.Text = Text1.Text + nl$ + Format$(n)     ' Let us know where we
stand.
        Text2.Text = Text2.Text + nl$ + Format$(m)
    Loop Until r = 0
End Sub
```

Text Box Formatting Issues

This section discusses some general matters about these functions. Much of each function's code is used for formatting setup and output. Note that the new line assignments (`Text2.Text = nl$` and `Text1.Text = nl$`) are necessary to ensure that the output is multiline. Although the text box `Multiline` property has been set to True for the progress display (to show the past and the current status, not just the results of the current status), the output does not automatically use the multiline capability of the text box unless you insert the new lines (that is, carriage returns).

Note also that the `Val` function is used to get the numerical value of the contents of a text box. The content of a text box is always a string variable. Therefore, if you want to use it as something other than a string (a number, for example), you will have to convert it. `Val` converts a string to a double-precision floating-point number, which is what this application (and most mathematical functions) needs.

Also, you must convert the number back to a string if you want to display it in a text box; use either a `Format$` or `Str$` function to do this. `Format$` is the more versatile and complex of the two because it formats and converts the number. `Str$` simply converts it. When you omit formatting instructions as done here, `Format$` works just like `Str$`.

It is necessary also to implement the event code to inform the application that a function has been selected. Use the event code for function menu clicks.

For a SquareRoot menu item click:

```
Sub SquareRootCom_Click ()          ' Event procedure.
    LastFType = FType               ' Note the previous function type.
    FType = 1                       ' Set this function type.
    ControlCenter                   ' Let the ControlCenter set controls.
End Sub
```

For a GCD menu item click:

```
Sub GCDCom_Click ()                 ' Event procedure.
    LastFType = FType               ' Note the previous function type.
    FType = 2                       ' Set this function type.
    ControlCenter                   ' Let the ControlCenter set controls.
End Sub
```

Each of these functions does three things:

1. Notes the previous function type so that the `ControlCenter` can show and hide controls.
2. Sets the current function type (using `FType`).
3. Calls the `ControlCenter` to show and hide controls based on the previous (`LastFType`) and current (`FType`) function types.

The code for `ControlCenter()` looks like this:

```
Sub ControlCenter ()
    Select Case LastFType        ' Hide the Last function's controls.
        Case 1                   ' Function 1 = SquareRoot
            SRL3.Visible = 0
            SRL4.Visible = 0
        Case 2                   ' Function 2 = GCD
            InNumber2.Visible = 0
            GCDL3.Visible     = 0
            GCDL1.Visible     = 0
            GCDL2.Visible     = 0
    End Select

    Select Case FType            ' Show this function's controls.
        Case 1                   ' Function 1 = SquareRoot
            InNumber1.Visible = -1
            Command1.Visible = -1
            SRFixedErr.Visible = -1
            Text1.Visible = -1
            Text2.Visible = -1
            SRL1.Visible = -1
            SRL2.Visible = -1
            SRL3.Visible = -1
            SRL4.Visible = -1
        Case 2                   ' Function 2 = GCD
            InNumber1.Visible = -1
            InNumber2.Visible = -1
            Command1.Visible = -1
            GCDL1.Visible = -1
            GCDL2.Visible = -1
            GCDL3.Visible = -1
            SRL1.Visible = -1
            Text1.Visible = -1
            Text2.Visible = -1
    End Select
End Sub
```

At this point, you might be thinking that you don't need a `ControlCenter` and that instead you could have each function handle its own controls. That's really not a good solution, however, unless the application is very simple. By designating a `ControlCenter`, all control manipulation is isolated in a single procedure. You easily can add new functionality to the application and add its control information to a single procedure: `ControlCenter`.

Listing 4.1 shows the complete code for MATH1.

LISTING 4.1. MATH1.

```
General Declarations


Dim FType As Integer     ' FTypes: SqrRoot = 1
                         '         GCD     = 2
Dim LastFType As Integer' Used to turn off preceding function's controls.


Procedures


Sub Command1_Click ()
        If FType = 1 Then
            SquareRoot
        End If
        If FType = 2 Then
            GCD
        End If
End Sub


Sub SquareRoot ()
Dim g1 As Double
Dim g2 As Double
Dim num As Double
Dim CurEr As Double

    nl$ = Chr$(13) + Chr$(10)
    Text2.Text = nl$
    Text1.Text = nl$
    num = Val(InNumber1.Text)
    g2 = num / 2
    Do
        g1 = g2
        g2 = (g1 + num / g1) / 2
        Text2.Text = Text2.Text + nl$ + Format$(g2)
        CurEr = Abs(g1 - g2)
        Text1.Text = Text1.Text + nl$ + Format$(CurEr)
        i = i + 1
    Loop Until CurEr < Val(SRFixedErr.Text) Or i = 15
End Sub


Sub SquareRootCom_Click ()
    LastFType = FType
    FType = 1                ' Set Function type.
    ControlCenter            ' Set controls.
End Sub
```

```
Sub GCDCom_Click ()
    LastFType = FType
    FType = 2               ' Set Function type.
    ControlCenter           ' Set controls.
End Sub


Sub GCD ()
Dim r As Long
Dim n As Long
Dim m As Long

    nl$ = Chr$(13) + Chr$(10)
    Text2.Text = nl$
    Text1.Text = nl$
    n = Val(InNumber1.Text)
    m = Val(InNumber2.Text)
    Do
        r = n Mod m
        n = m
        m = r
        Text1.Text = Text1.Text + nl$ + Format$(n)
        Text2.Text = Text2.Text + nl$ + Format$(m)
    Loop Until r = 0
End Sub


Sub ControlCenter ()
    Select Case LastFType      ' Hide controls.
        Case 1
            SRL3.Visible = 0
            SRL4.Visible = 0
        Case 2
            InNumber2.Visible = 0
            GCDL3.Visible = 0
            GCDL1.Visible = 0
            GCDL2.Visible = 0
    End Select

    Select Case FType          ' Show controls.
        Case 1
            InNumber1.Visible = -1
            Command1.Visible = -1
            SRFixedErr.Visible = -1
            Text1.Visible = -1
            Text2.Visible = -1
            SRL1.Visible = -1
            SRL2.Visible = -1
            SRL3.Visible = -1
            SRL4.Visible = -1
```

continues

LISTING 4.1. CONTINUED

```
        Case 2
            InNumber1.Visible = -1
            InNumber2.Visible = -1
            Command1.Visible = -1
            GCDL1.Visible = -1
            GCDL2.Visible = -1
            GCDL3.Visible = -1
            SRL1.Visible = -1
            Text1.Visible = -1
            Text2.Visible = -1
    End Select
End Sub
```

RECAP: TAB ORDER OF CONTROLS

Remember that you can set the tab order of a form's controls to make it easier for users to move easily (by way of tabs) from one control to another. Visual Basic assigns tab order to controls in the order in which you draw them on a form. Each new control is placed last in the tab order. You can change this order at design time with the Properties bar, or at runtime through code.

To change the tab order at design time:

1. Click a control to select it.
2. Select `TabIndex` from the Properties list box. (Visual Basic displays the current tab position in the Settings box.)
3. Enter the number for the tab order position you want the control to have.
4. Click the Enter button or press Enter.

For example, in this GCD function, if you want the user to move easily between the input number boxes, set the tab order for the number input boxes to 0 and 1 using each box's `TabIndex` property. You might also want to disable the Tab Stop on controls the user never uses for input, such as the two answer boxes on this form. Figure 4.5 shows the Properties bar settings for the selected input box (Number 1 TabIndex = 0; Number 2 TabIndex = 1).

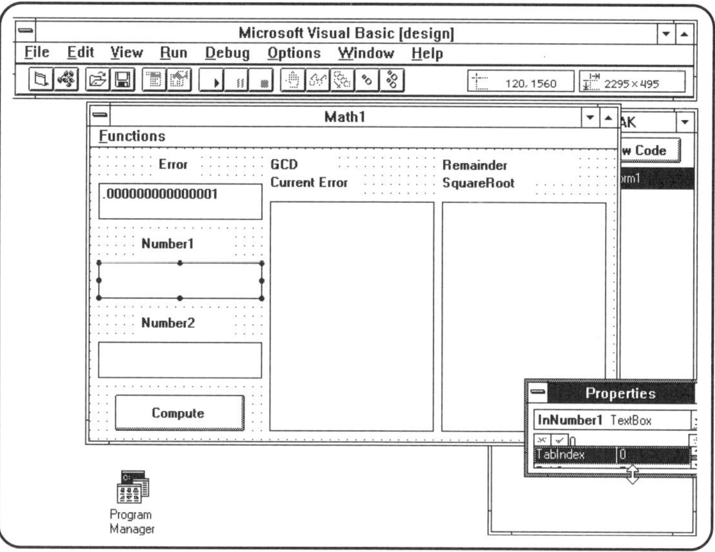

Figure 4.5. Tab.

A Multiform Version of Math Functions

The first version of the math application used a single form to perform more than one function. Although it worked, eventually a single form becomes more than a little crowded during design mode; it can be cumbersome to turn all those controls on and off. A more versatile version of the math application could implement each function on a separate form. Each form then could be shown whenever the function it implements is requested. The next example, MATH2, demonstrates this version.

Step 1. Create the forms.

First, create a `StartUp` form to manage the application (use the one Visual Basic supplies by default) and change the `Name` and `Caption` (using the Properties bar) to MATH2 (see Figure 4.6). Note that its name and caption properties are always `Form1` (by default).

Note that you can resize and move any form you create for an application during design mode and that it appears at runtime in the new size at the new location.

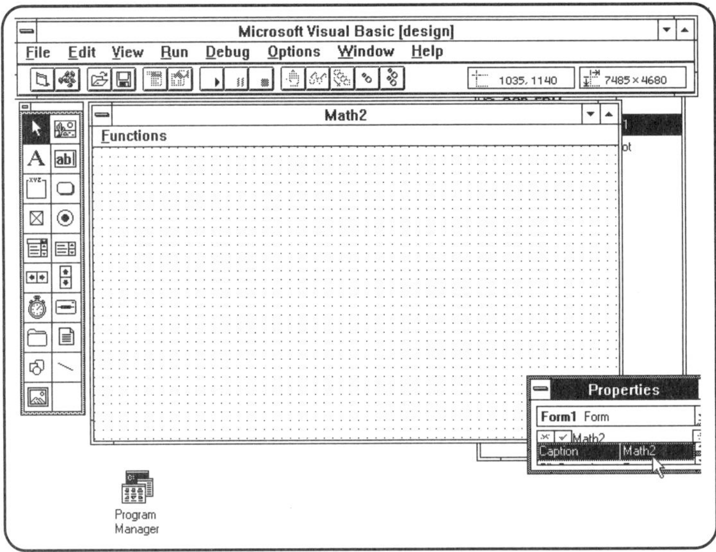

Figure 4.6. StartUp form for MATH2 in the design mode.

The next step is to create forms for each function: Select NewForm from the File menu and add a `SquareRoot` form, and then select NewForm again and add a Greatest Common Divisor form.

Step 2. Add controls to the `SquareRoot` form.

Figure 4.7 shows the `SquareRoot` form after its controls have been added using the toolbox.

Figure 4.8 shows this form and controls. Add controls to the Greatest Common Divisor form.

Step 3. Add a menu to the `StartUp` form. Note that any form, not just the `StartUp` form, can have a menu.

Make the MATH2 (the `StartUp`) form active by selecting it (either from the Project window or by clicking it with the mouse, if it's on-screen). Add the menu items for the two functions (see Figure 4.9).

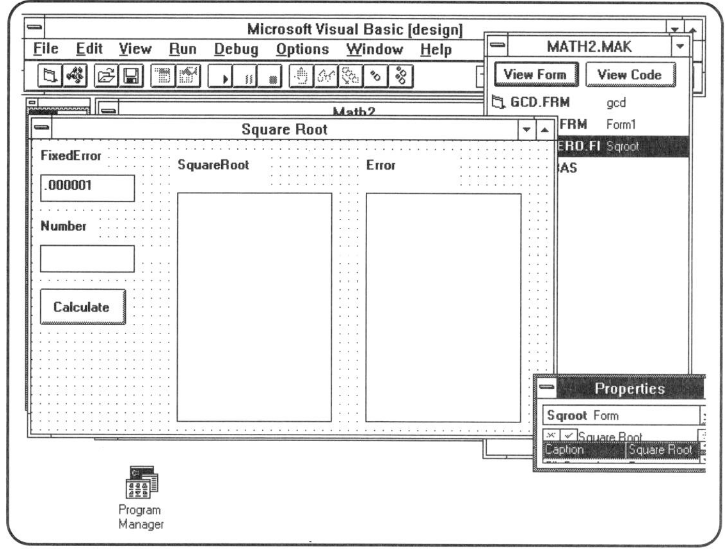

Figure 4.7. The SquareRoot form in design view.

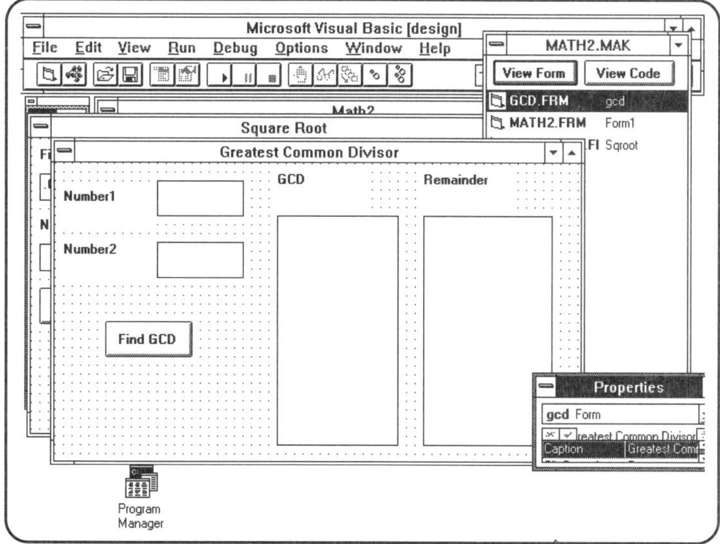

Figure 4.8. The Greatest Common Devisor form in design view.

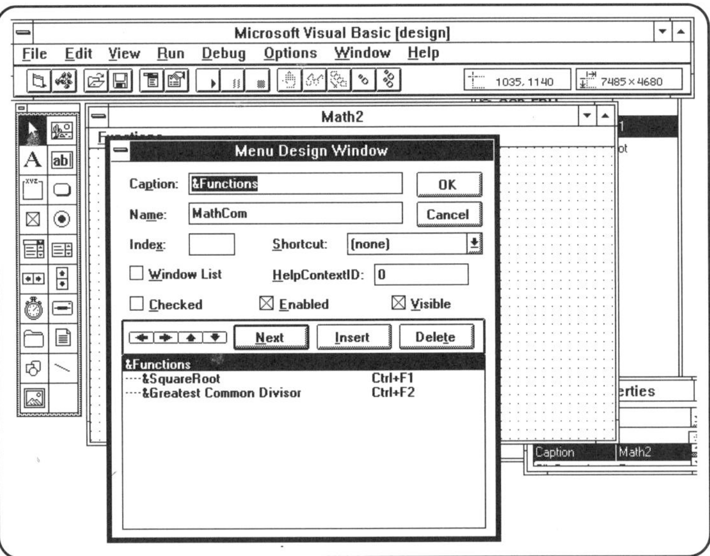

Figure 4.9. Menu design for MATH2 (StartUp).

Make the User's Life Easier: Use Keyboard Shortcuts

You may have noticed that something else is new in Figure 4.9. I used the accelerator box to create keyboard shortcuts for the functions (Ctrl-F1 and Ctrl-F2). When you click the accelerator box, it displays a drop-down list of keyboard combination options. Select the combinations you want to use for each menu item (you can give one item a shortcut without giving all items in the menu shortcuts). You can set keyboard shortcuts for any menu item and give the user the option of using the keyboard or the mouse to select menu items. The complete applications (MATH2 and MATH2b on the disk) use these keyboard shortcuts.

> *Step 4.* Set the form and control properties. If you haven't already done so, you might want to load the project from the *Secrets* disk so you can see the property changes I've chosen for this project.

Use the Properties bar to change the settings for the text boxes and the labels. Figure 4.10 shows the form after these settings have been changed. Make sure, however, that you set the output text boxes on both the GCD and the Square Root forms to `"Multiline = True"` (using the Properties bar).

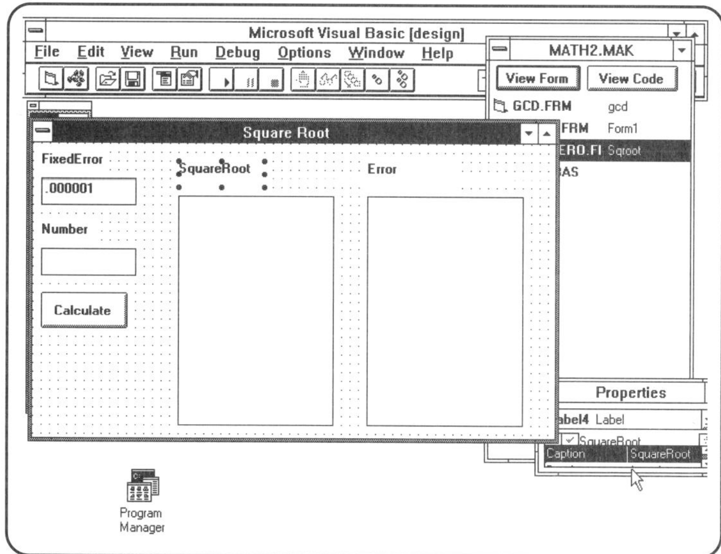

Figure 4.10. The Greatest Common Divisor form (stage 2).

Step 5. Write event and general procedure code.

Let's begin this step by reconsidering MATH1 (shown earlier in this chapter). In that application, the two functions were coded as general procedures, and a general procedure called `ControlCenter()` was coded to show and hide controls.

MATH2 contains a slight variation. Rather than make the two functions general procedures of the `StartUp` form, code them as general procedures for the forms that will use them. In this way, the Square Root form and the GCD form will be attached to and responsible for executing these procedures. After the form is shown (or loaded) by the `StartUp` form's `ControlCenter()`, it is up to the Function form to respond to its own controls and to carry out functions.

This is another important design consideration. Although Visual Basic is not entirely object-oriented, and will let you think as non-object-orientedly as you want, it still makes sense to think in terms of objects. Each form is an object that consists of the controls and code it needs to handle itself. Therefore, if a form is intended to carry out a task, give it the code that it needs to handle it. You can think about this another way, as a one-task, one-form system. Keep in mind, however, that you don't have to. I do it because it makes sense for me and my applications.

Design Considerations

How you organize code and forms in a project becomes increasingly more important as your projects get larger. The one-task, one-form system puts an object's (the forms's) data and characteristics in one place. In this scenario (very object-oriented), if you want something done on or by a form, you load the form and let it handle the task. This is the safest way to organize a project, but not necessarily the most efficient.

Suppose you place a text box on a form and want to read the contents of a file into the text box. It's safest to put the code that actually changes the textbox `Text` property in the form module. However, the code that reads the contents of the file into a variable is general, so you should only write it once. File I/O routines should be in a code module that any form can use. Thus, the following describes how you might use two forms and one code module to generalize the reading of a file into a text box. This description assumes:

- A startup form
- A task (`EditForm`)
- A general (or global module) that contains file I/O procedures.

The form contains a text box that has a `Text` property:

Form	(an object)
-> Text box	(an object contained within the form)
-> Text	(property of the text box)

The file I/O module contains procedures:

File I/O Module	(a code object)
-> OpenFile	(procedure contained within the code module)
-> CloseFile	(" ")
-> etc...	(" ")
Form (StartUpForm)	You request the task here: 1. Read the contents of a file; 2. Put the contents in text box.

-> StartUp	Loads Form (EditForm) containing the text box.
-> EditForm	Handles the user interface part, for example, by showing a File dialog to get the name of a file. It then sends that information to a general Read routine in the file I/O module.
	1. Read contents into a variable.
-> Textbox	2. Put contents in the text box.

Notice that each object is responsible for itself.

Note also that Visual Basic does not require this "safer approach." You can, alternatively, manipulate a text box, for example, directly from a form that does not contain it, by using the "!" notation. For example:

```
SomeVar$ =EditForm!Text1.Text
```

Accessing control properties remotely is really handy. But beware; freedom can be costly. Setting control properties remotely in large projects can make the project harder to debug and maintain.

You can also more efficiently (but less safely) access the value of a control directly without using its property name. The value of a control varies depending on the control, corresponding to the likely most commonly used property of the control. Table 4.1 lists controls and their relative values.

Table 4.1. Control properties that coincide with their values.

Control	*Property that Coincides with its Value*
Check box	Value
Combo box	Text
Command button	Value
Common dialog	Action
Data	Caption
Directory list box	Path
Drive list box	Drive
File list box	FileName

continues

Table 4.1. continued

Control	*Property that Coincides with its Value*
Frame	Caption
Grid	Text
Horizon scrollbar	Value
Image	Picture
Label	Caption
Line	Visible
List box	Text
Menu	Enabled
Option button	Value
Picture box	Picture
Shape	Shape
Text box	Text
Timer	Enabled
Vertical scrollbar	Value

Math2, Details

Code the forms one at a time. First, code the `StartUp` form: `GCDCom_Click` (the menu event procedure for the menu item GCD) looks the way it did in MATH1:

```
Sub GCDCom_Click ()
    LastFType = FType
    FType = 2                   ' Set Function type.
    ControlCenter               ' Set controls.
End Sub
```

Again, the application begins responding to the menu click event by setting some form-level variables: the previous function type and the current function type. Next, call the `ControlCenter`. `LastFType` and `FType` are still form-level variables. They don't need to be made global (that is, application level) because only this one form (MATH2, the StartUp form) needs to know about them. After the ControlCenter interprets these variables, it transfers control (at least until it regains the focus) to the function or form the user requested.

SquareRootCom_Click (the menu event procedure for the menu item SqRoot) also looks like it did in MATH1:

```
Sub SquareRootCom_Click ()
    LastFType = FType
    FType = 1                   'Set Function type.
    ControlCenter               'Set controls.
End Sub
```

The ControlCenter has been changed, however. Instead of showing and hiding controls, it shows a form:

```
Sub ControlCenter ()
    Select Case LastFType        ' Test LastFType.
        Case 1
                                 ' Disregard for now.
        Case 2

    End Select

    Select Case FType            ' Show form.
        Case 1
            SqRoot.Show
        Case 2
            GCD.Show
    End Select
End Sub
```

By using the ControlCenter this way, you can add new functions and new ways of showing and hiding forms and controls by recoding all of the form and control code here. Each new form, function, or task can be added in the ControlCenter as a Case; within a Select...Case statement, specific instructions for loading, hiding, and showing the form also can be held in the ControlCenter.

The general declarations for the StartUp form (MATH2) are identical to those in MATH1:

```
Dim FType As Integer         ' FTypes: SqrRoot = 1
                             '         GCD     = 2
Dim LastFType As Integer     ' Used to turn off previous function's controls.'
```

Next, add the code for the two function and task forms.

The GCD form now uses the same code that the set of controls in MATH1 (for GCD) used:

```
Sub Command1_Click ()
    GCDiv                   ' Invoke GCDiv.
End Sub

Sub GCDiv ()                ' Now a GCD form general procedure.
Dim r As Long
Dim n As Long
Dim m As Long

    nl$ = Chr$(13) + Chr$(10)
    Text2.Text = nl$
    Text1.Text = nl$
    n = Val(InNumber1.Text)
    m = Val(InNumber2.Text)
    Do
        r = n Mod m
        n = m
        m = r
        Text1.Text = Text1.Text + nl$ + Format$(n)
        Text2.Text = Text2.Text + nl$ + Format$(m)
    Loop Until r = 0
End Sub
```

The Square Root form also uses the same code as the set of controls in MATH1 (for `SqRoot`):

```
Sub Command1_Click ()
    SquareRoot                  ' Invoke SquareRoot().
End Sub

Sub SquareRoot ()               ' Now a SqRoot form general procedure.
Dim g1 As Double
Dim g2 As Double
Dim num As Double
Dim CurEr As Double

    nl$ = Chr$(13) + Chr$(10)
    Text2.Text = nl$
    Text1.Text = nl$
    num = Val(InNumber1.Text)
    g2 = num / 2
    Do
        g1 = g2
        g2 = (g1 + num / g1) / 2
        Text2.Text = Text2.Text + nl$ + Format$(g2)
        CurEr = Abs(g1 - g2)
        Text1.Text = Text1.Text + nl$ + Format$(CurEr)
        i = i + 1
    Loop Until CurEr < Val(SRFixedError.Text) Or i = 15
End Sub
```

Listing 4.2 shows the complete listing for MATH2. Figures 4.11 and 4.12 show MATH2 in operation.

Listing 4.2. MATH2.

```
' StartUp Form (MATH2)


' general declarations

Dim FType As Integer             ' FTypes: SquareRoot = 1
                                 '         GCD        = 2
Dim LastFType As Integer         ' Used to turn off preceding functions
                                 ' controls.


' general procedures

Sub ControlCenter ()
    Select Case LastFType        ' Test LastFType.
        Case 1
                                 ' Disregard for now.
        Case 2

    End Select

    Select Case FType            ' Show form.
        Case 1
            SqRoot.Show
        Case 2
            GCD.Show
    End Select
End Sub


' event procedures

Sub GCDCom_Click ()
    LastFType = FType
    FType = 2                    ' Set Function type.
    ControlCenter                ' Set controls.
End Sub


Sub SquareRootCom_Click ()
    LastFType = FType
    FType = 1                    'Set Function type.
```

continues

LISTING 4.2. CONTINUED

```
    ControlCenter                   'Set controls.
End Sub


' GCD Form


' event procedures

Sub Command1_Click ()
    GCDiv                           ' Invoke GCDiv.
End Sub


' general procedures

Sub GCDiv ()                        ' Now a GCD form general procedure.
Dim r As Long
Dim n As Long
Dim m As Long

    nl$ = Chr$(13) + Chr$(10)
    Text2.Text = nl$
    Text1.Text = nl$
    n = Val(InNumber1.Text)
    m = Val(InNumber2.Text)
    Do
        r = n Mod m
        n = m
        m = r
        Text1.Text = Text1.Text + nl$ + Format$(n)
        Text2.Text = Text2.Text + nl$ + Format$(m)
    Loop Until r = 0
End Sub



' SqRoot Form


' event procedures

Sub Command1_Click ()
    SquareRoot                      ' Invoke SquareRoot().
End Sub
' general procedures

Sub SquareRoot ()                   ' Now a SqRoot form general procedure.
Dim g1 As Double
```

```
Dim g2 As Double
Dim num As Double
Dim CurEr As Double

    nl$ = Chr$(13) + Chr$(10)
    Text2.Text = nl$
    Text1.Text = nl$
    num = Val(InNumber1.Text)
    g2 = num / 2
    Do
        g1 = g2
        g2 = (g1 + num / g1) / 2
        Text2.Text = Text2.Text + nl$ + Format$(g2)
        CurEr = Abs(g1 - g2)
        Text1.Text = Text1.Text + nl$ + Format$(CurEr)
        i = i + 1
    Loop Until CurEr < Val(SRFixedError.Text) Or i = 15
End Sub
```

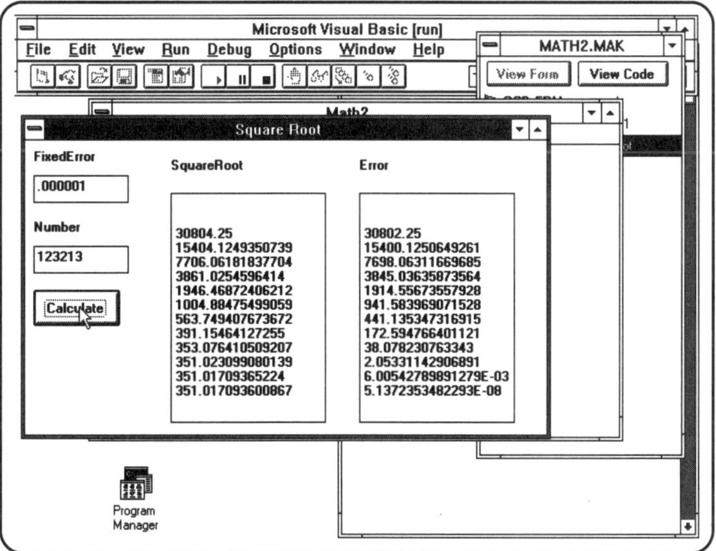

Figure 4.11. MATH2.

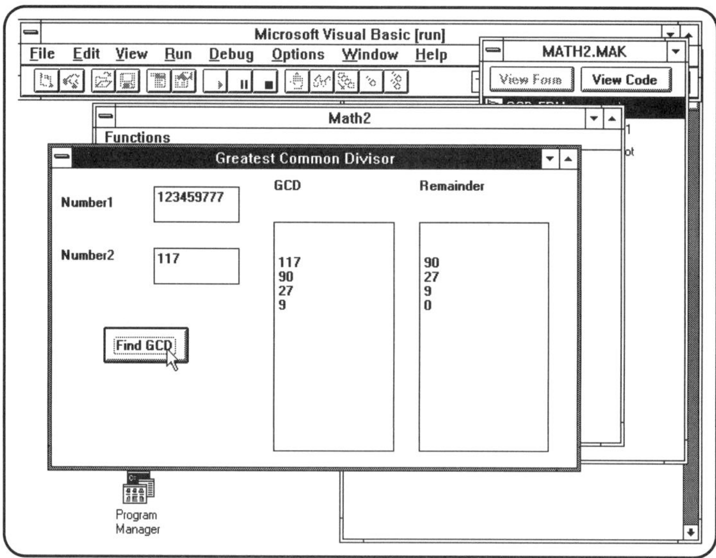

Figure 4.12. Another Stage of MATH2.

SHOW AND HIDE MULTIFORMS: MEMORY AND ACCESS CONSIDERATIONS

In the preceding application (MATH2), after a form is shown, it remains onscreen, even if another function form is requested. If you try to run the form again (after it's been shown), the focus simply switches back to the form; a second instance of a form is not loaded. This action effectively makes any form, after it is loaded, a separate entity within the application because the function form (if it hasn't been closed through its own command system) remains active even if the main form is closed.

However, you may want the `ControlCenter` to have a little more control over the forms. A simple modification to the MATH2 code accomplishes this. Change the `ControlCenter()` (remember that it's attached to the `StartUp` form) so that it hides the `LastForm` after it shows the `CurrentForm`:

```
Sub ControlCenter ()
    Select Case LastFType        ' Hide LastFType's form.
        Case 1
            SqRoot.Hide
```

```
        Case 2
            CGD.Hide
    End Select

    Select Case FType           ' Show current FType's form.
        Case 1
            SqRoot.Show
        Case 2
            GCD.Show
    End Select
End Sub
```

That's all there is to it. Now, each time one function form is shown, the one shown previously is hidden. Alternatively, you can show and unload the form and recover any memory being used by the form. Each time a form is hidden, it remains in memory. Each time a form is unloaded, it's removed from memory. Each time a form is shown, it's loaded if it's not already in memory. Listing 4.3 shows the complete listing for MATH2b.

Listing 4.3. The complete listing for MATH2b.

```
' StartUp Form (MATH2b)


' general declarations

Dim FType As Integer            ' FTypes: SqrRoot = 1
                                '         GCD     = 2
Dim LastFType As Integer        ' Used to turn off preceding function's
                                ' controls.


' general procedures

Sub ControlCenter ()
    Select Case LastFType       ' Hide LastFType's form.
        Case 1
           SqRoot.Hide
        Case 2
           CGD.Hide
    End Select

    Select Case FType           ' Show current FType's form.
        Case 1
            SqRoot.Show
```

continues

LISTING 4.3. CONTINUED

```
        Case 2
            GCD.Show
    End Select
End Sub


' event procedures

Sub GCDCom_Click ()
    LastFType = FType
    FType = 2                         ' Set Function type
    ControlCenter                     ' Set controls.
End Sub


Sub SquareRootCom_Click ()
    LastFType = FType
    FType = 1                         'Set Function type.
    ControlCenter                     'Set controls.
End Sub


' GCD Form


' event procedures

Sub Command1_Click ()
    GCDiv                             ' Invoke GCDiv.
End Sub


' general procedures

Sub GCDiv ()                          ' Now a GCD form general procedure.
Dim r As Long
Dim n As Long
Dim m As Long

    nl$ = Chr$(13) + Chr$(10)
    Text2.Text = nl$
    Text1.Text = nl$
    n = Val(InNumber1.Text)
    m = Val(InNumber2.Text)
    Do
        r = n Mod m
        n = m
        m = r
```

```
        Text1.Text = Text1.Text + nl$ + Format$(n)
        Text2.Text = Text2.Text + nl$ + Format$(m)
    Loop Until r = 0
End Sub



' SqRoot Form


' event procedures

Sub Command1_Click ()
    SquareRoot                      ' Invoke SquareRoot().
End Sub


' general procedures

Sub SquareRoot ()                   ' Now a SqRoot form general procedure.
Dim g1 As Double
Dim g2 As Double
Dim num As Double
Dim CurEr As Double

    nl$ = Chr$(13) + Chr$(10)
    Text2.Text = nl$
    Text1.Text = nl$
    num = Val(InNumber1.Text)
    g2 = num / 2
    Do
        g1 = g2
        g2 = (g1 + num / g1) / 2
        Text2.Text = Text2.Text + nl$ + Format$(g2)
        CurEr = Abs(g1 - g2)
        Text1.Text = Text1.Text + nl$ + Format$(CurEr)
        i = i + 1
    Loop Until CurEr < Val(SRFixedError.Text) Or i = 15
End Sub
```

You might want to consider the following items, however, before you decide whether to hide or unload a form:

- If you want to access values on a form even when the form is not being shown (for example, to check a value in another form's text box), the form will be loaded (implicitly) whenever that value is needed. It will not be implicitly unloaded, however. You can save time therefore by hiding the form, not unloading it. If that's the only reason you are keeping the form in memory, however, have the form save the value you need to check (from another form) in a global variable, and save the loading time.

- To conserve memory, unload and load (or show) the form each time it's needed. This works particularly well when the form is seldom used. Keep in mind, though, that a bug in Visual Basic Version 1.0 (but not Versions 2.0 and 3.0) can make this loading and unloading a non-memory-saving affair. If your application contains a multiline text box and you unload the form, the memory in use by the text box is lost. The solution, however, is simple: empty the text box before you unload a form containing a multiline text box. Of course, don't forget to save the contents somewhere if you expect to see them again.
- Consider making a form modal if it is shown for a specific purpose and then removed. A modal form must be closed before another form can get the focus. You make a form modal when you show it with a form's Show method. Show can have a MODALSTATE argument of 0 or 1. If MODALSTATE is 1, the form is modal. See the *Microsoft Visual Basic Programmer's Guide* (your Visual Basic manual) for other details.

Build a Simple Memory Check Application

To demonstrate how memory is used (and recovered) every time I load or unload a form, I wrote a simple application that uses the Clipboard's About the Clipboard command to return the status of Windows' memory use. You can use almost any Microsoft Windows 3.1 application, including the Program Manager, to get this information. I used the Clipboard because it loads and unloads quickly. (Note: Windows 3.0 lacks this capability and many other features that have been added in Windows 3.1. If you haven't upgraded to Windows 3.1, I urge you to do so in order to get the most out of Windows, Visual Basic, and this book.)

First, load it with the Visual Basic `Shell` command:

```
X = Shell("\Win31\Clipbrd.exe",1)
```

and then send commands with the Visual Basic `SendKeys` command. `SendKeys` enables you to send keystrokes to the active (or activated) application. The following SendKeys statement tells the Clipboard (and many other Microsoft applications) to display information about current memory use:

```
SendKeys "%HA", -1
```

The % indicates the Alt key; pressing Alt-H-A gets the Help menu item and the About menu item; -1 indicates that you want to remain in the application receiving keystrokes by way of SendKeys.

Finally, press the OK command button and press Alt-F4 to close the Clipboard.

Alternatively, you can use the ActivateApp command to access a running application rather than use the Shell command to start it. To activate the Program Manager:

```
AppActivate ("Program manager")
SendKeys "%HA", -1
```

or, to activate the Recorder:

```
AppActivate("Recorder")
SendKeys "%HA", -1
```

Although AppActivate saves a small amount of time because it doesn't require the loading of the application, it's more complicated to use. Because the application must be running in order for it to be activated, you must verify in some way that the application is running. Additionally, your application does not automatically return from the activated application; therefore, you must write some more code to set up the return or use the Program Manager to switch back to your application. In this example, it is more convenient to use the Shell command.

In addition to checking form Load/Unload memory use and recovery, I thought it would be interesting to use this application (called MEMCHK on the disk) to determine whether Visual Basic recovers memory allocated for some variables. For example, I created a 64K variable-length string:

```
V1$ = String$(64000, " ")
```

and checked the status of memory using the Clipboard:

```
Sub MemCheck ()
    x = Shell("\Win31\Clipbrd.exe", 1)
    SendKeys "%HA", -1
End Sub
```

The application consists of the main form (MEMCHK), which has no controls—just menu items for checking memory; creating and deleting a 64K variable-length string; loading and unloading an additional form (FORM2) that contains a text box; and loading a form with a text box containing text. The complete application is shown in Listing 4.4. Figures 4.13 and 4.14 show the application before and after loading a form containing a text box that has no text.

Figures 4.15 and 4.16 show the application before and after creating and deleting a 64K variable-length string. Figures 4.18 and 4.19 show the application after loading and unloading the form with a text box containing text. Figures 4.19 and 4.21 show the application before and after creating and deleting a dynamic array of 16,000 integer elements. I ran this test several times, and in each test all or 1K less than all of the memory was recovered. A Visual Basic quirk? Or is this a round off error?

Listing 4.4. MEMCHK.

```
' general declarations
Dim V1$


Sub MemCheck ()
    x = Shell("\Win31\CLipbrd.exe", 1)
    SendKeys "%HA", -1
End Sub


Sub CreateStrCom_Click ()
    V1$ = String$(64000, " ")
    MemCheck
End Sub


Sub MemCheckCom_Click ()
    MemCheck
End Sub


Sub DeleteStrCom_Click ()
    V1$ = String$(64000, " ")
    V1$ = String$(1, " ")
    MemCheck
End Sub
```

```
Sub LoadFormCom_Click ()
    Load Form2
    MemCheck
End Sub


Sub LoadTextCom_Click ()
    Load Form2
    For I% = 1 To 100
        AStr$ = AStr$ + "TenLetters"
    Next I%
    Form2.Text1.Text = AStr$
    MemCheck
End Sub


Sub UnloadFormCom_Click ()
    Unload Form2
    MemCheck
End Sub


Sub DynArrayCom_Click ()
    Size = 16000
    ReDim TestArray(Size) As Integer
    MemCheck
End Sub
```

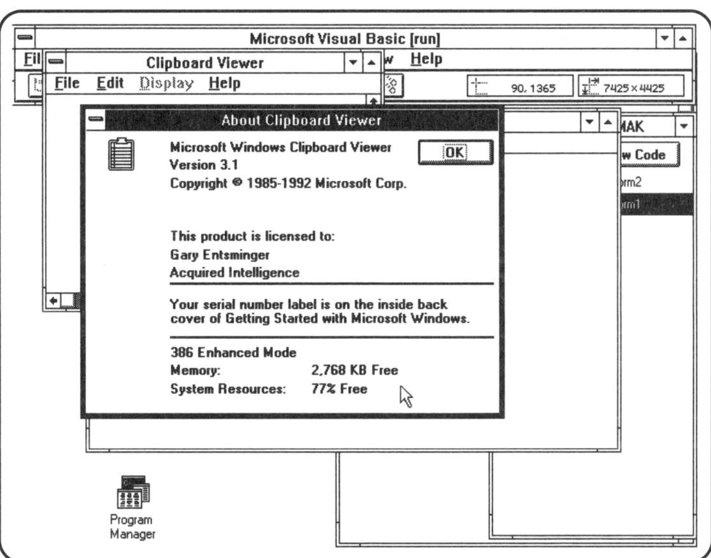

Figure 4.13. The application before loading a form containing a text box that has no text.

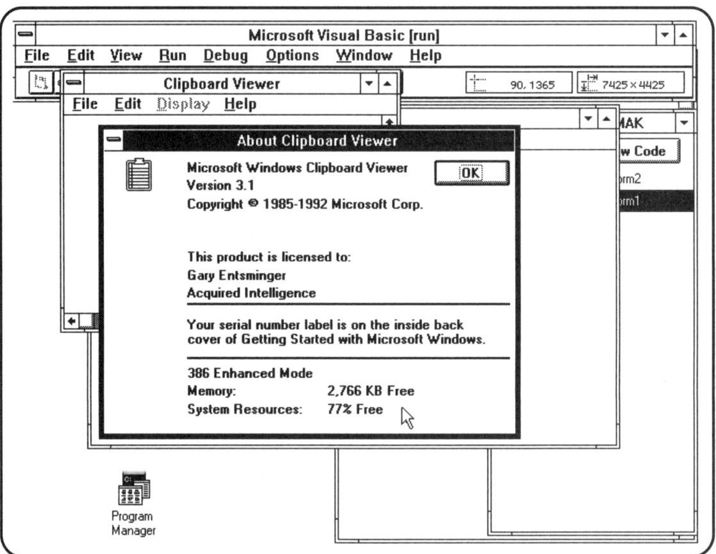

Figure 4.14. The application after loading a form containing a text box that has no text.

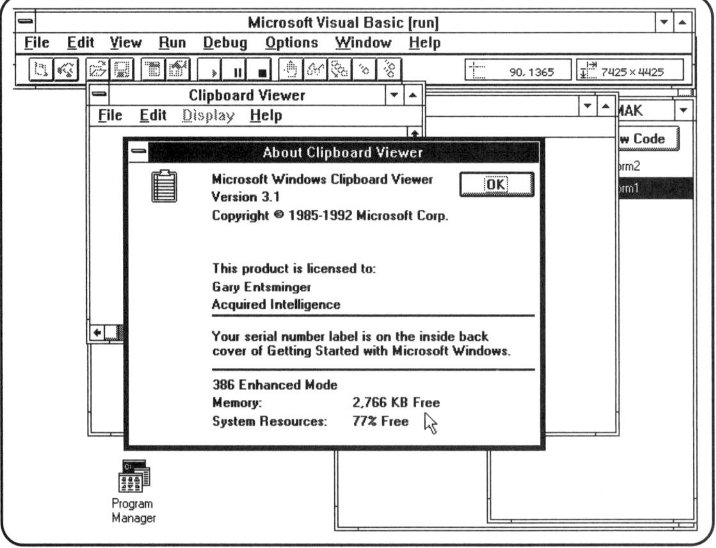

Figure 4.15. The application before creating and deleting a 64K variable-length string.

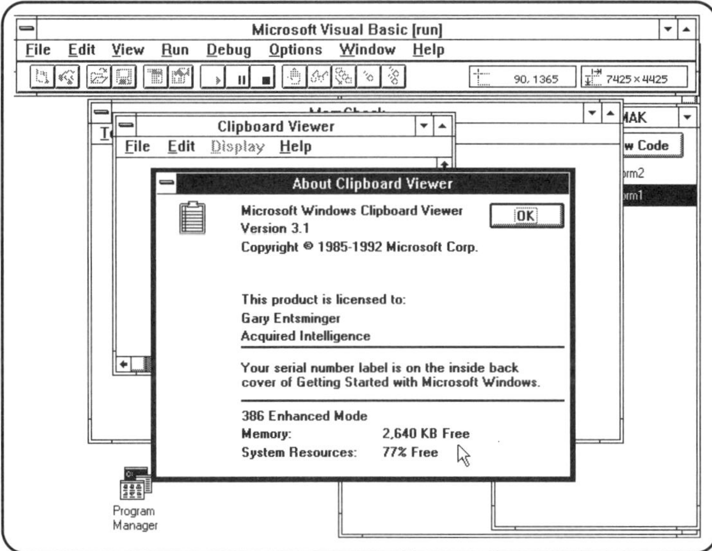

Figure 4.16. The application after creating and deleting a 64K variable-length string.

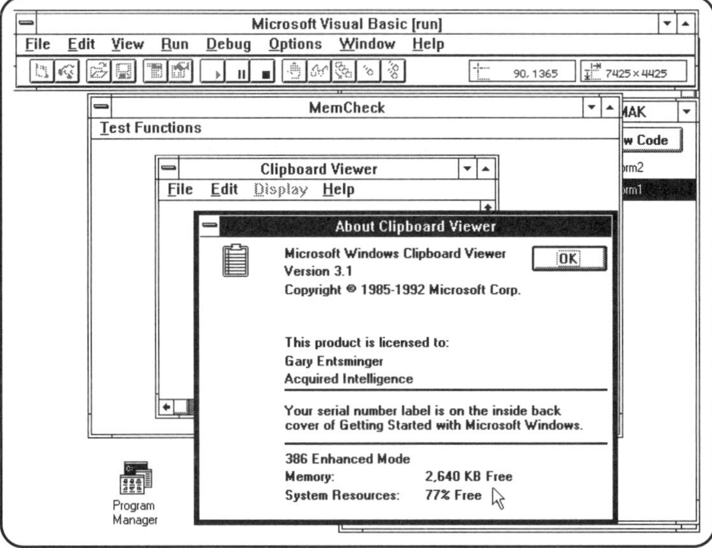

Figure 4.17. The application before loading and unloading the form with a text box containing text.

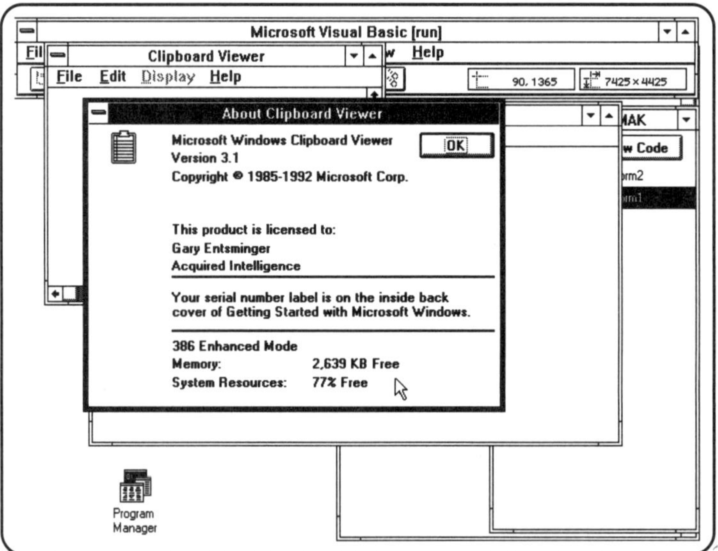

Figure 4.18. The application after loading and unloading the form with a text box containing text.

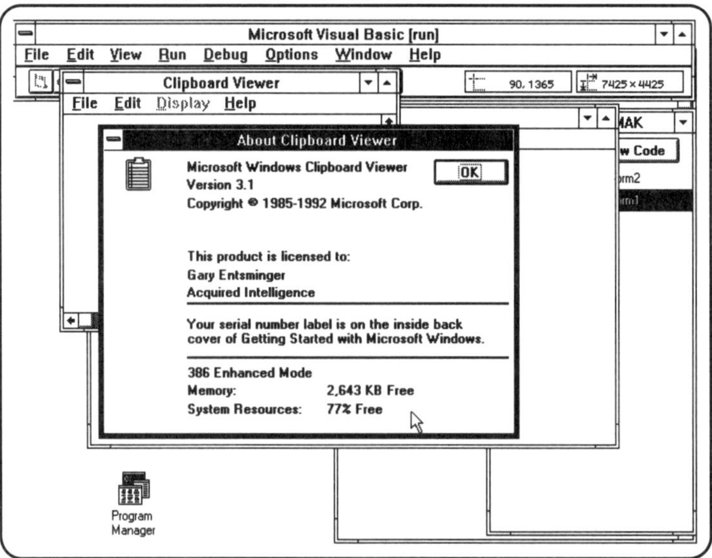

Figure 4.19. The application before creating and deleting a dynamic array of 16,000 integer elements.

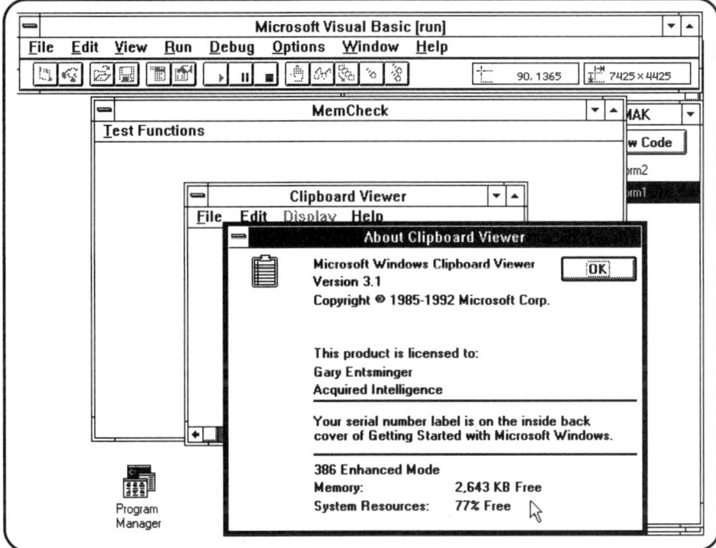

Figure 4.20. The application after creating and deleting a dynamic array of 16,000 integer elements.

When you run this code, you may see some interesting results. First, the results of the form test indicate that a form and one (multiline) text box require about 2K of memory (the 2K in this case is fully recoverable each time the form is unloaded). If the multiline text box contains text, however, not all of the memory is recoverable when the form is unloaded. The amount of memory that's recoverable in this example is about 40 percent. Therefore, if you are using multiline text boxes, you should clear the text box (by setting the `Text` property to "0") before unloading the form.

Note also that the memory for the variable-length string isn't recovered even after it's deleted. Remember the study of the memory allocation for string problems in Chapter 3, "Dynamic Events: Controls, Menus, and Dynamic Arrays"? It was concluded there that variable-length strings were useful for better memory management. This further evidence indicates, however, that variable-length strings help you to squeeze out another data segment's worth of strings; however, this does not necessarily save memory because the memory for the variable-length string is not recovered, as you might expect, after the procedure returns. It is recovered only after the application terminates.

Finally, the test to determine whether memory allocated for a dynamic array is recovered after the procedure is exited (and the dynamic array is no longer in use) produces good results. This memory is recovered. Hooray! Dynamic arrays therefore can be the memory savers you expect (and need) them to be.

SUMMARY

Multiforms open up a brave new world of multitasking capability. You can use multiforms, in fact, to create applications that look and behave like any mainstream Windows application. Figure 4.21 is a good example. It shows a screen I captured during one of my programming/writing sessions for this book.

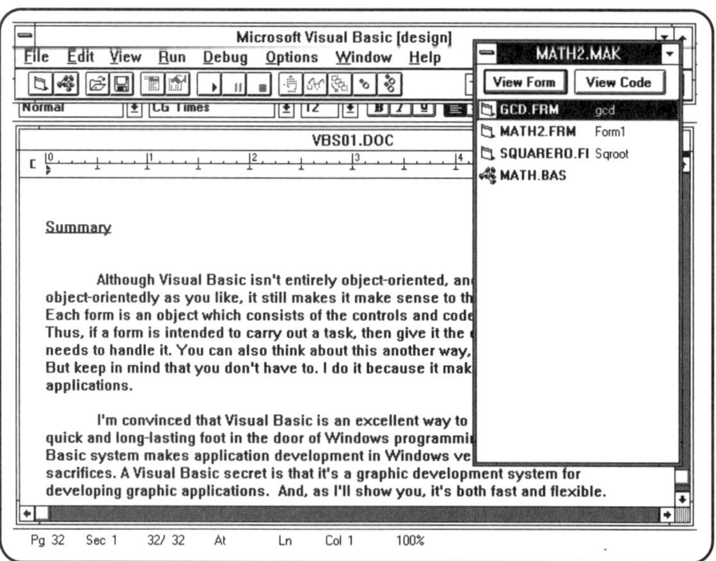

Figure 4.21. Multitasking, Windows, and Visual Basic style.

Note that the applications (Visual Basic, Microsoft Word, and MATH2) share the screen and interact beautifully with each other; Collage, my screen-capture application, is in the background taking the picture.

Each form of your application can be a task, which, after being started by a `StartUp` (or main) module, can determine its own fate. As shown in this chapter (using the MATH2 application), the `StartUp` module can be closed without closing other modules in the application. In this scenario, the `StartUp` module acts as a Windows-like Program Manager—a *bootstrapper*, in the programming lingo of the early 1980s. You can make the `StartUp` form more of a "form manager" also (as shown in MATH2b) that shows and hides forms rather than leaves them visible after they are shown.

Chapter 5, "Multitasking Via Interrupt Loops and *DoEvents*," continues the discussion of design and extends the techniques you learned in this chapter to create graphics forms for displaying the results of calculations and models. Along the way, I'll uncover a few more Visual Basic secrets to help you design efficient, smooth applications.

Multitasking Via Interrupt Loops and DoEvents

Add a Graphics Form to a Project

Chaos and Strange Attractors

Add a Scale to a Form

Plot Strange Attractors in a Picture Box

Resize a Picture Box Automatically When a Form Is Resized

Henon, Rossler, and Lorenz Attractors

I use the Windows environment and Visual Basic primarily for graphics and multitasking. (Because I often have to graphically display the results of much of my work, I have found that switching back and forth between text and graphics modes in DOS can be cumbersome as well as annoying.) This chapter continues the exploration of strings, forms, and applications and goes deeper into the heart of both graphics and multitasking using multiforms and idle loops with `DoEvents()`. The eight applications developed in this chapter enable you to do the following:

1. Add a graphics form to the MATH2b application in Chapter 4, "Using Numbers and Forms," (MATH3).
2. Plot strange attractors (those elegant versions of chaotic shapes) (ATTRACT1).

3. Plot strange attractors (as tasks) using multiforms (ATTRACT2).
4. Add a scale label to the graphics form (ATTRACT3).
5. Plot strange attractors as part of a multitasking environment using `DoEvents()` (ATTRACT4).
6. Add resize events (ATTRACT5).
7. Determine whether a number is a prime (PRIMES).
8. Use new attractors for the second edition (ATTRACT6).

ADD A GRAPHICS FORM TO A PROJECT

Let's begin by adding some new functionality to one of the applications, MATH2b, discussed in Chapter 4. MATH2b uses a multiform design to enable each function to maintain its own form. This application (and many applications) can be improved by adding a graphics element. An application often is improved when it can show the results of a function (or task) using graphics. Many times, of course, the graphics steal the show.

It is relatively easy to plot points, lines, and shapes using Visual Basic. Let's start with points by making the square root function of MATH2b display the values of the square root in a Cartesian plane. In other words, simply plot the latest guess (see the code for details) in a time series.

How is this done? Visual Basic displays graphics (points, lines, and so on) in either a form or a picture box. Because this example deals with points, plotting is trivial. Use the `PSet` method for the form or picture box object you use for the display. For example:

```
Form1.PSet X, Y
```

or

```
Picture1.PSet X, Y
```

Now, where do you use `PSet`? You could add a picture box to the square root form, but there's really no room for it there. You could expand the size of the square root form to include a picture box, but this could be limiting if the user wants the picture box to be as large as possible. For the picture box to be large enough to fill the screen, therefore, it must be either a form or a picture box that takes up most of a form.

You could create a separate form just to handle square root graphics. But what about GCD graphics? What about the functions that might be added to the application? Do you really want each function to have its own graphics form? I don't think so. Why not create a general graphics form that modifies itself when it's invoked in order to satisfy any function? MATH3 uses a single form for graphics that gets information (scale, label, X, Y location, and so on) from the function that calls it.

Step 1. Add a form using File/Add New Form.

Step 2. Add controls. I've chosen to add a picture box to my graph form in this project. I'll show you how to use it later in the chapter in the section "Plot Strange Attractors in a Picture Box."

Step 3. Although this form doesn't get a menu, any form can have its own menu (rather than command buttons) that can be used to initiate events.

Step 4. Set form properties. Set both the `FormName` and `Caption` properties to Graph using the Properties bar. Figure 5.1 shows the new Graph form with these changes after I resized and moved it around using the mouse pointer. Click any edge of a form to stretch or shrink it. Click the command menu's Move command to move the form.

Step 5. Add event and general procedures.

HOW TO USE CHECK BOXES

You will want to reuse all the code you can from MATH2b without compromising yourself. Here's one approach: Skip back to Step 2 (there's no law about the order you use) and add a control check box to the square root form. The check box indicates whether graphics are On or Off. If the check box is checked, graphics are On. If the graphics are On, the output of the square root function is displayed in graphics and text forms. In other words, there still is a text display in addition to a graphics display in the graphics form. Figure 5.2 shows the check box added to the square root form.

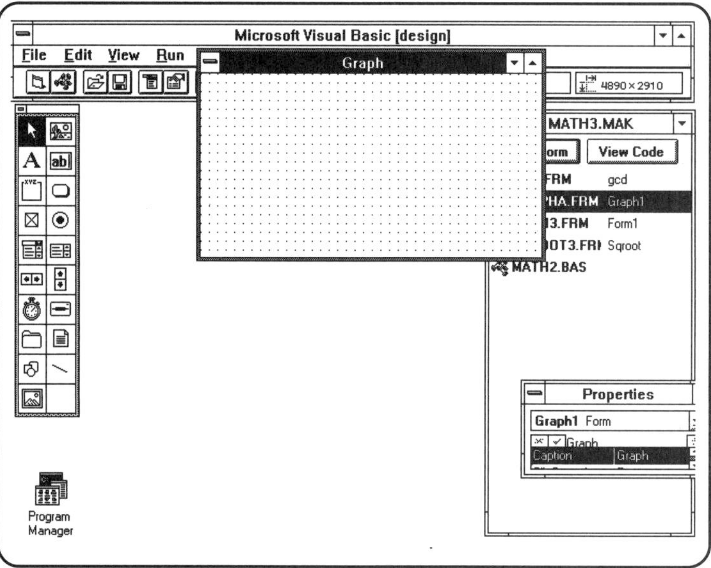

Figure 5.1. The Graph form.

A check box displays an option that can be turned On or Off. Use this control to give the user a True/False or Yes/No option. Check boxes can be used in groups also to display multiple choices from which the user can choose one or more options.

Although check boxes and option buttons may appear to function similarly, there is an important difference. When a user selects an option button, the other option buttons in the same group are cancelled automatically. Any number of check boxes can be selected, however.

To display text next to the check box, set the `Caption` property. To determine the state of the box (cleared, selected, or disabled) set the `Value` property. Table 5.1 shows the properties, events, and methods for the check box control (in Version 3.0).

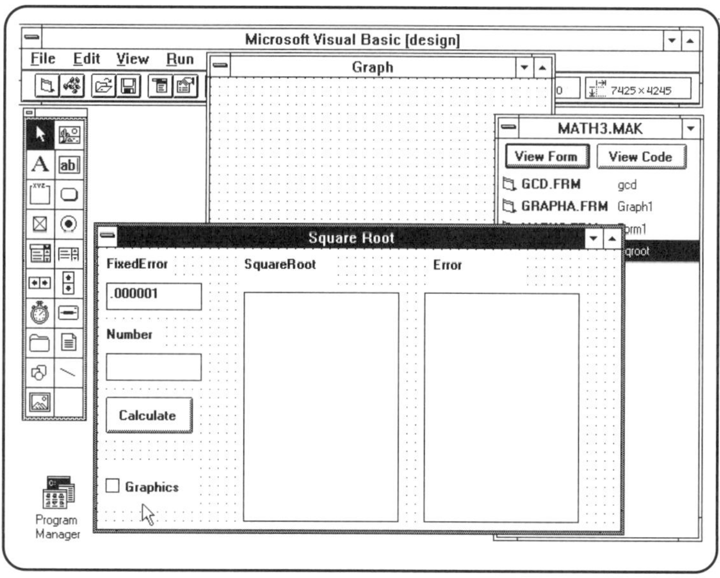

Figure 5.2. A check box added to the Square Root form.

Table 5.1. Check box.

Properties		
Alignment	BackColor	Caption
DragIcon	DragMode	Enabled
FontBold	FontItalic	FontName
FontSize	FontStrikethru	FontUnderline
ForeColor	Height	HelpContextID
hwnd	Index	Left
MousePointer	Name	Parent
TabIndex	TabStop	Tag
Top	Value	Visible
Width		

continues

TABLE 5.1. CONTINUED

	Events	
Click	DragDrop	DragOver
GotFocus	KeyDown	KeyPress
KeyUp	LostFocus	MouseDown
MouseMove	MouseUp	
	Methods	
Drag	Move	Refresh
SetFocus	ZOrder	

For example, in this application, you will want to inspect the value of the check box (Check1) to determine whether the user wants to implement graphics. If the check box is checked, indicating that the user wants to implement graphics, show the graph form, change its caption to indicate that the square root function invoked it, clear the graph form, and set a scale for the form. The following code handles it:

```
If Check1.Value = 1 Then
   Graph1.Show
   Graph1.Caption = "Graph -> Square Root"
   Graph1.Cls
   ScaleY2 = Val(InNumber1.Text) / 4' Let the graph be self-scaling
   Graph1.Scale (0, ScaleY2)-(15, 0)' depending on the input number
   X = 1                             ' Also initialize first point
End If
```

SCALES

Note that the graph scales itself depending not only on the function calling it but also on the value of the input number (the square). For square root, you will want to see the relative slopes as the function finds the square roots of different numbers. If you don't scale, a large number's graph bunches up at one end of the graph, and that is not very illuminating. Scaling, therefore, is another important design consideration for your applications. The Visual Basic scaling system is very flexible; explore it and vary it to suit your needs.

Now that the graph form is set up, you need to plot points in it. The following code does this:

```
If Check1.Value = 1 Then
    Graph1.PSet (X, g2)      ' g2 is the value of a guess!
    X = X + 1                ' This is a time series; X = an increment of time
End If
```

If the check box is checked, plot a point. Increment the time series by 1. If the check box is not checked, don't plot the point (but still calculate it).

The following code shows both of these fragments added to the general procedure `SquareRoot ()`:

```
Sub SquareRoot ()
Dim g1 As Double
Dim g2 As Double
Dim num As Double
Dim CurEr As Double

  If Check1.Value = 1 Then
     Graph1.Show
     Graph1.Caption = "Graph -> Square Root"
     Graph1.Cls
     ScaleY2 = Val(InNumber1.Text) / 4
     Graph1.Scale (0, ScaleY2)-(15, 0)
     X = 1
  End If

  nl$ = Chr$(13) + Chr$(10)
  Text2.Text = nl$
  Text1.Text = nl$
  num = Val(InNumber1.Text)
  g2 = num / 2
  Do
    g1 = g2
    g2 = (g1 + num / g1) / 2
    Text2.Text = Text2.Text + nl$ + Format$(g2)
    CurEr = Abs(g1 - g2)
    Text1.Text = Text1.Text + nl$ + Format$(CurEr)
    i = i + 1

    If Check1.Value = 1 Then'   Plot the point if checked.
       Graph1.PSet (X, g2)
       X = X + 1
    End If
  Loop Until CurEr < Val(SRFixedError.Text) Or i = 15
End Sub
```

Note that points are plotted to the Graph form, and text is written alternately to the text boxes in the SquareRoot. The visual display therefore is "real time" relative to the text display—a neat effect and one not easily accomplished in most environments. Windows and Visual Basic make this effect seem routine.

To add graphics capability to other functions in this application (GCD and so on), add a check box to each of their forms, and add similar code to their general function procedures. Note that the StartUp form is the same one used in MATH2b. You don't have to do anything to it to indicate this new form (GRAPH). The individual functions maintain it. Listing 5.1 shows the complete code for MATH3, the StartUp form, the modified square root form, the new graph form, and the unchanged GCD form.

LISTING 5.1. MATH3.

```
' general declarations

Dim FType As Integer        ' FTypes: SqrRoot = 1
                            '         GCD     = 2
Dim LastFType As Integer    ' Used to turn off previous function's controls.

' event procedures for StartUp form

Sub SquareRootCom_Click ()
  LastFType = FType
  FType = 1                'Set Function type.
  ControlCenter            'Set controls.
End Sub

Sub GCDCom_Click ()
  LastFType = FType
  FType = 2                ' Set Function type.
  ControlCenter            ' Set Controls.
End Sub

' general procedures for StartUp

Sub ControlCenter ()
  Select Case LastFType      'Hide form.
     Case 1
       SqRoot.Hide
     Case 2
       GCD.Hide
  End Select
```

```
  Select Case FType           'Show form.
     Case 1
       SqRoot.Show

     Case 2
       GCD.Show
  End Select
End Sub

' general procedures for GCD form

Sub GCDiv ()
Dim r As Long
Dim n As Long
Dim m As Long

  nl$ = Chr$(13) + Chr$(10)
  Text2.Text = nl$
  Text1.Text = nl$
  n = Val(InNumber1.Text)
  m = Val(InNumber2.Text)
  Do
    r = n Mod m
    n = m
    m = r
    Text1.Text = Text1.Text + nl$ + Format$(n)
    Text2.Text = Text2.Text + nl$ + Format$(m)
  Loop Until r = 0
End Sub

' events for GCD form

Sub Command1_Click ()
  GCDiv
End Sub

' events for Sq Root form

Sub Command1_Click ()
  SquareRoot
End Sub

' general procedures for Sq Root form

Sub SquareRoot ()
Dim g1 As Double
Dim g2 As Double
Dim num As Double
Dim CurEr As Double
```

continues

LISTING 5.1. CONTINUED

```
 If Check1.Value = 1 Then
    Graph1.Show
    Graph1.Caption = "Graph -> Square Root"
    Graph1.Cls
    ScaleY2 = Val(InNumber1.Text) / 4
    Graph1.Scale (0, ScaleY2)-(15, 0)
    X = 1
 End If

 nl$ = Chr$(13) + Chr$(10)
 Text2.Text = nl$
   Text1.Text = nl$
   num = Val(InNumber1.Text)
   g2 = num / 2
   Do
     g1 = g2
     g2 = (g1 + num / g1) / 2
     Text2.Text = Text2.Text + nl$ + Format$(g2)
     CurEr = Abs(g1 - g2)
     Text1.Text = Text1.Text + nl$ + Format$(CurEr)
     i = i + 1

     If Check1.Value = 1 Then
        Graph1.PSet (X, g2)
        X = X + 1
     End If
  Loop Until CurEr < Val(SRFixedError.Text) Or i = 15
End Sub
```

Figure 5.3 shows the application running (with its check box checked), displaying text in one form and graphics in another.

CHAOS AND STRANGE ATTRACTORS

Now for something a little strange. In recent years, researchers in various fields that involve dynamics have used computers to model nonlinear systems (in a nonlinear system, the parameters of the system do not vary proportionally) that exhibit behavior that's not easily visualized or understood by just looking at the numbers. The key to understanding many of these systems is to uncover the attractors of the system. Generally, an attractor is a state or set of states toward which a system evolves. Attractors are found in a computer-generated phase (or state) space. In state space, a point represents all the information known about a system's state; the space itself is a picture of a system's current state plotted against its next state (see Figure 5.4).

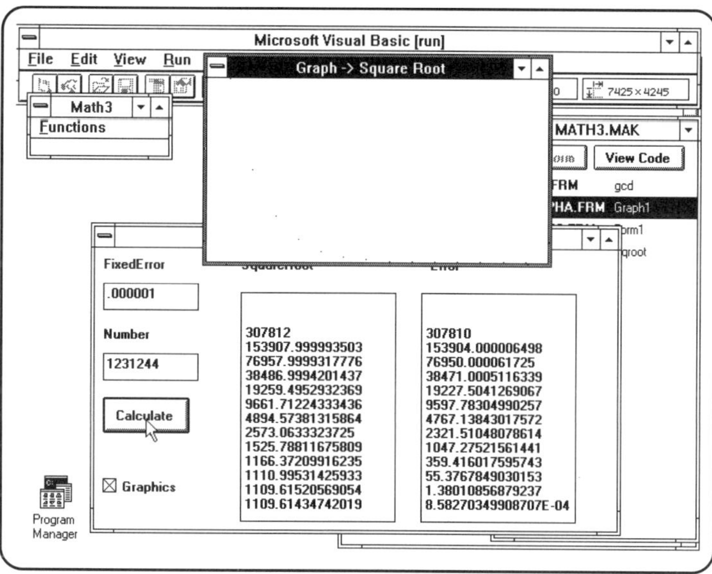

Figure 5.3. MATH3 in motion with Graphics checked.

The key to understanding the system is to determine what state (or states) the system is evolving toward. Attractors "attract" a system. As the system evolves, the collection of points that represent successive states can do one of the following:

1. Settle to one point (a point attractor) (see Figure 5.5).
2. Repeatedly return to a set of points (a periodic attractor) (see Figure 5.6).
3. Not return to a well-defined group of points, or return to a strange set of points (see Figure 5.7).

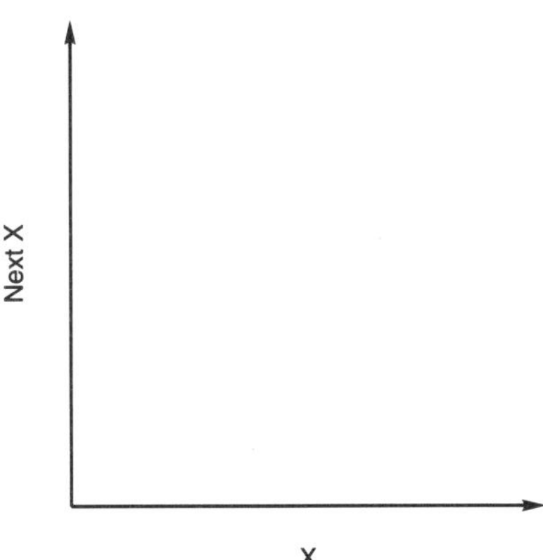

Figure 5.4. State space.

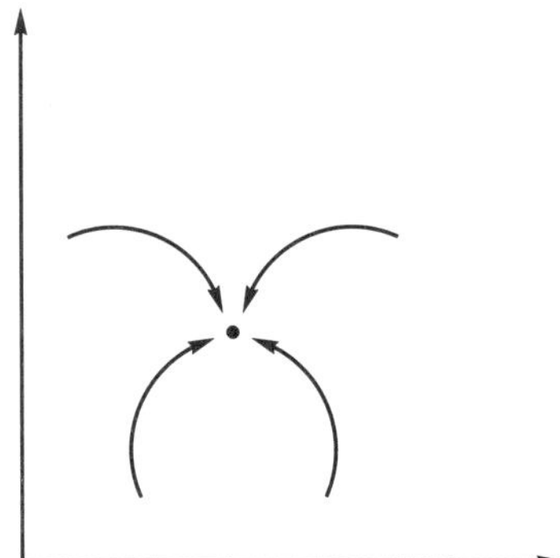

Figure 5.5. A point attractor.

Dynamic Modeling Systems

The system evolves as the values of the current state become the initial values of the next state. Each time, before each loop into the next state, the model records or plots the current system's state in phase space.

For several reasons, modeling systems (like tasking systems in general) are easily described with object-oriented techniques. It is easy to generalize the characteristics that models have in common. Any model is a type of model related to other models. From a computing perspective, models share low-level graphics primitives such as points. They're all plotted in some kind of space, although they differ in the way they generate states in that space.

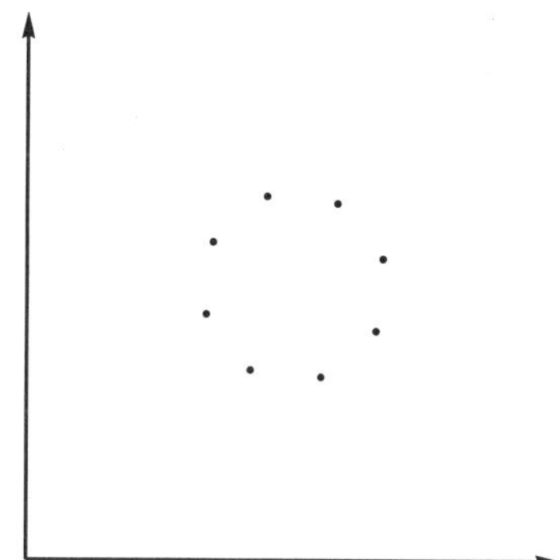

Figure 5.6. A periodic attractor.

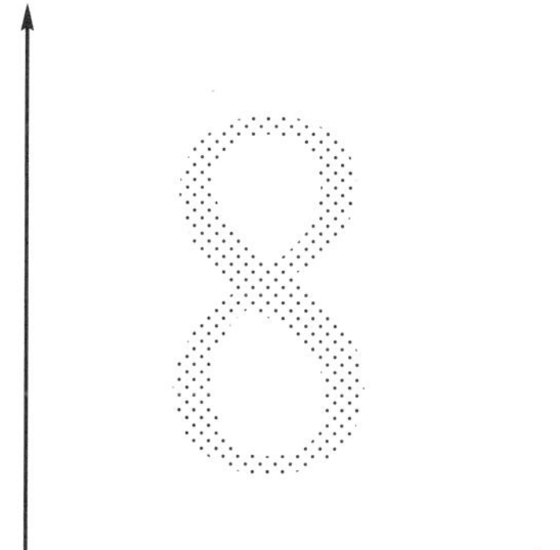

Figure 5.7. A strange attractor.

A dynamic system (which a model represents) can be anything you can describe by knowing the values of variables and whose current state depends on its previous states. The state of the system can be something measured on a continuous scale, something with logical changes (Is it Yes? Is it On? Has something happened since we checked last?) and so on.

In a speech recognition system, one of my favorite examples, each word in the sentence carries some individual weight and affects (and is affected by) all the other words in the sentence. In a sense, one can consider a sentence to be a dynamic system that changes state through the addition of words and punctuation marks. Initially, a sentence is empty; add a word (that word is the new sentence), add another word (the two words are the new sentence), add another word (the three words are the new sentence), add a punctuation mark (the three words plus the punctuation mark equals a new sentence), and so on.

When you speak, words necessarily follow each other. When you write, they follow or displace one another (by replacing or being inserted between words). Each new state represents your attempt to clarify the state of the sentence. (But, as many of you know, each new state can clarify or confuse—one reason that parsing sentences is so difficult.)

The sentence in its next state is very sensitive to its current state (or condition) and to its previous states. You might say that "meanings" are the attractors in the dynamic system "sentence." At any state the sentence may have no meaning (an extinction state), one meaning (a stable state), or many meanings (possibly a chaotic state), depending on any number of things (point of view, reading or writing skill, and so on).

Mathematic Attraction

Scientists (in mathematics, physics, engineering, biology, computer science, business, economics, and so on) are trying to understand dynamic systems. Their discoveries have led to at least one agreeable conclusion: anything of interest that changes state is beautifully complex.

Mathematicians and computer scientists try to get meaning from complex systems by representing them with equations (or rules), and they visualize the system in pictures.

Some particularly interesting pictures exist in phase (or state) space, where each point holds all the information needed to describe a dynamic system at any time (or state). For example, suppose that a system varies (changes state) depending on a variable such as size or number. Call the variable X, and call its rate of change *R*, and then equations such as

```
Nextx = R * X * (1-X)
```

can describe the system.

In this case, 1 represents the system at some maximum state, and 0 represents the system at some minimum state. Either extreme state (when `Nextx` = 1 or 0) translates into an infinite state (because there's either nothing left to act on the current state—when `Nextx` = 0—or nothing left to act on when `Nextx` = 1 and `Nextx` is everything) that our mathematical model can no longer act on.

The preceding equation, the "standard map" or "logistic equation," has been explored for many years by mathematically inclined people in many fields. They have discovered that it (and presumably the dynamic system it describes) behaves unpredictably. In general, any system described with any nonlinear equation or equations behaves unpredictably because it's extremely sensitive to initial conditions. Nearby values of X in one state may lead to values (of `Nextx`) that are far apart in the next state.

You can complicate matters even more by increasing the number of variables in a system (that is, your representation of a system). For example, these two coupled nonlinear equations for changes in state

```
Nextx = AX - (1-(Y*Y*Y))
Nexty = 1 - BY
```

can present an "infinite" number of states (`Nextx` values) responding to "infinitely" small changes in the condition of the previous state (or X value). This infinity of values is the chaotic set for this dynamic system. You can see this chaos by plotting the values of each state (`Nextx`) in time. (The X axis is time; the Y axis is the value of each X.) (See Figure 5.8.)

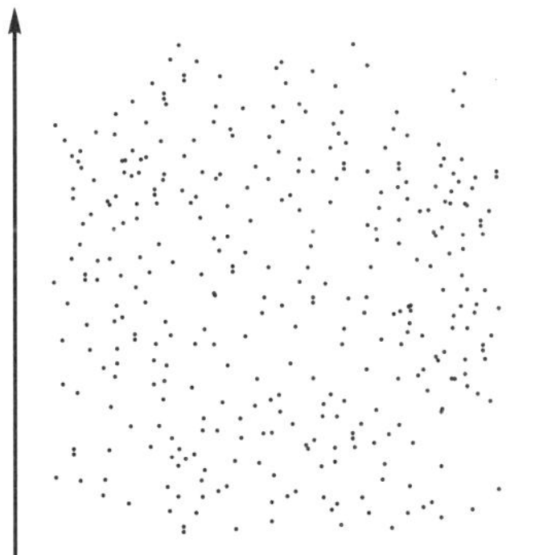

Figure 5.8. Chaos.

Order in Chaos

There's an intriguing and often surprising order in even the most chaotic systems, and one way to see this order is in phase space. When you plot values of `Nextx` against values of current X, you uncover the attractor for the chaotic set. This attractor "lives" in phase space and is made up of all the points in the chaotic set. By mutual agreement it's called "strange." Figure 5.9 shows the strange attractor corresponding to the chaotic set in Figure 5.8.

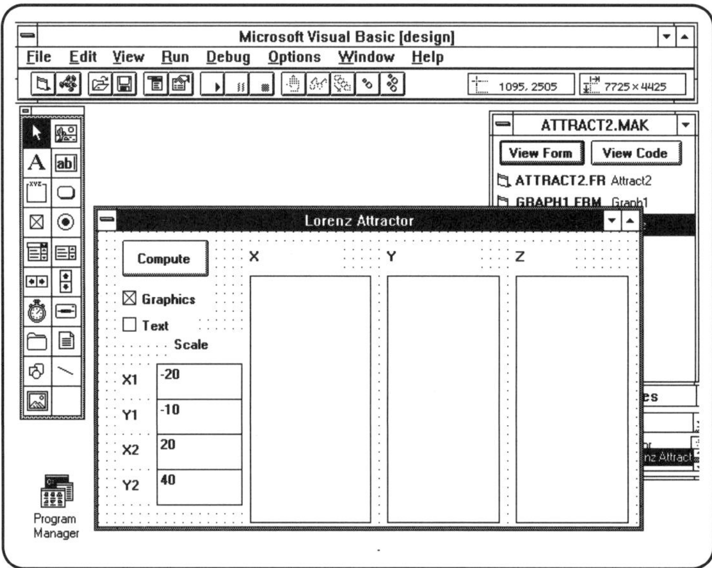

Figure 5.9. The Lorenz attractor.

The strange attractor in Figure 5.9 is the Lorenz attractor. First explored by Edward Lorenz in 1963, the Lorenz attractor is a graphic description of a weather prediction model based on the interaction of three variables:

```
Dx = 10 * (Y - X)
Dy = X * (28 - Z) - Y
Dz = X * Y - (8 / 3) * Z
```

(Although I won't explain the nature of those variables here, for detailed information see *Chaos*, by James Gleick.)

The code in Listing 5.2 (ATTRACT1 on the Visual Basic programming disk) is all you need in order to show the attractor.

Listing 5.2. The Lorenz attractor.

```
Sub Form_Click ()
    Scale (-20, -10)-(20, 40)      ' Set a scale
    X = 1
    Y = 1
    Z = 1
    I = 1
```

```
    For I = 1 To 6000               ' Number of iterations can vary.
        LorenzAttractor X, Y, Z     ' Call general procedure
    Next I
End Sub

Sub LorenzAttractor (X, Y, Z)       ' General procedure
    Dx = 10 * (Y - X)               ' Change equations
    Dy = X * (28 - Z) - Y
    Dz = X * Y - (8 / 3) * Z
    X = X + .01 * Dx
    Y = Y + .01 * Dy
    Z = Z + .01 * Dz
    PSet (X, Z)                     ' Plot in X,Z plane
End Sub
```

This code is simple and it illustrates how easily you can use Visual Basic to produce quick results. It uses only one form and has no menu or controls. Because the attractor is displayed whenever the user clicks the form, the only procedures are the two in Listing 5.2: the `Click` event procedure for the form and the general procedure for displaying the attractor. You can even omit the general procedure and put the Lorenz code right in the `Click` event procedure. I did not do that, however, because I want to build a general-purpose model displayer; it goes much easier (as you will see) if I keep the model-generating code from the interface code.

The general-purpose attractor display application I have in mind, in fact, is similar to the function application (MATH3) developed earlier in this chapter. Each model (in this case, an attractor) can be added to a menu (using the Menu Design window), and then each menu event (a `Click`) causes the attractor selected to be displayed in the Graph form.

Although I'm not going to detail every step used to create this application (ATTRACT2) because it's so much like MATH3, you can build it similarly by creating a form for each task (attractor), adding specific controls for the task, adding the task to the menu, and writing the event and general procedure code. Figure 5.10 shows the form I created for the Lorenz attractor.

Note the controls for text output for the three variables and for modifying the scale in Figure 5.10. Note also the two check boxes (one to indicate graphics display; one to indicate text display); both check boxes can be on simultaneously.

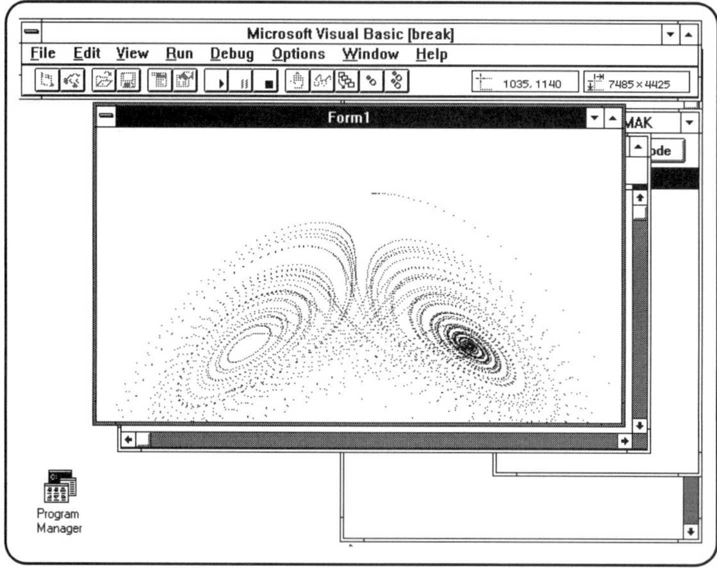

Figure 5.10. The Lorenz form.

Figure 5.11 shows the application running with the graphics output directed to the Graph form and the text output directed to the Lorenz form.

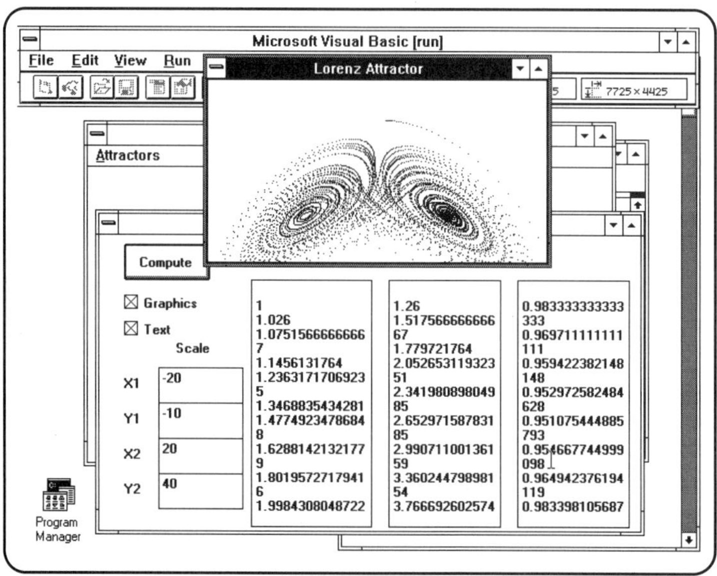

Figure 5.11. ATTRACT2.

The complete code for ATTRACT2 is in Listing 5.3. Note that `Check1` and `Check2` are check boxes on the main form; `Command1` is a command button on the main form; Graph1 is the graphics form; `X`, `Y`, `Z` are the Lorenz equation variables in the `Lorenz Attractor` procedure; and `Text5`, `Text6`, and `Text7` are text boxes on the main form.

Listing 5.3. ATTRACT2.

```
' events

Sub LorenzCom_Click ()
    Lorenz.Show
End Sub

' Lorenz events

Sub Command1_Click ()
    If Check1.Value = 1 Then
        Graph1.Show
        Graph1.Cls
        Graph1.Caption = "Lorenz Attractor"
        Graph1.Scale (Val(Text1.Text), Val(Text2.Text)) -
        ➥ (Val(Text3.Text), Val(Text4.Text))
    End If
    X = 1
    Y = 1
    Z = 1
    I = 1
    For I = 1 To 6000
        LorenzAttractor X, Y, Z
    Next I
    Beep
End Sub

' Lorenz general procedures

Sub LorenzAttractor (X, Y, Z)
    nl$ = Chr$(13) + Chr$(10)
    Dx = 10 * (Y - X)
    Dy = X * (28 - Z) - Y
    Dz = X * Y - (8 / 3) * Z
    X = X + .01 * Dx
    Y = Y + .01 * Dy
    Z = Z + .01 * Dz
    If Check2.Value = 1 Then
        Text5.Text = Text5.Text + nl$ + Format$(X)
        Text6.Text = Text6.Text + nl$ + Format$(Y)
        Text7.Text = Text7.Text + nl$ + Format$(Z)
```

continues

LISTING 5.3. CONTINUED

```
    End If
    If Check1.Value = 1 Then
        Graph1.PSet (X, Z)
    End If
End Sub
```

Real Multitasking via *DoEvents()*

Let's make a minor and a significant improvement to the attractor application, one that goes a long way toward making ATTRACT2 (and any other application you design) a true multitasking application. Begin by reconsidering ATTRACT—particularly the code for `COMMAND1.Click()`. It looks like this:

```
Sub Command1_Click ()
    If Check1.Value = 1 Then
        Graph1.Show
        Graph1.Cls
        Graph1.Caption = "Lorenz Attractor"
        Graph1.Scale (Val(Text1.Text), Val(Text2.Text)) -
        ➥ (Val(Text3.Text), Val(Text4.Text))
    End If
    X = 1
    Y = 1
    Z = 1
    I = 1
    For I = 1 To 6000
        LorenzAttractor X, Y, Z
    Next I
    Beep
End Sub
```

The first part of this code initializes the graph form if the graphics check box is checked. It then initializes the Lorenz model's variables (X, Y, Z). Finally, it calls the Lorenz attractor general procedure, which calculates new values for X, Y, and Z based on equations. The Lorenz attractor general procedure also handles all the output to the Graphics form and text output to the text boxes on the Lorenz form (see Listing 5.3). Any model you want to add to this application can follow a simple pattern.

Add a Scale to a Form

Before going too much further, let's make the minor modification to ATTRACT2. Let the graph form show the scale it has passed. Add two text box controls (or, alternately, add two labels) to the Graph form for displaying the scale (you could also add four text boxes, or labels, if you want to display the maximum and minimum values of the scale in separate text boxes or labels). (See Figure 5.12.)

Then add code to the Graph form (using the `Load` event procedure) to show the scale:

```
Sub Form_Load ()
    Graph1.Scale (X1, Y1)-(X2, Y2)
    UpperLeft$ = Str$(X1) + "," + Str$(Y1)
    Text1.Text = UpperLeft$
    LowerRight$ = Str$(X2) + "," + Str$(X2)
    Text4.Text = LowerRight$
End Sub
```

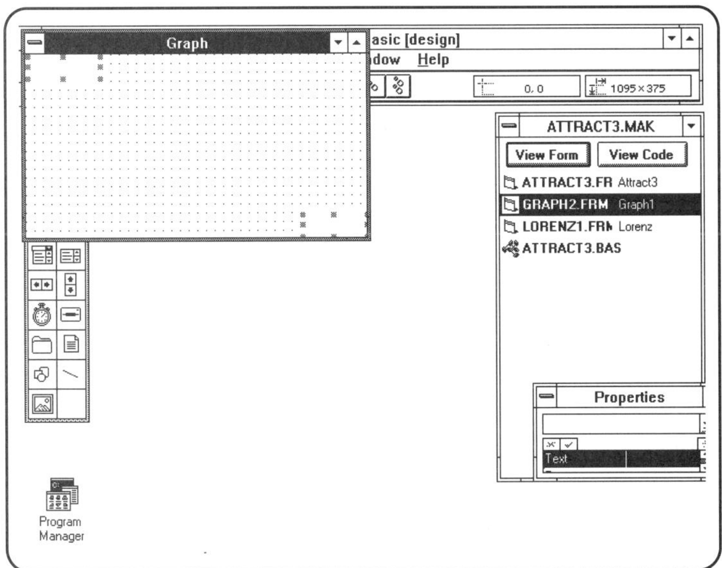

Figure 5.12. Adding a scale to the Graph form.

Listing 5.4 shows the complete new version of ATTRACT (ATTRACT3 on the disk), and Figure 5.13 shows ATTRACT3 in motion.

LISTING 5.4. ATTRACT3.

```
' Graph form events

Sub Form_Load ()
    Graph1.Scale (X1, Y1)-(X2, Y2)
    UpperLeft$ = Str$(X1) + "," + Str$(Y1)
    Text1.Text = UpperLeft$
    LowerRight$ = Str$(X2) + "," + Str$(X2)
    Text4.Text = LowerRight$
End Sub

' StartUp form events

Sub LorenzCom_Click ()
    Lorenz.Show
End Sub

' Lorenz general procedures

Sub LorenzAttractor (X, Y, Z)
    nl$ = Chr$(13) + Chr$(10)
    Dx = 10 * (Y - X)
    Dy = X * (28 - Z) - Y
    Dz = X * Y - (8 / 3) * Z
    X = X + .01 * Dx
    Y = Y + .01 * Dy
    Z = Z + .01 * Dz
    If Check2.Value = 1 Then
        Text5.Text = Text5.Text + nl$ + Format$(X)
        Text6.Text = Text6.Text + nl$ + Format$(Y)
        Text7.Text = Text7.Text + nl$ + Format$(Z)
    End If
    If Check1.Value = 1 Then
        Graph1.PSet (X, Z)
    End If
End Sub
```

At this point, it is important to note that in order to plot a sufficient number of points for an attractor, it's often necessary to plot a very large number of points. In this case, an acceptable number of points for the Lorenz attractor is 6,000. Note also that if the user checks both the text and graphics check boxes on the Lorenz form, it takes a little time to calculate, plot, and output as text 6,000 points and 6,000 values for X, Y, and Z. If you were modeling a sophisticated system of one-half of a dozen variables and more complex calculations, this process could tie up the system for a very long time.

Because multitasking is not preemptive in Windows, an application must voluntarily yield time (and focus) before another application can take control. Visual Basic supplies a simple solution: idle loops with `DoEvents`.

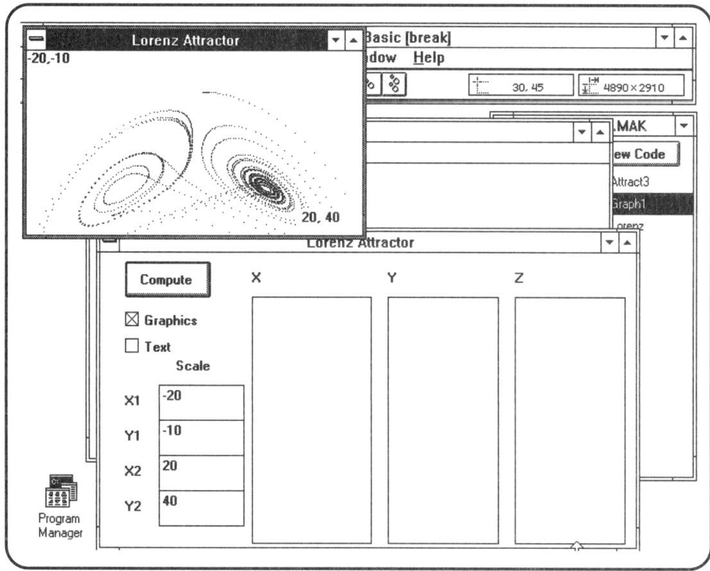

Figure 5.13. ATTRACT3: the scale labels in action.

DOEVENTS()

The `DoEvents()` function switches control to the operating system. If another application has requested control, it gets it. When it is finished, or if no other application wants control, focus shifts back to the application that yielded control.

But there's more to it than that. The yielding application actually continues processing. For example, let's say that the Lorenz attractor yields control to some other application, Microsoft Word, for example, when you click the Word icon. When you begin editing again in Word, the Lorenz attractor continues to calculate and draw points on the Graph form. Note that this multitasking works only if the other application (Word, in this case) relinquishes control, using its equivalent of `DoEvents()`.

There you have it: multitasking, pure and sweet. Figure 5.14 shows you what I mean. I added the `DoEvent()` procedure (to be discussed shortly) and opened Word (to write this paragraph), and the Lorenz attractor kept working.

So, how do you do it? Revise the code as follows:

1. Create a new form (File/New Form) with no controls and no menu.
2. Add the following general procedure:

```
Sub Main ()
    Attract2.Show
    Done = -1
    Do While DoEvents()
    Loop
End Sub
```

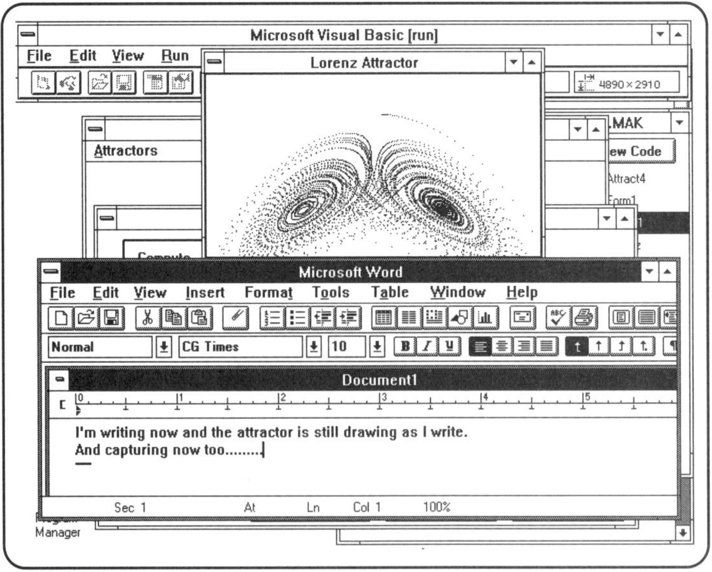

Figure 5.14. Multitasking with `DoEvents()`.

The application now should start with this procedure (you may have to specify it as a `StartUp` form; to do this, select `Set StartUp Form` from the Visual Basic Run menu). First, it shows the form previously designated as a `StartUp` form (ATTRACT2). Now it shows that form and sets the `DoEvents` loop in motion. You can, if you want, add code within the loop:

```
Sub Main ()
    Attract2.Show
    Done = -1
    Do While DoEvents()
     ' idle loop code here
    Loop
End Sub
```

Our application (ATTRACT4) doesn't need any code here because all it wants to do is to allow another application to process in the foreground if the user chooses it. But remember that ATTRACT4 continues to process in the background.

The variable `Done` also is of interest—it is global (declared in the Global module). The `Command1_Click()` event procedure uses it to prevent the restarting of a calculation after the calculation yields control. In other words, if `Command_Click()` yields control, but is still processing, and if you allow `Command_Click()` to start again, you will have two copies of this procedure running simultaneously. In all but the wildest application, this is definitely not what you would want.

`Done`, therefore, is used as a flag (or watch) to indicate whether the application is still running (Not Done) or not running (Done). The following revision of `Command_Click()` tests to see whether it's already running (in the background). If not, it initializes the Graphics form (`Graph1`), Lorenz variables (`X, Y, Z`), and initializes its part of the `DoEvents()` process (`Dummy=DoEvents()`):

```
Sub Command1_Click ()
    If Done = 0 Then Exit Sub
    Done = 0
    If Check1.Value = 1 Then
        Graph1.Show
        Graph1.Cls
        Graph1.Caption = "Lorenz Attractor"
        Graph1.Scale (Val(Text1.Text), Val(Text2.Text)) -
        ➥ (Val(Text3.Text), Val(Text4.Text))
    End If
    X = 1
    Y = 1
    Z = 1
    I = 1
    For I = 1 To 6000
        C = C + 1
        LorenzAttractor X, Y, Z
        If C = 100 Then
            C = 0
            Dummy = DoEvents()
        End If
```

```
    Next I
    Beep
    Done = -1
End Sub
```

`Command1_Click` uses a counter (`c`) to check `DoEvents()`. Every 100 loops, `Command1_Click` gives `DoEvents()` a chance to respond to another application's request for the operating system. When the calculation is complete, a beep lets you know (if it's in the background) that it is done. It then sets `Done` to True (–1), which allows the process to restart if a user clicks the command button.

Note that you put the `DoEvents()` function call where it's needed the most: in the calculation part of the application. As a rule, use the `DoEvents()` function only when you need it because it slows down the system somewhat (as the counter is checked). `DoEvents()` is particularly useful when an application is doing long calculations.

The complete code for ATTRACT4, a true multitasking version of this application, is in Listing 5.5.

LISTING 5.5. ATTRACT4.

```
' StartUp form events

Sub LorenzCom_Click ()
    Lorenz.Show
End Sub

Sub Form_Load ()
    Done = -1
End Sub


'  Lorenz general procedures

Sub LorenzAttractor (X, Y, Z)
    nl$ = Chr$(13) + Chr$(10)
    Dx = 10 * (Y - X)
    Dy = X * (28 - Z) - Y
    Dz = X * Y - (8 / 3) * Z
    X = X + .01 * Dx
    Y = Y + .01 * Dy
    Z = Z + .01 * Dz
    If Check2.Value = 1 Then
        Text5.Text = Text5.Text + nl$ + Format$(X)
        Text6.Text = Text6.Text + nl$ + Format$(Y)
        Text7.Text = Text7.Text + nl$ + Format$(Z)
    End If
```

```
    If Check1.Value = 1 Then
        Graph1.PSet (X, Z)
    End If
End Sub

' Main general procedure

Sub Main ()
    Attract2.Show
    Done = -1
    Do While DoEvents()
    Loop
End Sub

' Lorenz events

Sub Command1_Click ()
    If Done = 0 Then Exit Sub
    Done = 0
    If Check1.Value = 1 Then
        Graph1.Show
        Graph1.Cls
        Graph1.Caption = "Lorenz Attractor"
        Graph1.Scale (Val(Text1.Text), Val(Text2.Text)) -
        ➥ (Val(Text3.Text), Val(Text4.Text))
    End If
    X = 1
    Y = 1
    Z = 1
    I = 1
    For I = 1 To 6000
        C = C + 1
        LorenzAttractor X, Y, Z
        If C = 10 Then
            C = 0
            Dummy = DoEvents()
        End If
    Next I
    Beep
    Done = -1
End Sub
```

PLOT STRANGE ATTRACTORS IN A PICTURE BOX

Up to this point, graphics output has been limited to a form. Graphics certainly are not limited to a form, however; you can plot them in a picture box also. To modify the code in ATTRACT4 to print attractors in a picture box rather than in a form, add a picture box control to the Graph form and then redirect the plotting to the picture box:

```
Graph1.Picture1.PSet (X, Z)
```

There's almost nothing to it, really. Figure 5.15 shows the new display with points drawn in the picture box rather than directly on the form.

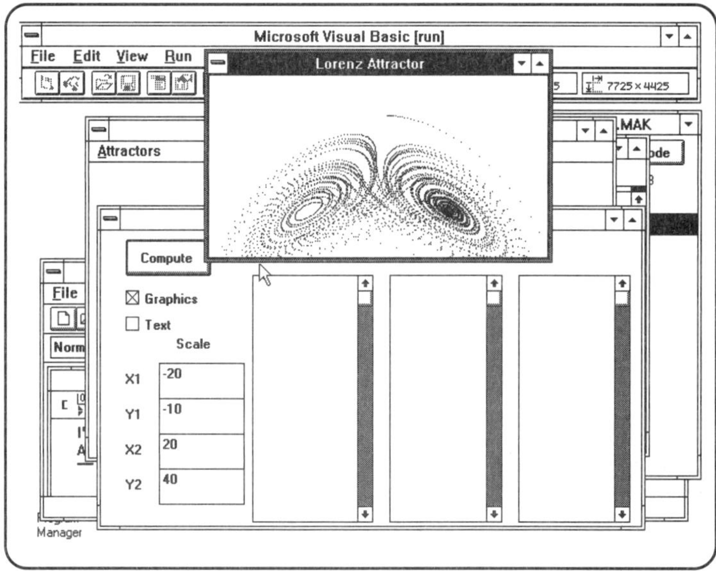

Figure 5.15. A picture display of a Lorenz attractor.

Resize a Picture Box When a Form Is Resized

Consider what happens to the picture box (or a picture plotted directly on a form) when a user resizes the form. Unless you anticipate the resizing event, you will get the results shown in Figure 5.16, which shows the picture after the user has resized the form.

The picture isn't automatically resized to fit the new form size, which is probably not what you want. In most circumstances, you will want to resize the picture (whether in a picture box or on the form) to fill the form. Fortunately, you can easily handle this by using the form's `Resize` event procedure to resize the picture.

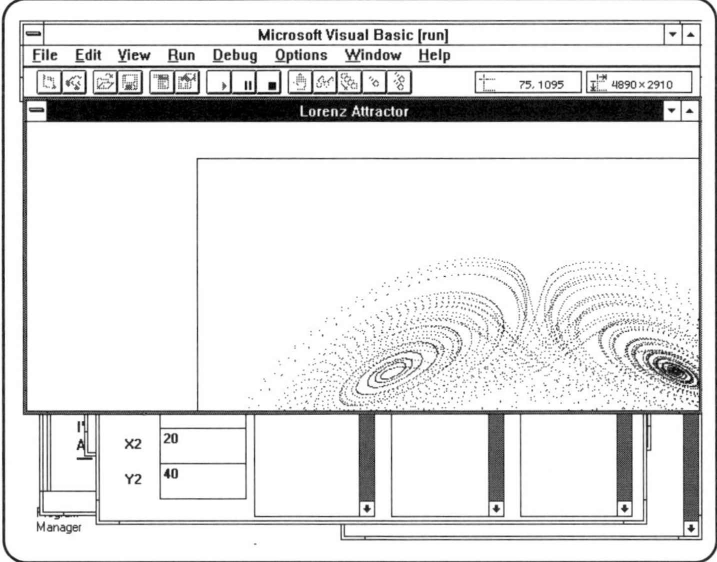

Figure 5.16. A picture display after a resize event.

Because the `Resize` event procedure for the form is automatically invoked each time the form is resized, put any resize response code in the `Resize` event procedure. The following code resets the picture size to fill the form and resets the picture scale to reflect the new picture size:

```
Sub Form_Resize ()
   Picture1.Move 0, 0, ScaleWidth, ScaleHeight
   Graph1.Scale (Val(Lorenz.Text1.Text), Val(Lorenz.Text2.Text)) -
    ➥ (Val(Lorenz.Text3.Text), Val(Lorenz.Text4.Text))
   Graph1.Picture1.Scale (Val(Lorenz.Text1.Text), Val(Lorenz.Text2.Text)) -
    ➥ (Val(Lorenz.Text3.Text), Val(Lorenz.Text4.Text))
End Sub
```

Note that this fragment includes code to reset the scale for the entire form and for the picture box. If you are using the picture box only to display the picture, omit the form scale code. Note also that if you don't change the scale, the picture box is resized correctly, but the picture itself is not rescaled.

ATTRACT5 on the disk adds the `Resize` event procedure to ATTRACT4.

FIND PRIME NUMBERS + DOEVENTS()

Just for fun, let's write another quick application that uses `DoEvents()` to enable the user to interrupt processing and go to another task.

The application is relatively simple. When a form is clicked, the user is presented with an input box and a prompt to enter a number the user wants to test for primality. If the input is valid, the `FindPrime` function is called. It looks like this:

```
Function FindPrimes (Number As Long) As Long
    Dim Limit As Long
    If Done = 0 Then Exit Sub
    Done = 0
    FindPrimes = 0              ' 0 = is a prime
    Limit = Sqr(Number)
    For Index = 2 To Limit
        If Number Mod Index = 0 Then
            FindPrimes = Index   ' >0 isn't prime
            Exit For
        End If
        x = DoEvents()          ' Yield to other applications.
    Next Index
    Done =-1
End Function
```

This application determines whether a number is prime by repeatedly dividing it by an incremented index. Because this find-primes version is primitive (really, it's a brute force method), you enable the user to interrupt processing by inserting the `DoEvents` statement `x = DoEvents()`. Figure 5.17 shows the application in progress. Listing 5.6 shows the complete application (PRIMES on the disk).

Note that this little application can easily bomb because user input (the number to test) isn't checked before it is passed to the `Val` function:

```
NumStr$ = InputBox$("Enter a number to test for Prime.")
Number = Val(NumStr$)
```

If `Number` is greater than 2,147,483,647—the maximum value for a long integer—Visual Basic generates an error message. Chapter 9, "Extending Visual Basic: Custom Controls and DLLs," returns to this problem and improves the Primes application (and others) by using the Windows API to control user input.

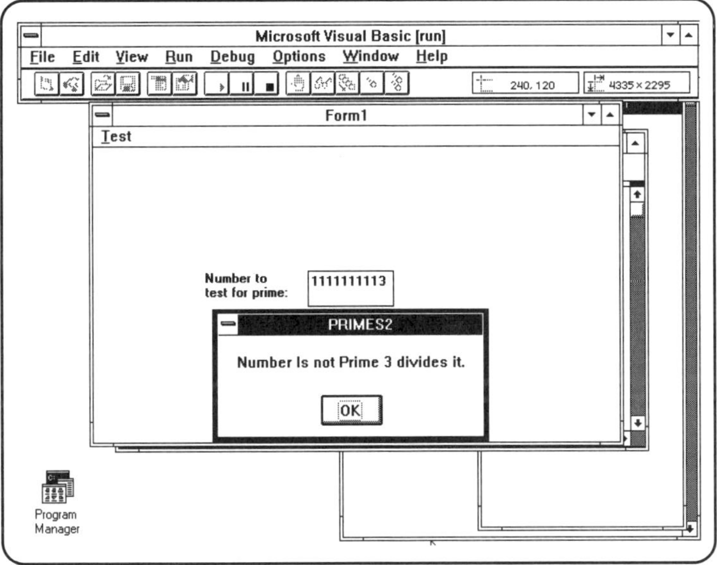

Figure 5.17. Primes.

Listing 5.6. Primes.

```
' general declarations
  Done As Integer
Sub Form_Load ()
  Done = -1
End Sub
Sub Form_Click ()
    Dim Number As Long
    NumStr$ = InputBox$("Enter a number to test for Prime.")
    Number = Val(NumStr$)
    If Number > 0 Then
        Prime% = FindPrimes(Number)
        If Prime% > 0 Then
            Msg$ = "Number Is not Prime" + Str$(Prime%) + " divides it."
        Else
            Msg$ = "Number Is a Prime."
        End If
    Else
        Msg$ = "Number is invalid."
    End If
    MsgBox Msg$
End Sub
```

continues

LISTING 5.6. CONTINUED

```
Function FindPrimes (Number As Long) As Long
    Dim Limit As Long
    If Done = 0 Then Exit Sub
    Done = 0
    FindPrimes = 0
    Limit = Sqr(Number)
    For Index = 2 To Limit
        If Number Mod Index = 0 Then
            FindPrimes = Index
            Exit For
        End If
        x = DoEvents()
    Next Index
    Done = -1
End Function
```

Before abandoning Primes, let's make one slight improvement that doubles its speed. As it stands, the `FindPrimes` routine divides the test number by every number from 1 to the square root of the test number. This process is a waste of time, however, because you know that if the number 2 doesn't divide evenly into the test number, no other even number does. Let's revise the code, therefore, to first test the number 2, and if that doesn't divide evenly, to proceed to test every odd number until the square root of the test number is reached. The following revised `FindPrimes()` function does this:

```
Function FindPrimes (Number As Long) As Long
    Dim Limit As Long
    If Done = 0 Then Exit Sub
    Done = 0
    FindPrimes = 0
    Limit = Sqr(Number)
    If Number Mod 2 = 0 Then
        FindPrimes = 2
        Exit Function
    End If
    For Index = 3 To Limit Step 2
        If Number Mod Index = 0 Then
            FindPrimes = Index
            Exit For
        End If
        x = DoEvents()
    Next Index
    Done = -1
End Function
```

On my Zeos 386 Notebook, the first version of `FindPrimes()` required 59 seconds using Visual Basic Version 1.0 and 30 seconds using Version 2.0 or Version 3.0 to determine that 2,147,483,647 was indeed prime. The revised `FindPrimes()` required 29 seconds to make the same determination using Visual Basic Version 1.0 and 15 seconds using Version 2.0 and Version 3.0. Again, you can see the significant speed improvement using Version 2.0 or Version 3.0. The revised version of `FindPrimes()` is included in the PRIMES2 application on the disk (see Chapter 9 for a PRIMES3 application).

HENON, ROSSLER, AND LORENZ ATTRACTORS

Since the first edition of *Secrets of the Visual Basic Masters*, I've been exploring other fascinating strange attractors with Visual Basic. The code in Listing 5.7 (called ATTRACT6 on the disk) shows the basic Growth attractor, the Lorenz attractor discussed earlier, and the Rossler and Henon Attractors. This listing includes `DoEvents()` and picture box resize code.

Each of these strange attractors has its own form to enable you to vary the scaling at runtime. The main form (Attract6) is menu-driven. Each time you select a new attractor, the corresponding form for the attractor is shown. Figure 5.18 shows the Henon form in design view. Figure 5.19 shows the Henon attractor displayed on the graphics form at runtime. Figure 5.20 shows the Rossler attractor displayed at runtime.

The design of each of these forms is similar to the Lorenz form, so you should have little trouble using this general design to add other strange attractors to your projects. Simply follow the one form-one attractor plan to setup parameters for the attractor; then use the graphics form designed earlier to display.

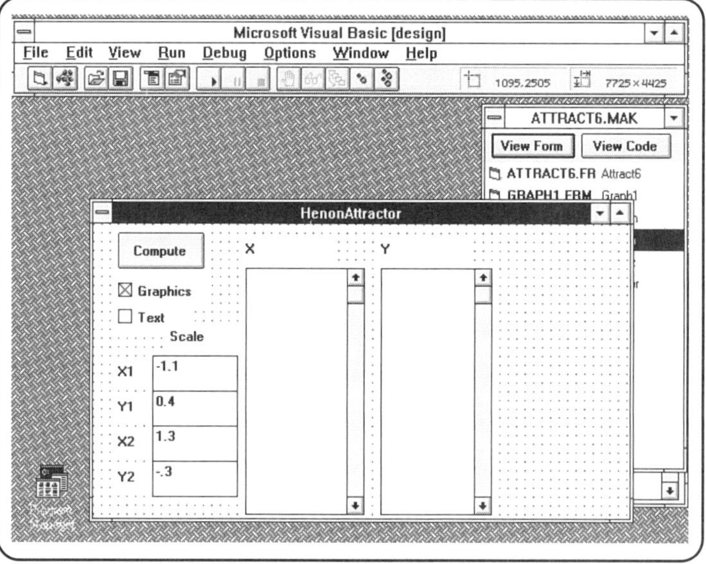

Figure 5.18. Henon attractor form in design view.

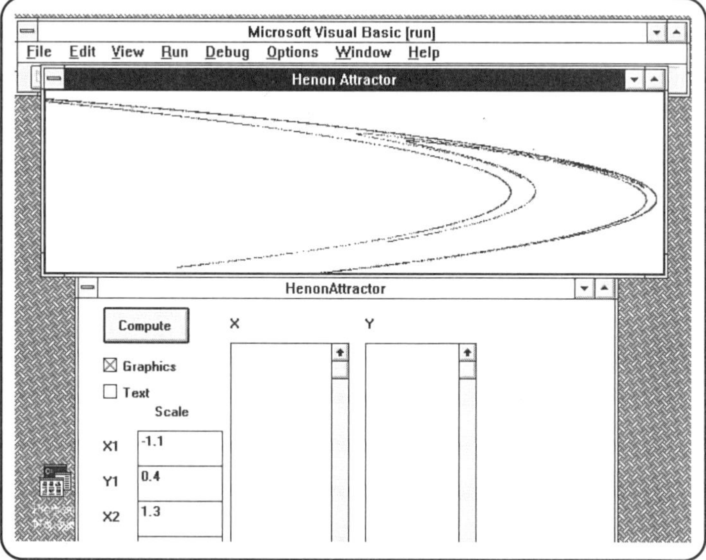

Figure 5.19. Henon attractor displayed on the graphics form.

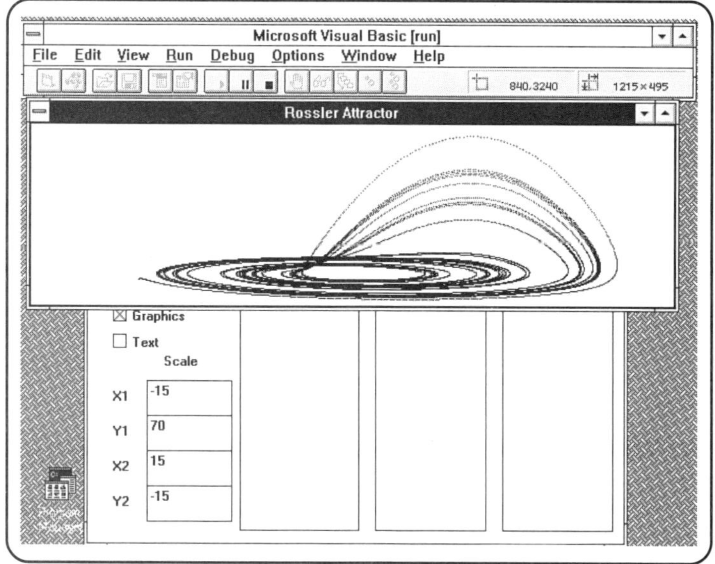

Figure 5.20. Rossler attractor displayed on the graphics form.

Listing 5.7. Attract6.

```
' Attract.Bas
Global Done As Integer
Global X1 As Double
Global X2 As Double
Global Y1 As Double
Global Y2 As Double

'Attract6.frm

Sub Form_Load ()
    Done = -1
End Sub

Sub mnuGrowth_Click ()
    Growth.Show
End Sub

Sub MnuHenon_Click ()
    Henon.Show
End Sub
```

continues

LISTING 5.7. CONTINUED

```
Sub MnuLorenz_Click ()
    Lorenz.Show
End Sub

Sub MnuRossler_Click ()
    Rossler.Show
End Sub

Sub Parabola (I)
    NextX = R * X * (1 - X)
    CurX = X * 4575 ' conversion necessary for picturebox
    CurY = NextX * 3255
    Graph1.PSet (CurX, CurY)
    X = NextX
End Sub

' Graph1.frm

Sub Form_Resize ()
    Picture1.Move 0, 0, ScaleWidth, ScaleHeight
    Picture1.Scale (X1, Y1)-(X2, Y2)
    Picture1.Refresh
End Sub


'Growth.frm

Sub Attract1 (X, y)
    y = X
    X = 4 * X * (1 - X)
    If Check2.Value = 1 Then
        Text5.Text = Text5.Text + nl$ + Format$(X)
        Text6.Text = Text6.Text + nl$ + Format$(y)
    End If
    If Check1.Value = 1 Then
        Graph1.Picture1.PSet (X, y)
    End If
End Sub

Sub Command1_Click ()
    A = 1
    If Done = 0 Then Exit Sub
    Done = 0
    If Check1.Value = 1 Then
        X1 = Val(Text1.Text)
        Y1 = Val(Text2.Text)
        X2 = Val(Text3.Text)
```

```
        Y2 = Val(Text4.Text)
        Graph1.Show
        Graph1.Cls
        Graph1.Caption = "Growth Attractor"
        Graph1.Picture1.Scale (X1, Y1)-(X2, Y2)
    End If
    X = .04
    y = .04
    I = 1
    For I = 1 To 6000
        C = C + 1
        Attract1 X, y
        If C = 100 Then
            C = 0
            Dummy = DoEvents()
        End If
    Next I
    Beep
    Done = -1
End Sub

'Henon.frm


Sub Command1_Click ()
    A = 1
    If Done = 0 Then Exit Sub
    Done = 0
    If Check1.Value = 1 Then
        X1 = Val(Text1.Text)
        Y1 = Val(Text2.Text)
        X2 = Val(Text3.Text)
        Y2 = Val(Text4.Text)
        Graph1.Show
        Graph1.Cls
        Graph1.Caption = "Henon Attractor"
        Graph1.Picture1.Scale (X1, Y1)-(X2, Y2)
    End If
    X = 1
    Y = 1
    I = 1
    For I = 1 To 6000
        C = C + 1
        HenonAttractor X, Y
        If C = 100 Then
            C = 0
            Dummy = DoEvents()
        End If
```

continues

LISTING 5.7. CONTINUED

```
    Next I
    Beep
    Done = -1
End Sub

Sub HenonAttractor (X, Y)
    Dx = Y - 1.4 * X * X + 1
    Dy = .3 * X
    If Check2.Value = 1 Then
        Text5.Text = Text5.Text + nl$ + Format$(X)
        Text6.Text = Text6.Text + nl$ + Format$(Y)
    End If
    If Check1.Value = 1 Then
        Graph1.Picture1.PSet (Dx, Dy)
        'Graph1.PSet (Dx, Dy)
    End If
    X = Dx
    Y = Dy
End Sub

'Lorenz.frm

Sub Command1_Click ()
    If Done = 0 Then Exit Sub
    Done = 0
    If Check1.Value = 1 Then
        X1 = Val(Text1.Text)
        Y1 = Val(Text2.Text)
        X2 = Val(Text3.Text)
        Y2 = Val(Text4.Text)
        Graph1.Show
        Graph1.Cls
        Graph1.Caption = "Lorenz Attractor"
        Graph1.Picture1.Scale (X1, Y1)-(X2, Y2)
    End If
    X = 1
    Y = 1
    Z = 1
    I = 1
    For I = 1 To 6000
        C = C + 1
        LorenzAttractor X, Y, Z
        If C = 10 Then
            C = 0
            Dummy = DoEvents()
        End If
    Next I
    Beep
    Done = -1
End Sub
```

```
Sub LorenzAttractor (X, Y, Z)
    nl$ = Chr$(13) + Chr$(10)
    Dx = 10 * (Y - X)
    Dy = X * (28 - Z) - Y
    Dz = X * Y - (8 / 3) * Z
    X = X + .01 * Dx
    Y = Y + .01 * Dy
    Z = Z + .01 * Dz
    If Check2.Value = 1 Then
        Text5.Text = Text5.Text + nl$ + Format$(X)
        Text6.Text = Text6.Text + nl$ + Format$(Y)
        Text7.Text = Text7.Text + nl$ + Format$(Z)
    End If
    If Check1.Value = 1 Then
        Graph1.Picture1.PSet (X, Z)
    End If
End Sub

'Rossler.frm

Sub Command1_Click ()
    If Done = 0 Then Exit Sub
    Done = 0
    If Check1.Value = 1 Then
        X1 = Val(Text1.Text)
        Y1 = Val(Text2.Text)
        X2 = Val(Text3.Text)
        Y2 = Val(Text4.Text)
        Graph1.Show
        Graph1.Cls
        Graph1.Caption = "Rossler Attractor"
        Graph1.Picture1.Scale (X1, Y1)-(X2, Y2)
    End If
    X = -10
    Y = -1
    Z = -1
    I = 1
    For I = 1 To 30000
        C = C + 1
        RosslerAttractor X, Y, Z
        If C = 100 Then
            C = 0
            Dummy = DoEvents()
        End If
    Next I
    Beep
    Done = -1
End Sub
```

continues

LISTING 5.7. CONTINUED

```
Sub RosslerAttractor (X, Y, Z)
    Dx = -(Y + Z)
    Dy = X + (Y / 5)
    Dz = (1 / 5) + Z * (X - 5.7)
    X = X + Dx * .005
    Y = Y + Dy * .005
    Z = Z + Dz * .005
    If Check2.Value = 1 Then
        Text5.Text = Text5.Text + nl$ + Format$(X)
        Text6.Text = Text6.Text + nl$ + Format$(Y)
        Text7.Text = Text7.Text + nl$ + Format$(Z)
    End If
    If Check1.Value = 1 Then
        Graph1.Picture1.PSet (X, (Y + Z + Z))
    End If
End Sub
```

SUMMARY

That's about it for this chapter, except for this closing aside. I should note that I really needed the `DoEvents()` function throughout the creation of this book. As noted elsewhere, I'm using several applications simultaneously as I write: Visual Basic, the applications I'm working on for the book, Microsoft Word, Collage (a nice screen-capture utility), and Nemesis (a delightful Go game that diverts my attention from time to time). Fortunately, everything works well together, with the occasional exception of my code. For example, to capture some of the screens you see in this book, I had to run my application and then switch to the screen-capture utility to grab the image for a figure. But, when a graphic (the Lorenz attractor, for example) is calculating and drawing in a long loop, I can't switch from it without going through a Ctrl-Break sequence.

Pressing Ctrl-Break, of course, brings me out of the application and back to Visual Basic. But that's not what I want. I want to capture the application as it's processing so that you can see it in this book.

The solution that's worked many times for me is a good old `DoEvents()` loop. Sometimes I temporarily add a `DoEvents()` loop to a simple application (for example, most of the applications in Chapters 8, 9, 10, and 11) just to capture a screen. Then I edit it out, to simplify the application for its current stage in the book.

Thanks, `DoEvents()`.

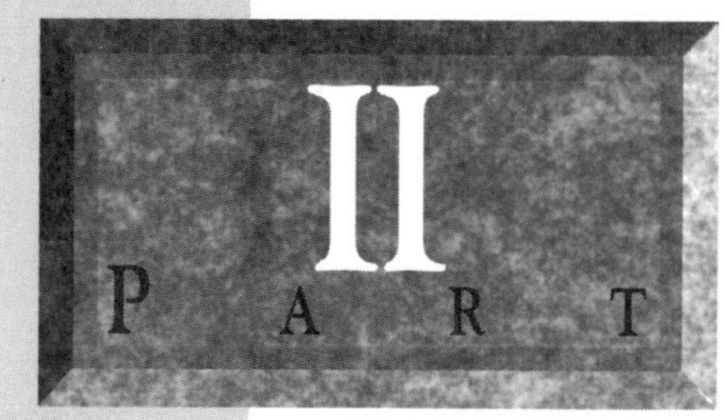

Exploiting Visual Basic 3.0

FILES, DIRECTORIES, AND A CODE WIZARD

Everything else being equal, you should always try to minimize the size of your .EXE applications. A quirk of Visual Basic is that it doesn't always remove the items deleted from your code. In other words, just because you delete an item of code doesn't mean that Visual Basic has removed it from the file. The code works and Visual Basic has made the changes, but as a bookkeeping matter, the old code still exists in the file—Visual Basic saves your code in an internal format if you don't specify otherwise. Therefore, as you proceed through a development or debugging cycle, you might find that the subsequently compiled application (in .EXE form) gets larger and larger.

Fortunately, you can get around Visual Basic's bookkeeping quirk quite easily: Save your code to text using Code/Save Text and then reload that code (using Code/Load Text) into the application. It looks like you're simply replacing existing code with identical code, but that's not really the case. You're cleaning up the residue Visual Basic retained when you made a change.

Build a Generic File I/O Form

Trigger and Use Change Events

Conserve Your Energy: Reuse Code and Forms

Build a File I/O Module

Use Binary Gets and Puts to Optimize File I/O

You're also saving your code in a second format (text), which makes it useful both as a backup and for use in other applications that might not be capable of reading Visual Basic's internal format. I feel safer knowing that the code is there somewhere in a simple ASCII format I can view from any number of ASCII (text) editors, including the text controls (for example, a text box) in Visual Basic.

If you try to load the text associated with a Visual Basic form (saved in an .FRM file in Visual Basic's internal format), you discover that the text box, as is, doesn't display it correctly. Any number of non-ASCII characters stop it cold. The GREP-like application (Wizard) developed in this chapter demonstrates this behavior (you can check it out by running Wizard and viewing a .FRM file or two).

For those of you not familiar with GREP, it's a search-and-view utility that lets a user (typically a programmer) search a group or groups of files for specific strings. Typically, C and Pascal programmers and UNIX-heads (and others, I presume) use GREPs to locate variables, functions, constants, and so on in projects that contain many files or in libraries that contain many routines and variables.

Visual Basic doesn't come with a GREP-like tool; and, because it is something I can't do without, I wrote one to help me manage my projects. This chapter fills you in on all the design details and discusses file I/O and file I/O optimization. I've discovered a thing or two that I think you might find interesting. I call my Visual Basic GREP-like tool Wizard; it's derived from a DOS-based version I wrote (and contributed to the shareware domain) several years ago. I wrote that version in Turbo Pascal and, interestingly, I can run it within a window in the Windows environment. It is text-based, however, and not as pretty or as user-friendly as the one I will show you in Visual Basic.

You may be surprised to learn that the Visual Basic .EXE file is smaller than the Turbo Pascal (DOS) .EXE version (without the VBRUN100.DLL, VBRUN200.DLL, or VBRUN300.DLL), and it's just as fast. I will show you some speed tests at the end of this chapter. As I've said (and continue to say throughout this book), Visual Basic lets you easily write complex and user-friendly applications. In addition, these benefits usually don't require you to pay a price in speed or size.

Although it's the first substantial code example in this book, Wizard cuts only a few corners. Later, as we go along, and as needed, I add features to Wizard. In particular, I substantially extend Wizard into a Visual Basic project editor in Chapter 9, "Extending Visual Basic: Custom Controls, and DLLs." The Wizard project editor greatly simplifies debugging and maintaining your Visual Basic code; I suggest that you compile it (WIZARD7 on the disk) and begin using it even before it is discussed in detail in Chapter 10 "A Wizard Project Editor and a Wizard Clipboard."

Wizard is multiform (consisting initially of three forms) and menu-driven, and it interacts with the Clipboard (the simplest form of DDE) and illustrates a number of key concepts (such as list processing) that are reused throughout this book. The first version of Wizard (called WIZARD1 on the disk) focuses on the interaction of multiforms and on building forms and modules that can be reused. Chapter 7, " Bulletproof at Runtime: Into the Real World of Error and Error Handling," adds to Wizard (WIZARD2) a fourth form, some error-handling, and Chapter 9 completes the project (WIZARD7) by adding many spiffy features.

Each of these Wizards lets a user search a specifiable group of files for a string. Every time a string is found in a file, the filename and position is recorded and saved. The user also has the option of viewing the file at the position where the string was found and copying selected text from the file to the Clipboard.

Because Wizard uses binary input to read files, it isn't limited (in theory) to ASCII. I have more to say about that later. Whether to use text, binary, sequential, or random input for file I/O is a key decision you have to make whenever your application works with files. The file handler developed quickly in this chapter is generic because it can read (and write) files in several formats including text, binary, and sequential, and it is reusable by other applications. The reason that Wizard uses binary file I/O is for speed and flexibility. I demonstrate this speed improvement by showing a couple of file I/O options. Chapter 9 returns to flexibility and adds some features that enable Wizard to discriminate among file types.

The plan for this chapter is five-fold:

- Build a flexible and expandable file I/O handler that can read and write any Visual Basic-supported file type.
- Build the Wizard form—the Visual Basic GREP—which will be the application control form and will use the file I/O handler (and other forms).

- Discuss multiform design.
- Compare binary and sequential file I/O (with some benchmarks thrown in for fun).
- Build a list-handling form that will be a model for any list-handling application. Wizard uses the list-handling form to maintain, record, and report its activity.

Wizard is a tool I always use (whether I'm programming or writing). I run it first thing every time I load Windows. I use it throughout my development and debugging cycle and when I'm trying to explain what I'm doing (now, for example). I think that you will find many uses for it. After you've explored it, add your own features and send me an update—we can exchange Wizards.

A Code Wizard: Take 1

Wizard has many components, so let's get started. The best way to get the most out of the many details and components of this project is to load the Wizard project (on the disk) into Visual Basic and run the project. Then experiment with Wizard as you read the accompanying text in this chapter. The first version of Wizard (WIZARD1) uses three forms: one to control the application, one to control file I/O, and one to record and report results. One good reason for separating these functions into forms (you don't *have* to separate them) is to make it easier to use the file I/O controls and the list-handling form without Wizard. For example, you might want to let a user browse through the files on a disk without actually searching for a string or let a user search for a string without loading a selected file into the editor maintained on the Wizard form. Or, you might want to use the file I/O form to get the name and path of a file to run an application or to compare files. The uses of the file I/O and the list-handling form are diverse.

As a general practice, let each of your applications have a main or start-up form (with a control menu) that is more or less specific to a task. Then, whenever possible, let the main form direct operations on other forms. I use this approach throughout this book.

Build a Generic File I/O Form

Putting task-specific controls on a separate form is a general, reusable design approach (for example, all of the file I/O controls are on a separate form that Wizard, or any other application, loads when necessary). The file I/O form then takes care of any file-related tasks and returns drive, directory, and file information. It's up to the application that called the file I/O form to use the returned information.

In this application, the Wizard form uses that information to load files containing the specified string into a text box for viewing and copying. Any general information that you want to find out about files, drives, or directories can be retrieved from this file information form.

Let's start by building this form, adding controls and routines, and returning information from the form to any application that might use it. Building the form is simple. You should enable a user to specify a drive, directory, file, and file pattern. Because Visual Basic supplies three ready-to-go controls (drive, dir, and file), you simply plug them in and add a text box to enable the user to change the file pattern. Figure 6.1 shows the results.

Use Change Events

The Visual Basic developers designed the Drive, Directory, and File list boxes to work together, so it's trivial to work with them. Primarily, you need to know when change events are triggered; then update each list box accordingly.

A drive change event is triggered by a single click. When the user clicks a drive, the drive change event is triggered automatically. Therefore, you indicate anything that you want to happen after a single click in the drive change event procedure. The only thing you have to do after a drive change is pass that new drive information to the directory list box so it can be updated. You handle this by assigning the Directory list box Path property the value of the drive list box's Drive property.

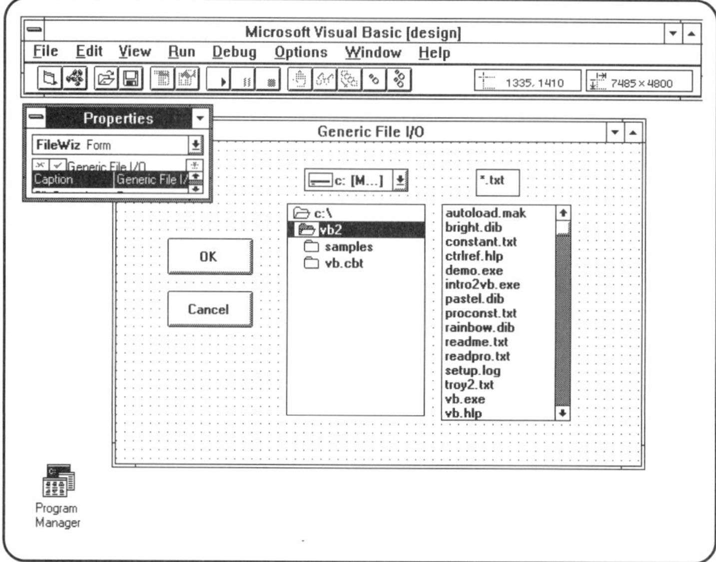

Figure 6.1. A generic file I/O form.

The drive change event procedure looks like this:

```
Sub Drive1_Change ()
    Dir1.Path = Drive1.Drive
End Sub
```

TRIGGER AND USE CHANGE EVENTS

Changing the value of any directory list box's Path property automatically triggers a change event (in the directory list box). If you want to indicate anything to happen in response to this change in the directory list box, therefore, you do it here in the directory list box's Change event procedure. The only thing you have to specify in this generic form is to assign the file directory Path property the value of the directory list box Path property.

The Dir change event procedure looks like this:

```
Sub Dir1_Change ()
    File1.Path = Dir1.Path
End Sub
```

When the file list box Path property is changed, a `PathChange` event for the file list box is generated automatically. If you want to, therefore, you can specify action to occur in the `PathChange` event procedure for the file list box. In the generic file I/O form, you don't have to specify any new behavior, but you can continue the string of behavior changes.

To sum up, when the drive list box is clicked, a drive list box change event is triggered, which in turn can be used to specify behavior that triggers a directory list box change event, which in turn is used to trigger a file list box change event. Figure 6.2 shows this string of events.

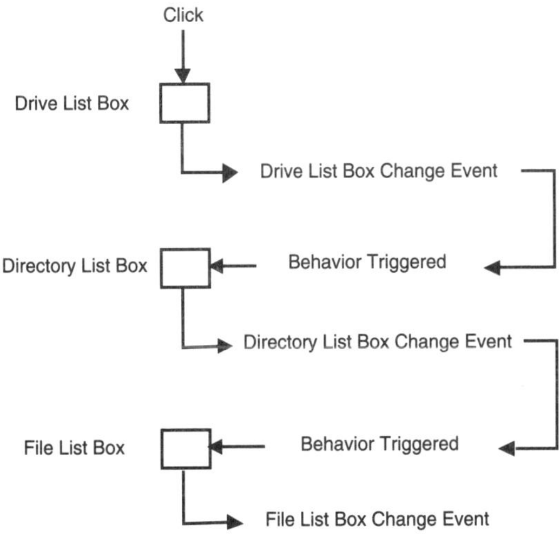

Figure 6.2. Triggered events.

Typically, when a user double-clicks a file within a file list box, an action is initiated (for example, opening the file the user specifies). Because you want this file I/O form to be general, simply let the double-click record the current file I/O form settings (the directory path and the filename), and then hide the file I/O form. Alternatively, you can unload the form if you don't anticipate reusing it soon or if you want to conserve memory. (Note: If you choose to unload a form rather than hide it, keep in mind that a "bug" in Visual Basic 1.0 doesn't free the memory used by any multiline text box on the form.) In this case, because you're using a single-line text box, it's no problem. If you are using a multiline text box as a screen-type editor or viewer, however, as the Wizard `Startup` form does, this could quickly become a problem.

The file double-click event procedure looks like this (note that `TheFileName` in the code must be a global variable):

```
Sub File1_DblClick ()
    TheNewPath = Dir1.Path
    If Right$(TheNewPath, 1) <> "\" Then
        TheNewPath = TheNewPath + "\"
    End If
    TheFileName = File1.FileName
    FileInfo.Hide
End Sub
```

SET THE FILE PATTERN

Although it isn't necessary, it's convenient to let users specify which file patterns to list when a file list box is displayed. The file list box Pattern property keeps track of the file pattern and can be changed at both design time and runtime. Typically, you set a default file pattern (*.* or *.doc, for example) at design time, and then let the user use a text box to change the pattern. An easy way to show the user how the text box works from the beginning is to indicate a default pattern at design time in the text box, and then assign the value of the text box Text property to the file list box File property when the file I/O form is loaded. The following code makes the assignment:

```
Sub Form_Load ()
    File1.Pattern = Text1.Text
End Sub
```

Now, whenever the user changes the value of the text box, the results can be seen immediately by updating the file list box Pattern property, which automatically generates a `PatternChange` event for the file list box. The assignment is identical to the one just made in the `Form_Load` event procedure:

```
Sub Text1_Change ()
    File1.Pattern = Text1.Text
End Sub
```

That's really about it for the general file I/O form. Save this form and add new controls and behaviors to it—as you will do now to develop the file I/O form for Wizard.

Derive a New File I/O Form

Wizard gets its file information from the file I/O form. In addition, it's convenient (I think) for the user to change the search string on the same form (that is, in the same window) as file patterns, directories, drives, and so on are changed. I've elected, therefore, to add an additional text box for editing the search string, and two command buttons to let the user indicate whether to proceed with the search or to cancel.

Figure 6.3 shows the revised file I/O form derived from the generic file I/O form by simply adding the new controls to the existing file I/O form and saving it under a new name (WIZFILE on the disk).

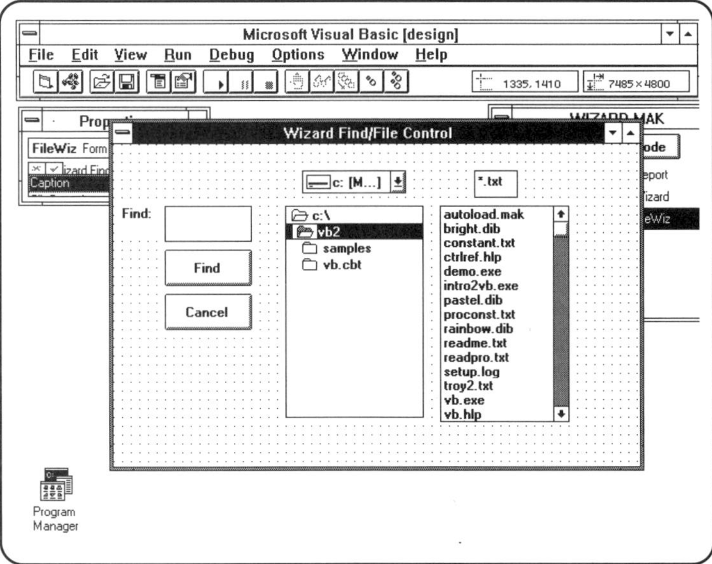

Figure 6.3. Wizard file I/O form.

Note that you use the existing controls and control behavior for the Wizard file I/O form—just add the new controls and behavior as needed.

There are no new events or behaviors to define for the text box. You use it merely to enable the user to enter or edit a search string. The value of the Text property of the text box is used subsequently by the Wizard `Startup` (or Control) form when it carries out its search. Note again that this text box can be anywhere—on the Wizard form, for example, or on its own distinct form. I put it here because I think it works best here.

The Cancel button behavior also is simple. If the user decides to cancel the search, record the Cancel (in a global variable) and hide (or unload) the form. I've elected to record all the variable information that needs to be used by several forms in global variables for the project. Alternatively, you can record this behavior in local variables and pass them between procedures on different forms. For me, because global variables are simpler to keep up, I usually use them to hold project-level information. Unless you have a good reason not to, I suggest that you use global variables in this manner.

The Cancel command click event procedure looks like the following, where `CancelFind` is the global variable that can be used by any procedure in the project. I use True (–1) and False (0) to indicate action. Thus, –1 = Cancel the Search:

```
Sub Command2_Click ()
    FileInfo.Hide
    CancelFind = -1
End Sub
```

The second command button is effectively an OK button. If it's clicked by the user, the current file and directory information is recorded:

```
Sub Command1_Click ()
    TheNewPath = Dir1.Path
    If Right$(TheNewPath, 1) <> "\" Then
        TheNewPath = TheNewPath + "\"
    End If
    TheFileName = File1.FileName
    FileInfo.Hide
End Sub
```

CONSERVE YOUR ENERGY: REUSE CODE AND FORMS

That discussion takes care of the derived Wizard file I/O form (WIZFILE). In sum, it lets a user specify the drive, directory, file pattern, and search string for a search. The search is controlled by the Wizard form, which I'll explain in the section "Into the Heart of a Wizard" later in this chapter. First, let's consider a few more general routines that accompany the file I/O form and that you will need to use in many applications: the routines for opening, closing, saving files, and so on.

Because all these routines are reusable, they should be centralized in a module that is visible to the entire application. Although your first thought might be that these routines should be in the file I/O form, that's not a good place for them for a simple reason: if they're attached (locally) to a form, they can be accessed only from within the form. To use them outside the form, therefore (for example, from any control form that accesses the file I/O form), you would have to trigger an event in the file I/O form that opens, closes, saves, and so on. Triggering an event this way works, but it's so strange-sounding to me. I prefer to put these routines in a code module (called FILE.BAS) that I can add to any project that needs file I/O. This module is handy for another reason as well. If you don't want to use the file I/O form, but you still want to open a file, you can use the code module without the expense (in terms of memory) of loading a form. Keep this in mind because forms are more expensive than code without a form.

BUILD A FILE I/O MODULE

In this first version of FILES.BAS, I keep things very simple. Chapter 7 (and later chapters) add more general-purpose routines to the module. For starters, let's simply code a general `OpenAFile` function that gets a free file number (from Windows or DOS) and then opens the file in an indicated mode. If you will write applications that open files in only a single mode, you might want to simplify even further. Because Wizard eventually uses three file modes (sequential, binary, and random), and other applications in this book use additional modes, I make this function as general as possible. Again, note that this preliminary version excludes any sophisticated error handling (it's added in Chapter 7).

To open a file, you have to indicate a filename, a mode, and a record length if the mode is random. The file mode indicates how you access the file (get at the data). The differences among these file modes are described in detail in Chapter 21 of the *Visual Basic Programmer's Guide*. In short, a sequential file is usually a text file (ASCII) in which each byte is assumed to be a character. Sequential file access can be used also for handling variable-length record data. If record data length is fixed, you typically use random access. If you want to access the data in a file at the byte level, where any byte can contain any kind of data, binary access works best. These file access modes are discussed later in this chapter in the section "Use Binary Gets and Puts to Optimize File I/O."

Let's first create a file-opening function that can handle these various kinds of access. The following simple function gets a file access number from DOS (using the Visual Basic `FreeFile` function). Use `FreeFile()` to guarantee that you don't use a file number that's already in use. `FreeFile()` verifies the validity of the file number before it returns it.

Next, open a file (using the Visual Basic Open statement) in the indicated mode. Visual Basic recognizes five keywords for indicating the mode: random (the default mode), binary, input, output, and append (the three sequential access modes). A case statement handles the selection.

Mode is an integer variable where:

```
Output = 1
Input  = 2
Append = 3
Random = 4
Binary = 5
```

The Visual Basic CONSTANT.TXT file supplies the following global `const` replacements for these modes, which you can use by adding these lines to a project module (or the global module in Version 1.0):

```
Global Const SAVEFILE = 1
Global Const REPLACEFILE = 1
Global Const LOADFILE = 2
Global Const READFILE = 2
Global Const ADDTOFILE = 3
Global Const RANDOMFILE = 4
Global Const BINARYFILE = 5
```

(`SAVEFILE` and `REPLACEFILE` indicate sequential output; `LOADFILE` and `READFILE` indicate sequential input; `ADDTOFILE` indicates sequential append; `RANDOMFILE` indicates random I/O; and `BINARYFILE` indicates binary access.)

The bare-bones `OpenAFile()` function using these global constants (without error checking) looks like this:

```
Function OpenAFile (FName$, Mode%, RecordLen%) As Integer
    FileNum% = FreeFile
    Select Case Mode%
        Case REPLACEFILE
            Open FName For Output As FileNum%
```

```
        Case READFILE
            Open FName For Input As FileNum%
        Case ADDTOFILE
            Open FName For Append As FileNum%
        Case RANDOMFILE
            Open FName For Random As FileNum% Len = RecordLen%
        Case BINARYFILE
            Open FName For Binary As FileNum%
        Case Else
            MsgBox "Invalid File Mode."
            FileNum%
    End Select
    OpenAFile = FileNum%
End Function
```

The function opens the file and returns the file number to the calling function. The calling function then can use the file number for subsequent access to the file.

Because the first version of Wizard is a file viewer that can access any kind of file (including .EXE), it's safer not to allow a user to modify the files and save them. The user can modify a copy of the file (the one in the viewer) and copy selected text to the Clipboard, but cannot save the file. Use a text box to view the file, and the text box handles text. Any non-ASCII file therefore can be loaded incorrectly into the text box. For now, however, don't worry about that because you can search non-ASCII files for string matches and get that information. Later, as more features are added to Wizard, this problem is discussed. For now, the FILES.BAS module simply contains a file-opening function. Later, routines are added for saving, copying, and so on.

The basic flow of control in Wizard is shown in these steps:

1. The user requests a search and is shown the file I/O form to specify drive, directory, file pattern to search, and a search string.
2. Every time a file containing the string is found, the filename and position are recorded (and saved) in two lists (one for name, one for position), the file containing the desired string is read into the text box, and the text box scrolls to the first occurrence of the string.
3. The user then can continue the search for the next file containing the string, start a new search, or report all the searched files containing the string.

This flow is based on menu selections with one exception: you use a command button to let the user indicate whether a search should continue to the next file.

INTO THE HEART OF A WIZARD

Now that you have the flow of control worked out and a file I/O form, let's move to the heart of the application, the Wizard start-up (or control) form.

First, add controls. The form uses two controls—a text box for viewing files and a command button to let the user continue a search. Then create a control menu for the form. The form needs a menu item to instigate a search (called Find), an item for copying selected text to the Clipboard (Copy), an item to show the lists that contain file and position information (Report), and an Exit item. Figure 6.4 shows the first Wizard with menu.

How to Find Matching Patterns in Files

Let's begin with the Find menu item. When the user clicks Find, you want to set up for a search and then show the file I/O form (WIZFILE) to enable the user to manipulate the search string, directory, file pattern, and so on.

To set up for the search, I've used global variables to indicate the state of the application. For example, if a user cancels the search on the file I/O form, you want the Wizard form to know about it and cancel the search. I've used a `CancelFind` global variable, which the file I/O form changes when the user indicates that the search should be canceled. Wizard checks this variable before it continues a search. During setup, therefore, set the `CancelFind` value to False (because the user wants to search). Now, when the procedure continues after calling the file I/O form, it checks again to make sure that the user still wants to continue the search.

I've used also a global variable called `Current` to indicate the number of the current file being searched, beginning with 0. This global variable is used to let the user interrupt a search to view a file that contains the search string and then to continue the search at the next file. `Current` initially is set to 0 and then incremented every time a new file is found. `Current` is a form-level variable because it needs to be used by more than one procedure in the project but it doesn't need to be used by other forms. It's a good practice, in general, to determine the scope the variable requires and declare it at the narrowest level you can. In other words, if a variable is used by only a procedure or function, declare it locally to the procedure or function. If it needs to be used by procedures and functions only within a form, declare the variable in the declarations section of the form. If it needs to be used by more than one form in the project, declare it as a global variable. This declaration reduces the likelihood that the variable will be manipulated incorrectly.

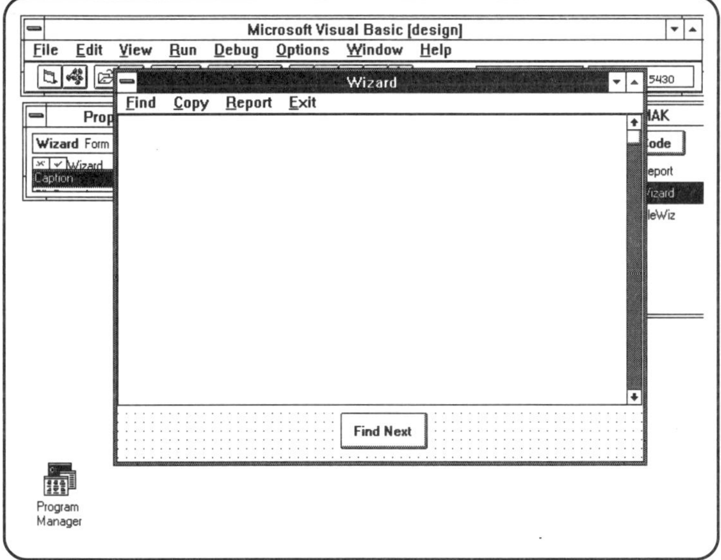

Figure 6.4. Wizard form.

How to Hide a Command Button

Whenever a search is in progress, you want to hide the command button that says "Find Next" (that additional information may confuse the user). Set the command button's Visible property to False. When a search string is found in a file, make the command button visible so the user can indicate a preference for continuing or starting a new search.

Dynamic Maintenance and Storage Using Lists

The last items discussed in greater detail in this chapter are the lists on the Report form. These lists record file and position information, and for convenience I've put them on a separate form to make the Wizard form less cluttered and give the user the option of viewing or not viewing the lists. That form (called Report) is built later in this chapter, and it contains two lists (List1 and List2) that must be emptied before every search. It makes sense to let the form that contains the lists manage the lists. In this way, if you decide to optimize the removal of items in a list, you can optimize once, and any form that uses the list benefits.

Suppose you write a routine for deleting items from the two lists on the Report (that is, the list) form. If the routine is local to the form (which you want it to be), other forms can't call it directly (it's beyond another form's scope). How do you manage the call?

One good way is to create a command button on the (list) form that calls the routine. Why use a command button? The command button might be useful later to control the list form, but for now it's useful because you can trigger a command button's Click event procedure from another form. You can circumvent the direct call problem, therefore, via an indirect call (or event). Trigger a command button's Click event by setting its `Value` property to True (–1). Click events can be triggered for both command buttons and option buttons by setting their `Value` properties to True (–1). See the *Microsoft Visual Basic Language Reference* `Click Event` for other ways to trigger click events. Note that the event is triggered and the routine to clear lists is run, all behind the scenes. The List (Report) form is not shown to the user until a report is requested following a search.

The command's (`Command1_Click()`) event procedure looks like this:

```
Sub Command1_Click ()
        Do While Report.List1.ListCount
            Report.List1.RemoveItem 0
        Loop
        Do While Report.List2.ListCount
            Report.List2.RemoveItem 0
        Loop
End Sub
```

The event procedure simply uses the Visual Basic List `RemoveItem` routines to empty the lists. Although this way of emptying lists is fairly quick, there is a better way (using the Windows API), discussed in Chapter 9.

After all this setup, show the file I/O form (in MODAL to make sure that it's not left stranded on the screen) and return. When you return, Wizard makes a quick check for a `Cancel`. If it finds a `CancelFind`, it doesn't continue, but exits the Find click event procedure. This action effectively leaves the main menu on the control form, but doesn't exit from the application. The user can proceed either by instigating another search, viewing the last file of the preceding search (which is still in the text box), selecting and copying text to the Clipboard, generating a report, or exiting.

How to Write an Efficient Search Procedure

If `CancelFind` is False, continue the Find event procedure by determining how many files are in the list to be searched (this information comes from the file I/O form). Then set `Found` to False because you haven't found anything, and begin searching the files via a loop that calls a `Srch()` procedure which opens the file, reads it into a string, searches, reads files containing the string into a text box, and so on. Because it's complicated enough to warrant its own procedure, you will give it one.

The loop looks like this:

```
For I% = Current To MaxI
            Found = 0
            Srch (I%)
            If Found = -1 Then
                   Current = I% + 1
                   Command1.Visible = -1
                   Exit Sub
            End If
    Next I%
```

Note that you exit from the loop every time you find a string in a file. The exit leaves the text box displayed for viewing, selecting, copying, and so on. Note also that the loop uses two variables, `Current` and `MaxI`, to determine the loop boundaries. These boundaries represent the file you're on (because when you continue a search you want to continue with the next unsearched file, not with the first file), and `MaxI` indicates the last file. Every time you initiate a search, `Current` is set to 0.

The complete Find menu item Click event looks like this:

```
Sub FindCom_Click ()
        Report.Command1.Value = -1
        CancelFind = 0
        Current = 0
        Command1.Visible = 0
        FileInfo.Show MODAL          'Load File I/)O Form
        If CancelFind = -1 Then
            Exit Sub
        End If
        MaxI = FileInfo.File1.ListCount
        For I% = Current To MaxI
             Found = 0
             Srch (I%)
```

```
            If Found = -1 Then
                Current = I% + 1
                Command1.Visible = -1
                Exit Sub
            End If
        Next I%
End Sub
```

(Note that `MODAL` is a defined constant that equals 1. You must define this constant somewhere in your code or specify the 1 here. For example, `FileInfo.Show1`.)

What happens in `Srch()`? This beans and potatoes part of Wizard takes all the information accumulated by the file I/O form and Wizard and opens a file (using the previously acquired filename and the FILES.BAS `OpenAFile()` routine). `Srch()` actually reads the file into a string. Using the Visual Basic `InStr()` function, get the file into a string to search for a substring. `InStr()` does all the work and returns the position of the substring within the string (the file) if it finds a match. If it doesn't find a match, it returns a 0.

`Srch()` then checks to see whether there was a match; if there was a match, `Srch()` adds the file and position to the Report list, sets the `Found` variable, and loads the file (via its string representation) into the text box for viewing. It then relinquishes control to the calling procedure (the `FileCom_Click` event procedure).

The flow of the `Srch()` procedure is straightforward, but there's one aspect of it that should be discussed in detail: how to read the file and get it into a string that `InStr` can use for its substring search.

USE BINARY GETS AND PUTS TO OPTIMIZE FILE I/O

The *Microsoft Visual Basic Programmer's Guide* (Version 1.0 and Version 2.0) suggests that you read text files in sequential mode a line at a time using `Line Input#`:

```
Ln$= " "
Do Until EOF(FileNum%)
    Line Input #FileNum%, NextLine$
    Ln$ = Ln$ + NextLine$ + Chr$(13) + Chr$(10)
Loop
```

Note that you have to build the string a line at a time and insert carriage returns after each line because `Line Input#` strips them automatically. Because putting the carriage return back in takes practically no time, it's not really a problem.

Building the string a line at a time in this manner is slow, however. Some comparative benchmarks are described at the end of this section and in the following note.

In Version 3.0, you can use `Input$` to read an entire file into a variable in a single statement as follows:

```
EntireFile$ = Input$(LOF(FileNumber),FileNumber)
```

This is much more efficient than reading a file a line at a time. To test its relative efficiency, I created a small project (Files1.Mak on the disk) to compare three methods of reading files: `Input#` (a line at a time), `Input$` (in one gulp), and `Get` (using binary input). The code for the project is in the sidebar listing. Note that the main form uses the common dialog control, standard in Visual Basic 3.0, and three text boxes: one to hold the file contents, and two to record the beginning and ending times for the comparisons. This project also includes some primitive (but functional) error checking. See Chapter 7 for more information about handling errors.

```
'Global declarations and Open File in Files1.bas

Global Filename As String
Global FileVar As String

Sub GetFileName ()
    On Error GoTo Err1
    Form1!CMDialog1.Filter = "Text Files (*.txt)¦*.txt"
'Use the Common dialog
    Form1!CMDialog1.FilterIndex = 1
    Form1!CMDialog1.Action = 1
    Filename = Form1!CMDialog1.Filename
    Exit Sub
Err1:
    Exit Sub
End Sub



'Form1

Sub mnuBinary_Click ()
```

```
    Dim Lines As String
    On Error GoTo Err4
    GetFileName
    FNum = FreeFile
    Open FileName For Binary As FNum
    Text2.Text = Time
    Length = LOF(FNum)
    If Length < 32000 Then
        Lines = String$(Length, " ")
        Get FNum, , Lines
        Text3.Text = Time
        Close
        Text1.Text = Lines
    End If
    Close           'Make certain the file is closed.
    Exit Sub
Err4:
    Close
    Exit Sub
End Sub

Sub mnuInput_Click ()
    Dim Lines, NextLine As String
    On Error GoTo Err3
    GetFileName
    FNum = FreeFile
    Open FileName For Input As FNum
    Text2.Text = Time
    Do Until EOF(FNum)
        Line Input #FNum, NextLine
        Lines = Lines + NextLine + Chr(13) + Chr(10)
    Loop
    Text3.Text = Time
    Close
    Text1.Text = Lines
    Exit Sub



Err3:
    Close
    Exit Sub
End Sub

Sub mnuInVar_Click ()
```

```
    Dim Lines As String
    On Error GoTo Err2
    GetFileName
    FNum = FreeFile
    Open FileName For Input As FNum
    Text2.Text = Time
    Lines = Input$(LOF(FNum), FNum)
    Text3.Text = Time
    Close
    Text1.Text = Lines
    Exit Sub
Err2:
    Close
    Exit Sub
End Sub
```

The results are illuminating. For example, to read one 30K file into a text box using `Input#` took 5 seconds on my Zeos 386 Notebook, running at 20 Mhz. It took 1 second to read the file using `Input$`, and 1 second using `Get`.

I built the first Visual Basic 1.0 version of Wizard using `Line Input#` to read the file in sequential mode. Then, I rethought the problem and decided that I wanted to read more than just text files (`Line Input#` is designed for text files) and that I wanted to make the routine faster.

The best solution I've found is to read the file using binary access mode:

```
VarString$ = String$(Length, " ")
Get FileNum%, , VarString$
```

Notice, however, that in the previous note, `Input$` is also an excellent solution for reading text files.

There's no loop because `Get` reads the number of bytes specified by the third parameter in the argument to it in (effectively) one gulp. In this case, determine the number of bytes you want to get by finding the file length and creating a string of that length. First, create an empty string (using spaces) of the length you want, and then read the entire file a byte at a time into the string.

It's probably not obvious, but this routine is as much as 13 times faster than the preceding one, which used `Line Input#`. I tested both routines by running the same search on a couple of directories (one containing 160 files and a total of 4.5 megabytes and one containing 30 files and a total of 1 megabyte). The search string consisted of 6 garbage characters (asdasd) that I knew could not be found. The search continues, therefore, through all 160 files (or 30 files) before terminating. Each time it doesn't find a string, it prints this information to the text box. In addition, it updates the form caption to keep you posted on the current file being searched. The complete `Srch()` routine follows (it shows both search options, with one of them commented out; to test the other option, I commented out the other search routine):

```
Sub Srch (I As Integer)
        TheFileName = FileInfo.File1.List(I)
        FileP = TheNewPath + TheFileName

        If FileP <> "" Then
            Editor.Caption = "Searching: " + FileP
            OpenMode% = BINARYFILE    ' Comment out this line or the next.
          ' OpenMode% = LOADFILE
            FileNum% = OpenAFile(FileP, OpenMode%, 0)
        End If

        If FileNum% = 0 Then
            ViewBox.Text = "String not found."
            Exit Sub
        End If

        Length = LOF(FileNum%)
        If Length < 65535 Then
                        ' Comment out these 2 lines or the next 5.
           VarString$ = String$(Length, " ")
           Get FileNum%, , VarString$

'          Ln$= " "
'          Do Until EOF(FileNum%)       ' We have a good file, so read it.
'              Line Input #FileNum%, NextLine$
'              Ln$ = Ln$ + NextLine$ '+ Chr$(13) + Chr$(10)
'          Loop
```

```
            Close FileNum%
            Search$ = FileInfo.Text2.Text
            A% = InStr(VarString$, Search$)
            If A% > 0 Then
                Found = -1
                Report.List2.AddItem Str$(A%)
                Report.List1.AddItem FileP
                Editor.Caption = Search$ +
                ➥" found at character position: " +
                ➥Str$(A%) + " in " + FileP

                ViewBox.Text = VarString$
                ViewBox.SelStart = A% - 1
                ViewBox.Sellength = Len(Search$)
            Else
                ViewBox.Text = "String not found."
            End If
        Else
            ViewBox.Text = "File too large"
        End If
End Sub
```

I tested the two routines on my Zeos 20 MHz 386 notebook computer. Table 6.1 shows the results. It took 15 seconds to search all 4.5 megabytes of files using the binary function, and 55 seconds to search them using `Line Input#`—about 3 1/2 times faster. It took 7 seconds for the binary routine to search the 1 megabyte directory and 90 seconds for the `Line Input#` routine—about 13 times faster. The extra time results from building larger strings (because the average file size is larger). In the 4.5 megabyte directory and 160-file directory, more time is spent opening and closing files.

TABLE 6.1. FILE SEARCH BENCHMARKS.

Directory Size	*# of Files*	*Binary*	*Line Input #*
4.5 megabytes	160	15 seconds	55 seconds
1 megabyte	30	7 seconds	90 seconds

USE THE CLIPBOARD TO CUT, COPY, AND PASTE TEXT

It's always good, even in a view-only-type application to enable users to manipulate information. Because WIZARD1 can read any kind of file (including .EXE files), the safest way to let a user manipulate information in the file without changing the file is to make a copy of the information the user wants to manipulate. This process is straightforward in Visual Basic because the text box control already has built-in facilities for selecting text.

Therefore, let the user select (or mark) and copy the desired text to the Clipboard. From there, the user is free to manipulate it in any way. At times, of course, you might want to let a user use the Wizard Viewer as an editor, a feature added in this chapter. For now, let's build a Clipboard copy routine.

As you might expect, Visual Basic literally does all except one line of work for you. The Visual Basic system has a built-in Clipboard object that already has a routine (`SetText`) which copies any selected text from a specified text box to the Clipboard. All you do is send the `SetText` message. Therefore, the copy to the Clipboard routine looks like this:

```
Sub CopyCom_Click ()
    Clipboard.SetText ViewBox.SelText
End Sub
```

It's simple, right?

Although WIZARD1 is only a viewer and copier, for completeness let me now show you the cut-and-paste routines that a later version of Wizard uses (see Chapter 9). The cut routine works identically to the paste routine with one exception—it sets the selected text in the Clipboard to an empty string, thereby erasing the text:

```
Sub CutCom_Click ()
    Clipboard.SetText ViewBox.SelText
    ViewBox.SelText = ""
End Sub
```

The paste routine simply gets the text from the Clipboard and places it in the text box at the current cursor position:

```
Sub PasteCom_Click ()
    ViewBox.SelText = Clipboard.GetText()
End Sub
```

As you can see, using the Clipboard is trivial with Visual Basic, and most of the applications you build can add this functionality with very little effort on your part.

A Wild Sheep Chase

For those of you who enjoy watching a programmer fumble around, let me share one of the experiences I had in developing this project. You might find it a useful lesson in your own programming practice.

During the first go at Wizard, while I was still using sequential I/O to read the files for searching, I kept getting a strange error message, `Out of string space.` Also, Visual Basic left the cursor at this line:

```
Ln$ = Ln$ + NextLine$ + Chr$(13) + Chr$(10)
```

in the following loop:

```
Do Until EOF(FileNum%)
   Line Input #FileNum%, NextLine$
   Ln$ = Ln$ + NextLine$ + Chr$(13) + Chr$(10)
Loop
```

I pressed F1 to get help for the error and read the following:

Error 14

Possible causes:

You tried to exceed the 64K string space allowed for all your global and module-level string variables.

You tried to exceed the 64K string space allowed for all your local (procedure-level) string variables.

You tried to create a single string array larger than 64K.

You may have run out of memory, which has prevented a 64K string space from being allocated.

What was going on? If you look at the listing at the end of this chapter, you see that Wizard checks to make sure that it's not trying to read a greater-than-64K file. So, that wasn't the problem. I then quickly looked over the code to see whether I was exceeding 64K in the total string variables for the procedure (because I was building a local string). No. A few bytes at most were being used, and the application was misbehaving, sometimes as early as 40K, a number that didn't make that much sense to me (32K might have).

I restarted Wizard and pressed Break to enter debug mode just after loading it (before I selected a menu item). I then set a break point just before the loop that generated the error message. After the break I used single-step mode to follow the loop. Every time I encountered a new string assignment, I switched to the Immediate window and checked its value. At first, nothing seemed to be amiss. Everything seemed to work fine—the new lines were being added correctly—but the total length of `Ln$` was greater than the length of the file (they should have been equal, of course).

Then, by pure luck, I stumbled on the problem. `Ln$` had an uncertain value at the beginning of the loop. I had committed a fundamental mistake: I had used a variable without initializing it to a known value. So, I added the line

```
Ln$ = " "
```

to the code before entering the loop:

```
Ln$ = " "
Do Until EOF(FileNum%)
    Line Input #FileNum%, NextLine$
   Ln$ = Ln$ + NextLine$ + Chr$(13) + Chr$(10)
Loop
```

Then, of course, Wizard could read 64K files before it ran out of string space.

One lesson I learned was not to ignore details. More often than not, it's the simple things, such as initializing a variable, that get you in trouble. Unfortunately, because the mistake is so trivial, it's not easy to locate. (The out-of-string-space problem, however, reoccurs in Chapter 9 for a different reason.)

THE REPORT FORM

Now you have to fill in the Report form details and you're finished.

The Report form consists of six controls (and no menu because it typically is called by a control form). Refer to Figure 6.5 to see the Report form. The six controls are in this list:

- The command button (used to clear the lists).
- An OK button for continuation.

- Two list boxes for holding the positions and filenames.
- Two labels for identifying the lists.

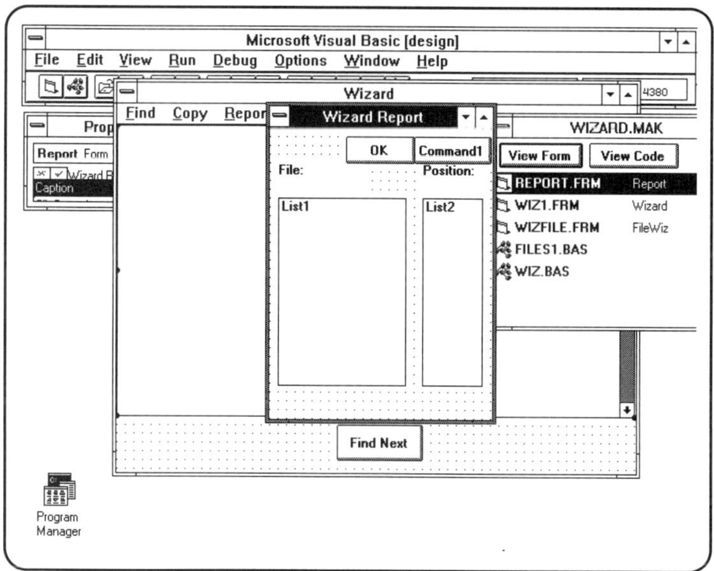

Figure 6.5. The Report form.

The Report form is used to display the lists when the user requests a report. The `Command_Click()` event procedure developed earlier is the only procedure added now. Keep in mind, however, that you can add new general-purpose list functionality at any time by adding it to this form.

Figures 6.6 and 6.7 show Wizard in action. Listing 6.1 shows the code for the complete application. This code can be loaded into the Visual Basic system by loading the WIZARD.MAK file.

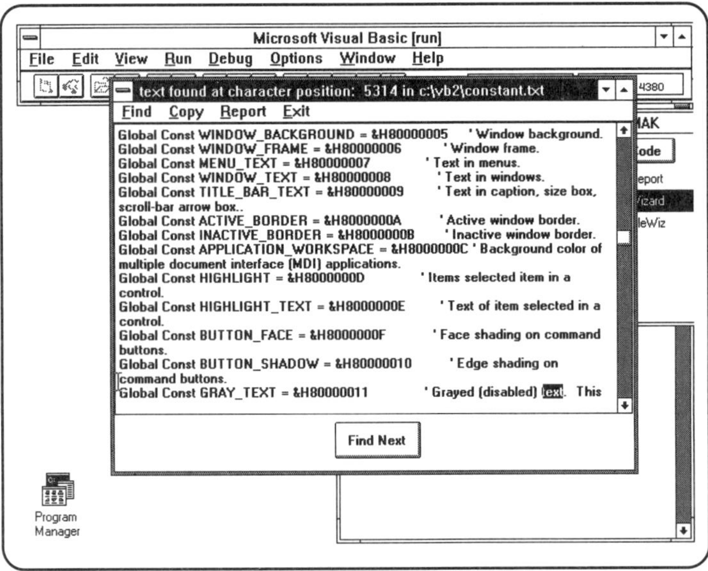

Figure 6.6. A Wizard search.

LISTING 6.1. THE COMPLETE LISTING FOR WIZARD.

```
' (global module — WIZ.BAS)

' Types

Type FileRecord
    FileName As String * 30
    Position As Long
End Type


' Constants to hold project level information

Global CancelFind As Integer
Global TheFileName As String
Global TheNewPath As String
Global EditFile As String * 30
Global TempEditFile As String * 30
Global ProjectFile As String * 30
Global Position&
Global Cancel
Global ReplaceLoop
Global VarString$
```

```
Global Search$
Global Replace$
Global LeftPart$
Global RightPart$
Global ReplaceState%


Global SaveErr%
Global Server$

' Constants to rerepresent the file-access modes.

Global Const SAVEFILE = 1
Global Const REPLACEFILE = 1
Global Const LOADFILE = 2
Global Const READFILE = 2
Global Const ADDTOFILE = 3
Global Const RANDOMFILE = 4
Global Const BINARYFILE = 5

' Constant for MODAL

Global Const MODAL = 1


' Constants to represent error conditions

Global Const Err_DeviceUnavailable = 68
Global Const Err_DiskNotReady = 71
Global Const Err_FileAlreadyExists = 58
Global Const Err_TooManyFiles = 67


' (WIZFILE FORM — WIZFILE.FRM)

Sub Drive1_Change ()
    Dir1.Path = Drive1.Drive
End Sub

Sub Dir1_Change ()
    File1.Path = Dir1.Path
End Sub

Sub Dir1_Click ()
    'LastChange = DIRSBOXCLICK
    ' Dir1_Change
End Sub

Sub File1_DblClick ()
    Command1_Click
End Sub
```

continues

LISTING 6.1. CONTINUED

```
Sub Command1_Click ()
    TheNewPath = Dir1.Path
    If Right$(TheNewPath, 1) <> "\" Then
        TheNewPath = TheNewPath + "\"
    End If
    TheFileName = File1.FileName
    FileWiz.Hide
End Sub

Sub Command2_Click ()
    FileWiz.Hide
    CancelFind = -1
End Sub

Sub Text1_Change ()
    File1.Pattern = Text1.Text
End Sub

Sub Form_Load ()
    File1.Pattern = Text1.Text
End Sub


' ( FILES.BAS )


Function OpenAFile (NameToUse$, Mode%, RecordLen%) As Integer
    FileNum% = FreeFile
    On Error GoTo OpenFileError

    Select Case Mode
        Case LOADFILE
            Open NameToUse For Input As FileNum%
        Case REPLACEFILE
            Open NameToUse For Output As FileNum%

        Case RANDOMFILE
            Open NameToUse For Random As FileNum% Len = RecordLen%
        Case BINARYFILE
            Open NameToUse For Binary As FileNum%
        Case Else
            Exit Function
    End Select
    OpenAFile = FileNum%
    Exit Function
```

```
OpenFileError:
    Action% = FileErrors(Err)
    Select Case Action%
        Case 0
            Resume
        Case Else
            OpenAFile = 0   'Open failed
            Exit Function
        End Select
End Function

Function FileErrors (errVal As Integer) As Integer
    msgType% = MB_EXCLAIM
    Select Case errVal
        Case Err_DeviceUnavailable  ' Error #68
            Msg$ = "Device unavailable"
            msgType% = MB_EXCLAIM + 4
        Case Err_DiskNotReady       ' Error #71
            Msg$ = "Drive not ready."
        Case Err_DeviceIO           ' Error #57
            Msg$ = "Internal disk error"
            msgType% = MB_EXCLAIM + 4
        Case Err_DiskFull           ' Error #61
            Msg$ = "Disk full."
            msgType% = 35
        Case Err_BadFileName        ' Error #64
            Msg$ = "File name is illegal"
        Case Err_BadFileNameOrNumber 'Error #52
            Msg$ = "File name is illegal"
        Case Err_PathDoesNotExist   ' Error #76
            Msg$ = "Path does not exist."
        Case Err_BadFileMode        ' Error #54
            Msg$ = "Can't open file in current mode."
        Case Err_FileAlreadyOpen    ' Error #55
            Msg$ = "File already open"
        Case Err_InputPastEndOfFile ' Error #62
            Msg$ = "Attempting to read past EOF"
        Case Else
            FileErrors = 3
            Exit Function
    End Select

    Response% = MsgBox(Msg$, msgType%, "Disk Error")
    Select Case Response%
        Case 1, 4   ' OK, Retry buttons
            FileErrors = 0
        Case 5      ' Ignore buttons
            FileErrors = 1
        Case 2, 3   ' Cancel, abort buttons
            FileErrors = 2
```

continues

LISTING 6.1. CONTINUED

```
        Case Else
            FileErrors = 3
    End Select
End Function


(' REPORT.FRM )

Sub Command1_Click ()
        Do While Report.List1.ListCount
            Report.List1.RemoveItem 0
        Loop
        Do While Report.List2.ListCount
            Report.List2.RemoveItem 0
        Loop

End Sub

Sub Command2_Click ()
    Hide
End Sub

' (WIZARD MAIN — WIZ1.FRM )

Dim Current As Integer
Dim Found As Integer
Dim Ln As String
Dim MaxI As Integer
Dim Length As Long

Sub ExitCom_Click ()
    End
End Sub

Sub CopyCom_Click ()
    Clipboard.SetText ViewBox.SelText
End Sub

Sub Srch (I As Integer)
     TheFileName = FileWiz.File1.List(I)
     EditFile = TheNewPath + TheFileName

     If EditFile <> "" Then
         Wizard.Caption = "Searching: " + EditFile
         OpenMode% = BINARYFILE 'LOADFILE
         FileNum% = OpenAFile(EditFile, OpenMode%, 0)
     End If
```

```
    If FileNum% = 0 Then
        ViewBox.Text = "Open Failed."
        Exit Sub
    End If

    Length = LOF(FileNum%)
    If Length < 65535 Then
       VarString$ = String$(Length, " ")
       Get FileNum%, , VarString$

  'Ln$ = " "
  ' Do Until EOF(FileNum%)    ' We have a good file. So read it.
  '    Line Input #FileNum%, NextLine$
  '   Ln$ = Ln$ + NextLine$ '+ Chr$(13) + Chr$(10)
  ' Loop

        Close FileNum%
        Search$ = FileWiz.Text2.Text
        A% = InStr(VarString$, Search$)
        If A% > 0 Then
         Found = -1
         Report.List2.AddItem Str$(A%)
         Report.List1.AddItem EditFile
         Wizard.Caption = Search$ + " found at character
         ➥     position: " + Str$(A%) + " in " + EditFile
         'Need error handling here.
         ViewBox.Text = VarString$
         ViewBox.SelStart = A% - 1
         ViewBox.Sellength = Len(Search$)
        Else
         ViewBox.Text = "String not found."
        End If
    Else
        ViewBox.Text = "File too large"
    End If

End Sub

Sub FindCom_Click ()
    Report.Command1.Value = -1
    CancelFind = 0
    Current = 0
    Command1.Visible = 0
    FileWiz.Show MODAL
    If CancelFind = -1 Then
        Exit Sub
    End If
    MaxI = FileWiz.File1.ListCount
    Command1.Visible = 0
```

continues

LISTING 6.1. CONTINUED

```
     For I% = Current To MaxI
         Found = 0
         Srch (I%)
         If Found = -1 Then
          Current = I% + 1
          Command1.Visible = -1
          Exit Sub
         End If
     Next I%
End Sub

Sub Command1_Click ()
     Find
End Sub

Sub Find ()
    Command1.Visible = 0
    For I% = Current To MaxI
     Found = 0
     Srch (I%)
     If Found = -1 Then
          Current = I% + 1
          Command1.Visible = -1
          Exit Sub
     End If
    Next I%
End Sub

Sub ReportCom_Click ()
    Report.Show
End Sub
```

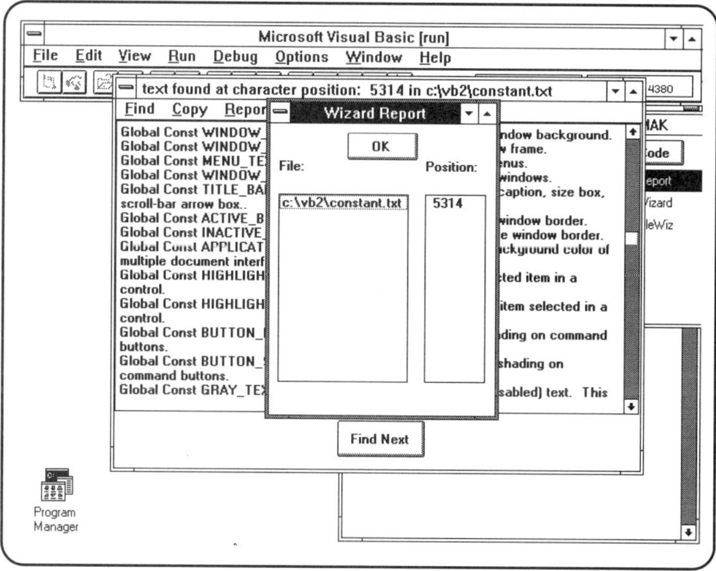

Figure 6.7. Wizard in motion.

Summary

This discussion covered this first Wizard application. I hope that you found it as useful as I did. Chapter 9 adds some important functionality to Wizard after digressing a bit to discuss error handling, interrupt loops via `DoEvents()`, custom controls, and DDE. The complete Wizard application is, I think, an exceptionally handy Visual Basic programming tool; one I hope you find useful in your own development. You should jump to Chapter 10 and get it up and running as you explore the following chapters.

Bullet-proof at Runtime: Into the Real World of Errors and Error Handling

In Chapter 6, "Files, Directories, and a Code Wizard," you used a multiform design to create a file I/O system and a file viewer that use the file I/O system to open files. That system works fine *if* there are no disk or file errors. What if the system encounters one of these "unexpected" errors?

Unfortunately, as the Wizard application stands, the system crashes after a disk or file error, and the application grinds to a halt. This is not good; in fact, it is downright irritating.

Fortunately, however, you can avert some disasters by using Visual Basic's extensive error-handling capability to trap and recover from disk and file errors, as well as from other runtime errors.

You can trap runtime errors by setting up an error handler that takes control of the application when an error occurs. Then, if the error handler can "handle" the error, the application resumes at or just after the point of the error. Visual Basic simplifies this kind of error handling by supplying several functions to handle the low-level work. The functions communicate with the operating system for you. You decide how you want the application to proceed.

In this chapter, you develop a complete error-handling system that you can plug into any system with very little effort.

This chapter discusses runtime errors in general and develops two versions of the error handler. The first is an error simulator and the second is an all-purpose error handler you can plug in "as is" to your application. You use it throughout the rest of this book by adding it to the Wizard you implemented in Chapter 6.

Because the error handler uses many of Visual Basic's error-handling techniques and demonstrates a general approach to error handling, you should be able to build from or readily adapt it to your applications. (This application—WIZARD + Error Handler—is called WIZARD2 on the disk). But before we go into it, let's talk just a bit about errors in general and the various kinds of errors you should expect to encounter with your Visual Basic applications.

Compile-Time Errors Defined

Errors fall into two broad categories: compile time and runtime. A compile-time error occurs when you run an application. It may be caused by an incorrectly blocked control structure, such as an `EndIf` statement used without a corresponding `If` statement. Syntax errors (that is, misuse of the Visual Basic language) also are compile-time errors. For example, if you misspell a word or omit a separator—syntax or compile-time errors occur.

When syntax checking is selected in the Visual Basic Code menu, the Visual Basic "interpreter" checks each line of your code as you work. Every time you enter a return (by pressing Enter), Visual Basic checks the line you have just typed for errors and notifies you if it finds any.

When you select the Make Exe File command from the File menu or the Start command from the Run menu, Visual Basic automatically checks your code for errors. If a line contains code that Visual Basic does not understand, it displays an error message.

When a compile-time error occurs, you must correct it before the application can continue. You also can get context-sensitive help about an error by pressing F1 while the error message is on-screen. The help is particularly useful when you don't know what's going on.

In response to pressing F1, Visual Basic displays a topic with possible causes for the error. It also suggests ways to resolve the type of error it detected. It doesn't suggest anything about your particular error; it simply responds to the "type" of error.

You can also get Help about the syntax of Visual Basic functions, statements, properties, events, and methods while you're working in the Code window. Type or select the keyword, property, event, or method name, and press the F1 key.

Runtime Errors Defined

A runtime error can be a little more complicated. A runtime error occurs while an application is running, which might be long after you've published or sold the application (and even longer after the checks for it have stopped coming in).

When Visual Basic encounters an untrapped runtime error, it halts the application, displays an error message, and places the insertion point within a box that surrounds the statement in which the error occurred. As with compile-time errors, you can use online Help for information about the possible causes of the error and suggestions for resolving it. (Note that the insertion point is the location within a form or window where the cursor appears after a form or window gets the focus.)

While your application is halted, you can open files or change variable values in the Immediate window, correct your code, modify the next statement to be executed, and so on. After you have corrected the error, continue running the application by pressing F5 at the statement after the stop. You can restart the application from the beginning by pressing Shift-F5.

To change the form (controls, properties, and so on) or make major changes to your code, select the End command from the Run menu to end execution and return to design mode. Often when you try to make a change, Visual Basic notifies you that you must restart the application and dumps back to design mode.

These coding and debugging design mode sessions can generate runtime errors (file and disk problems), but it's easy to recover from them. Pressing Ctrl-Break gets you out of almost anything.

When a runtime error occurs while you (or someone else) are running an executable file (that is, a .EXE version of the application), you can't recover unless you have prepared for it in advance. To keep an application running at this juncture calls for an error-handling routine. That brings us to the hands-on part of this chapter.

TRAPPABLE ERRORS DEFINED

The kinds of errors discussed here are fortunately "trappable errors." Again, these errors may occur while an application is running, whether it's running within the Visual Basic environment or as a stand-alone executable. You can test and respond to the errors by using the `On Error` statement and the `Err` function (discussed later in this chapter). Trappable errors can be generated during file and disk I/O, while manipulating object properties, with control arrays and timer functions, and so on. In other words, you can trap just about anything.

To get all of Visual Basic's (Version 3.0) trappable errors in one place (a file), I created a little project (GetError on the disk) to cycle through the first 32,765 integers and return a corresponding error message. The code in Listing 7.1 uses a form (consisting of a text box and a command button) and a module to do the following:

- Get each error message
- Decide if the error message is a user-defined error
- If the message is not a user-defined error, write the error message and its corresponding number to a file, using binary output

Notice that `GetError` uses an `On Error GoTo` statement to prevent the project from crashing if there's a file error. `On Error GoTo` is discussed in greater detail later in this chapter.

LISTING 7.1. GETERROR.

```
'Global declaration in module GetError.Bas

Global CurrentTxt As String

' GetError Form
Dim Txt As String

Sub Command1_Click ()
Dim I As Integer
NL = Chr$(13) + Chr$(10)
On Error GoTo CloseErr
CurrentTxt = ""
Txt = ""
FileNum = FreeFile
Open "ErrFile.txt" For Binary As FileNum
For I = 1 To 32765
Txt = GetErrors(I)
If Txt <> "User-defined error" Then
CurrentTxt = NL & Str$(I) & " " & Txt
Put FileNum, , CurrentTxt
End If
Next I
Close FileNum
Beep
Text1.Text = Str$(I)
Exit Sub
CloseErr:
Close FileNum
MsgBox "File Error"
Exit Sub
End Sub

Function GetErrors (ErrNum As Integer) As String
Msg$ = Error(ErrNum)
'MsgBox Msg$ & " " & Str$(ErrNum)
GetErrors = Msg$
End Function
```

Table 7.1 lists the Visual Basic Version 3.0 trappable errors generated by the code in Listing 7.1. This is the contents of ErrFile.txt on the disk. Note that this list does not include any error messages that are .VBX specific. .VBX errors are considered user-defined errors. For example, the error messages from 31001-31039 are OLE2 specific error messages. The `GetError` project recognizes these numbers as user-defined errors. Similarly, the error messages between 30000-30019 are Grid control specific (i.e., user-defined from Visual Basic's perspective). The common dialog control's error messages are between 20476-32765. Notice that all Data Access error messages do appear in this list.

All numbers do not have an error message associated with them. User-defined error messages have been omitted. Microsoft suggests that, when you are implementing your own error-handling messages, you begin with 32767 and work down, using available error messages as you encounter them. In theory, doing so prevents your error messages and Visual Basic's error messages from colliding, because Visual Basic is working up from 0. However, keep in mind that you might conflict with a .VBX using a user-defined error message.

TABLE 7.1. VISUAL BASIC VERSION 3.0 ERROR MESSAGES (EXCLUDING .VBX ERROR MESSAGES).

Error Code	*Message*
	Compile Time/Runtime Errors
3	Return without GoSub
5	Illegal function call
6	Overflow
7	Out of memory
9	Subscript out of range
10	Duplicate definition
11	Division by zero
13	Type mismatch
14	Out of string space
16	String formula too complex
17	Can't continue

Error Code	*Message*
19	No Resume
20	Resume without error
28	Out of stack space
35	Sub or Function not defined
48	Error in loading DLL
49	Bad DLL calling convention
51	Internal error
52	Bad file name or number
53	File not found
54	Bad file mode
55	File already open
57	Device I/O error
58	File already exists
59	Bad record length
61	Disk full
62	Input past end of file
63	Bad record number
64	Bad file name
67	Too many files
68	Device unavailable
70	Permission denied
71	Disk not ready
74	Can't rename with different drive
75	Path/File access error
76	Path not found
91	Object variable not Set

continues

Table 7.1. continued	
Error Code	*Message*
92	For loop not initialized
93	Invalid pattern string
94	Invalid use of Null
95	Cannot destroy active form instance
260	No timer available
280	DDE channel not fully closed; awaiting response from foreign application
281	No more DDE channels
282	No foreign application responded to a DDE initiate
283	Multiple applications responded to a DDE initiate
284	DDE channel locked
285	Foreign application won't perform DDE method or operation
286	Timeout while waiting for DDE response
287	User pressed Escape key during DDE operation
288	Destination is busy
289	Data not provided in DDE operation
290	Data in wrong format
291	Foreign application quit
292	DDE conversation closed or changed
293	DDE Method invoked with no channel open
294	Invalid DDE Link format
295	Message queue filled; DDE message lost
296	PasteLink already performed on this control
297	Can't set `LinkMode`; invalid `LinkTopic`

Error Code	*Message*
298	DDE requires ddeml.dll
320	Can't use character device names in file names: *item*
321	Invalid file format
340	Control array element *item* doesn't exist
341	Invalid control array index
342	Not enough room to allocate control array *item*
343	Object not an array
344	Must specify index for object array
345	Reached limit: cannot create any more controls for this form
360	Object already loaded
361	Can't load or unload this object
362	Can't unload controls created at design time
363	Custom control *item* not found
364	Object was unloaded
365	Unable to unload within this context
366	No MDI Form available to load
380	Invalid property value
381	Invalid property array index
382	*item* property cannot be set at run time
383	*item* property is read-only
384	A form can't be moved or sized while minimized or maximized
385	Must specify index when using property array
386	*item* property not available at run time
387	*item* property can't be set on this control

continues

Table 7.1. continued	
Error Code	*Message*
388	Can't set Visible property from a parent menu
389	Invalid key
390	No Defined Value
391	Name not available
392	MDI child forms cannot be hidden
393	*item* property cannot be read at run time
394	*item* property is write-only
395	Can't use separator bar as menu name
400	Form already displayed; can't show modally
401	Can't show non-modal form when modal form is displayed
402	Must close or hide topmost modal form first
403	MDI forms cannot be shown modally
404	MDI child forms cannot be shown modally
420	Invalid object reference
421	Method not applicable for this object
422	Property *item* not found
423	Property or control *item* not found
424	Object required
425	Invalid object use
426	Only one MDI Form allowed
427	Invalid object type; Menu control required
428	Popup menu must have at least one submenu
429	OLE Automation server cannot create object

Error Code	*Message*
430	Class does not support OLE Automation
431	OLE Automation server cannot load file
432	OLE Automation file or object name syntax error
433	OLE Automation object does not exist
434	Access to OLE Automation object denied
435	OLE initialization error
436	OLE Automation method returned unsupported type
437	OLE Automation method did not return a value
438	OLE Automation no such property or method
439	OLE Automation argument type mismatch
440	OLE Automation error
441	Error loading VBOA300.DLL
442	OLE Automation Lbound or Ubound on non Array value
443	OLE Automation Object does not have a default value
444	Method not applicable in this context
460	Invalid Clipboard format
461	Specified format doesn't match format of data
480	Can't create AutoRedraw image
481	Invalid picture
482	Printer error
520	Can't empty Clipboard
521	Can't open Clipboard
600	Set value not allowed on collections
601	Get value not allowed on collections
602	General ODBC error: *item*

continues

TABLE 7.1. CONTINUED

Error Code	*Message*
603	ODBC - SQLAllocEnv failure
604	ODBC - SQLAllocConnect failure
605	OpenDatabase - invalid connect string
606	ODBC - SQLConnect failure *item*
607	Access attempted on unopened Database
608	ODBC - SQLFreeConnect error
609	ODBC - GetDriverFunctions failure
610	ODBC - SQLAllocStmt failure
611	ODBC - SQLTables (TableDefs.Refresh) failure: *item*
612	ODBC - SQLBindCol failure
613	ODBC - SQLFetch failure: *item*
614	ODBC - SQLColumns (Fields.Refresh) failure: *item*
615	ODBC - SQLStatistics (Indexes.Refresh) failure: *item*
616	Table exists - append not allowed
617	No fields defined - cannot append table
618	ODBC - SQLNumResultCols (CreateDynaset) failure: *item*
619	ODBC - SQLDescibeCol (CreateDynaset) failure: *item*
620	Dynaset is open - CreateDynaset method not allowed
621	Row-returning SQL is illegal in ExecuteSQL method
622	CommitTrans/Rollback illegal - Transactions not supported
623	Name not found in this collection
624	Unable to Build Data Type Table
625	Data type of field *item* not supported by target database

Error Code	*Message*
626	Attempt to Move past EOF
627	Dynaset is not updatable or Edit method has not been invoked
628	*item* Dynaset method illegal - no scrollable cursor support
629	Warning: (ODBC - SQLSetConnectOption failure)
630	Property is read-only
631	Zero rows affected by Update method
632	Update illegal without previous Edit or AddNew method
633	Append illegal - Field is part of a TableDefs collection
634	Property value only valid when Field is part of a Dynaset
635	Cannot set the property of an object which is part of a Database object
636	Set field value illegal without previous Edit or AddNew method
637	Append illegal - Index is part of a TableDefs collection
638	Access attempted on unopened Dynaset
639	Field type is illegal
640	Field size illegal for specified Field Type
641	Illegal - no current record
642	Reserved parameter must be FALSE
643	Property Not Found
644	ODBC - SQLConfigDataSource error *item*
645	ODBC Driver does not support exclusive access to Dynasets
646	GetChunk: Offset/Size argument combination illegal
647	Delete method requires a name argument
648	Data access objects require VBDB300.DLL

continues

TABLE 7.1. CONTINUED	
Error Code	*Message*
2420	Syntax error in number
2421	Syntax error in date
2422	Syntax error in string
2423	Invalid use of '.', '!', or '()'
2424	Unknown name
2425	Unknown function name
2426	Function isn't available in expressions
2427	Object has no value
2428	Invalid arguments used with domain function
2429	In operator without ()
2430	Between operator without And
2431	Syntax error
2432	Syntax error
2433	Syntax error
2434	Syntax error
2435	Extra
2436	Missing)]
2437	Invalid use of vertical bars
2438	Syntax error
2439	Wrong number of arguments used with function
2440	IIF function without ()
2442	Invalid use of parentheses
2443	Invalid use of Is operator
2445	Expression too complex

Error Code	*Message*
2446	Out of memory during calculation
2447	Invalid use of '.', '!', or '()'
2448	Can't set value
2449	Invalid method in expression
2450	Invalid reference to form *item*
2451	Invalid reference to report *item*
2452	Invalid reference to Parent property
2453	Invalid reference to control *item*
2454	Invalid reference to '! '
2455	Invalid reference to property *item*
2456	Invalid form number reference
2457	Invalid report number reference
2458	Invalid control number reference
2459	Can't refer to Parent property in Design view
2460	Can't refer to Dynaset property in Design view
2461	Invalid section reference
2462	Invalid section number reference
2463	Invalid group level reference
2464	Invalid group level number reference
2465	Invalid reference to field *item*
2466	Invalid reference to Dynaset property
2467	Object referred to in expression no longer exists
2468	Invalid argument used with DatePart, DateAdd or DateDiff function
2469	1 in validation rule: ' | 2'
2470	in validation rule

continues

TABLE 7.1. CONTINUED	
Error Code	*Message*
2471	in query
2472	in linked master field
2473	1 in '|2' expression
2474	No control is active
2475	No form is active
2476	No report is active
2477	Invalid subclass *item* referred to in TypeOf function
3000	Reserved error ( ); there is no message for this error
3001	Invalid argument
3002	Couldn't start session
3003	Couldn't start transaction; too many transactions already nested
3004	Couldn't find database *item*
3005	*item* isn't a valid database name
3006	Database *item* is exclusively locked
3007	Couldn't open database *item*
3008	Table *item* is exclusively locked
3009	Couldn't lock table *item*; currently in use
3010	Table *item* already exists
3011	Couldn't find object *item*
3012	Object *item* already exists
3013	Couldn't rename installable ISAM file
3014	Can't open any more tables
3015	*item* isn't an index in this table
3016	Field won't fit in record

Error Code	*Message*
3017	Field length is too long
3018	Couldn't find field *item*
3019	Operation invalid without a current index
3020	Update without AddNew or Edit
3021	No current record
3022	Can't have duplicate key; index changes were unsuccessful
3023	AddNew or Edit already used
3024	Couldn't find file *item*
3025	Can't open any more files
3026	Not enough space on disk
3027	Couldn't update; database is read-only
3028	Couldn't initialize data access because file 'SYSTEM.MDA' couldn't be opened
3029	Not a valid account name or password
3030	*item* isn't a valid account name
3031	Not a valid password
3032	Can't delete account
3033	No permission for *item*
3034	Commit or Rollback without BeginTrans
3035	Out of memory
3036	Database has reached maximum size
3037	Can't open any more tables or queries
3038	Out of memory
3039	Couldn't create index; too many indexes already defined
3040	Disk I/O error during read

continues

TABLE 7.1. CONTINUED	
Error Code	*Message*
3041	Incompatible database version
3042	Out of MS-DOS file handles
3043	Disk or network error
3044	*item* isn't a valid path
3045	Couldn't use *item*; file already in use
3046	Couldn't save; currently locked by another use
3047	Record is too large
3048	Can't open any more database
3049	*item* is corrupted or isn't a Microsoft Access database
3050	Couldn't lock file; SHARE.EXE hasn't been loaded
3051	Couldn't open file *item*
3052	MS-DOS file sharing lock count exceeded. You need to increase the number of locks installed with SHARE.EXE
3053	Too many client tasks
3054	Too many Memo or Long Binary fields
3055	Not a valid file name
3056	Couldn't repair this database
3057	Operation not supported on attached tables
3058	Can't have Null value in index
3059	Operation canceled by user
3060	Wrong data type for parameter *item*
3061	1 parameters were expected, but only | 2 were supplied
3062	Duplicate output alias *item*
3063	Duplicate output destination *item*

Error Code	*Message*
3064	Can't open action query *item*
3065	Can't execute a non-action query
3066	Query must have at least one output field
3067	Query input must contain at least one table or query
3068	Not a valid alias name
3069	Can't have action query *item* as an input
3070	Can't bind name *item*
3071	Can't evaluate expression
3073	Operation must use an updatable query
3074	Can't repeat table name *item* in FROM clause
3075	1 in query expression '|2'
3076	in criteria expression
3077	in expression
3078	Couldn't find input table or query *item*
3079	Ambiguous field reference *item*
3080	Joined table *item* not listed in FROM clause
3081	Can't join more than one table with the same name ( )
3082	JOIN operation *item* refers to a non-joined table
3083	Can't use internal report query
3084	Can't insert into action query
3085	Undefined function *item* in expression
3086	Couldn't delete from specified tables
3087	Too many expressions in GROUP BY clause
3088	Too many expressions in ORDER BY clause
3089	Too many expressions in DISTINCT output

continues

Table 7.1. continued	
Error Code	*Message*
3090	Resultant table may not have more than one Counter field
3091	HAVING clause ( ) without grouping or aggregation
3092	Can't use HAVING clause in TRANSFORM statement
3093	ORDER BY clause ( ) conflicts with DISTINCT
3094	ORDER BY clause ( ) conflicts with GROUP BY clause
3095	Can't have aggregate function in expression ( )
3096	Can't have aggregate function in WHERE clause (
3097	Can't have aggregate function in ORDER BY clause ( )
3098	Can't have aggregate function in GROUP BY clause ( )
3099	Can't have aggregate function in JOIN operation ( )
3100	Can't set field *item* in join key to Null
3101	Join is broken by value(s) in fields *item*
3102	Circular reference caused by *item*
3103	Circular reference caused by alias *item* in query definition's SELECT list
3104	Can't specify Fixed Column Heading *item* in a crosstab query more than onc
3105	Missing destination field name in SELECT INTO statement ( )
3106	Missing destination field name in UPDATE statement ( )
3107	Couldn't insert; no insert permission for table or query *item*
3108	Couldn't replace; no replace permission for table or query *item*
3109	Couldn't delete; no delete permission for table or query *item*

Error Code	*Message*
3110	Couldn't read definitions; no read definitions permission for table or query *item*
3111	Couldn't create; no create permission for table or query *item*
3112	Couldn't read; no read permission for table or query *item*
3113	Can't update *item*; field not updatable
3114	Can't include Memo or Long Binary when you select unique values ( )
3115	Can't have Memo or Long Binary in aggregate argument ( )
3116	Can't have Memo or Long Binary in criteria ( ) for aggregate function
3117	Can't sort on Memo or Long Binary ( )
3118	Can't join on Memo or Long Binary ( )
3119	Can't group on Memo or Long Binary ( )
3120	Can't group on fields selected with '*' ( )
3121	Can't group on fields selected with '*'
3122	*item* not part of aggregate function or grouping
3123	Can't use '*' in crosstab query
3124	Can't input from internal report query ( )
3125	*item* isn't a valid name
3126	Invalid bracketing of name *item*
3127	INSERT INTO statement contains unknown field name *item*
3128	Must specify tables to delete from
3129	Invalid SQL statement; expected 'DELETE', 'INSERT', 'PROCEDURE', 'SELECT', or 'UPDATE'

continues

TABLE 7.1. CONTINUED

Error Code	*Message*
3130	Syntax error in DELETE statement
3131	Syntax error in FROM clause
3132	Syntax error in GROUP BY clause
3133	Syntax error in HAVING clause
3134	Syntax error in INSERT statement
3135	Syntax error in JOIN operation
3136	Syntax error in LEVEL clause
3137	Missing semicolon (;) at end of SQL statement
3138	Syntax error in ORDER BY clause
3139	Syntax error in PARAMETER clause
3140	Syntax error in PROCEDURE clause
3141	Syntax error in SELECT statement
3142	Characters found after end of SQL statement
3143	Syntax error in TRANSFORM statement
3144	Syntax error in UPDATE statement
3145	Syntax error in WHERE clause
3146	ODBC--call failed
3147	ODBC--data buffer overflow
3148	ODBC--connection failed
3149	ODBC--incorrect DL
3150	ODBC--missing DL
3151	ODBC--connection to *item* failed
3152	ODBC--incorrect driver version ' 1'; expected version '| 2'

Error Code	*Message*
3153	ODBC--incorrect server version ' 1'; expected version ' 2'
3154	ODBC--couldn't find DLL *item*
3155	ODBC--insert failed
3156	ODBC--delete failed
3157	ODBC--update failed
3158	Couldn't save record; currently locked by another user
3159	Not a valid bookmark
3160	Table isn't open
3161	Couldn't decrypt file
3162	Null is invalid
3163	Couldn't insert or paste; data too long for field
3164	Couldn't update field
3165	Couldn't open .INF file
3166	Missing memo file
3167	Record is deleted
3168	Invalid .INF file
3169	Illegal type in expression
3170	Couldn't find installable ISAM
3171	Couldn't find net path or user name
3172	Couldn't open PARADOX.NET
3173	Couldn't open table 'MSysAccounts' in SYSTEM.MDA
3174	Couldn't open table 'MSysGroups' in SYSTEM.MDA
3175	Date is out of range or is in an invalid format
3176	Couldn't open file *item*

continues

TABLE 7.1. CONTINUED

Error Code	*Message*
3177	Not a valid table name
3178	Out of memory
3179	Encountered unexpected end of file
3180	Couldn't write to file *item*
3181	Invalid range
3182	Invalid file format
3183	Not enough space on temporary disk
3184	Couldn't execute query; couldn't find linked table
3185	SELECT INTO remote database tried to produce too many fields
3186	Couldn't save; currently locked by user ' 2' on machine '|1'
3187	Couldn't read; currently locked by user ' 2' on machine '|1'
3188	Couldn't update; currently locked by another session on this machine
3189	Table ' 1' is exclusively locked by user '|3' on machine '|2'
3190	Too many fields defined
3191	Can't define field more than once
3192	Couldn't find output table *item*
3193	(unknown)
3194	(unknown)
3195	(expression)
3196	Couldn't use *item*; database already in use

Error Code	*Message*
3197	Data has changed; operation stopped
3198	Couldn't start session. Too many sessions already active
3199	Couldn't find reference
3200	Can't delete or change record. Since related records exist in table *item*, referential integrity rules would be violated
3201	Can't add or change record. Referential integrity rules require a related record in table *item*
3202	Couldn't save; currently locked by another user
3203	Can't specify subquery in expression ( )
3204	Database already exists
3205	Too many crosstab column headers ( )
3206	Can't create a relationship between a field and itself
3207	Operation not supported on Paradox table with no primary key
3208	Invalid Deleted entry in [dBASE ISAM] section in INI file
3209	Invalid Stats entry in [dBASE ISAM] section in INI file
3210	Connect string too long
3211	Couldn't lock table *item*; currently in use
3212	Couldn't lock table ' 1'; currently in use by user ' | 3' on machine ' | 2'
3213	Invalid Date entry in [dBASE ISAM] section in INI file
3214	Invalid Mark entry in [dBASE ISAM] section in INI file
3215	Too many Btrieve tasks
3216	Parameter *item* specified where a table name is required
3217	Parameter *item* specified where a database name is required

continues

Table 7.1. continued

Error Code	*Message*
3218	Couldn't update; currently locked
3219	Can't perform operation; it is illegal
3220	Wrong Paradox sort sequence
3221	Invalid entries in [Btrieve ISAM] section in WIN.INI
3222	Query can't contain a Database parameter
3223	*item* isn't a valid parameter name
3224	Btrieve--data dictionary is corrupted
3225	Encountered record locking deadlock while performing Btrieve operation
3226	Errors encountered while using the Btrieve DLL
3227	Invalid Century entry in [dBASE ISAM] section in INI file
3228	Invalid Collating Sequence entry in [Paradox ISAM] section in INI file
3229	Btrieve--can't change field
3230	Out-of-date Paradox lock file
3231	ODBC--field would be too long; data truncated
3232	ODBC--couldn't create table
3233	ODBC--incorrect driver version
3234	ODBC--remote query timeout expired
3235	ODBC--data type not supported on server
3236	ODBC--encountered unexpected Null value
3237	ODBC--unexpected type
3238	ODBC--data out of range
3239	Too many active users

Error Code	*Message*
3240	Btrieve--missing WBTRCALL.DLL
3241	Btrieve--out of resources
3242	Invalid reference in SELECT statement
3243	None of the import field names match fields in the appended table
3244	Can't import password-protected spreadsheet
3245	Couldn't parse field names from first row of import table
3246	Operation not supported in transactions
3247	ODBC--linked table definition has changed
3248	Invalid NetworkAccess entry in INI file
3249	Invalid PageTimeout entry in INI file
3250	Couldn't build key
3251	Feature not available
3252	Illegal reentrancy during query execution
3254	ODBC--Can't lock all records
3255	ODBC--Can't change connect string parameter
3256	Index file not found
3257	Syntax error in WITH OWNERACCESS OPTION declaration
3258	Query contains ambiguous (outer) joins
3259	Invalid field data type
3260	Couldn't update; currently locked by user ' 2' on machine ' | 1'
3263	Invalid database object
3264	No fields defined - cannot append table
3265	Name not found in this collection

continues

TABLE 7.1. CONTINUED

Error Code	*Message*
3266	Append illegal - Field is part of a TableDefs collection
3267	Property value only valid when Field is part of a recordset
3268	Cannot set the property of an object which is part of a Database object
3269	Append illegal - Index is part of a TableDefs collection
3270	Property not found
3271	Invalid property value
3272	Object is not an array
3273	Method not applicable for this object
3274	External table isn't in the expected format
3275	Unexpected error from external database driver ( )
3276	Invalid database ID
3277	Can't have more than 10 fields in an index
3278	Database engine has not been initialized
3279	Database engine has already been initialized
3280	Can't delete a field that is part of an index
3281	Can't delete an index that is used in a relationship
3282	Can't perform operation on a nontable
3283	Primary key already exists
3284	Index already exists
3285	Invalid index definition
3286	Invalid type for Memo field
3287	Can't create index on Memo field or Long Binary field

Error Code	*Message*
3288	Invalid ODBC driver
3289	Paradox: No primary index
3290	Syntax error
3291	Syntax error in CREATE TABLE statement
3292	Syntax error in CREATE INDEX statement
3293	Syntax error in column definition
3294	Syntax error in ALTER TABLE statement
3295	Syntax error in DROP INDEX statement
3296	Syntax error in DROP statement
3297	Operation not supported in Version 1.1
3298	Couldn't import. No records found or all records contained errors
3299	Several tables exist with that name; please specify owner, as in 'owner.table'

HOW TO SET AND SPRING THE ERROR-HANDLING TRAP

How do you set up the error handler and spring the trap? Here's one set of steps:

1. Set an error trap that tells the application where to "GoTo" when it encounters an error. Use the `On Error GoTo` statement to set (or enable) the trap. For example:

```
Sub AProcedure
On Error GoTo ErrorHandler
.
.
.
End Sub
```

2. Write a routine (within the procedure) to handle the specific errors you expect your application to encounter. For example:

```
Sub AProcedure
On Error GoTo ErrorHandler ' Turn on error trap
.
. (other code here )
.
Exit Sub
ErrorHandler: ' Branch to here if error
If ... Then
.
.
End If
End Sub
```

3. Exit the error-handling procedure (using a `Resume` or `Resume Next` statement). For example:

```
Sub AProcedure
On Error GoTo ErrorHandler ' Turn on error trap
.
.
.
ErrorHandler: ' Branch here if error
If ... Then
.
.
End IfResume ' Resume after error
```

Note that `Resume` returns to the statement with the error that caused the jump to the error handler. `Resume Next` (another option) returns to the statement following the one with the error. Figure 7.1 shows how the error handler's flow of control works.

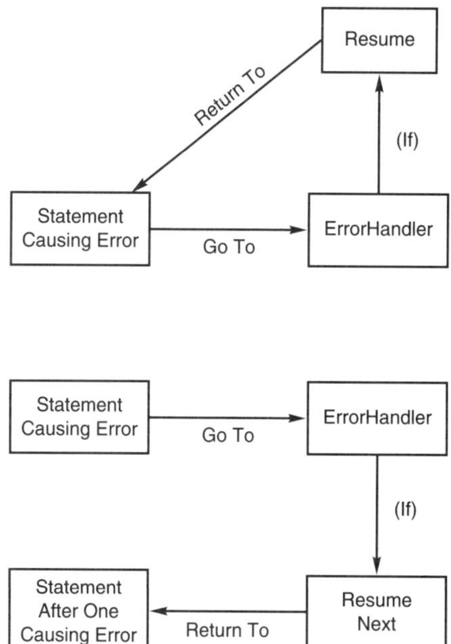

Figure 7.1. The error handler: flow of control.

To see this flow of control in motion, look at the following code (included in the RESUMES application on the disk):

```
Sub ResumeCom_Click ()
    On Error GoTo ErrorHandler
        Error 13
        Print " We'll never get here with a Resume."
        Exit Sub
ErrorHandler:
        Msg$ = Error$
        MsgBox Msg$
        Resume
End Sub
```

This code sets up the error handler with the `On Error GoTo` statement, and then simulates an error using the `Error` statement, which redirects the flow of control to the error handler. The error handler prints an error message corresponding to the specific error simulated (using the `Error$` function). Finally, the error handler concludes with the `Resume` statement, which returns control to the line of code that caused the error (`Error 13`).

The `Error 13` statement is re-executed, which simulates the error again (and again and again), until you press Break if you're working in design mode, or until you turn off the computer if you're running the application. Figure 7.2 shows this routine in motion. Note that an `On Error GoTo` statement applies to the entire procedure or function it appears within. Any error generated during the procedure, therefore, invokes the error handler unless the error handler is disabled (with a `GoTo 0` statement).

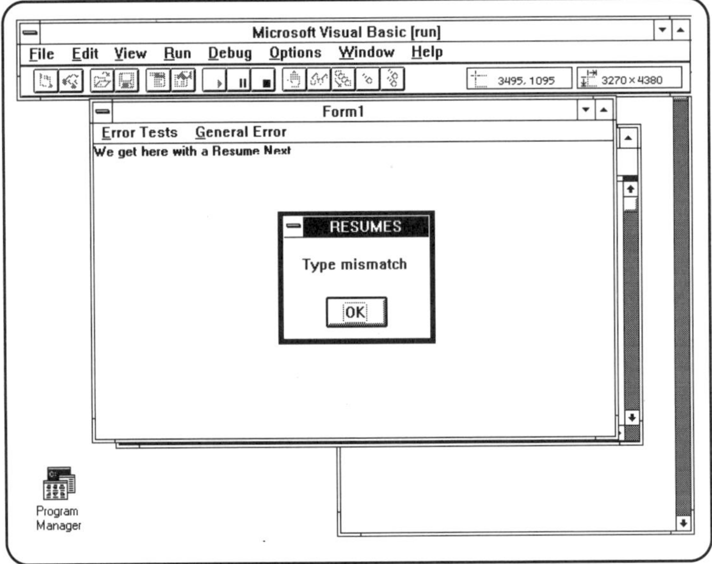

Figure 7.2. RESUMES in motion.

To move past the error, you must either correct the error before the statement is re-executed or use a `Resume Next` statement to continue execution at the next line of code:

```
Sub ResumeCom_Click ()
    On Error GoTo ErrorHandler2
        Error 13
        Print "We will get here with a Resume Next."
        Exit Sub
ErrorHandler2:
        Msg$ = Error$
        MsgBox Msg$
        Resume Next
End Sub
```

Typically, you use the Resume statement only for runtime errors that the user can correct immediately. For example, if a drive door is open, which prevents the application from reading a file, the user can close the door.

In sum, the `On Error GoTo` statement enables error handling and tells the application where to go within the procedure to analyze the error.

A Resume statement indicates that control returns to the statement that generated the error. A `Resume Next` statement indicates that control returns to the statement immediately following the statement where the error occurred. To obtain the runtime error code, use the `Err` function, which returns the runtime error code.

Use a `GoTo 0` statement to disable an enabled error handler:

```
Sub DisableCom_Click ()
    0 On Error GoTo ErrorHandler3 ' Note the 0 line label here.
        Error 13
        Print " We get here with a Resume Next."
        Exit Sub
ErrorHandler3:
            Msg$ = Error$
        MsgBox Msg$
        GoTo 0 ' Disable the error handler.
        Resume
End Sub
```

Note that a `0` must be placed on the line which enables the error handler, `On Error GoTo ErrorHandler3`. In this example, the error handler is invoked the first time through the procedure, but is disabled the second time through. Run this code (called RESUMES on the disk) and see for yourself how this works. The second time through the procedure, the application crashes. It is important to remember that, in general, if you don't use an `On Error GoTo` statement to implement an error handler, any runtime error will crash your application. Visual Basic generates an error message (after the error), but then halts the application (see Figure 7.3).

The `On Error GoTo 0` statement disables error handling, but it does not specify line 0 as the start of the error-handling code as you might expect. It specifies line 0 as the "enabling" of the error handler.

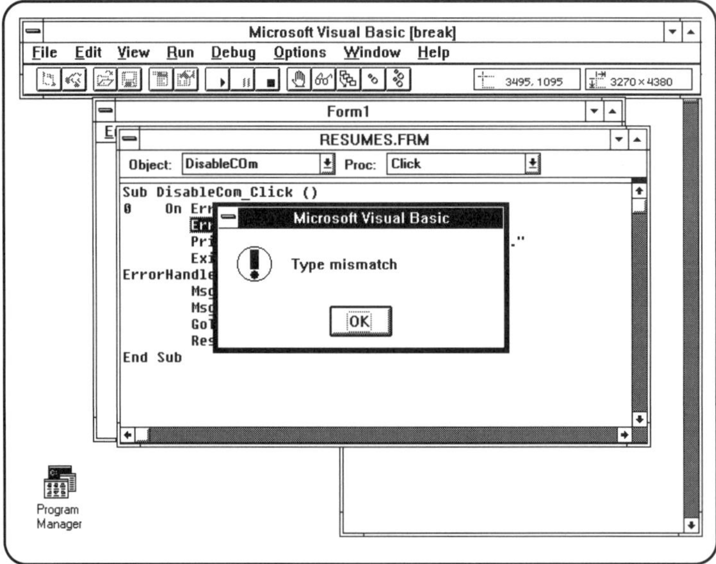

Figure 7.3. An application crash.

On Error: Some Nitty-Gritty Details

Some folks, including the ones at Microsoft, use the term enabled to indicate that an error handler is implemented (or enabled) by an `On Error GoTo` line statement. After an error handler is enabled, a runtime error causes application control to jump to the enabled error-handling routine. The error handler then has control of the application. An error handler is "active" (that is, in control) from the time a runtime error is trapped until the error handler reaches a Resume or Resume Next statement.

It's important to keep in mind that error handling can become complicated. A procedure with error trapping can call other procedures with error trapping. Thus, you need to understand how Visual Basic keeps track of these procedures. In general, the flow of control of error handlers is as follows. If an error occurs while an error handler is active (after the error and before the Resume statement is reached), the current procedure's error handler is automatically disabled. If the calling procedure has an enabled error handler, control is returned to the calling procedure, and its error handler is activated to handle the error. (If not, the application likely will crash.)

If the calling procedure's error handler also is active, control is passed back through any previous calling procedures until an inactive error handler is located. If no inactive error handler is found, the error is fatal at the point where it actually occurred. (Again, at this point the system likely will crash.)

At each point where the error handler passes control back to the calling procedure, the calling procedure becomes the current procedure. After an error handler handles an error in any procedure, the application resumes in the current procedure at the point designated by the `Resume` or `Resume Next` statement.

Whew! This is the "error within the error within the error" scenario that you hope your applications never reach. Note, however, that at least all of this recasting of control can enable an application to recover from virtually any error.

Error-handling routines can use the error status returned by the Err function to determine the cause of the error. The error-handling routine should test or save this value before doing anything else, because another error corrupts this value. The value in Err reflects only the last error that occurred. The following code does not work correctly because the error code is corrupted before it is used (see Figure 7.4):

```
Sub ErrCom_Click ()
    On Error GoTo ErrorHandler4
        Error 13
        Print "We'll get here with a Resume Next."
        If Err = 13 Then
            Msg$ = "Error number wasn't corrupted."
        Else
            Msg$ = "Error corrupted."
        End If
        MsgBox Msg$
        Exit Sub
ErrorHandler4:
        Msg$ = Error$
        MsgBox Msg$
        Resume Next
End Sub
```

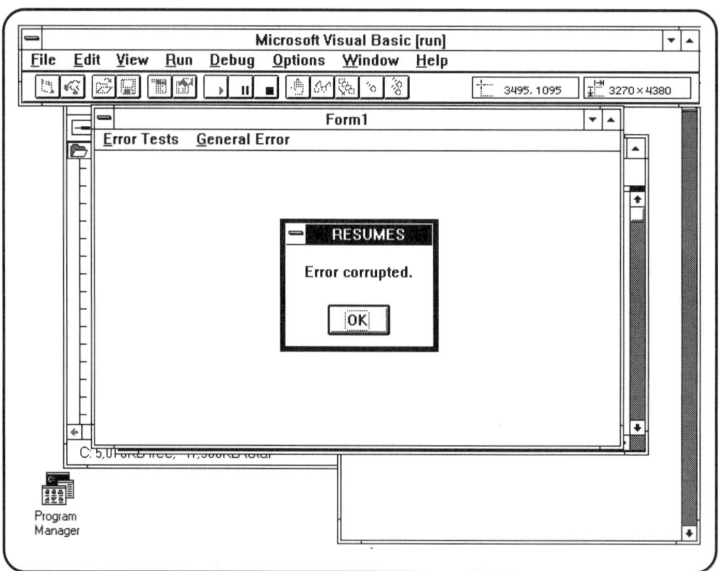

Figure 7.4. The result (error corruption) of not saving the error number (`Err`).

To preserve the error number, save the error (`Err`) as demonstrated by the following code (see Figure 7.5):

```
Sub Err2Com_Click ()
    On Error GoTo ErrorHandler5
    Error 13
    Print "We'll get here with a Resume Next."
    If SaveErr = 13 Then ' Test the Saved error, not Err
        Msg$ = "Error number wasn't corrupted."
    Else
        Msg$ = "Error corrupted."
    End If
    MsgBox Msg$
Exit Sub
ErrorHandler5:
    SaveErr = Err ' Save the error number
    Msg$ = Error$
    MsgBox Msg$
    Resume Next
End Sub
```

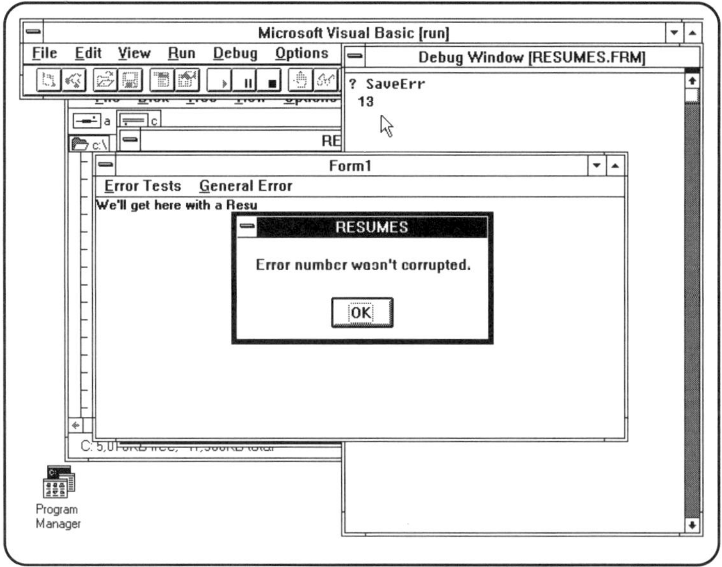

Figure 7.5. The error number is saved and translated into an error message using Error$.

Note that the `Error$` function was used to produce the error message associated with any runtime error number returned by `Err` and that the error number was preserved in the first line of the error handler before it was corrupted.

Keep in mind that the error handler is code within the procedure. The procedure, therefore, can reach the error handler by executing sequential statements, as well as by a jump. As a general practice, don't let the procedure reach the error handler by sequential statements. The error handler should be reachable only when an error occurs; the application should jump into the error handler, not fall into it. You can avoid a fall, as was done in each of these short code examples, by putting an `Exit Sub` or `Exit Function` statement immediately before the error-handling routine. For example:

```
Sub DoSomething(Var1, Var2, Var3)
      On Error GoTo ErrorHandler
      TheNextProcedure          ' Resume here
      .
      .
      Exit Sub                  ' Exit here before falling into
ErrorHandler:                   ' the error handler.
      .
      .
      .
      Resume Next
End Sub
```

In this example, the error handler is called if an error occurs. When the error handler is finished processing, control returns to the statement following the call to the error handler. Then, just before the error handler code, if the procedure gets this far, the procedure is exited. If the `Exit Sub` statement is not there, the error handler is called again (although there's no error). Even if the error handler is successful, the procedure loops indefinitely— not good. You want to handle the error and proceed, not loop indefinitely. Thus, the `Exit Sub` statement is necessary to prevent the procedure from falling into the error handler again and again.

USING *ERR* AND *ERL*: A FEW MORE DETAILS

After an error, the `Err` function returns an integer indicating the runtime error code for the error that occurred. The `Erl` function returns an integer indicating the line number where the error occurred (or the nearest line number before the line where the error occurred).

Because `Err` and `Erl` return meaningful values only after an error has occurred, you should use them in error-handling routines only when you need to determine error-status values. The values returned by `Err` and `Erl` are also not meaningful across procedure calls (either `Sub` or `Function`).

If you implement an error handler using `On Error GoTo`, and that error handler calls another procedure, the value of `Err` and `Erl` might be reset to 0. The value of `Err` and `Erl` definitely is reset to 0 if you execute `On Error GoTo`, `On Error Resume Next`, or a `Resume` or `Resume Next` statement. Be sure, therefore, that you save the values returned by `Err` or `Erl` in variables before calling another procedure or before executing any of the three statements that reset `Err` and `Erl`.

Note also that the `Erl` function returns only a line number, not a line label. If your application has no line numbers or if there's no line number in the application before the point where an error occurs, `Erl` returns `0`.

Because I don't use line numbers, the `Erl` function isn't useful to me, and I don't use it in any applications in this book. Instead, I have borrowed a simple example from the *Microsoft Visual Basic Programmer's Guide* that demonstrates how you can use it.

The example uses the `Err` function to return the runtime error code for a division-by-zero error. It uses the `Erl` function to report the line number where the error occurred. You should note the number 1020 on the procedure line that is most likely to encounter an error. If you use a line number in this way, you can determine precisely where an error occurred. For example:

```
Sub ErrErlDemo ()
1000   On Error GoTo ErrHandler   ' Set up an error handler.
1010   B% = 1
1020   A% = B% \ C%       ' Cause a "Divide by Zero" error.
1030   Exit Sub

ErrHandler:
      Msg$ = "Error number " + Ltrim$(Str$(Err)) + " occurred at line "
      Msg$ = Msg$ + Ltrim$(Str$(Erl))
      MsgBox Msg$      ' Display error information.
      Resume Next
End Sub
```

BACK TO THE WIZARD

Now you can implement an error handler for the Wizard application you created in Chapter 6. Because the Wizard uses the `FileInfo` form to get the filename and path, begin there.

One problem is obvious immediately: if the user changes the drive and selects a floppy disk drive, it's possible that the drive either does not have a disk in it or the drive door is open. The simplest solution is to use an `On Error Resume Next` statement during the drive change event procedure:

```
Sub Drive1_Change ()
    On Error Resume Next          ' Set the error trap
    Dir1.Path = Drive1.Drive      ' If no error, allow the drive change
    If Err Then                   ' If Err
        MsgBox Error$             ' Report error
        Drive1.Drive = Dir1.Path  ' Reset drive to previous state before error
    End If
End Sub
```

What's going on here? Supposedly, you implemented an error handler with the `On Error` statement, but the procedure does not contain one. This Visual Basic shortcut enables the application to effectively ignore the error and continue at the next statement.

If an error has occurred, the next line, immediately following the error, is executed after the procedure resumes execution. If an error is returned by `Err`, the drive status is reset to its previous state (that is, its state before the error). This code works just as well as the following, which uses an `On Error GoTo`:

```
Sub Drive1_Change ()
  On Error GoTo ErrorHandler          ' Set the error trap
  Dir1.Path = Drive1.Drive            ' If no error, allow the drive change
  Exit Sub                            ' Exit before error handler is reached

ErrorHandler:                         ' Error handler
      MsgBox Error$                   ' Report error
      Drive1.Drive = Dir1.Path        ' Reset drive to previous state before error
  Resume Next                         ' Resume application
End Sub
```

This code is verbose, but it is probably the one you will use most often if you want to correct or handle the error in a more complex way.

The File-Handling Problem

The other immediate potential problem in the Wizard application is a general one concerning files. Many things can go wrong when an application tries to open a file: the file might not exist; the operating system might not allow another file to be opened; and if a user saves a file with the same name as an existing file, the old file is overwritten. The list goes on.

The *Visual Basic Programmer's Guide* suggests a general-purpose error handler to handle file errors and to decide what action to take after an error. WIZARD2 takes this approach, adding two functions to the application: `FileErrors`, which determines the error, and `ConfirmFile`, which takes action.

Because the entire application needs access to both functions, code them in a module accessible to the entire application. WIZARD2 simply adds them to the FILES1.BAS module (a module in the project).

The `FileErrors` function looks like this:

```
Function FileErrors (errVal As Integer) As Integer
  msgType% = MB_EXCLAIM                    ' Constant in CONSTANT.TXT
  Select Case errVal
     Case Err_DeviceUnavailable            ' Error #68
       Msg$ = "Device unavailable"
       msgType% = MB_EXCLAIM + 4
     Case Err_DiskNotReady                 ' Error #71
       Msg$ = "Drive not ready."
     Case Err_DeviceIO                     ' Error #57
       Msg$ = "Internal disk error"
       msgType% = MB_EXCLAIM + 4
     Case Err_DiskFull                     ' Error #61
       Msg$ = "Disk full."
       msgType% = 35
```

```
    Case Err_BadFileName                    ' Error #64
      Msg$ = "File name is illegal"
    Case Err_BadFileNameOrNumber            ' Error #52
      Msg$ = "File name is illegal"
    Case Err_PathDoesNotExist               ' Error #76
      Msg$ = "Path does not exist."
    Case Err_BadFileMode                    ' Error #54
      Msg$ = "Can't open file in current mode."
    Case Err_FileAlreadyOpen                ' Error #55
      Msg$ = "File already open"
    Case Err_InputPastEndOfFile             ' Error #62
      Msg$ = "Attempting to read past EOF"
    Case Else
      FileErrors = 3
      Exit Function
  End Select

  Response% = MsgBox(Msg$, msgType%, "Disk Error")
  Select Case Response%
    Case 1, 4                             ' OK, Retry buttons
      FileErrors = 0                      ' Send this info back to the
    Case 5                                ' Ignore buttons
      FileErrors = 1                      ' calling procedure: 0, 1, 2, or 3
    Case 2, 3                             ' Cancel, abort buttons
      FileErrors = 2
    Case Else
      FileErrors = 3
  End Select
End Function
```

`FileErrors` puts all the file errors that the application can identify in one place rather than within each function. Therefore, you don't have to repeat code in your application, if several functions need this information.

`FileErrors` identifies the error using constants declared in the CONSTANT.TXT file and returns a response to the error. The calling procedure (that is, the one that called `FileErrors`) still sets up the error trap, which calls the `FileErrors` function. It then decides what to do with this error information returned by `FileErrors`. For example, `OpenAFile` in the Wizard application sets up the error trap (using the `On Error GoTo`), which calls the `FileError` function:

```
Function OpenAFile (NameToUse$, Mode%, RecordLen%) As Integer
  FileNum% = FreeFile
  On Error GoTo OpenFileError             ' Set up error trap

  Select Case Mode
    Case ReplaceFile
      Open NameToUse For Output As FileNum%
    Case READFILE
      Open NameToUse For Input As FileNum%
```

```
      Case ADDTOFILE
        Open NameToUse For Append As FileNum%
      Case RANDOMFILE
        Open NameToUse For Random As FileNum% Len = RecordLen%
      Case BINARYFILE
        Open NameToUse For Binary As FileNum%
      Case Else
        Exit Function
  End Select
  OpenAFile = FileNum%
  Exit Function                         ' Don't bump into the error handler

OpenFileError:                          ' Error handler
  Action% = FileErrors(Err)             ' Identify the error
  Select Case Action%                   ' Act accordingly
     Case 0                             ' OK, continue
       Resume
     Case Else
       OpenAFile = 0                    'Open failed
       Exit Function
     End Select
End Function
```

Note that `OpenFileError`, the error handler, is still in the procedure. The error handler calls `FileErrors`; `FileErrors` does not call the error handler. Also note that the `Resume` statement now depends on the type of error encountered. If the file cannot be opened now, the `Resume` does not occur. Instead, the function exits without opening the file.

The complete code for the WIZARD2 application is in Listing 7.2.

LISTING 7.2. WIZARD2.

```
' ( Wiz.Bas )


' Types

Type FileRecord
    FileName As String * 30
    Position As Long
End Type


' Constants to hold project level information

Global CancelFind As Integer
Global TheFileName As String
Global TheNewPath As String
```

```
Global EditFile As String * 30
Global TempEditFile As String * 30
Global ProjectFile As String * 30
Global Position&
Global Cancel
Global ReplaceLoop
Global VarString$
Global Search$
Global Replace$
Global LeftPart$
Global RightPart$
Global ReplaceState%


Global SaveErr%
Global Server$

' Constants to rerepresent the file-access modes.

Global Const SAVEFILE = 1
Global Const REPLACEFILE = 1
Global Const LOADFILE = 2
Global Const ReadFile = 2
Global Const ADDTOFILE = 3
Global Const RANDOMFILE = 4
Global Const BINARYFILE = 5

' Constant for MODAL

Global Const MODAL = 1


' Constants to represent error conditions

Global Const Err_DeviceUnavailable = 68
Global Const Err_DiskNotReady = 71
Global Const Err_FileAlreadyExists = 58
Global Const Err_TooManyFiles = 67


'(Report.frm)

Sub Command1_Click ()
        Do While Report.List1.ListCount
            Report.List1.RemoveItem 0
        Loop
        Do While Report.List2.ListCount
            Report.List2.RemoveItem 0
        Loop

End Sub
```

continues

LISTING 7.2. CONTINUED

```
Sub Command2_Click ()
    Hide
End Sub


' (Wiz1.frm )

Dim Current As Integer
Dim Found As Integer
Dim Ln As String
Dim MaxI As Integer
Dim Length As Long

Sub ExitCom_Click ()
    End
End Sub

Sub CopyCom_Click ()
    Clipboard.SetText ViewBox.SelText
End Sub

Sub Srch (I As Integer)
     TheFileName = FileWiz.File1.List(I)
     EditFile = TheNewPath + TheFileName

     If EditFile <> "" Then
         Wizard.Caption = "Searching: " + EditFile
         OpenMode% = BINARYFILE 'LOADFILE
         FileNum% = OpenAFile(EditFile, OpenMode%, 0)
     End If

     If FileNum% = 0 Then
         ViewBox.Text = "Open Failed."
         Exit Sub
     End If

     Length = LOF(FileNum%)
     If Length < 65535 Then
        VarString$ = String$(Length, " ")
        Get FileNum%, , VarString$

    'Ln$ = " "
    ' Do Until EOF(FileNum%)     ' We have a good file. So read it.
    '    Line Input #FileNum%, NextLine$
    '   Ln$ = Ln$ + NextLine$ '+ Chr$(13) + Chr$(10)
    ' Loop

         Close FileNum%
         Search$ = FileWiz.Text2.Text
         A% = InStr(VarString$, Search$)
```

```
        If A% > 0 Then
         Found = -1
         Report.List2.AddItem Str$(A%)
         Report.List1.AddItem EditFile
         Wizard.Caption = Search$ + " found at character position: "
         ➥+ Str$(A%) + " in " + EditFile
         'Need error handling here.
         ViewBox.Text = VarString$
         ViewBox.SelStart = A% - 1
         ViewBox.Sellength = Len(Search$)
        Else
         ViewBox.Text = "String not found."
        End If
    Else
        ViewBox.Text = "File too large"
    End If

End Sub

Sub FindCom_Click ()
     Report.Command1.Value = -1
     CancelFind = 0
     Current = 0
     Command1.Visible = 0
     FileWiz.Show MODAL
     If CancelFind = -1 Then
         Exit Sub
     End If
     MaxI = FileWiz.File1.ListCount
     Command1.Visible = 0
     For I% = Current To MaxI
         Found = 0
         Srch (I%)
         If Found = -1 Then
          Current = I% + 1
          Command1.Visible = -1
          Exit Sub
         End If
     Next I%
End Sub

Sub Command1_Click ()
     Find
End Sub

Sub Find ()
    Command1.Visible = 0
    For I% = Current To MaxI
     Found = 0
     Srch (I%)
     If Found = -1 Then
          Current = I% + 1
```

continues

LISTING 7.2. CONTINUED

```
          Command1.Visible = -1
          Exit Sub
     End If
    Next I%
End Sub

Sub ReportCom_Click ()
    Report.Show
End Sub


' ( Wizfile.frm )

Sub Drive1_Change ()
    Dir1.Path = Drive1.Drive
End Sub

Sub Dir1_Change ()
    File1.Path = Dir1.Path
End Sub

Sub Dir1_Click ()
    'LastChange = DIRSBOXCLICK
    ' Dir1_Change
End Sub

Sub File1_DblClick ()
    Command1_Click
End Sub

Sub Command1_Click ()
    TheNewPath = Dir1.Path
    If Right$(TheNewPath, 1) <> "\" Then
        TheNewPath = TheNewPath + "\"
    End If
    TheFileName = File1.FileName
    FileWiz.Hide
End Sub

Sub Command2_Click ()
    FileWiz.Hide
    CancelFind = -1
End Sub

Sub Text1_Change ()
    File1.Pattern = Text1.Text
End Sub

Sub Form_Load ()
    File1.Pattern = Text1.Text
End Sub
```

```
' (Errors1.bas)

Function GeneralErrors (ErrNum As Integer)
    Msg$ = Error$
    MsgBox Msg$
End Function

' ( Files.bas )

Function OpenAFile (NameToUse$, Mode%, RecordLen%) As Integer
    On Error GoTo ErrorHandler
    FileNum% = FreeFile
    Select Case Mode
        Case ReplaceFile
            Open NameToUse For Output As FileNum%
        Case READFILE
            Open NameToUse For Input As FileNum%
        Case ADDTOFILE
            Open NameToUse For Append As FileNum%
        Case RANDOMFILE
            Open NameToUse For Random As FileNum% Len = RecordLen%
        Case BINARYFILE
            Open NameToUse For Binary As FileNum%
        Case Else
            Exit Function
    End Select
    OpenAFile = FileNum%
    Exit Function
ErrorHandler:
    Response% = GeneralErrors(Err)
    If Response% = 2 Then
        OpenAFile = 0
        Exit Function
    Else Resume Next
    End If

End Function

Sub SaveAFile (ThisTextBox As Control)
    If FileNum% = 0 Then
        Exit Sub
    End If
    Print #FileNum%, ThisTextBox.Text
    Close FileNum%
End Sub
```

Figures 7.6, 7.7, and 7.8 show WIZARD2 in various stages of development.

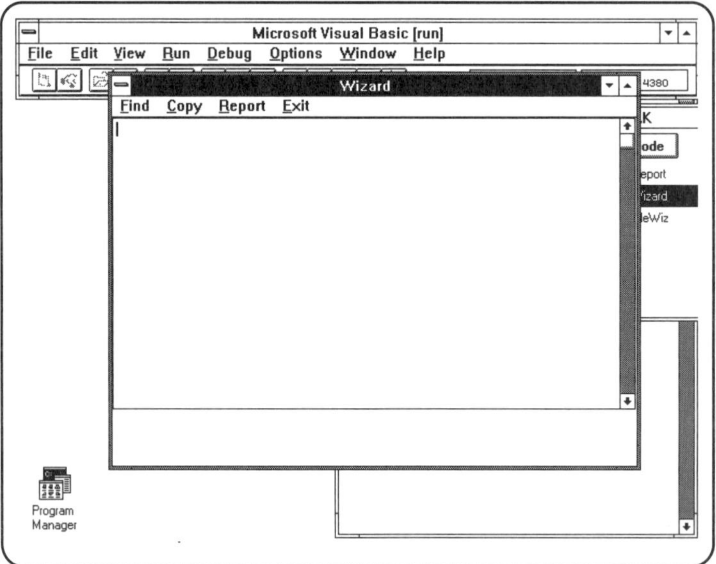

Figure 7.6. WIZARD2.

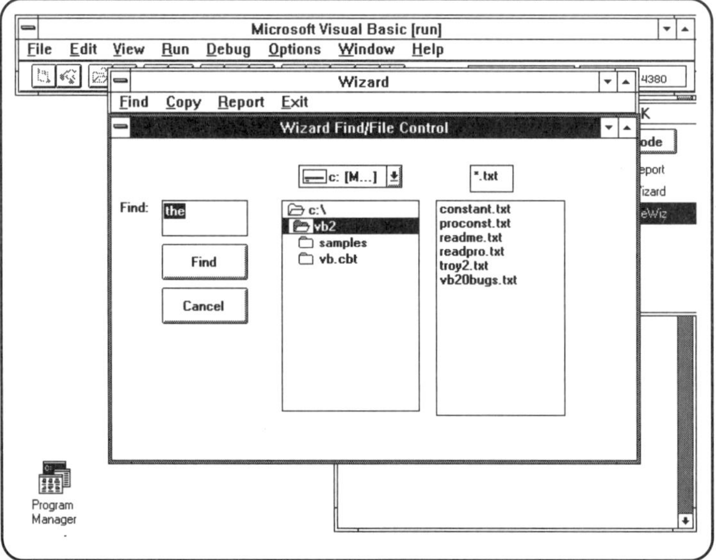

Figure 7.7. WIZARD2.

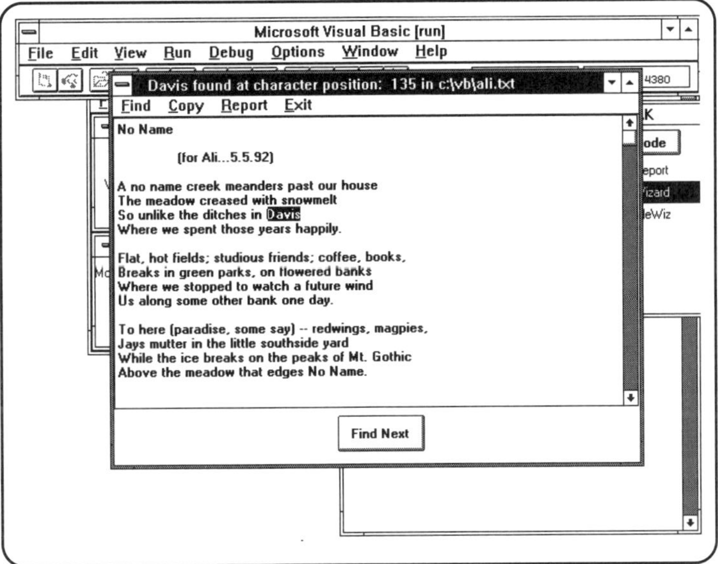

Figure 7.8. WIZARD2.

Build a General-Purpose Error Handler

So far, each of these attempts to build an error handler (the examples in RESUMES and in WIZARD2) has led to a rather slapdash approach to error handling, with the creation of an error handler for each routine. This approach is both cumbersome and code-consuming. A better approach combines the error-handling information used by several functions into a single routine that is invoked by each procedure's "personal" error handler. Note that the error handler must be within each procedure, but it can, in turn, invoke procedures not contained within itself. For example, the following code passes the error number to a general-purpose routine that simply reports the corresponding message for the error:

```
Sub ErrHandleCom_Click ()
    On Error GoTo ErrorHandler6
        Error 13
        Print "We'll get here with a Resume Next."
        If Err = 13 Then
            Msg$ = "Error number wasn't corrupted."
        Else
            Msg$ = "Error corrupted."
```

```
        End If
        MsgBox Msg$
        Exit Sub
ErrorHandler6:
        GeneralError (Err)
        Resume Next
End Sub


Sub GeneralError (ErrNum As Integer)
    Msg$ = Error$(ErrNum)
    MsgBox Msg$
End Sub
```

Now you can build into the `GeneralError` routine a `Select Case` statement to handle any specific error you choose. For example, the following code invokes the File Manager (WINFILE) if the application generates a disk full error. The user then has the option to create some disk space by deleting a file or files before the application continues:

```
Sub GeneralError (ErrNum As Integer)
  Msg$ = Error$(ErrNum)
  MsgBox Msg$

  Select Case ErrNum
     Case 61                              ' Disk full error
       x = Shell("\win31\winfile.exe", 1) ' Let the user create some space.
     Case Else
       Exit Sub
  End Select
End Sub
```

In this example, if the error is `disk full`, the error handler invokes the File Manager (WINFILE.EXE) using the shell command and lets the user attempt to correct the problem before resuming operation.

By using a general-purpose error handler in this way, you can save time and code, and selectively decide which errors you want your application to handle specifically. The `Else` allows the application to `Resume` (or `Resume Next`) if it does not take care of the error itself.

Also, this general-purpose approach does not limit applications by preventing them from handling the error themselves. For example, you can still do something specific in the error handler part of the procedure, before or after calling the general-purpose error-handling routine:

```
Sub ErrHandleCom_Click ()
  On Error GoTo ErrorHandler6
```

```
    Error 13
    Print "We'll get here with a Resume Next."
    If Err = 13 Then
       Msg$ = "Error number wasn't corrupted."
    Else
       Msg$ = "Error corrupted."
    End If
    MsgBox Msg$
    Exit Sub
ErrorHandler6:
      ' Do something here before calling the GeneralError routine
      ' For example, preserve the error number for later use.
      SaveErr = Err
     GeneralError (Err)
     ' Or Do something here before resuming.
     Resume Next
End Sub


Sub GeneralError (ErrNum As Integer)
  Msg$ = Error$(ErrNum)
  MsgBox Msg$

  Select Case ErrNum
     Case 61
       x = Shell("\win31\winfile.exe", 1)
     Case Else
       Exit Sub
  End Select
End Sub
```

Let's attempt to generalize the general-purpose error handler. First, to be on the safe side, save each generated error before calling the general errors routine (`GeneralErrors`):

```
ErrorHandler1:
    SaveErr% = Err
    GeneralErrors
```

Also make the `SaveErr%` variable global so you don't have to pass it around. You are not required to do this, but it simplifies the code. To declare it in the global module for the project:

```
Global SaveErr%
```

`GeneralErrors` does two things:

- Reports the error using the `Error$` function
- Branches to a more specific error routine when appropriate

The following version of `GeneralErrors` uses a `Select Case` statement to determine whether the error is DDE-related or disk- or OLE-related:

```
Sub GeneralErrors ()
  Msg$ = Error$(SaveErr%)
  MsgBox Msg$
  Select Case SaveErr%
      Case 280 To 297
             DDEErrors
      Case 48 To 76
            DiskErrors
      Case 30000 to 31015
            OLE Errors
  End Select
End Sub
```

Note that the `Select Case` statement uses a range of values to test for the `Case`. Note also the use of separate procedures for specific error-handling tasks.

For example, a first version of `DDEErrors` looks like this:

```
Sub DDEErrors ()
     Select Case SaveErr%

        Case 282
          App% = Shell(Server$, 1)
          App% = DoEvents()
        Case 283
          Msg$ = "Suggest you open Program Manager "
          Msg$ = Msg$ + " NOW and use End Task "
          Msg$ = Msg$ + " to terminate the LAST "
          Msg$ = Msg$ + " INSTANCE of " + Server$
          MsgBox Msg$

     End Select
End Sub
```

This version handles two specific cases of DDE errors:

282	No foreign application responded to a DDE initiate.
283	Multiple applications responded to a DDE initiate.

In this version of `DDEErrors`, any error except 282 or 283 is ignored.

I handled these two errors first because they were the first two problems I encountered when I began developing a DDE application. (The details of DDE and some of the errors you must anticipate are discussed in Chapter 8, "Stretching Your Visual Basic Applications: DDE in Depth.") This type of general-purpose error handling is efficient because you have to respond specifically to only the errors you want.

This "little" application, ERRORST on the disk, tests this version of the `GeneralErrors` error handler (see Listing 7.3). Figures 7.9 and 7.10 show the application in motion.

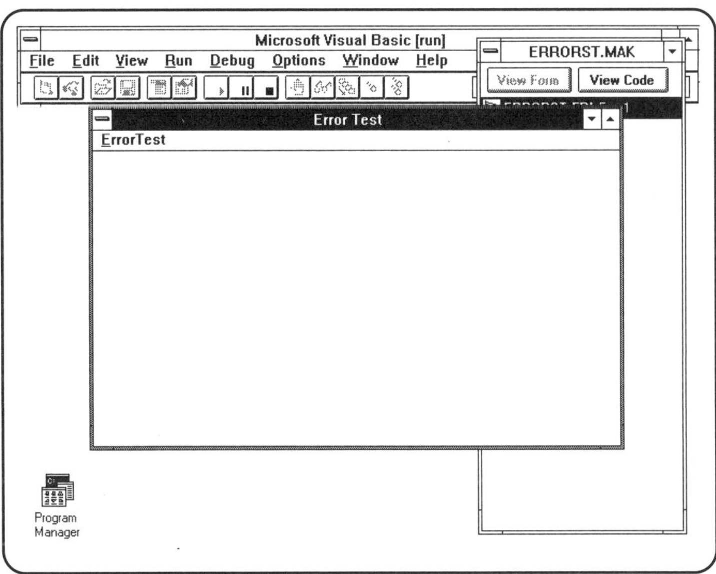

Figure 7.9. ERRORST.

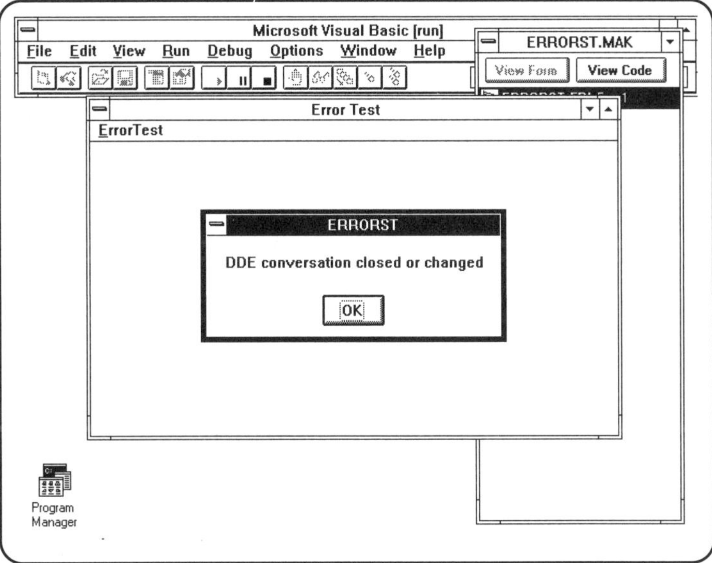

Figure 7.10. More of ERRORST in action.

LISTING 7.3. ERRORST.

```
' global module


Global Server$
Global App%
Global Topic$
Global Item$
Global SaveErr%


' Errorst.frm


Sub DDECom_Click ()
On Error GoTo E1
    Randomize Number%
    ErrCode% = Int(18 * Rnd + 279)
    Error ErrCode%
    Exit Sub
E1:
    SaveErr% = Err
    GeneralErrors
    Resume Next
End Sub



Sub GeneralErrors ()
    Msg$ = Error$(SaveErr%)
    MsgBox Msg$
    Select Case SaveErr%
        Case 280 To 297
            DDEErrors
        Case 48 To 76
            DiskErrors
        Case 30000 To 31015
            OLEErrors
    End Select
End Sub


' Errorsb.bas

Sub DDEErrors ()
        Select Case SaveErr%
```

```
            Case 282
                Msg$ = "Starting Server " + Server$
                MsgBox Msg$
                App% = Shell(Server$, 1)
                App% = DoEvents()
            Case 283
                Msg$ = "Suggest you open Program Manager "
                Msg$ = Msg$ + " NOW and use End Task "
                Msg$ = Msg$ + " to terminate the LAST "
                Msg$ = Msg$ + " INSTANCE of " + Server$
                MsgBox Msg$

        End Select
End Sub

Sub OLEErrors ()
        Select Case SaveErr%

            Case 30005
                Msg$ = "OLE_Error_Stream"
                MsgBox Msg$
            ' Other cases here.
        End Select

End Sub

Sub DiskErrors ()
        Select Case SaveErr%

            Case 48
                Msg$ = "Disk Error"
                MsgBox Msg$
            ' Other cases here.
        End Select

End Sub
```

Summary

Let's wrap up this error-handling chapter with a few general observations:

- If your application (like the Wizard in this chapter) can use a drive or open a file, implement an error handler.
- If your application does calculations that can lead to division by zero and so on, you should implement an error handler or write code at the point of the calculation to test for mathematical errors.

- If your application tries to talk to other applications by way of DDE and OLE, use an error handler.
- If you are planning to distribute your application, use an error handler.
- In other words, if you are doing anything at all substantial, use an error handler.
- If you can, make the error handler as general as possible. If you do, you can easily reuse it in other applications and not have to rewrite a lot of code. For example, the `GeneralErrors` procedure implemented at the end of this chapter is a great place to begin your general-purpose error handler, and it is the one used and expanded in the following chapters.
- Try to determine the simplest way to catch the errors you need to catch. You should avoid error loops that call other procedures because they are prone to errors.
- If you implement an error handler similar to the one implemented earlier in this chapter (which uses constants), you must code the constant yourself or use the CONSTANT.TXT file that comes with Visual Basic. When I develop applications, I usually copy the constants I need from the CONSTANT.TXT into the global module for the project.
- Note again that the error handler must be a routine within the procedure generating the error. The `GoTo` statement doesn't allow you to "go to" code outside the current procedure; because the error handler depends on a `GoTo`, this is always a restriction. From a designer's view, however, it's not much of a limitation. You want to handle the code as near to the problem as possible and you don't want to be `GoTo`ing all over an application because that usually leads to trouble.

Chapter 8 discusses DDE in depth and extends the error handler again. In Chapter 10 you extend the Wizard again and expand its error handling as well, using the general-purpose error-handling approach you began at the end of this chapter.

Stretching Your Visual Basic Applications: DDE in Depth

Prepare a Server

Create a Client

Use a Control's Link Properties to Establish the Link

Create Hot Links for Automatic Updating

Poke User-Selected Excel Cells

This book has emphasized how easy it is to design useful, friendly applications with Visual Basic. Visual Basic alone or in conjunction with the Clipboard is more than sufficient for most users. But some of you who have grander applications in mind might want even more power. No problem: Visual Basic was designed with power-hungry folks in mind.

The first part of this chapter discusses DDE in depth and shows how to connect a Visual Basic application to other Visual Basic applications, as well as how to create dynamic links between control arrays in two separate applications. Then you can build a general-purpose DDE form that enables users to specify various applications, link topics, items, and so on. You use that form to connect to Microsoft Excel in the last part of this chapter. When numerous features are added to Wizard in Chapter 10, "A Wizard Project Editor and a Wizard Clipboard," use that form to create dynamic links to the Wizard Clipboard, as well as to create a specialized Clipboard application.

INSIDE DDE

Dynamic data exchange (DDE) is a way, provided by Windows, for applications to exchange data with each other. Typically, a Client application initiates a conversation (that is, an exchange) between two applications, and a Server application responds to a Client's request for a conversation. For example, if your Visual Basic application wants to engage Excel in a conversation, it might initiate the conversation by starting Excel and specifying a spreadsheet as the "topic" of conversation. In this case, the Visual Basic application initiating the conversation is the Client, and Excel is the Server.

Before an application can engage in a conversation with any other application, however, it must establish a link to the application. If your Visual Basic application is the client (it can be either Client or Server), you first must decide which control or controls on which form or forms will participate in the conversation.

Any Visual Basic picture box, label, or text box can be the Client in the Client application's conversation. Generally, a form is the Server when an application is a server application. In both Client and Server applications, however, the actual exchange of data is between controls on the relative applications.

When an application initiates a DDE conversation, it must indicate:

- The name of the Server application with which it wants to engage in a conversation
- The topic of conversation, such as a spreadsheet, a document, or a control on the Server application
- The item of the conversation (such as a spreadsheet cell)
- The link type or mode of the conversation (either a hot or cold link)

The Client application must indicate also which Client control will engage in the conversation. As you will see in the CLIENT2 application, which links two control arrays in a conversation, more than one control can participate in a conversation.

Although the *Microsoft Visual Basic Programmer's Guide* shows how to make DDE connections, I struggled through it before finally understanding how DDE, Visual Basic-style, works. For that reason, the first applications (CLIENT1, 1B, 1C, and 1D) step through simple connections between two Visual Basic applications. The second Client application (CLIENT2) moves to a more complex conversation between multiple controls. Then I discuss some potential problems and how to add some error handling to your DDE applications. At that point, you build a generic DDE form to plug into any application to enable quick DDE connections. You use that generic form in this chapter to connect to Excel; use a modified version of it again in Chapter 10 with an advanced Wizard; and use it again in the stock market modeling application in Chapter 12, "DDE, Custom Controls, and DLLs: Intimate Details."

Connect Two Visual Basic Applications

Let's start by using Visual Basic to create two applications: one Server and one Client. You need both for a DDE connection.

Prepare a Server

Because the Server is the simpler application to build, create it first. Start up Visual Basic and use the default form. Add a text box, which will participate in the link with the Client application. Then change the form's `LinkMode` property to the Server. This step is absolutely necessary because it enables the form to respond to a DDE initiative from a Client application. Note also that you specify only the `LinkMode` for the form (to the Server); do nothing to the text box control's link properties. The Client application sets them as needed.

There's no code in the application. The DDE conversation in this example is run entirely from the Client. Note, however, that this is just one way to handle the conversation. The Server can double also as Client; more on that later in this chapter. Figure 8.1 shows the server application.

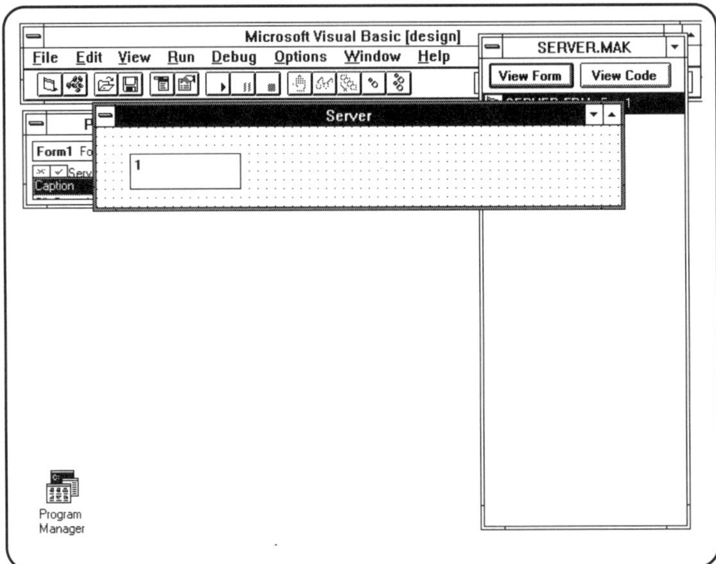

Figure 8.1. The Server application.

Create a Client

Now let's create the Client application. Start up Visual Basic and use the default form. Add a text box control (which serves as the client control in the conversation); two option buttons to indicate the type of link the user wants to make (hot or cold); and two command buttons for sending and receiving messages. I have ignored error checking, which you soon will discover can be a serious problem.

Because this first Client application is used only to demonstrate a DDE exchange, we can forego most niceties and simply have it automatically set up a DDE exchange when it's loaded. It needs to:

1. Run the Server application.
2. Clear any current DDE link before establishing a new link (a safety check).
3. Set up a link to the Server application.
4. Set up a link to text box control on the Server application (for the DDE conversation).
5. Establish the DDE link (by way of `LinkMode`).

Step 1 uses the Visual Basic `Shell` command to run the Server application:

```
x% = Shell("C:\VB\SERVER", 1)
```

In addition, Step 1 has Windows finish processing the `Shell` command by invoking `DoEvents()`:

```
x% = DoEvents()
```

If you don't use the line `x% = DoEvents()`, and you invoke `Shell` with the `1` window style, `x% = Shell("C:\VB\SERVER", 1)`, the "shelled" application retains the focus. Use `DoEvents()` to "grab" the focus from the server. Alternatively, the following code achieves the same effect:

```
x% = Shell("C:\VB\SERVER", 4)
```

The `4` window style indicates a normal window without the focus. The shelled application can have the focus or not have it and still respond to a DDE initiative.

You can run the shelled application also as a maximized or minimized application and exchange data with it. For example, you can start the application, give it the focus, and minimize it with the following line:

```
x% = Shell("C:\VB\SERVER", 2)
```

Figure 8.2 shows a Client and a minimized Server conversing in a DDE exchange.

You must always include the call to `DoEvents()`, however, or the DDE connection isn't made properly. I single-stepped through the code in Listing 8.1 later in this chapter in hopes of obtaining a clue about how `Shell` and `DoEvents()` work. As you might expect, this doesn't accomplish much because most of what happens in `Shell` and `DoEvents()` occurs behind the scenes. My guess is that the `Shell` command alone doesn't return control to Windows in a manner that lets it respond properly to other events. A DDE connection requires Windows to work properly. `DoEvents()` enables the operating system to respond to other events, such as a DDE connection attempt by the Client. Notice again that the Client, not the Server, initiates the DDE connection.

`Shell` is a function and, therefore, returns a value that indicates the task identification number for the shelled application. This example doesn't really use the returned value, but you still must put it in a variable.

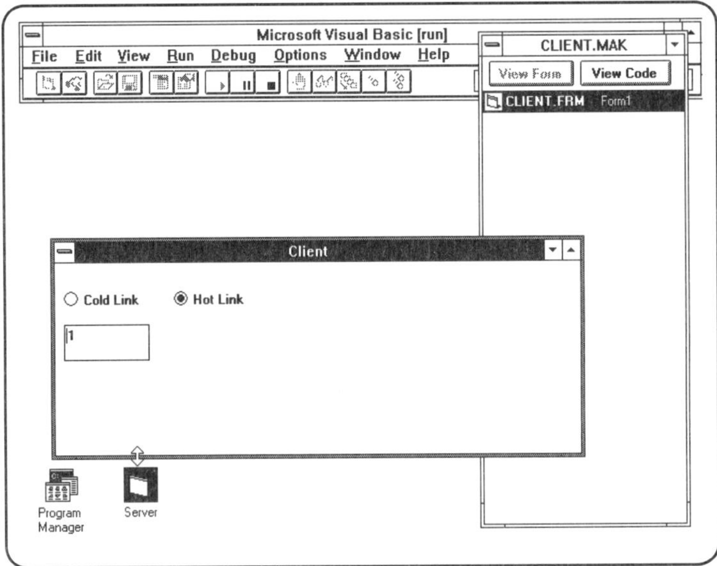

Figure 8.2. A minimized Server-Client link.

Use a Control's Link Property to Establish the Link

Before continuing, let me show you the general declarations for this project. Alternatively, they could be coded in a module in the project (or in the Global module in Version 1.0). The general declarations are extracted from the CONSTANT.TXT file and simply give names to numbers to make them easier to remember:

```
Const HOT = 1
Const COLD = 2
Const NONE = 0
```

Steps 2 through 5 listed earlier use the link properties of the client control's text box because the text box is engaging in the DDE conversation. It, therefore, clears any current link the Client text box might have by setting its `LinkMode` property to 0, the default link mode (or NONE):

```
Text1.LinkMode = NONE     'NONE = 0 if you don't use Const
```

Next, indicate the topic the Client text box wants to use for the conversation by setting its `LinkTopic`. The topic consists of the application name (the name preceding .EXE) and the document type. Because Visual Basic applications must use a form as the server, that is the document type (although "document" might sound a little strained in this case):

```
Text1.LinkTopic = "Server¦Form1"
```

In this case the document type is `Form1` with no path specification. `Form1` is assumed to exist in the current directory. If the topic had been an Excel spreadsheet, the following would be a possible topic (that is, `LinkTopic`) specification:

```
Text1.LinkTopic = "Excel¦C:\Excel\Sheet1"
```

In this case the spreadsheet exists in the Excel directory on drive C. If the topic isn't in the default directory, you must specify its location. Now indicate the specific item within the topic (within the application) with which the client control wants to link. Recall that the Server application created earlier has a single control: a text box named `Text1`. This text box (`Text1`) is the item:

```
Text1.LinkItem = "Text1"
```

A comparable Excel item is a cell:

```
Text1.LinkItem = "R1C1"
```

Then establish the link. In this case, make it a *hot* link, which means that the Client is updated automatically when the contents of the Server's text box changes:

```
Text1.LinkMode = HOT
```

Finally, set the value of the option button on the Client form to Hot, thus triggering a Click event for the Hot option button (note that in this example I'm calling the Hot Link option button `HotLink` and the Cold Link option button `ColdLink` by changing the `CtlName` properties for the two option buttons on the form):

```
HotLink.Value = TRUE          'TRUE = -1 if you don't use CONST
```

The complete `Form_Load` event procedure looks like this:

```
Sub Form_Load ()
      ' Run the Server application.
      z% = Shell("C:\VB\SERVER", 1)      ' Normal, focused window style.

      'Finish processing the Shell command.
      'You must use DoEvents() for this to work!

      z% = DoEvents()
```

```
      'Clear DDE link.
      Text1.LinkMode = NONE


      'Set up link with VB server.
      Text1.LinkTopic = "Server¦Form1"


      'Set link to text box server.
             Text1.LinkItem = " Text1 "

      'Set hot link button which establishes a hot DDE link.
      HotLink.Value = TRUE
End Sub
```

Create Hot Links for Automatic Updating

To create hot links, you must first disconnect any current link:

```
Text1.LinkMode = NONE     'NONE = 0 if you don't use CONST
```

and then establish a hot link:

```
Text1.LinkMode = HOT     'HOT = 1 if you don't use CONST
```

You don't have to do anything else to establish a hot link. When you make a cold link, you must use `LinkRequest` to get the data from the Server. Here's the minimal hot link event procedure:

```
Sub HotLink_Click ()

      'Clear DDE Link.
      Text1.LinkMode = NONE

      'Reestablish new LinkMode.
        Text1.LinkMode = HOT

End Sub
```

Create a Cold Link

Creating a cold link is just as simple. You must first disconnect any current link:

```
Text1.LinkMode = NONE     'NONE = 0 if you don't use CONST
```

Then establish the cold link:

```
Text1.LinkMode = COLD     'COLD = 2 if you don't use CONST
```

Here's the minimal cold link procedure:

```
Sub ColdLink_Click ()

      'Clear DDE Link.
      Text1.LinkMode = NONE

      'Reestablish new LinkMode.
      Text1.LinkMode = COLD
End Sub
```

With a cold link, no data is exchanged without a `LinkRequest` or `LinkPoke` message. With a hot link, the `LinkRequest` is automatic: Data is sent automatically from Server to Client. Data never is poked automatically from Client to Server, however. Regardless of the link type, the Client (or the Server) must ask for a `LinkPoke` operation.

Request Data from the Link (If You Have Made a Cold Link)

In a cold link, to request data from the server, simply ask for it:

```
Sub Request_Click ()
      Text1.LinkRequest
End Sub
```

Of course, you must specify the object (`Text1`) that is participating in the DDE conversation. In the world of object-oriented programming, the `LinkRequest` method "belongs" to the control that is making the DDE connection. Every time the control participating in the DDE conversation wants to be updated by the Server, it must ask for the data using its `LinkRequest` method.

SEND DATA VIA A LINK

To poke data to the Server, regardless of the type of link (hot or cold), simply reverse the process every time you want to poke data. Use the `LinkPoke` method of the Client object that is participating in the DDE connection:

```
Sub Send_Click ()
     Text1.LinkPoke
End Sub
```

That's all there is to it. Listing 8.1 shows a complete Client including code to turn on the hot link (default in this example) button and to disable the Send button (needed only with a cold link.)

Listing 8.1. Client.

```
' general declarations (not necessary, but used here to improve
' readability)

Const HOT = 1
Const COLD = 2
Const NONE = 0


Sub Form_Load ()
      z% = Shell("C:\VB\SERVER", 1)

      'Finish processing the Shell command.

      z% = DoEvents()

      'Clear DDE link.
      Text1.LinkMode = NONE


      'Set up link with VB server.
      Text1.LinkTopic = "Server¦Form1"


      'Set link to text box server.
              Text1.LinkItem = " Text1 "

      'Set hot link button and establish a hot DDE link.
      HotLink.Value = TRUE
End Sub


Sub ColdLink_Click ()
      'Make request button valid.
      Request.Visible = TRUE
      ' Enable Send command button.
      Send.Visible = TRUE
      'Clear DDE Link.
      Text1.LinkMode = NONE

      'Reestablish new LinkMode.
      Text1.LinkMode = COLD
End Sub
```

```
Sub HotLink_Click ()
      Request.Visible = FALSE
      ' Disable Send command button
      Send.Visible = FALSE
      'Clear DDE Link.
      Text1.LinkMode = NONE

      'Reestablish new LinkMode.
        Text1.LinkMode = HOT

      ' Request
      Request.Value = -1
End Sub


Sub Send_Click ()
     Text1.LinkPoke
End Sub


Sub Request_Click ()
      Text1.LinkRequest
End Sub
```

Figure 8.3 shows the Client application in operation with a simple Server.

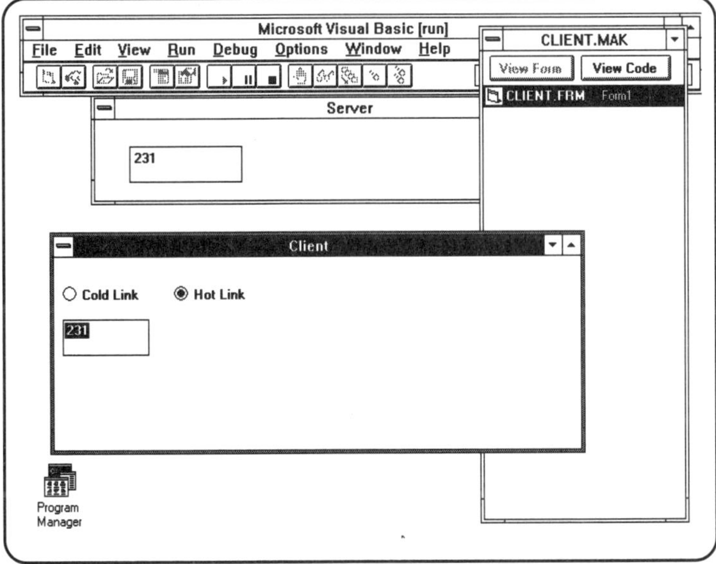

Figure 8.3. The Client application.

ADD AN ERROR HANDLER (CLIENT1B)

If you run the Client application and play with it, switching from cold to hot link, sending and receiving data, and switching between the Server and the Client, you're bound to be favorably impressed. It's magic the way these two applications communicate with each other, as though they were part of the same application.

What happens, though, if you quit the Server application before you quit the Client application? And, what happens if the Client can't find the Server? As the applications stand in both cases, Client crashes to a halt—not good.

Fortunately, you can redesign Client to avoid virtually any unsuspected circumstance by adding an error handler based on the one you began developing at the end of Chapter 7, "Bullet-proof at Runtime: Into the Real World of Errors and Error Handling." Start by specifying some global variables for the Server, application number, `LinkTopic`, `LinkItem`, and `Saved Error` value:

```
global declarations

Global Server$
Global App%
Global Topic$
Global Item$
Global SaveErr%
```

You are not required to make these variables global (or general). If you don't, be sure to pass them to any procedure that needs them. I know that it's a little old-fashioned to make variables global rather than pass them, but I prefer it and use them whenever several procedures need to use a variable.

Recall from Chapter 7 the `GeneralErrors` procedure that implemented one class of special errors: `DDEErrors`—just what you need for this error handler:

```
Sub GeneralErrors ()
    Msg$ = Error$(SaveErr%)
    MsgBox Msg$
    Select Case SaveErr%
        Case 280 To 297
            DDEErrors
    End Select
End Sub
```

The `DDEErrors()` procedure looks like this:

```
Sub DDEErrors ()
     Select Case SaveErr%
```

```
        Case 282
          App% = Shell(Server$, 1)
          App% = DoEvents()
        Case 283
          Msg$ = "Suggest you open Program Manager "
          Msg$ = Msg$ + " NOW and use End Task "
          Msg$ = Msg$ + " to terminate the LAST "
          Msg$ = Msg$ + " INSTANCE of " + Server$
          MsgBox Msg$

    End Select
End Sub
```

This `DDEError` procedure handles two errors:

282 No foreign application responded to a DDE initiate
283 Multiple applications responded to a DDE initiate

In this version of `DDEErrors`, any error except 282 or 283 is ignored.

I chose to handle these two errors first because they were the first two problems I encountered when I began developing this DDE application. Error 282 occurs when the DDE link cannot be made because no application responds to the DDE request specified by Client. This error occurs when Client attempts to make the link in the `Text1.LinkMode = HOT` statement.

It's easy to handle error 282—just run the application using the `Shell` command as illustrated here. Error 283 is a little more difficult to handle. I chose the easiest way—to send the user a message telling how to handle the error by removing the last instance of the Server application.

Although the Visual Basic documentation doesn't say that a DDE link is always attempted with the first instance of the Server application, my tests have determined that the first instance listed in the Program Manager's task list is a safe bet to save for a DDE link in this situation. To test this, end the first instance of the Server application in the Program Manager Task List and see what happens. In all my test cases, no DDE link is established if you end the first instance.

This particular method of handling error 283 is user-dependent, but it's the safest way I have found to handle the error. Note that you generally can modify this response without affecting the error handler, or you can add new responses to errors (such as error 284) without changing any other code. This type of general-purpose error handling is efficient because you have to respond specifically to only the errors you want.

The code in Listing 8.2 shows the complete Client application with this first version of an error handler. Figures 8.4 and 8.5 show CLIENT1B in various stages of operation.

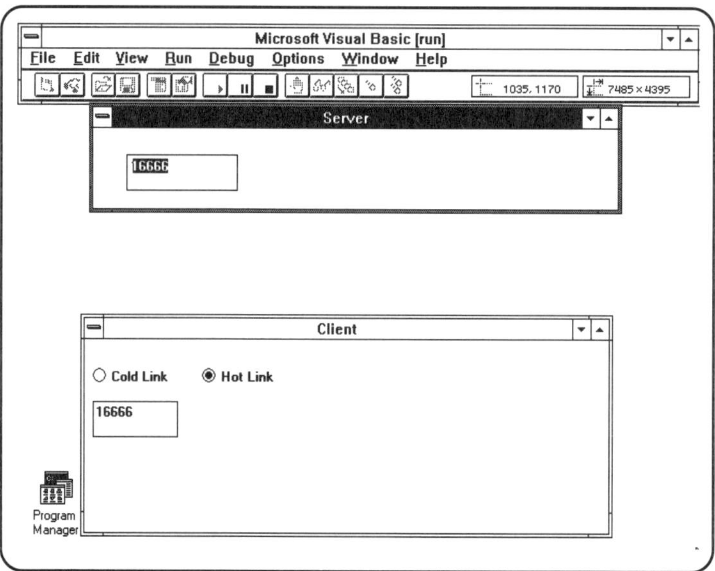

Figure 8.4. Client 1B.

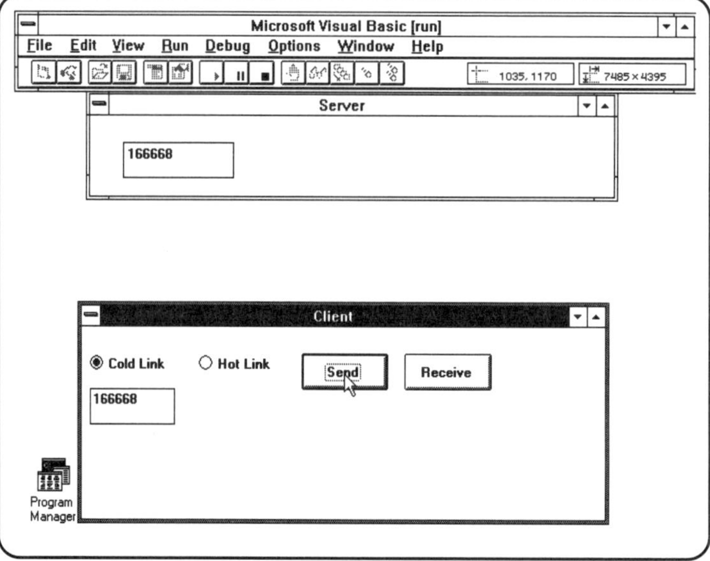

Figure 8.5. Client 1B, in another stage of operation.

Listing 8.2. CLIENT1B.

```
' Global declarations

Global SaveErr%

' General Declarations at form-level

Const HOT = 1
Const COLD = 2
Const NONE = 0

' Client form

Sub Form_Load ()
      On Error GoTo E1:
      ' Simple, hard-coding of Server application
      z% = Shell("C:\VB\SERVER", 1)

      'Allow Windows to finish processing the Shell command.
      'Necessary for DDE connection to work.
      z% = DoEvents()

      'Clear DDE link.
      Text1.LinkMode = NONE


      'Set up link with VB server.
      Text1.LinkTopic = "Server¦Form1"


      'Set link to text box server,

      Text1.LinkItem = " Text1 "


      'Sets hot link button.
      HotLink.Value = TRUE
      Exit Sub
E1:
      SaveErr% = Err
      GeneralErrors
      Resume Next
End Sub

Sub ColdLink_Click ()
      On Error GoTo ErrorHandler1

      'Enable request and send buttons.
```

continues

LISTING 8.2. CONTINUED

```
      Request.Visible = TRUE
      Send.Visible = TRUE

      'Clear DDE Link.

      Text1.LinkMode = NONE

      'Reestablish new LinkMode.

      Text1.LinkMode = COLD
      Exit Sub
ErrorHandler1:
      SaveErr% = Err
      GeneralErrors
      Resume
End Sub

Sub HotLink_Click ()
      On Error GoTo E2

      Request.Visible = FALSE
      Send.Visible = FALSE

      'Clear DDE Link.
      Text1.LinkMode = NONE

      'Reestablish new LinkMode.

      Text1.LinkMode = HOT

      ' Request button on
      Request.Value = -1
Exit Sub
E2:
      SaveErr% = Err
      GeneralErrors ' optionally you can fix the error
      Resume Next   ' and resume.

End Sub

Sub Request_Click ()
      On Error GoTo E3

      Text1.LinkRequest
      Exit Sub
```

```
E3:
      SaveErr% = Err
      GeneralErrors ' optionally you can fix the error
      Resume Next   ' and resume.

End Sub

Sub Send_Click ()
      On Error GoTo E4
      Text1.LinkPoke
      Exit Sub
E4:
      SaveErr% = Err
      GeneralErrors ' optionally you can fix the error
      Resume Next   ' and resume.

End Sub


' Errors Module

Sub GeneralErrors ()
  Msg$ = Error$(SaveErr%)
  MsgBox Msg$
  Select Case SaveErr%
     Case 280 To 297
       DDEErrors
  End Select
End Sub


Sub DDEErrors ()
  Select Case SaveErr%

     Case 282
       App% = Shell(Server$, 1)
       App% = DoEvents()
     Case 283
       Msg$ = "Suggest you open Program Manager "
       Msg$ = Msg$ + " NOW and use End Task "
       Msg$ = Msg$ + " to terminate the LAST "
       Msg$ = Msg$ + " INSTANCE of " + Server$
       MsgBox Msg$

  End Select
End Sub
```

DESIGN NOTES: REVISE A CLIENT—MENU ITEMS RATHER THAN CONTROLS (CLIENT1C)

With the CLIENT1C application, you've made the DDE connection and provided a general way to handle DDE errors. So far, so good, but from a design standpoint, you can see that it might be handy to have a DDE client use menu items rather than controls to indicate links and handle poke, receive requests, and so on. In addition, CLIENT1C adds an important feature you will want to include in many of your DDE applications. It enables the user to specify a Server, a link topic, and a link item. These features also create some error-handling problems.

LET THE USER SPECIFY A SERVER (CLIENT1C)

To let the user specify Server, link topic, and link item, add a new procedure called `EstablishLink`, which uses an input box to get the user's request:

```
Sub EstablishCom_Click ()
On Error GoTo E6:

       Msg$ = "Enter Server for link."
       Server$ = InputBox$(Msg$, "Establish New Link", "C:\VB¦SERVER")
       z% = Shell(Server$, 1)

       'Allow Windows to finish processing the Shell command.

       z% = DoEvents()

       'Clear DDE link.
       Text1.LinkMode = NONE


       'Sets up link with VB server.
       Msg$ = "Enter Topic for link."
       Topic$ = InputBox$(Msg$, "Establish New Topic", "SERVER¦Form1")

       Text1.LinkTopic = Topic$


       'Set link to text box server.
       Msg$ = "Enter Item for link."
       Item$ = InputBox$(Msg$, "Establish New Item", " Text1 ")
```

```
        Text1.LinkItem = Item$

        'Establish a hot DDE link.

        Text1.LinkMode = HOT

        Exit Sub
E6:
        SaveErr% = Err
        GeneralErrors ' optionally you can fix the error
        Resume Next   ' and resume.

End Sub
```

The CLIENT1C application on the disk and in Listing 8.3 shows the menu look and the additional `EstablishLink` event procedure. Figure 8.6 shows CLIENT1C in operation.

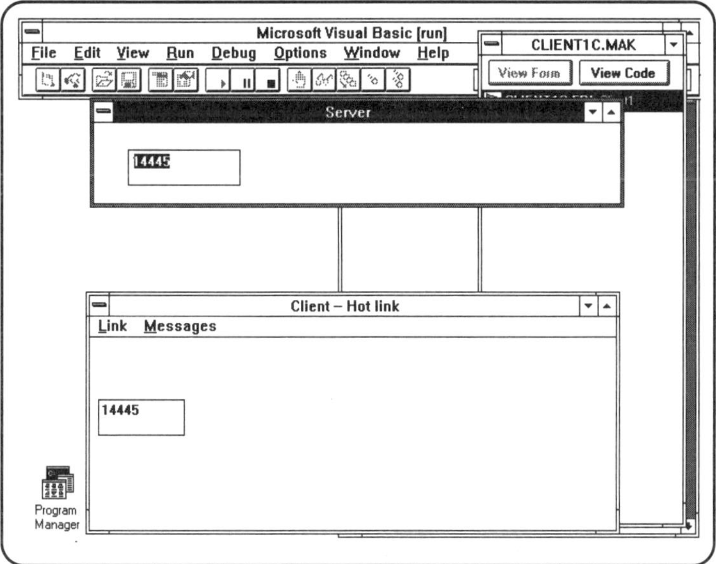

Figure 8.6. CLIENT1C.

LISTING 8.3. CLIENT1C.

```
' global declarations

Global SaveErr%


' Client1c.frm


Const HOT = 1
Const COLD = 2
Const NONE = 0


Sub Form_Load ()
     On Error GoTo E1:

     z% = Shell("C:\VB\SERVER", 1)

     'Causes Windows to finish processing the Shell command.

     z% = DoEvents()

     'Clears DDE link.
     Text1.LinkMode = NONE

     'Sets up link with VB server.
     Text1.LinkTopic = "Server¦Form1"


     'Set link to text box server

          Text1.LinkItem = "Text1"

     'Set hot link button & establishes hot link
     HotLinkCom_Click
     Exit Sub
E1:
     SaveErr% = Err
     GeneralErrors
     Resume Next
End Sub


Sub SendCom_Click ()
     On Error GoTo E4
            Text1.LinkItem = "Text1"
         Text1.LinkPoke
     Exit Sub
```

```
E4:
     SaveErr% = Err
     GeneralErrors
     Resume Next
End Sub


Sub ReceiveCom_Click ()
     On Error GoTo E3

     Text1.LinkRequest
     Exit Sub
E3:
     SaveErr% = Err
     GeneralErrors
     Resume Next
End Sub


Sub HotLinkCom_Click ()
     On Error GoTo E2

     ReceiveCom.Enabled = FALSE
     SendCom.Enabled = FALSE
     Client1.Caption = "Client -- Hot link"

     'Clear DDE Link.
     Text1.LinkMode = NONE

     'Reestablish new LinkMode.
            Text1.LinkMode = HOT

     ' Request
     ReceiveCom_Click
     Exit Sub
E2:
     SaveErr% = Err
     GeneralErrors
     Resume Next
End Sub


Sub ColdLinkCom_Click ()
     On Error GoTo ErrorHandler1

     'Make request button valid.

     ReceiveCom.Enabled = TRUE
     SendCom.Enabled = TRUE
     Client1.Caption = "Client -- Cold link"
```

continues

LISTING 8.3. CONTINUED

```
     'Clear DDE Link.
     Text1.LinkMode = NONE

     'Reestablish new LinkMode.

     Text1.LinkMode = COLD
     Exit Sub
ErrorHandler1:
     SaveErr% = Err
     GeneralErrors
     Exit Sub
End Sub


Sub EstablishCom_Click ()
     On Error GoTo E6:

     Msg$ = "Enter Server for link."
     Server$ = InputBox$(Msg$, "Establish New Link", "C:\VB¦SERVER")
     z% = Shell(Server$, 1)

     'Causes Windows to finish processing the Shell command.

     z% = DoEvents()

     'Clears DDE link.
     Text1.LinkMode = NONE

     'Sets up link with VB server.
     Msg$ = "Enter Topic for link."
     Topic$ = InputBox$(Msg$, "Establish New Topic", "SERVER¦Form1")

     Text1.LinkTopic = Topic$


     'Set link to text box server
     Msg$ = "Enter Item for link."
     Item$ = InputBox$(Msg$, "Establish New Item", "Text1")

         Text1.LinkItem = Item$

     'Establish a hot DDE link.
          'Sets hot link button.
     HotLinkCom_Click
     Exit Sub
E6:
     SaveErr% = Err
     GeneralErrors
     Resume Next
End Sub
```

```
' Errorsb module


Sub GeneralErrors ()
    Msg$ = Error$(SaveErr%)
    MsgBox Msg$
    Select Case SaveErr%
        Case 280 To 297
            DDEErrors
        Case 40 To 76
            DiskErrors
        Case 30000 To 31015
            OLEErrors
    End Select
End Sub


Sub DDEErrors ()
        Dim App%
        Select Case SaveErr%

            Case 282
                Msg$ = "Starting Server " + Server$
                MsgBox Msg$
                App% = Shell(Server$, 1)
                App% = DoEvents()
            Case 283
                Msg$ = "Suggest you open Program Manager "
                Msg$ = Msg$ + " NOW and use End Task "
                Msg$ = Msg$ + " to terminate the LAST "
          Msg$ = Msg$ + " INSTANCE of " + Server$
                MsgBox Msg$
        End Select
End Sub


Sub OLEErrors ()
        Select Case SaveErr%

            Case 30005
                Msg$ = "OLE_Error_Stream"
                MsgBox Msg$
            ' Other cases here.
        End Select

End Sub

Sub DiskErrors ()
        Select Case SaveErr%
```

continues

LISTING 8.3. CONTINUED

```
        Case 48
            Msg$ = "Disk Error"
            MsgBox Msg$
        ' Other cases here.
    End Select

End Sub
```

HANDLING SERVER, LINKTOPIC, AND LINKITEM ERRORS

So far, you've given the user some freedom to specify Server, `LinkTopic`, and `LinkItem` in the DDE connection, but you haven't added any error checking. If the user specifies this trio, the system may crash, or at least behave unpredictably, unless you have implemented some error checking.

One approach to this problem is to let the `GeneralErrors` error handler report the error and then, on -return to the procedure that generates the error, `EstablishCom_Click`, handle the specific error using a `Select Case` statement. The following `Select Case` statement handles three common errors generated by incorrect Server, `LinkTopic`, and `LinkItem`:

```
Select Case SaveErr%
      Case 380
        Msg$ = "Topic error: Reenter Topic for link."
        Topic$ = InputBox$(Msg$, "Establish New Topic", "SERVER¦Form1")
      Case 53
        Msg$ = "Application error: Reenter Server for link."
        Server$ = InputBox$(Msg$, "Establish New Link", "C:\VB\SERVER")
      Case 285
        Msg$ = "Item error: Reenter Topic for link."
        Item$ = InputBox$(Msg$, "Establish New Topic", "Text1")
        SetUpLink
End Select
```

The `SetUpLink` procedure looks like this:

```
Sub SetUpLink()
     Text1.LinkMode = NONE
     Text1.LinkTopic = Topic$
     Text1.LinkItem = Item$
End Sub
```

Because error 285 is generated by the time the `LinkMode` property is set, it's necessary to reset the `LinkMode` to 0 (NONE) before you attempt another link.

The completely revised `EstablishCom_Click()` event procedure looks like this:

```
Sub EstablishCom_Click ()
On Error GoTo E6:

  Msg$ = "Enter Server for link."
  Server$ = InputBox$(Msg$, "Establish New Link", "C:\VB\SERVER")
  App% = Shell(Server$, 1)

  'Causes Windows to finish processing the Shell command.

  App% = DoEvents()

  'Clears DDE link.
  Text1.LinkMode = NONE


  'Sets up link with VB server.
  Msg$ = "Enter Topic for link."
  Topic$ = InputBox$(Msg$, "Establish New Topic", "SERVER¦Form1")

  Text1.LinkTopic = Topic$


  'Set link to text box server
  Msg$ = "Enter Item for link."
  Item$ = InputBox$(Msg$, "Establish New Item", "Text1")

     Text1.LinkItem = Item$

  'Establish a hot DDE link.

     Text1.LinkMode = HOT


  'Sets hot link button.
  HotLinkCom_Click
  Exit Sub
 E6:
  SaveErr% = Err
  GeneralErrors
  Select Case SaveErr%
     Case 380
       Msg$ = "Topic error: Reenter Topic for link."
       Topic$ = InputBox$(Msg$, "Establish New Topic", "SERVER¦Form1")
```

```
      Case 53
        Msg$ = "Application error: Reenter Server for link."
        Server$ = InputBox$(Msg$, "Establish New Link", "C:\VB\SERVER")
      Case 285
        Msg$ = "Item error: Reenter Topic for link."
        Item$ = InputBox$(Msg$, "Establish New Topic", "Text1")
        SetUpLink

  End Select
  Resume
End Sub
```

The complete CLIENT1D application is in Listing 8.4. Figures 8.7 and 8.8 show the CLIENT1D application in operation.

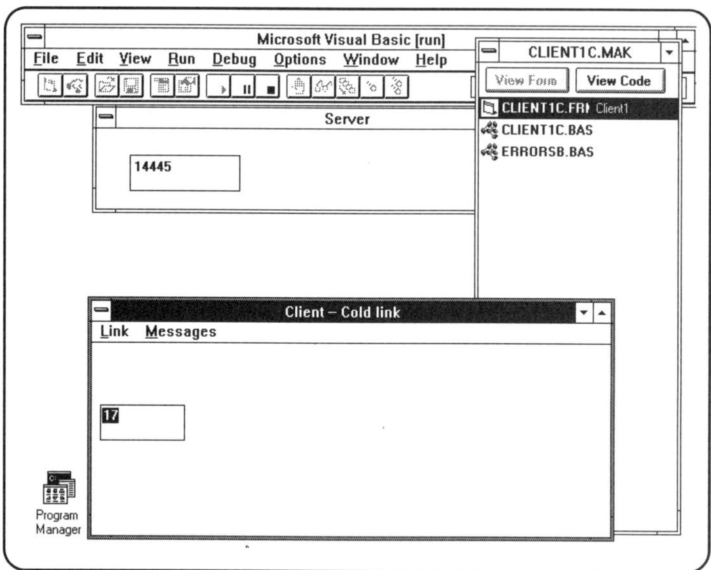

Figure 8.7. CLIENT1D: Making a cold link with the server.

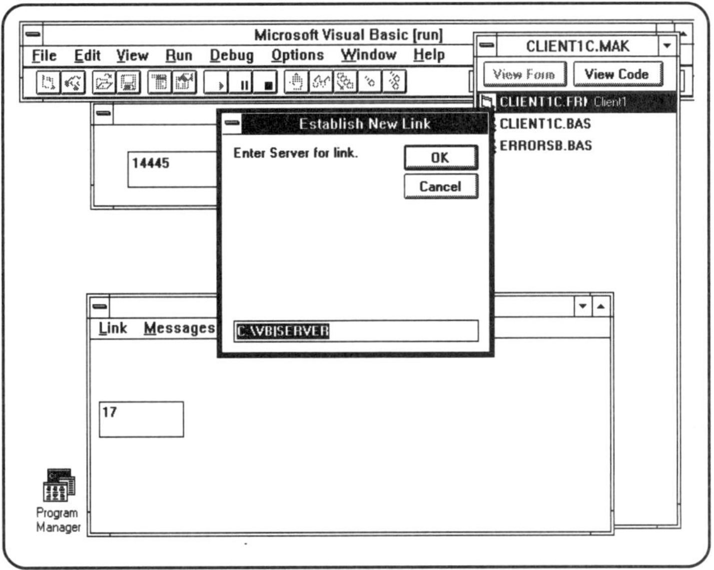

Figure 8.8. CLIENT1D: Establishing a new link with the server.

Listing 8.4. CLIENT1D.

```
' Global declarations
Global Server$
Global ZApp%
Global Topic$
Global Item$
Global SaveErr%
Const HOT = 1
Const COLD = 2
Const NONE = 0

Sub Form_Load ()
On Error GoTo E1:

     Server$ = "Server"
     Topic$ = "Server¦Form1"
     Item$ = "Text1"
     ZApp% = Shell(Server$, 1)
     ZApp% = DoEvents()
```

continues

LISTING 8.4. CONTINUED

```
     SetUpLink
     Text1.LinkMode = HOT
     HotLinkCom_Click
     Exit Sub
E1:
     SaveErr% = Err
     GeneralErrors
     SetUpLink
     Resume
End Sub

Sub SendCom_Click ()
On Error GoTo E4
     Text1.LinkItem = "Text1"
     Text1.LinkPoke
  Exit Sub
E4:
  SaveErr% = Err
  GeneralErrors
  Resume

End Sub

Sub ReceiveCom_Click ()
On Error GoTo E3

  Text1.LinkRequest
  Exit Sub
E3:
  SaveErr% = Err
  GeneralErrors
  Resume Next

End Sub

Sub HotLinkCom_Click ()
On Error GoTo E2

  ReceiveCom.Enabled = FALSE
  SendCom.Enabled = FALSE
  Client1.Caption = "Client -- Hot link"
  'Clear DDE Link.
  Text1.LinkMode = NONE

  'Reestablish new LinkMode.

     Text1.LinkMode = HOT
```

```
  ' Request
  ReceiveCom_Click
  Exit Sub
E2:
  SaveErr% = Err
  GeneralErrors
  Text1.LinkMode = NONE
  Resume

End Sub

Sub ColdLinkCom_Click ()
On Error GoTo EH1

'Make request button valid.

ReceiveCom.Enabled = TRUE
SendCom.Enabled = TRUE
Client1.Caption = "Client -- Cold link"

'Clear DDE Link


  Text1.LinkMode = NONE

'Reestablish new LinkMode.


  Text1.LinkMode = COLD
  Exit Sub

EH1:
  SaveErr% = Err
  GeneralErrors
  Text1.LinkMode = NONE
  Resume
End Sub

Sub EstablishCom_Click ()
On Error GoTo E6:

  Msg$ = "Enter Server for link."
  Server$ = InputBox$(Msg$, "Establish New Link", "C:\VB\SERVER")
  ZApp% = Shell(Server$, 1)

  'Causes Windows to finish processing the Shell command.

  ZApp% = DoEvents()
```

continues

LISTING 8.4. CONTINUED

```
  'Clears DDE link.
  Text1.LinkMode = NONE


  'Sets up link with VB server.
  Msg$ = "Enter Topic for link."
  Topic$ = InputBox$(Msg$, "Establish New Topic", "SERVER¦Form1")

  Text1.LinkTopic = Topic$


  'Set link to text box server.
  Msg$ = "Enter Item for link."
  Item$ = InputBox$(Msg$, "Establish New Item", "Text1")

     Text1.LinkItem = Item$

  'Establish a hot DDE link.

     Text1.LinkMode = HOT


  'Sets hot link button.
  HotLinkCom_Click
  Exit Sub
E6:
  SaveErr% = Err
  GeneralErrors
  Select Case SaveErr%
     Case 380
       Msg$ = "Topic error: Reenter Topic for link."
       Topic$ = InputBox$(Msg$, "Establish New Topic", "SERVER¦Form1")
     Case 53
       Msg$ = "Application error: Reenter Server for link."
       Server$ = InputBox$(Msg$, "Establish New Link", "C:\VB\SERVER")
     Case 285
       Msg$ = "Item error: Reenter Topic for link."
       Item$ = InputBox$(Msg$, "Establish New Topic", "Text1")
       SetUpLink

  End Select
  Resume
End Sub

Sub SetUpLink()
     Text1.LinkMode = NONE
     Text1.LinkTopic = Topic$
     Text1.LinkItem = Item$
End Sub
```

```
' Errors Module

Sub GeneralErrors ()
  Msg$ = Error$(SaveErr%)
  MsgBox Msg$
  Select Case SaveErr%
     Case 280 To 297
       DDEErrors
  End Select
End Sub


Sub DDEErrors ()
     Select Case SaveErr%

        Case 282
          ZApp% = Shell(Server$, 1)
          ZApp% = DoEvents()
        Case 283
          Msg$ = "Suggest you open Program Manager "
          Msg$ = Msg$ + " NOW and use End Task "
          Msg$ = Msg$ + " to terminate the LAST "
          Msg$ = Msg$ + " INSTANCE of " + Server$
          MsgBox Msg$

     End Select
End Sub
```

DDE Connections between Control Arrays (CLIENT2)

Until now, you have been limited to establishing DDE links between single controls (one on the Client form and one on the Server form). But you can, with just a little more effort, establish a connection between more than one control in both Server and Client applications.

One DDE connection you might make between more than one control in Server and Client applications is between control arrays. Use the application form for CLIENT1D and Server, and change the text box control on both to a control array of text boxes called `Text1()`. Then create three text boxes (for this example) as members of the control array. First make the change in the Server and save it as SERVER2. Then make SERVER2 a stand-alone executable application. Figure 8.9 shows the revised Server with a text box control array of three text boxes.

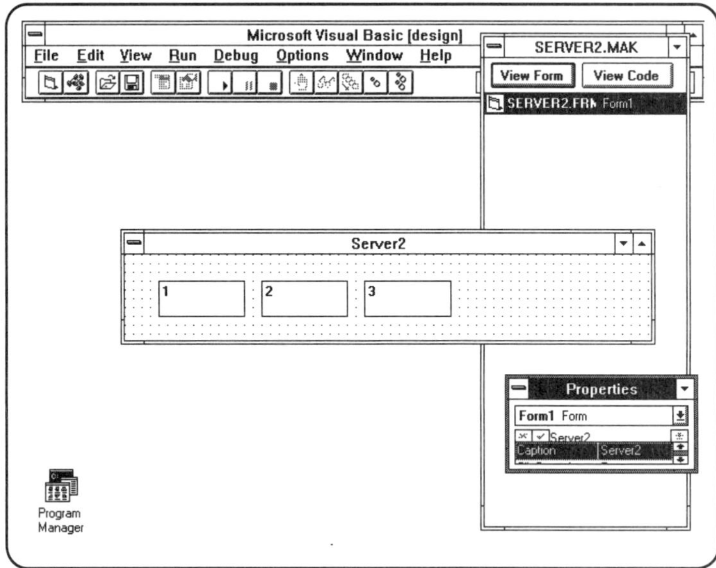

Figure 8.9. SERVER2: An array of text boxes.

Next, revise the text box control to a text box control array in the Client and also add two more text boxes (for a total of three) to the control array. Figure 8.10 shows the revised Client.

The first change you have to make (basing the changes on the CLIENT1D application) is to establish the DDE link between the first control in the Client's control array and the Server. By first establishing the link with a single control of the control array, you can test the link before trying to complete the link with the entire array. If you are connecting a large control array, this step saves time if an error occurs.

Implement your general-purpose error handler again to handle link errors so that the first part of the attempted connection looks like the following:

```
Sub Form_Load ()
      On Error GoTo E1
      I% = 0
      Text1(I%).LinkTopic = "Server2¦Form1"
      Text1(I%).LinkItem = "Text1" + "(" + Str$(I%) + ")"
      Text1(I%).LinkMode = HOT
      '....procedure will continue here....
      '........
E1:   '       Error handler
  SaveErr% = Err
```

```
   GeneralErrors
   Resume Next

End Sub
```

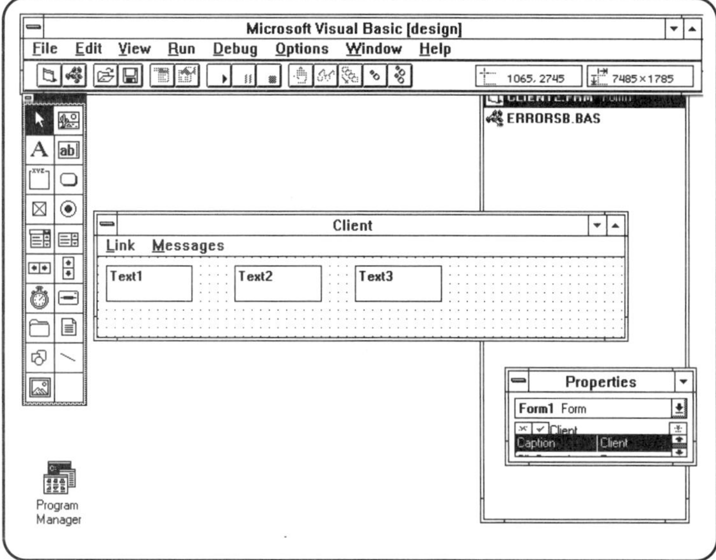

Figure 8.10. CLIENT2: An array of text boxes.

If a DDE connection error occurs, you can try to resolve it in the error handler before you proceed. If there's no error, the procedure continues to establish the DDE link by looping through the Client's control array and, in this example, connecting each text box of the control array to a text box of the control array in the Server. First it clears any previous links:

```
'Clears DDE link.
For I% = 0 To 2
   Text1(I%).LinkMode = NONE
Next I%
```

Then the procedure establishes the new link to the `LinkTopic` and `LinkItem`:

```
'Sets up link with VB server.
'Set link to text box server
'Establish a hot DDE link.

For I% = 0 To 2
   Text1(I%).LinkTopic = "Server2¦Form1"
   Text1(I%).LinkItem = "Text1 " + "(" + Str$(I%) + ")"
   Text1(I%).LinkMode = HOT
Next I%
```

```
SendCom.Enabled = 0
Exit Sub
```

Note the line `Text1(I%).LinkItem = "Text1" + "(" + Str$(I%) + ")"`. It enables the `LinkItem` to be the next item in the Server's control array.

The hot link event procedure similarly establishes a link by looping through the control array:

```
Sub HotLinkCom_CLick ()
  ' Disable Send Message
  SendCom.Enabled = 0
  'Clear DDE Link.
  'Reestablish new LinkMode
  For I% = 0 To 2
    Text1(I%).LinkMode = NONE
    Text1(I%).LinkMode = HOT
  Next I%
End Sub
```

The cold link also works similarly:

```
Sub ColdLinkCom_Click ()

'Clear DDE Link.
'Reestablish new LinkMode.

For I% = 0 To 2
   Text1(I%).LinkMode = NONE
   Text1(I%).LinkMode = COLD
Next I%
```

Use a similar technique to request data:

```
Sub RequestCom_Click ()
  For I% = 0 To 2
     Text1(I%).LinkItem = "Text1" + "(" + Str$(I%) + ")"
     Text1(I%).LinkRequest
  Next I%

End Sub
```

And, to send data:

```
Sub SendCom_Click ()
  For I% = 0 To 2
     Text1(I%).LinkItem = "Text1" + "(" + Str$(I%) + ")"
     Text1(I%).LinkPoke
  Next I%

End Sub
```

The complete CLIENT2 application is in Listing 8.5. Figures 8.11 and 8.12 show SERVER2 and CLIENT2 making a DDE connection.

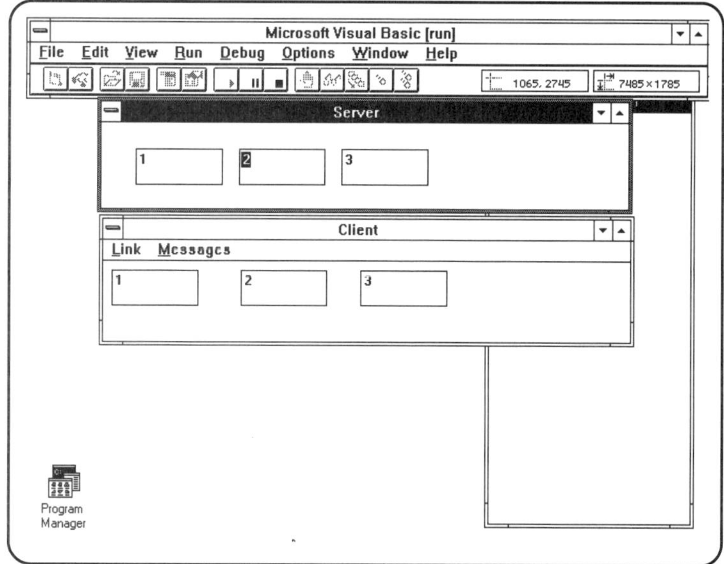

Figure 8.11. CLIENT2 and SERVER2 making a link.

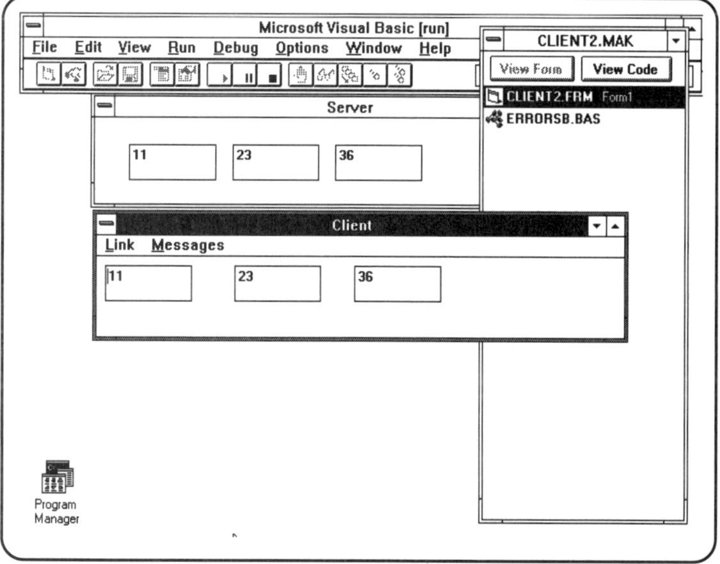

Figure 8.12. CLIENT2 and SERVER2 after a new DDE exchange.

LISTING 8.5. CLIENT2.

```
' Global declarations

Global SaveErr%
Const HOT = 1
Const COLD = 2
Const NONE = 0

Sub Form_Load ()
On Error GoTo E1
    I% = 0
    Text1(I%).LinkTopic = "Server2¦Form1"
    Text1(I%).LinkItem = "Text1" + "(" + Str$(I%) + ")"
    Text1(I%).LinkMode = HOT

  'Clears DDE link.
  For I% = 0 To 2
    Text1(I%).LinkMode = NONE
  Next I%

  'Sets up link with VB server.
  'Set link to text box server
  'Establish a hot DDE link.

  For I% = 0 To 2
    Text1(I%).LinkTopic = "Server2¦Form1"
    Text1(I%).LinkItem = "Text1" + "(" + Str$(I%) + ")"
    Text1(I%).LinkMode = HOT
  Next I%

  SendCom.Enabled = 0
  Exit Sub

E1:
  SaveErr% = Err
  GeneralErrors
  Resume Next

End Sub

Sub Form_GotFocus()
  HotLink Com_Click
End Sub

Sub HotLinkCom_CLick ()
  ' Disable Send Message
  SendCom.Enabled = 0
  'Clear DDE Link.
  'Reestablish new LinkMode
```

```
  For I% = 0 To 2
    Text1(I%).LinkMode = NONE
    Text1(I%).LinkMode = HOT
  Next I%
End Sub

Sub ColdLinkCom_Click ()

'Clear DDE Link.
'Reestablish new LinkMode.

For I% = 0 To 2
  Text1(I%).LinkMode = NONE
  Text1(I%).LinkMode = COLD
Next I%

'Show Send menu item.
   SendCom.Enabled = -1
End Sub

Sub RequestCom_Click ()
  For I% = 0 To 2
    Text1(I%).LinkItem = "Text1 " + "(" + Str$(I%) + ")"
    Text1(I%).LinkRequest
  Next I%

End Sub

Sub SendCom_Click ()
  For I% = 0 To 2
    Text1(I%).LinkItem = "Text1" + "(" + Str$(I%) + ")"
    Text1(I%).LinkPoke
  Next I%

End Sub

Sub Form_Click ()
  HotLinkCom_CLick
End Sub


' Errors Module

Sub GeneralErrors ()
  Msg$ = Error$(SaveErr%)
  MsgBox Msg$
  Select Case SaveErr%
     Case 280 To 297
        DDEErrors
  End Select
End Sub
```

continues

LISTING 8.5. CONTINUED

```
Sub DDEErrors ()
     Select Case SaveErr%

        Case 282
          App% = Shell(Server$, 1)
          App% = DoEvents()
        Case 283
          Msg$ = "Suggest you open Program Manager "
          Msg$ = Msg$ + " NOW and use End Task "
          Msg$ = Msg$ + " to terminate the LAST "
          Msg$ = Msg$ + " INSTANCE of " + Server$
          MsgBox Msg$

     End Select
End Sub
```

AVOID MULTIPLE INSTANCES TAKE 2: APPACTIVATE AND ERROR HANDLING

If you've explored the Client applications, you no doubt have noticed that the error handler implemented earlier prevents your CLIENT from crashing, but reports that `Multiple Applications Are Responding` to the DDE request every time you run the Client without closing the Server.

What's happening is that every time the Client application starts, it automatically runs the Server. It doesn't check first to see whether the Server is running. You may, therefore, get many instances of Server executing simultaneously, which is probably not what you want.

Earlier, the error handler you implemented handled this error (#283) by suggesting that the user end the last instance of the Server until only one instance of Server is running. Alternatively, the Client might attempt to activate the Server before executing it using a `Shell` command. The Client can do this using the `AppActivate` command:

```
AppActivate Server$
```

Note that if the Server, specified by `Server$`, isn't running, Visual Basic generates an illegal function call error (error #5). Therefore, you must implement the error handler and test for the specific error for this technique to work.

You use the error (if there is one) to find out what you want to know about how many instances of the application are running. If Visual Basic generates error #5, the Client starts the Server; otherwise, it doesn't. The following `Form_Load()` event procedure takes this approach:

```
Sub Form_Load ()
On Error GoTo E1:

     Server$ = "Server"
     Topic$ = "Server¦Form1"
     Item$ = "Text1"
     AppActivate Server$
     If SaveErr% = 5 Then
         App% = Shell(Server$, 1)
         App% = DoEvents()
     End If
     SetUpLink
     Text1.LinkMode = HOT
     HotLinkCom_Click
     Exit Sub
E1:
     SaveErr% = Err
     GeneralErrors
     SetUpLink
     If SaveErr% = 5 Then
         Resume Next
     Else
         Resume
     End If
End Sub
```

Notice the conditional test for the error in the error handler within the procedure, after the return from `GeneralErrors`. Notice also that the procedure `Resumes` (retries) the statement that generated the error unless the error is #5, the illegal function call. If it's the error you want, proceed to the next statement after the error, which runs the Server.

You might consider two things at this point: You can add a `Select Case` statement rather than the `If` test, if you're testing several errors; and that this approach to the problem is fairly tricky and consequently requires some care on your part.

Create a Generic DDE Form

Before concluding this chapter's study of DDE, I want to generalize the DDE connection in a form that enables you to:

- Connect to any application (that supports DDE)
- Let the user specify at runtime the application, link topic, and link item for the DDE connection
- Reuse the form in any application with a minimum of changes

You've basically met most of these requirements. The generic DDE form needs a menu or command/option buttons similar to the ones you've been using to allow sending and receiving messages; option buttons to enable the user to indicate the type of link (hot or cold); text boxes to enable the user to specify the Server application, link topic, and link item; labels; a text box or control array of text boxes for making the link; and OK and Cancel command buttons for good measure. Figure 8.13 shows this generic DDE form before you add a menu system to it.

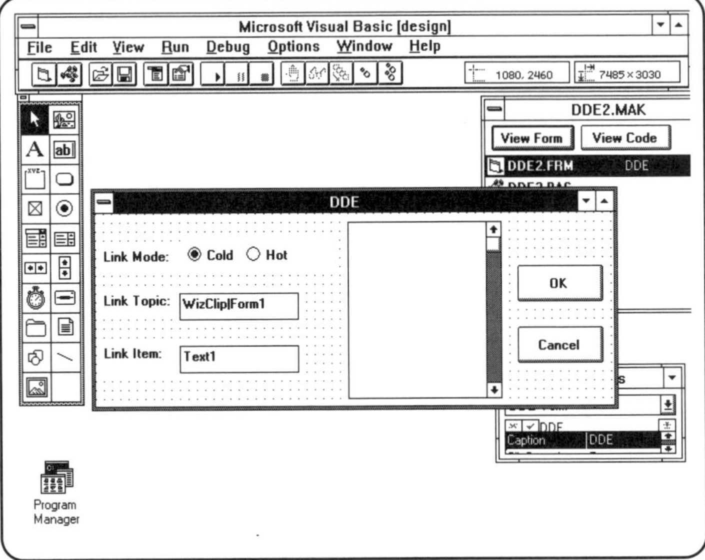

Figure 8.13. The generic DDE form.

To establish any DDE connection, an application using this form gets its server and link information from the appropriate text boxes. For example, the `LinkTop` text box contains the `LinkTopic` information:

```
'Set up link with VB server.
Text1.LinkTopic = LinkTop.Text
```

The `LinkIt` text box contains the `LinkItem` information:

```
'Set link to text box server
Text1.LinkItem = LinkIt.Text
```

The option buttons determine the type of link:

```
If ColdLink.Value = -1 Then
   Text1.LinkMode = 2

Else
   Text1.LinkMode = 1

End If
```

Poke User-Selected Excel Cells

Because the `LinkItem` text box enables the user to indicate at runtime which item to link, the user can change the text box, cell, or other Server topic while the application is running. For example, the code in Listing 8.6 automatically runs Excel, but enables the user to change the Excel spreadsheet, row, and cell number at will. Figures 8.14 and 8.15 show this exchange changing. Notice again that the general error-handling module works well in this scenario.

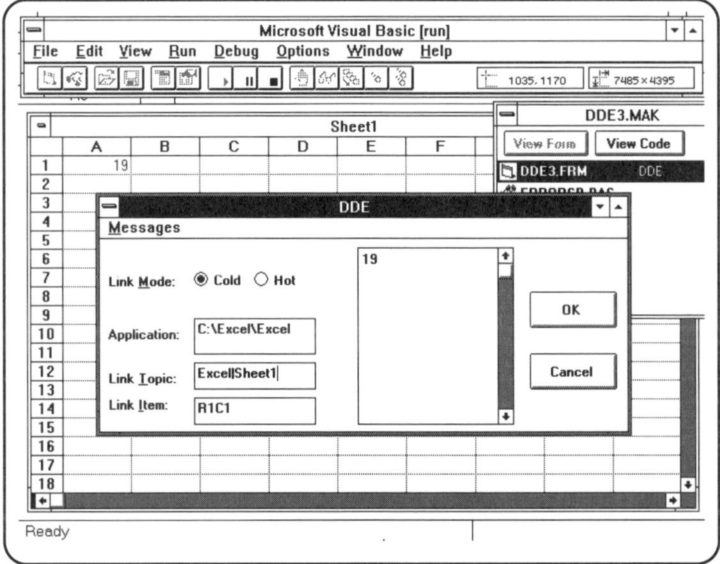

Figure 8.14. Excel as a Server.

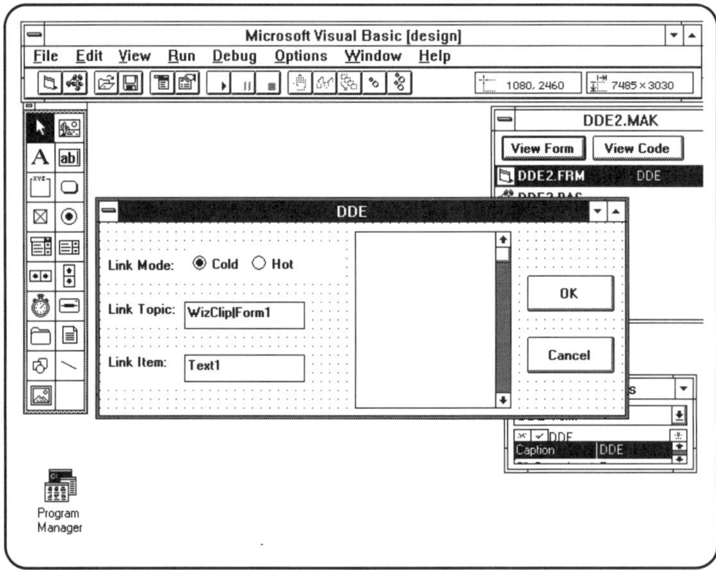

Figure 8.15. Excel as a Server: Updating the Client application.

LISTING 8.6. A PRELIMINARY VERSION OF DDE3.

```
Global declarations

Global Server$
Global App%
Global Topic$
Global Item$
Global SaveErr%

' Global Declarations

Const HOT = 1
Const COLD = 2
Const NONE = 0


Sub Command1_Click () 'OK button.
  On Error GoTo Errors

  'Clear DDE link.
  Text1.LinkMode = 0
```

```
  'Set up link with VB server.
  Text1.LinkTopic = LinkTop.Text

  'Set link to text box server
  Text1.LinkItem = LinkIt.Text

  'Determine and establish a DDE link.

  If ColdLink.Value = -1 Then
     Text1.LinkMode = 2

  Else
     Text1.LinkMode = 1

  End If

  If SaveErr% = 282 Or SaveErr%= 293 Then
     z% = Shell("C:\EXCEL\EXCEL", 1)
     z% = DoEvents()
  'Clear DDE link.
  Text1.LinkMode = 0


  'Set up link with VB server.
  Text1.LinkTopic = LinkTop.Text
  'Set link to text box server
  Text1.LinkItem = LinkIt.Text

  'Establish a DDE link.

  If ColdLink.Value = -1 Then
     Text1.LinkMode = 2

  Else
     Text1.LinkMode = 1

  End If
  End If

  Exit Sub

Errors:
   SaveErr% = Err
   GeneralErrors
   Resume Next


End Sub

Sub Command2_Click ()
  Unload DDE
End Sub
```

continues

LISTING 8.6. CONTINUED

```
Sub RequestCom_Click ()
  Command1_Click
  Text1.LinkRequest
End Sub

Sub SendCom_Click ()
  Command1_Click
  Text1.LinkPoke
End Sub


' Error Module



Sub GeneralErrors ()
  Msg$ = Error$(SaveErr%)
  MsgBox Msg$
  Select Case SaveErr%
     Case 280 To 297
       DDEErrors
  End Select
End Sub

Sub DDEErrors ()
     Select Case SaveErr%

        Case 282
          App% = Shell("c:\Excel\Excel", 1))
          App% = DoEvents()
        Case 283
          Msg$ = "Suggest you open Program Manager "
          Msg$ = Msg$ + " NOW and use End Task "
          Msg$ = Msg$ + " to terminate the LAST "
          Msg$ = Msg$ + " INSTANCE of " + Server$
          MsgBox Msg$

     End Select
End Sub
```

One final item completes the generic DDE form. As it stands, the application, DDE2, automatically loads Excel. Because this application should be under the user's control as well, however, add another text box and label to the form. Then revise the `Command1_Click` event procedure to get the application name, the Server, from this text box:

```
Server$ = Text2.Text
If SaveErr% = 282 Or SaveErr%= 293 Then
z% = Shell(Server$, 1)
z% = DoEvents()
'....rest of code here.
```

Figure 8.16 shows this chapter's final version of the DDE form (called DDE3 on the disk). Listing 8.7 shows the complete DDE3 listing.

LISTING 8.7. DDE3.

```
' DDE3.frm

' General Declarations
Const HOT = 1
Const COLD = 2
Const NONE = 0

Sub Poke_Click ()
          Text1.LinkItem = "Text1"
          Text1.LinkPoke
End Sub

Sub Request_Click ()
     Text1.LinkRequest
End Sub


Sub Command1_Click ()
     On Error GoTo Errors

     'Clear DDE link.
     Text1.LinkMode = 0

     'Set up link with VB server.
     Text1.LinkTopic = LinkTop.Text

     'Set link to text box server
     Text1.LinkItem = LinkIt.Text

     'Determine & Establish a DDE link.

     If ColdLink.Value = -1 Then
               Text1.LinkMode = 2
     Else
               Text1.LinkMode = 1
     End If
```

continues

Listing 8.7. continued

```
     Server$ = Text2.Text
     If SaveErr = 282 Or SaveErr = 293 Then
               z% = Shell(Server$, 1)
               z% = DoEvents()
          'Clear DDE link.
          Text1.LinkMode = 0

               'Set up link with VB server.
          Text1.LinkTopic = LinkTop.Text

          'Set link to text box server
          Text1.LinkItem = LinkIt.Text

          'Establish a DDE link.

          If ColdLink.Value = -1 Then
                    Text1.LinkMode = 2
          Else
                    Text1.LinkMode = 1
          End If
     End If
     Exit Sub

Errors:
     SaveErr = Err
     Msg$ = Error$
     MsgBox Msg$
     Resume Next
End Sub


Sub Command2_Click ()
     Unload DDE
End Sub


Sub RequestCom_Click ()
     Command1_Click
     Text1.LinkRequest
End Sub


Sub SendCom_Click ()
     Command1_Click
     Text1.LinkPoke
End Sub


' Errorsb module
```

```
Sub GeneralErrors ()
    Msg$ = Error$(SaveErr%)
    MsgBox Msg$
    Select Case SaveErr%
        Case 280 To 297
            DDEErrors
        Case 48 To 76
            DiskErrors
        Case 30000 To 31015
            OLEErrors
    End Select
End Sub

Sub DDEErrors ()
        Select Case SaveErr%

            Case 282
                Msg$ = "Starting Server " + Server$
                MsgBox Msg$
                App% = Shell(Server$, 1)
                App% = DoEvents()
            Case 283
                Msg$ = "Suggest you open Program Manager "
                Msg$ = Msg$ + " NOW and use End Task "
                Msg$ = Msg$ + " to terminate the LAST "
                Msg$ = Msg$ + " INSTANCE of " + Server$
                MsgBox Msg$

        End Select
End Sub

Sub OLEErrors ()
        Select Case SaveErr%

            Case 30005
                Msg$ = "OLE_Error_Stream"
                MsgBox Msg$
            ' Other cases here.
        End Select

End Sub

Sub DiskErrors ()
        Select Case SaveErr%

            Case 48
                Msg$ = "Disk Error"
                MsgBox Msg$
            ' Other cases here.
        End Select

End Sub
```

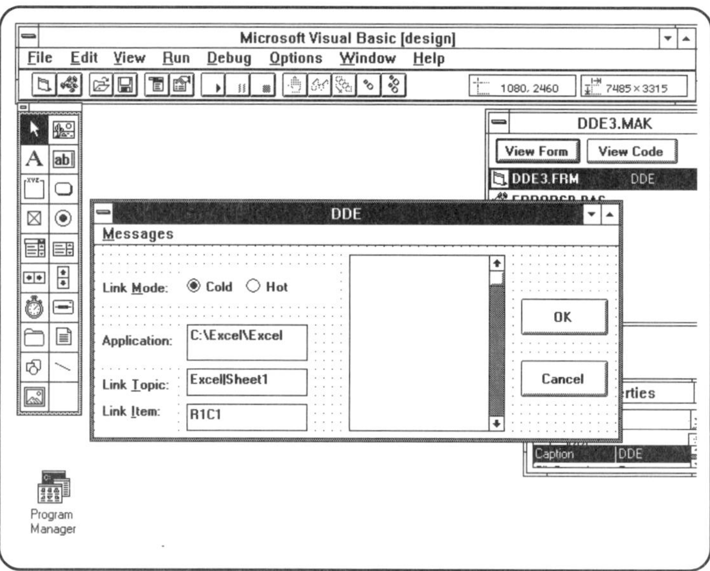

Figure 8.16. The DDE3 form.

The code on the disk titled DDE3 shows the complete DDE3 form application.

SUMMARY

That's enough for this chapter's study of DDE. The generic form developed at the end of this chapter is a model for your own applications, and you will use it again in later chapters of this book.

From a design perspective, it's important to remember to give users a flexible, easy way to manipulate the components of the DDE connection. It's just as important for you to be prepared to handle any errors caused by the user. The more freedom you give the user to manipulate the application at a low level, as done here in the generic DDE form, the better the chance that the application's execution life will be threatened.

In other words, freedom for the user and error handling on your part go together like, well, Mr. and Mrs.—or was that soup and sandwich? I can't remember.

Extending Visual Basic: Custom Controls and DLLs

Call a DDL Routine Just Like a Visual Basic Routine

Pass (Carefully) Array Elements to a DDL

Optimize Control Operations with the API

Use Assembly Language Routines Not in the API

Chapter 8, "Stretching Your Visual Basic Applications: DDE In Depth," discussed DDE, an important way to extend your Visual Basic applications by building your applications to communicate with each other and other applications that support DDE. But Visual Basic is not limited, of course, to DDE. You can also extend Visual Basic by:

- Loading and using custom control files
- Calling routines in the operating system
- Calling routines within dynamic link libraries (DLLs)

You can't create DLLs or custom controls within Visual Basic, but you can access the DLLs that you or someone else creates in C, C++, Turbo Pascal for Windows, and so on. A DLL can be packaged with Windows (the Windows API is a DLL) or added to the system by way of your own DLLs, third-party DLLs, and so on.

This ability to add functionality to your applications by adding custom controls or DLLs is fantastically far-reaching. For example, if you want to optimize a function already supplied by Visual Basic (for example, by recoding it in assembly language), you can. Code the function, put it in a DLL, and call that new function in your code rather than in Visual Basic's. Or, if you want to add a specialized functionality to your application, such as a database, expert system, or neural network, without writing the code from scratch in Visual Basic, there are lots of C-based database applications, Pascal expert system shells, and so on, already out there. Never (never say never, though) recode anything you don't have to. Invest that coding time in design, features, optimization, and so forth. Visual Basic lets you make the connection to existing code written in other languages. All it takes is a little setup, and you must follow a few rules for exchanging data with the DLL.

The early part of this chapter tells you how to load custom controls and how to declare and call DLLs, and describes generally how custom controls and DLLs are used. Later in this chapter you will build several applications using custom controls, the Windows API (a free DLL), and third-party support from MicroHelp and Crescent Software, two leading vendors of Visual Basic add-on packages.

Connecting to any DLL from Visual Basic is straightforward, especially if the DLL has been designed to interact with Visual Basic. Loading and using a custom control in a Visual Basic application is simple if the custom control is well-designed. Because working with DDE is somewhat more complicated, a good portion of this chapter discusses its ins and outs. Several small code examples are developed to illustrate DDE, and DLLs and custom controls are used generously in applications in the remaining chapters of this book.

Let's begin with a general custom control and DLL introduction, and then move into some more specific aspects of extending your applications through DDE.

FUNDAMENTALS REVIEW: HOW TO LOAD CUSTOM CONTROLS

A custom control file contains the information needed by Visual Basic to make a new control available for any Visual Basic application. In other words, you (or a third party) can create (in some other language's code, probably C or C++)

a new kind of control (for example, a quadruple-bordered window or a different kind of picture box).

When you add a custom control file to the Visual Basic environment, the file appears in the project window, and the new control (or controls) contained in the file appear in the Toolbox. The Toolbox automatically grows to accommodate the new controls.

After these controls are loaded, you can use them just as you would any built-in control. Each control has its own set of properties and events. You manipulate the controls as usual using these control attributes. (You cannot create custom controls within Visual Basic; you can load them only after they've been created in another language.)

Loading a custom control file is straightforward:

1. Select Add File from the File menu.
2. Enter the filename. By convention, any custom control file will have a .VBX extension, although it's not required.

That's all there is to it. A number of custom-control packages for Visual Basic already have appeared in the software marketplace. Later in this chapter and throughout the rest of this book, you will use custom controls from the Microsoft Professional Toolkit, Ward Systems, MicroHelp, Inc., and Crescent Software to improve and speed up the development of your applications.

INSIDE DLLS: EXTENDING VISUAL BASIC

Even if you never explicitly use a DLL in a Visual Basic application, DLL use is fundamental to Visual Basic programming. For example, the Visual Basic runtime library is a DLL, which you include when you pass an .EXE application along to your clients. When you're working (just for yourself) within Visual Basic, it lets you ostensibly ignore this aspect of its system. But it's still important to keep in mind that DLLs are fundamental to Visual Basic. DLLs are fundamental to Windows also. The Windows API, for example, is a DLL. Finally, DLLs are an excellent way to add specialized functionality to your applications—the focus of this section and subsequent sections in this chapter.

To use a DLL, it first must exist in the system, usually in the Windows system subdirectory (and be capable of communicating with other applications). If it exists, declare in your application any routines you want to use (that are in the DLL). The DLL contains system information (which enables you to use it) and routines you can use just as you would another Visual Basic statement or procedure. In short, to use a DLL routine, declare the routine within your Visual Basic code and then call it.

You use a `Declare` statement in the global module of your application to declare the routine. For example, if the routine in the DLL returns a value, declare it as a `Function`:

```
Declare Function IsWindowVisible Lib "User" (ByVal hWnd%) As Integer
```

If it doesn't return a value, declare it as a `Sub`:

```
Declare Sub DoSpecial Lib "Special" (ByVal AnIndex%)
```

Note that `ByVal` is a keyword. Properties and handles to forms and controls must be passed to DLLs by value using the `ByVal` keyword. `ByVal` indicates that the argument is passed by value rather than by reference. Note that you can't use the `ByVal` keyword with a variable of a user-defined type—that is, a variable you declare in the global module using the `Type` keyword.

When `ByVal` appears in front of a numeric variable, the variable is converted to the numeric type indicated in the `Declare` statement before being passed to the DLL. When `ByVal` appears in front of a string variable, the address of the null-terminated string data is sent to the procedure in the DLL. Without the `ByVal` keyword, a string descriptor (used only with the Visual Basic External API) is sent to the called DLL procedure.

Visual Basic doesn't normally terminate strings with a null character, but that's the way C does it, and the way the DLL routines in Windows do it. When you use `ByVal`, Visual Basic automatically converts the Visual Basic variable-length string to a "standard" C string. If you don't use the `ByVal` keyword when working for typical DLLs such as Windows, the behavior of the function or procedure to which you're passing the string will be unpredictable.

Some DLLs, however, are designed to work specifically with Visual Basic. Most of these expect to receive a Visual Basic-type string. In this case, therefore, you don't want to use the `ByVal` keyword. Check the documentation of the third-party DLLs you're using to make sure which kind of string the DLL expects.

Some other `ByVal` rules also can apply, depending on how the DLL you're using expects to receive a value. Because this discussion is fairly specific to the DLL, I won't go into detail until applications are developed later in this chapter and later in the book. In general, whenever you use a DLL, consult its documentation to determine the rules that might apply to the DLL.

> You can't pass fixed-length strings in the parameter list of a `Declare` statement; Visual Basic allows variable-length strings to be passed only to procedures. If you try to pass fixed-length strings as variables to procedures, they are converted to variable-length strings before being passed. You can, however, use the elements of arrays of fixed-length strings as variables in the `Declare` statement's variable list. Note, however, that you can't pass an entire array to a DLL routine in one gulp. There's more on that in this chapter's section called "Pass (Carefully) Array Elements to a DLL."

A `Declare` statement for an external procedure in a DLL can appear only in the global module (in Version 1.0) or in the Declarations section of a form or module. If you declare DLL procedures in a form, they are available only to other procedures within that form. If you declare DLL procedures in the global module (in Version 1.0), they're available to all procedures in all modules, including any forms in the project. If you declare DLL procedures in any module in Version 2.0 or 3.0, they're available to all procedures in all modules.

The way you form the variable (or argument) list determines how variable type checking is handled. Use empty parentheses to indicate that the `Sub` or `Function` procedure doesn't pass any variables to the DLL, and that variable type checking should be enabled to ensure that no variables are being passed to the DLL. For example, the following DLL procedure, `SomePro1`, doesn't expect to receive any variables:

```
Declare Sub SomePro1 "YourLib" ()
```

In this case, if you try to pass a variable to `SomeLib()`, Visual Basic generates an error.

When you declare a variable list, the number and type of variables in the list are checked (by Visual Basic) every time you invoke the procedure. For example, `SomePro2` in the following code expects to receive one long-integer variable:

```
Declare Sub SomePro2 "YourLib" (X&)
```

USE THE WINDOWS API (THE USER DLL) TO FIND THE NUMBER OF LINES IN A TEXT BOX

To give you a feel for how easy it is to use DLLs, let's use the Windows "user" DLL (part of the API) to determine the number of lines in a text box. The user DLL contains a function, called `SendMessage`, that enables you to send various messages to the Windows API. These messages are also called "control messages" because they return information about or change the state of controls.

You can use `SendMessage` to send button-control, edit-control, list box, combo box, and various other control messages. To use `SendMessage`, you must first declare it:

```
Declare Function SendMessage% Lib "user" (ByVal hWd%, ByVal wMsg%,
ByVal wParam%, ByVal lParam&)
```

The message you send (by way of `SendMessage`) is a hexadecimal number, which must be specified as such. You might find it convenient to specify these hexadecimal numbers as constants that correspond to the message requests. For example:

```
Const EM_GETLINECOUNT = &H40A
```

After you've declared the DLL function, `SendMessage` in this example, you must declare also one other function, `GetFocus`, which obtains the handle for the control you want to get information about or manipulate. This function also is in the "user" DLL:

```
Declare Function GetFocus% Lib "user" ()
```

After these functions are declared, you're ready to use them.

CALL A DLL ROUTINE JUST LIKE A VISUAL BASIC ROUTINE

When you've declared a DLL routine, you use it by calling it. When you call any procedure (whether in a DLL or not), the application transfers control to the procedure.

The call looks like any other call in Visual Basic. For example, suppose that you declared an `IsIconic` function in the global module:

```
Declare Function IsIconic Lib "User" (ByVal hWnd%) As Integer
```

You then can use that function in another routine in your code:

```
Sub Form_Resize()
      If IsIconic(hWnd) Then
            MsgBox "The form is minimized."
      End If
End Sub
```

Let's return to the line count problem and set up a simple application that consists of a text box (`Text1`), a label for reporting the number of lines (note that I've changed the label `Caption` property to `Number of lines`), and a menu item for obtaining the number of lines in the text box. The menu item is called `LineCtCom` in this example. Figure 9.1 shows the form.

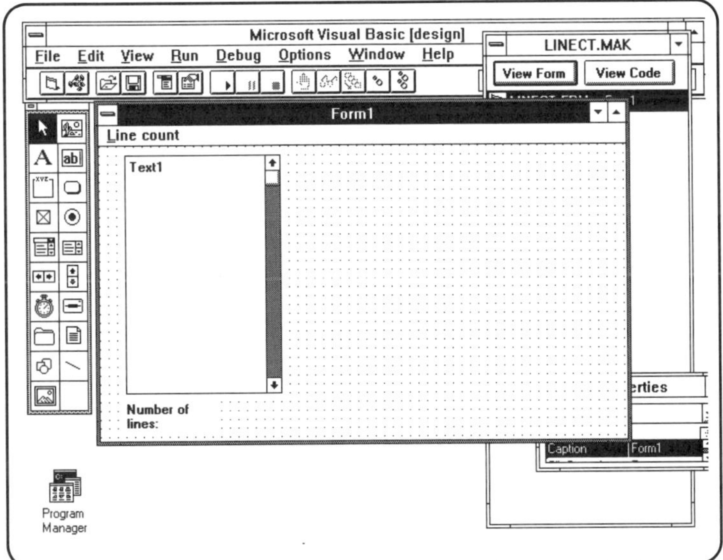

Figure 9.1. The line count form in the design mode.

The `LineCtCom` event procedure:

- Sets the focus to the control you want information about (`Text1`)
- Gets the handle for the text box
- Sends the line count message and reports the result in a label

Here it is:

```
Sub LineCtCom_Click ()

    Text1.SetFocus              'Make sure the text box has the focus.
    hWd% = GetFocus()           'Get the text box handle.
    Label1.Caption = Str$(SendMessage(hWd%, EM_GETLINECOUNT, 0, 0))
End Sub
```

Every time the user clicks the `LineCtCom` menu item, the number of lines are quickly reported in the label.

Before we move on, let's make one addition to this trivial application, which you might find handy in other applications. Let's have the application automatically update the line count every time the contents of the text box change. To accomplish this, copy the code you just implemented to the `Text1_Change` event procedure for the text box—voila, you have automatic line count updating. Listing 9.1 shows the code for this application (LINECT on the disk), including the `Text_Change` event procedure. Figure 9.2 shows the application in motion.

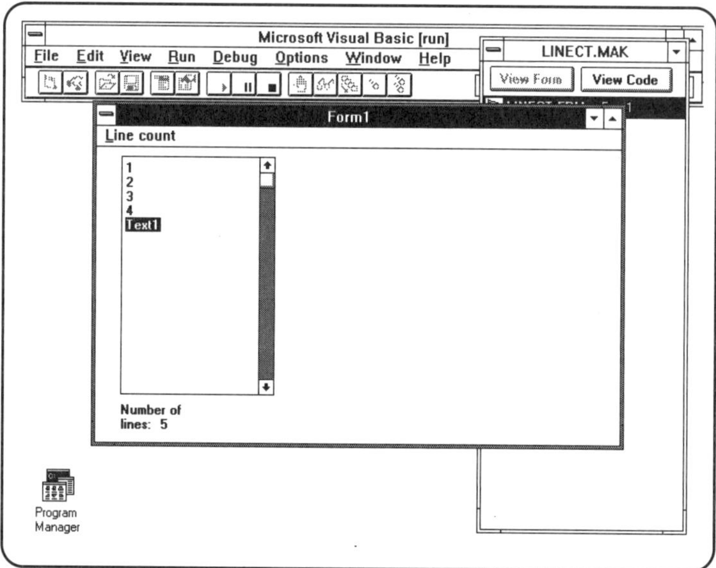

Figure 9.2. LINECT.

Listing 9.1. LINECT.

```
Declare Function SendMessage% Lib "user" (ByVal hWd%,
➥ByVal wMsg%, ByVal wParam%, ByVal lParam&)

Declare Function GetFocus% Lib "user" ()

Const EM_GETLINECOUNT = &H40A         ' in Windows.h


" LineCt Menu Click event

Sub LineCtCom_Click ()

      Text1.SetFocus              'Make sure the text box has the focus.
      hWd% = GetFocus()           'Get the text box handle.
      Msg$ = "Number of lines: "

                                       ' Report results to a label.
      Label1.Caption = Str$(SendMessage(hWd%, EM_GETLINECOUNT, 0, 0))
End Sub


Sub Text1_Change ()
      Text1.SetFocus              'Make sure the text box has the focus.
      hWd% = GetFocus()           'Get the text box handle.
      Msg$ = "Number of lines: "
      Label1.Caption = Msg$ +
          Str$(SendMessage(hWd%, EM_GETLINECOUNT, 0, 0))
End Sub
```

Pass (Carefully) Array Elements to a DLL

You can pass an array of elements to a DLL function, but you must pass the array one element at a time. In effect, you detach the element from the array before sending the element to the DLL function. For example, let's modify the last application (LINECT) to consist of a control array of three text boxes rather than a single text box. You need to add an additional label for each text box to report the line counts (see Figure 9.3).

Although you now want information about a control array of text boxes, you must get that information one text box at a time. You accomplish this by simply looping through the control array, changing the focus to each successive text box, sending a message (by way of `SendMessage`) to obtain the line count, and updating the text box's label, which reports the line count. As before, the

`LineCtCom` event procedure and the `TextChange` event procedure contain the same code:

```
Sub Text1_Change (Index As Integer)
      'Make sure the text box has the focus.
      For I% = 0 To 2
        Text1(I%).SetFocus
        'Get the text box handle.
        hWd% = GetFocus()
        Label1(I%).Caption =
           Str$(SendMessage(hWd%, EM_GETLINECOUNT, 0, 0))
      Next I%
End Sub
```

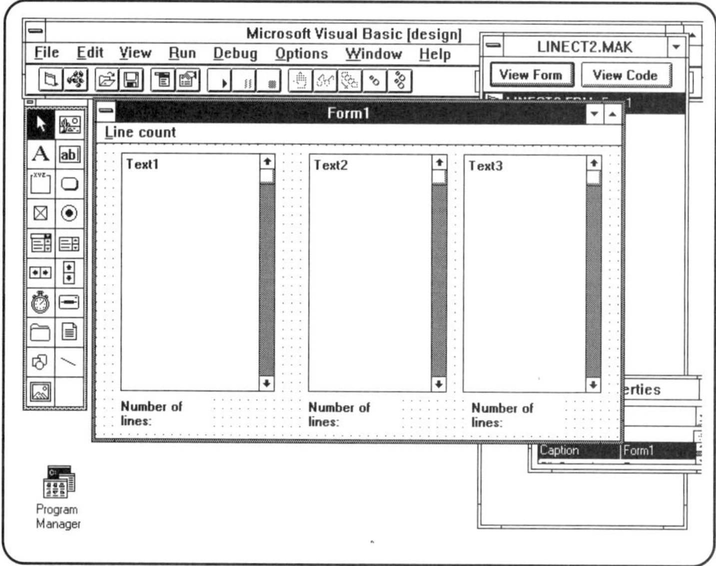

Figure 9.3. An array of text boxes.

Now, every time the contents of any text box in the control array change, the line count is updated automatically for all the text boxes. Note that each time you get the line count for the array of text boxes you move from text box 0 to text box 1 to text box 2. Thus, each sequence of line counts will leave you in the third text box (text box 2). This might not be what you want; usually you want to return to the text box that had the focus before you counted lines. To ensure that you always end up where you started, use the `GotFocus` event procedure for the text boxes to save the index of the text box that currently has the focus. Then when the line counts are done, set the focus for the text boxes back to the text box that originally had the focus. You'll need to use a form- (or global-) level variable as I've done in this example. Here, I've called this variable, which saves the index of the text box that currently has the focus, `TextFocus`. Listing 9.2 shows the complete listing for `LineCt2`. Figure 9.4 shows the automatic updating of a control array of text boxes.

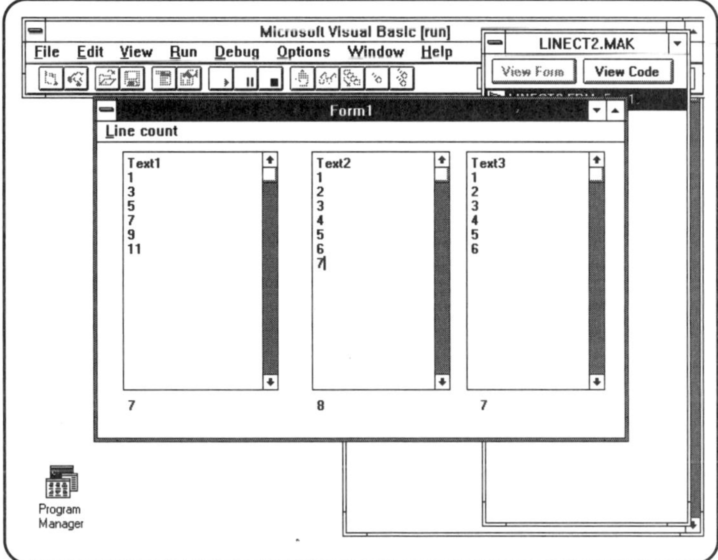

Figure 9.4. LineCt2.

Listing 9.2. LineCt2.

```
' General declarations

Declare Function SendMessage% Lib "user" (ByVal hWd%,
➥ByVal wMsg%, ByVal wParam%, ByVal lParam&)

Declare Function GetFocus% Lib "user" ()

Const EM_GETLINECOUNT = &H40A
Dim TextFocus As Integer


' Event procedures

Sub LineCtCom_Click ()
```

continues

LISTING 9.2. CONTINUED

```
'Make sure the text box has the focus.

For I% = 0 To 2
      Text1(I%).SetFocus

      'Get the text box handle.

      hWd% = GetFocus()

      Label1(I%).Caption =
         Str$(SendMessage(hWd%, EM_GETLINECOUNT, 0, 0))
Next I%
End Sub


Sub Text1_Change (Index As Integer)

      'Make sure the text box has the focus.
      SaveFocus% = TextFocus
      For I% = 0 To 2
         Text1(I%).SetFocus

         'Get the text box handle.

         hWd% = GetFocus()

         Label1(I%).Caption =
             Str$(SendMessage(hWd%, EM_GETLINECOUNT, 0, 0))
      Next I%
      Text 1 (SaveFocus%). SetFocus
End Sub
Sub Text1_GotFocus (Index As Integer)
      TextFocus = Index
End Sub
```

OPTIMIZE CONTROL OPERATIONS WITH THE API

Let's use the Windows API for another important purpose: to speed up an application. This example uses only the Windows API (GDI.EXE), so (again) you can do this example without any third-party support. You need only Windows and Visual Basic.

Suppose that you want to find the length and height of a string. This process is simple enough in Visual Basic—just use two of the built-in Visual Basic functions to accomplish this task:

```
Sub Form_Click()
      TxtHeight = TextHeight(AString$)
      TxtWidth = TextWidth(AString$)
End Sub
```

This procedure works just fine, but it doesn't work as fast as it might if you accessed the Windows API directly. To get the same results directly from the Windows API, first declare the subroutine in the global module for the project:

```
Declare Function GetTextExtent& Lib "Gdi" (ByVal hDC%,
➥ByVal lpString$, ByVal nCount%)
```

Then call the subroutine just as you would any Visual Basic subroutine:

```
Value& = GetTextExtent(hDC, AString$, Len(AString$))
TxtHeight = Value& \ 65536
TxtWidth = Value& Mod 65536
```

It's a little more complicated, but about twice as fast. The code in Listing 9.3 tests these two versions. The test example (GETEXT on the disk) uses several controls for displaying the results.

Listing 9.3. Benchmark Windows API versus Visual Basic controls.

```
' General Declarations

Declare Function GetTextExtent& Lib "Gdi" (ByVal hDC%,
➥ByVal lpString$, ByVal nCount%)


' Events

Sub Form_Load ()
  ' Make a call to GetTextExtent to ensure that the DLL is loaded.
  ' Otherwise, the timing test isn't a fair test.
  A& = GetTextExtent&(hDC, (APITime.Caption), Len(APITime.Caption))
End Sub

Sub Command1_Click ()
  Dim CycleCount%, I%
  VBTime.Caption = "Wait"
  APITime.Caption = ""
  Refresh
  CycleCount% = Val(Text1.Text)

  ' First test TextWidth and TextHeight _ the Visual Basic procedures
  AString$ = APITime.Caption
  VBTime.Caption = Time$                          ' Timer start.
```

continues

LISTING 9.3. CONTINUED

```
  For I = 1 To CycleCount
      A& = TextWidth(AString$)
      B& = TextHeight(AString$)
  Next
  VBTime.Caption = VBTime.Caption + "  " + Time$ ' Timer end.

  'Next test the API _ GetTextExtent
  APITime.Caption = Time$                        ' Timer start.
  Length% = Len(AString$)
  For I = 1 To CycleCount
      A& = GetTextExtent&(hDC, AString$, Length%)
      B& = A& \ 65536                                   ' Text height
      A& = A& Mod 65536                                 ' Text width
  Next
  APITime.Caption = APITime.Caption + "  " + Time$      ' Timer end.

End Sub
```

Figure 9.5 shows the application (called GETEXT on the disk) after a test of 6,000 iterations. On a Zeos 386 notebook computer running at 20 MHz, it takes about 8 seconds and 4 seconds, respectively, to complete the 6,000 iterations using Version 2.0 or Version 3.0. Therefore, the API is about twice as fast in this case.

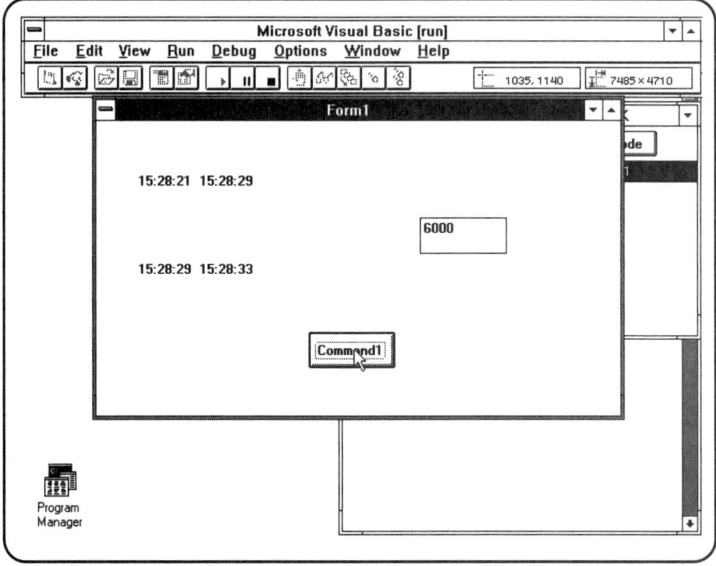

Figure 9.5. The GETEXT benchmarking application running.

Use Assembly Language Routines Not in the API

Now let's diverge away from the ready-to-use Windows API support and delve deeper into third-party support packages that are already on the market. The next two applications in this chapter use this third-party support to:

- Add functionality to Visual Basic applications
- Optimize or ease the use of existing Visual Basic functionality

The assembly language routines and custom controls used in this chapter are available on the Visual Basic programming disks (contained in the back of this book so that you can use them freely in your own application) and from MicroHelp and Crescent Software (their addresses and phone numbers are in Appendix A of this book).

> I'm going to use only a few of MicroHelp's and Crescent Software's custom controls and assembly language routines in this book. The packages MicroHelp sells (VBTools, Muscle, HighEdit, 3-D Gizmos, and so on) have hundreds of useful tools, and the Crescent Software QuickPak Professional package are exceptional developer values. Check them out.

MicroHelp Muscle is a collection of assembly language routines you can use to speed up and add functionality to your Visual Basic applications. In addition, it contains numerous application development tips and ideas. Because the assembly language routines are in a DLL, you can access any of them, as you've been doing, by:

1. Declaring the routine you need in the global module for the project.
2. Calling the routine just as you would any Visual Basic routine.

In other words, call third-party DLLs just as you call Windows DLLs. One method serves all.

> The third-party support routines don't have to be written in assembly language.

The Windows DLL system is efficient and easy to use. If you need to use a subroutine that's in a DLL, don't load all the code in the DLL into your application—just load (and use) the subroutine you need. Your applications don't pay a size penalty, therefore, for using a DLL subroutine.

Let's expand a little and use assembly language routines that aren't in the Windows API to add functionality to an application. The following example uses two assembly language subroutines in the MicroHelp Muscle and MicroHelp VBTools packages to load a file in binary format directly into an array, and to save the array in binary format to a file.

This application (called BLOAD on the disk) is very simple. It uses the `Bload` and `BSave` functions (located in `prhall.vbx`, a DLL) to first load a file, in binary format, directly into an array. Then, it saves the array, in binary format, into a file.

To use these functions, first declare them globally for the project:

```
Declare Function Bload% Lib "prhall.vbx"
    (ByVal Lin$, X As Any,ByVal Length&)

Declare Function Bsave% Lib "prhall.vbx"
    (ByVal Lin$, X As Any,ByVal Length&)
```

Then call them from the application when you need them, just as you would any Visual Basic function:

```
Result% = Bsave((Text1.Text), WriteArray%(1), Length&)
'...other code here
'...other code here
'...other code here
Result% = Bload((Text1.Text), ReadArray%(1), Length&)
```

Application BLOAD consists of a single form and several controls (a command button, three labels, and a text box). Most of the action occurs in the text box `KeyPress` event procedure. The `KeyPress` event occurs every time the user presses a key in the text box.

Other controls also can respond to the `KeyPress` event.

The code for `Text1_KeyPress` looks like this:

```
Sub Text1_KeyPress (KeyAscii As Integer)
  Randomize
  Elements = Int(200 * Rnd + 1)      ' Number of array elements.
  If KeyAscii = 13 Then
```

```
      KeyAscii = 0                        ' Disable beep.
                                          ' Filename is in Text1.Text.
      Text1.SelStart = 0
      Text1.SelLength = Len(Text1.Text) ' Select all for next entry.
      ReDim WriteArray%(1 To Elements) ' Dimension arrays.
      ReDim ReadArray%(1 To Elements)
      For I% = 1 To Elements
         WriteArray%(I%) = I%             ' Put elements in the array.
      Next
      Length& = UBound(WriteArray%) * 2
      Result% = Bsave((Text1.Text), WriteArray%(1), Length&) ' Save the array
                                                             ' to a file.
      If Result% Then                                        ' If error
         Label3.Caption = "Error" + Str$(Result%) + " attempting Bsave"
         Exit Sub
      End If
      Result% = Bload((Text1.Text), ReadArray%(1), Length&)
                          ' Now load the file back into an array.
      If Result% Then                                   ' If error
         Label3.Caption = "Error" + Str$(Result%) + " attempting Bload"
         Exit Sub
      End If
                                                  ' Compare the arrays.
      OK% = -1                                    ' Assume OK.
      For I% = 1 To UBound(ReadArray%)
        If ReadArray%(I%) <> WriteArray%(I%) Then
           OK% = 0
           Exit For
        End If
      Next
      If OK% Then
        Label3.Caption = "Success!" +
        ➥"# of Array Elements = " + Str$(Elements)
      Else
        Label3.Caption = "Error on array compare!"
      End If
   End If
End Sub
```

This code is fairly straightforward. The user enters a filename in the text box and concludes entry by entering a carriage return (ASCII 13). Then an array of random size is created. The array is written in binary format to a file. The file then is reloaded and its contents are written back into another array. Finally, the two arrays are compared to test for errors, and the results (including the size of the arrays) are reported.

Figures 9.6 and 9.7 show the application before and after a test run. The complete listing for the application is in Listing 9.4.

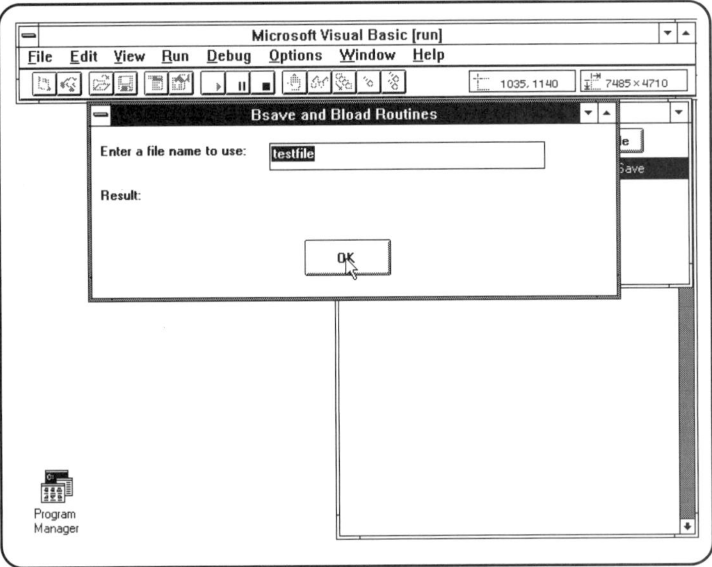

Figure 9.6. BLOAD before the test.

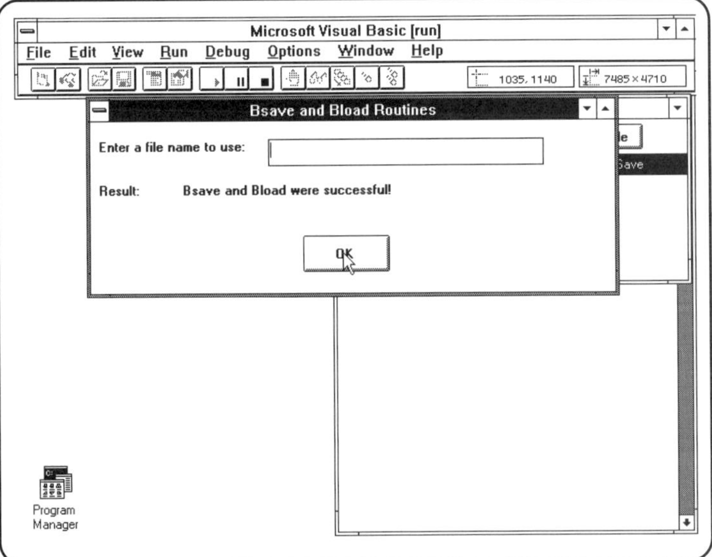

Figure 9.7. BLOAD after the test run.

Listing 9.4. The BLOAD application.

```
' Global declarations.

   Declare Function Bload% Lib "vbtools.vbx" (ByVal Lin$,
   ➥ X As Any, ByVal Length&)
   Declare Function Bsave% Lib "vbtools.vbx" (ByVal Lin$,
   ➥ X As Any, ByVal Length&)


' Events

Sub Text1_KeyPress (KeyAscii As Integer)
  Randomize
  Elements = Int(200 * Rnd + 1)           ' Generate random array size.
  If KeyAscii = 13 Then
     KeyAscii = 0                         ' Avoid beep.
     Text1.SelStart = 0
     Text1.SelLength = Len(Text1.Text)    ' Select all for next entry.
     ReDim WriteArray%(1 To Elements)
     ReDim ReadArray%(1 To Elements)
     For I% = 1 To Elements
        WriteArray%(I%) = I%
     Next
     Length& = UBound(WriteArray%) * 2
     Result% = Bsave((Text1.Text), WriteArray%(1), Length&)
     If Result% Then                    ' If an error occurred
        Label3.Caption = "Error" + Str$(Result%) + " attempting Bsave"
        Exit Sub
     End If
     Result% = Bload((Text1.Text), ReadArray%(1), Length&)
     If Result% Then                    ' If an error occurred
        Label3.Caption = "Error" + Str$(Result%) + " attempting Bload"
        Exit Sub
      End If
                                        ' Test the results
      OK% = -1                                ' Assume OK.
      For I% = 1 To UBound(ReadArray%)        ' Compare arrays.
        If ReadArray%(I%) <> WriteArray%(I%) Then
           OK% = 0
           Exit For
        End If
      Next
      If OK% Then
        Label3.Caption = "Success!" + "# of ArraryElements = "+ Str$ (Elements)"
      Else
        Label3.Caption = "Error on array compare!"
      End If
```

continues

LISTING 9.4. CONTINUED

```
    Text1.Text = Str$(Elements)
  End If
End Sub

Sub Command1_Click ()                    ' End example.
  Unload BloadSave                       ' Unload form.
End Sub
```

MORE CUSTOM CONTROLS AND ALL THAT JAZZ

Now let's return to custom controls. As discussed earlier in this chapter, a custom control file contains the information needed by Visual Basic to make a new control available for any Visual Basic application. In other words, you (or a third party) can create (in some other language's code: C, C++, Turbo Pascal for Windows, and so on) a new kind of control—a fancy-bordered window or a different kind of picture box, for example.

When you add a custom control file to the Visual Basic environment, the file appears in the project window, and the new control (or controls) contained in the file appear in the Toolbox. The Toolbox automatically grows to accommodate the new controls.

After these controls are loaded, you can use them just as you would any other built-in control. Each control has its own set of properties and events. You manipulate the controls as usual using these control attributes. (Again, note that you cannot create custom controls within Visual Basic; you can load them only after they've been created in another language.)

Remember that loading a custom control file is almost trivial:

1. Select Add File from the File menu.
2. Enter the filename. By convention, any custom control file will have a .VBX extension, although it's not required.

Figures 9.8, 9.9, and 9.10 show examples of what happens to the Visual Basic toolbar before and after custom controls are added to a project.

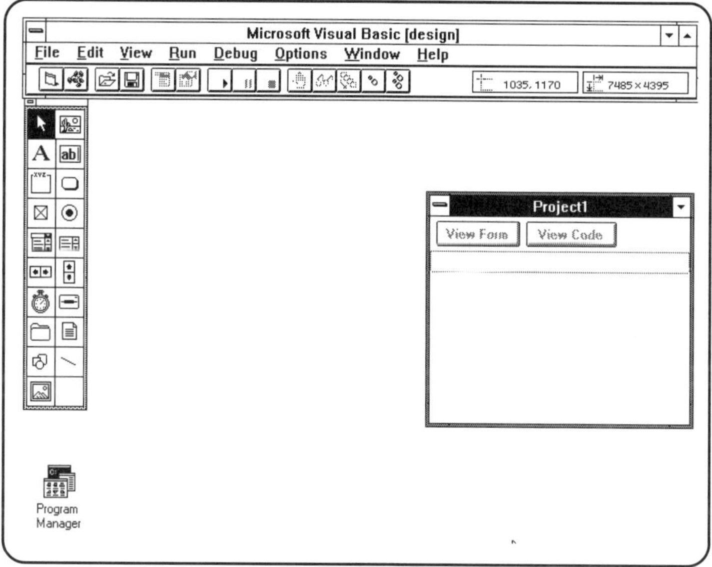

Figure 9.8. The Visual Basic toolbar before you add a custom control file.

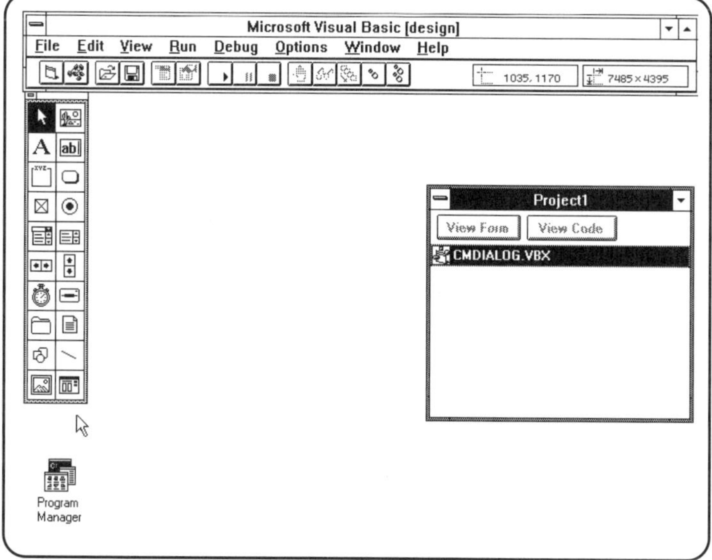

Figure 9.9. The Visual Basic toolbar after you add a custom control file.

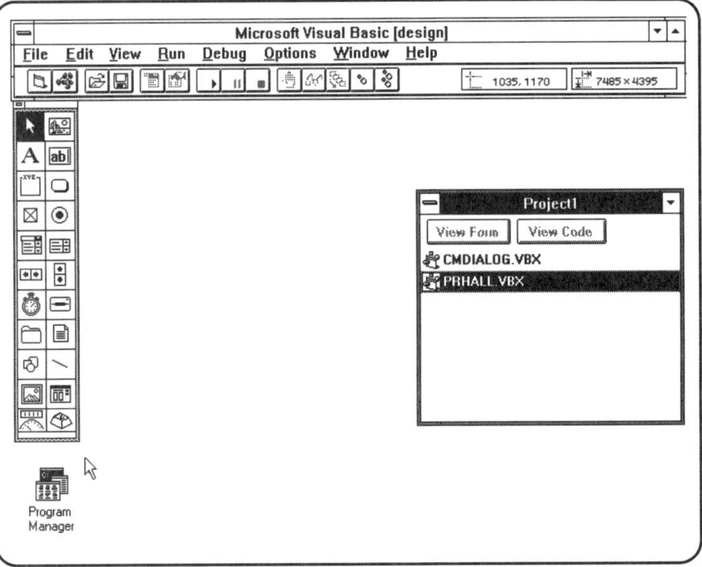

Figure 9.10. Add another custom control file to the toolbar.

Custom Control Application: Custom Key States

As I've tried to emphasize throughout this book, one of the most important aspects of Windows and Visual Basic is that applications are built around graphics components. Applications can "naturally" mix text and pictures, therefore, without any major shift in mode (from text to pixel and back) or perspective. Any Visual Basic application can use pictures just as easily as text, on the same screen, interactively.

Custom controls are important because they expand this concept. If you can create a bitmap of something (that is, make it a picture) and give it functionality (properties, procedures, and so on), you can add it to your Visual Basic Toolbox. This means that you have a lot of power as a Visual Basic developer to create unusual, creative, or specialized applications built around your own "unique" tools. The key to creating new "graphically oriented" tools is custom controls.

In this section, let's create a simple application based on a custom control that's available in the MicroHelp VBTools package. The control I use is *MhState*

Custom Control, made up of four controls for displaying and modifying the state of the Caps Lock, Num Lock, Insert, and Scroll Lock keys.

The application in this section (called STATE on the disk) displays these keys "graphically," enabling a user to change the state of the keys by clicking a command button with a mouse. The controls themselves change (Off and On) to reflect the current state of the keys. You might find this to be a handy addition to applications designed for users who want to avoid the keyboard as much as possible. Rather than pressing the Num Lock key, for example, the user can click the mouse to get the same result.

Let's quickly step through developing the application:

1. Open a new project (remember that you don't have to do anything to begin a new project: Visual Basic automatically opens a new project—with a new form and global module—for you when you start up Visual Basic). This project has only one form, so you're ready to go.
2. Draw the controls for each form.

This part of this application is interesting, yet simple. Because you want to use a custom control for this application, you have to make the custom control file that contains the custom control accessible. In this case, the custom control you need is called KeyState (it is on the *Secrets* DLL as PRHALL.VBX the disk). To make this custom control accessible, add the DLL to the application from the Visual Basic menu bar. Press Alt-F-Add to do it.

> A modified version of VBTOOLS.VBX, the complete MicroHelp custom control package, is included on the disk, so you can create this example in its entirety. MicroHelp has generously donated two custom controls from its VBTools package. The complete package, however, contains many more custom controls.

As soon as you add the custom control file, the Visual Basic toolbar is updated to reflect the new custom controls (refer to Figure 9.10).

Add four `KeyState` custom controls to a frame, eight command buttons to represent On and Off for each Keystate, one command button (for exit), and six labels to supply information to the user (Figure 9.11 shows the form in design state). These labels have the following `Caption` property settings:

- Set Caps Lock.
- Set Num Lock.
- Set Insert State.
- Set Scroll Lock.
- Key States can be set from code.
- State keys will reflect the current state for that key, whether set from the keyboard, set from code, or by clicking directly on that button.

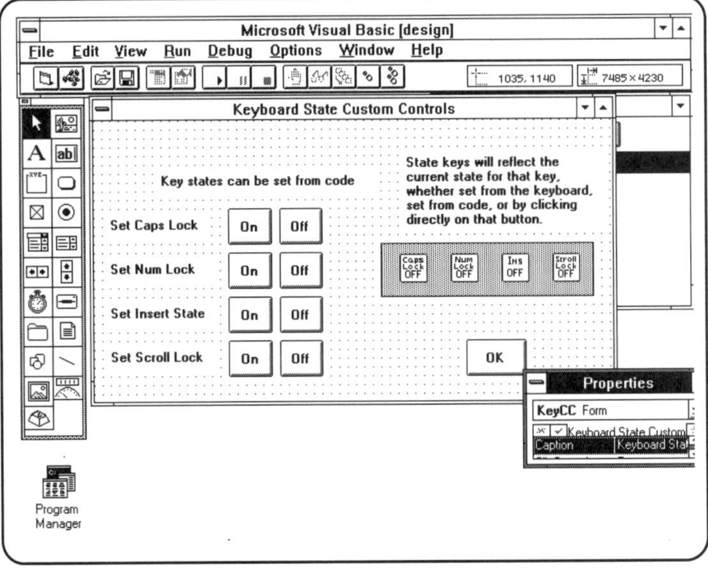

Figure 9.11. STATE in design mode.

3. Design a menu bar for the main form. (There's no menu bar for `STATE`, so continue to Step 4.)
4. Set form and control properties. With the exception of the `Keystate` custom controls and label captions, the rest of the application uses default form and control properties. The `Keystate` style property indicates the type (or style) of `Keystate` control: Num Lock, Scroll Lock, Caps Lock, or Insert keys. To indicate each of these keys, therefore, you must set the style property for each instance of the `Keystate` control. Figure 9.12 shows the style setting for one of these `Keystate` controls. Figure 9.13 shows the `Name` setting for the Num Lock key.

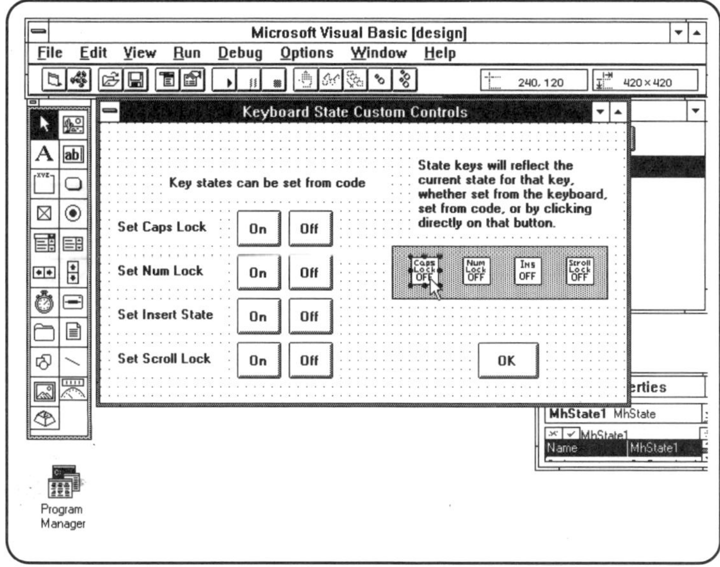

Figure 9.12. Keystate style property 1.

5. Write event and general procedures.

Basically, you have to write events to indicate state changes in each key for the command buttons that indicate whether a key is On or Off. For example:

```
Sub Command2_Click ()
  MhState1.Value = 1
End Sub
```

This code indicates that when `Command2` is clicked, the state of `MhState1` changes to On (1). (`Command2` is the command button that controls the On part of the Caps Lock key. Recall that each command button is associated with either the On or Off state of a key. Each key therefore has two command buttons: one for On and one for Off.)

Similarly, the following code controls the Off state of the Caps Lock key, indicating that when it's down, the Caps Lock key is Off (0):

```
Sub Command6_Click ()
  MhState1.Value = 0
End Sub
```

The values 1 and 0 for On and Off are defined in the custom controls themselves. Similarly, the value property is part of the custom control. You manipulate the custom control just as you would a Visual Basic control

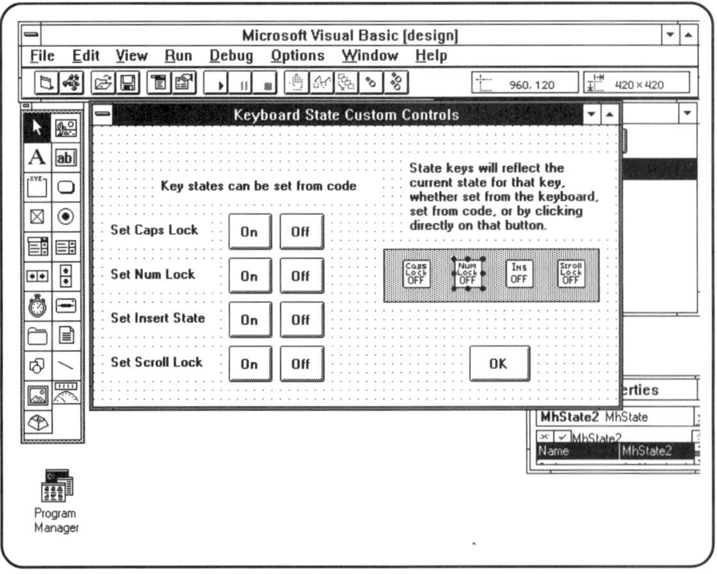

Figure 9.13. Keystate style property 2.

The complete listing for the STATE application is in Listing 9.5.

Listing 9.5. STATE.

```
' Events

Sub Command2_Click ()              ' Use command to change states.
  MhState1.Value = 1               ' Caps Lock on.
End Sub

Sub Command3_Click ()
  MhState2.Value = 1               ' Num Lock on.
End Sub

Sub Command4_Click ()
  MhState3.Value = 1               ' Insert State on.
End Sub

Sub Command5_Click ()
  MhState4.Value = 1               '  Scroll Lock on.
End Sub

Sub Command6_Click ()
  MhState1.Value = 0               ' Caps Lock off.
End Sub
```

```
Sub Command7_Click ()
  MhState2.Value = 0                ' Num Lock off.
End Sub

Sub Command8_Click ()
  MhState3.Value = 0                ' Insert State off.
End Sub

Sub Command9_Click ()
  MhState4.Value = 0                ' Scroll Lock off.
End Sub

Sub Command1_Click ()
  Unload KeyCC                      ' Unload form.
End Sub
```

Figure 9.14 shows the application running.

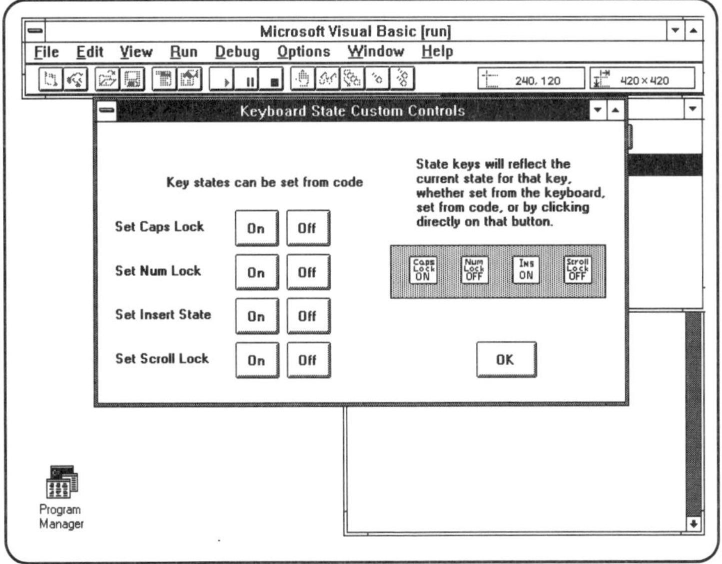

Figure 9.14. STATE.

CUSTOM CONTROL APPLICATION: CUSTOM GAUGES

Again, thanks to MicroHelp, I can easily demonstrate one additional custom control you might find useful in your applications. This custom control is called *Gauge*, and it enables your application to display information in various analog-style gauges (for example, fuel gauges, thermometers, percent-complete gauges, circular gauges, semicircular gauges, and so on). To use these gauges, add the PRHALL.VBX custom control (as in the last example), and then use these custom controls just as you would Visual Basic controls. Again, note the modified Toolbox in Figure 9.15.

This example application (GAUGE on the disk) simply demonstrates how you might use gauges to monitor information. I'm not going to step through the development of the application in much detail here. It's very straightforward. But note in particular that GAUGE uses the mouse down event procedures to increase and decrease the values in the gauges. The `Command1` button increases the values of all the gauges in the GAUGE control array. The `Command2` button decreases the values of all the gauges in the GAUGE control array. The complete code is in Listing 9.6 and on the *Secrets* disk along with the custom control, so you can experiment with it.

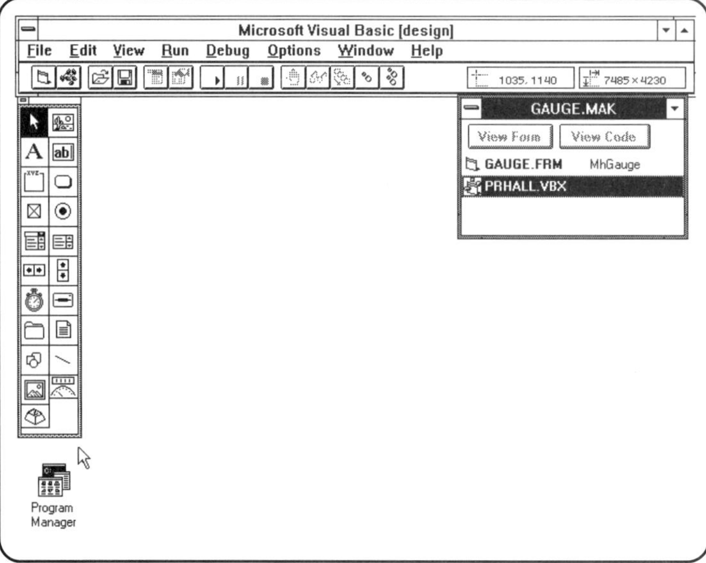

Figure 9.15. The modified Toolbox.

The application consists primarily of the gauges and two command buttons for increasing and decreasing the values of the gauges. For example, to increase the value of the gauges, the following code does the trick (note the use of `DoEvents()` to allow user interrupts and the `DoEvents()` protection—the `If Done = 0 Then Exit Sub` line at the beginning of the procedure; `Done` must be either a form-level or global variable):

```
Sub Command1_MouseDown (Button As Integer, Shift As Integer,
➥X As Single, Y As Single)
  If Done = 0 Then Exit Sub
  If Button And 1 Then
     MDown1 = TRUE
     Do
       For I = 0 To 3                       ' Control array of 4 gauges.
       MhGauge1(I).Value = MhGauge1(I).Value + 1   ' Increase value.
      Next
      Dummy% = DoEvents()                    ' Allow interrupts.
    Loop While MDown1 And MhGauge1(0).Value < MhGauge1(0).Max
   End If
   Done = -1
End Sub
```

Conversely, to decrease the value of the gauges, the application uses the following event code:

```
Sub Command2_MouseDown (Button As Integer, Shift As Integer,
➥X As Single, Y As Single)
  If Done = 0 Then Exit Sub
  If Button And 1 Then
     MDown2 = TRUE
     Do
       For I = 0 To 3                       ' Control array of 4 gauges.
          MhGauge1(I).Value = MhGauge1(I).Value - 1 ' Decrease value.
        Next
        Dummy% = DoEvents()                  ' Allow interrupts.
      Loop While MDown2 And MhGauge1(0).Value > MhGauge1(0).Min
    End If
    Done = -1
End Sub
```

CREATE A CONTROL ARRAY OF GAUGES

Note that each gauge can be part of a control array of gauges, as indicated by the index property of each gauge (see Figure 9.16). Note also the use of `DoEvents()`, which allow the processes to be interrupted by other applications.

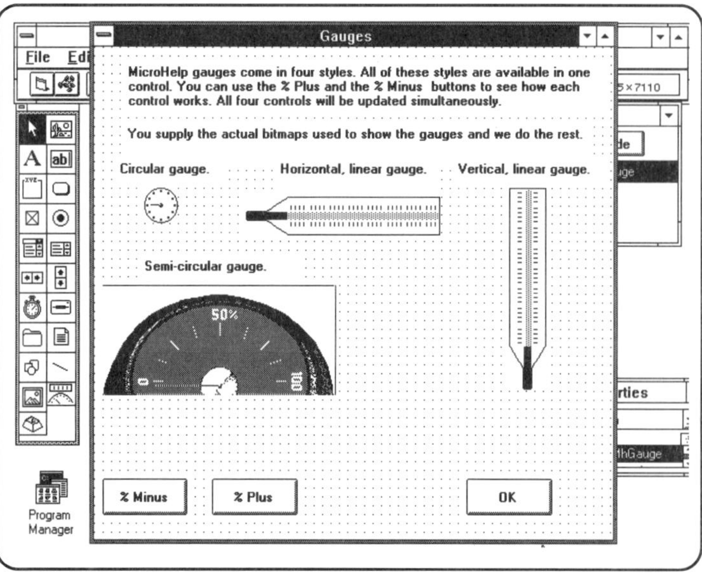

Figure 9.16. Gauge control array.

Experiment with the complete listing (9.6). Figures 9.17 and 9.18 show the GAUGE application running in two different states.

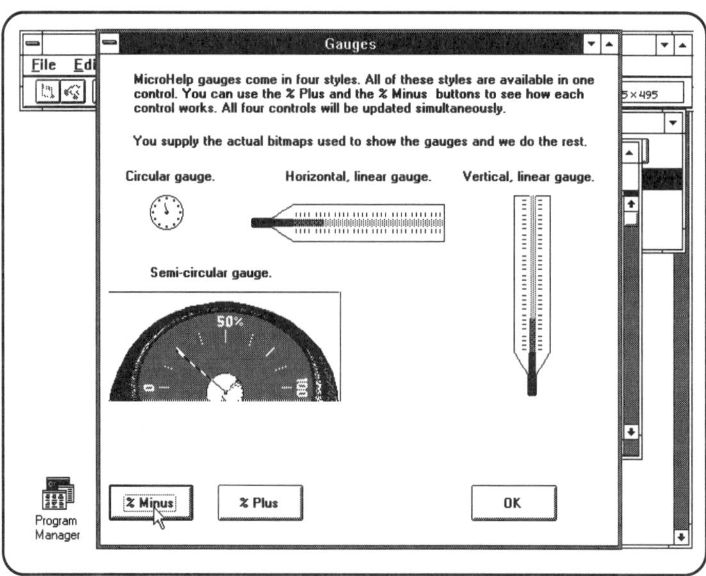

Figure 9.17. Gauge running.

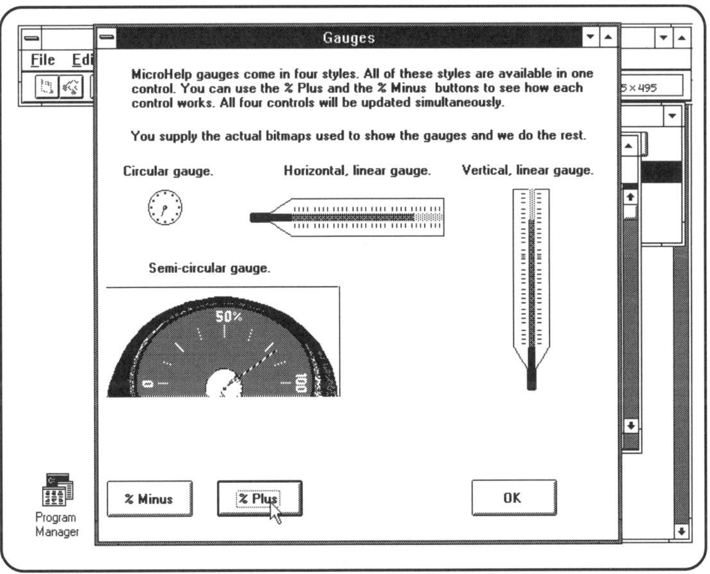

Figure 9.18. GAUGE running.

LISTING 9.6. GAUGE.

```
' form declarations

DefInt A-Z
Dim MDown1%, MDown2%
Const TRUE = -1, FALSE = 0
Dim Done As Integer


' form events
Sub Form_Load()
  Done = -1
End Sub
Sub Command3_Click ()
  Unload MhGauge
End Sub


Sub Command1_MouseDown (Button As Integer, Shift As Integer,
➥X As Single, Y As Single)
  If Done = 0 Then Exit Sub
```

continues

LISTING 9.6. CONTINUED

```
  If Button And 1 Then
     MDown1 = TRUE
     Do
       For I = 0 To 3
          MhGauge1(I).Value = MhGauge1(I).Value + 1
       Next
       X = DoEvents()
     Loop While MDown1 And MhGauge1(0).Value < MhGauge1(0).Max
    End If
    Done = -1
End Sub

Sub Command2_MouseDown (Button As Integer, Shift As Integer;
 ➥X As Single, Y As Single)
  If Done = 0 Then Exit Sub
  If Button And 1 Then
     MDown2 = TRUE
     Do
       For I = 0 To 3
          MhGauge1(I).Value = MhGauge1(I).Value - 1
       Next
       X = DoEvents()
     Loop While MDown2 And MhGauge1(0).Value > MhGauge1(0).Min
    End If
    Done = -1
End Sub


Sub Command1_MouseUp (Button As Integer, Shift As Integer,
 ➥X As Single, Y As Single)
  MDown1 = FALSE
End Sub


Sub Command2_MouseUp (Button As Integer, Shift As Integer,
 ➥X As Single, Y As Single)
  MDown2 = FALSE
End Sub
```

CONTROL USER INPUT USING THE API

Remember the Prime application from Chapter 5? In that application (PRIMES on the disk), you used an input box to let a user enter a number as a prime-number test. In that example, you used a long-integer variable to store the user's input. To avoid one type of error, you then tested the user's input to make sure that the number had been entered using the `Number > 0` test.

If the user entered a number larger than the largest possible long integer—2,147,483,647—Visual Basic generated an `overflow` error message and the application crashed. By now, you know that you can implement an error handler to handle this error message. You can reduce the likelihood of error in another way as well, however—by limiting the number of characters the user can input as the number to test.

To limit the number of characters, you can send a message to the Windows API setting the character limit for some controls (combo and text boxes, for example). When this limit is set, whenever the user tries to enter additional characters in the control, Windows "beeps" and refuses the extra character.

You can easily revise the PRIMES code to include both an error handler and the character limit. To add the error handler, add the errors form (ERRORSb on the disk) to the project and add the `On Error GoTo` statement and an error handler (`E1`) within the procedure:

```
Sub TestCom_Click ()
On Error GoTo E1
  Dim Number As Long
  Number = Val(Text1.Text)
  If Number > 0 And Number < (2147483648#) Then
      Prime% = FindPrimes(Number)
      If Prime% > 0 Then
         Msg$ = "Number Is not Prime" + Str$(Prime%) + " divides it."
      Else
         Msg$ = "Number Is a Prime."
      End If
  Else
      Msg$ = "Number is invalid."
  End If
  MsgBox Msg$
  Exit Sub
E1:
  SaveErr% = Err
  GeneralErrors
  Resume Next
End Sub
```

To limit character input, use the Windows API `SendMessage` function and the Windows API `GotFocus` function. First declare them in the general declarations section of the form:

```
Declare Function GetFocus% Lib "user" ()

Declare Function SendMessage& Lib "user" (ByVal hWnd%,
➥ByVal wMsg%, ByVal wParam%, lp As Any)
```

Then send the EM_LIMITTEXT message (by way of SendMessage) to the API. Note again that the API expects a hexadecimal value in the wParam% of the SendMessage function. The EM (text box control messages) are easily calculated from &H400, the WM_USER constant:

```
Const WM_USER = &H400
Const EM_LIMITTEXT = WM_USER + 21
```

For future reference, other EM_...hexadecimal values are as follows:

```
EM_GETSEL = WM_USER + 0

EM_SETSEL = WM_USER + 1

EM_GETLINECOUNT = WM_USER + 10

EM_LINEINDEX = WM_USER + 11

EM_LINELENGTH = WM_USER + 17

EM_REPLACESEL = WM_USER + 18

EM_GETLINE = WM_USER + 20

EM_LIMITTEXT = WM_USER + 21

EM_LINEFROMCHAR = WM_USER + 25
```

Next, because this application is simple (and uses only the text box for the limited input you specify), let's send the Windows API the LimitText message when the form loads:

```
Sub Form_Load ()

'Must show form to work on it

       Form1.Show

'Set the focus to the text box

       Text1.SetFocus

'Get the handle to the text box

       cbhWnd% = GetFocus()

'Specify the largest string

       TextLimit% = 10
       retVal = SendMessage(cbhWnd%, EM_LIMITTEXT, TextLimit%, 0)

End Sub
```

Now when the user inputs the prime number into the text box, the character limit will always be in place. Listing 9.7 shows the new version of PRIMES (PRIMES2), and Figures 9.19 and 9.20 show PRIMES2 in motion.

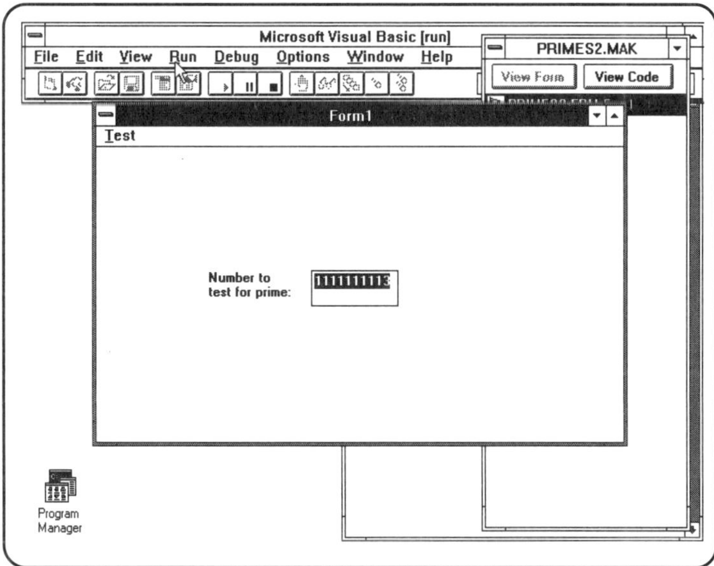

Figure 9.19. PRIMES2: user dialog.

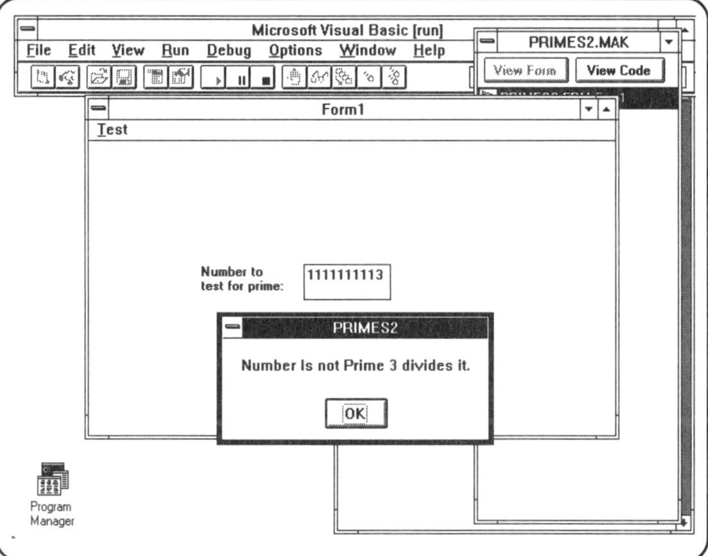

Figure 9.20. PRIMES2: results.

LISTING 9.7. PRIMES2.

```
' Global declaration


Global SaveErr%      'Must be global so that errors module can see it.


' General Declarations
Dim Done As Integer
Declare Function GetFocus% Lib "user" ()


Declare Function SendMessage& Lib "user" (ByVal hWnd%,
➥ ByVal wMsg%, ByVal wParam%, lp As Any)

Const WM_USER = &H400
Const EM_LIMITTEXT = WM_USER + 21

Function FindPrimes (Number As Long) As Long
  Dim Limit As Long

  FindPrimes = 0
  Limit = Sqr(Number)
  If Number Mod 2 = 0 Then
      FindPrimes = 2
      Exit Function
  End If
  For Index = 3 To Limit Step 2
      If Number Mod Index = 0 Then
         FindPrimes = Index
         Exit For
      End If
      x = DoEvents()
  Next Index
End Function


Sub Form_Load ()
  'Must show form to work on it
  Form1.Show
  Done = -1  'DoEvents protection
  'Set the focus to the text box
  Text1.SetFocus

  'Get the handle to the text box
  cbhWnd% = GetFocus()

  'Specify the largest string
  TextLimit% = 10
```

```
  retVal = SendMessage(cbhWnd%, EM_LIMITTEXT, TextLimit%, 0)

End Sub


Sub TestCom_Click ()
On Error GoTo E1
     Dim Number As Long
     Number = Val(Text1.Text)
     If Number > 0 And Number < (2147483648#) Then
         Prime% = FindPrimes(Number)
         If Prime% > 0 Then
            Msg$ = "Number Is not Prime" + Str$(Prime%) + " divides it."
     Else
        Msg$ = "Number Is a Prime."
     End If
  Else
        Msg$ = "Number is invalid."
  End If
  MsgBox Msg$
  Exit Sub
E1:
  SaveErr% = Err
  GeneralErrors
  Resume Next
End Sub


' Error  module


Sub GeneralErrors ()
  Msg$ = Error$(SaveErr%)
  MsgBox Msg$
  Select Case SaveErr%
     Case 280 To 297
       DDEErrors
  End Select
End Sub

Sub DDEErrors ()
     Dim App%
     Select Case SaveErr%

        Case 282
          If Done = 0 Then Exit Sub
          App% = Shell(Server$, 1)
          App% = DoEvents()
          Done = -1
```

continues

LISTING 9.7. CONTINUED

```
        Case 283
          Msg$ = "Suggest you open Program Manager "
          Msg$ = Msg$ + " NOW and use End Task "
          Msg$ = Msg$ + " to terminate the LAST "
          Msg$ = Msg$ + " INSTANCE of " + Server$
          MsgBox Msg$

      End Select
End Sub
```

USING THE CRESCENT.VBX TO EXPLORE YOUR SYSTEM

The final example in this chapter uses the bonus Crescent.Vbx (on the disk) to explore the Windows system. The Crescent.Vbx contains seven useful routines (donated by Crescent Software) that get information about the current version of Windows, operating ModeInfo, and so on. Here are the declarations for the seven routines:

```
Declare Function WinVer% Lib "Crescent.Vbx" ()
Declare Function SysDir$ Lib "Crescent.Vbx" ()
Declare Function GetSystemResources% Lib "Crescent.Vbx" ()
Declare Function ModeInfo$ Lib "Crescent.Vbx" ()
Declare Function Inp% Lib "Crescent.Vbx" (ByVal PortNo%)
Declare Sub Out Lib "Crescent.Vbx" (ByVal PortNo%, ByVal Word%)
Declare Sub ReadSect Lib "Crescent.Vbx" (ByVal Drive$, Info$, ByVal Sector&)
```

The project, Crescent.Mak, on the disk demonstrates how to use these routines. The complete code for the project is in Listing 9.8. Figure 9.21 shows the results of using this code.

Note again that these seven routines are a very modest sampling of the nifty low-level tools and custom controls available from Crescent Software in the QuickPak Professional package for Visual Basic for Windows. Check out this amazing package.

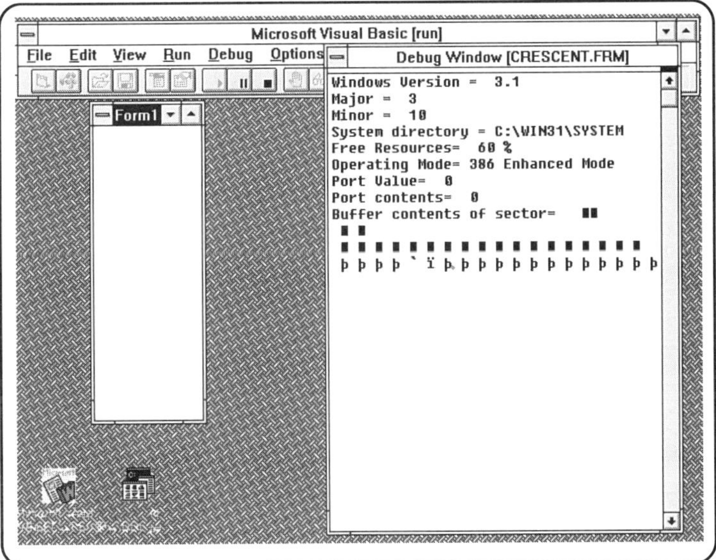

Figure 9.21. CRESCENT: results.

Listing 9.8. CRESCENT.

```
Declare Function WinVer% Lib "Crescent.Vbx" ()
Declare Function SysDir$ Lib "Crescent.Vbx" ()
Declare Function GetSystemResources% Lib "Crescent.Vbx" ()
Declare Function ModeInfo$ Lib "Crescent.Vbx" ()
Declare Function Inp% Lib "Crescent.Vbx" (ByVal PortNo%)
Declare Sub Out Lib "Crescent.Vbx" (ByVal PortNo%, ByVal Word%)
Declare Sub ReadSect Lib "Crescent.Vbx" (ByVal Drive$, Info$, ByVal Sector&)

Sub Form_Click ()
  UseWinVer
  UseSysDir
  UseGetSys
  UseModeInfo
  UseInp
  UseOut
  UseReadSect
End Sub

Sub UseGetSys ()
  FreeResources% = GetSystemResources%()
  Debug.Print "Free Resources= "; Str$(FreeResources%); " %"
End Sub
```

```
Sub UseInp ()
  PortNo% = 1
  Word% = Inp%(PortNo%)
  Debug.Print "Port Value= "; Str$(Word%)
End Sub

Sub UseModeInfo ()
  OperatingMode$ = ModeInfo$()
  Debug.Print "Operating Mode= "; OperatingMode$
End Sub

Sub UseOut ()
  PortNo% = 1
  Word% = Inp%(PortNo%)
  Out PortNo%, Word%
  Debug.Print "Port contents= "; Str$(Word%)
End Sub

Sub UseReadSect ()
  Drive$ = "C:"
  Sector& = 1223 'Arbitrarily selected sector.
  '---- Read in a 512 byte sector into Buffer$
  BUFFER$ = Space$(512)
  ReadSect Drive$, BUFFER$, Sector&
  Debug.Print "Buffer contents of sector= "; BUFFER$
End Sub

Sub UseSysDir ()
  SystemDirectory$ = SysDir$()
  Debug.Print "System directory = "; SystemDirectory$
End Sub

Sub UseWinVer ()
  Version! = WinVer%() / 100
  Major% = WinVer%() \ 100
  Minor% = WinVer%() Mod 100
  Debug.Print "Windows Version = "; Str$(Version!)
  Debug.Print "Major = "; Str$(Major%)
  Debug.Print "Minor = "; Str$(Minor%)
End Sub
```

Summary

That does it for this chapter's intermediate study of DLLs and custom controls. By now, you should get the impression that I'm convinced that Visual Basic plus custom control and other DLL support is an amazingly powerful combination. Visual Basic is both easy and fun to use and alone is powerful enough to meet most developers' needs. Combined with third-party support, it becomes even more powerful.

If you need more speed (although Visual Basic is very fast), you can get it by calling the Windows API directly or by utilizing assembly language routines. This chapter has described how easily assembly language routines can be added.

If you need additional functionality (although Visual Basic already has considerable power), you can add it by way of custom controls or DLLs written in many languages. You're not limited to assembly language. If you have existing C code, for example, put it in a DLL and call it from Visual Basic.

Left to you and your imagination, the combinations of languages and the potential power of the Visual Basic programming system are virtually limitless.

A Wizard Project Editor and a Wizard Clipboard

Use the Common Dialog Control

Use the API to Set the Text Box to Greater Than 32K

Open a Project

In Chapter 6, "Files, Directories, and a Code Wizard," you built the first version of Wizard, a GREP-like file manager. In this chapter, as promised in Chapter 6, Wizard is expanded to a full-featured project editor. The final version of Wizard (by the end of this chapter) does the things in the following list:

- Enables a user to create, open, and save projects. (A Wizard project is similar to a Visual Basic project, consisting of a group of files the user specifies for inclusion in the project.)
- Enables a user to edit any file that is text. Wizard uses binary file I/O to examine the individual bytes of a file to determine the kind of file it is. If it's a text file, Wizard enables editing functions (Save, Cut, Paste, Undo, Replace, and so on). If it's an executable file

(.DLL, .EXE, .COM), a Visual Basic form file, or any other non-ASCII text file, the user can view, but not alter, the file. The development of this functionality illustrates how you can enable and disable menu commands. The use of binary file I/O serves as a blueprint for examining any individual byte in a file, saving records, and so on.

- Keeps track of where a user is currently editing in the file. Every time the user saves a file, Wizard notes the current position in the file and saves that information in a Wizard position database. This database uses random I/O (to save and read records) and therefore illustrates how to set up, read, and write a database file. In addition, maintaining the current editing position utilizes several sophisticated edit box functions.
- Implements and optimizes search and search-and-replace functions within a file. Recall that the earlier version of Wizard in Chapter 6 found string matches in any (or all) of the files on a disk. This version extends that capability to finding any matches within the currently edited file as well and, in addition, "remembers" any search or replace string for future use. The replace function is relatively complicated and illustrates a number of limitations (and alternative coding strategies) of Visual Basic.
- Implements an Undo so the user can undo the last edit command in the edit window. This function requires (and illustrates) the use of a Windows API call.
- Increases the size of the edit window (a text box) to 60K using a Windows API call. By increasing the size of a file that the text box can handle (the default is 32K), you can greatly expand the usefulness of a text box; however, this action can create a number of problems, which are discussed in detail. (I'll show you how to work around them.)
- Adds handy debug utilities by connecting Wizard to Recorder, the Windows Macro Editor. This illustrates how to use the Shell command and greatly enhances Visual Basic debugging in general, by saving you hundreds of keystrokes.
- Uses the Common Dialog custom control to simplify opening and saving files.
- Uses the Windows API to increase the performance of list box handling.

In other words, this chapter covers many interesting (and problematic) topics. The final Wizard (at the end of this chapter) is useful indeed; it's an application I always run concurrently with Visual Basic when I'm developing an application. It makes it easier for me to keep track of my code (as I'll discuss), and it simplifies debugging.

In addition, I use Wizard—as a Notepad substitute—for fundamental text editing. For example, I used it to make notes for this book while I was writing example applications, including Wizard. Because Wizard keeps track of your position in a file even after you've exited Wizard, you don't have to pay a premium for exiting your text editor. Not even Word for Windows is this flexible. I think that you will find it an important addition to your Visual Basic toolbox. Because you have the code as well, you can modify it or add other features.

Use the Common Dialog Control

You begin updating Wizard from Chapter 6 by making it into a project editor. The project editor lets the user create, open, and save work projects—presumably, Visual Basic code or text files. I'm restricting the project editor to text files for two reasons:

1. The Visual Basic text box control, which is used in the Wizard application, displays only text reliably. It attempts to display binary files, but control characters can knock it for a loop.
2. Presumably, you maintain your Visual Basic code in text (to optimize .EXE size).

This final version of Wizard, the project editor, therefore, lets the user edit any file that's text. If it's an executable file (.DLL, .EXE, .COM), a Visual Basic form file, or any other non-ASCII text file, the user can view, but not alter, the file.

To determine the kind of file the user is attempting to display in the editor, Wizard uses binary file I/O to examine the individual bytes of each before loading it. If it's a text file, it enables editing functions (Save, Cut, Paste, Undo, Replace, and so on).

Wizard also lets users add and remove files from the project, which it displays in a dynamic menu. In addition, it keeps track of where a user is currently editing in the file every time it's saved. When the user saves a file, Wizard notes the current position in the file (using the `SelText` property) and saves that information in a Wizard position database. This database consists of records that are accessed using random file I/O.

For starters you need an efficient file I/O dialog, which is used to enable the user to add files to the project, save files, and save projects. Although you can easily build your own file dialog forms and routines, the easiest way to implement file I/O is to use the Common Dialog custom control.

Add the Common Dialog custom control by:

1. Selecting Add File from the File menu.
2. Entering the filename or selecting the Common Dialog custom control from the VBX menu:

```
CMDIALOG.VBX
```

This adds the Common Dialog custom control to the project, and displays the icon for the Common Dialog in the toolbar (see Figure 10.1).

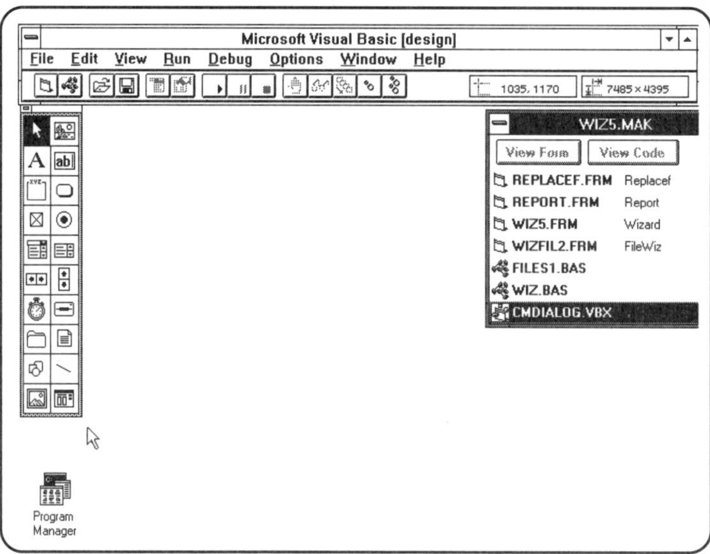

Figure 10.1. The Common Dialog icon in the toolbar.

Next, add it to the Wizard main form. It appears as an icon on the form (see Figure 10.2).

Now you can use it throughout the project by simply setting its properties. For example, the following fragment sets the file filter for the dialog to `*.prj` for project files and sets the Action property to open a file:

```
CMDialog1.Filter = "Project files(*.prj)¦*.prj"
CMDialog1.FilterIndex = 1
CMDialog1.Action = 1
```

The following fragment sets the Common Dialog for a Save:

```
CMDialog1.Filter = "Project files(*.prj)¦*.prj"
CMDialog1.FilterIndex = 1
CMDialog1.Action = 2
```

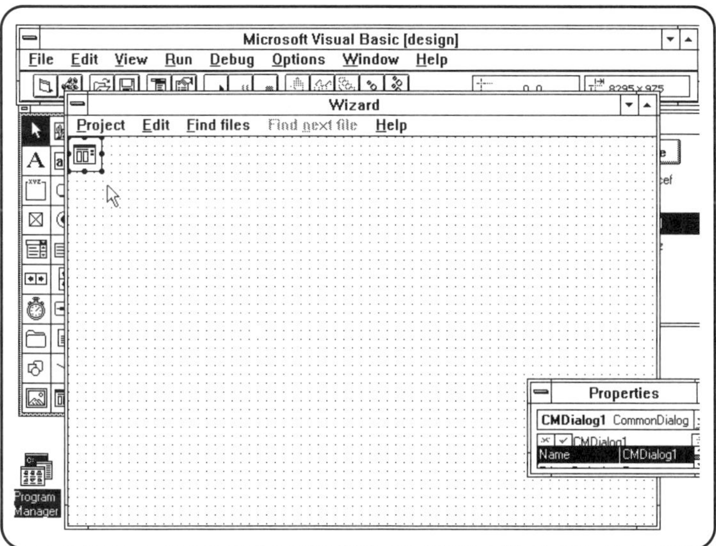

Figure 10.2. The Common Dialog on the form.

That's really all there is to using the Common Dialog custom control. Other Common Dialog properties enable you to create other, more complex tasks, but you use it in this project for just opening and saving files and project files.

When you add a file to a project, you get the filename from the user. Using the Common Dialog, read the file from disk into the edit window and update the dynamic project menu so the user can easily select the file again (after it's closed) without searching the file directory. In other words, every time the user opens a file for editing, it should be easy to close and reopen it. If you've used Word for Windows, its dynamic file menu works this way.

The following `AddFileCom_Click` event procedure, a menu click event procedure, handles the management of these tasks:

```
Sub AddFileCom_Click ()
Dim TempEditFile As String * 30
On Error Resume Next
      CMDialog1.Filter = "All files(*.*)¦*.*¦Text files(*.txt)¦*.txt"
      CMDialog1.FilterIndex = 2
      CMDialog1.CancelError = -1
      CMDialog1.Action = 1
      TempEditFile = CMDialog1.FileName
      If Err = 32755 Then Exit Sub
      If Err = 0 Then
         SaveDialog
         EditFile = TempEditFile
         ReadFile
         MenuNum% = MenuNum% + 1
         Load Files(MenuNum%)
         Files(MenuNum%).Caption = EditFile
         Files(MenuNum%).Visible = -1
      End If
End Sub
```

When the user selects the Add File menu item, the Common Dialog is shown; if the user selects a file, it is read and the dynamic project menu is updated.

Although `ReadFile` occupies a single line in the `AddFileCom_Click` event procedure, it does a lot:

- Increases the size of text that the text box will accept—from the default 32K to 60K. (You will see how it does that in the section "Use the API to Set the Text Box to Greater Than 32K" later in this chapter.)
- Attempts to open the file using binary file I/O, just as the Wizard in Chapter 6 did. (See that chapter for a discussion of the merits of binary file I/O.)
- Reads the file.

- Reads the first two bytes of the file to determine what kind of file it's attempting to read. After some mucking around at the byte level, I discovered that all the files I was attempting to type (.FRM, .MAK, .EXE, .COM, .DLL, and so on) can be typed by reading and evaluating the first two bytes of the file—the `GetFileType` procedure, which I'll show you at the end of this section, handles the evaluation.
- Opens the project position database to determine the last position where the user was editing the last time the file was opened in a project. If the file hasn't been opened in a project, position 1 is assumed to be the last position.

Looking up the position in a position database naturally assumes that you already have a project file position database where you've been saving positions.

The saving of positions in the database is handled when the user saves a file. First the file is saved; then the edit file position is saved. Here's the `SaveFileCom_Click` event procedure:

```
Sub SaveFileCom_Click ()
On Error GoTo SaveError
  If EditFlag% = 0 Then
      SaveFileAsCom_Click
  End If
  If EditFile <> "" Then
      Wizard.Caption = EditFile
      OpenMode% = BINARYFILE
      FileNum% = OpenAFile(EditFile, OpenMode%, 0)
  End If

      If FileNum% = 0 Then
          FileInfo.Caption = "Open Failed."
          FindNextCom.Enabled = 0
          Exit Sub
      End If

      Length = Len(EditWindow.Text)
      FileInfo.Caption = "Saving " + Str$(Length) + " bytes."
      SaveStr$ = EditWindow.Text
      Put #FileNum%, , SaveStr$
      Close (FileNum%)

      ' Save position

      RecLength% = Len(FileRec)
      OpenMode% = RandomFILE
```

```
      FileNum% = OpenAFile("wizard.pos", OpenMode%, Len(FileRec))
      For Index% = 1 To LOF(FileNum%) \ RecLength%
         Get #(FileNum%), Index%, FileRec
         If FileRec.FileName = EditFile Then
              FileRec.FileName = EditFile
              FileRec.Position = EditWindow.SelStart
              Put #(FileNum%), Index%, FileRec
              Close FileNum%
              Exit Sub
         End If
      Next Index%
      FileRec.FileName = EditFile
      FileRec.Position = EditWindow.SelStart
      Index% = Index% + 1
      Put #(FileNum%), Index%, FileRec
      Close FileNum%
      Exit Sub
SaveError:
      SaveErr% = Err
      GeneralErrors
      Resume Next

End Sub
```

The Save position part of this procedure uses random file I/O to save each file's position information as a record, using the `SelStart` property of the edit window to determine where the user is when the file is saved, and a user-defined record Type to define record information.

The Type must be declared in a module (or the Global module in Version 1.0):

```
Type FileRecord
  FileName As String * 30
  Position As Long
End Type
```

Here's the Save position part:

```
RecLength% = Len(FileRec)
OpenMode% = RandomFILE

FileNum% = OpenAFile("wizard.pos", OpenMode%, Len(FileRec))
For Index% = 1 To LOF(FileNum%) \ RecLength%
   Get #(FileNum%), Index%, FileRec
   If FileRec.FileName = EditFile Then
        FileRec.FileName = EditFile
        FileRec.Position = EditWindow.SelStart
        Put #(FileNum%), Index%, FileRec
        Close FileNum%
        Exit Sub
   End If
Next Index%
```

```
FileRec.FileName = EditFile
FileRec.Position = EditWindow.SelStart
Index% = Index% + 1
Put #(FileNum%), Index%, FileRec
Close FileNum%
```

This simple routine could be used to easily maintain any database by adding different Types or different fields to the current record Type.

`ReadFile()` looks like this:

```
Sub ReadFile ()
      SetTextBox
      If EditFile <> "" Then
         Wizard.Caption = EditFile
         OpenMode% = BINARYFILE
         FileNum% = OpenAFile(EditFile, OpenMode%, 0)
      End If

      If FileNum% = 0 Then
         FileInfo.Caption = "Open Failed."
         FindNextCom.Enabled = 0
         Exit Sub
      End If

      Length = LOF(FileNum%)

      If Length < 60000 And Length > 1 Then
         VarString$ = String$(Length, " ")
         Get FileNum%, , VarString$
         Close FileNum%
         EditWindow.Text = ""
         EditWindow.Text = VarString$
         If EditWindow.Text = "" Then
             FileInfo.Caption = "Problem loading file."
             VarString$ = String$(1, " ")
             Exit Sub
         End If
         FirstTwo$ = Left$(VarString$, 2)
         Number2$ = Right$(FirstTwo$, 1)
         One% = Asc(FirstTwo$)
         Two% = Asc(Number2$)
         VarString$ = String$(1, " ")
         GetFileType One%, Two%

      ' Read position database
         RecLength% = Len(FileRec)
         OpenMode% = RandomFILE
         FileNum% = OpenAFile("wizard.pos", OpenMode%, Len(FileRec))
         For Index% = 1 To LOF(FileNum%) \ RecLength%
             Get #(FileNum%), Index%, FileRec
             If FileRec.FileName = EditFile Then
```

```
                FilePos& = FileRec.Position
                EditWindow.SelStart = FilePos&
                EditWindow.SelLength = 2
                Close FileNum%
                Exit Sub
             End If
         Next Index%
         Close FileNum%
      Else
             FileInfo.Caption = "File size out of range."
             Wizard.Caption = "No file."
      End If
End Sub
```

The `GetFileType` procedure uses a `SelectCase` statement to evaluate the first two bytes of each file to determine its Type:

```
Sub GetFileType (One As Integer, Two As Integer)
  Select Case One%
             Case 77
               If Two% = 90 Then FileInfo.Caption = ".EXE, .DLL, .VBX, .DRV"
             Case 233
               FileInfo.Caption = ".COM"
             Case 35
               If Two% = 204 Then FileInfo.Caption = "Visual Basic.FRM"
             Case 190
               If Two% = 186 Then FileInfo.Caption = "Visual Basic.MAK"
             Case 63
               If Two% = 95 Then FileInfo.Caption = ".HLP"
             Case 255
               If Two% = 255 Then FileInfo.Caption = ".SYS"
             Case 66
               If Two% = 77 Then FileInfo.Caption = ".BMP"
             Case 0
               If Two% = 0 Then FileInfo.Caption = ".ICO"
             Case 155
               If Two% = 165 Then FileInfo.Caption = "Word for Windows 1.1"
             Case 219
               If Two% = 165 Then FileInfo.Caption = ".Word for Windows 2.0"
             Case 9
               If Two% = 2 Then FileInfo.Caption = "Excel (or related) data"
             Case 80
               If Two% = 77 Then FileInfo.Caption = "Windows .GRP"
             Case Else
             FileInfo.Caption =
               ➥"Probably a text file. Edit capability enabled."
               EditEnable (-1)
               Exit Sub
         End Select
         EditEnable (0)
End Sub
```

Note that the preceding procedure `GetFileType` uses the `Case Else` part of the `Select Case` statement to conclude, by default, that the examined file is a text file. Alternatively, you could have an additional test for control characters in general for determining whether a file is text. If it contains no control characters, Wizard assumes that the file is text.

Use the API to Set the Text Box to Greater Than 32K

Before we stray too far, let's look at the `SetTextBox` procedure that sends a message to the Windows API to set the text box length to greater than 32K.

First, declare the `SendMessage` and `GetFocus` functions where this form-level procedure can see it. For example, the declarations section of the Wizard main form follows:

```
Declare Function GetFocus% Lib "user" ()
Declare Function SendMessage& Lib "user" (ByVal hWnd%,
➥ ByVal wMsg%, ByVal wParam%, lp As Any)
```

Also, declare the constant offsets for the `EM_LIMITTEXT` message. The following is a convenient way to declare these message constants because it offsets each message from a single `WM_USER` constant:

```
Const WM_USER = &H400
Const EM_LIMITTEXT = WM_USER + 21
Const EM_UNDO = WM_USER + 23
```

Alternatively, you can put the hexadecimal values directly in your code if you don't mind it being a little less readable.

Now, to send a message to the Windows API, you must first set the focus to the control that you want affected by the message—in this case, `EditWindow`. Next, get the handle to the focused control using `GetFocus`. Then you can send the message and it acts on the control referred to by the handle. Here's the procedure:

```
Sub SetTextBox ()
  If SetBox% = 0 Then
      EditWindow.Text = ""
      EditWindow.SetFocus
      cbhWnd% = GetFocus()
      TextLimit% = &HFAAA
      RetVal = SendMessage(cbhWnd%, EM_LIMITTEXT, TextLimit%, 0)
```

```
      SetBox% = -1
   End If
End Sub
```

By calling this procedure, before using the `EditWindow` text box the first time, you can establish it as a greater-than-32K (in this case, 60K) text box every time it's used. If you don't set the length, Visual Basic generates an error every time you try to read a file greater than 32K into a text box control.

While working with this function, I first pondered why there is a 32K limit. (By the way, earlier versions of the Microsoft Visual Basic documentation imply in examples that the default text box control can handle 64K of text. But this is not true, as you discover if you don't set the text using an API procedure.) After loading a few large files into the expanded text box, I discovered one good reason for the 32K limit.

As Windows attempts to load larger and larger files, it seems to run into a "memory thrashing" problem. (Remember that Windows and Visual Basic are doing all the complicated work of getting the text into the text box for you.) Windows seems to build a text-box string one step at a time (or something similar). I decided to investigate further by first calling other developers; they confirmed that the problem I was encountering was normal. None of them could explain exactly why the problem was occurring, but they all agreed that it was "memory thrashing." Next, I called the Microsoft support number, and explained the problem to an incredulous technician who agreed to check it out. He called back to say that I was right—a memory thrashing problem seems to exist, and it occurs in not only the text-box control, but also in any control (such as the grid custom control) as it approaches 64K or so. If you experiment, you'll find that 32K is the peak performance size for these controls. Exactly what this memory thrashing problem is continues to elude me; in any case, the problem exists.

There it is in a nutshell. You can increase the size of the text box's text capability, but you probably will sacrifice control performance. If you've used Notepad with large files, you no doubt have encountered a similar problem because it too uses a text-box control to handle text.

In case you're wondering why Word for Windows and other "expensive" editors efficiently handle text greater than 32K, it's because they don't use text-box controls for editing. These "word processors" build their own controls, essentially from scratch, usually in C or assembly language. In my opinion, this size problem is one of Visual Basic's primary weaknesses and should keep you from attempting to build a competitor to Word, WordPerfect, and Ami Professional.

The Wizard project editor, therefore, is intended not to replace Word, but to complement it.

Finally, someone (MicroHelp) has come to the rescue and created a text box (editor) that can efficiently read files greater than 64K. This custom control is called "HighEdit" and it's an exceptional product. You buy it, add it to your project, and then build the custom editing features you need around it. I built a Text Editor with the HighEdit custom control and it works great as a better-than Notepad substitute. A useable executable (.EXE) version of the HighEditWizard is included on the disk. Check it out. You can use it as is to edit files greater than 64K. To modify it to suit your custom needs, however, you'll need to purchase your own copy of the HighEdit custom control from MicroHelp.

Open a Project

Now that you have the procedural tools built, opening and saving projects is straightforward. Use the Common Dialog to let the user specify the project, and then build the dynamic project menu from the filenames in the project file. Note that you don't read the position database when you open or close a project, only when you open or close a file in the project. Here's the `OpenProjectCom_Click` event procedure:

```
Sub OpenProjectCom_Click ()
  Dim App$
  While MenuNum% > 0
     Unload Files(MenuNum%)
     MenuNum% = MenuNum% - 1
  Wend

  On Error Resume Next
  CMDialog1.Filter = "Project files(*.prj)¦*.prj"
  CMDialog1.FilterIndex = 1
  CMDialog1.CancelError = -1
  CMDialog1.Action = 1

  If Err = 32755 Then
      SaveErr% = Err
      GeneralErrors
      Exit Sub
  End If
  If Err = 0 Then
```

```
        ProjectFile = CMDialog1.FileName
  End If

  If ProjectFile <> "" Then
     OpenMode% = LOADFILE
     FileNum% = OpenAFile(ProjectFile, OpenMode%, 0)
  End If

     If FileNum% = 0 Then
        FileInfo.Caption = "Open Failed."
        Exit Sub
     End If

     FileInfo.Caption = "Opening project."
        While Not EOF(FileNum%)
           Input #FileNum%, App$
           MenuNum% = MenuNum% + 1
           Load Files(MenuNum%)
           Files(MenuNum%).Caption = App$
           Files(MenuNum%).Visible = -1
        Wend
        Close FileNum%

End Sub
```

Here's the `SaveProjectCom_Click` event procedure:

```
SaveProjectCom_Click ()
  On Error Resume Next
  CMDialog1.Filter = "Project files(*.prj)¦*.prj"
  CMDialog1.FilterIndex = 1
  CMDialog1.FileName = ProjectFile
  CMDialog1.DefaultExt = "PRJ"
  CMDialog1.CancelError = -1
  CMDialog1.Action = 2
  If Err = 32755 Then Exit Sub
  If Err = 0 Then
        ProjectFile = CMDialog1.FileName
  End If

  If ProjectFile <> "" Then
        OpenMode% = REPLACEFILE
        FileNum% = OpenAFile(ProjectFile, OpenMode%, 0)
  End If

  If FileNum% = 0 Then
        FileInfo.Caption = "Open Failed."
        Exit Sub
  End If
  FileInfo.Caption = "Saving project."
  For I% = 1 To MenuNum%
        Print #FileNum%, Files(I%).Caption
```

```
  Next I%
  Close FileNum%
End Sub
```

It would also be nice to enable the user to selectively remove items (files) from the project menu. To let the user decide which items to remove, use an input box to get the selection, and then unload the selected menu item:

```
Sub RemoveFileCom_Click ()
  Msg$ = "Enter the number of the menu item to remove. 25 to remove all."
  Num% = Val(InputBox$(Msg$, "Remove Files From Project", Str$(25)))
  If Num% = 25 Then
      While MenuNum% > 0
        Unload Files(MenuNum%)
        MenuNum% = MenuNum% - 1
      Wend
      Exit Sub
End If

  If Num% > MenuNum% Then
        MsgBox "Number is out of range."
        Exit Sub
  End If
  End If
  For I% = Num% To MenuNum% - 1
      Files(I%).Caption = Files(I% + 1).Caption
  Next I%
  Unload Files(MenuNum%)
  MenuNum% = MenuNum% - 1
End Sub
```

Search and Replace

Two more features I can't do without are search and search-and-replace routines. Search is trivial; simply use the Visual Basic `InStr` function to determine whether the search string (`Search$`) is in the `EditWindow.Text`. Then use the `SelStart` and `SelLength` properties of the `EditWindow` to move the mouse pointer (or cursor) to the first occurrence of the string:

```
Sub FindCurrentCom_Click ()
         FindForm.Show MODAL
         If Cancel <> -1 Then
             Position& = InStr(EditWindow.Text, Search$)
             If Position& > 0 Then
                EditWindow.SelStart = Position& - 1
                EditWindow.SelLength = Len(Search$)
             End If
         End If
End Sub
```

Figure 10.3 shows the Find form in action.

What about a `FindNext` routine? That's a little more complicated because you have to begin a `FindNext` search at the current position in the `EditWindow`. If you simply use `InStr` as you did before, you will find the first occurrence again. Therefore, you have to create a string that consists of everything to the right of the current position. Then search that string for the search string. The Visual Basic `Right$` function returns the number of characters specified in the right part of the string—it creates the string for us. Then use `InStr` for the search, which returns it to the position in the string where the string was found.

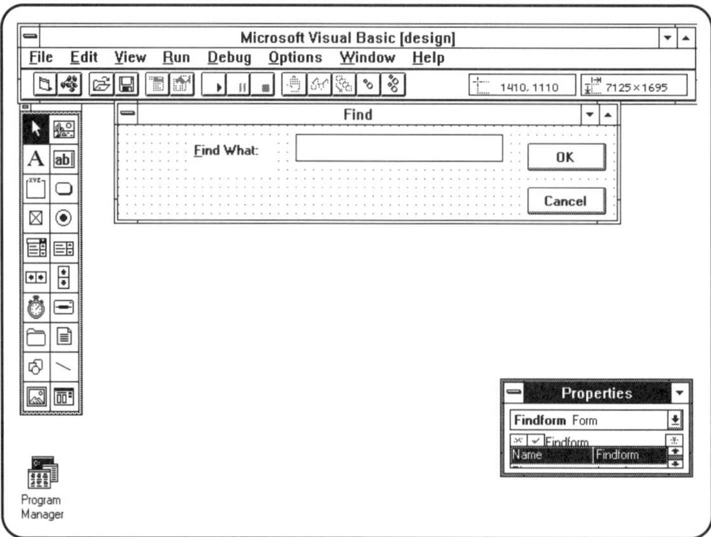

Figure 10.3. The Find form.

Note that this position isn't the position you ultimately want, however; it's the position in the right string. Therefore, add the length of the left string to the position to get the position in the edit window where you will put the mouse pointer. The `FindNext` procedure looks like the following:

```
Sub FindNextCurrentCom_Click ()
        Search$ = FindForm.Text1.Text
        RLength& = Len(EditWindow.Text) - (EditWindow.SelStart + 1)
        LLength& = Len(EditWindow.Text) - RLength&
        Rest$ = Right$(EditWindow.Text, RLength&)
        Position& = InStr(Rest$, Search$)
```

```
           If Position& > 0 Then
              EditWindow.SelStart = LLength& + Position& - 1
              EditWindow.SelLength = Len(Search$)
           Else
              FileInfo.Caption = "String not found."
          End If
End Sub
```

It doesn't matter where you begin a `FindNext` search—simply divide the `EditWindow`'s text into two strings, before and after the current position.

The search-and-replace procedure gave me several fits and starts before I finally stumbled on a solution that worked efficiently: essentially, it's the `FindNext` procedure—plus replace the string you find with a replace string. Sound simple? It's problematic, however, for a couple of reasons.

Suppose, for example, that you want to replace all occurrences of a string with a replace string, and suppose that the text string in the `EditWindow` is 60K in length. If you divide it into a left and right string of 30K and 30K, for example, you've used up 120K of string space in the current module. Presuming that you're using variable-length strings, this doesn't work (refer to Chapter 6). In addition, you're probably going to want to keep track of whatever is left of the string after the replacement—that's some more kilobytes as well.

Also, if you simply update the `EditWindow` (the text box) every time you replace an instance of the string, performance nearly grinds to a halt. Updating a 60K string with 150 replacements, for example, takes forever.

Getting around the text-box update problem is easy: simply write the contents of the text box into another string and search that string, updating it with the replacement string instead of updating the text box. After all the replacements have been made, write the updated string back to the text box. Updating a string this way is very fast; in fact, it's many times faster than updating the `EditWindow` directly and, therefore, well worth the trouble.

There's a catch, however, if you need to create another string of 60K, for example, in length. Without burdening you any longer with this string-space problem (which is discussed in depth in Chapter 6), let me show you one efficient solution, although it's ultimately limited to doing search and replace on a maximum of 32K worth of strings:

```
Sub ReplaceCom_Click ()
  ReplaceState% = -1
  Length = Len(EditWindow.Text)
   If Length > 32767 Then
```

```
        Msg$ = " Can't do replace on > 32767. File is " +
           ➥Str$(Length) + " bytes."
        FileInfo.Caption = Msg$
        Exit Sub
   End If
   VarString$ = String$(Length, " ")
   VarString$ = EditWindow.Text
   Replacef.Show MODAL
   If Search$ = Replace$ Then Exit Sub
   If Cancel <> -1 Then
        DoReplace
   End If
   Unload Replacef
End Sub


Sub DoReplace ()
   Dim LeftPart$
        Start& = Wizard.EditWindow.SelStart
        RLength& = Len(VarString$) - (Wizard.EditWindow.SelStart)
        LLength& = Len(VarString$) - RLength&
        If RLength& > 0 Then
           PreRest$ = Left$(VarString$, LLength&)
           OpenMode% = BINARYFILE
           FileNum% = OpenAFile("~temp.wiz", OpenMode%, 0)
           Put FileNum%, , PreRest$
           P& = Len(PreRest$)
           PreRest$ = String$(1, " ")
           VarString$ = Right$(VarString$, RLength&)
        Else
           ReplaceState% = 0
           Exit Sub
        End If

        SLength& = Len(Search$)

        Position& = 99
        ReplaceState% = -1
        While Position& <> 0 And ReplaceState% <> 0
          If Replacef.Option1.Value = -1 Then
              ReplaceState% = 0
          End If
          Position& = InStr(VarString$, Search$)
          If Position& > 0 Then
              RLength& = Len(VarString$)
              LeftPart$ = Left$(VarString$, Position& - 1)
              Rightlength& = RLength& - (Position& + SLength&)
              VarString$ = Right$(VarString$, Rightlength& + 1)
              Wanted$ = Left$(VarString$, SLength&)
```

```
            Wanted$ = Replace$
            VarString$ = LeftPart$ + Wanted$ + VarString$
        End If
      Wend
      LeftPart$ = String$(1, " ")
      RightPart$ = String$(1, " ")
      PreRest$ = String$(P&, " ")
      Get FileNum%, , PreRest$
      Close FileNum%
      Wizard.EditWindow.Text = PreRest$ + VarString$
      Wizard.EditWindow.SelStart = Start&
      VarString$ = String$(1, " ")
      Wizard.FileInfo.Caption = "String not found."
End Sub
```

Note that this code saves one string to a temporary file to manipulate the limited Visual Basic string space. If your hard disk is even normally fast, this isn't much of a trade-off, and it's a method typically used by "expensive" applications. Figure 10.4 shows the Replace form in action.

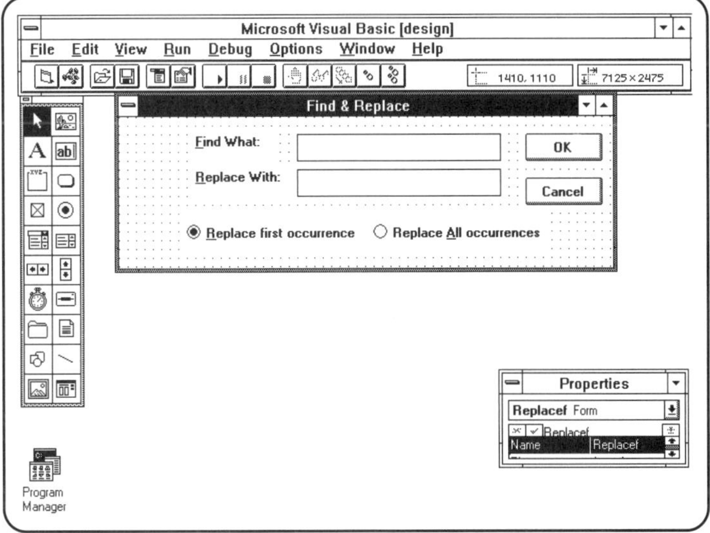

Figure 10.4. The Replace form.

USE THE API TO UNDO

What feature do you want next? How about an Undo? That's simple enough—just send a message to the Windows API and it automatically undoes the last action in the text box. As before, make sure that the Windows API functions SendMessage and GetFocus are declared. If you're using constants, make sure that the EM_UNDO constant is declared. Then, set the focus to the text box, get a handle to the text box, and send the Undo message to the Windows API, which takes care of the rest because it has maintained the most recent keyboard activity in a buffer. It simply reads the contents of that buffer and acts accordingly—if you delete a character, it keeps track of the text you delete; if you add text, it keeps track of the last character; if you select a block of text and do something to the block, it undoes the block operation:

```
Sub UndoCom_Click ()
  EditWindow.SetFocus
  cbhWnd% = GetFocus()
  RetVal = SendMessage(cbhWnd%, EM_UNDO, 0, 0)
End Sub
```

DEBUGGING

At this point, the Wizard project editor can handle dynamic projects and files. It also can search and replace within files, keep track of your position in a file and save it for reloading the next time you open the project, do searches across files (GREP-style), perform undos, and so on. What's next?

Because one of my primary uses of Wizard is as a Visual Basic support tool, I thought that it might be nice to use it to improve one aspect of the Visual Basic development process I'm not entirely thrilled with: debugging. Note that if you're using Version 2.0 or Version 3.0 of Visual Basic, the debugging process has been significantly improved. Version 2.0 and Version 3.0 allow watch and break expressions, instant watches, active procedure call displays, and the editing of watchpoints. However, typing and printing of variables in the Debug window (called the Immediate window in Version 1.0) still works the same way in Version 2.0 and Version 3.0 that I describe here.

Essentially, I don't like going into the Debug window every time I'm trying to track variables and type in the variable names, the number of question marks, and a comparable number of Returns. Therefore, I use Wizard with the Windows Recorder, a Macro editor, to duplicate much of the debugging task.

I reasoned that if I could get my hands on a variable list for a code file, I could automate such tasks as adding the question marks and Returns to the variable names.

To obtain all the variables in a code file, therefore, so I can work with them in the Recorder, I wrote the following extract variable loop, which is incorporated in the `Scan` routine in Wizard:

```
Do Until EOF(FileNum%)
   Line Input #FileNum%, NextLine$
   GPos% = InStr(NextLine$, "Global")
   DPos% = InStr(NextLine$, "Dim")
   GCPos% = InStr(NextLine$, "Global Const")
   If (GPos% > 0 And GCPos% = 0) Or DPos% > 0 Then
      NextLine$ = NextLine$ + Chr$(13) + Chr$(10) + Chr$(13) + Chr$(10)
      Print #FileNum2%, NextLine$
   End If
Loop
```

This loop uses sequential file I/O to read a code file one line at a time. It then tests the line for the occurrence of a `Dim`, `Global`, or `Global Const` statement. When it finds one of these statements, it adds it to a file and then dumps the file into the `EditWindow` for processing.

`Scan` looks like this:

```
Sub ScanCom_Click ()
      On Error Resume Next
      CMDialog1.Filter = "All files(*.*)¦*.*¦Text files(*.txt)¦
                ➥*.txt¦Basic files(*.bas)¦*.bas"
      CMDialog1.FilterIndex = 3
      CMDialog1.CancelError = -1
      CMDialog1.Action = 1
      TempEditFile = CMDialog1.FileName
      If Err = 32755 Then Exit Sub
      If Err = 0 Then
         SaveDialog
         EditFile = TempEditFile
      End If
      If EditFile <> "" Then
         Wizard.Caption = EditFile
         OpenMode% = LOADFILE
         FileNum% = OpenAFile(EditFile, OpenMode%, 0)
      End If

      If FileNum% = 0 Then
         FileInfo.Caption = "Open Failed."
         FindNextCom.Enabled = 0
         Exit Sub
      End If
```

```
        Length = LOF(FileNum%)

        If Length < 60000 And Length > 1 Then
           OpenMode% = REPLACEFILE
           FileNum2% = OpenAFile("~1temp.bas", OpenMode%, 0)

           Do Until EOF(FileNum%)
              Line Input #FileNum%, NextLine$
              GPos% = InStr(NextLine$, "Global")
              DPos% = InStr(NextLine$, "Dim")
              GCPos% = InStr(NextLine$, "Global Const")
              If (GPos% > 0 And GCPos% = 0) Or DPos% > 0 Then
                 NextLine$ = NextLine$ + Chr$(13) + Chr$(10) +
                    ➥Chr$(13) + Chr$(10)
                 Print #FileNum2%, NextLine$
              End If
           Loop
           Close FileNum2%
           Close FileNum%
    End If
           FromScan% = -1
           LoadFileCom_Click
End Sub
```

LoadFile looks like this:

```
Sub LoadFileCom_Click ()
        If FromScan% = 0 Then
           On Error Resume Next
           CMDialog1.Filter = "All files(*.*)¦*.*¦Text files(*.txt)¦
           ➥ *.txt¦Basic files(*.bas)¦*.bas"
           CMDialog1.FilterIndex = 3
           CMDialog1.CancelError = -1
           CMDialog1.Action = 1
           TempEditFile = CMDialog1.FileName
           If Err = 32755 Then Exit Sub
           If Err = 0 Then
               SaveDialog
               EditFile = TempEditFile
               ReadFile
```

```
        End If
      Else
        FromScan% = 0
        EditFile = "~1temp.bas"
        ReadFile
      End If
End Sub
```

USE THE SHELL COMMAND AND RECORDER TO AUTOMATE DEBUGGING

After the file is in the Wizard editor, you have the search-and-replace routines needed to strip these lines down to variable names with question marks that you can use in the Debug window. Rather than repeat this conversion of variable names to names suitable for the Debug window each time, I call Recorder to handle the task one time:

```
Sub MacroCom_Click ()
On Error GoTo E2
     x = Shell("\win31\recorder.exe", 1)
E2:
     SaveErr% = Err
     GeneralErrors
     Resume Next
End Sub
```

With Recorder running, I simply convert the variables the different ways necessary and record my actions in various macros, which I can reuse when needed. These macros, included on the disk, make debugging more convenient. Wizard virtually automates all these tasks for you—just select them from the Wizard menu. Because even the multimacros have been reduced to a single macro, you have to run only one to convert all the lines to Debug window usable variable names. Figures 10.5, 10.6, 10.7, and 10.8 show several phases of this process. The possibilities for this Wizard-macro connection are virtually endless; experiment with Wizard and see how you can simplify your debugging tasks.

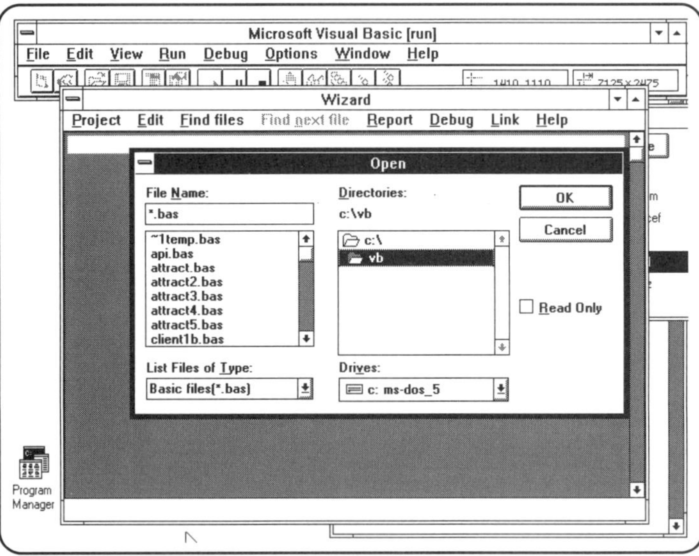

Figure 10.5. Wizard and Recorder: open a file for scanning.

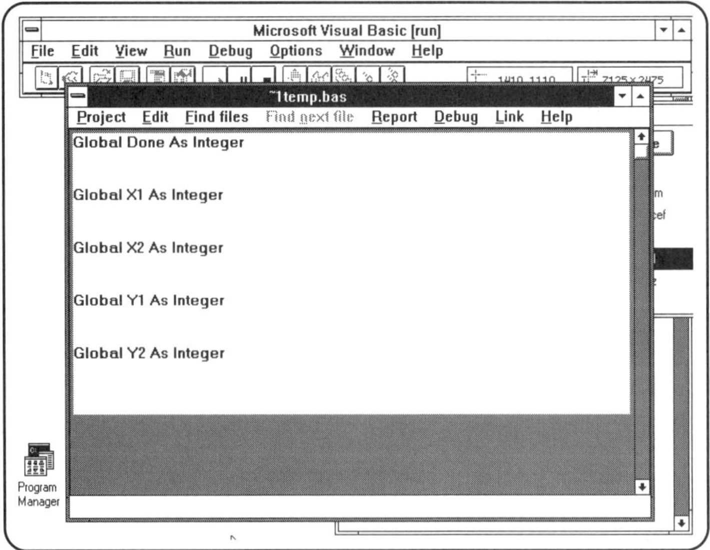

Figure 10.6. Wizard and Recorder: result of scanning a file for global variables.

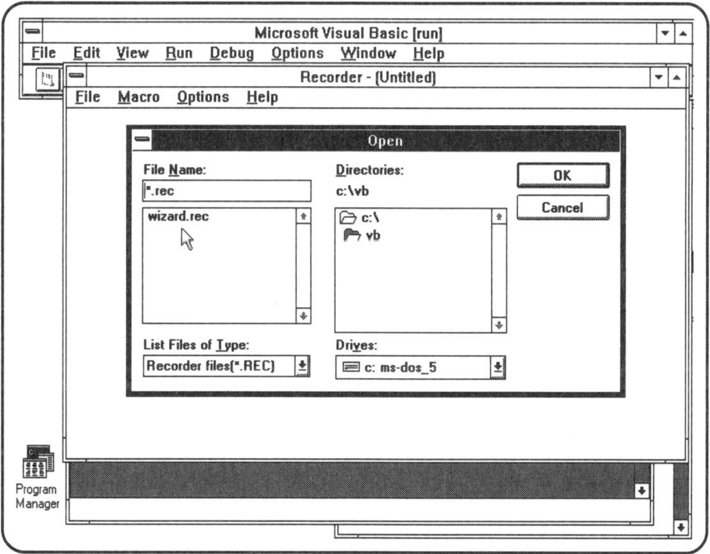

Figure 10.7. Wizard and Recorder: open a macro file for recording.

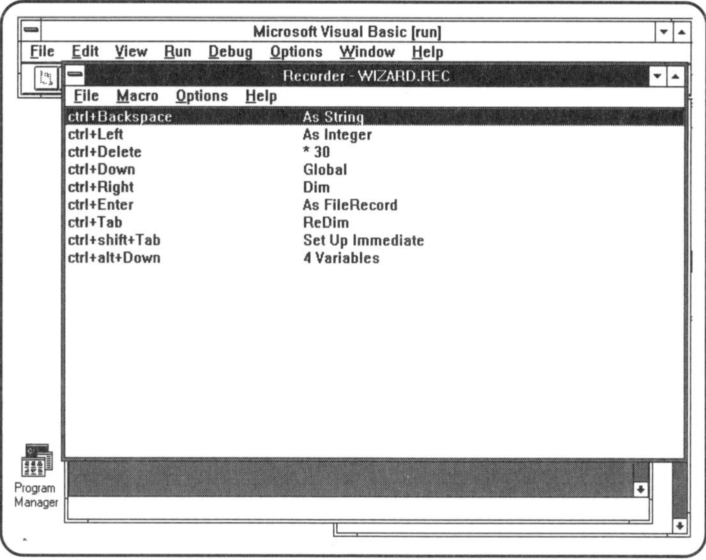

Figure 10.8. Wizard and Recorder: the Recorder macro file for Wizard showing elements that are typically scanned.

BUILDING A SPECIALIZED CLIPBOARD (WIZARD CLIPBOARD)

As usual at this point in a project, I thought I was nearly finished. Wizard seemed relatively complete to me. Then I lost some data I had copied to the Clipboard—I overwrote it with other data before I had a chance to use it. I wanted a modified Clipboard that I could access easily from Wizard (one that could simply retain all the text copied to it until I chose to reset it for new text). I also wanted it to work as simply as the regular Clipboard.

Connecting Wizard to the Wizard Clipboard by DDE seemed to be a reasonable solution. Creating a Wizard Clipboard was easy. It's only a text box and a Copy menu item that lets its contents be copied to the regular Clipboard, if necessary. Because I intended it to be a server, I set its Server property (see Chapter 9, "Extending Visual Basic: Custom Controls and DLLs") and made it into an .EXE. Here's the code for the Copy command:

```
Sub CopyCom_Click ()
     Clipboard.SetText Text1.SelText
End Sub
```

Figure 10.9 shows the Wizard Clipboard in Design mode.

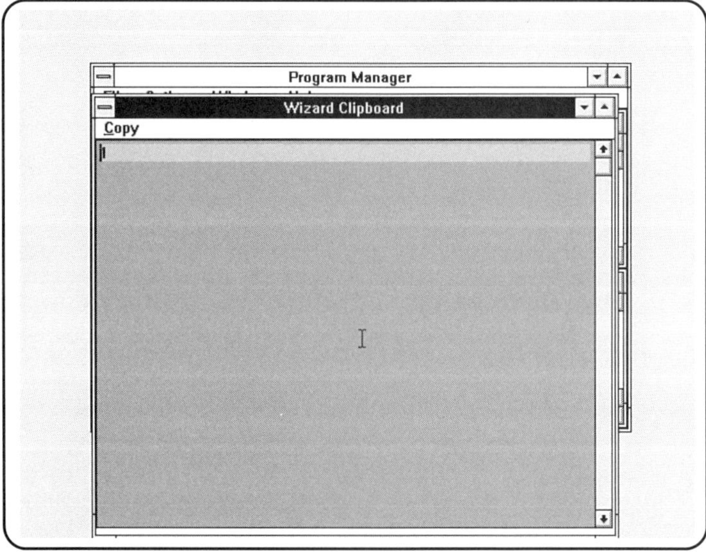

Figure 10.9. The Wizard Clipboard.

Connect Wizard to the Wizard Clipboard Using the DDE Form

Because you already have a generic DDE form (from Chapter 9), it's easy to connect a Client to a Server using that form. Then, when the user wants to copy selected text to the Wizard Clipboard, simply clicking the `CopyLink` menu item does the trick.

Note, however, that you don't want the entire `EditWindow` to be the DDE link. If it were, all the text in the window would be copied to the Server. Instead, you want only the text the user selects to be copied to the Server. You can accomplish this by adding a multiline text box to the DDE form that makes the DDE link to the Wizard Clipboard. Just copy the text the user selects to this temporary text box. Then, to get this text copied to the Server—the Wizard Clipboard—write a text change event procedure that pokes the contents of the DDE temporary text box (which maintains the DDE link, not the `EditWindow`) to the Server every time the temporary text box contents change:

```
Sub Text1_Change ()
On Error GoTo E1
     Command1_Click
     Text1.LinkPoke
     Exit Sub
E1:
     SaveErr% = Err
     GeneralErrors
     Resume Next
End Sub
```

You can also easily clear the DDE text box when the user decides to:

```
Sub ResetCom_Click ()
On Error GoTo E5
     DDE.Text1.Text = ""
     Exit Sub
E5:
     SaveErr% = Err
     GeneralErrors
     Resume Next
End Sub
```

To retain the current text in the DDE text box so you don't lose any text, which is the main reason you created this link in the first place, write the `CopyLinkCom_Click` event procedure so it adds text to the text box rather than replaces it:

```
Sub CopyLinkCom_Click ()
     On Error GoTo Errors
     DDE.Text1.Text = DDE.Text1.Text + Chr$(13) + Chr$(10) +
        ➥EditWindow.SelText
     LinkCom_Click
     Exit Sub
Errors:
     SaveErr% = Err
     GeneralErrors
     Exit Sub
End Sub
```

Finally, allow the user to manipulate the DDE form directly—to change settings with a `SettingsCom_Click` event procedure:

```
Sub SettingsCom_Click ()
On Error GoTo E6
     DDE.Show 1
     Exit Sub
E6:
     SaveErr% = Err
     GeneralErrors
     Resume Next
End Sub
```

One interesting problem I encountered while developing this DDE component of Wizard was a number of errors: channel locked, DDE-busy, and so on. These errors were created because I was trying to allow both hot and cold links to the Wizard Clipboard. Because of the way I implemented the `DDETextbox` change event procedure, however, it updates the Clipboard automatically. If there's a hot link between the Wizard Clipboard and the DDE text box, data is trying to go both ways—from the Wizard Clipboard to the DDE text box and vice versa. As far as I know, you can't have it both ways. Therefore, I made the Hot Link button on the generic DDE form invisible for this application, and effectively disabled it. By default, the DDE form now maintains a cold link, and text goes from the DDE text box to only the Wizard Clipboard.

Figures 10.10, 10.11, and 10.12 show the Wizard-to-Wizard Clipboard connection in operation.

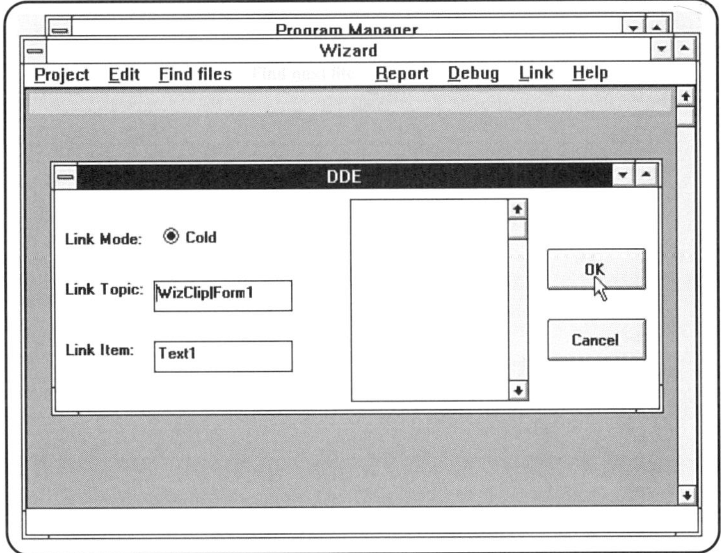

Figure 10.10. The Wizard-to-Wizard Clipboard connection: setting up the DDE connection between Wizard and the Wizard Clipboard.

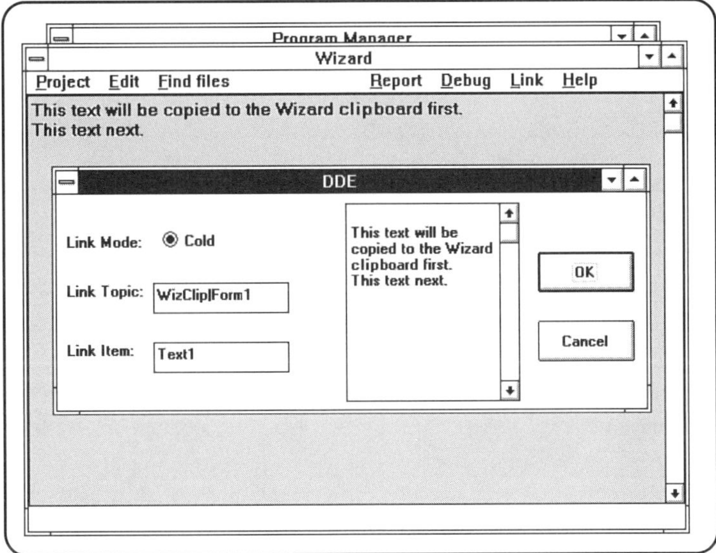

Figure 10.11. The Wizard-to-Wizard Clipboard connection: text copied from Wizard to the intermediate text box on the DDE form.

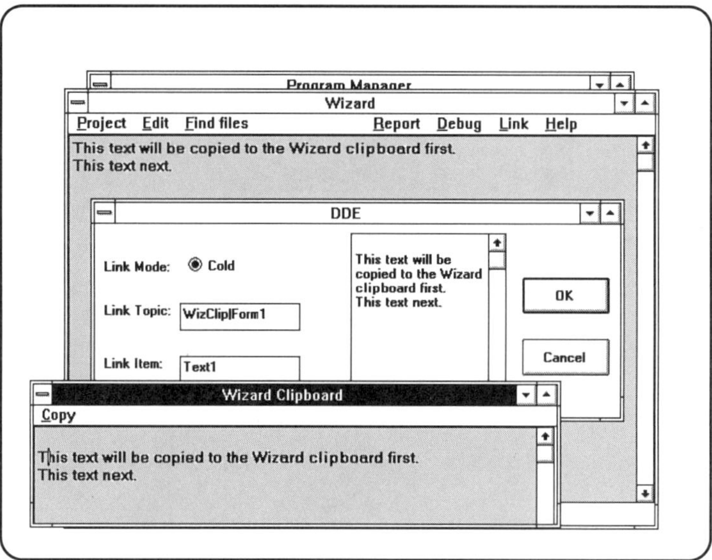

Figure 10.12. The Wizard-to-Wizard Clipboard connection: text copied from Wizard to the DDE form and on to the Wizard Clipboard. (Note that each line of copied text is saved.)

The complete Wizard, as I use it, with relatively strong error checking, is on the *Secrets* disk and in Listing 10.1. Listing 10.2 shows the Wizard Clipboard.

Listing 10.1. The complete listing of the Wizard project editor with DDE.

```
' Wizard Global declarations


' Types

Type FileRecord
     FileName As String * 30
     Position As Long
End Type


' Constants to hold project level information

Global CancelFind As Integer
Global TheFileName As String
Global TheNewPath As String
Global EditFile As String * 30
Global TempEditFile As String * 30
Global ProjectFile As String * 30
```

```
Global Cancel
Global ReplaceLoop
Global VarString$
Global Search$
Global Replace$
Global LeftPart$
Global RightPart$
Global ReplaceState%


Global SaveErr%
Global Server$

' Constants to represent the file-access modes.

Global Const SAVEFILE = 1
Global Const REPLACEFILE = 1
Global Const LOADFILE = 2
Global Const READFILE = 2
Global Const ADDTOFILE = 3
Global Const RANDOMFILE = 4
Global Const BINARYFILE = 5

' Constant for MODAL

Global Const MODAL = 1


' Constants to represent error conditions

Global Const Err_DeviceUnavailable = 68
Global Const Err_DiskNotReady = 71
Global Const Err_FileAlreadyExists = 58
Global Const Err_TooManyFiles = 67



' Revised DDE Form


Const HOT = 1
Const COLD = 2
Const NONE = 0

Sub Poke_Click ()
     Text1.LinkItem = "Text1"
     Text1.LinkPoke
End Sub

Sub Request_Click ()
     Text1.LinkRequest
```

continues

LISTING 10.1. CONTINUED

```
End Sub

Sub Text1_Change ()
On Error GoTo E1
     Command1_Click
     Text1.LinkPoke
     Exit Sub
E1:
     SaveErr% = Err
     GeneralErrors
     Resume Next
End Sub

Sub Command1_Click ()
     Server$ = "C:\VB\wizclip"
     On Error GoTo Errors

     'Clear DDE link.
     Text1.LinkMode = 0


     'Set up link with VB server.
     Text1.LinkTopic = LinkTop.Text

     'Set link to text box server
     Text1.LinkItem = LinkIt.Text

     'Determine & Establish a DDE link.

     If ColdLink.Value = -1 Then
        Text1.LinkMode = 2

     Else
        Text1.LinkMode = 1

     End If

     If SaveErr% = 282 Then

        ' If error we'll be here next."
        'Clear DDE link. And try to reestablish link.
        Text1.LinkMode = 0


        'Set up link with VB server.
        Text1.LinkTopic = LinkTop.Text
```

```
        'Set link to text box server
        Text1.LinkItem = LinkIt.Text
        'ReEstablish a DDE link.

        If ColdLink.Value = -1 Then
        Text1.LinkMode = 2

     Else
        Text1.LinkMode = 1
     End If
     End If
        Hide

     Exit Sub

Errors:
     SaveErr% = Err
     GeneralErrors
     Resume Next


End Sub

Sub Command2_Click ()
     Hide
End Sub


' Findform


Sub Command1_Click ()
     Search$ = Text1.Text
     Hide
End Sub

Sub Command2_Click ()
     Unload FindForm
     Cancel = -1
End Sub

Sub Form_Load ()
     Text1.Text = Search$
End Sub



' Replaceform
```

continues

LISTING 10.1. CONTINUED

```
Sub Command1_Click ()
     Search$ = Text1.Text
     Replace$ = Text2.Text
     Hide
     Cancel = 0
End Sub

Sub Command2_Click ()
     Hide
     Cancel = -1
End Sub

Sub Form_Load ()
     Text1.Text = Search$
     Text2.Text = Replace$
End Sub


' Report form


Sub Command1_Click ()
     Do While Report.List1.ListCount
       Report.List1.RemoveItem 0
     Loop
     Do While Report.List2.ListCount
       Report.List2.RemoveItem 0
     Loop

End Sub

Sub Command2_Click ()
  Hide
End Sub


' Wizard Main form


Dim Current%
Dim Found%
Dim MaxI%
Dim MenuNum%
Dim EditFlag%
Dim ReplaceState%
Dim Length&
Dim FileRec As FileRecord
Dim SetBox%
Dim FromScan%
```

```
Declare Function GetFocus% Lib "user" ()
Declare Function SendMessage& Lib "user" (ByVal hWnd%, ByVal wMsg%,
➥ ByVal wParam%, lp As Any)

Const WM_USER = &H400
Const EM_LIMITTEXT = WM_USER + 21
Const EM_UNDO = WM_USER + 23


' Exit

Sub ExitCom_Click ()
     CloseCom_Click
     End
End Sub


' Copy to clipboard

Sub CopyCom_Click ()
     Clipboard.SetText EditWindow.SelText
End Sub


' Search routine

Sub Srch (I As Integer)
      SetTextBox
      FindNextCom.Enabled = 0
      TheFileName = FileWiz.File1.List(I)
      EditFile = TheNewPath + TheFileName

      If EditFile <> "" Then
         Wizard.Caption = "Searching: " + EditFile
         OpenMode% = BINARYFILE 'LOADFILE
         FileNum% = OpenAFile(EditFile, OpenMode%, 0)
      End If

      If FileNum% = 0 Then
         FileInfo.Caption = "Open Failed."
         FindNextCom.Enabled = 0
         Exit Sub
      End If

      Length = LOF(FileNum%)

      If Length < 60000 And Length > 1 Then
         VarString$ = String$(Length, " ")
         Get FileNum%, , VarString$
         Close FileNum%
```

continues

LISTING 10.1. CONTINUED

```
         A& = InStr(VarString$, Search$)
         If A& > 0 Then
             EditWindow.Text = VarString$
             If EditWindow.Text = "" Then
                FileInfo.Caption = " Problem loading file."
                VarString$ = String$(1, " ")
                Exit Sub
             End If
             Found% = -1
             Report.List2.AddItem Str$(A&)
             Report.List1.AddItem EditFile
             Wizard.Caption = Search$ +
                 ➥" found at character position: " +
                 ➥Str$(A&) + " in " + EditFile
             FirstTwo$ = Left$(VarString$, 2)
             Number2$ = Right$(FirstTwo$, 1)
             One% = Asc(FirstTwo$)
             Two% = Asc(Number2$)
             GetFileType One%, Two%

             EditWindow.SelStart = A& - 1
             EditWindow.SelLength = Len(Search$)

             VarString$ = String$(1, " ")
        Else
             FileInfo.Caption = "String not found."
        End If
      Else
         FileInfo.Caption = "File out of range."
         Wizard.Caption = " No file."
      End If
End Sub



' Report

Sub ReportCom_Click ()
On Error GoTo E3
     Report.Show MODAL
     Exit Sub
E3:
     SaveErr% = Err
     GeneralErrors
     Resume Next
End Sub
```

```
' Form load

Sub Form_Load ()
     MenuNum% = 0
     EditEnable (-1)
     EditFlag% = 0
     FromScan% = 0
End Sub



'Files

Sub Files_Click (Index As Integer)
     SaveDialog
     EditFile = Files(Index).Caption
     ReadFile
End Sub


' Edit Enable routine

Sub EditEnable (Index As Integer)
     If Index = -1 Then
        SaveFileCom.Enabled = -1
        SaveFileAsCom.Enabled = -1
        CutCom.Enabled = -1
        PasteCom.Enabled = -1
        ReplaceCom.Enabled = -1
        UndoCom.Enabled = -1
     Else
        SaveFileCom.Enabled = 0
        SaveFileAsCom.Enabled = 0
        CutCom.Enabled = 0
        PasteCom.Enabled = 0
        ReplaceCom.Enabled = 0
        UndoCom.Enabled = 0
     End If
End Sub


' Close

Sub CloseCom_Click ()
     SaveDialog
     EditFlag% = 0
     EditWindow.Text = ""
     Wizard.Caption = ""
     EditFile = ""
End Sub
```

continues

Listing 10.1. continued

```
' Resize form

Sub Form_Resize ()
     If WindowState <> 1 Then
        If ScaleHeight - 600 > 1 Then
           EditWindow.Height = ScaleHeight - 300
        End If
        If ScaleWidth < 6000 Then
           EditWindow.Width = 6000
        ElseIf ScaleWidth - 200 > 1 Then
           EditWindow.Width = ScaleWidth
        End If
     End If
     FileInfo.Top = EditWindow.Height
End Sub


' Find files


Sub FindNextCurrentCom_Click ()
     Search$ = FindForm.Text1.Text
     RLength& = Len(EditWindow.Text) - (EditWindow.SelStart + 1)
     LLength& = Len(EditWindow.Text) - RLength&
     Rest$ = Right$(EditWindow.Text, RLength&)
     Position& = InStr(Rest$, Search$)
     If Position& > 0 Then
        EditWindow.SelStart = LLength& + Position& - 1
        EditWindow.SelLength = Len(Search$)
     Else
        FileInfo.Caption = "String not found."
     End If

End Sub


Sub FindNextCom_Click ()
     Find
End Sub

Sub FindFilesCom_Click ()
     Report.Command1.Value = -1
     CancelFind = 0
     Current% = 0
     FindNextCom.Enabled = 0
     FileWiz.Show MODAL
     If CancelFind = -1 Then
         Exit Sub
```

```
        End If
        MaxI = FileWiz.File1.ListCount
        FindNextCom.Enabled = -1
        For I% = Current% To MaxI
            Found% = 0
            Srch (I%)
            If Found% = -1 Then
                Current% = I% + 1
                FindNextCom.Enabled = -1
                Exit Sub
            End If
        Next I%
End Sub


' Find match in files

Sub Find ()
        For I% = Current% To MaxI
            Found% = 0
            EditWindow.Text = ""
            Srch (I%)
            If Found% = -1 Then
                Current% = I% + 1
                FindNextCom.Enabled = -1
                Exit Sub
            End If
        Next I%
End Sub


' Cut to clipboard

Sub CutCom_Click ()
        Clipboard.SetText EditWindow.SelText
        EditWindow.SelText = ""
End Sub



' Project procedures

Sub OpenProjectCom_Click ()
        Dim App$
        While MenuNum% > 0
            Unload Files(MenuNum%)
            MenuNum% = MenuNum% - 1
        Wend
```

continues

LISTING 10.1. CONTINUED

```
    On Error Resume Next
    CMDialog1.Filter = "Project files(*.prj)¦*.prj"
    CMDialog1.FilterIndex = 1
    CMDialog1.CancelError = -1
    CMDialog1.Action = 1

    If Err = 32755 Then
       SaveErr% = Err
       GeneralErrors
       Exit Sub
    End If
    If Err = 0 Then
       ProjectFile = CMDialog1.FileName
    End If

    If ProjectFile <> "" Then
       OpenMode% = LOADFILE
       FileNum% = OpenAFile(ProjectFile, OpenMode%, 0)
    End If

    If FileNum% = 0 Then
       FileInfo.Caption = "Open Failed."
       Exit Sub
    End If

    FileInfo.Caption = "Opening project."
       While Not EOF(FileNum%)
          Input #FileNum%, App$
          MenuNum% = MenuNum% + 1
          Load Files(MenuNum%)
          Files(MenuNum%).Caption = App$
          Files(MenuNum%).Visible = -1
       Wend
       Close FileNum%

End Sub


Sub AddFileCom_Click ()
Dim TempEditFile As String * 30
On Error Resume Next
      CMDialog1.Filter = "All files(*.*)¦*.*¦Text files(*.txt)¦*.txt"
      CMDialog1.FilterIndex = 2
      CMDialog1.CancelError = -1
      CMDialog1.Action = 1
      TempEditFile = CMDialog1.FileName
      If Err = 32755 Then Exit Sub
      If Err = 0 Then
         SaveDialog
```

```
          EditFile = TempEditFile
          ReadFile
          MenuNum% = MenuNum% + 1
          Load Files(MenuNum%)
          Files(MenuNum%).Caption = EditFile
          Files(MenuNum%).Visible = -1
        End If
End Sub



Sub RemoveFileCom_Click ()
  Msg$ = "Enter the number of the menu item to remove. 25 to remove all."
  Num% = Val(InputBox$(Msg$, "Remove Files From Project", Str$(25)))
  If Num% = 25 Then
      While MenuNum% > 0
        Unload Files(MenuNum%)
        MenuNum% = MenuNum% - 1
      Wend
  Exit Sub

  If Num% > MenuNum% Then
        MsgBox "Number is out of range."
        Exit Sub
  End If
  End If
  For I% = Num% To MenuNum% - 1
      Files(I%).Caption = Files(I% + 1).Caption
  Next I%
  Unload Files(MenuNum%)
  MenuNum% = MenuNum% - 1


End Sub



Sub SaveProjectCom_Click ()
  On Error Resume Next
  CMDialog1.Filter = "Project files(*.prj)¦*.prj"
  CMDialog1.FilterIndex = 1
  CMDialog1.FileName = ProjectFile
  CMDialog1.DefaultExt = "PRJ"
  CMDialog1.CancelError = -1
  CMDialog1.Action = 2
  If Err = 32755 Then Exit Sub
  If Err = 0 Then
         ProjectFile = CMDialog1.FileName
  End If
```

continues

LISTING 10.1. CONTINUED

```
  If ProjectFile <> "" Then
          OpenMode% = REPLACEFILE
          FileNum% = OpenAFile(ProjectFile, OpenMode%, 0)
  End If

  If FileNum% = 0 Then
         FileInfo.Caption = "Open Failed."
         Exit Sub
  End If
  FileInfo.Caption = "Saving project."
  For I% = 1 To MenuNum%
         Print #FileNum%, Files(I%).Caption
  Next I%
  Close FileNum%
End Sub



' Paste to clipboard

Sub PasteCom_Click ()
  EditWindow.SelText = Clipboard.GetText()
End Sub



' Print

Sub PrintFileCom_Click ()
On Error GoTo PrintError
  Printer.Print EditWindow.Text
  Exit Sub
PrintError:
  SaveErr% = Err
  GeneralErrors
  Resume Next
End Sub



' Save file

Sub SaveFileAsCom_Click ()
  On Error Resume Next
  CMDialog1.FileName = EditFile
  CMDialog1.CancelError = -1
  CMDialog1.Action = 2
  If Err = 0 Then
```

```
            EditFile = CMDialog1.FileName
            EditFlag% = -1
            SaveFileCom_Click
    Else If Err = 32755 Then Exit Sub
    End If
End Sub


Sub SaveFileCom_Click ()
On Error GoTo SaveError
    If EditFlag% = 0 Then
            SaveFileAsCom_Click
    End If
    If EditFile <> "" Then
          Wizard.Caption = EditFile
          OpenMode% = BINARYFILE
          FileNum% = OpenAFile(EditFile, OpenMode%, 0)
    End If

          If FileNum% = 0 Then
              FileInfo.Caption = "Open Failed."
              FindNextCom.Enabled = 0
              Exit Sub
          End If

          Length = Len(EditWindow.Text)
          FileInfo.Caption = "Saving " + Str$(Length) + " bytes."
          SaveStr$ = EditWindow.Text
          Put #FileNum%, , SaveStr$
          Close (FileNum%)

          RecLength% = Len(FileRec)
          OpenMode% = RandomFILE

          FileNum% = OpenAFile("wizard.pos", OpenMode%, Len(FileRec))
          For Index% = 1 To LOF(FileNum%) \ RecLength%
             Get #(FileNum%), Index%, FileRec
             If FileRec.FileName = EditFile Then
                  FileRec.FileName = EditFile
                  FileRec.Position = EditWindow.SelStart
                  Put #(FileNum%), Index%, FileRec
                  Close FileNum%
                  Exit Sub
             End If
           Next Index%
           FileRec.FileName = EditFile
           FileRec.Position = EditWindow.SelStart
           Index% = Index% + 1
           Put #(FileNum%), Index%, FileRec
           Close FileNum%
           Exit Sub
```

continues

LISTING 10.1. CONTINUED

```
SaveError:
       SaveErr% = Err
       GeneralErrors
       Resume Next

End Sub



Sub SaveDialog ()
      If SaveFileCom.Enabled = -1 Then
         If EditWindow.Text <> "" Then
             Msg$ = "Save the text in the EditWindow?"
             Response% = MsgBox(Msg$, 4)
             If Response% = 6 Then
                SaveFileCom_Click
             End If
         End If
       End If
End Sub



' Read a file subroutine


Sub ReadFile ()
      SetTextBox
      If EditFile <> "" Then
         Wizard.Caption = EditFile
         OpenMode% = BINARYFILE
         FileNum% = OpenAFile(EditFile, OpenMode%, 0)
      End If

      If FileNum% = 0 Then
         FileInfo.Caption = "Open Failed."
         FindNextCom.Enabled = 0
         Exit Sub
      End If

      Length = LOF(FileNum%)

      If Length < 60000 And Length > 1 Then
         VarString$ = String$(Length, " ")
         Get FileNum%, , VarString$
         Close FileNum%
         EditWindow.Text = ""
         EditWindow.Text = VarString$
         If EditWindow.Text = "" Then
```

```
            FileInfo.Caption = "Problem loading file."
            VarString$ = String$(1, " ")
            Exit Sub
        End If
        FirstTwo$ = Left$(VarString$, 2)
        Number2$ = Right$(FirstTwo$, 1)
        One% = Asc(FirstTwo$)
        Two% = Asc(Number2$)
        VarString$ = String$(1, " ")
        GetFileType One%, Two%
        RecLength% = Len(FileRec)
        OpenMode% = RandomFILE
        FileNum% = OpenAFile("wizard.pos", OpenMode%, Len(FileRec))
        For Index% = 1 To LOF(FileNum%) \ RecLength%
            Get #(FileNum%), Index%, FileRec
            If FileRec.FileName = EditFile Then
               FilePos& = FileRec.Position
               EditWindow.SelStart = FilePos&
               EditWindow.SelLength = 2
               Close FileNum%
               Exit Sub
            End If
        Next Index%
        Close FileNum%
      Else
            FileInfo.Caption = "File size out of range."
            Wizard.Caption = "No file."
      End If
End Sub



' Set Text Limit to 60K

Sub SetTextBox ()
  If SetBox% = 0 Then
      EditWindow.Text = ""
      EditWindow.SetFocus
      cbhWnd% = GetFocus()
      TextLimit% = &HFAAA
      RetVal = SendMessage(cbhWnd%, EM_LIMITTEXT, TextLimit%, 0)
      SetBox% = -1
  End If
End Sub


' Determine file type

Sub GetFileType (One As Integer, Two As Integer)
  Select Case One%
            Case 77
```

continues

LISTING 10.1. CONTINUED

```
        If Two% = 90 Then FileInfo.Caption = ".EXE, .DLL, .VBX, .DRV"
      Case 233
        FileInfo.Caption = ".COM"
      Case 35
        If Two% = 204 Then FileInfo.Caption = "Visual Basic.FRM"
      Case 190
        If Two% = 186 Then FileInfo.Caption = "Visual Basic.MAK"
      Case 63
        If Two% = 95 Then FileInfo.Caption = ".HLP"
      Case 255
        If Two% = 255 Then FileInfo.Caption = ".SYS"
      Case 66
        If Two% = 77 Then FileInfo.Caption = ".BMP"
      Case 0
        If Two% = 0 Then FileInfo.Caption = ".ICO"
      Case 155
        If Two% = 165 Then FileInfo.Caption = "Word for Windows 1.1"
      Case 219
        If Two% = 165 Then FileInfo.Caption = ".Word for Windows 2.0"
      Case 9
        If Two% = 2 Then FileInfo.Caption = "Excel (or related) data"
      Case 80
        If Two% = 77 Then FileInfo.Caption = "Windows .GRP"
      Case Else
        FileInfo.Caption =
          ➥"Probably a text file. Edit capability enabled."
        EditEnable (-1)
        Exit Sub
    End Select
    EditEnable (0)
End Sub


' Implement Further Help here.


Sub HelpCom_Click ()
  FileInfo.Caption = "Help hasn't been implemented yet."
End Sub



' Undo


Sub UndoCom_Click ()
  EditWindow.SetFocus
  cbhWnd% = GetFocus()
  RetVal = SendMessage(cbhWnd%, EM_UNDO, 0, 0)
End Sub
```

```
' Find

Sub FindCurrentCom_Click ()
        FindForm.Show MODAL
        If Cancel <> -1 Then
            Position& = InStr(EditWindow.Text, Search$)
            If Position& > 0 Then
               EditWindow.SelStart = Position& - 1
               EditWindow.SelLength = Len(Search$)
            End If
        End If
End Sub




' Replace


Sub ReplaceCom_Click ()
  ReplaceState% = -1
  Length = Len(EditWindow.Text)
  If Length > 32767 Then
      Msg$ = " Can't do replace on > 32767. File is " + Str$(Length) + " bytes."
      FileInfo.Caption = Msg$
      Exit Sub
  End If
  VarString$ = String$(Length, " ")
  VarString$ = EditWindow.Text
  Replacef.Show MODAL
  If Search$ = Replace$ Then Exit Sub
  If Cancel <> -1 Then
      DoReplace
  End If
  Unload Replacef
End Sub



Sub DoReplace ()
  Dim LeftPart$
     Start& = Wizard.EditWindow.SelStart
     RLength& = Len(VarString$) - (Wizard.EditWindow.SelStart)
     LLength& = Len(VarString$) - RLength&
     If RLength& > 0 Then
```

continues

LISTING 10.1. CONTINUED

```
        PreRest$ = Left$(VarString$, LLength&)
        OpenMode% = BINARYFILE
        FileNum% = OpenAFile("~temp.wiz", OpenMode%, 0)
        Put FileNum%, , PreRest$
        P& = Len(PreRest$)
        PreRest$ = String$(1, " ")
        VarString$ = Right$(VarString$, RLength&)
    Else
        ReplaceState% = 0
        Exit Sub
    End If

    SLength& = Len(Search$)

    Position& = 99
    ReplaceState% = -1
    While Position& <> 0 And ReplaceState% <> 0
      If Replacef.Option1.Value = -1 Then
          ReplaceState% = 0
      End If
      Position& = InStr(VarString$, Search$)
      If Position& > 0 Then
          RLength& = Len(VarString$)
          LeftPart$ = Left$(VarString$, Position& - 1)
          Rightlength& = RLength& - (Position& + SLength&)

          VarString$ = Right$(VarString$, Rightlength& + 1)
          Wanted$ = Left$(VarString$, SLength&)
          Wanted$ = Replace$
          VarString$ = LeftPart$ + Wanted$ + VarString$
      End If
    Wend
    LeftPart$ = String$(1, " ")
    RightPart$ = String$(1, " ")
    PreRest$ = String$(P&, " ")
    Get FileNum%, , PreRest$
    Close FileNum%

    Wizard.EditWindow.Text = PreRest$ + VarString$
    Wizard.EditWindow.SelStart = Start&
    VarString$ = String$(1, " ")
    Wizard.FileInfo.Caption = "String not found."

End Sub



' Scan / Macro Procedures
```

```
Sub LoadFileCom_Click ()
      If FromScan% = 0 Then
         On Error Resume Next
         CMDialog1.Filter = "All files(*.*)¦*.*¦Text files(*.txt)¦
            ➥*.txt¦Basic files(*.bas)¦*.bas"
         CMDialog1.FilterIndex = 3
         CMDialog1.CancelError = -1
         CMDialog1.Action = 1
         TempEditFile = CMDialog1.FileName
         If Err = 32755 Then Exit Sub
         If Err = 0 Then
              SaveDialog
              EditFile = TempEditFile
              ReadFile
         End If
      Else
         FromScan% = 0
         EditFile = "~1temp.bas"
         ReadFile
      End If
End Sub


Sub MacroCom_Click ()
On Error GoTo E2
  x = Shell("\win31\recorder.exe", 1)
E2:
  SaveErr% = Err
  GeneralErrors
  Resume Next
End Sub

Sub ScanCom_Click ()
      On Error Resume Next
      CMDialog1.Filter = "All files(*.*)¦*.*¦Text files(*.txt)¦
         ➥*.txt¦Basic files(*.bas)¦*.bas"
      CMDialog1.FilterIndex = 3
      CMDialog1.CancelError = -1
      CMDialog1.Action = 1
      TempEditFile = CMDialog1.FileName
      If Err = 32755 Then Exit Sub
      If Err = 0 Then
         SaveDialog
         EditFile = TempEditFile
      End If
      If EditFile <> "" Then
         Wizard.Caption = EditFile
         OpenMode% = LOADFILE
         FileNum% = OpenAFile(EditFile, OpenMode%, 0)
      End If
```

continues

LISTING 10.1. CONTINUED

```
      If FileNum% = 0 Then
         FileInfo.Caption = "Open Failed."
         FindNextCom.Enabled = 0
         Exit Sub
      End If

      Length = LOF(FileNum%)

      If Length < 60000 And Length > 1 Then
         OpenMode% = REPLACEFILE
         FileNum2% = OpenAFile("~1temp.bas", OpenMode%, 0)

         Do Until EOF(FileNum%)
            Line Input #FileNum%, NextLine$
            GPos% = InStr(NextLine$, "Global")
            DPos% = InStr(NextLine$, "Dim")
            GCPos% = InStr(NextLine$, "Global Const")
            If (GPos% > 0 And GCPos% = 0) Or DPos% > 0 Then
               NextLine$ = NextLine$ + Chr$(13) + Chr$(10) +
                  ➥Chr$(13) + Chr$(10)
               Print #FileNum2%, NextLine$
            End If
         Loop
         Close FileNum2%
         Close FileNum%
  End If
         FromScan% = -1
         LoadFileCom_Click
End Sub



' DDE, Link procedures


Sub LinkCom_Click ()

End Sub

Sub SettingsCom_Click ()
On Error GoTo E6
  DDE.Show 1
  Exit Sub
E6:
  SaveErr% = Err
  GeneralErrors
```

```
  Resume Next
End Sub

Sub ResetCom_Click ()
On Error GoTo E5
  DDE.Text1.Text = ""
  Exit Sub
E5:
  SaveErr% = Err
  GeneralErrors
  Resume Next
End Sub

Sub CopyLinkCom_Click ()
  On Error GoTo Errors
  DDE.Text1.Text = DDE.Text1.Text + Chr$(13) + Chr$(10) + EditWindow.SelText
  LinkCom_Click
  Exit Sub
Errors:
  SaveErr% = Err
  GeneralErrors
  Exit Sub

End Sub



' Revised WizFile form

Sub Drive1_Change ()
  Dir1.Path = Drive1.Drive
End Sub

Sub Dir1_Change ()
  File1.Path = Dir1.Path
End Sub

Sub Dir1_Click ()
  'LastChange = DIRSBOXCLICK
  ' Dir1_Change
End Sub

Sub File1_DblClick ()
  Command1_Click
End Sub

Sub Command1_Click ()
  TheNewPath = Dir1.Path
  If Right$(TheNewPath, 1) <> "\" Then
     TheNewPath = TheNewPath + "\"
  End If
```

continues

LISTING 10.1. CONTINUED

```
  TheFileName = File1.FileName
  Search$ = Text2.TExt
  FileWiz.Hide
End Sub

Sub Command2_Click ()
  FileWiz.Hide
  CancelFind = -1
End Sub

Sub Text1_Change ()
  File1.Pattern = Text1.TExt
End Sub

Sub Form_Load ()
  File1.Pattern = Text1.TExt
End Sub



' Files 2 module



Function OpenAFile (NameToUse$, Mode%, RecordLen%) As Integer
  FileNum% = FreeFile
  On Error GoTo OpenFileError

  Select Case Mode
     Case LOADFILE
       Open NameToUse For Input As FileNum%
     Case REPLACEFILE
       Open NameToUse For Output As FileNum%

     Case RANDOMFILE
       Open NameToUse For Random As FileNum% Len = RecordLen%
     Case BINARYFILE
       Open NameToUse For Binary As FileNum%
     Case Else
       Exit Function
  End Select
  OpenAFile = FileNum%
  Exit Function

OpenFileError:
  Action% = ErrorHandler(Err)
  Select Case Action%
     Case 0
       Resume
     Case Else
```

```
      OpenAFile = 0       'Open failed
      Exit Function
     End Select
End Function

Function ErrorHandler (errVal As Integer) As Integer
  Msg$ = Error$(errVal)

  Response% = MsgBox(Msg$, 2, "Potentially fatal Error!")
  Select Case Response%
     Case 1, 4    ' OK, Retry buttons
       ErrorHandler = 0
     Case 5       ' Ignore buttons
       ErrorHandler = 1
     Case 2, 3    ' Cancel, abort buttons
       ErrorHandler = 2
     Case Else
       ErrorHandler = 3
  End Select
End Function



' Errors Module



Sub GeneralErrors ()
  Msg$ = Error$(SaveErr%)
  MsgBox Msg$
  Select Case SaveErr%
     Case 280 To 297
       DDEErrors
  End Select
End Sub

Sub DDEErrors ()
     Select Case SaveErr%

        Case 282
          App% = Shell(Server$, 1)
          App% = DoEvents()
        Case 283
          Msg$ = "Suggest you open Program Manager "
          Msg$ = Msg$ + " NOW and use End Task "
          Msg$ = Msg$ + " to terminate the LAST "
          Msg$ = Msg$ + " INSTANCE of " + Server$
          MsgBox Msg$

    End Select
End Sub
```

LISTING 10.2. WIZCLIP.

```
Sub CopyCom_Click ()
    Clipboard.SetText Text1.SelText
End Sub
```

SUMMARY

That about wraps up Wizard and the Wizard Clipboard. This (temporarily) final version of Wizard demonstrates a number of development techniques, but in addition provides a useful tool that should make your Visual Basic projects easier to develop.

I suggest that you experiment with Wizard and the Wizard Clipboard and find your own ways to improve and optimize them. I'm still trying to improve them, so get in touch with me if you have any ideas or faster code.

Into the Heart of OLE (Object Linking and Embedding)

Although OLE (Object Linking and Embedding) was included in earlier versions of Visual Basic, it becomes especially powerful and easy-to-use in OLE 2.0 (the version of OLE shipped with Visual Basic Version 3.0).

This chapter begins with an introduction to OLE and the OLE custom control, steps through procedural details you need to know to establish and maintain OLE connections, and concludes by developing two OLE applications, OLE2a and OLE2b.

OLE2a is an introductory application that demonstrates fundamental OLE techniques:

- Creating OLE objects
- Using the OLE Insert Object dialog

- Embedding new (or empty) objects and objects from files
- Linking objects

OLE2b demonstrates a more complex and more powerful approach to creating OLE objects using MDI (Multi-Document Interface). Use OLE2b as the basis for your more sophisticated OLE applications. Because error handling is critical with OLE, OLE2b contains some important error handling capability.

The routines in this chapter illustrate the main components of OLE that you use every time you add an OLE control to a Visual Basic application.

The OLE 2.0 custom control is called the "OLE client control" in OLE 1.0.

The OLE2b application, an OLE Object Editor, enables you to do the following:

- Use the OLE Insert Object dialog box to get a list of any OLE object applications in the Windows system and create OLE objects.

In OLE 1.0, Visual Basic programmers had to write code to get a list of OLE object applications. These object applications registered their OLE objects with Windows. In OLE 2.0, this task is much easier because you use the Insert Object dialog box to get the OLE registered objects for your Windows system and to create the OLE object.

- Edit the objects in the application that created them
- Cut, copy, and paste objects to and from the Clipboard
- Load and save objects from and to disk using binary file I/O
- Delete objects
- Interact with applications such as Object Packager, Word for Windows, and Microsoft Excel
- Maintain OLE objects dynamically using `New` to create new forms that contain OLE objects
- Use MDI to build a container for child OLE forms

The disk in the back of this book contains three OLE example applications. Two of these were written with OLE 1.0 and are described in the first edition of *Secrets of the Visual Basic Masters*. I won't discuss them in this chapter, because this edition is aimed primarily at Visual Basic 3.0 programmers, and OLE 2.0 ships with Visual Basic 3.0.

However, if you're still using OLE 1.0, the Object Editor applications on the disk will be useful. For the majority of you, Visual Basic programmers, who have moved on to OLE 2.0, I'll describe the OLE2b (Object Editor) application in this chapter (it's also on the disk).

Also, when appropriate, I'll discuss how OLE 1.0 and 2.0 differ. References to the term *OLE* in general will always refer to OLE 2.0 and usually to OLE 1.0.

OLE, THE BASICS

You use OLE (object linking and embedding) in much the same way as you use DDE, but with some important differences. OLE lets you create applications that display data as they appear in other applications. In addition, OLE lets the user edit that data from within the application they used to create the data.

With DDE, your applications exchange data with other applications, but control never switches (at least automatically) to the linked application. OLE goes a step further; it does the following:

- Enables the user to edit data with the application that created the data.
- Enables the user to view data in a foreign application, that is, in an application that did not create the data.

When your applications are using DDE, they exchange data with other applications by way of links. With OLE, the applications don't necessarily exchange data, at least in the DDE sense. Instead, you continue to use the application that created the data to edit and manipulate the data.

When you finish editing, if the OLE object is embedded, use that application (the object application) to update the object in your Visual Basic OLE control. If the OLE object is linked, use the object application to maintain the edited data.

Your Visual Basic application is responsible for maintaining the data if the object is embedded in the Visual Basic OLE control. If the object is linked, the object is maintained by the object application (the one that created it and continues to manipulate it).

Because this explanation might sound confusing, this chapter continues to clarify with text and examples. OLE 2.0 is indeed a major breakthrough—making OLE an easy-to-use and powerful tool for connecting applications and data.

In short, the Visual Basic OLE custom control that ships with Visual Basic provides a nifty interface to this technology. Use the OLE custom control to "connect" to other applications and to maintain the object.

The object (that is, the OLE object), that this chapter discusses refers to an item or chunk of data referenced (or maintained) by the OLE custom control. This object can be a single spreadsheet cell, a range of cells, an entire spreadsheet, a drawing, a Microsoft Word document, and so on.

Similar to the DDE applications you create in Visual Basic, an OLE application requires a *Client* (the OLE 1.0 term) or *Container application* (the OLE 2.0 term) and a *Server* (the OLE 1.0 term) or *Object application* (the OLE 2.0 term). From now on, this chapter uses the the OLE 2.0 terms without the corresponding OLE 1.0 equivalent.

The Container application creates the OLE object, receives and displays the Object application's data (the object), or asks the Object aplication to maintain or display the data.

LINKED AND EMBEDDED OBJECTS

You can create an OLE application by linking or by embedding data from the Container application into an object (maintained by the OLE custom control). These two approaches to OLE differ primarily in where the data are stored during the OLE connection.

When you link an object, the data associated with the linked object are stored and maintained in the application that created the data. Only a placeholder for the data, not the data itself, is stored in the OLE custom control.

When you embed an object, the data associated with the embedded object are stored in an OLE custom control and can be saved to a file, cut or copied to the Clipboard, and edited (by way of the Container application).

An important distinction between linked and embedded objects is the way in which applications other than your Visual Basic Container application have access to the data.

When you link an object to your Visual Basic Container application, the linked object's data can be accessed by any application that maintains a link to that data. Consequently, the linked object's data can be modified by any of these applications.

For example, a Microsoft Excel spreadsheet file (Microsoft Excel = the Object application) linked to both your Visual Basic Container application and to another Container application (not necessarily a Visual Basic application) could be modified by the other application as well as by Microsoft Excel. The modified version of the spreadsheet then appears in any documents (or Container applications) that have links to the spreadsheet.

Linking, therefore, is an important technique if you are supporting real-time links between applications, or if you're using several applications to modify data, yet want the results to show up automatically in several applications.

In contrast, embedding is useful when you want your application to have exclusive control over the embedded object's data; Visual Basic lets you edit the data (by way of the Container application).

When you use an OLE custom control to create an embedded object, all the data associated with the object are maintained in the OLE Container application. For example, if a range of Excel spreadsheet cells is embedded in your Visual Basic Container application, all the data associated with the cells are maintained in the OLE custom control.

Because the data are maintained in the OLE custom control, not in the Container application, applications maintaining links to the Container application do not automatically have access to the data in the embedded object. Your Visual Basic application has exclusive control over the data.

If you want your application to have exclusive control over an object's data, therefore, embed the object in the Container application. If you don't want your application to have complete control over an object's data, link the object with the Container application. If you embed the object, the Container application is responsible for saving the object's data because the data must be maintained in the OLE custom control. If you link the object, the Class application (or application that created the data) is responsible for saving the data.

How to Create Objects With the OLE Custom Control At Design Time

In OLE 2.0, linking or embedding an object's data in a Visual Basic application is much easier than in OLE 1.0. You can either create OLE objects at design time or runtime.

To create an OLE object (either at design time or runtime), begin by adding the OLE custom control file (MSOLE2.VBX) to your project:

1. Select Add File from the File menu.
2. Select the file (MSOLE2.VBX) from the ensuing dialog.

After Visual Basic loads the OLE custom control into the project, use the Visual Basic Toolbox to add an OLE control to the main form of the application. Note that it won't look like much on the form. It's there to establish the link and to hold data; the Object application it connects to will do most of the work.

The OLE 2.0 custom control has 44 properties, 5 methods, and 14 event procedures. It's one complex custom control. Table 11.1 shows these properties, methods, and events.

Table 11.1. OLE custom control properties.

	Action
AppIsRunning	Drag Mode
AutoActivate	FileNumber
AutoVerbMenu	Format
BackColor	Height
BorderStyle	HelpContextID
Class	HostName
Data	hWnd
DataText	Index
DisplayType	Left
DragIcon	lpOleObject

Name	PasteOK
Object	Picture
ObjectAcceptFormats	SizeMode
ObjectAcceptFormatCounts	SourceDoc
ObjectGetFormats	SourceItem
ObjectGetFormatsCount	Tag
ObjectVerbFlags	Top
ObjectVerbs	UpdateOptions
ObjectVerbsCount	Verb
OleType	Visible
OleTypeAllowed	Width
Parent	

Events

Click	KeyUp
DblClick	LostFocus
DragDrop	MouseDown
DragOver	MouseMove
GotFocus	MouseUp
KeyDown	Resize
KeyPress	Updated

Methods

Drag
Move
Refresh
SetFocus
ZOrder

You set properties, use methods, and respond to events to accomplish tasks with the OLE custom control.

Much of what you do with an OLE custom control consists of changing the `Class`, `OleTypeAllowed`, `SourceDoc`, and `SourceItem` properties, and then setting the `Action` property for the task you want to accomplish.

About the Action Property

The `Action` property handles most of the fundamental OLE custom control operations for you.

In OLE 2.0, `Action` can have any of 18 settings (OLE 1.0 allowed 12 settings), and each of these settings determines how the object in the OLE custom control is created, manipulated, and maintained. `Action` isn't available at design time and is write-only at runtime. Table 11.2 briefly notes these settings, which you will use throughout this chapter.

Table 11.2. Values of the Action property.

Value	*Description*
0	CreateEmbed (insert an embedded object in the OLE custom control)
1	CreateLink (insert a linked object into the OLE custom control)
2	Reserved setting (not used by Visual Basic)
3	Reserved setting (not used by Visual Basic)
4	Copy an object to the Clipboard
5	Paste an object from the Clipboard
6	Update data from the Object application
7	Activate an object (for editing, for example)
8	Reserved
9	Close an OLE object
10	Delete the object from the OLE custom control

11	SaveToFile (save the object to a file using binary I/O)
12	ReadFromFile (read an object using binary I/O)
13	Reserved
14	InsertObjDialog (display the Insert Object dialog)
15	PasteSpecialDlg (display the Paste Special dialog)
16	Reserved
17	Fetch Verbs (get or update the list of verbs an object supports)
18	Save an object in OLE1 format.

These settings are translated into "English" constants in a CONSTANT file included with Visual Basic 3.0. For convenience, I maintain all the OLE2 constants for a project in a module (called OLE2CONS.TXT). This module, listed within the complete listings for the OLE2a and OLE2b projects, Listings 11.1 and 11.2, later in this chapter, is included in the code on the disk.

About the Class, OleTypeAllowed, SourceDoc, and SourceItem Properties

Before you can set the `Action` property to request an OLE task, you must set any properties needed by the OLE control to carry out the task. In particular, you need to know how to use the `Action`, `Class`, `OleType`, `OleTypeAllowed`, `SourceDoc`, and `SourceItem` properties.

Briefly, a `Class` indicates the application that creates an object for a Container application and the type of data an object contains. Some applications can support more than one type of data. For example, Microsoft Excel can support spreadsheets, charts, and macrosheets.

Fortunately, you don't have to memorize every type (also called *class name*) that an object application (such as Microsoft Excel) supports.

When you create an object at design time using the Insert Object or Paste Special dialogs, the class of the new object is automatically entered in the Properties window.

To view a list of class names available on your system, select the `Class` property in the Properties window and click the three dots (...) in the Settings box (see Figure 11.1).

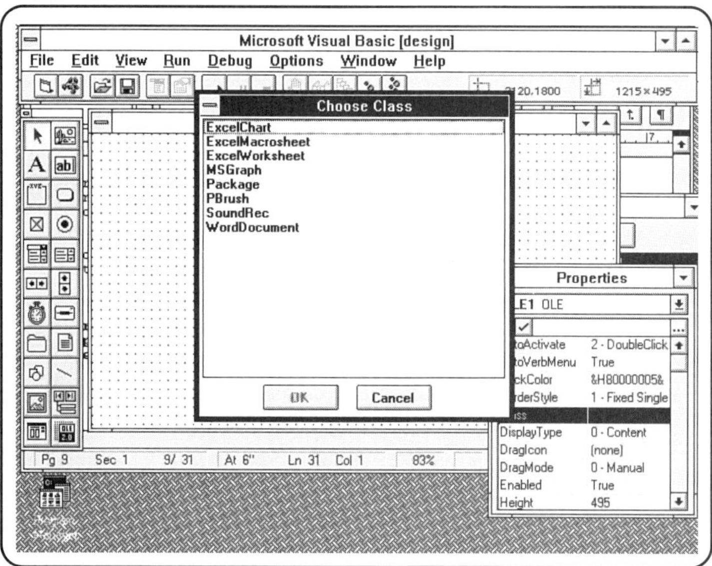

Figure 11.1. In Design view, to obtain the class names for any particular Object application, highlight the Class property in the Properties window and click the three dots (...) in the settings box.

Visual Basic updates the OLE Control's `Class` property whenever the type of object in the OLE control changes. For example, the `Class` property is updated when you copy an object into an OLE control from the Clipboard.

For example, if you paste a Microsoft Excel chart from the Clipboard to an OLE object that previously contained a Microsoft Excel worksheet, the `Class` property changes from "ExcelWorksheet" to "ExcelChart." Interacting with the Clipboard is straight-forward: Use the `Action` property. You can paste an object from the Clipboard by setting Action to 5 (Paste) or Action to 15 (Paste Special Dialog).

OLETYPE AND OLETYPEALLOWED PROPERTIES

The OLE control's `OLEType` property indicates the status of the object in an OLE control.

The `OleType` property settings are listed in Table 11.3.

Table 11.3. `OleType` property settings.

Setting	*Description*
0	Linked. The OLE control contains a linked object. All the object's data is maintained by the application that created it. When you save the object (by setting Action to 11 or Action to Save To File), only link information such as the values of the SourceDoc and SourceItem properties is saved in the save file.
1	Embedded. The OLE control contains an embedded object. All the OLE object's data is maintained by the Visual Basic application. When you save the object (by setting Action to 11 or Action to Save To File), all data associated with the object are saved in the save file.
3	No object. The OLE control doesn't contain an object.

Use the `OLEType` property to determine 1) if the OLE control contains an object or 2) the type of object the OLE control contains.

The OLE control's `OLETypeAllowed` property indicates the type of object an OLE control can contain.

The `OleTypeAllowed` property settings are listed in Table 11.4.

Table 11.4. `OleTypeAllowed` property settings.

Setting	*Description*
0	Linked. The OLE control can contain a linked object.
1	Embedded. The OLE control can contain an embedded object.
2	(default) The OLE control can contain either an embedded or linked object.

ABOUT THE SOURCEDOC AND SOURCEITEM PROPERTIES

Use the `SourceDoc` property to indicate the file name to use for creating an embedded or linked OLE object.

Use the `SourceItem` property to indicate an item or range of data within a file when linking an object.

When you create an embedded object (set Action to 0 or Action to OLE Create Embed), and the `SourceDoc` property is set to a valid file name, Visual Basic creates an embedded object using the specified file as a template.

When you create a linked object (by setting Action to 1 or Action to OLE Create Link), Visual Basic concatenates the `SourceItem` property to the `SourceDoc` property.

Note that you must set the `OleTypeAllowed` property to 0 (Linked) or to 2 (Either) when you set the `SourceItem` property. Either (2) is the default.

Each object application (Microsoft Excel, Word for Windows, etc.) has its own syntax to describe units of data. To set this property, specify a unit of data recognized by the object application. For example, when you link to Microsoft Excel, indicate the `SourceItem` using a cell or cell-range reference such as "R1C1" or "R4C6:R8C15," or a designated range such as "Expenses."

Usually, to determine the syntax for describing a unit (a cell or character) of data for an object, consult the manuals for the Object application (the application that created the object).

However, you might be able to determine the syntax for the object by creating a linked object at design time using the Paste Special command (click the OLE control with the right mouse button). After creating the object, select the `SourceDoc` property for the OLE control in the Properties window; then view the `SourceDoc` string in the Settings box.

For most objects, the `SourceDoc` string is a path to a linked file, followed by an exclamation point (`!`), or a backslash (`\`) and the syntax for the linked data.

In OLE Verion 1.0, you had to write code to show the user a list of the class types in the registration database at runtime. In OLE 2.0, OLE dialogs do most of the work for you.

Anytime (whether at design time or runtime), you want to insert (create) an OLE object, you can use the Insert Object dialog box.

At design time, when you create a new OLE object (by placing an OLE control on a form), Visual Basic automatically displays the Insert Object dialog box (see Figure 11.2).

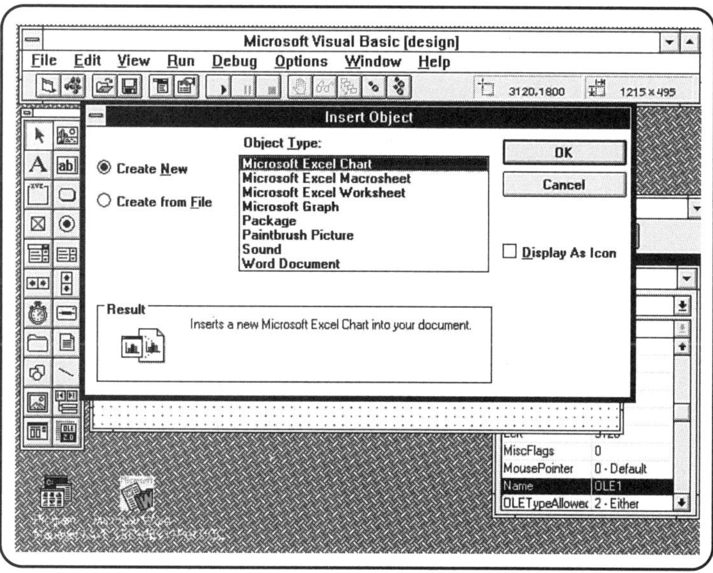

Figure 11.2. At design time, when you create a new OLE object (by placing an OLE control on a form), Visual Basic automatically displays the Insert Object dialog box.

When you select an object to create from the Insert Object Dialog box, Visual Basic automatically sets the appropriate properties for the OLE custom control (see Figure 11.3).

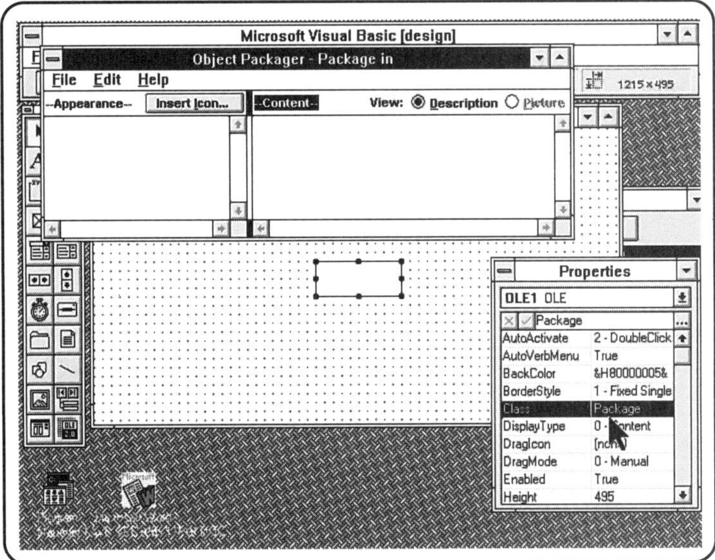

Figure 11.3. When you select an object to create from the Insert Object Dialog box, Visual Basic automatically sets the appropriate properties for the OLE custom control.

At runtime, to insert an embedded object in an OLE custom control, set the object type (the Class property), invoke the OLE `CREATE_EMBED` action, and then activate the newly created object:

```
Sub SomeSub()
     ' Set class.
     Ole1.Class = "ExcelWorksheet"

     ' Create an embedded object
     Ole1.Action = OLE_CREATE_EMBED

     ' Activate object.
     Ole1.Action = OLE_ACTIVATE
End Sub
```

At runtime, to insert an embedded object in an OLE custom control from a file, set the object type (the Class property), specify the source file, and then invoke the OLE `CREATE_EMBED` action:

```
Sub SomeSub2 ()
     ' Specify class.
     Ole1.Class = "ExcelWorksheet"

     ' Specify source file.
```

```
    Ole1.SourceDoc = "C:\EXCEL\RMBL\rmbl1.XLS"

    ' Create an embedded object using rmbl1.xls.
    Ole1.Action = OLE_CREATE_EMBED
End Sub
```

At runtime, to link an object with the OLE custom control, set the object type (the Class property), specify the source file, optionally, set the SourceItem property, and then invoke the OLE `CREATE_LINK` action:

To link an object into an OLE custom control:

```
Sub SomeSub3 ()
    ' Specify class.
    Ole1.Class = "ExcelWorksheet"

    ' Specify source file.
    Ole1.SourceDoc = "C:\EXCEL\RMBL\rmbl1.XLS"

    ' Optionally, specify the data within the file to be linked.
    Ole1.SourceItem = "R1C1:R5C5"

    ' Create a linked object using rmbl1.xls.
    Ole1.Action = OLE_CREATE_LINK
End Sub
```

Verbs

A verb indicates an operation or task that an Object application can perform. Most Object applications support a default verb, usually the `edit` verb, which is at position 0 in the verb count (the verb count can be obtained with the `ObjectVerbsCount` property). `Play` and `Activate Contents` are examples of other verbs.

In OLE 1.0, you had to write code to obtain a list of verbs for display. In OLE 2.0, you can automatically display the verbs for an object at runtime by setting the `AutoVerbMenu` property for the OLE control to True. When this property is True, the user can click the right mouse button (while on the object), and a popup menu of verbs is displayed.

OLE2a, Embedding and Linking Objects

The first OLE application in this chapter, OLE2a, uses one form and several menu choices to allow a user to do the following with one OLE control:

- Embed a new object
- Embed an object from a file
- Link an object

OLE2a uses a one-OLE-control-to-many-potential-objects approach, one that works, but as you'll soon see, is limited. OLE2b solves these limitations.

Begin the OLE2a application by opening a new project. Use the File/Add menu item to add the MSOLE2.VBX to the project. Then use the Toolbox to add an OLE control to the form (see Figure 11.4).

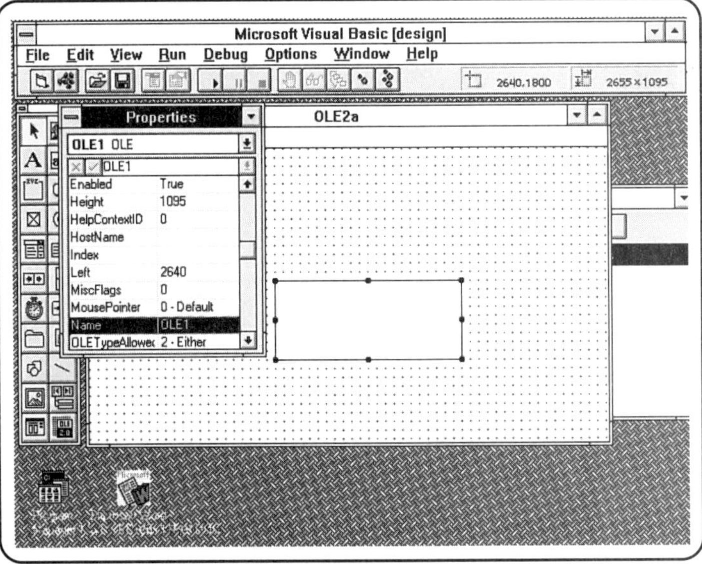

Figure 11.4. Use the File/Add menu item to add the MSOLE2.VBX to the project. Then use the Toolbox to add an OLE control to the form.

Next, use the menu design window to add menu items for embedding and linking objects (see Figure 11.5).

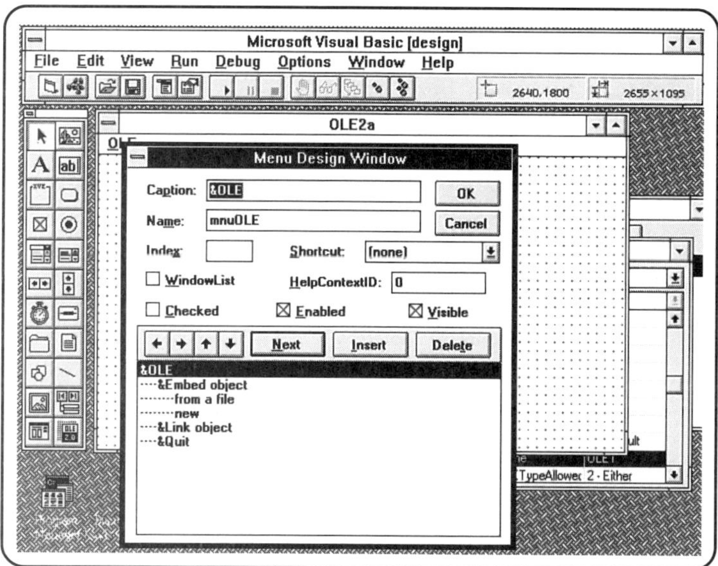

Figure 11.5. Next, use the menu design window to add menu items for embedding and linking objects.

Then write code (as follows) for each menu click event procedure.

To insert an embedded object in an OLE custom control at runtime, write the following code:

```
Sub mnuEmbedNew_Click ()
    ' Set class.
    Ole1.Class = "ExcelWorksheet"
    ' Create an embedded object using rmbl1.xls
    Ole1.Action = OLE_CREATE_EMBED
    ' Activate object.
    Ole1.Action = OLE_ACTIVATE
End Sub
```

To insert an embedded object from a file at runtime, write the following code:

```
Sub mnuEmbedFromfile_Click ()
    ' Specify class.
    Ole1.Class = "ExcelWorksheet"
    ' Specify source file.
    Ole1.SourceDoc = "C:\EXCEL\RMBL\rmbl1.XLS"
    ' Create an embedded object using rmbl1.xls.
    Ole1.Action = OLE_CREATE_EMBED
End Sub
```

To link an object at runtime, write the following code:

```
Sub mnuLink_Click ()
    ' Specify class.
    Ole1.Class = "ExcelWorksheet"
    ' Specify source file.
    Ole1.SourceDoc = "C:\EXCEL\RMBL\rmbl1.XLS"
    ' Specify the data within the file to be linked.
    Ole1.SourceItem = "R1C1:R5C5"
    ' Create a linked object using rmbl1.xls.
    Ole1.Action = OLE_CREATE_LINK
End Sub
```

Listing 11.1 contains the complete code for OLE2a.

LISTING 11.1. OLE2A.

```
'OLE2CONS.TXT

' Constants and error IDs for OLE 2.0 Client Control

' Actions

Global Const OLE_CREATE_EMBED = 0
Global Const OLE_CREATE_NEW = 0              ' ole1 control
Global Const OLE_CREATE_LINK = 1
Global Const OLE_CREATE_FROM_FILE = 1        ' ole1 control
Global Const OLE_COPY = 4
Global Const OLE_PASTE = 5
Global Const OLE_UPDATE = 6
Global Const OLE_ACTIVATE = 7
Global Const OLE_CLOSE = 9
Global Const OLE_DELETE = 10
Global Const OLE_SAVE_TO_FILE = 11
Global Const OLE_READ_FROM_FILE = 12
Global Const OLE_INSERT_OBJ_DLG = 14
Global Const OLE_PASTE_SPECIAL_DLG = 15
Global Const OLE_FETCH_VERBS = 17
Global Const OLE_SAVE_TO_OLE1FILE = 18

' OLEType

Global Const OLE_LINKED = 0
Global Const OLE_EMBEDDED = 1
Global Const OLE_NONE = 3

' OLETypeAllowed

Global Const OLE_EITHER = 2
```

```
' UpdateOptions

Global Const OLE_AUTOMATIC = 0
Global Const OLE_FROZEN = 1
Global Const OLE_MANUAL = 2

' AutoActivate modes

Global Const OLE_ACTIVATE_MANUAL = 0
Global Const OLE_ACTIVATE_GETFOCUS = 1
Global Const OLE_ACTIVATE_DOUBLECLICK = 2

' SizeModes

Global Const OLE_SIZE_CLIP = 0
Global Const OLE_SIZE_STRETCH = 1
Global Const OLE_SIZE_AUTOSIZE = 2

' DisplayTypes

Global Const OLE_DISPLAY_CONTENT = 0
Global Const OLE_DISPLAY_ICON = 1

' Update Event Constants

Global Const OLE_CHANGED = 0
Global Const OLE_SAVED = 1
Global Const OLE_CLOSED = 2
Global Const OLE_RENAMED = 3

' Special Verb Values

Global Const VERB_PRIMARY = 0
Global Const VERB_SHOW = -1
Global Const VERB_OPEN = -2
Global Const VERB_HIDE = -3

' VerbFlag Bit Masks

Global Const VERBFLAG_GRAYED = &H1
Global Const VERBFLAG_DISABLED = &H2
Global Const VERBFLAG_CHECKED = &H8
Global Const VERBFLAG_SEPARATOR = &H800

' OLE Client Error IDs
'This first set are carried over from OLE 1.0 control

Global Const OLEERR_OutOfMem = 31001
Global Const OLEERR_CantOpenClipboard = 31003
Global Const OLEERR_NoObject = 31004
Global Const OLEERR_CantClose = 31006
```

continues

LISTING 11.1. CONTINUED

```
Global Const OLEERR_CantPaste = 31007
Global Const OLEERR_InvProp = 31008
Global Const OLEERR_CantCopy = 31009
Global Const OLEERR_InvFormat = 31017
Global Const OLEERR_NoClass = 31018
Global Const OLEERR_NoSourceDoc = 31019

' InvAction is our first new error for the OLE2.0 control
Global Const OLEERR_InvAction = 31021
Global Const OLEERR_OleInitFailed = 31022
Global Const OLEERR_InvClass = 31023
Global Const OLEERR_CantLink = 31024
Global Const OLEERR_SourceTooLong = 31026
Global Const OLEERR_CantActivate = 31027
Global Const OLEERR_NotRunning = 31028
Global Const OLEERR_DialogBusy = 31029
Global Const OLEERR_InvalidSource = 31031
Global Const OLEERR_CantEmbed = 31032
Global Const OLEERR_CantFetchLinkSrc = 31033
Global Const OLEERR_InvalidVerb = 31034
Global Const OLEERR_NoCompatClipFmt = 31035
Global Const OLEERR_ErrorSavingFile = 31036
Global Const OLEERR_ErrorLoadingFile = 31037
Global Const OLEERR_BadVBVersion = 31038
Global Const OLEERR_CantAccessSource = 31039

' Arrange Method
' for MDI Forms

Global Const CASCADE = 0
Global Const TILE_HORIZONTAL = 1
Global Const TILE_VERTICAL = 2
Global Const ARRANGE_ICONS = 3

Global Const VerbMax = 10


' OLE2a.frm

Sub mnuEmbedFromfile_Click ()
    ' Specify class.
    Ole1.Class = "ExcelWorksheet"
    ' Specify source file.
    Ole1.SourceDoc = "C:\EXCEL\RMBL\rmbl1.XLS"
    ' Create an embedded object using rmbl1.xls.
    Ole1.Action = OLE_CREATE_EMBED
End Sub

Sub mnuEmbedNew_Click ()
```

```
    ' Set class.
    Ole1.Class = "ExcelWorksheet"
    ' Create an embedded object using rmbl1.xls
    Ole1.Action = OLE_CREATE_EMBED
    ' Activate object.
    Ole1.Action = OLE_ACTIVATE
End Sub

Sub mnuLink_Click ()
    ' Specify class.
    Ole1.Class = "ExcelWorksheet"
    ' Specify source file.
    Ole1.SourceDoc = "C:\EXCEL\RMBL\rmbl1.XLS"
    ' Specify the data within the file to be linked.
    Ole1.SourceItem = "R1C1:R5C5"
    ' Create a linked object using rmbl1.xls.
    Ole1.Action = OLE_CREATE_LINK
End Sub
```

Run this code and insert (or link) an object. Figure 11.6 shows a successful link to Microsoft Excel.

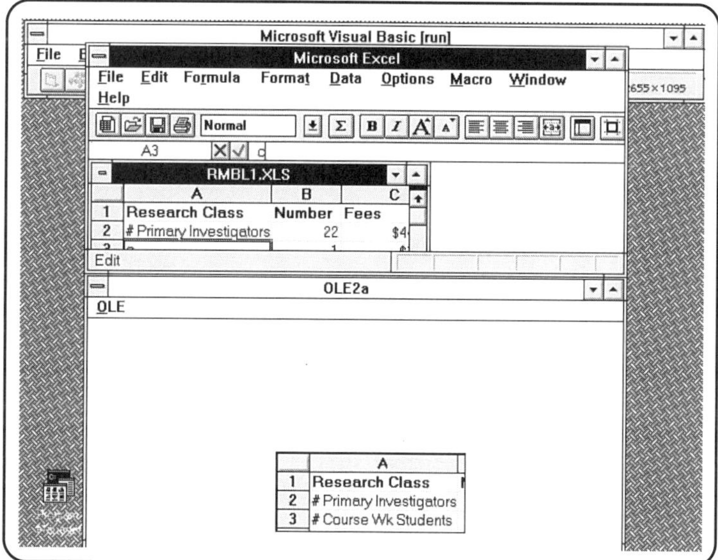

Figure 11.6. A successful OLE2a link to Microsoft Excel.

Next, link or embed a second (and third) object. Then double-click the OLE control (double-clicking an OLE control switches control to the object). Control switches to Microsoft Excel, *to the last object you created.* In other words, each time you create a new object in a control, it *replaces* the last object.

Although this behavior might be the kind you want in an application, it's limiting. A more flexible system might allow an application to maintain several objects at once, allowing a user to switch among these objects. OLE2b takes this approach.

OLE2B—OLE AND MDI

The approach you take in the next OLE example emphasizes the one-OLE control-per-form technique. OLE2b uses an OLE form that contains one OLE control. This form is the child form in the MDI application.

If you're unfamiliar with MDI (Multiple-Document Interface), see Chapter 13 for an introduction to MDI techniques. This chapter will use the MDI techniques discussed in that chapter.

CREATE AN MDI FORM

Begin the OLE2b project by creating two forms, an MDI and a Child (OLE) form.

To create an MDI form, select New MDI Form from the File menu. An MDI form (note the form Caption) appears in the project (see Figure 11.7).

An application can have only one MDI form but can have many MDI child forms. Although you design MDI child forms independently of the MDI form, MDI child forms always appear (contained) within the MDI form at runtime.

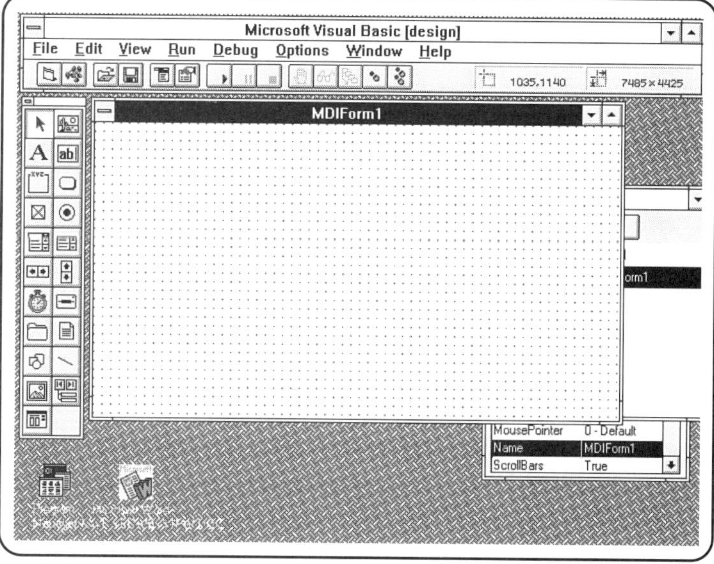

Figure 11.7. Use New MDI Form to create an MDI Form.

Create a menu bar (called Files) for the MDI form with New, Open, and Exit menu items. These commands will do the following:

- Create a new object
- Open an existing object
- Exit the application

CREATE AN EDITOR CHILD FORM

Before developing any code, create the child form type. Use the Files/New form menu command to create the form. Call this form, "frmOLE." Then change its MDI child property to True to indicate that the form will appear as an MDI child form inside an MDI form.

The child form will continue to be displayed as a separate form at design time, but at run time, it will appear inside an MDI form. Note that an MDI child form can be maximized, minimized, and moved, all inside the parent MDI form.

At runtime, the Windows environment controls the initial size and placement of MDI child forms unless you manually place the child in the `Form_Load` procedure. The following `Form_Load` event procedure for the child form invokes the `OLE_INSERT_OBJ_DIALOG` to let the user indicate the type of OLE object wanted, and places the new child form within the MDI container form:

```
Sub Form_Load ()
     On Error Resume Next

     Ole1.Move 0, 0

     ' Only display Insert Object dialog if File New was selected.
     If MDINew Then
         Ole1.Action = OLE_INSERT_OBJ_DLG
     Else
         Ole1.Height = Me.Height
         Ole1.Width = Me.Width
     End If
     Ole1.HostName = "OLE2b"
End Sub
```

Next, create the child form's menu. Add File, Edit, and Window menu items to the horizontal menu bar. Add New, SaveAs, Open, and Exit items to the File menu. Add Object, Cut, Copy, Paste, Paste Special, and Update items to the Edit menu. Add Cascade, Tile, and Arrange Icons items to the Window menu. Make sure to check WindowList when you create the Window menu to enable a display of open child forms (or child windows). See Figure 11.8.

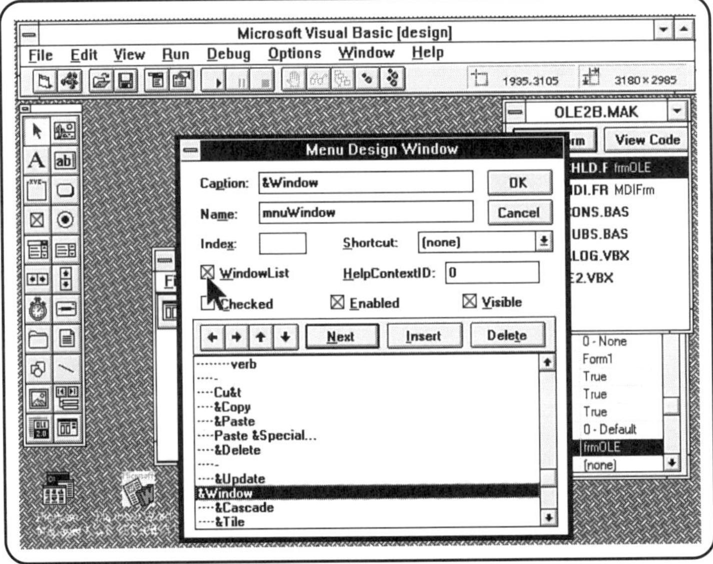

Figure 11.8. Check WindowList during Menu Design to enable a display of open child forms.

Finally, add a common dialog box (which you'll use to open and save objects) and an OLE control (to contain the object). Figure 11.9 shows the child form during design view.

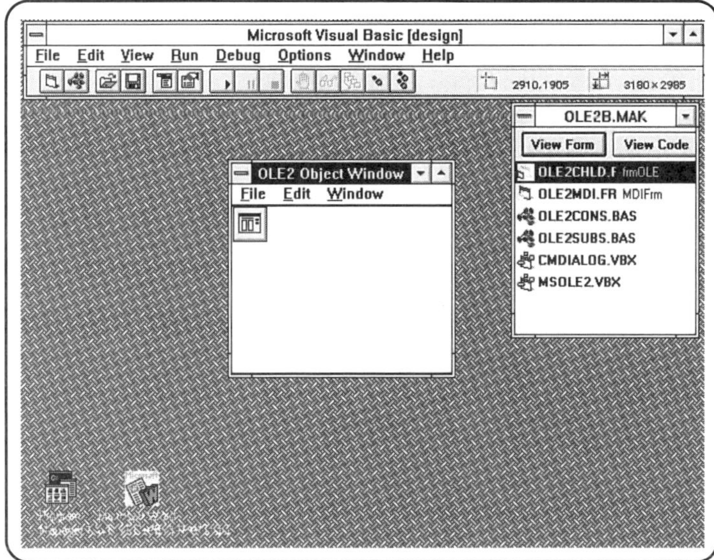

Figure 11.9. The child form during design view.

Create Objects

To create a new OLE object, create a new instance of the child form that contains the OLE control. (For a discussion of creating instances of forms with New, see Chapter 13, "Objects, Instances, and MDI.")

```
Sub CreateOLE ()
    Dim Newform As New frmOLE
    Newform.Show
    UpdateCaption
End Sub
```

Then, insert a new object into the OLE control by creating a new form (by invoking the `CreateOLE()` `Sub` procedure) and then use the `OLEType` property to make sure the object was created properly:

```
Sub InsertObject ()
    MDINew = True
```

```
     CreateOLE
     If MDIfrm.ActiveForm.Ole1.OLEType <> OLE_NONE Then
          MDIfrm.ActiveForm.Ole1.Action = OLE_ACTIVATE
     Else
          Unload MDIfrm.ActiveForm
     End If
End Sub
```

To handle File I/O, use the Open and Save dialogs in the common dialog. The following OpenSave() Sub procedure handles both opening and saving files, depending on whether it's invoked in Open or Save mode. Note that the error-handling routine, FileErr1, tries to identify anticipated errors. If the error is an anticipated one, it notifies the user of the error, and resumes gracefully:

```
Sub OpenSave (Action As String)
     Dim Filenum
     Filenum = FreeFile

     ' Set common dialog options.
     MDIfrm.ActiveForm.CMDialog1.Filter = "OLE 2.0 Objects¦*.OLE"
     MDIfrm.ActiveForm.CMDialog1.FilterIndex = 1
     MDIfrm.ActiveForm.Ole1.FileNumber = Filenum

     On Error GoTo FileErr1
     Select Case Action
     Case "Save"
          ' Display Save As dialog.
          MDIfrm.ActiveForm.CMDialog1.Action = 2
          ' Open and save the file.
          Open MDIfrm.ActiveForm.CMDialog1.Filename For Binary As Filenum
             MDIfrm.ActiveForm.Ole1.Action = OLE_SAVE_TO_FILE
     Case "Open"
          ' Display File Open dialog.
          MDIfrm.ActiveForm.CMDialog1.Action = 1
          ' Open the file.
          Open MDIfrm.ActiveForm.CMDialog1.Filename For Binary As Filenum
          ' Display hourglass.
          Screen.MousePointer = 11
          MDIfrm.ActiveForm.Ole1.Action = OLE_READ_FROM_FILE

     ' Set form properties now that OLE control contains an object.
        UpdateCaption
     ' Restore mouse pointer.
        Screen.MousePointer = 0
     End Select
     Close Filenum
     Exit Sub
FileErr1:
     If Err = 30015 Then
          Unload MDIfrm.ActiveForm
     End If
```

```
    If Err = 32755 Then 'User pressed cancel.
        Exit Sub
    Else
        MsgBox (Error)
    End If
    Screen.MousePointer = 0
    Exit Sub
End Sub
```

To open a new OLE object, set the MDI to invoke the `CreateOLE()` procedure to create a new instance of the child form and the `OpenSave() Sub` procedure in Open mode to open a file specified by a user in the File Open dialog:

```
Sub OpenObject ()
    MDINew = False
    CreateOLE
    OpenSave ("Open")
    If MDIfrm.ActiveForm.Ole1.OLEType = OLE_NONE Then
        Unload MDIfrm.ActiveForm
    End If
End Sub
```

To save an object, invoke the `OpenSave() Sub` procedure in Save mode:

```
Sub mnuSave_Click ()
    OpenSave ("Save")
End Sub
```

MDI Update and Edit Routines

The UpdateCaption Sub procedure sets the `Caption` property of the Active MDI form and loads the verbs menu. If there's an error getting the object's verbs, it doesn't show the verb menu:

```
Sub UpdateCaption ()
    Dim Verb
    ' Set Form properties now that it contains an object.
    MDIfrm.ActiveForm.Caption = MDIfrm.ActiveForm.Ole1.Class + " Object"
    MDIfrm.ActiveForm.mnuObject.Caption = MDIfrm.ActiveForm.Ole1.Class + " " +
    ➥ MDIfrm.ActiveForm.mnuObject.Caption

    On Error Resume Next
    For Verb = 1 To VerbMax
        Load MDIfrm.ActiveForm.mnuVerbs(Verb)
        If Err = 360 Then ' Object already loaded.
                Unload MDIfrm.ActiveForm.mnuVerbs(Verb)
                Load MDIfrm.ActiveForm.mnuVerbs(Verb)
                Err = 0
        End If
    Next Verb
    MDIfrm.ActiveForm.mnuVerbs(0).Visible = False
End Sub
```

To edit an object (when the user clicks the Edit menu item):

- Verify that there's an OLE object in the OLE control
- Use the OLE Action property = OLE FETCH VERBS to get the object's verbs
- Show the verb menu (allowing the user to select one of the verbs from a menu)
- If appropriate, enable the Paste and Paste Special menu items.

```
Sub mnuEdit_Click ()
     Dim Verb
     Dim LargestCurrentVerb As Integer
     On Error Goto EditError
     Ole1.Action = OLE_FETCH_VERBS
     LargestCurrentVerb = Ole1.ObjectVerbsCount - 1

     If MDIfrm.ActiveForm.Ole1.OLEType <> OLE_NONE Then
          For Verb = 1 To LargestCurrentVerb
                    mnuVerbs(Verb).Caption = Ole1.ObjectVerbs(Verb)
                    mnuVerbs(Verb).Visible = True
               Next Verb

          For Verb = LargestCurrentVerb + 1 To VerbMax
                    mnuVerbs(Verb).Visible = False
          Next Verb
     End If

     If MDIfrm.ActiveForm.Ole1.PasteOK Then
          MDIfrm.ActiveForm.mnuPaste.Enabled = True
          MDIfrm.ActiveForm.mnuSpecial.Enabled = True
     Else
          MDIfrm.ActiveForm.mnuPaste.Enabled = False
          MDIfrm.ActiveForm.mnuSpecial.Enabled = False
     End If
     Exit Sub
EditError:
     MsgBox (Error)
End Sub
```

MDI WINDOW MANAGEMENT

Use the MDI Arrange method to allow the user to arrange MDI children (see Chapter 13, "Objects, Instances, and MDI," for more details):

```
Sub mnuArrange_Click ()
     MDIfrm.Arrange ARRANGE_ICONS
End Sub

Sub mnuCascade_Click ()
     MDIfrm.Arrange CASCADE
End Sub

Sub mnuTile_Click ()
    MDIfrm.Arrange TILE_HORIZONTAL
End Sub
```

CLIPBOARD ROUTINES

To paste the contents of the CLipboard into an existing object, set the MDI flag to False, use the OLE PASTE action to automatically paste the object into the object, and update the caption:

```
Sub mnuPaste_Click ()
     If Ole1.PasteOK Then
          MDINew = False
          ' Display new form.
          ' Paste Clipboard contents.
          Ole1.Action = OLE_PASTE
          ' Set form properties.
          UpdateCaption
     Else
          MsgBox "Can't Paste"
     End If
End Sub
```

To invoke the PasteSpecial dialog and to allow a user to embed or link the contents of the Clipboard into the object, do the following:

```
Sub mnuSpecial_Click ()
     If Ole1.PasteOK Then
          MDINew = False
          Ole1.Action = OLE_PASTE_SPECIAL_DLG
          Screen.MousePointer = 11
          UpdateCaption
          Screen.MousePointer = 0
     End If
End Sub
```

To cut an object from the OLE control to the Clipboard, first copy the object to the Clipboard; then delete it:

```
Sub mnuCut_Click ()
     mnuCopy_Click   ' Copy object to the clipboard.
     mnuDelete_Click ' Delete object and unload the form.
End Sub
```

Use the OLE Action property (OLE Delete) to delete the object:

```
Sub mnuDelete_Click ()
     If Ole1.OLEType <> OLE_NONE Then  ' If OLE control contains a valid object.
          Ole1.Action = OLE_DELETE      ' Delete the object,
                                        ' then unload the form.
     End If
     Unload Me
End Sub
```

To copy an object to the Clipboard, make sure the OLE control contains an object; check to see if the Object application is active (if not, activate it); then use the Action property = OLE COPY to do the copy:

```
Sub mnuCopy_Click ()
     If Ole1.OLEType <> OLE_NONE Then  ' If the control contains a valid object.
          ' Display hourglass
          Screen.MousePointer = 11
          If Ole1.AppIsRunning Then
                   Ole1.Action = OLE_COPY          ' Copy object to
                                                   ' the Clipboard.
          Else
                   ' Set Verb to hidden
                   Ole1.Verb = VERB_HIDE
                   Ole1.Action = OLE_ACTIVATE
                   Ole1.Action = OLE_COPY          ' Copy object to
                                                   ' the Clipboard.
                   ' Set verb back to default.
                   Ole1.Verb = VERB_PRIMARY
          End If
          ' Restore mouse cursor.
          Screen.MousePointer = 0
     End If
End Sub
```

Listing 11.2 shows the complete application, including a few other self-explanatory procedures. Figure 11.10 shows OLE2b in operation.

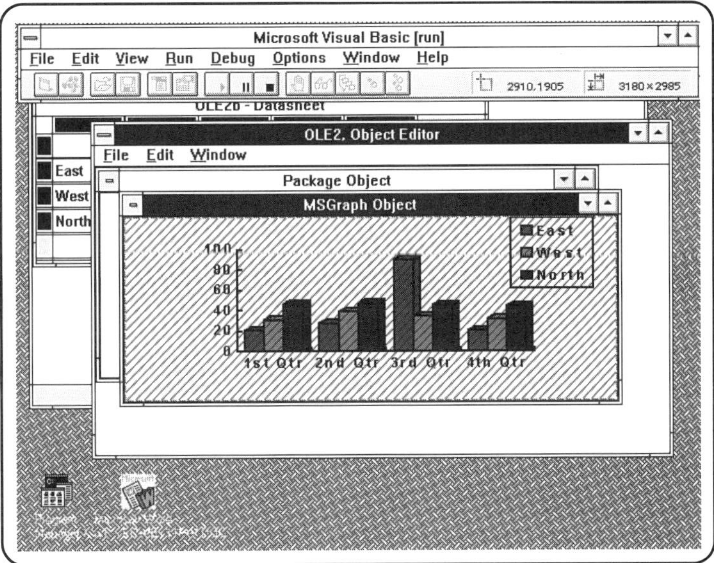

Figure 11.10. OLE2b in operation.

Listing 11.2. OLE2b.

```
'OLE2CONS.TXT

' Constants and error IDs for OLE 2.0 Client Control

' Actions

Global Const OLE_CREATE_EMBED = 0
Global Const OLE_CREATE_NEW = 0              ' ole1 control
Global Const OLE_CREATE_LINK = 1
Global Const OLE_CREATE_FROM_FILE = 1       ' ole1 control
Global Const OLE_COPY = 4
Global Const OLE_PASTE = 5
Global Const OLE_UPDATE = 6
Global Const OLE_ACTIVATE = 7
Global Const OLE_CLOSE = 9
Global Const OLE_DELETE = 10
Global Const OLE_SAVE_TO_FILE = 11
Global Const OLE_READ_FROM_FILE = 12
Global Const OLE_INSERT_OBJ_DLG = 14
Global Const OLE_PASTE_SPECIAL_DLG = 15
```

continues

Listing 11.2. continued

```
Global Const OLE_FETCH_VERBS = 17
Global Const OLE_SAVE_TO_OLE1FILE = 18

' OLEType

Global Const OLE_LINKED = 0
Global Const OLE_EMBEDDED = 1
Global Const OLE_NONE = 3

' OLETypeAllowed

Global Const OLE_EITHER = 2

' UpdateOptions

Global Const OLE_AUTOMATIC = 0
Global Const OLE_FROZEN = 1
Global Const OLE_MANUAL = 2

' AutoActivate modes

Global Const OLE_ACTIVATE_MANUAL = 0
Global Const OLE_ACTIVATE_GETFOCUS = 1
Global Const OLE_ACTIVATE_DOUBLECLICK = 2

' SizeModes

Global Const OLE_SIZE_CLIP = 0
Global Const OLE_SIZE_STRETCH = 1
Global Const OLE_SIZE_AUTOSIZE = 2

' DisplayTypes

Global Const OLE_DISPLAY_CONTENT = 0
Global Const OLE_DISPLAY_ICON = 1

' Update Event Constants

Global Const OLE_CHANGED = 0
Global Const OLE_SAVED = 1
Global Const OLE_CLOSED = 2
Global Const OLE_RENAMED = 3

' Special Verb Values
```

```
Global Const VERB_PRIMARY = 0
Global Const VERB_SHOW = -1
Global Const VERB_OPEN = -2
Global Const VERB_HIDE = -3

' VerbFlag Bit Masks

Global Const VERBFLAG_GRAYED = &H1
Global Const VERBFLAG_DISABLED = &H2
Global Const VERBFLAG_CHECKED = &H8
Global Const VERBFLAG_SEPARATOR = &H800

' OLE Client Error IDs
'This first set are carried over from OLE 1.0 control

Global Const OLEERR_OutOfMem = 31001
Global Const OLEERR_CantOpenClipboard = 31003
Global Const OLEERR_NoObject = 31004
Global Const OLEERR_CantClose = 31006
Global Const OLEERR_CantPaste = 31007
Global Const OLEERR_InvProp = 31008
Global Const OLEERR_CantCopy = 31009
Global Const OLEERR_InvFormat = 31017
Global Const OLEERR_NoClass = 31018
Global Const OLEERR_NoSourceDoc = 31019

' InvAction is our first new error for the OLE2.0 control
Global Const OLEERR_InvAction = 31021
Global Const OLEERR_OleInitFailed = 31022
Global Const OLEERR_InvClass = 31023
Global Const OLEERR_CantLink = 31024
Global Const OLEERR_SourceTooLong = 31026
Global Const OLEERR_CantActivate = 31027
Global Const OLEERR_NotRunning = 31028
Global Const OLEERR_DialogBusy = 31029
Global Const OLEERR_InvalidSource = 31031
Global Const OLEERR_CantEmbed = 31032
Global Const OLEERR_CantFetchLinkSrc = 31033
Global Const OLEERR_InvalidVerb = 31034
Global Const OLEERR_NoCompatClipFmt = 31035
Global Const OLEERR_ErrorSavingFile = 31036
Global Const OLEERR_ErrorLoadingFile = 31037
Global Const OLEERR_BadVBVersion = 31038
Global Const OLEERR_CantAccessSource = 31039

' Arrange Method
' for MDI Forms
```

continues

LISTING 11.2. CONTINUED

```
Global Const CASCADE = 0
Global Const TILE_HORIZONTAL = 1
Global Const TILE_VERTICAL = 2
Global Const ARRANGE_ICONS = 3

Global Const VerbMax = 10

' OLESubs.Bas

Option Explicit

Global MDINew As Integer

Sub CreateOLE ()
     Dim Newform As New frmOLE
     Newform.Show
     UpdateCaption
End Sub

Sub OpenObject ()
     MDINew = False
     CreateOLE
     OpenSave ("Open")
     If MDIfrm.ActiveForm.Ole1.OLEType = OLE_NONE Then
          Unload MDIfrm.ActiveForm
     End If
End Sub

Sub OpenSave (Action As String)
     Dim Filenum
     Filenum = FreeFile

     ' Set common dialog options.
     MDIfrm.ActiveForm.CMDialog1.Filter = "OLE 2.0 Objects¦*.OLE"
     MDIfrm.ActiveForm.CMDialog1.FilterIndex = 1
     MDIfrm.ActiveForm.Ole1.FileNumber = Filenum

     On Error GoTo FileErr1
     Select Case Action
     Case "Save"
          ' Display Save As dialog.
          MDIfrm.ActiveForm.CMDialog1.Action = 2
          ' Open and save the file.
          Open MDIfrm.ActiveForm.CMDialog1.Filename For Binary As Filenum
             MDIfrm.ActiveForm.Ole1.Action = OLE_SAVE_TO_FILE
     Case "Open"
          ' Display File Open dialog.
          MDIfrm.ActiveForm.CMDialog1.Action = 1
```

```
            ' Open the file.
            Open MDIfrm.ActiveForm.CMDialog1.Filename For Binary As Filenum
            ' Display hourglass.
            Screen.MousePointer = 11
            MDIfrm.ActiveForm.Ole1.Action = OLE_READ_FROM_FILE

        ' Set form properties now that OLE control contains an object.
          UpdateCaption
        ' Restore mouse pointer.
          Screen.MousePointer = 0
        End Select
        Close Filenum
        Exit Sub
FileErr1:
        If Err = 30015 Then
            Unload MDIfrm.ActiveForm
        End If
        If Err = 32755 Then 'User pressed cancel.
            Exit Sub
        Else
            MsgBox (Error)
        End If
        Screen.MousePointer = 0
        Exit Sub
End Sub

Sub UpdateCaption ()
        Dim Verb
        ' Set Form properties now that it contains an object.
        MDIfrm.ActiveForm.Caption = MDIfrm.ActiveForm.Ole1.Class + " Object"
        MDIfrm.ActiveForm.mnuObject.Caption = MDIfrm.ActiveForm.Ole1.Class +
                  " " +      MDIfrm.ActiveForm.mnuObject.Caption

        On Error Resume Next
        For Verb = 1 To VerbMax
            Load MDIfrm.ActiveForm.mnuVerbs(Verb)
            If Err = 360 Then ' Object already loaded.
                      Unload MDIfrm.ActiveForm.mnuVerbs(Verb)
                      Load MDIfrm.ActiveForm.mnuVerbs(Verb)
                      Err = 0
            End If
        Next Verb
        MDIfrm.ActiveForm.mnuVerbs(0).Visible = False
End Sub

Sub InsertObject ()
        MDINew = True
        CreateOLE
        If MDIfrm.ActiveForm.Ole1.OLEType <> OLE_NONE Then
            MDIfrm.ActiveForm.Ole1.Action = OLE_ACTIVATE
        Else
```

continues

Listing 11.2. continued

```
          Unload MDIfrm.ActiveForm
     End If
End Sub

'OLE2chld.frm

Option Explicit

Sub Form_Load ()
     On Error Resume Next
     Ole1.Move 0, 0

     ' Only display Insert Object dialog if File New was selected.
     If MDINew Then
          Ole1.Action = OLE_INSERT_OBJ_DLG
     Else
          Ole1.Height = Me.Height
          Ole1.Width = Me.Width
     End If

     Ole1.HostName = "OLE 2.0b "
End Sub

Sub Form_Resize ()
     Ole1.SizeMode = OLE_SIZE_STRETCH
     Ole1.Height = Me.ScaleHeight
     Ole1.Width = Me.ScaleWidth
End Sub

Sub mnuArrange_Click ()
     MDIfrm.Arrange ARRANGE_ICONS
End Sub

Sub mnuCascade_Click ()
     MDIfrm.Arrange CASCADE
End Sub

Sub mnuTile_Click ()
     MDIfrm.Arrange TILE_HORIZONTAL
End Sub

Sub mnuCopy_Click ()
     If Ole1.OLEType <> OLE_NONE Then  ' If the control contains a
                                       ' valid object.
          ' Display hourglass
          Screen.MousePointer = 11
          If Ole1.AppIsRunning Then
                  Ole1.Action = OLE_COPY          ' Copy object to
                                                  ' the Clipboard.
```

```
        Else
                ' Set Verb to activate hidden
                Ole1.Verb = VERB_HIDE
                Ole1.Action = OLE_ACTIVATE
                Ole1.Action = OLE_COPY          ' Copy object to
                                                ' the Clipboard.
                ' Set verb back to default.
                Ole1.Verb = VERB_PRIMARY
            End If
        ' Restore mouse cursor.
        Screen.MousePointer = 0
    End If
End Sub

Sub mnuCut_Click ()
    mnuCopy_Click   ' Copy object to the clipboard.
    mnuDelete_Click ' Delete object and unload the form.
End Sub

Sub mnuDelete_Click ()
    If Ole1.OLEType <> OLE_NONE Then  ' If OLE control contains a
                                      ' valid object.
        Ole1.Action = OLE_DELETE      ' Delete the object, then
                                      ' unload the form.
    End If
    Unload Me
End Sub

Sub mnuEdit_Click ()
    Dim Verb
    Dim LargestCurrentVerb As Integer
    On Error Goto EditError
    Ole1.Action = OLE_FETCH_VERBS
    LargestCurrentVerb = Ole1.ObjectVerbsCount - 1

    If MDIfrm.ActiveForm.Ole1.OLEType <> OLE_NONE Then
        For Verb = 1 To LargestCurrentVerb
                mnuVerbs(Verb).Caption = Ole1.ObjectVerbs(Verb)
                mnuVerbs(Verb).Visible = True
           Next Verb

        For Verb = LargestCurrentVerb + 1 To VerbMax
                mnuVerbs(Verb).Visible = False
        Next Verb
    End If

    If MDIfrm.ActiveForm.Ole1.PasteOK Then
        MDIfrm.ActiveForm.mnuPaste.Enabled = True
        MDIfrm.ActiveForm.mnuSpecial.Enabled = True
    Else
        MDIfrm.ActiveForm.mnuPaste.Enabled = False
```

continues

LISTING 11.2. CONTINUED

```
          MDIfrm.ActiveForm.mnuSpecial.Enabled = False
     End If
     Exit Sub
EditError:
     MsgBox (Error)
End Sub

Sub mnuExit_Click ()
     End
End Sub

Sub mnuFileNew_Click ()
     InsertObject
End Sub

Sub mnuOpen_Click ()
     OpenObject
End Sub

Sub mnuPaste_Click ()
     If Ole1.PasteOK Then
          MDINew = False
          ' Display new form.
          ' Paste Clipboard contents.
          Ole1.Action = OLE_PASTE
          ' Set form properties.
          UpdateCaption
     Else
          MsgBox "Can't Paste"
     End If
End Sub

Sub mnuSave_Click ()
     OpenSave ("Save")
End Sub

Sub mnuSpecial_Click ()
     If Ole1.PasteOK Then
          MDINew = False
          Ole1.Action = OLE_PASTE_SPECIAL_DLG
          Screen.MousePointer = 11
          UpdateCaption
          Screen.MousePointer = 0
     End If
End Sub
```

```
Sub mnuUpdate_Click ()
     Screen.MousePointer = 11
     Ole1.Action = OLE_UPDATE
     Screen.MousePointer = 0
End Sub

Sub mnuVerbs_Click (index As Integer)
     Ole1.Verb = index
     Ole1.Action = OLE_ACTIVATE
End Sub

Sub Ole1_Resize (NewHeight As Single, NewWidth As Single)
     'The form and OLE control are in TWIPS
     'Me = OLE1
     On Error GoTo ResizeErr
     Me.Height = Me.Height + (NewHeight - Me.ScaleHeight)
     Me.Width = Me.Width + (NewWidth - Me.ScaleWidth)
     Exit Sub
ResizeErr:
     MsgBox "OLE Control has either been Maxed or Mined;" +
     ➥ " unable to complete function."
     Exit Sub
End Sub

Sub Ole1_Updated (Code As Integer)
     Ole1.SizeMode = OLE_SIZE_AUTOSIZE
End Sub
```

```
'OLE2MDI.frm

Option Explicit

Sub MDIForm_Load ()
     ChDir app.Path
End Sub

Sub mnuExit_Click ()
     End
End Sub

Sub mnuFileNew_Click ()
     InsertObject
End Sub

Sub mnuOpen_Click ()
     OpenObject
End Sub
```

SUMMARY

That's it for this introduction to OLE. I assume that you're convinced by now that OLE is a powerful tool you can use to extend your Visual Basic applications. Use OLE2b, the MDI Object Editor, to build more sophisticated Object Editors.

In a documented-centered (or object-based) application, Visual Basic doesn't try to do everything to and for the document (or object). Instead, it invokes other applications (usually with OLE) to handle editing, viewing, and so on.

OLE 2.0 and the Visual Basic OLE custom control makes powerful OLE techniques easy to use.

DDE, Custom Controls, and DLLs: Intimate Details

Build a Neural Network Application

Handle Neural Network Errors

Maintain an OLE Link to Excel with the Object Editor

Throughout this book I've tried to impress on you how flexible and powerful the Visual Basic development system is. If you simply use Visual Basic without any custom controls, DDE, or OLE connections, you still will have an amazingly easy-to-use and powerful system. In particular, it takes significantly less time to develop a Windows application with Visual Basic than it does with any of the so-called developer's languages—C, C++, Pascal, and so on.

But, by adding custom controls, DLL routines, DDE, and OLE connections to your Visual Basic applications, you can greatly extend them. In short, if you judiciously enhance Visual Basic, you can develop almost any Windows application you want in Visual Basic.

You can use the Windows API or third-party DLLs to optimize the Visual Basic routines that aren't fast enough for you; use custom controls to add functionality and DDE and OLE connections to create a powerful Visual Basic task control center. The possibilities are limited only by your imagination.

In this chapter, I want to demonstrate Visual Basic's flexibility by putting many of these "extended" components to work in a relatively ambitious application for modeling the stock market. Although this application sounds specific, it really demonstrates the way to connect these components. You should be able to use the techniques developed in this chapter for your own applications.

The stock market modeling application does the following:

- Uses a DDE form to maintain a link to Microsoft Excel. The data used in the model is maintained by Excel.
- Uses a third-party neural network DDL (from Ward Systems) to analyze the data and graph the results.
- Uses the Object Editor developed in Chapter 11 to make an OLE connection to the data in Excel.

The analysis component of the application is based on a hot neural network DLL called NEUROWINDOWS. I use NEUROWINDOWS for this application example, but you can use the techniques used in this application as a general example for creating other applications that access DLLs and link other applications using DDE and OLE. Connecting to any DLL from Visual Basic is straightforward, especially if the DLL is specifically designed to interact with Visual Basic.

I chose NEUROWINDOWS for several reasons:

- It's a well-behaved DLL.
- Because it was written especially to communicate with Visual Basic, you don't have to worry about Visual Basic compatibility.
- It utilizes one of the most popular and exciting topics in computing philosophy: the design and use of neural networks.

In addition to using a third-party DLL, the application you create with NEUROWINDOWS (NEURO on the disk) utilizes two other powerful features of Windows and Visual Basic that have already been discussed in this book: DDE and OLE. NEURO demonstrates how to obtain data from another application (Excel), analyze it with a third-party DLL (the neural network), and maintain it through an OLE connection.

NEURO uses a specialized DDE form (based on the one developed earlier in this book) to set up a dynamic link to Microsoft Excel. It then uses the values in an Excel spreadsheet's cells to solve the stock market modeling problem posed for the neural network. This application is fairly complex because it puts several Visual Basic components to work, and it uses some interesting new technology (neural networks, maintained in a DLL) to handle data analysis. Because I think that neural networks are particularly useful for solving many kinds of problems that can't be solved easily with other technology, I will spend some time explaining how they work before I get to the code.

Because the complete application (NEURO) contains some proprietary third-party information (the NEUROWINDOWS DLL), you won't be able to recompile the entire project on your own system without purchasing a copy of NEUROWINDOWS from Ward Systems. You will be able, however, to step through more than 99 percent of the code to see exactly how it works, and you will be able to run and explore NEURO (as an .EXE on the *Secrets* disk), use the OLE connection to modify the Excel-maintained data, and experiment and re-analyze the data using the network. In short, you can run the entire application, but you cannot recompile it unless you own a copy of the DLL.

NEURO also requires Microsoft Excel because it reads data from Excel into the neural network. If you don't have Microsoft Excel, you can still experiment with a neural network by running a similar neural network demo, called MODEL, on the disk. MODEL is in the compressed file DISK.EXE, and it will automatically decompress the neural network demo files. You can then run MODEL to see a new Excel version of NEURO in action. This version of a neural network reads data from a file instead of Excel.

I've chosen to show the more complex code in this chapter because anyone implementing a complex neural network system will typically use a spreadsheet or database to maintain the input data for the network. In this example (NEURO), the neural network model automatically uses the data maintained in Excel to predict the state of the stock market. To change the data, simply edit the spreadsheet in Excel. NEURO, thus, is a view of this Excel data which you manipulate in Excel. In order to appreciate this example, consider the document-centered view of computing, where the document or data is central to a project, and where any different applications operate on the data. In this case, data is maintained in Excel but viewed graphically after being filtered through a neural network.

> Thanks a bunch to Steve Ward and Ward Systems Group for some of the ideas and code they contributed to this chapter. For details about Ward Systems, refer to Appendix A.

About Neural Networks

In recent years, the computer has become the preeminent representational (or modeling) tool. One excellent example of how scientists use computers to represent an aspect of the world is the neural network, which attempts to capture aspects of how they believe the brain works.

A neural network is a dynamic system consisting of layers of connected neurons. Each neuron's state is determined by the messages sent to it by all the neurons connected to it. These messages tell the neuron the state of each connecting neuron sending a message and the weight (or strength) of the connection between them. In most commercial neural network systems on the PC, the neurons in one layer connect only to the neurons in adjoining layers. Neurons within a layer don't connect to each other.

Each layer of neurons can be one of three types:

- Input layer (consisting of a pattern to classify or match, a problem to solve, and so on)
- Hidden layer (the network's internal representation of connections)
- Output layer (a resulting classification, pattern, or solution)

In most neural network models, all the neurons in a single input layer are connected to all the neurons in a hidden layer, and all the neurons in the hidden layer are connected to all the neurons in an output layer (see Figure 12.1). A neural network can have more than one hidden layer, but the connection scheme is similar in that the neurons in the second hidden layer are connected to the neurons in the first hidden layer and the neurons in the output layer.

A neuron can be in one of two states: On or Off. The combined, weighted states (the messages from those neurons) of the neurons connected to a neuron determine its state.

The neurons in the input layer are connected to sources (devices, a program, and so on) outside the network, and the initial states of these neurons are determined by the messages sent to the neuron from the outside world (for example, from a communication port or from a data file).

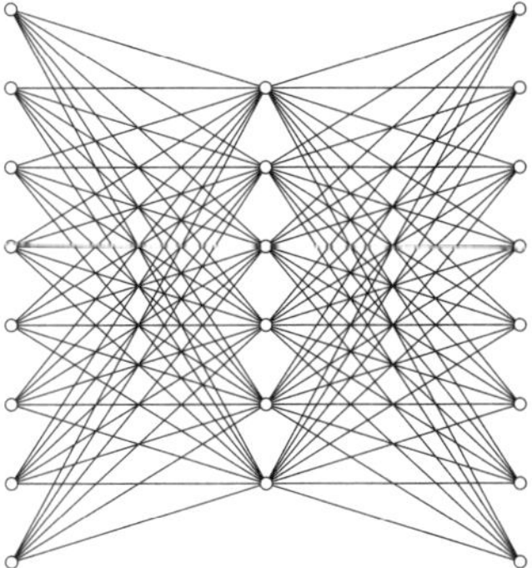

Figure 12.1. Connections between layers.

The states of neurons in the hidden layer are determined first by the messages sent from the neurons in the input layer.

The states of neurons in the output layer are determined by the messages sent to them from the hidden layer. These messages are generated by several factors: the network model that calculates the weights of the inputs (back propagation, counter propagation, feed-forward, functional link, Hopfield, perceptron, bidirectional associate memory, self-organizing, and so on), an activation function, and a transfer function (see Figure 12.2).

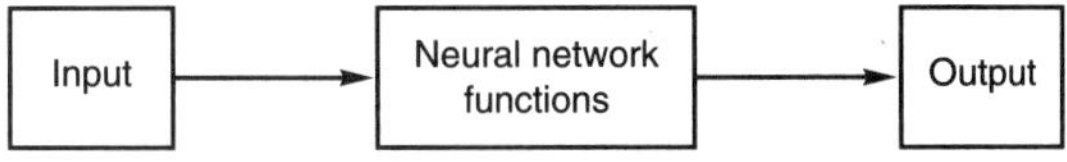

Figure 12.2. Input messages produce output messages.

When messages have been sent to all the output neurons in the network, the network has reached a temporary "state." The network then evaluates its state (by comparing it to some desired state) to determine how much error it contains. The total error in the network is equal to the sum of the errors in individual neurons. The total error determines what the network does next.

In a back-propagation network, for example, if the error is too large (determined by comparing its error to an acceptable error value), it sends a message back through the network from neuron to neuron (to the hidden layer, back to the input layer, forward again to the hidden layer, and then on to the output layer), telling every neuron, in effect, to adjust itself a little to reduce the total error in the network.

After the network has iterated (looped back to the output layer), it again recalculates its error. Eventually, the network settles into a stable state and sends an output message identifying its state. This output signal is the "result" of or "solution" to the problem the network is trying to solve.

In general, neural networks are information processors based on mathematical models of how we think the brain works. Although neural networks are similar to expert systems in that they solve (or classify) a new problem by matching its characteristics to an existing problem, they differ in two important aspects: expert systems use rules to generate output (neural networks use examples); and expert systems require complete information (neural networks can produce results from incomplete information).

These two differences give a neural network considerably more power to do the following:

- Solve problems where If/Then rules are either unknown or difficult to compile.
- Classify new problems using "fuzzy" logic.
- Predict (or "infer," in logistic language) new results from previous trends or patterns (in other words, to be creative).

Because neural network technology is still new and expanding, researchers haven't yet agreed on one model that they think works just right. In fact, because research goes on all over the world, much of it in isolation and with different premises and goals, distinct approaches to developing neural network models continue to appear and evolve.

In a neural network, the smallest unit is a neuron, which has a state and the capability to receive and send messages to the neurons to which it's connected. The state of any neuron is determined by incoming messages (that is, its connections) from other neurons. Connections have weights, and neurons change state by comparing the incoming message to a value determined by an activation function. Usually, this means that if the message coming to a neuron is higher than a certain value, the neuron is in an On or 1 state. If not, the neuron is in an Off or 0 state.

Each neuron's state is coupled with its connection weight to adjoining neurons in a message that is sent to each adjoining neuron. Depending on the message, each neuron receiving a message turns itself on or off. Typically, a message consists of a value determined by a function (for example, weight times state).

After all the neurons have received messages and changed states accordingly, the network asks itself if its current state is stable (or correct). It decides the status of its state by comparing it to a value determined by an error function. If its state is within some error boundary, it sends a message to the system that it's okay, for example, by printing a result. If its state (result) isn't stable (correct enough), it adjusts its state (using a function to compare its state to a desired state) and sends messages back through the network, neuron by neuron, changing the states of neurons as it goes until it settles into an acceptable state.

Each neural network model has its own methods, equations, connection schemes, activation functions, and so on, to determine its state and stability, but all networks generally share the characteristics just described. Beginning with data, you might ask these questions when you are setting up a neural network:

- How many neurons are in each layer?
- How many layers are there?
- How can I describe error?
- How can I describe connection weights?

You also must specify where the first input message to the network comes from and where the network will send its output message (its interactions with the outside world—this could be a message to a database to update a data file, a message to a communications port, and so on). After the network gets started, it generates its own messages.

Build a Neural Network Application

NEURO starts with a main Visual Basic form and calls the NEUROWINDOWS DLL to create (or make) the neural network. It then calls Excel to get data for the network to evaluate. Because the application is relatively straightforward, you don't have to get mired in too many details. Its primary purpose is to show you how to use any DLL in your application and how to maintain DDE and OLE links to other application data. It demonstrates the capability of neural networks—in particular, the NEUROWINDOWS DLL, the best Windows neural network tool I know.

NEURO has a multiform design—it has a `StartUp` (or Main) form with a menu for invoking the Object Editor (for OLE), opening and saving network files, and loading, training, and running the neural network.

In short, NEURO uses the data it obtains from Excel to model one aspect of the stock market, the S&P, through a multiyear period. The modeling system predicts stock market prices using several fundamental and technical stock market indicator variables including:

- The treasury bill rate
- The New York gold price
- The value of the Swiss franc
- The current Standard & Poor's (S&P) monthly average
- The difference between this month's and last month's S&P

These market indicators, selected by researchers at Ward Systems, aren't intended to be definitive. (If you're planning to create a similar system, contact Ward Systems for a detailed update. Stock market analysis and other modeling problems are great topics for neural networks because they handle multivariate systems very well, and they perform admirably well with incomplete information.) Each of these market indicator variables is maintained in a Microsoft Excel spreadsheet that NEURO can access whenever it needs data (for training the network, for example).

DEVELOPMENT STEPS

Now, it's time to create the NEURO main form. This form consists of the main menu and is used for graphing the results of the network analysis. Figure 12.3 shows the main form in design mode.

> As has been the practice in this book, you generally should use a separate form for each DDE connection.

NEURO is completely menu-driven, so pay particular attention to the menu click event procedures (`StartMenu_Click`, `InterruptMenu_Click`, `ResetMenu_Click`, `LoadMenu_Click`, and `SaveMenu_Click`). Also note that the network is built when the main form is loaded (`Form_Load`). The procedure, `Excelread()`, which I'll discuss in the next section, reads the Excel cells one at a time. The `StartMenu_Click` event procedure indicates the training of the network. The `Graph_Results` procedure graphs both the training output and the predicted output on the main form.

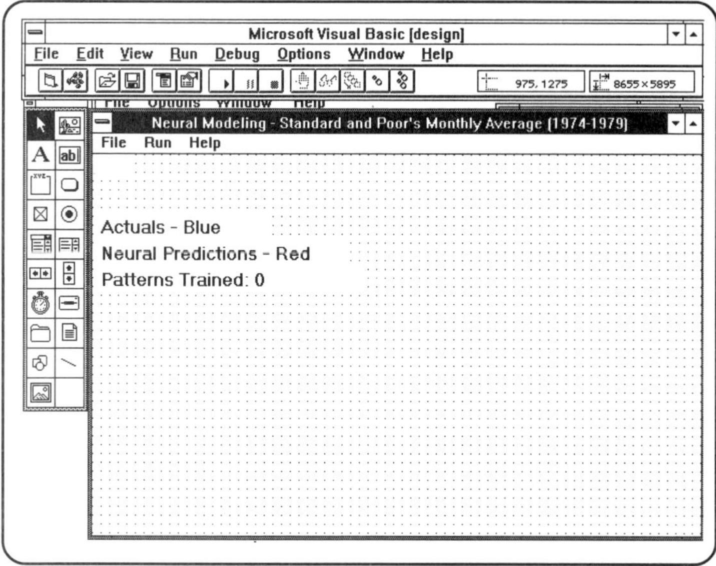

Figure 12.3. The NEURO main form.

You also can use a form to handle the DDE connection to Microsoft Excel. Figure 12.4 shows that form (with controls).

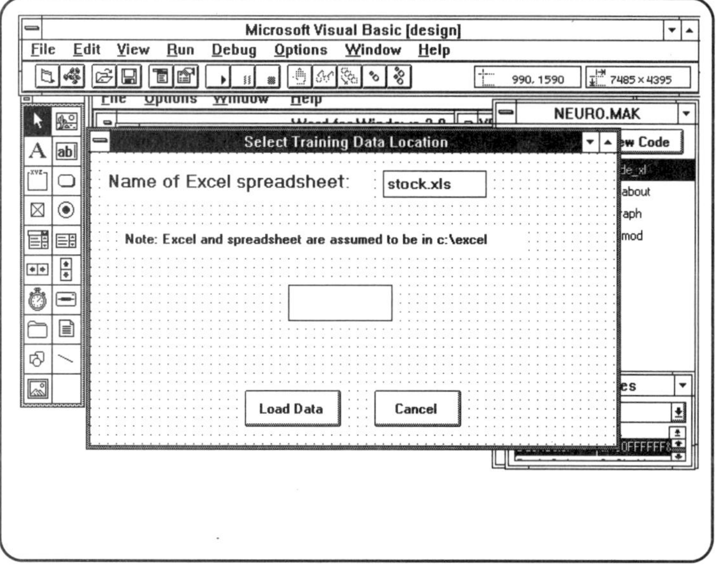

Figure 12.4. The DDE form.

Now for the code.

CONNECT YOUR APPLICATION TO A DLL

All of the neural network functionality resides in NEUROWIN.DLL. Therefore, you must declare the routines (in the DLL) needed for this application. Listing 12.1 shows the module (NEUROWIN.BAS) that contains these declarations and a number of other constants that the DLL (the neural network part of the application) needs.

LISTING 12.1. NEUROWIN.BAS.

```
' Neural Network Type Constants

Const BpVanilla% = 1      ' Vanilla backpropagation
Const BpMomentum% = 2     ' Backpropagation with momentum
Const BpBatch% = 3        ' Weights not updated after every event
Const LvqVanilla% = 4     ' Vanilla Learning Vector Quantizer
Const LvqNormalized% = 5 ' Input vectors are normalized instead of mapped on to
                           [0,1]


' Layer Constants

Const InputLayer% = 0      ' For a slab in the input layer
Const HiddenLayer% = 1     ' For a slab in any hidden layer
Const OutputLayer% = 2     ' For a slab in the output layer


' Constants for SetMath

Const Floating% = 0
Const Fixed% = 1


'
' ____________________________________________________________________________
' !!!!!!!!!!!!!   here's the declarations part   !!!!!!!!!!!!!


' Neural Network Function Declarations


Declare Function GetNextNet% Lib "NEUROWIN.DLL" (net%)

Declare Function MakeSlab% Lib "NEUROWIN.DLL" (net%, slab%,neurons%, layer%)

Declare Function MakeLink% Lib "NEUROWIN.DLL" (net%, link%, weight!,
```

```
➥fromslab%, toslab%)

Declare Function PutSlab% Lib "NEUROWIN.DLL" (net%, slab%, array!)

Declare Function GetSlab% Lib "NEUROWIN.DLL" (net%, slab%, array!)

Declare Function PutSlabInteger% Lib "NEUROWIN.DLL" (net%, slab%, array%)

Declare Function GetSlabInteger% Lib "NEUROWIN.DLL" (net%, slab%, array%)

Declare Function Putneuron% Lib "NEUROWIN.DLL" (net%, slab%,neuron%, value!)

Declare Function Getneuron% Lib "NEUROWIN.DLL" (net%, slab%,neuron%, value!)

Declare Function PutLink% Lib "NEUROWIN.DLL" (net%, link%, array!)

Declare Function GetLink% Lib "NEUROWIN.DLL" (net%, link%, array!)

Declare Function PutWeight% Lib "NEUROWIN.DLL" (net%, link%, fromneuron%,
➥toneuron%, weight!)

Declare Function GetWeight% Lib "NEUROWIN.DLL" (net%, link%, fromneuron%,
➥toneuron%, weight!)


Declare Function BpPropagate% Lib "NEUROWIN.DLL" (net%, toslab%)

Declare Function BpEvaluate% Lib "NEUROWIN.DLL" (net%, slab%,
➥actuals!,errorfactor!)

Declare Function BpEvaluateInteger% Lib "NEUROWIN.DLL" (net%, slab%,
➥actuals%, errorfactor!)

Declare Function BpTrain% Lib "NEUROWIN.DLL" (net%, fromslab%,learnrate!,
➥Momentum!,updateswitch%)

Declare Function LvqPropagate% Lib "NEUROWIN.DLL" (net%, toslab%)

Declare Function LvqEvaluate% Lib "NEUROWIN.DLL" (net%, slab%, winner%,adjust%)

Declare Function LvqTrain% Lib "NEUROWIN.DLL" (net%, fromslab%,
➥learnrate!, neighborhood%,cols%)


Declare Function CopySlab% Lib "NEUROWIN.DLL" (fromnet%, fromslab%,
➥tonet%, toslab%)

Declare Function SetSlab% Lib "NEUROWIN.DLL" (net%, slab%, value!)

Declare Function SlideSlab% Lib "NEUROWIN.DLL" (net%, slab%, value!)

Declare Function InitLink% Lib "NEUROWIN.DLL" (net%, link%, weight!)
```

continues

Listing 12.1. continued

```
Declare Function KillNet% Lib "NEUROWIN.DLL" (net%)

Declare Function KillSlab% Lib "NEUROWIN.DLL" (net%, slab%)

Declare Function KillLink% Lib "NEUROWIN.DLL" (net%, link%)

Declare Function SetMath% Lib "NEUROWIN.DLL" (mathtype%)

Declare Function LoadShell% Lib "NEUROWIN.DLL" (net%, ByVal path$)



' Error  codes for the Network error handler

 Const noerror = 0              ' No errors detected.
 Const nomemory = 1             ' Not enough global memory was available
                                ' for the request.
 Const badnettype = 2           ' Unknown network type.
 Const badnetnum = 3            ' Invalid network number.
 Const netactive = 4            ' Network is already in use.
 Const netinactive = 5          ' Network is not in use.
 Const badslabtype = 6          ' Invalid slab type (layer).
 Const badslabnum = 7           ' Invalid slab number.
 Const slabactive = 8           ' Slab is already in use.
 Const slabinactive = 9         ' Slab is not in use.
 Const noneurons = 10           ' At least one neuron must be specified
                                ' in every slab.
 Const slablinked = 11          ' All of a slab's links must be killed
                                ' before the slab can be killed.
 Const badlinknum = 12          ' Invalid link number.
 Const toomanylinks = 13        ' Slab already has maximum number of links to it.
 Const linkactive = 14          ' Link is already in use.
 Const linkinactive = 15        ' Link is not in use.
 Const wrongnettype = 16        ' Network was not the right type for
                                ' the function requested.
 Const notoslabs = 17           ' No slabs are linked to the specified slab.
 Const badeval = 18             ' Evaluation function may only be requested
                                ' for an Output layer slab.
 Const badfromneuron = 19       ' Bad from neuron number passed to GetWeight
                                ' or PutWeight
 Const badtoneuron = 20         ' Bad to neuron number passed to GetWeight
                                ' or PutWeight
 Const badserial = 21           ' Serial number was not correct
 Const badmath = 22             ' Unknown math type specified in SetMath
 Const badneighbor = 23         ' Neighborhood for Lvq must be >= 0
 Const badneuron = 24           ' Bad neuron number passed to
                                ' Getneuron or Putneuron.
 Const badfile = 25             ' I/O error opening or reading neuroShell
                                ' .NET file
```

As you can see in the listing, the NEUROWINDOWS DLL contains a large number of functions, procedures, and constants that you must declare before attempting to use the application. Note, however, that you don't need to declare all the functions in a DLL—just the ones you intend to use in your specific application. For example, in Chapter 10, "A Wizard Project Editor and a Wizard Clipboard," you used several Windows API functions (from the Windows DLLs), and you declared only those functions you needed. You didn't have to declare the numerous other functions contained in those DLLs.

In this example, you use (and consequently declare) many more DLL routines than you did in earlier chapters because you're using most of the functionality of the DLL.

The events for the main form are straightforward. `LoadMenu_Click()` sets up and loads a pretrained network, checks for errors, and reads patterns and links. The other menu Click events maintain aspects of the network. All of these procedures are included in Listing 12.2 at the end of this chapter. In that listing, note the many calls to DLL functions and procedures.

Connect the Network to Microsoft Excel

The DDE connection to Microsoft Excel begins with a call to the procedure `Excelread` and ends after `Excelread` returns. When you finish getting the data from Excel (by way of the DDE connection), unload the DDE form:

```
Sub Command1_Click ()
  Excelread
  Unload dde_xl          ' Unload the DDE form
End Sub
```

`Excelread` contains all the code needed to set up the link. It specifies these three things:

- A `LinkTopic` (the application plus spreadsheet topic):

  transfer.LinkTopic = "Excel | c:\excel\" + sheetname.text

- The `Linkitem`, which is an Excel cell:

  transfer.linkitem = "R1C1"

- The `LinkMode`:

  transfer.linkmode = COLD

Notice that because you're performing a one-time read of the cells, you maintain a cold link to Excel. Here's the code for the `Excelread` procedure:

```
Sub Excelread ()
' Read training data from the Excel spreadsheet using a DDE link.


 On Error GoTo StartExcel  ' If Excel not up, load it


 transfer.linkmode = NONE
 ' Before running this application, put the spreadsheet into
 ' the C:\excel directory _ that's where it expects to find it.


' If linkmode generated an error come back here and try to relink.
tryagain:
 transfer.LinkTopic = "Excel¦c:\excel\" + sheetname.text
 transfer.linkitem = "R1C1"
 transfer.linkmode = COLD


' First read minimums and maximums for training set
i% = 4 '  First row has minimums

  For j% = 1 To Inputs
    InMin(j%) = getcell(i%, j% + 1)' Get the data from sheet
  Next j%
  j% = Inputs + 1
  ' There is only one output
    Outmin = getcell(i%, j% + 1)

i% = 5 '  Next row has maximums
  For j% = 1 To Inputs
    Inmax(j%) = getcell(i%, j% + 1)
  Next j%
  j% = Inputs + 1
  ' There is only one output
    Outmax = getcell(i%, j% + 1)


' Now read the patterns

For i% = 1 To patterns
      For j% = 1 To Inputs
      temp! = getcell(i% + 5, j% + 1)' Starts on third row
      Training_Input(j%, i%) = Map(temp!, InMin(j%), Inmax(j%), 0!, 1!)
                                  ' Map to [0,1]
      Next j%
      j% = Inputs + 1
      temp! = getcell(i% + 5, j% + 1)
      Training_Output(i%) = Map(temp!, Outmin, Outmax, .1!, .9!)
                                  ' Map to [.1,.9]
Next i%
```

```
transfer.linkmode = NONE    ' Close it out
Exit Sub      ' Don't fall into the error handler

StartExcel:          ' A user-defined error handler for starting Excel
 If timeshere% > 0 Then
  MsgBox "Having trouble loading EXCEL or the proper spreadsheet.
  ➥Please make sure both are in C:\EXCEL", 16, ""
  i% = KillNet(netnum)
  End
 Else
  timeshere% = 1  ' A dynamic variable
  If Err = 282 Then       ' Load Excel with the sheet if not loaded
    MsgBox "Excel is not up with that spreadsheet. I will load a copy.",
    ➥48, ""
    excelid = Shell("c:\EXCEL\excel.exe c:\excel\" + sheetname.text, 7)
                          ' Load excel minimized
    Resume tryagain
   End If
 End If
End Sub
```

Note (in the `Excelread` procedure) that the cells are read with the `getcell` function. Because you want to read all the cells in the spreadsheet by way of the DDE link, you must increase the row and column with each call to `getcell`, and then build the row and column names using the `LTrim` procedure:

```
Function getcell (row%, col%) As Single
 '  Make a cell name, e.g. R1C1, for LinkItem
  transfer.linkitem = "R" + LTrim$(Str$(row%)) + "C" + LTrim$(Str$(col%))
  transfer.LinkRequest
  getcell = Val(transfer.text)          ' Get the next cell value
End Function
```

Note that `getcell` uses a `Linkrequest` to obtain the value in the cell. The cell value is returned through the text property of the transfer text box. You must use a `LinkRequest` because you're maintaining a cold link to Excel. To maintain a hot link, you would have to create a control array of cells as large as the Excel spreadsheet for the hot link transfer to work. You cannot hot-link an entire spreadsheet to a single cell!

A Few Details: *DoEvents()*, Updating the Report Form, and so on

You should note a couple of other important aspects of the application. First, because network training can take a long time, you want the user to be able to interrupt training to perform other tasks. In the training routine, therefore, within the `StartMenu_Click` event procedure, use a `DoEvents()` statement to enable the user to interrupt:

```
If Done = 0 Then Exit Sub
Done = 0
 i% = DoEvents()  ' allow screen updates, menu selections
 If KeepTraining = 1 Then Exit For  ' stop training immediately

Next j%   ' start on the next pattern now
Events = Events + patterns
Done = -1
```

By using `DoEvents()`, you can allow the user to interrupt training and, for example, view the Report window (form). This form keeps the user posted on the number of training loops and the relative amount of error still left in the system (see Figure 12.5).

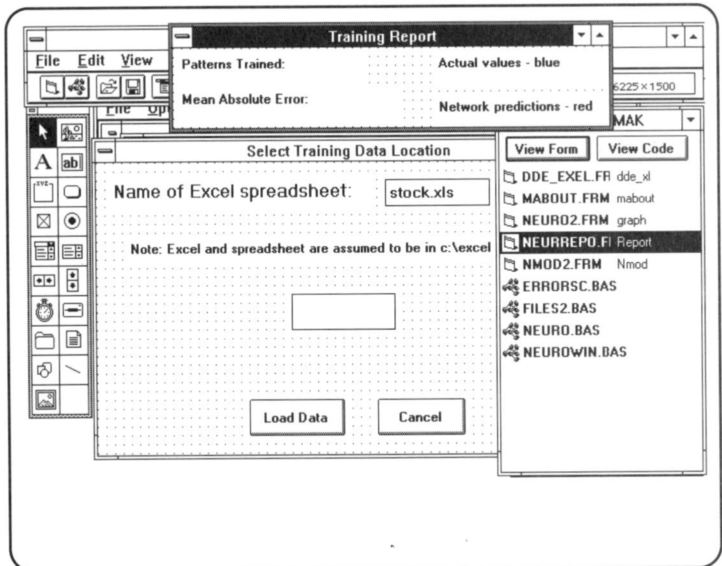

Figure 12.5. The Report form.

The Report form uses no code; it's used to store information as the network progresses. The Report form labels are updated with each training loop:

```
......
 i% = DoEvents()  ' allow screen updates, menu selections
 If KeepTraining = 1 Then Exit For  ' stop training immediately
```

```
Next j%   ' start on the next pattern now
Events = Events + patterns

If KeepTraining = 0 Then
  Report.label3.caption = "Patterns Trained: " + Str$(Events)
  Report.label4.caption = "Mean Absolute Error: " +
  ➥ Str$(meanerror / patterns)
  Graph_Results
End If
Wend
.........
```

Using a separate Report form is a handy way to maintain information (without cluttering the main form).

Handle Neural Network Errors

Any DLL, such as NEUROWIN.DLL, is capable of generating errors that Visual Basic can't handle automatically. When you're using any third-party DLL, therefore, you likely will have to implement a specialized error handler for the DLL.

The following procedure handles specific NEUROWIN.DLL errors:

```
Sub NetworkErrors ()
  Select Case NetwkError%
   Case noerror
     Msg$ = "No errors detected."
   Case nomemory
     Msg$ = "Not enough global memory was available for the request."
   Case badnettype
     Msg$ = "Unknown network type."
   Case badnetnum
     Msg$ = "Invalid network number."
   Case netactive
     Msg$ = "Network is already in use."
   Case netinactive
     Msg$ = "Network is not in use."
   Case badslabtype
     Msg$ = "Invalid slab type (layer)."
   Case badslabnum
     Msg$ = "Invalid slab number."
   Case slabactive
     Msg$ = "Slab is already in use."
   Case slabinactive
     Msg$ = "Slab is not in use."
   Case noneurons
     Msg$ = "At least one neuron must be specified in every slab."
   Case slablinked
```

```
    Msg$ = "All of a slab's links must be killed before
    ➥the slab can be killed."
  Case badlinknum
    Msg$ = "Invalid link number."
  Case toomanylinks
    Msg$ = "Slab already has maximum number of links to it."
  Case linkactive
    Msg$ = "Link is already in use."
  Case linkinactive
    Msg$ = "Link is not in use."
  Case wrongnettype
    Msg$ = "Network was not the right type for the function requested."
  Case notoslabs
    Msg$ = "No slabs are linked to the specified slab."
  Case badeval
    Msg$ = "Evaluation function may only be requested
    ➥for an Output layer slab."
  Case badfromneuron
    Msg$ = "Invalid from neuron index passed to GetWeight or Putweight."
  Case badtoneuron
    Msg$ = "Invalid to neuron index passed to GetWeight or Putweight."
  Case badserial
    Msg$ = "Serial number is incorrect."
  Case badmath
    Msg$ = "Unknown math type specified in SetMath."
  Case badneighbor
    Msg$ = "Neighborhood for Lvq must be >= 0."
  Case badneuron
     Msg$ = "Bad neuron number passed to Getneuron or Putneuron."
  Case badfile
     Msg$ = "I/O error opening or reading neuroShell .NET file."
  Case brdnospace
     Msg$ = "Not enough memory on neuroBoard for requested operation."
  Case brdbadfile
     Msg$ = "Problems reading neuroBoard .CDE initialization file."
  Case maxbrderror
     Msg$ = "No more than 10 neuroBoards may be used at once."
  Case brdnoreponse
     Msg$ = "The neuroBoard is not responding to commands
     ➥(Check the address)."
  Case brdslower
     Msg$ = "Warning: PutSlab & GetSlab may be slow
     ➥due to low neuroBoard memory."
  Case badpattern
     Msg$ = "Pattern number passed to Pnn for change
     ➥did not already exist."
  Case badsmoothing
     Msg$ = "Smoothing factor must be greater than zero"
  Case Else
    Msg$ = "Unknown error code: " + Str$(errornum)
End Select
```

```
    MsgBox Msg$
End Sub
```

The `NetwkError%` variable is global so that any routine in the project using the DLL can see and set it. This variable is similar to the `SaveErr%` global variable you have used throughout this book with the `GeneralErrors` error handler. Every time an error is generated by a procedure or function specific to the DLL, the error handler within the procedure is called and this variable is set before the network error handler is set. For example:

```
errors:
    NetwkError% = i%
    NetworkErrors
End Sub
```

Note that this specific DLL error handler isn't part of the typical `On Error GoTo` general error handling you have been implementing. You're therefore not required to use a `Resume` or `Resume Next` statement to continue processing.

Maintain an OLE Link to Excel with the Object Editor

One last component completes the application: an OLE link to the Excel data. You can, of course, run Excel directly, but it's handy to enable the network application to control Excel when it wants. You can accomplish this direct control by way of an OLE connection such as the one developed in Chapter 11.

You can either incorporate the Object Editor (on the disk) into the application by adding the appropriate menu items to the NEURO main menu or (more simply) run the Object Editor as a "shelled" application:

```
Sub ObjCom_Click ()
On Error GoTo E1
    x% = Shell("C:\vb\Objedit", 1)
    Exit Sub
E1:
    SaveErr% = Err
    GeneralErrors
    Resume Next
End Sub
```

(Take note of the error handling just in case NEURO can't find the Object Editor.)

This "shelled" solution is the simplest because it requires no extra work on your part. After the Object Editor is up and running, copy into the Excel client object the Excel spreadsheet (in this case, STOCK.XLS) you want to edit. Then edit the object with Excel. When you finish editing the spreadsheet (object), note that you will have to save it with the Object Editor, not with Excel. Then, when you reload the object into Excel for editing, you will have to resave it as STOCK.XLS.

If this process sounds odd, experiment with the NEURO application on the disk to see what I mean. (If you don't have Excel, you won't be able to edit the spreadsheet with the Object Editor or run the application. You can, however, run the compiled version of NEURO, on the disk. If you don't have Excel, however, you won't get the full benefit of NEURO, but you can understand the general idea, and you can still see the network in operation by first running the compressed neural network file DISTR.EXE on the disk. Then run MODEL.EXE from the program manager.)

Figures 12.6, 12.7, and 12.8 show various aspects of the application at run-time. The code is shown in Listing 12.2.

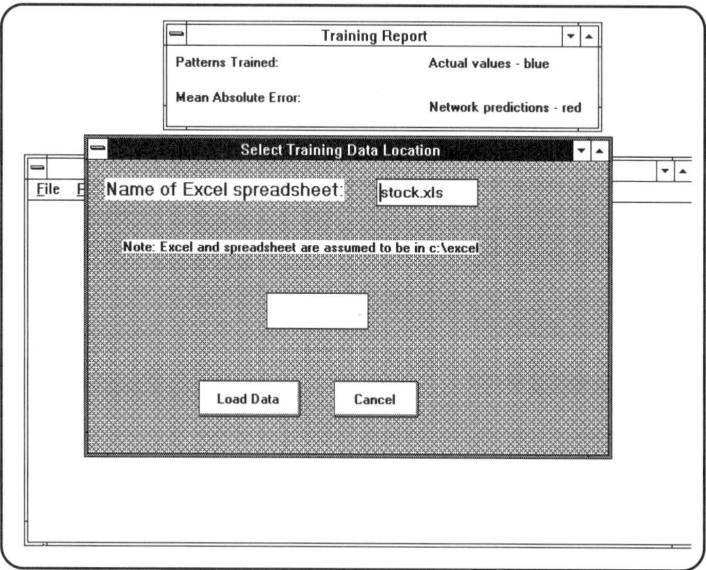

Figure 12.6. NEURO: Select Training Data Location.

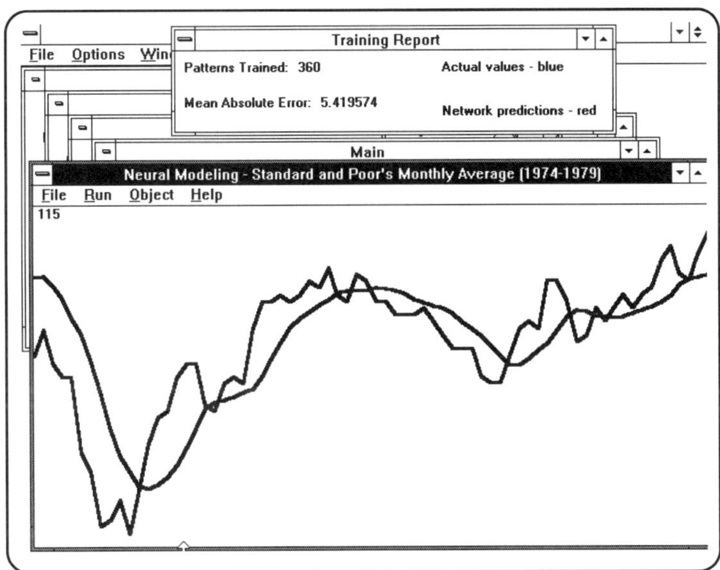

Figure 12.7. NEURO: graphic results and training report.

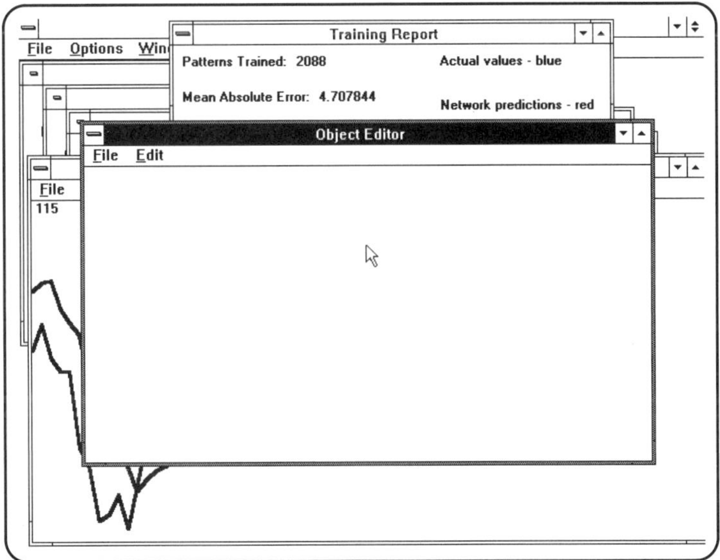

Figure 12.8. NEURO: invoking the Object Editor.

LISTING 12.2. NEURO.

```
' Note this listing includes all the code necessary to run
' NEURO except for some priority initialization code
' required by neurowindows.
' Check with Ward Systems for details.
' In addition, this code requires Excel in order to load the training data.
' If you don't have Excel you can still see a similar neural network in action.
' Run DISTR.EXE from the second Secrets disk; then run MODEL.EXE.
' neuro.BAS

Global Done As Integer
Global NetwkError%
Global CancelFlag%
Global SaveErr%


Global Const Patterns% = 72
Global Const Inputs% = 7
Global Const Outputs% = 1
Global Const Hiddens% = 10
Global Const Maxweights% = 300  ' This ought to do it
Global Const learning_rate! = .6
Global Const momentum = .35



Global Training_Input!(1 To Inputs, 1 To Patterns)
                                ' Allocate arrays for the training set
Global Training_Output!(Patterns)    ' Only 1 output
Global Predicted_Output(Patterns)
Global Linkarray(0 To Maxweights)    ' Weights saved here

Global Inmax!(1 To Inputs)
Global InMin!(1 To Inputs)
Global Outmin!
Global Outmax!

' LinkMode (controls)
Global Const NONE = 0                ' 0 - None
Global Const HOT = 1                 ' 1 - Hot
Global Const COLD = 2                ' 2 - Cold

Global netnum%  ' this is our network number


' neuro ABOUT

Sub Command1_Click ()
    Unload neuroAbout
```

```
End Sub


' neuro MAIN


Const True% = -1
Const False% = 0

' Colors

Const RED = &HFF&
Const GREEN = &HFF00&
Const YELLOW = &HFFFF&
Const BLUE = &HFF0000
Const MAGENTA = &HFF00FF
Const CYAN = &HFFFF00
Const WHITE = &HFFFFFF

' Neural Network Type Constants (you may want these
' in declarations proc of a form or global module)

Const BpVanilla% = 1    ' Vanilla backpropagation
Const BpMomentum% = 2   ' backpropagation with momentum
Const BpBatch% = 3      ' Weights not updated after every event

' Layer Constants (you may want these in declarations
' proc of a form or global module)

Const InputLayer% = 0      ' For a slab in the input layer
Const HiddenLayer% = 1     ' For a slab in any hidden layer
Const OutputLayer% = 2     ' For a slab in the output layer




Dim KeepTraining% ' Set to 1 when you want to stop
Dim Events&       ' Keeps track of patterns trained

Dim dataloaded%   ' Keeps track of whether data was loaded yet

Sub AboutMenu_Click ()
    neuroAbout.Show
End Sub

Sub StartMenu_Click ()

If KeepTraining = 2 Then
  Events = 0
  i% = InitLink(netnum, 0, .3)
     If i% Then GoTo errors
```

continues

LISTING 12.2. CONTINUED

```
  i% = InitLink(netnum, 1, .3)
     If i% Then GoTo errors
  i% = InitLink(netnum, 2, .3)
     If i% Then GoTo errors
End If

' Do the screen that loads the data

If Not dataloaded Then ' First time load
 neuroDDE.Show 1
 If CancelFlag <> -1 Then
    dataloaded = True
 End If
End If



label5.caption = Str$(Outmax)
label6.caption = Str$(Outmin)

Trainmore:
KeepTraining = 0


' Now we train the network until the user stops it
While KeepTraining = 0

' Each time we train it we load Slab 0 with a new training pattern.
' For the first pattern of an epoch, we clear the recurrent slab.

  i% = SetSlab(netnum, 1, 0!)
    If i% Then GoTo errors

meanerror = 0

For j% = 1 To patterns  ' This is a training event
 i% = PutSlab(netnum, 0, Training_Input(1, j%))  ' col j% of the array
    If i% Then GoTo errors

 i% = BpPropagate(netnum, 2)    ' propagate to the Hidden layer
    If i% Then GoTo errors
 i% = BpPropagate(netnum, 3)    ' propagate to the Output layer
    If i% Then GoTo errors

 ' Compare to actuals in output part of training set

 i% = BpEvaluate(netnum, 3, Training_Output(j%), errorfactor!)
    If i% Then GoTo errors
```

```
 i% = GetSlab(netnum, 3, Predicted_Output(j%))
     If i% Then GoTo errors

 ' To get the absolute error, first Map both outputs back to scale
 t1 = Map(Training_Output(j%), .1!, .9!, Outmin, Outmax)
 t2 = Map(Predicted_Output(j%), .1!, .9!, Outmin, Outmax)
 meanerror = meanerror + Abs(t1 - t2)

 ' Now the backward error propagation pass (training)

 ' LastPattern is set true if this is the last in the set
 ' but it is ignored by BpTrain unless the nettype is
 ' BpBatch

 i% = BpTrain(netnum, 2, learning_rate, momentum, False)
                                         ' Train to Hidden layer
    If i% Then GoTo errors

 i% = BpTrain(netnum, 0, learning_rate, momentum, False)
                                         ' Train to Input layer
    If i% Then GoTo errors

 i% = BpTrain(netnum, 1, learning_rate, momentum, False)
                                         ' Train to Input layer
    If i% Then GoTo errors


 i% = CopySlab(netnum, 2, netnum, 1)
                    ' Copy Hidden layer into second slab of input layer
    If i% Then GoTo errors


 i% = DoEvents()  ' allow screen updates, menu selections
 If KeepTraining = 1 Then Exit For      ' stop training immediately

Next j%   ' start on the next pattern now
Events = Events + patterns

If KeepTraining = 0 Then
  Report.label3.caption = "Patterns Trained: " + Str$(Events)
  Report.label4.caption = "Mean Absolute Error: " +
  ➥Str$(meanerror / patterns)
  Graph_Results
End If
Wend

Exit Sub

errors:
    NetwkError% = i%
```

continues

Listing 12.2. continued

```
    NetworkErrors
End Sub

Sub Form_Load ()
'Set up DoEvents
Done = -1
' Build the network and all 3 layers (2 slabs in input layer)

' First get a network number
i% = GetNextNet(netnum)
  If i% Then GoTo Errors2     ' in case it didn't work

  If i% Then GoTo Errors2     ' in case it didn't work
i% = MakeSlab(netnum, 0, Inputs, InputLayer)
                              ' Make net 0, slab 0 the size of the inputs
  If i% Then GoTo Errors2
i% = MakeSlab(netnum, 1, Hiddens, InputLayer)
                              ' This is where we'll copy the
                              ' Hidden layer from last pattern
  If i% Then GoTo Errors2

i% = MakeSlab(netnum, 2, Hiddens, HiddenLayer) '  The Hidden layer
  If i% Then GoTo Errors2
i% = MakeSlab(netnum, 3, Outputs, OutputLayer) ' The Output layer
  If i% Then GoTo Errors2


' Now link the Hidden layer(Slab2) to the Input slabs0 and 1
i% = MakeLink(netnum, 0, .3!, 0, 2) ' initial weights are between +-.3
    If i% Then GoTo Errors2
i% = MakeLink(netnum, 1, .3!, 1, 2) ' initial weights are between +-.3
    If i% Then GoTo Errors2


' Now link the Output layer (Slab3) to the Hidden layer
i% = MakeLink(netnum, 2, .3!, 2, 3)
     ' Remember the first arguments are the network and link numbers (0,1)
   If i% Then GoTo Errors2

    Report.Show

Exit Sub

Errors2:
    NetwkError% = i%
    NetworkErrors
End Sub

Sub InterruptMenu_Click ()
    KeepTraining = 1  ' this only interrupts
End Sub
```

```
Sub ExitMenu_Click ()
    i% = KillNet(netnum)
    Unload Report
    End
End Sub

Sub Form_Unload (Cancel As Integer)
    i% = KillNet(netnum)
    End
End Sub

Sub Graph_Results ()
' Graphs both the Training_Output (blue) and Predicted_Output (red)

Dim actual!, predicted!
Dim oldactual!, oldpredicted!

ScaleWidth = patterns - 1
ScaleHeight = Outmin - Outmax   ' this is negative
ScaleTop = Outmax
ScaleLeft = 1
Drawwidth = 3

Cls
For i% = 1 To patterns
  actual = Map(Training_Output(i%), .1, .9, Outmin, Outmax)
  predicted = Map(Predicted_Output(i%), .1, .9, Outmin, Outmax)
  If i% = 1 Then    ' no history for the first pattern
    oldactual = actual
    oldpredicted = predicted
  End If
  CurrentY = oldactual
  DrawStyle = 0
  Line -(i%, actual), BLUE
  CurrentY = oldpredicted
  Currentx = i% - 1' The line above moved it
  DrawStyle = 2
  Line -(i%, predicted), RED
  oldactual = actual
  oldpredicted = predicted
Next i%
End Sub

Sub ResetMenu_Click ()
    KeepTraining = 2 ' Make it start all over again
End Sub

Sub SaveMenu_Click ()
```

continues

LISTING 12.2. CONTINUED

```
    Filename$ = InputBox$("Name the file where network
    ➥will be saved:", "Save Network", "stockxls.net")

    If Filename$ = "" Then Exit Sub

    Open Filename$ For Binary As #1

    Screen.mousepointer = 11   ' make an hourglass

' Write the patterns trained out first
    Put #1, , Events

' We'll store all link weights until written in the same array

' first write link 0 of net
    k% = GetLink(netnum, 0, Linkarray(0))
    For i% = 0 To (Inputs + 1) * Hiddens
       ' That's how many in the weight array (+1 is for bias weight)
        Put #1, , Linkarray(i%)              ' write it out
    Next i%

' now write link 1 of net
    k% = GetLink(netnum, 1, Linkarray(0))
    For i% = 0 To (Hiddens + 1) * Hiddens    ' That's how many
                                             ' in the weight array
        Put #1, , Linkarray(i%)              ' Write it out
    Next i%

' finally write link 2 of net
    k% = GetLink(netnum, 2, Linkarray(0))
    For i% = 0 To (Hiddens + 1) * Outputs    ' That's how many
                                             ' in the weight array
        Put #1, , Linkarray(i%)              ' Write it out
    Next i%
    Close #1
    Screen.mousepointer = 0   ' restore cursor
    Exit Sub

Errors4:
    NetwkError% = k%
    NetworkErrors
    Close #1
    Screen.mousepointer = 0   ' restore cursor


End Sub

Sub LoadMenu_Click ()
    Filename$ = InputBox$("Name the file where networks
```

```
    ➥will be found:", "Load Network", "stockxls.net")
    If Filename$ = "" Then Exit Sub

    Open Filename$ For Binary As #1

    If LOF(1) = 0 Then
        MsgBox "Error opening file: " + Filename$, 16, ""
        Close #1
        Screen.mousepointer = 0    ' restore cursor
        Exit Sub
    End If


Screen.mousepointer = 11    ' make an hourglass

' Read the patterns trained out first
  Get #1, , Events


' first read link 0 of net

For i% = 0 To (Inputs + 1) * Hiddens     ' That's how many
                                         ' in the weight array
                                         ' (+1 is for bias weight)
   Get #1, , Linkarray(i%)               ' Read in
Next i%

k% = PutLink(netnum, 0, Linkarray(0))    ' Give it to the net
If k% Then GoTo errors5


' next read link 1 of net

For i% = 0 To (Hiddens + 1) * Hiddens     ' That's how many
                                          ' in the weight array
                                          ' (+1 is for bias weight)
   Get #1, , Linkarray(i%)                ' Read in
Next i%

k% = PutLink(netnum, 1, Linkarray(0))     ' Give it to the net
If k% Then GoTo errors5


' finally read link 2 of net

For i% = 0 To (Hiddens + 1) * Outputs     ' That's how many
                                          ' in the weight array
                                          ' (+1 is for bias weight)
   Get #1, , Linkarray(i%)                ' Read in
Next i%
```

continues

LISTING 12.2. CONTINUED

```
k% = PutLink(netnum, 2, Linkarray(0))    ' Give it to the net
If k% Then GoTo errors5


    Close #1
    Screen.mousepointer = 0   ' restore cursor
    Exit Sub

errors5:
    NetwkError% = k%
    NetworkErrors
End Sub

Sub ObjCom_Click ()
On Error GoTo E1
    x% = Shell("C:\vb\Objedit", 1)
    Exit Sub
E1:
    SaveErr% = Err
    GeneralErrors
    Resume Next
End Sub


' neuro DDE

Sub Command1_Click ()
    Excelread
    CancelFlag% = 0
    Unload neuroDDE
End Sub

Sub Excelread ()
' Reads training data from spreadsheet


  On Error GoTo startit  ' If Excel not up load it


 transfer.linkmode = NONE
 ' Note before running this application, put sheetname
 ' into C:\excel.

tryagain:
 transfer.LinkTopic = "Excel¦c:\excel\" + sheetname.text
 transfer.linkitem = "R1C1"
 transfer.linkmode = COLD


' First read minimums and maximums for training set
```

```
i% = 4 '  First row has minimums

  For j% = 1 To Inputs
    InMin(j%) = getcell(i%, j% + 1)' Get the data from sheet
  Next j%
  j% = Inputs + 1
  ' There is only one output
    Outmin = getcell(i%, j% + 1)

i% = 5 '  Next row has maximums
  For j% = 1 To Inputs
    Inmax(j%) = getcell(i%, j% + 1)
  Next j%
  j% = Inputs + 1
  ' There is only one output
    Outmax = getcell(i%, j% + 1)


' Now read the patterns themselves

For i% = 1 To patterns
  For j% = 1 To Inputs
    temp! = getcell(i% + 5, j% + 1)' Starts on third row
    Training_Input(j%, i%) = Map(temp!, InMin(j%),
      ➥Inmax(j%), 0!, 1!)  ' Map to [0,1]
  Next j%
    j% = Inputs + 1
    temp! = getcell(i% + 5, j% + 1)
    Training_Output(i%) = Map(temp!, Outmin, Outmax, .1!, .9!)
                                            ' Map to [.1,.9]

Next i%

transfer.linkmode = NONE    ' Close it out
Exit Sub

startit:
 If timeshere% > 0 Then
    MsgBox "Having trouble loading EXCEL or the proper spreadsheet.
      ➥Please make sure both are in C:\EXCEL", 16, ""
    i% = KillNet(netnum)
    End
 Else
    timeshere% = 1  ' A dynamic variable
    If Err = 282 Then ' Load Excel with the sheet if not loaded
      MsgBox "Excel is not up with that spreadsheet. I will load a copy.",
        ➥48, ""
      excelid = Shell("c:\EXCEL\excel.exe c:\excel\" +
        ➥sheetname.text, 7)      ' Load excel minimized
      Resume tryagain
    End If
```

continues

LISTING 12.2. CONTINUED

```
 End If
End Sub

Function getcell (row%, col%) As Single
    '  Make a cell name, e.g. R1C1, for LinkItem
    transfer.linkitem = "R" + LTrim$(Str$(row%)) + "C" + LTrim$(Str$(col%))
    transfer.LinkRequest
    getcell = Val(transfer.text)
End Function

Sub Command2_Click ()
    CancelFlag% = -1
    Unload neuroDDE
End Sub


' Errors Module


Sub GeneralErrors ()
    Msg$ = Error$(SaveErr%)
    MsgBox Msg$
    Select Case SaveErr%
        Case 280 To 297
            DDEErrors
        Case 30000 To 31015
            OLEErrors
    End Select
End Sub

Sub DDEErrors ()
        Select Case SaveErr%
            Dim App%
            Case 282
                App% = Shell(Server$, 1)
                App% = DoEvents()
            Case 283
                Msg$ = "Suggest you open Program Manager "
                Msg$ = Msg$ + " NOW and use End Task "
                Msg$ = Msg$ + " to terminate the LAST "
                Msg$ = Msg$ + " INSTANCE of " + Server$
                MsgBox Msg$

        End Select
End Sub

Sub OLEErrors ()
        Select Case SaveErr%

            Case 30005
                Msg$ = "OLE_Error_Stream"
```

```
                MsgBox Msg$
            ' Other cases here.
        End Select

End Sub

Sub NetworkErrors ()
  Select Case NetwkError%
   Case noerror
     Msg$ = "No errors detected."
   Case nomemory
     Msg$ = "Not enough global memory was available for the request."
   Case badnettype
     Msg$ = "Unknown network type."
   Case badnetnum
     Msg$ = "Invalid network number."
   Case netactive
     Msg$ = "Network is already in use."
   Case netinactive
     Msg$ = "Network is not in use."
   Case badslabtype
     Msg$ = "Invalid slab type (layer)."
   Case badslabnum
     Msg$ = "Invalid slab number."
   Case slabactive
     Msg$ = "Slab is already in use."
   Case slabinactive
     Msg$ = "Slab is not in use."
   Case noneurons
     Msg$ = "At least one neuron must be specified in every slab."
   Case slablinked
     Msg$ = "All of a slab's links must be killed
        ➥before the slab can be killed."
   Case badlinknum
     Msg$ = "Invalid link number."
   Case toomanylinks
     Msg$ = "Slab already has maximum number of links to it."
   Case linkactive
     Msg$ = "Link is already in use."
   Case linkinactive
     Msg$ = "Link is not in use."
   Case wrongnettype
     Msg$ = "Network was not the right type for the function requested."
   Case notoslabs
     Msg$ = "No slabs are linked to the specified slab."
   Case badeval
     Msg$ = "Evaluation function may only be requested
        ➥for an Output layer slab."
   Case badfromneuron
     Msg$ = "Invalid from neuron index passed to GetWeight or Putweight."
   Case badtoneuron
     Msg$ = "Invalid to neuron index passed to GetWeight or Putweight."
```

continues

LISTING 12.2. CONTINUED

```
   Case badserial
     Msg$ = "Serial number is incorrect."
   Case badmath
     Msg$ = "Unknown math type specified in SetMath."
   Case badneighbor
     Msg$ = "Neighborhood for Lvq must be >= 0."
   Case badneuron
      Msg$ = "Bad neuron number passed to Getneuron or Putneuron."
   Case badfile
      Msg$ = "I/O error opening or reading neuroShell .NET file."
   Case brdnospace
      Msg$ = "Not enough memory on neuroBoard for requested operation."
   Case brdbadfile
      Msg$ = "Problems reading neuroBoard .CDE initialization file."
   Case maxbrderror
      Msg$ = "No more than 10 neuroBoards may be used at once."
   Case brdnoreponse
      Msg$ = "The neuroBoard is not reponding to commands
         ➥(Check the address)."
   Case brdslower
      Msg$ = "Warning: PutSlab & GetSlab may be slow
         ➥due to low neuroBoard memory."
   Case badpattern
      Msg$ = "Pattern number passed to Pnn for change
         ➥did not already exist."
   Case badsmoothing
      Msg$ = "Smoothing factor must be greater than zero"
   Case Else
     Msg$ = "Unknown error code: " + Str$(errornum)
 End Select

    MsgBox Msg$
End Sub


' neuroWIN2 SUPPORT  Note proprietary information
' has been removed from this file, so it will not compile
' without the NEUROWINDOWS DLL

' General Use Constants



' Neural Network Type Constants  (you may want these in
' declarations proc of a form or global module)

Const BpVanilla% = 1      ' Vanilla backpropagation
Const BpMomentum% = 2     ' backpropagation with momentum
Const BpBatch% = 3        ' Weights not updated after every event
Const LvqVanilla% = 4     ' Vanilla Learning Vector Quantizer
```

```
Const LvqNormalized% = 5 ' Input vectors are normalized instead of
                         ' mapped on to [0,1]
Const PnnVanilla% = 6    ' Vanilla Probabilistic Neural Network
Const PnnNormalized% = 7 ' Input vectors are normalized instead of
                         ' mapped on to [0,1]

' Layer Constants (you may want these in declarations
' proc of a form or global module)

Const InputLayer% = 0     ' For a slab in the input layer
Const HiddenLayer% = 1    ' For a slab in any hidden layer
Const OutputLayer% = 2    ' For a slab in the output layer

' Constants for SetMath

Const Floating% = 0
Const Fixed% = 1


' Constants for reference only to document release 1.0

Const MaxNets = 128    ' maximum number of networks per program
Const MaxSlabs = 32    ' maximum number of slabs per net
Const MaxLinks = 32    ' maximum number of links per net
Const MaxSlabLinks = 8 ' maximum number of slabs any slab can
                       ' be linked to or from

' Neural Network Function Declarations

Declare Function GetNextNet% Lib "NEUROWIN.DLL" (net%)

Declare Function MakeSlab% Lib "NEUROWIN.DLL" (net%, slab%,
➥ neurons%, layer%)
Declare Function MakeLink% Lib "NEUROWIN.DLL" (net%, link%,
➥ weight!, fromslab%, toslab%)

Declare Function PutSlab% Lib "NEUROWIN.DLL" (net%, slab%, array!)
Declare Function GetSlab% Lib "NEUROWIN.DLL" (net%, slab%, array!)

Declare Function PutSlabInteger% Lib "NEUROWIN.DLL" (net%, slab%, array%)
Declare Function GetSlabInteger% Lib "NEUROWIN.DLL" (net%, slab%, array%)

Declare Function Putneuron% Lib "NEUROWIN.DLL" (net%, slab%,
➥ neuron%, value!)
Declare Function Getneuron% Lib "NEUROWIN.DLL" (net%, slab%,
➥ neuron%, value!)

Declare Function PutLink% Lib "NEUROWIN.DLL" (net%, link%, array!)
Declare Function GetLink% Lib "NEUROWIN.DLL" (net%, link%, array!)

Declare Function PutWeight% Lib "NEUROWIN.DLL" (net%, link%,
➥ fromneuron%, toneuron%, weight!)
```

continues

LISTING 12.2. CONTINUED

```
Declare Function GetWeight% Lib "NEUROWIN.DLL" (net%, link%,
➥ fromneuron%, toneuron%, weight!)

Declare Function BpPropagate% Lib "NEUROWIN.DLL" (net%, toslab%)
Declare Function BpEvaluate% Lib "NEUROWIN.DLL" (net%, slab%,
➥ actuals!, errorfactor!)
Declare Function BpEvaluateSum% Lib "NEUROWIN.DLL" (net%, slab%, actuals!)
Declare Function BpGetSum% Lib "NEUROWIN.DLL" (net%, slab%, errorfactor!)
Declare Function BpEvaluateInteger% Lib "NEUROWIN.DLL" (net%, slab%,
➥ actuals%, errorfactor!)
Declare Function BpTrain% Lib "NEUROWIN.DLL" (net%, fromslab%,
➥ learnrate!, Momentum!, updateswitch%)

Declare Function LvqPropagate% Lib "NEUROWIN.DLL" (net%, toslab%)
Declare Function LvqEvaluate% Lib "NEUROWIN.DLL" (net%, slab%,
➥ Winner%, adjust%)
Declare Function LvqTrain% Lib "NEUROWIN.DLL" (net%, fromslab%, learnrate!,
➥ neighborhood%, cols%)

Declare Function PnnPropagate% Lib "NEUROWIN.DLL" (net%, toslab%,
➥ smoothing!)
Declare Function PnnEvaluate% Lib "NEUROWIN.DLL" (net%, slab%,
➥ actuals!, pattern%)
Declare Function PnnTrain% Lib "NEUROWIN.DLL" (net%, fromslab%,
➥ pattern%)


Declare Function CopySlab% Lib "NEUROWIN.DLL" (fromnet%, fromslab%,
➥ tonet%, toslab%)
Declare Function SetSlab% Lib "NEUROWIN.DLL" (net%, slab%, value!)
Declare Function SlideSlab% Lib "NEUROWIN.DLL" (net%, slab%, value!)
Declare Function InitLink% Lib "NEUROWIN.DLL" (net%, link%, weight!)

Declare Function KillNet% Lib "NEUROWIN.DLL" (net%)
Declare Function KillSlab% Lib "NEUROWIN.DLL" (net%, slab%)
Declare Function KillLink% Lib "NEUROWIN.DLL" (net%, link%)

Declare Function SetMath% Lib "NEUROWIN.DLL" (mathtype%)
Declare Function SetCPU% Lib "NEUROWIN.DLL" (cpu%)
Declare Function LoadShell% Lib "NEUROWIN.DLL" (net%, ByVal path$)

' Error returns (See Neterror$)

 Const noerror = 0          ' No errors detected.
 Const nomemory = 1         ' Not enough global memory was
                            ' available for the request.
 Const badnettype = 2       ' Unknown network type.
 Const badnetnum = 3        ' Invalid network number.
 Const netactive = 4        ' Network is already in use.
 Const netinactive = 5      ' Network is not in use.
```

```
Const badslabtype = 6   ' Invalid slab type (layer).
Const badslabnum = 7    ' Invalid slab number.
Const slabactive = 8    ' Slab is already in use.
Const slabinactive = 9  ' Slab is not in use.
Const noneurons = 10    ' At least one neuron must be specified
                        ' in every slab.
Const slablinked = 11   ' All of a slab's links must be killed
                        ' before the slab can be killed.
Const badlinknum = 12   ' Invalid link number.
Const toomanylinks = 13 ' Slab already has maximum number of links to it.
Const linkactive = 14   ' Link is already in use.
Const linkinactive = 15 ' Link is not in use.
Const wrongnettype = 16 ' Network was not the right type
                        ' for the function requested.
Const notoslabs = 17    ' No slabs are linked to the specified slab.
Const badeval = 18      ' Evaluation function may only be requested
                        ' for an Output layer slab.
Const badfromneuron = 19 ' Bad from neuron number passed to
                         ' GetWeight or PutWeight
Const badtoneuron = 20   ' Bad to neuron number passed to
                         ' GetWeight or PutWeight
Const badserial = 21     ' Serial number was not correct
Const badmath = 22       ' Unknown math type specified in SetMath
Const badneighbor = 23   ' Neighborhood for Lvq must be >= 0
Const badneuron = 24     ' Bad neuron number passed to
                         ' Getneuron or Putneuron
Const badfile = 25       ' I/O error opening or reading neuroShell .NET file
Const brdnospace = 26    ' No memory left on neuroBoard
Const brdbadfile = 27    ' Problems reading neuroBoard .CDE
                         ' initialization file
Const maxbrderror = 28   ' No more than 10 neuroBoards allowed at once.
Const brdnoreponse = 29  ' neuroBoard is not responding (check the address)
Const brdslower = 30     ' Warning: PutSlab and GetSlab may be slow
                         ' due to low neuroBoard memory
Const badpattern = 31    ' Pattern number passed to Pnn for change
                         ' did not already exist
Const badsmoothing = 32  ' Smoothing factor must be greater than zero

Function Map! (ByVal value!, min!, max!, x1!, x2!)
'  maps value from [min,max] into [x1,x2]
' This function can be used to map neural net inputs from
'  their [min,max] ranges into [.0,1.0] and actual values
'  from their [min, max] ranges to [.1, .9] (or [.0,1.0])
' Then the output layer can be mapped back from [.1, .9]
  If min = max Then
    MsgBox "Min and max are equal in Map: " + Str$(min) + ", " +
    ➥Str$(max), 16, ""
    Map = 0!
    Exit Function
  End If
  If value < min Then value = min
  If value > max Then value = max
```

continues

LISTING 12.2. CONTINUED

```
  Map = (x2 - x1) * (value - min) / (max - min) + x1


End Function

Sub Normalize (array() As Single, count As Integer)
' This function normalizes a vector(array) for Lvq or Pnn
' Count is the count of elements in the array
' This function assumes the first element has index 1

sum! = 0
For i% = 1 To count
  sum = sum + array(i%) * array(i%)   ' sum of the squares
Next i%

If sum = 0 Then Exit Sub   '  nothing to do
sum = Sqr(sum)   '  take the square root

For i% = 1 To count
  array(i%) = array(i%) / sum
Next i%

End Sub

Function Winner% (array() As Single, count As Integer)
' This function searches a vector(array) for the index
'  of the largest value in the array.
' This function is useful in classification problems
'   for both Pnn and Backprop to find the "winning"
'   classification in the output layer.
' Count is the count of elements in the array
' This function assumes the first element has index 1

j% = 1
For i% = 2 To count
  If array(i%) > array(j%) Then j% = i%
Next i%

Winner% = j%

End Function

Function SD3 (array() As Single, count As Integer, mean As Single) As Single
' This function finds the mean and 3 times the standard
'  deviation of the data in array. The number of array
'  elements is in count. Three times the standard deviation
'  is returned by the function, and the mean is placed in
'  the variable mean passed to the function.
' If your data is in a column of an array, just use this
```

```
'  code in your own program to make the computation.
' SD3 might be used in conjunction with Map if you want
'  to clip your data at +- 3 standard deviations from the
'  mean. After you determine min=mean-DS3 and max=mean+DS3,
'  just use them as [min, max] in the MAP function.

Dim sumx, sumx2, hold As Single
For i% = 1 To count
  hold = array(i%)'  more efficient to reference array once
  sumx = sumx + hold
  sumx2 = sumx2 + hold * hold
Next i%
mean = sumx / count
SD3 = 3 * Sqr((count * sumx2 - sumx * sumx) / (count * (count - 1)))
End Function
```

Summary

That does it for this extended example application connecting a Visual Basic application to a DLL using DDE and OLE. If you need more information about DDEs or DLLS, see Appendix A, "Third-Party Support and Custom Controls," in this book or the *Microsoft Visual Basic Language Reference*. For the latest scoop on NEUROWINDOWS, contact Ward Systems (its address is in the Reference section).

If you want to connect any DLL or make a DDE or OLE link to your application, check the documentation for the software you're attempting to use with your Visual Basic application. The popularity of Visual Basic is leading many third-party vendors to develop DDLs that interact directly with Visual Basic. I've worked with much of their support software, and I find much of it just as amazing as Visual Basic.

Objects, Instances, and MDI

In Version 3.0, Visual Basic extends its object-orientation in a major way, providing *object variables* that correspond to "key" objects—forms or controls. You can use object variables to create new instances of forms and to manipulate forms and controls at runtime. This is an exciting new feature that you can use to build applications that don't "know" the precise number (or even) types of forms needed until runtime.

Create New Instances of Objects at Runtime

Using the Forms Collection

Menus Instead of Command Buttons

How MDI works

Create An MDI Form

In this chapter, you'll develop four applications that explore the dynamic manipulation of objects through object variables: *Multinst*, *Multins2*, *Multins3*, and *MDIWiz*.

Create New Instances of Objects At Runtime

Object variables allow you to create new instances of forms in an application during runtime. To create a new instance of a specific object type, such as a form, you first create the form; then use the keyword, `New`, to create an *instance* of the form when you need it at runtime.

`New` is a "new" keyword in Version 3.0, and is used only to create instances of *specific* forms or *generic* controls. You can't use it to create new variables of any fundamental data types (integer, string, etc.), variables of any generic object type (MDIForm, form, or control) or any specific control type (commandbutton, textbox, and so on).

To create a new instance of a form (called Form1), use `New` with a `Dim`, `ReDim`, `Static`, or `Global` declaration. For example:

```
Dim Frm As New Form1            'One new instance
Frm.Show
```

or

```
ReDim Frms(5) As New Form1      ' An array of new instances
Dim I As Integer
For I = 0 to UBound(Frms)
     Frms(I).Show
Next I
```

Note that Visual Basic doesn't actually create the new instance of the form until you reference the form, for example, by showing the form.

To see this for yourself, let's create an application (Multinst) that creates and destroys new instances of forms. Multinst consists of the following:

- A form
- Three command buttons
- A label

Use the default names for the form (Form1), the command buttons (command1, command2, command3), and the label. Use the command buttons to do the following:

- Create a new instance of a form (command1)
- Unload or destroy an instance of a form (command2)
- Create an array of form instances (command3)
- Show the current use of system resources (label1)

Figure 13.1 shows the layout of Form1 in design view.

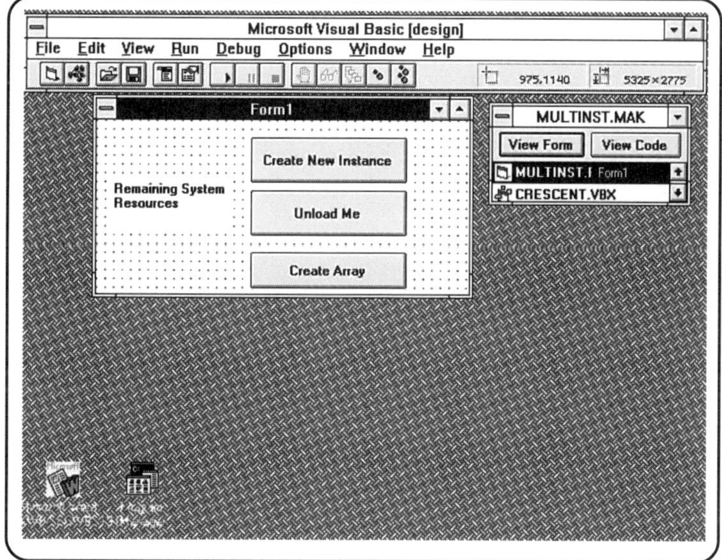

Figure 13.1. The layout of Form1 in design view.

Command1_Click: Creating a New Instance of a Form

Use a `Command1_click` event to create and show a new instance of the form:

```
Sub Command1_Click ()
    Dim Frm As New Form1        ' Declare form variable
    Frm.Show                    ' Load and display new instance
End Sub
```

Use the form's `Move` and and `BackColor` properties to align the form relative to the current form and to randomly color the form:

```
Sub Command1_Click ()
    Dim Frm As New Form1        ' Declare form variable
    Frm.Show                    ' Load and display new instance

                                ' Move and color new instance
    Frm.Move Left + (Width \ 10), Top + (Height \ 10)
    Frm.BackColor = RGB(Rnd * 256, Rnd * 256, Rnd * 256)
End Sub
```

Use the external `GetSystemsResources()` function (in the Crescent.Vbx on the disk and described in Chapter 9) to show the percent of currently available system resources:

```
Sub Command1_Click ()
    Dim Frm As New Form1        ' Declare form variable
    Dim Res As Integer
    Frm.Show                    ' Load and display new instance

                                ' Move and color new instance
    Frm.Move Left + (Width \ 10), Top + (Height \ 10)
    Frm.BackColor = RGB(Rnd * 256, Rnd * 256, Rnd * 256)
    Res = GetSystemResources()     ' What % resources are remaining?
    Frm!Label1.Caption = Frm!Label1.Caption & " = " & Str$(Res) & "%"
End Sub
```

(On my system, I use about one percent of my systems resources every two new forms or so—of type form1; a more complex form would use more resources.)

ME

`Me` is a new reserved word in Visual Basic Version 3.0. `Me` is automatically available to every Sub or Function procedure in a form. When an application has more than one instance of a form, `Me` lets you refer to the specific instance of the form where the code is currently executing. Using `Me` is also useful when you want to pass information about the current instance of a form to a procedure in another module. For example, suppose you have the following procedure in a module:

```
Sub SubUnload (ThisForm As Form)
    Unload ThisForm
End Sub
```

You can call the procedure and pass the current instance of the form as an argument using the following statement in one of the procedures in your form:

```
SubUnload Me
```

> In most cases the form referred to by `Me` is the same as the form referred to by `Screen.ActiveForm`. However, `Me` and `Screen.ActiveForm` can refer to different forms. `Screen.ActiveForm` always refers to the form that has the focus; `Me` always refers to the form where code is executing.

> For example, a Timer event in an application can occur in a form that doesn't have the focus. In this situation, `Me` refers to the form where the Timer event occurs (or occurred). `Screen.ActiveForm` refers to the form that currently has the focus.

Command2_Click: Unloading An Instance of a Form

The simplest way to unload an instance of a form is to unload `Me`:

```
Sub Command2_Click ()
     Unload Me
End Sub
```

Command3_Click: Verifying When Instances Are Created

Let's next return to a point raised earlier in the chapter: that instances of forms aren't created until the instance is referenced.

To verify that this is indeed the case, create an array of forms (using `ReDim`), but don't show (or otherwise reference) the forms, as follows:

```
Sub Command3_Click ()
     ReDim Frms(5) As New Form1
     Dim I As Integer
     Dim PreI As Integer
     Dim Res As Integer
     PreI = 0
     For I = 0 To UBound(Frms)
          Res = GetSystemResources()
          If I > 0 Then PreI = I - 1 Else PreI = I
          Debug.Print Res
     Next I
End Sub
```

Run the application. Figure 13.2 shows the results. Notice that even after creating five new instances of the form, system resource usage remains unchanged.

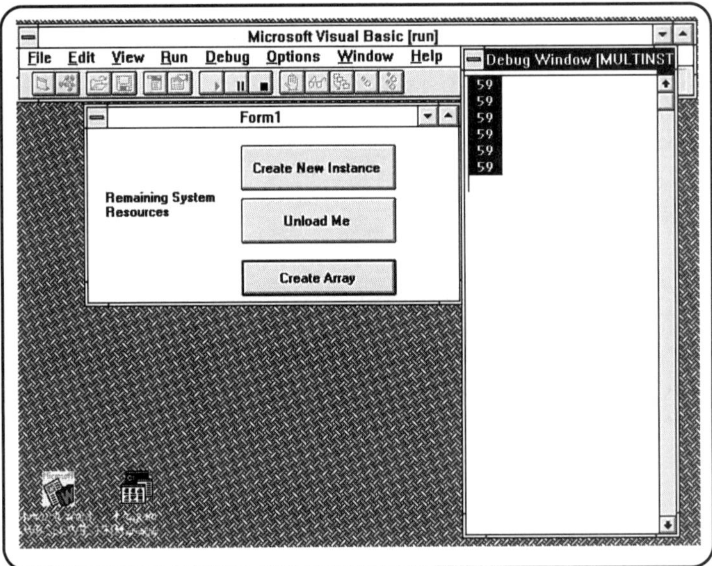

Figure 13.2. Notice that even after creating five new instances of the form, system resource usage remains unchanged.

Next, revise the code for `Command3_click` as follows to move and show the form:

```
Sub Command3_Click ()
    ReDim Frms(5) As New Form1
    Dim I As Integer
    Dim PreI As Integer
    Dim Res As Integer
    PreI = 0
    For I = 0 To UBound(Frms)
        Frms(I).Move Frms(PreI).Left + (Width \ 10), Frms(PreI).Top + (Height\10)
        Frms(I).BackColor = RGB(Rnd * 256, Rnd * 256, Rnd * 256)
        Res = GetSystemResources()
       Frms(I)!Label1.Caption = Frms(I)!Label1.Caption & " = " & Str$(Res) & "%"
        Frms(I).Show
        If I > 0 Then PreI = I - 1 Else PreI = I
        Debug.Print Res
    Next I
End Sub
```

Figure 13.3 shows these results.

Notice the use of system resources when the form is referenced.

Note also the use of the variable, `PreI`, in the code for `Command3_click`. We use this variable to align the next instance of the form slightly down and to the right of the current instance of the form. In this specific example, not using `PreI` to maintain the position of the last instance results in all the new instances of the form (except the first new instance) being placed on top of each other. Verify this by changing all occurrences of `PreI` to `I` in the `frms()` array in this event procedure:

```
Sub Command3_Click ()
    ReDim Frms(5) As New Form1
    Dim I As Integer
    Dim PreI As Integer
    Dim Res As Integer
    PreI = 0
    For I = 0 To UBound(Frms)
        Frms(I).Move Frms(I).Left + (Width \ 10), Frms(I).Top + (Height \ 10)
        Frms(I).BackColor = RGB(Rnd * 256, Rnd * 256, Rnd * 256)
        Res = GetSystemResources()
        Frms(I)!Label1.Caption = Frms(I)!Label1.Caption & " = " & Str$(Res) & "%"
        Frms(I).Show
        If I > 0 Then PreI = I - 1 Else PreI = I
        Debug.Print Res
    Next I
End Sub
```

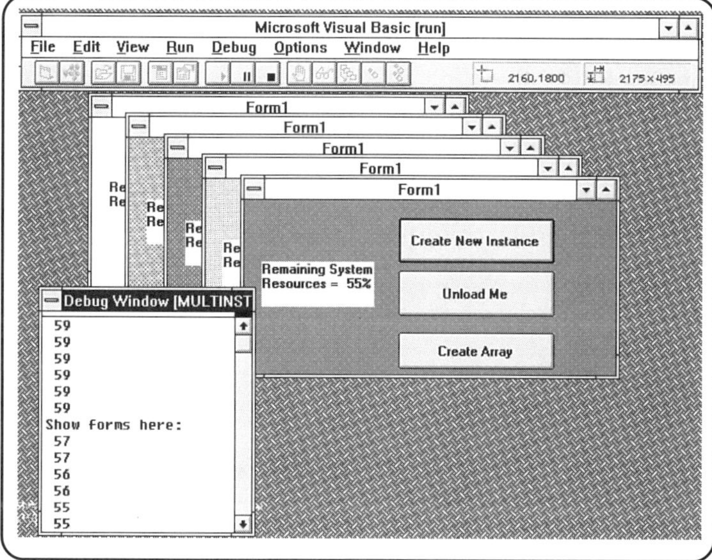

Figure 13.3. Note the using of system resources when the form is referenced.

Figure 13.4 shows the results. System resources are getting used, but all but the first new instance of the form are hidden (below the top instance of the form). Delete the top instance of the form (or move the top instance of the form) to reveal an almost indentical form below it.

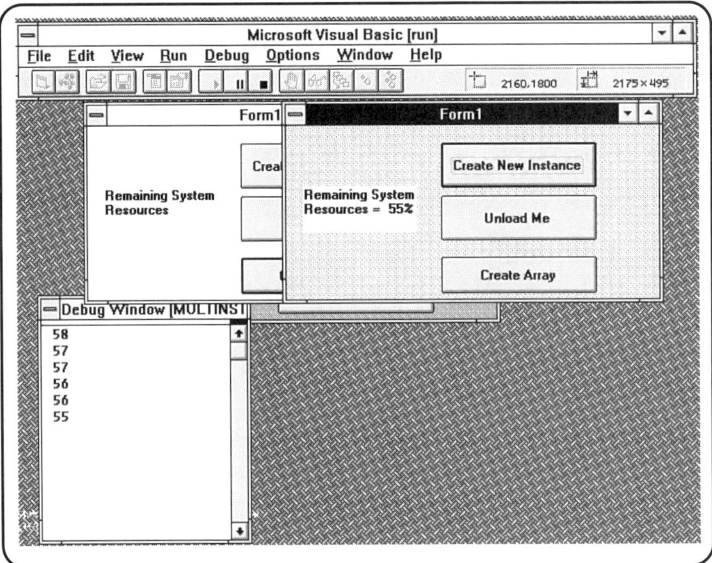

Figure 13.4. System resources are getting used, but all but the first new instance of the form are hidden (below the top instance of the form). The top instance of the form has been moved in this figure.

In short, you need to keep track of the location of the previous instance of a form if you want the new instances of the form to be cascaded.

Listing 13.1 shows the complete code for the Multinst application.

Listing 13.1. The Multinst application.

```
Option Explicit
Declare Function GetSystemResources% Lib "Crescent.Vbx" ()

Sub Command1_Click ()
    Dim Frm As New Form1          ' Declare form variable
    Dim Res As Integer
    Frm.Show                      ' Load and display new instance

                                  ' Move and color new instance
```

```
    Frm.Move Left + (Width \ 10), Top + (Height \ 10)
    Frm.BackColor = RGB(Rnd * 256, Rnd * 256, Rnd * 256)
    Res = GetSystemResources()     ' What % resources are remaining?
    Frm!Label1.Caption = Frm!Label1.Caption & " = " & Str$(Res) & "%"
End Sub

Sub Command2_Click ()
    Unload Me
End Sub

Sub Form_Load ()
    Randomize
End Sub
```

Collections

A collection is an ordered set of similarly typed objects. Collection objects are ordered numerically from zero to the Count of objects – 1.

Although a collection consistently maintains a set of objects, any object's position in the collection may change whenever a change occurs in the collection. In other words, an instant of a form in a form collection might initially be element number five in a collection. However, if an instant of a form below five is removed from the collection, form five might become form four in the collection. Thus, the position of any specific object in a collection is unpredictable. Contrast a collection with an array, where objects (or members) of an array maintain their positions in the array unless they are explicitly changed, even if members of the array are deleted.

The Forms collection maintains the count of each loaded instant of a form in an application. The collection includes the application's MDI form, MDI child forms, and non-MDI forms. Use the Forms collection's only property, `Count`, to return the number of elements in the collection.

The Forms collection is globally pre-defined by Visual Basic and can be accessed anywhere in an application, using the name, `Forms`.

Note that `Forms` is a keyword, but not a reserved word. It identifies a global variable named `Forms`. You can use `Forms(index)` as an argument to a procedure with a parameter of type Form.

MULTINS2: USING THE FORMS COLLECTION

The next application, Multins2, is a slight variation on Multinst. It does the following:

- Uses the forms collection to get the number (count) of currently active forms; then uses that count to display the number of active forms.
- Uses the getsystems resources function to check for existing resources before creating a new instance of a form.
- Uses `Me` and the current value of `Me`'s `Caption` property to decide whether to destroy the current instance of a form.
- Uses a command button's `Value` property to trigger a click event to remove several instances of a form as a process.

Multins2 uses five command buttons and three labels. Figure 13.5 shows this form in design view.

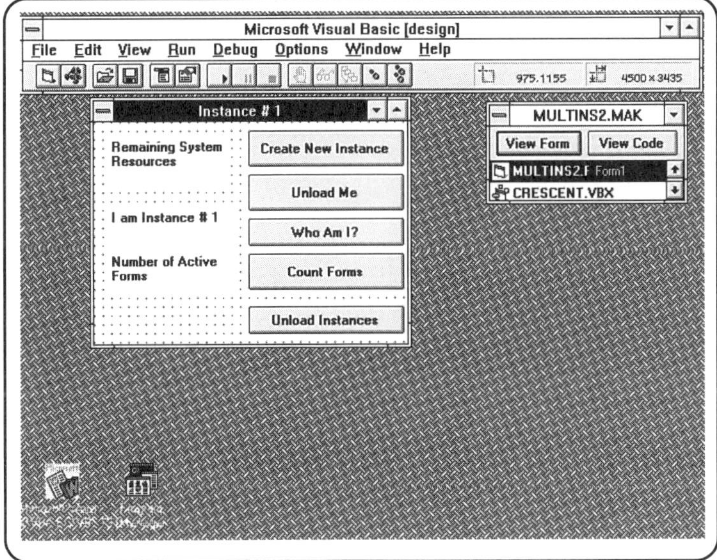

Figure 13.5. Multinst2 in design view.

The `Command1_click` event creates a new instance of the form after first checking the current systems resources. It also uses the forms collection to create a caption for the new instance:

```
Sub Command1_Click ()
    Dim Res As Integer
    Res = GetSystemResources()
    If Res > 65 Then           ' > than 65% (arbitrary %)
        Dim F As New Form1   ' Declare form variable

        F.Show           ' Load and display new instance

    ' Move and color new instance
        F.Move Left + (Width \ 10), Top + (Height \ 10)
        F.BackColor = RGB(Rnd * 256, Rnd * 256, Rnd * 256)
        F!Label1.Caption = F!Label1.Caption & " = " & Str$(Res) & "%"
        F.Caption = "Instance # " & Str$(Forms.Count)
        F.Label3.Caption = ""
    Else
```

```
        MsgBox "Not enough resources to create Instance."
    End If
End Sub
```

The `Command2_click` event unloads the current instance of the form:

```
Sub Command2_Click ()
    Unload Me
End Sub
```

The `Command3_click` event uses the forms collection to report (in label2) the number of currently active forms:

```
Sub Command3_Click ()
    Label2.Caption = Label2.Caption & " = " & Str$(Forms.Count)
End Sub
```

The `Command4_click` event uses `Me` and its caption to report (in label3) who the current form is:

```
Sub Command4_Click ()
    Label3.Caption = "I am " & Me.Caption
End Sub
```

The `Command5_click` event uses `Me` and its caption to determine the current form. If the caption indicates that this (`Me`) isn't the first instance of the form, it unloads itself and sends a message to the currently active form (the one that gets control after this instance is destroyed). This message is a trigger of the `Command5_click` event on that instance. If it is the first instance of the form, it doesn't unload itself:

```
Sub Command5_Click ()
    If Me.Caption <> "Instance # 1" Then
    Unload Me
    Screen.ActiveForm.Command5.Value = -1
    End If
End Sub
```

Figure 13.6 shows Multins2 during runtime.

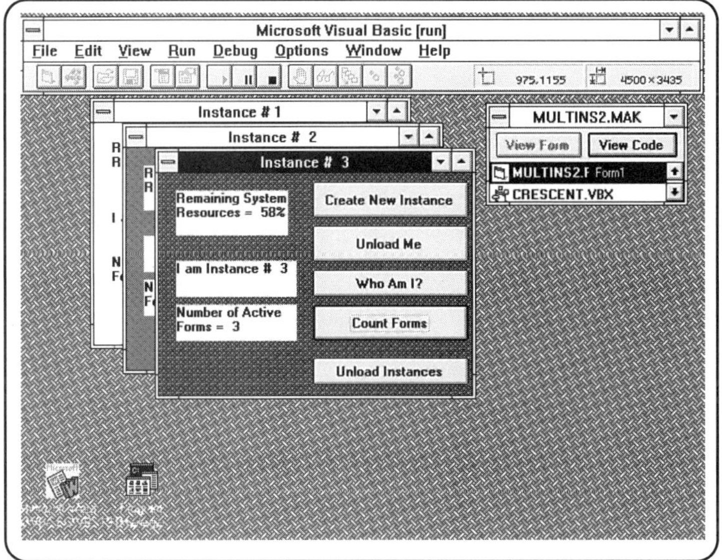

Figure 13.6. Multins2 during runtime.

Listing 13.2 shows the complete code for Multinst2.

Listing 13.2. Multins2.

```
Option Explicit
Declare Function GetSystemResources% Lib "Crescent.Vbx" ()

Sub Command1_Click ()
    Dim Res As Integer
    Res = GetSystemResources()
    If Res > 65 Then
        Dim F As New Form1   ' Declare form variable

        F.Show               ' Load and display new instance

    ' Move and color new instance
        F.Move Left + (Width \ 10), Top + (Height \ 10)
        F.BackColor = RGB(Rnd * 256, Rnd * 256, Rnd * 256)
        F!Label1.Caption = F!Label1.Caption & " = " & Str$(Res) & "%"
        F.Caption = "Instance # " & Str$(Forms.Count)
        F.Label3.Caption = ""
    Else
        MsgBox "Not enough resources to create Instance."
    End If
End Sub
```

continues

LISTING 13.2. CONTINUED

```
Sub Command2_Click ()
    Unload Me
End Sub

Sub Command3_Click ()
    Label2.Caption = Label2.Caption & " = " & Str$(Forms.Count)
End Sub

Sub Command4_Click ()
    Label3.Caption = "I am " & Me.Caption
End Sub

Sub Command5_Click ()
    If Me.Caption <> "Instance # 1" Then
    Unload Me
    UnloadFlag = -1
    Screen.ActiveForm.Command5.Value = -1
    End If
End Sub

Sub Form_Load ()
    Randomize
    UnloadFlag = 0
End Sub
```

MULTINS3: MENUS INSTEAD OF COMMAND BUTTONS

As you might have noticed, the Multins2 form is tad crowded. A simple way to unclutter the form without significantly revising the code is to make menu items to do the same tasks as the command buttons. This is straight-forward and since menus have already been discussed in detail in this book (in Chapter 3), I won't go into the details here, but simply show you the code with comments.

One item to note: to save time, I borrowed the code from Multins2 and didn't bother to remove the command buttons from the Multins3 when I created the menu. I simply hid the command buttons at runtime (by setting each command button's `Visible` property to False). Thus, the command buttons are still on the form (and can be used), but they can't be seen. For this "quick and dirty" example, this approach allows us to implement a menu that uses the `Command5_click` event (that already exists) to unload several instances of the form in one process:

```
Sub mnuUnload_Click ()
    If Me.Caption <> "Instance # 1" Then
    Unload Me
```

```
    Screen.ActiveForm.Command5.Value = -1
    End If
End Sub
```

Also, notice that the `mnuUnloadMe_click` event invokes another Sub procedure `SubUnload(ThisForm As Form)` to unload the current form (`Me`):

```
Sub mnuUnloadMe_Click ()
'    Unload Me       ' Could have just unloaded Me
    SubUnload Me          ' but passing Me is Ok too.
End Sub


Sub SubUnload (ThisForm As Form)
    Unload ThisForm
End Sub
```

These two procedures demonstrate that you can pass a form name as a parameter.

Figures 13.7 and 13.8 show the form in design view (with the command buttons visible) and during runtime (with the command buttons hidden.)

Listing 13.3 shows the complete code for Multins3.

Listing 13.3. Multins3.

```
Option Explicit
Declare Function GetSystemResources% Lib "Crescent.Vbx" ()

Sub Command1_Click ()
    Dim Res As Integer
    Res = GetSystemResources()
    If Res > 65 Then
        Dim F As New Form1   ' Declare form variable

        F.Show          ' Load and display new instance

    ' Move and color new instance
        F.Move Left + (Width \ 10), Top + (Height \ 10)
        F.BackColor = RGB(Rnd * 256, Rnd * 256, Rnd * 256)
        F!Label1.Caption = F!Label1.Caption & " = " & Str$(Res) & "%"
        F.Caption = "Instance # " & Str$(Forms.Count)
        F.Label3.Caption = ""
    Else
        MsgBox "Not enough resources to create Instance."
    End If
End Sub

Sub Command2_Click ()
    Unload Me
```

continues

Listing 13.3. continued

```
End Sub

Sub Command3_Click ()
    Label2.Caption = Label2.Caption & " = " & Str$(Forms.Count)
End Sub

Sub Command4_Click ()
    Label3.Caption = "I am " & Me.Caption
End Sub

Sub Command5_Click ()
    If Me.Caption <> "Instance # 1" Then
    Unload Me
    'UnloadFlag = -1
    Screen.ActiveForm.Command5.Value = -1
    End If
End Sub

Sub Form_Load ()
    Randomize
    'UnloadFlag = 0
End Sub

Sub mnuCountForms_Click ()
    Label2.Caption = Label2.Caption & " = " & Str$(Forms.Count)
End Sub

Sub mnuCreateNewInstance_Click ()
    Dim Res As Integer
    Res = GetSystemResources()
    If Res > 55 Then
        Dim F As New Form1  ' Declare form variable

        F.Show          ' Load and display new instance

    ' Move and color new instance
        F.Move Left + (Width \ 10), Top + (Height \ 10)
        F.BackColor = RGB(Rnd * 256, Rnd * 256, Rnd * 256)
        F!Label1.Caption = F!Label1.Caption & " = " & Str$(Res) & "%"
        F.Caption = "Instance # " & Str$(Forms.Count)
        F.Label3.Caption = ""
    Else
        MsgBox "Not enough resources to create Instance."
    End If
End Sub

Sub mnuExit_Click ()
    Unload Me
End Sub
```

```
Sub mnuUnload_Click ()
    If Me.Caption <> "Instance # 1" Then
    Unload Me
 '    UnloadFlag = -1
    Screen.ActiveForm.Command5.Value = -1
    End If
End Sub

Sub mnuUnloadMe_Click ()
'     Unload Me
    SubUnload Me
End Sub

Sub mnuWho_Click ()
    Label3.Caption = "I am " & Me.Caption
End Sub

Sub SubUnload (ThisForm As Form)
    Unload ThisForm
End Sub
```

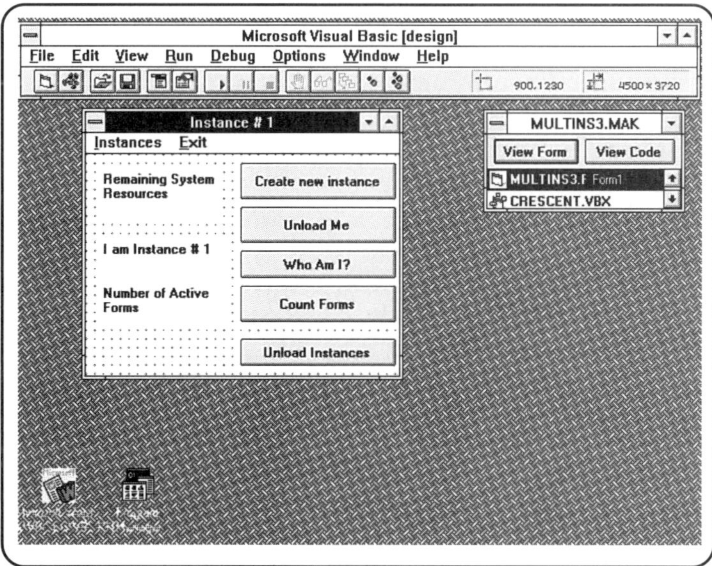

Figure 13.7. Multins3 in design view with the command buttons visible.

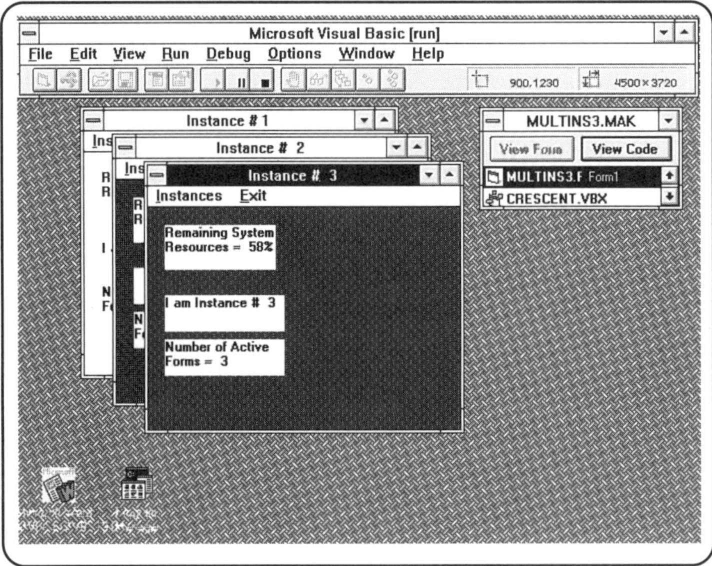

Figure 13.8. Multins3 at runtime with the command buttons hidden.

HOW MDI WORKS

And now for a variation on the multiple instance theme—MDI.

Visual Basic's multiple-document interface (MDI) lets you create applications in which one parent form (an MDI form) holds (or maintains) multiple child forms (a form is a child form if its `MDIChild` property is True).

Using MDI is basically a three-step process:

1. Create an MDI form to hold MDI child forms.
2. Create the form you want to use as an MDI child.
3. Write specific code to define the relationships between the MDI form and the child forms.

You create the MDI and child form separately during design time; then the child form (or forms) are displayed within the borders of the MDI form at runtime (see Figures 13.9 and 13.10).

The MDI form and any MDI child form can have their own menus. Visual Basic displays the menu you design for an MDI child form on the MDI form at run time when the MDI child form is active, even though it only appears on the child form at design time. In other words, an MDI form might have its own menu, one displayed when no MDI child form is active. However, if an MDI child form is active, and if it has a menu, that menu (not the MDI form menu) will be displayed at runtime (see Figures 13.11 and 13.12).

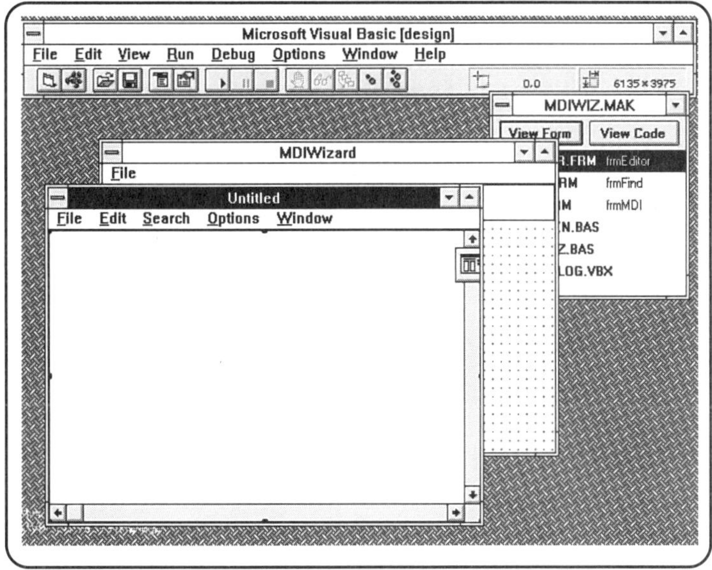

Figure 13.9. MDI form and MDI child during design view.

Unlike non-MDI forms, an MDI form can only contain a picture box or other custom controls that have an `Align` property. You can, however, place other controls within the picture box. For example, you might use the picture box to create a toolbar.

On an MDI form, you must align a picture box to the top or bottom of the MDI form client area. The picture box will always have the same width as the

`ScaleWidth` of the MDI form, but it can have any height up to the `ScaleHeight` of the MDI form.

If you want to place a common dialog control on an MDI form, you place it within a picture box's boundaries. (You will not be able to place a common dialog box directly on an MDI form.)

Typically, you want several MDI child forms in an MDI application to function similarly. For example, child forms might represent open files in an MDI text editor, spreadsheets in a spreadsheet application, or tables in a database. When form functionality is similar, you can use multiple instances of a single form type, or an array of forms of a single type, instead of designing more than one child form.

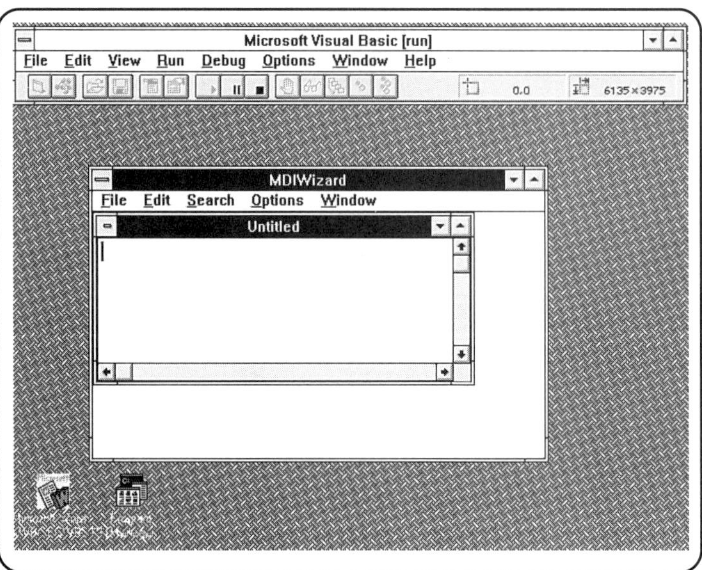

Figure 13.10. MDI form and MDI child during runtime.

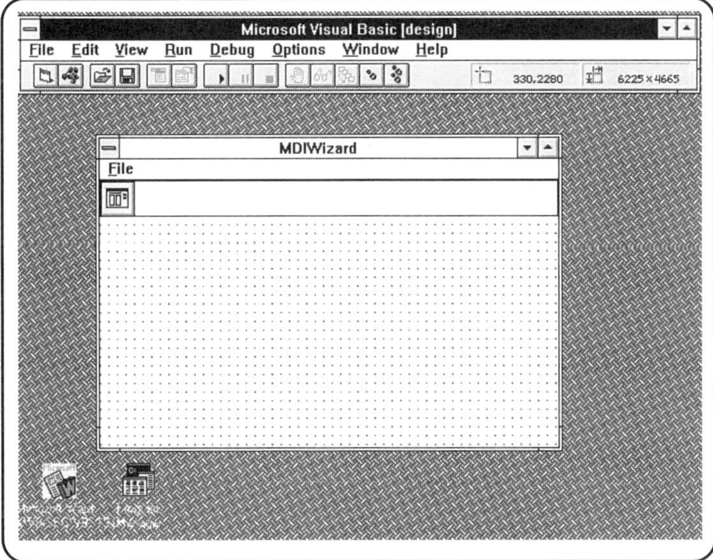

Figure 13.11. MDI form at runtime with its own menu.

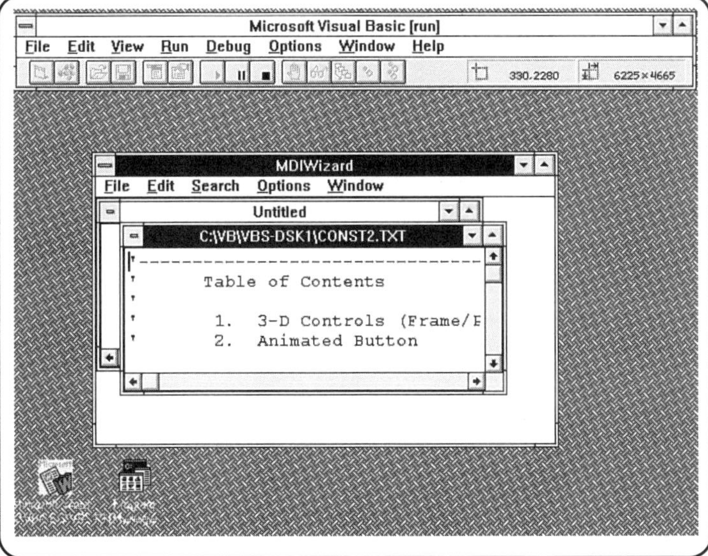

Figure 13.12. MDI form and Active child at runtime. Child menu is now shown.

You can load or instantiate MDI child forms dynamically at run time using the `Dim` or `ReDim` statement. After creating a new instance of a form (i.e., a child form), you can change that instance's properties without affecting the properties of other forms. Each instance of a form type has its own life.

As in the examples earlier in this chapter, the `Me` keyword is the "key" to referencing the currently active instance of a form or the currently active form array element. You can also use the `ActiveForm` property of an MDI form to determine which MDI child form has the focus (or was most recently active).

If you want an MDI form or MDI child's menu to display a list of open child forms at runtime, check the WindowList check box in the Menu Design window of the MDI form or the MDI child form. Then use the Arrange method to rearrange, tile, and cascade child forms and their icons.

Let's explore these (and other) aspects of MDI in more detail by developing a multi-file text editor application (called MDIWIZ on the disk).

CREATE AN MDI FORM

To create an MDI form, select New MDI Form from the File menu. An MDI form (note the form Caption) appears in the project (see Figure 13.13).

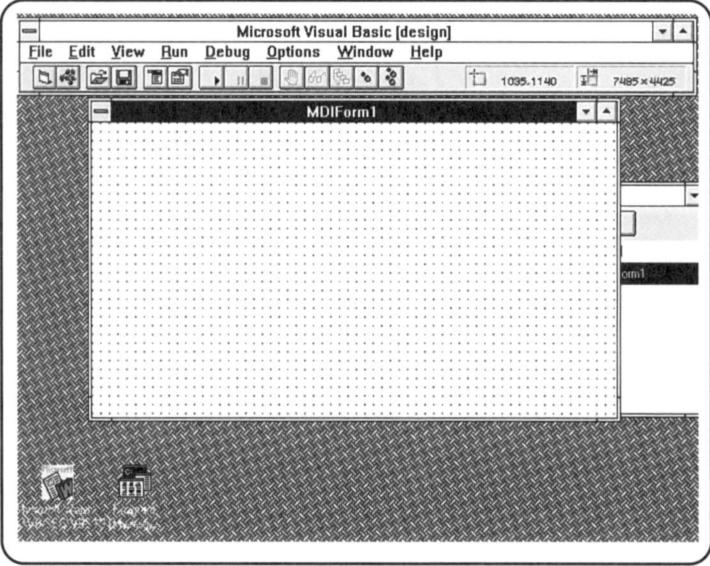

Figure 13.13. Use New MDI Form to Create an MDI Form.

An application can have only one MDI form but can have many MDI child forms. Although you design MDI child forms independently of the MDI form, MDI child forms always appear (contained) within the MDI form at runtime.

Create a menu bar (called Files) for the MDI form with New, Open, and Exit menu items. These commands will do the following:

- Create a new file
- Open an existing file
- Exit the application

Next, add a picture box to the MDI form. In this example, the picture box will only be used to hold a common dialog box. However, you could use this picture box to hold a toolbar (see Figure 13.14).

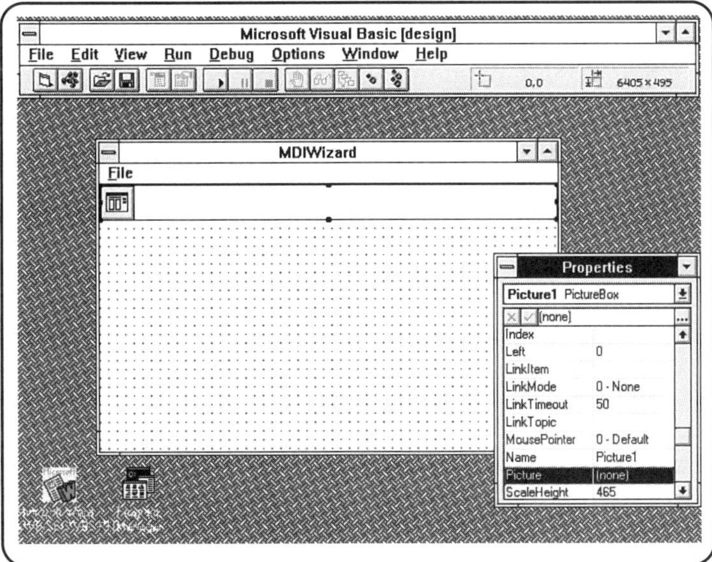

Figure 13.14. MDI form with menu bar, picture box, and common dialog box.

CREATE AN EDITOR CHILD FORM

Before developing any code, create the child form type. Use the Files/New form menu command to create the form. Call this form, "frmEditor." Then change its MDI child property to True to indicate that the form will appear as an MDI child form inside an MDI form.

The child form will continue to be displayed as a separate form at design time, but at run time, it will appear inside an MDI form. Note that an MDI child form can be maximized, minimized, and moved, all inside the parent MDI form.

At runtime, the Windows environment controls the initial size and placement of MDI child forms unless you manually place the child in the `Form_Load` procedure.

> If your application references an MDI child form before it loads the parent MDI form, Visual Basic automatically loads the parent MDI form before loading the MDI child form. However, if your application references the parent MDI form before loading an MDI child form, Visual Basic won't automatically load the child form.

Next, create the child form's menu. Add File, Edit, Search, Options, and Window menu items to the horizontal menu bar. Add New, Open Close, Save, Save As, and Exit items to the File menu. Add Cut, Copy, Paste, Delete, Select All, and Time/Date items to the Edit menu. Add Find and Find Next items to the Search menu. Add Font to the Options menu. Add Cascade, Tile, and Arrange Icons items to the Window menu. Make sure to check WindowList when you create the Window menu to enable a display of open child forms (or child windows). See Figure 13.15.

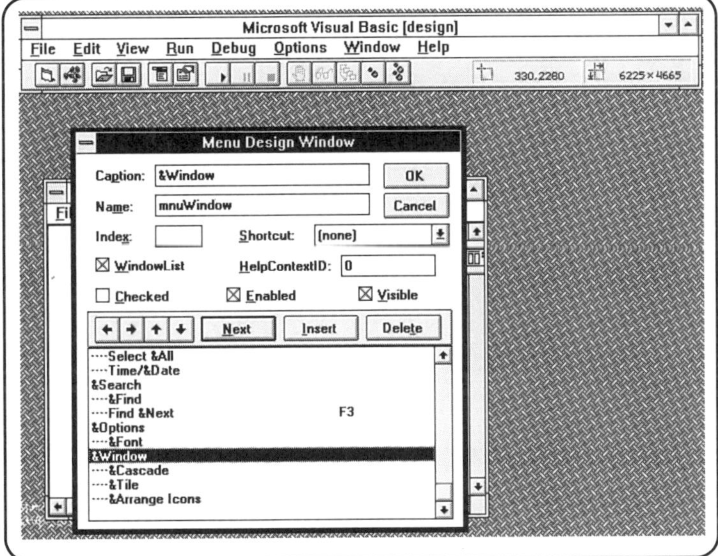

Figure 13.15. Check WindowList during Menu Design to enable a display of open child forms.

Finally, create a multi-line text box on the child form to handle text and add a common dialog box (which you'll use to display fonts for the text box). Figure 13.16 shows the child form during design view.

Creating a New Child at Runtime

Recall from earlier examples that you use `New` to create a new instance of a form at runtime. Since this MDI editor will want to optionally display more than one instance of a child form at a time during runtime, create a global array of new forms. Create a global module called MDIWiz.bas and declare an array of child forms (frmEditor forms) as follows:

```
Global Document() As New frmEditor
```

Then, each time a user requests a new child form (a new file to be edited), redimension the document array by preserving the existing array and adding a new item (ArrayCount + 1) to the array:

```
ReDim Preserve Document(ArrayCount + 1)
```

In order to make this MDI editor more useful for text editing (or word processing), you need to create code to open, close, and save files, to search for text within a text box, to copy and paste text to and from the Clipboard, to switch fonts, and to manage child windows. Opening, closing, and saving files and interacting with the Clipboard have been discussed earlier in this book, so I'll just show you the code here (in Listing 13.4).

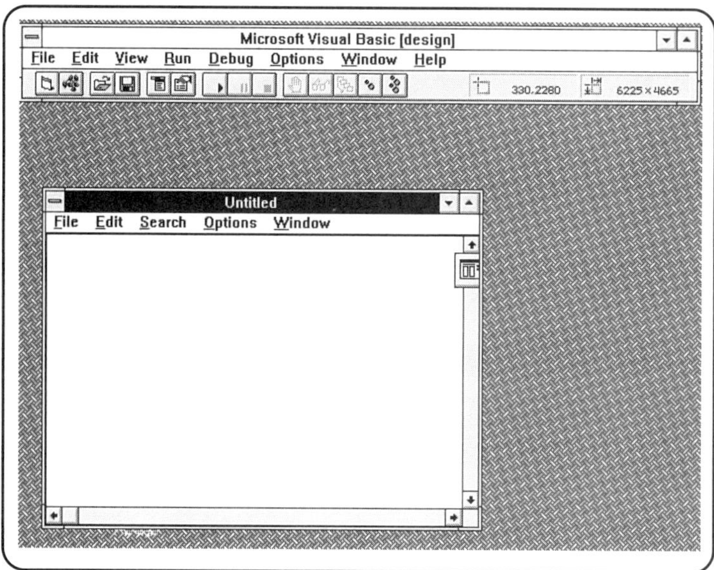

Figure 13.16. The child form during design view.

Maintaining child forms and closing the MDI text editor is a bit more complicated than maintaining and closing a single-file text editor. One way to manage each child form is through the use of a corresponding Form State record for each form. The one this example uses maintains Deleted and Dirty flags (to indicate whether a form has been deleted or its text changed) and a record of the form's Color:

```
Type FormState
    Deleted As Integer
    Dirty As Integer
    Color As Long
End Type
```

This record is created each time a new child form is created:

```
ReDim Preserve Document(ArrayCount + 1)
ReDim Preserve FState(ArrayCount + 1)
```

The application then uses this state record each time a new child form is created to determine whether any child forms have been deleted. If a chld form has been deleted, an existing index in the child form array is used. If no child forms have been deleted, the size of the array is dynamically increased using `ReDim`:

```
Function GetDocIndex () As Integer
    Dim i As Integer
    Dim ArrayCount As Integer

    ArrayCount = UBound(Document)

    ' Cycle through the document array. If one of the
    ' documents has been deleted, then return that
    ' index.
    For i = 1 To ArrayCount
        If FState(i).Deleted Then
            GetDocIndex = i
            FState(i).Deleted = False
            Exit Function
        End If
    Next

    ' If none of the elements in the document array have
    ' been deleted, then increment the document and the
    ' state arrays by one and return the index to the
    ' new element.

    ReDim Preserve Document(ArrayCount + 1)
    ReDim Preserve FState(ArrayCount + 1)
    GetDocIndex = UBound(Document)
End Function
```

The Form state's `Deleted` property is set to true when the form is unloaded:

```
Sub Form_Unload (Cancel As Integer)
    FState(Me.Tag).Deleted = True
End Sub
```

The form state is also used to determine if there are any open child forms when the MDI form closes:

```
Sub MDIForm_Unload (Cancel As Integer)
    ' If the Unload was not canceled
    ' (in the QueryUnload events for the Notepad forms)
    ' there will be no document windows left,
    ' so go ahead and end the application.
    If Not FindOpenDocuments() Then
        End
    End If
End Sub

Function FindOpenDocuments () As Integer
    Dim i As Integer

    ' Cycle through the document array.
```

```
    ' Return True if there is at least one
    ' open document remaining.
    For i = 1 To UBound(Document)
        If Not FState(i).Deleted Then
            FindOpenDocuments = True
            Exit Function
        End If
    Next
End Function
```

In order to maintain a list of recently used files, you can establish an initialization file (MDIWIZ.INI) for the editor and use external Functions (contained in the Windows Kernel) to get and write the private profile string for the file.

Declare the two external functions:

```
Declare Function GetPrivateProfileString Lib "Kernel"
➥ (ByVal lpApplicationName As String, ByVal lpKeyName As String,
➥ ByVal lpDefault As String, ByVal lpReturnedString As String,
➥ ByVal nSize As Integer, ByVal lpFileName As String) As Integer
Declare Function WritePrivateProfileString Lib "Kernel"
➥ (ByVal lpApplicationName As String, ByVal lpKeyName As String,
➥ ByVal lpString As String, ByVal lplFileName As String) As Integer
```

Then Get the most recently edited files:

```
Sub GetRecentFiles ()
  Dim retval, key, i, j
  Dim IniString As String

  ' This variable must be large enough to hold the return string
  ' from the GetPrivateProfileString API.
  IniString = String(255, 0)

  ' Get recent file strings from MDIWIZ.INI
  For i = 1 To 4
    key = "RecentFile" & i
    retval = GetPrivateProfileString("Recent Files", key, "Not Used",
➥ IniString, Len(IniString), "MDIWIZ.INI")
    If retval And Left(IniString, 8) <> "Not Used" Then
      ' Update the MDI form's menu.
      frmMDI.mnuRecentFile(0).Visible = True
      frmMDI.mnuRecentFile(i).Caption = IniString
      frmMDI.mnuRecentFile(i).Visible = True

      ' Iterate through all the notepads and update each menu.
      On Error GoTo E1
      For j = 1 To UBound(Document)
        If Not FState(j).Deleted Then
          Document(j).mnuRecentFile(0).Visible = True
          Document(j).mnuRecentFile(i).Caption = IniString
          Document(j).mnuRecentFile(i).Visible = True
        End If
```

```
      Next j
    End If
  Next i

E1:
    Exit Sub
End Sub
```

And write recent files:

```
Sub WriteRecentFiles (OpenFileName)
  Dim i, j, key, retval
  Dim IniString As String
  IniString = String(255, 0)

  ' Copy RecentFile1 to RecentFile2, etc.
  For i = 3 To 1 Step -1
    key = "RecentFile" & i
    retval = GetPrivateProfileString("Recent Files", key, "Not Used",
➥ IniString, Len(IniString), "MDIWIZ.INI")
    If retval And Left(IniString, 8) <> "Not Used" Then
      key = "RecentFile" & (i + 1)
      retval = WritePrivateProfileString("Recent Files", key, IniString,
➥ "MDIWIZ.INI")
    End If
  Next i

  ' Write openfile to first Recent File.
    retval = WritePrivateProfileString("Recent Files", "RecentFile1",
➥ OpenFileName, "MDIWIZ.INI")
End Sub
```

The application manages child windows using the MDI form's `Arrange` method with appropriate constants (defined in WizFile.bas):

```
Sub mnuWArrange_Click ()
    frmMDI.Arrange ARRANGE_ICONS
End Sub

Sub mnuWCascade_Click ()
    frmMDI.Arrange CASCADE
End Sub

Sub mnuWTile_Click ()
    frmMDI.Arrange TILE_HORIZONTAL
End Sub
```

Use the font dialog box to allow users to select different fonts. Set the common dialog box, Flags property and show the Fonts dialog box by setting the common dialog box's Action property to 4:

```
Sub mnuFont_Click ()
    CMDialog1.CancelError = True
```

```
    On Error GoTo FontError
    CMDialog1.Flags = &H3& Or &H100&
    CMDialog1.Action = 4
    Text1.FontName = CMDialog1.FontName
    Text1.FontSize = CMDialog1.FontSize
    Text1.FontBold = CMDialog1.FontBold
    Text1.FontItalic = CMDialog1.FontItalic
    Text1.FontUnderline = CMDialog1.FontUnderline
    Text1.FontStrikethru = CMDialog1.FontStrikethru
    Text1.ForeColor = CMDialog1.Color
    Exit Sub
FontError:
    Exit Sub
End Sub
```

Listing 13.4 contains the complete code for this project. Use this MDI Wizard as the start for more complex MDI applications.

Listing 13.4. MIDWIZ.

```
'MDIWiz.bas

' global declarations
Option Explicit

Global Const CASCADE = 0
Global Const TILE_HORIZONTAL = 1
Global Const TILE_VERTICAL = 2
Global Const ARRANGE_ICONS = 3

' type to maintain the state of each editor form
Type FormState
    Deleted As Integer
    Dirty As Integer
    Color As Long
End Type


Global FState()  As FormState
Global Document() As New frmEditor
Global gFindString, gFindCase As Integer, gFindDirection As Integer
Global gCurPos As Integer, gFirstTime As Integer
Global ArrayNum As Integer

' API functions used to read and write to MDIWIZ.INI.
' For handling the recent files list.
Declare Function GetPrivateProfileString Lib "Kernel"
➥ (ByVal lpApplicationName As String, ByVal lpKeyName As String,
➥ ByVal lpDefault As String, ByVal lpReturnedString As String,
```

```
➥ ByVal nSize As Integer, ByVal lpFileName As String) As Integer
Declare Function WritePrivateProfileString Lib "Kernel"
➥ (ByVal lpApplicationName As String, ByVal lpKeyName As String,
➥ ByVal lpString As String, ByVal lplFileName As String) As Integer

Sub CenterForm (frmParent As Form, frmChild As Form)
' This procedure centers a child form over a parent form.
' Calling this routine loads the dialog. Use the Show method
' to display the dialog after calling this routine ( ie MyFrm.Show 1)

Dim l, t
  ' get left offset
  l = frmParent.Left + ((frmParent.Width - frmChild.Width) / 2)
  If (l + frmChild.Width > screen.Width) Then
    l = screen.Width = frmChild.Width
  End If

  ' get top offset
  t = frmParent.Top + ((frmParent.Height - frmChild.Height) / 2)
  If (t + frmChild.Height > screen.Height) Then
    t = screen.Height - frmChild.Height
  End If

  ' center the child formfv
  frmChild.Move l, t

End Sub

Sub EditCopyProc ()
    ' Copy selected text to Clipboard.
    ClipBoard.SetText frmMDI.ActiveForm.ActiveControl.SelText
End Sub

Sub EditCutProc ()
    ' Copy selected text to Clipboard.
    ClipBoard.SetText frmMDI.ActiveForm.ActiveControl.SelText
    ' Delete selected text.
    frmMDI.ActiveForm.ActiveControl.SelText = ""
End Sub

Sub EditPasteProc ()
    ' Place text from Clipboard into active control.
    frmMDI.ActiveForm.ActiveControl.SelText = ClipBoard.GetText()
End Sub

Sub FileNew ()
    Dim fIndex As Integer
    fIndex = GetDocIndex()
    Document(fIndex).Tag = fIndex
    Document(fIndex).Caption = "Untitled:" & fIndex
    Document(fIndex).Show
End Sub
```

continues

Listing 13.4. continued

```
Sub FindIt ()
    Dim start, pos, findstring, sourcestring, msg, response, Offset

    If (gCurPos = frmMDI.ActiveForm.ActiveControl.SelStart) Then
        Offset = 1
    Else
        Offset = 0
    End If

    If gFirstTime Then Offset = 0

    start = frmMDI.ActiveForm.ActiveControl.SelStart + Offset

    If gFindCase Then
        findstring = gFindString
        sourcestring = frmMDI.ActiveForm.ActiveControl.Text
    Else
        findstring = UCase(gFindString)
        sourcestring = UCase(frmMDI.ActiveForm.ActiveControl.Text)
    End If

    If gFindDirection = 1 Then
        pos = InStr(start + 1, sourcestring, findstring)
    Else
        For pos = start - 1 To 0 Step -1
            If pos = 0 Then Exit For
            If Mid(sourcestring, pos, Len(findstring)) =
    ➥ findstring Then Exit For
        Next
    End If

    ' If string is found
    If pos Then
        frmMDI.ActiveForm.ActiveControl.SelStart = pos - 1
        frmMDI.ActiveForm.ActiveControl.SelLength = Len(findstring)
        frmFind.Top = 500

    Else
        msg = "Cannot find " & Chr(34) & gFindString & Chr(34)
        response = MsgBox(msg, 0, App.Title)
        frmFind.cmdcancel.Default = True
    End If

    gCurPos = frmMDI.ActiveForm.ActiveControl.SelStart
    gFirstTime = False
End Sub

Function FindOpenDocuments () As Integer
```

```
    Dim i As Integer

    ' Cycle through the document array.
    ' Return True if there is at least one
    ' open document remaining.
    For i = 1 To UBound(Document)
        If Not FState(i).Deleted Then
            FindOpenDocuments = True
            Exit Function
        End If
    Next
End Function

Function GetDocIndex () As Integer
    Dim i As Integer
    Dim ArrayCount As Integer

    ArrayCount = UBound(Document)

    ' Cycle through the document array. If one of the
    ' documents has been deleted, then return that
    ' index.
    For i = 1 To ArrayCount
        If FState(i).Deleted Then
            GetDocIndex = i
            FState(i).Deleted = False
            Exit Function
        End If
    Next

    ' If none of the elements in the document array have
    ' been deleted, then increment the document and the
    ' state arrays by one and return the index to the
    ' new element.

    ReDim Preserve Document(ArrayCount + 1)
    ReDim Preserve FState(ArrayCount + 1)
    GetDocIndex = UBound(Document)
End Function

Sub GetRecentFiles ()
  Dim retval, key, i, j
  Dim IniString As String

  ' This variable must be large enough to hold the return string
  ' from the GetPrivateProfileString API.
  IniString = String(255, 0)

  ' Get recent file strings from MDIWIZ.INI
  For i = 1 To 4
```

continues

LISTING 13.4. CONTINUED

```
    key = "RecentFile" & i
    retval = GetPrivateProfileString("Recent Files", key, "Not Used",
➥ IniString, Len(IniString), "MDIWIZ.INI")
    If retval And Left(IniString, 8) <> "Not Used" Then
      ' Update the MDI form's menu.
      frmMDI.mnuRecentFile(0).Visible = True
      frmMDI.mnuRecentFile(i).Caption = IniString
      frmMDI.mnuRecentFile(i).Visible = True

      ' Iterate through all the notepads and update each menu.
      On Error GoTo E1
      For j = 1 To UBound(Document)
        If Not FState(j).Deleted Then
          Document(j).mnuRecentFile(0).Visible = True
          Document(j).mnuRecentFile(i).Caption = IniString
          Document(j).mnuRecentFile(i).Visible = True
        End If
      Next j
    End If
  Next i

E1:
    Exit Sub
End Sub

Sub WriteRecentFiles (OpenFileName)
  Dim i, j, key, retval
  Dim IniString As String
  IniString = String(255, 0)

  ' Copy RecentFile1 to RecentFile2, etc.
  For i = 3 To 1 Step -1
    key = "RecentFile" & i
    retval = GetPrivateProfileString("Recent Files", key, "Not Used",
➥ IniString, Len(IniString), "MDIWIZ.INI")
    If retval And Left(IniString, 8) <> "Not Used" Then
      key = "RecentFile" & (i + 1)
      retval = WritePrivateProfileString("Recent Files", key, IniString,
➥ "MDIWIZ.INI")
    End If
  Next i

  ' Write openfile to first Recent File.
    retval = WritePrivateProfileString("Recent Files", "RecentFile1",
➥ OpenFileName, "MDIWIZ.INI")

End Sub
```

```
'FileOpen.bas

Sub FOpenProc ()
    Dim RetVal
    On Error Resume Next
    Dim OpenFileName As String
    frmMDI.CMDialog1.Filename = ""
    frmMDI.CMDialog1.Filter = "Txt files(*.txt)¦*.txt¦"
    frmMDI.CMDialog1.FilterIndex = 1
    frmMDI.CMDialog1.Action = 1
    If Err <> 32755 Then 'user pressed cancel
       OpenFileName = frmMDI.CMDialog1.Filename
       OpenFile (OpenFileName)
       UpdateFileMenu (OpenFileName)
   End If
End Sub

Function GetFileName ()
    'Displays a Save As dialog and returns a file name
    'or an empty string if the user cancels
    On Error Resume Next
    frmMDI.CMDialog1.Filename = ""
    frmMDI.CMDialog1.Action = 2
    If Err <> 32755 Then      'User cancelled dialog
     GetFileName = frmMDI.CMDialog1.Filename
    Else
     GetFileName = ""
    End If
End Function

Function OnRecentFilesList (Filename) As Integer
  Dim i

  For i = 1 To 4
    If frmMDI.mnuRecentFile(i).Caption = Filename Then
      OnRecentFilesList = True
      Exit Function
    End If
  Next i
    OnRecentFilesList = False
End Function

Sub OpenFile (Filename)
    Dim NL, TextIn, GetLine
    Dim fIndex As Integer

    NL = Chr$(13) + Chr$(10)

    On Error Resume Next
    'open the selected file
    Open Filename For Input As #1
```

continues

LISTING 13.4. CONTINUED

```
    If Err Then
     MsgBox "Can't open file: " + Filename
     Exit Sub
    End If
    ' change mousepointer to an hourglass
    screen.MousePointer = 11

    ' change form's caption and display new text
    fIndex = GetDocIndex()
    document(fIndex).Tag = fIndex
    document(fIndex).Caption = UCase$(Filename)
    document(fIndex).Text1.Text = Input$(LOF(1), 1)

    FState(fIndex).Dirty = False
    document(fIndex).Show
    Close #1
    ' reset mouse pointer
    screen.MousePointer = 0
End Sub

Sub SaveFileAs (Filename)
On Error Resume Next
    Dim Contents As String

    ' open the file
    Open Filename For Output As #1
    ' put contents of the notepad into a variable
    Contents = frmMDI.ActiveForm.Text1.Text
    ' display hourglass
    screen.MousePointer = 11
    ' write variable contents to saved file
    Print #1, Contents
    Close #1
    ' reset the mousepointer
    screen.MousePointer = 0
    ' set the Notepad's caption

    If Err Then
     MsgBox Error, 48, App.Title
    Else
     frmMDI.ActiveForm.Caption = UCase$(Filename)
     ' reset the dirty flag
     FState(frmMDI.ActiveForm.Tag).Dirty = False
    End If
End Sub
```

```
Sub UpdateFileMenu (Filename)
     Dim RetVal
     ' Check if OpenFileName is already on MRU list.
     RetVal = OnRecentFilesList(Filename)
     If Not RetVal Then
       ' Write OpenFileName to MDINOTEPAD.INI
       WriteRecentFiles (Filename)
     End If
     ' Update menus for most recent file list.
     GetRecentFiles
End Sub


'MDI form


Sub MDIForm_Load ()
    ' Application starts here (Load event of Startup form).
    Show
    ' Always set working directory to directory containing the application.
    ChDir App.Path

    'Initialize document form arrays, and show first document.
    ReDim Document(1)
    ReDim FState(1)
    Document(1).Tag = 1
    FState(1).Dirty = False
    Document(1).Show

    ' Read MDIWIZ.INI and set recent file menu items appropriately
    GetRecentFiles
End Sub

Sub MDIForm_Unload (Cancel As Integer)
    ' If the Unload was not canceled
    ' (in the QueryUnload events for the Notepad forms)
    ' there will be no document windows left,
    ' so go ahead and end the application.

    If Not FindOpenDocuments() Then
        End
    End If

End Sub

Sub mnuFExit_Click ()
    End
End Sub

Sub mnuFNew_Click ()
    FileNew
End Sub
```

continues

LISTING 13.4. CONTINUED

```
Sub mnuFOpen_Click ()
    FOpenProc
End Sub

Sub mnuRecentFile_Click (index As Integer)
  OpenFile (mnuRecentFile(index).Caption)
  ' Update recent files list.
  GetRecentFiles
End Sub

'Editor form


Sub Form_Load ()
'    Dim i As Integer

'    mnuFontName(0).Caption = screen.Fonts(0)
'    For i = 1 To screen.FontCount - 1
'        Load mnuFontName(i)
'        mnuFontName(0).Caption = screen.Fonts(i)
'    Next
End Sub

Sub Form_QueryUnload (Cancel As Integer, UnloadMode As Integer)
    Dim Msg, Filename, NL
    Dim Response As Integer

    If FState(Me.Tag).Dirty Then
     Filename = Me.Caption
     NL = Chr$(10) & Chr$(13)
     Msg = "The text in [" & Filename & "] has changed."
     Msg = Msg & NL
     Msg = Msg & "Do you want to save the changes?"
     Response = MsgBox(Msg, 51, frmMDI.Caption)
     Select Case Response
     ' User selects Yes
     Case 6
         'Get the filename to save the file
         Filename = GetFileName()
         'If the user did not specify a file name,
         'cancel the unload; otherwise, save it.
         If Filename = "" Then
          Cancel = True
         Else
          SaveFileAs (Filename)
         End If

     ' User selects No
     ' Ok to unload
```

```
        Case 7
            Cancel = False
        ' User selects Cancel
        ' Cancel the unload
        Case 2
            Cancel = True
        End Select
    End If
End Sub

Sub Form_Resize ()
    If windowstate <> 1 And ScaleHeight <> 0 Then
     Text1.Visible = False
     Text1.Height = ScaleHeight
     Text1.Width = ScaleWidth
     Text1.Visible = True
    End If
End Sub

Sub Form_Unload (Cancel As Integer)
    FState(Me.Tag).Deleted = True
End Sub

Sub mnuECopy_Click ()
    EditCopyProc
End Sub

Sub mnuECut_Click ()
    EditCutProc
End Sub

Sub mnuEDelete_Click ()
  ' If cursor is not at the end of the notepad.
  If screen.ActiveControl.SelStart <> Len(screen.ActiveControl.Text) Then
    ' If nothing is selected, extend selection by one.
    If screen.ActiveControl.SelLength = 0 Then
      screen.ActiveControl.SelLength = 1
      ' If cursor is on a blank line, extend selection by two.
      If Asc(screen.ActiveControl.SelText) = 13 Then
     screen.ActiveControl.SelLength = 2
      End If
    End If
    ' Delete selected text.
    screen.ActiveControl.SelText = ""
  End If
End Sub

Sub mnuEPaste_Click ()
    EditPasteProc
End Sub
```

continues

Listing 13.4. continued

```
Sub mnuESelectAll_Click ()
    frmMDI.ActiveForm.Text1.SelStart = 0
    frmMDI.ActiveForm.Text1.SelLength = Len(frmMDI.ActiveForm.Text1.Text)
End Sub

Sub mnuETime_Click ()
    Dim TimeStr As String, DateStr As String
    Text1.SelText = Now
End Sub

Sub mnuFClose_Click ()
    Unload Me
End Sub

Sub mnuFExit_Click ()
    ' Unloading the MDI form invokes the QueryUnload event
    ' for each child form, then the MDI form - before unloading
    ' the MDI form. Setting the Cancel argument to True in any of the
    ' QueryUnload events aborts the unload.

    Unload frmMDI
End Sub

Sub mnuFNew_Click ()
    FileNew
End Sub

Sub mnuFont_Click ()
    CMDialog1.CancelError = True
    On Error GoTo FontError
    CMDialog1.Flags = &H3& Or &H100&
    CMDialog1.Action = 4
    Text1.FontName = CMDialog1.FontName
    Text1.FontSize = CMDialog1.FontSize
    Text1.FontBold = CMDialog1.FontBold
    Text1.FontItalic = CMDialog1.FontItalic
    Text1.FontUnderline = CMDialog1.FontUnderline
    Text1.FontStrikethru = CMDialog1.FontStrikethru
    Text1.ForeColor = CMDialog1.Color
    Exit Sub
FontError:
    Exit Sub
End Sub

Sub mnuFontName_Click (index As Integer)
    'Text1.FontName = mnuFontName(index).Caption
End Sub

Sub mnuFOpen_Click ()
    FOpenProc
End Sub
```

```
Sub mnuFSave_Click ()
    Dim Filename As String

    If Left(Me.Caption, 8) = "Untitled" Then
     ' The file hasn't been saved yet,
     ' get the filename, then call the
     ' save procedure
     Filename = GetFileName()
    Else
     ' The caption contains the name of the open file
     Filename = Me.Caption
    End If
    ' call the save procedure, if Filename = Empty then
    ' the user selected Cancel in the Save As dialog, otherwise
    ' save the file
    If Filename <> "" Then
     SaveFileAs Filename
    End If
End Sub

Sub mnuFSaveAs_Click ()
    Dim SaveFileName As String

    SaveFileName = GetFileName()
    If SaveFileName <> "" Then SaveFileAs (SaveFileName)
    ' Update the recent files menu
    UpdateFileMenu (SaveFileName)
End Sub

Sub mnuRecentFile_Click (index As Integer)
  OpenFile (mnuRecentFile(index).Caption)
  ' Update recent files list for new notepad.
  GetRecentFiles
End Sub

Sub mnuSFind_Click ()
    If Me!Text1.SelText <> "" Then
     frmFind!Text1.Text = Me!Text1.SelText
    Else
     frmFind!Text1.Text = FindString
    End If
    gFirstTime = True
    frmFind.Show
End Sub

Sub mnuSFindNext_Click ()
    If Len(gFindString) > 0 Then
     FindIt
    Else
     mnuSFind_Click
    End If
```

continues

LISTING 13.4. CONTINUED

```
End Sub

Sub mnuWArrange_Click ()
    frmMDI.Arrange ARRANGE_ICONS
End Sub

Sub mnuWCascade_Click ()
    frmMDI.Arrange CASCADE
End Sub

Sub mnuWTile_Click ()
    frmMDI.Arrange TILE_HORIZONTAL
End Sub

Sub Text1_Change ()
    FState(Me.Tag).Dirty = True
End Sub

Sub Text1_GotFocus ()
    If frmFind.Visible Then
     frmFind.ZOrder 0
    End If
End Sub

'Find form


Sub chkCase_Click ()
    gFindCase = chkCase.Value
End Sub

Sub cmdcancel_Click ()
    gFindString = Text1.Text
    gFindCase = chkCase.Value
    Unload Frmfind
End Sub

Sub cmdFind_Click ()
    gFindString = Text1.Text
    FindIt
End Sub

Sub Form_Load ()
    cmdFind.Enabled = False
    gFindDirection = 1
End Sub

Sub optDirection_Click (index As Integer)
    gFindDirection = index
```

```
End Sub

Sub Text1_Change ()
    FirstTime = True

    If Text1.Text = "" Then
        cmdFind.Enabled = False
    Else
        cmdFind.Enabled = True
    End If
End Sub
```

Summary

And that wraps up this chapter's discussion of objects, object variables, and MDI. Using object variables in conjunction with MDI can make your applications both nifty and professional.

The capability of creating new instances of forms during runtime, dynamically, and of controlling multiple child forms from within a single MDI form are two of Visual Basic's most powerful features.

Using the Grid Custom Control and the Bonus PRHALL.VBX

This is a hands-on chapter that explores the grid control (a nifty custom control included with Visual Basic) and the external procedures included in prhall.vbx (on the disk in the back of this book).

In particular, if you're a spreadsheet developer, a music lover, plan to use the grid custom control, or need to declare procedures in external libraries, you'll benefit from the two applications, Compose1 and Compose2, in this chapter.

The prhall.vbx is a bonus .vbx file donated by MicroHelp that contains 13 low-level procedures. It's available on the disk in the back of this book.

Compose1 is a simple application that demonstrates the basic use of the grid control and prhall.vbx. Compose2 is a more complex application that shows how to use the grid control and prhall.vbx to create a useful composition based on a mandolin (or fiddle) fretboard. Use Compose1 and Compose2 as models for more complex grid applications or as a basis for other music composition applications.

Before we get to developing these applications, though, let's spend a few paragraphs introducing the grid custom control.

ABOUT THE GRID

The grid control is a powerful custom control that makes it easy for you to display a series of rows and columns that operate as a group on a form. The intersection of each row and column in the grid is a *cell*. You can read and write the contents of each cell programmatically.

You can put either text or a picture in any cell of a grid. The `Row` and `Col` properties specify the current cell in a grid. You can specify the current cell in code, or the user can dynamically specify the current cell at runtime using the arrow keys or the mouse. You use the `Text` property to reference the contents of the current cell. To read the contents of a cell, you indicate a current `Row` and current `Column` for reading:

```
Grid1.Col = 1       ' Set up a current cell.
Grid1.Row = 1
Grid1.Text = "Style"     ' Write to the cell.
```

If the text is too long to be displayed in the specified cell, the text automatically wraps to the next line within the same cell. To display the wrapped text, you must increase the cell's column width (using the `ColWidth` property) or row height (using the `RowHeight` property).

Use the `Cols` and `Rows` properties (note that these are different from the `Row` and `Col` properties) to determine the number of columns and rows in a grid. A grid is limited to 2000 rows by 400 columns.

In order to use a grid control in an application, you must add grid.vbx to the project. Use Files/Add File to add grid.vbx. After you add grid.vbx, the grid icon appears in the Toolbox (see Figure 14.1).

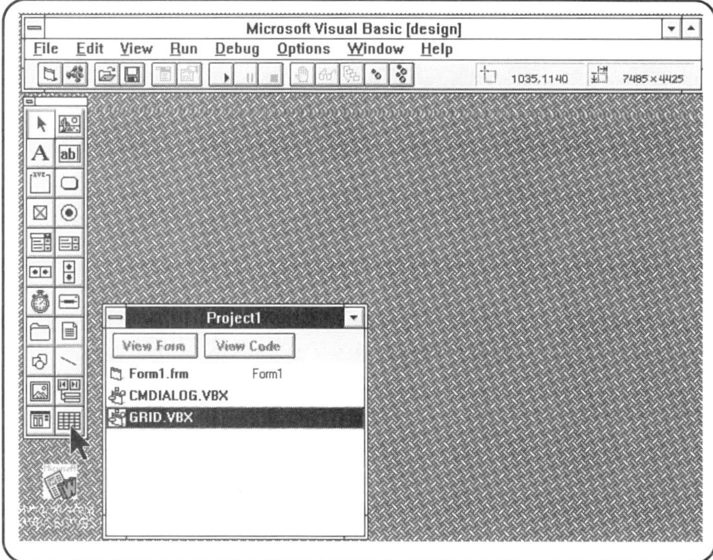

Figure 14.1. After you add grid.vbx, the grid icon appears in the Toolbox.

To automatically include grid.vbx in new projects, add it to the Visual Basic autoload.mak file. For example, here's the contents of an autoload.mak file that includes the grid control and a common dialog control:

```
CMDIALOG.VBX
GRID.VBX
ProjWinSize=152,402,248,215
ProjWinShow=9
```

When you distribute an application, you should install the grid.vbx file in the user's Microsoft Windows \SYSTEM subdirectory.

The Grid control has 49 properties:

BackColor	FontName	RowHeight
BorderStyle	FontSize	Rows
CellSelected	FontStrikethru	ScrollBars

```
Clip
Col
ColAlignment
Cols
ColWidth
DragICon
DragMode
Enabled
FillStyle
FixedAlignment
FixedCols
FixedRows
FontBold
FontItalic
FontUnderline
ForeColor
GridLines
Height
HelpContextId
HighLight
hWnd
Index
Left
LeftCol
Name
Parent
Picture
Row
SelEndCol
SelEndRow
SelStartCol
SelStartRow
TabIndex
TabStop
Tag
Text
Top
TopRow
Visible
Width
```

The Grid control has 14 events:

```
Click
DblClick
DragDrop
DragOver
GotFocus
KeyDown
KeyPress
KeyUp
LostFocus
MouseDown
MouseMove
MouseUp
RowColChange
SelChange
```

The Grid control has seven methods:

`AddItem`	`Refresh`	`ZOrder`
`Drag`	`RemoveItem`	
`Move`	`SetFocus`	

In general, you use four properties to set up a grid:

- `Rows` (the number of fixed and non-fixed rows)
- `Cols` (the number of fixed and non-fixed columns)
- `FixedRows` (the number of fixed rows)
- `FixedCols` (the number of fixed columns)

Unlike non-fixed rows and non-fixed cols, `fixedCols` and `fixedRows` don't scroll in grids that contain scroll bars.

Figure 14.2 shows a grid control. The fixed column and row are shaded.

Compose1—Declarations for PRHALL.VBX

The prhall.vbx file consists of 13 procedures (12 Functions and 1 Sub). In this chapter, you will only use two of these procedures (`Play` and `PlayStop`), yet for completeness, they're all declared in compose.bas on the disk.

In order to use any of the Sub or Function procedures in prhall.vbx (or any other external library), you must first declare them. Here are all the Sub and Function declarations for prhall.vbx:

```
Declare Function Bload% Lib "prhall.vbx" (ByVal Lin$, X As Any, ByVal Length&)
Declare Function Bsave% Lib "prhall.vbx" (ByVal Lin$, X As Any, ByVal Length&)
Declare Function MhDefaultDrive% Lib "prhall.vbx" ()
Declare Function MhDirectoryExists% Lib "prhall.vbx" (A$)
Declare Function MhEcode% Lib "prhall.vbx" ()
Declare Function MhExeName$ Lib "prhall.vbx" (ByVal Hwnd As Integer)
Declare Function MhExePath$ Lib "prhall.vbx" (ByVal Hwnd As Integer)
Declare Function MhFileExists% Lib "prhall.vbx" (A$)
Declare Function MhFileDateCompare% Lib "prhall.vbx" (ByVal F1$, ByVal F2$)
Declare Function MhKillFiles% Lib "prhall.vbx" (ByVal Attr%, A$)
```

```
Declare Function MhSetDefaultDrive% Lib "prhall.vbx" (ByVal A%)
Declare Function PLAY% Lib "prhall.vbx" (ByVal Lin$)
Declare Sub PlayStop Lib "prhall.vbx" ()
```

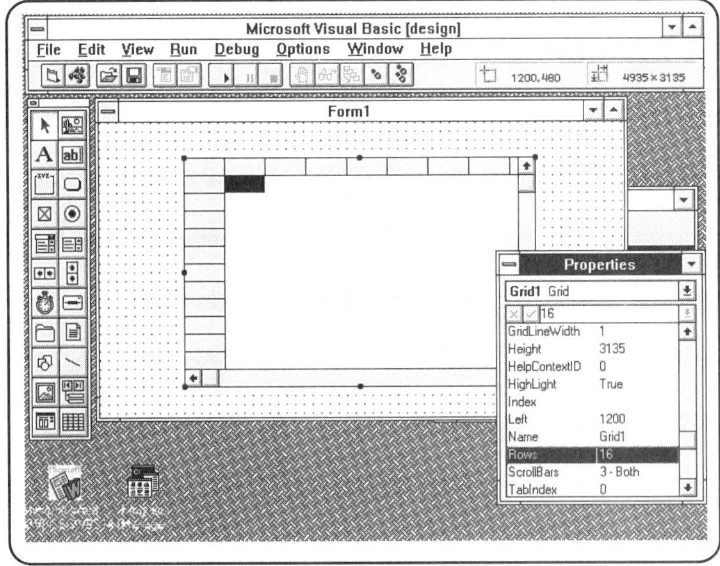

Figure 14.2. A grid control. The fixed column and row are shaded.

Create the Player Form

The Player form consists of the following:

- A text box for the note(s) string
- A text box for composition help information
- A label

The play command button plays the current string of notes in the text book each time the user presses Enter (`KeyAscii = 13`) while in the text box. When the tune has finished playing, focus is returned to the Composer form and more specifically, the grid on the Composer form. Note the use of the `Play` function contained within prhall.vbx; there is no comparable built-in `Play` function in Visual Basic:

```
Sub Text1_KeyPress (KeyAscii As Integer)
    If KeyAscii = 13 Then
       PlayStop
       KeyAscii = 0
       Temp$ = Text1.Text
       Result = PLAY(Temp$)       ' The Play Function from prhall.vbx
       Composer!Grid1.SetFocus    ' Give the grid the focus.
    End If
End Sub
```

When the Player form is loaded or unloaded, or if the user presses Exit or Stop, the tune is stopped using the `PlayStop` procedure contained within prhall.vbx:

```
Sub Form_Load ()
    PlayStop        ' in prhall.vbx
End Sub

Sub Form_Unload (Cancel As Integer)
    PlayStop        ' in prhall.vbx
End Sub

Sub mnuExit_Click ()
    PlayStop        ' in prhall.vbx
    Unload Player
End Sub

Sub mnuStop_Click ()
    PlayStop        ' in prhall.vbx
End Sub
```

Let's revise the default `Form_Load` event procedure to load help information (about composition notation) into the Help textbox (Text2) when the form loads:

```
Sub Form_Load ()
    PlayStop
    Txt$ = "o n : Sets the current octave. Octave range (0-7). Each C starts a
new  octave."
    Txt$ = Txt$ & ">   : Increase octave by 1"
    Txt$ = Txt$ & "<   : Decrease octave by 1"
    Txt$ = Txt$ & "A-G : Notes (# or + =sharp; - = flat."
    Txt$ = Txt$ & "N n : Play note in the range (n) 0-84. n=0 indicates a rest."
    Txt$ = Txt$ & "L n : Note length (L1 = whole; L2 = half; etc.)"
    Txt$ = Txt$ & "MN,ML,MS : Normal, Legato, Staccato."
    Txt$ = Txt$ & "P n : Pause (range 1-64 where 1 = whole; 2 = half; etc.)"
    Txt$ = Txt$ & "T n : tempo (range = 32-255; default = 120"
    Text2.Text = Txt$
End Sub
```

The help information for the Text2 textbox defines the notation expected by the Play function. For example, you can specify octave, note length, note style, rests (pauses), and tempo.

CREATE THE COMPOSER FORM

The Composer form consists of:

- A text box for editing the note(s) string
- A command button to play the string
- A grid to display/edit a series of notes

Add the grid to the form, using the fixed row (0) and columns 1,2,3, and 4 to indicate a Style, Octave, Length, and Note columns (see Figure 14.3).

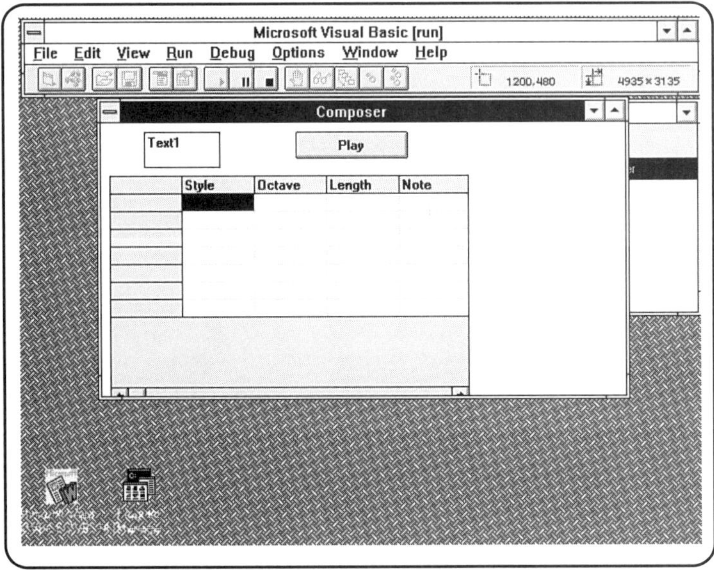

Figure 14.3. Grid at runtime with fixed row and columns.

A good time to set up any fixed columns and rows for a grid (contained within a form) is during the `Form_load` event procedure:

```
Sub Form_Load ()                        ' Set up form & grid
    Dim Count As Integer
    For Count = 0 To 4
        Grid1.ColWidth(Count) = Grid1.Width / 5
    Next Count
    Grid1.Col = 1         ' Set up text for fixed columns.
    Grid1.Row = 0
    Grid1.Text = "Style"
    Grid1.Col = 2
    Grid1.Text = "Octave"
    Grid1.Col = 3
    Grid1.Text = "Length"
    Grid1.Col = 4
    Grid1.Text = "Note"
End Sub
```

Although a user can't edit the contents of a grid cell directly, you can use a text box to allow editing; you can subsequently update the grid cell based on the contents of the text box.

To allow the user to click the mouse to edit:

```
Sub Grid1_Click ()                      ' Allow user to use the mouse
    Text1.Text = ""
    Text1.SetFocus
End Sub
```

To allow the user to press Enter:

```
Sub Grid1_KeyPress (KeyAscii As Integer)  'Allow user to use <enter>
    If KeyAscii = 10 Then
    Text1.Text = ""
    Text1.SetFocus
    End If
End Sub
```

Then use the `text_change` event to update the grid as the user edits the text box:

```
Sub Text1_Change ()                     ' Update grid with text box text
    ColNum = Grid1.SelStartCol
    RowNum = Grid1.SelStartRow
    Grid1.Col = ColNum
    Grid1.Row = RowNum
    Grid1.Text = Text1.Text
End Sub
```

It occurred to me while developing this project that it might be more efficient to update the grid after a text box edit when the text box lost the focus instead of after each text change. So I recast the `Text1_Change` and `Text1_LostFocus` event procedures as follows:

```
Sub Text1_Change ()     ' Update grid with text box text.
    Exit Sub
    ColNum = Grid1.SelStartCol
    RowNum = Grid1.SelStartRow
    Grid1.Col = ColNum
    Grid1.Row = RowNum
    Grid1.Text = Text1.Text
End Sub

Sub Text1_LostFocus ()  ' Update grid with text box text.
    ColNum = Grid1.SelStartCol
    RowNum = Grid1.SelStartRow
    Grid1.Col = ColNum
    Grid1.Row = RowNum
    Grid1.Text = Text1.Text
End Sub
```

Note the use of an `Exit Sub` statement at the beginning of the existing `Text1_Change` Sub procedure. When you're testing alternatives to a procedure that already works, and want to save the procedure but don't want to comment out a lot of code, you can use an `Exit Sub` statement at the beginning of the procedure. If you decide to use the alternative to the procedure, delete the procedure's code later if you don't need it. If you decide to abandon the alternative, simply remove the `Exit Sub` statement and your working code is still intact.

Unfortunately, the `Lost_Focus` alternative doesn't work quite the way I hoped. When the text box loses the focus, it updates the grid, but not in the cell that previously had the focus. Instead, the grid is updated in the cell that next has the focus. Explore this for yourself, using the Compose1 application on the disk. It contains both options (just uncomment the `Lost_Focus Exit Sub` statement to explore the alternative).

The command button "plays" the tune contained in the grid (combining the octave, length of note, and note). It reads the grid, building a text string that's passed to the Player form. The player form actually plays the tune.

Notice at the end of the `Command1_Click` code the use of `SendKeys` to send a return to the text box on the Player form. That text box (`Player!Text1`) receives the string:

```
Sub Command1_Click ()          ' Play
    Dim C As Integer
    Dim R As Integer
    Dim Txt As String
    Txt = ""
    For R = 1 To 7             ' Read rows and cols of grid.
        For C = 1 To 4
            Grid1.Row = R
            Grid1.Col = C
            Txt = Txt + Grid1.Text
        Next C
    Next R
    Player!Text1.Text = Txt
    Player.Show
    SendKeys "{ENTER}"         ' Play the tune by sending a command
                               ' to the text box on Player
End Sub
```

Using two forms (one to compose and one to play) isn't necessary as you'll learn in Compose2. I used two forms here because some applications will use a grid on one form and the data from the grid on another form, for example a graphic application. Using `SendKeys` is an excellent way to send commands from one form to another.

Listing 14.1 shows the complete code for Compose1.

Listing 14.1. Compose1.

```
' Listing 14.1

'Compose.Bas

DefInt A-Z

' SUB and FUNCTION declarations for prhall.vbx

    Declare Function Bload% Lib "prhall.vbx" (ByVal Lin$, X As Any,
    ➥ ByVal Length&)
```

continues

LISTING 14.1. CONTINUED

```
    Declare Function Bsave% Lib "prhall.vbx" (ByVal Lin$, X As Any,
    ➥ ByVal Length&)
    Declare Function MhDefaultDrive% Lib "prhall.vbx" ()
    Declare Function MhDirectoryExists% Lib "prhall.vbx" (A$)
    Declare Function MhEcode% Lib "prhall.vbx" ()
    Declare Function MhExeName$ Lib "prhall.vbx" (ByVal Hwnd As Integer)
    Declare Function MhExePath$ Lib "prhall.vbx" (ByVal Hwnd As Integer)
    Declare Function MhFileExists% Lib "prhall.vbx" (A$)
    Declare Function MhFileDateCompare% Lib "prhall.vbx" (ByVal F1$, ByVal F2$)
    Declare Function MhKillFiles% Lib "prhall.vbx" (ByVal Attr%, A$)
    Declare Function MhSetDefaultDrive% Lib "prhall.vbx" (ByVal A%)
    Declare Function PLAY% Lib "prhall.vbx" (ByVal Lin$)
    Declare Sub PlayStop Lib "prhall.vbx" ()


'Player.frm

Sub Form_Load ()
    PlayStop
    Txt$ = "o n : Sets the current octave. Octave range (0-7). " &
    ➥ "Each C starts a new octave."
    Txt$ = Txt$ & ">   : Increase octave by 1"
    Txt$ = Txt$ & "<   : Decrease octave by 1"
    Txt$ = Txt$ & "A-G : Notes (# or + =sharp; - = flat."
    Txt$ = Txt$ & "N n : Play note in the range (n) 0-84. " &
    ➥ " n=0 indicates a rest."
    Txt$ = Txt$ & "L n : Note length (L1 = whole; L2 = half; etc.)"
    Txt$ = Txt$ & "MN,ML,MS : Normal, Legato, Staccato."
    Txt$ = Txt$ & "P n : Pause (range 1-64 where 1 = whole; 2 = half; etc.)"
    Txt$ = Txt$ & "T n : tempo (range = 32-255; default = 120"
    Text2.Text = Txt$
End Sub

Sub Form_Unload (Cancel As Integer)
    PlayStop
End Sub

Sub mnuExit_Click ()
    PlayStop
    Unload Player
End Sub

Sub mnuStop_Click ()
    PlayStop
End Sub

Sub Text1_KeyPress (KeyAscii As Integer)
    If KeyAscii = 13 Then
       PlayStop
       KeyAscii = 0
```

```
        Temp$ = Text1.Text
        Result = PLAY(Temp$)
        Composer!Grid1.SetFocus          ' Give the grid the focus.
    End If
End Sub

'Compose1.frm

Sub Command1_Click ()                    ' Play
    Dim C As Integer
    Dim R As Integer
    Dim Txt As String
    Txt = ""
    For R = 1 To 7                   ' Read rows and cols of grid.
        For C = 1 To 4
            Grid1.Row = R
            Grid1.Col = C
            Txt = Txt + Grid1.Text
        Next C
    Next R
    Player!Text1.Text = Txt
    Player.Show
    SendKeys "{ENTER}"
End Sub

Sub Form_Load ()                     ' Set up form & grid
    Dim Count As Integer
    For Count = 0 To 4
        Grid1.ColWidth(Count) = Grid1.Width / 5
    Next Count
    Grid1.Col = 1
    Grid1.Row = 0
    Grid1.Text = "Style"
    Grid1.Col = 2
    Grid1.Text = "Octave"
    Grid1.Col = 3
    Grid1.Text = "Length"
    Grid1.Col = 4
    Grid1.Text = "Note"
End Sub

Sub Grid1_Click ()                   ' Allow user to use the mouse
    Text1.Text = ""
    Text1.SetFocus
End Sub

Sub Grid1_KeyPress (KeyAscii As Integer)   'Allow user to use <enter>
    If KeyAscii = 10 Then
    Text1.Text = ""
    Text1.SetFocus
```

continues

LISTING 14.1. CONTINUED

```
    End If
End Sub

Sub Text1_Change ()                  ' Update grid with text box text.
    ColNum = Grid1.SelStartCol
    RowNum = Grid1.SelStartRow
    Grid1.Col = ColNum
    Grid1.Row = RowNum
    Grid1.Text = Text1.Text
End Sub
```

COMPOSE2—USING THE GRID TO CREATE A MUSICAL FRETBOARD

Although Compose1 is useful and interesting, it's strictly a starting point as a composition application. Since I'm a string (guitar and mandolin) player, I compose with string instruments in mind. In addition, specifying such details as octave (in Compose1) is cumbersome. A better approach, Compose2, uses the grid control to create a fretboard (for mandolin or fiddle, but you can easily modify it for guitar, or even piano) that automatically determines the note and octave when a cell is clicked. Figure 14.4 shows the grid laid out as a fretboard.

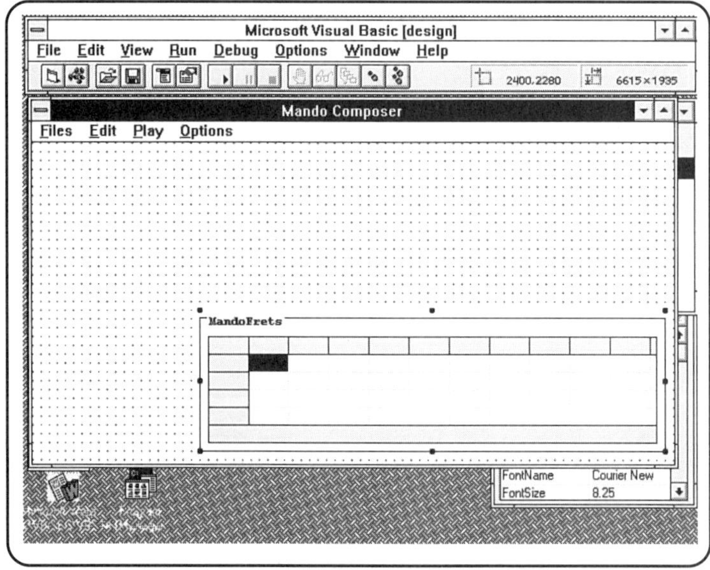

Figure 14.4. Grid As a Mandolin Fretboard.

Compose2 consists of six frames to contain:

- An option group for styles
- An option group for note lengths
- A text box for the current note
- A multiline text box for the tune
- A grid to represent the fretboard
- A menu bar consisting of Files, Edit, Play, and Options menus; these menus contain Open and Save File commands, Edit a tune, Clear note, and Clear tune commands, Play note and tune, and Stop Play commands, and the Options menu to set text change (to play a note or tune automatically) options.

Figure 14.5 shows the Compose2 form in design view.

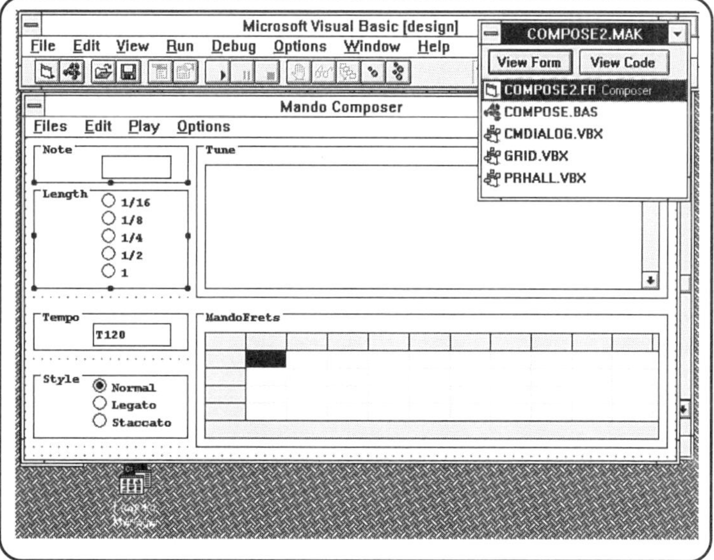

Figure 14.5. The Compose2 form in design view.

Compose2 differs from Compose1 in several ways:

- Compose2 combines Compose and Play functions on a single form.
- Compose2 interprets the data within the grid. For example, cell

position (i.e., a cell corresponds to a fret) indicates the octave a note lies in.

- Compose2 combines strings within several text boxes (e.g. the Style plus the Tempo plus the Length plus the Note) to produce a note.
- Compose2 allows tunes to be saved to files and loaded from files.
- Compose2 plays more efficiently because compose and play functions all occur on a single form.

Compose2, like Compose1, uses the `Play` and `PlayStop` procedures from prhall.vbx. `Play` is a particularly nifty function because:

- It allows a tune to play in the background.
- It's fully interruptable by the `PlayStop` procedure. `DoEvent()` capability is built-in.

CREATE THE COMPOSE2 CODE

As in Compose1, declare the procedures for the prhall.vbx:

```
Declare Function Bload% Lib "prhall.vbx" (ByVal Lin$, X As Any, ByVal Length&)
Declare Function Bsave% Lib "prhall.vbx" (ByVal Lin$, X As Any, ByVal Length&)
Declare Function MhDefaultDrive% Lib "prhall.vbx" ()
Declare Function MhDirectoryExists% Lib "prhall.vbx" (A$)
Declare Function MhEcode% Lib "prhall.vbx" ()
Declare Function MhExeName$ Lib "prhall.vbx" (ByVal Hwnd As Integer)
Declare Function MhExePath$ Lib "prhall.vbx" (ByVal Hwnd As Integer)
Declare Function MhFileExists% Lib "prhall.vbx" (A$)
Declare Function MhFileDateCompare% Lib "prhall.vbx" (ByVal F1$, ByVal F2$)
Declare Function MhKillFiles% Lib "prhall.vbx" (ByVal Attr%, A$)
Declare Function MhSetDefaultDrive% Lib "prhall.vbx" (ByVal A%)
Declare Function PLAY% Lib "prhall.vbx" (ByVal Lin$)
Declare Sub PlayStop Lib "prhall.vbx" ()
```

Add a common dialog control to the Compose2 form for file I/O dialogs (see Figure 14.6).

I use the common dialog control so frequently, I include it in my Visual Basic autoload.mak file. In general, if you frequently use a custom control, you should consider listing it in autoload.mak. This way it will be loaded automatically for you each time you load a new project in Visual Basic.

USE FORM_LOAD TO SET UP THE FRETBOARD

A user can specify whether to have each note played as it's clicked within the grid or have the entire current tune played each time a new note is added. The `mnuPlaynotes_Click` described later in this chapter checks and unchecks the two menu options. Set up the grid (the fretboard) and any option values during the Compose2 form `Form_Load` event. Notice that the initial values for the cell are maintained in a file. Thus, you can change initial values for a grid without recompiling the code, a nifty option in more complex applications. Use the `Input#` function to read one initial cell value (a note in this case) at a time:

```
Sub Form_Load ()
    Dim Count As Integer
    Dim Note As String * 2
    NumCols% = MandoFrets.Cols - 1
    For Count = 1 To NumCols%
        MandoFrets.ColWidth(Count) = MandoFrets.Width / NumCols% - 70
    Next Count
    Option2.Value = True
    mnuPlayNotes(0).Checked = True
    mnuPlayNotes(1).Checked = False

    MandoFrets.Col = 1
    MandoFrets.Row = 0
    MandoFrets.Text = " — "
    MandoFrets.Col = 4
    MandoFrets.Text = " 3 "
    MandoFrets.Col = 6
    MandoFrets.Text = " 5 "
    MandoFrets.Col = 8
    MandoFrets.Text = " 7 "
    MandoFrets.Col = 11
    MandoFrets.Text = " 10 "

    Open "C:\vb\vbs-dsk1\Notes.txt" For Input As #1   ' Grid values
                                                      ' maintained in a file.
    On Error GoTo FileError
    For r = 1 To 4
         For c = 1 To 13
            MandoFrets.Col = c
            MandoFrets.Row = r
            Note = Input$(2, #1)
            MandoFrets.Text = Note
         Next c
    Next r
    Close
    Exit Sub
FileError:
```

```
        MsgBox Error(Err)
        Close
        Exit Sub
End Sub
```

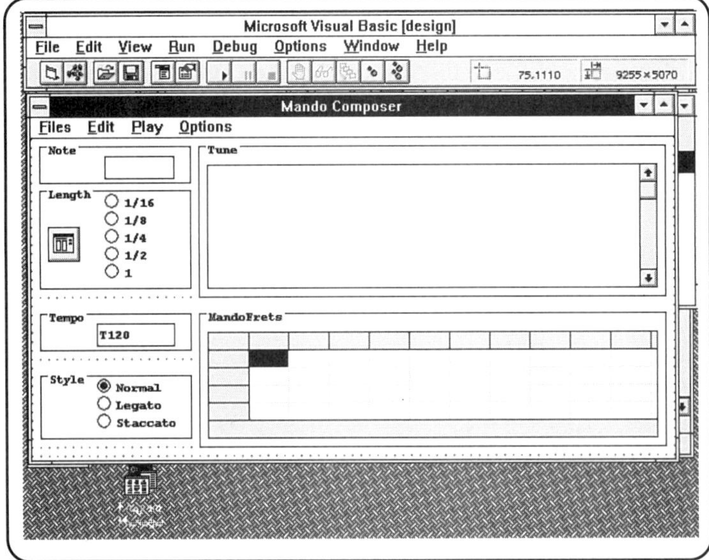

Figure 14.6. Compose2 form with common dialog control in design view.

Handling a Grid Click

Each time a user clicks a cell on the grid, pass that note to the current note text box (Text1) and then determine the length and octave of the note (in the `FindNote(ColNum,RowNum,Txt)` procedure.

```
Sub MandoFrets_Click ()
    Dim Index As Integer
    Dim Txt As String
    Dim ColNum As Integer
    Dim RowNum As Integer
    ColNum = MandoFrets.SelStartCol
    RowNum = MandoFrets.SelStartRow
    Txt = MandoFrets.Text
    FindNote ColNum, RowNum, Txt
End Sub
```

Find Note

The `FindNote` procedure looks up the note length value in the length option group, determines the octave (based on cell position), and combines the octave, length, and note to produce the playable note. The tune text box string is all the notes (the previous notes plus the new note); the note text box string is simply the current note:

```
Sub FindNote (ColNum As Integer, RowNum As Integer, Note As String)
    Dim Length As String
    Dim Octave As String
    If Option1.Value = True Then Length = "L16"
    If Option2.Value = True Then Length = "L8"
    If Option3.Value = True Then Length = "L4"
    If Option4.Value = True Then Length = "L2"
    If Option5.Value = True Then Length = "L1"
    Select Case RowNum
        Case 4
            If ColNum >= 1 And ColNum <= 5 Then
                Octave = "o1"
            Else
                Octave = "o2"
            End If
        Case 3
            If ColNum >= 1 And ColNum <= 10 Then
                Octave = "o2"
            Else
                Octave = "o3"
            End If
        Case 2
            If ColNum >= 1 And ColNum <= 3 Then
                Octave = "o2"
            Else
                Octave = "o3"
            End If
        Case 1
            If ColNum >= 1 And ColNum <= 8 Then
                Octave = "o3"
            Else
                Octave = "o4"
            End If
        End Select
    Text2.Text = Text2.Text & Octave & Length & Note
    Text1.Text = ""
    Text1.Text = Octave & Length & Note
End Sub
```

Clear Note, Clear Tune, Edit Tune

To clear the current note, clear the note (Text1) textbox:

```
Sub mnuClearNote_Click ()
    Text1.Text = ""
End Sub
```

To clear the current tune, clear the tune (Text2) textbox:

```
Sub mnuClearTune_Click ()
    Text2.Text = ""
End Sub
```

To edit a tune, set the focus to the tune (Text2) textbox:

```
Sub mnuEditTune_Click ()
    Text2.SetFocus
End Sub
```

The Play Note or Play Tune Option

A user can specify either that each note is played as it's clicked within the grid or that the entire current tune is played each time a new note is added to the tune. The following `mnuPlaynotes_Click` event checks and unchecks the two menu options:

```
Sub mnuPlaynotes_Click (Index As Integer)
    Select Case Index
        Case 0
            mnuPlayNotes(0).Checked = True
            mnuPlayNotes(1).Checked = False
        Case 1
            mnuPlayNotes(1).Checked = True
            mnuPlayNotes(0).Checked = False
        End Select
End Sub
```

Text_Change Events

Each time the text in Text1 changes (that is, each time there's a new note), play the note if the play note option is checked:

```
Sub Text1_Change ()
       If mnuPlayNotes(0).Checked = True Then
       Temp$ = Text1.Text
       Result = PLAY(Temp$)
       End If
       MandoFrets.SetFocus
End Sub
```

Each time the text in Text2 changes (that is, each time there's a new note added to the tune), play the tune if the play tune option is checked:

```
Sub Text2_Change ()
       If mnuPlayNotes(1).Checked = True Then
          Style$ = GetStyle()
          Temp$ = Style$ & Text3.Text & Text2.Text
        Result = PLAY(Temp$)
        MandoFrets.SetFocus
       End If
End Sub
```

`GetStyle()` determines the current style option by reading the style option group:

```
Function GetStyle ()
    If Option6.Value = True Then
        GetStyle = "MN"
    End If
    If Option7.Value = True Then
        GetStyle = "ML"
    End If
    If Option8.Value = True Then
        GetStyle = "MS"
    End If
End Function
```

File I/O

The `mnuOpen_Click` event procedure uses the common dialog to let the user select a file to open:

```
Sub mnuOpen_Click ()
    On Error GoTo OpenError
    CMDialog1.Filter = "Tune files(*.tne)¦*.tne"
    CMDialog1.FilterIndex = 1
    CMDialog1.Action = 1
    OpenFile (CMDialog1.Filename)
OpenError:
    Exit Sub
End Sub
```

Then the `OpenFile` procedure receives the filename and uses an `Input#` statement to read the contents of the file (a tune) into the tune text box (Text2):

```
Sub OpenFile (Filename As String)
    FileNum = FreeFile
    Open Filename For Input As FileNum
    Lines$ = Input$(LOF(FileNum), FileNum)
    Text2.Text = Lines$
    Close FileNum
End Sub
```

The `mnuSave_Click` event procedure uses the common dialog to let the user select a filename for the save:

```
Sub mnuSave_Click ()
    On Error GoTo SaveError
    CMDialog1.Filter = "Tune files(*.tne)¦*.tne"
    CMDialog1.FilterIndex = 1
    CMDialog1.Action = 2
    SaveFile (CMDialog1.Filename)
SaveError:
    Exit Sub
End Sub
```

Then the `SaveFile` procedure receives the filename and uses a `Print#` statement to save the contents of the tune text box (Text2):

```
Sub SaveFile (Filename As String)
    FileNum = FreeFile
    Open Filename For Output As FileNum
    Print #FileNum, Text2.Text
    Close FileNum
End Sub
```

Figure 14.7 shows the Compose2 application during runtime after a few notes have been selected from the grid.

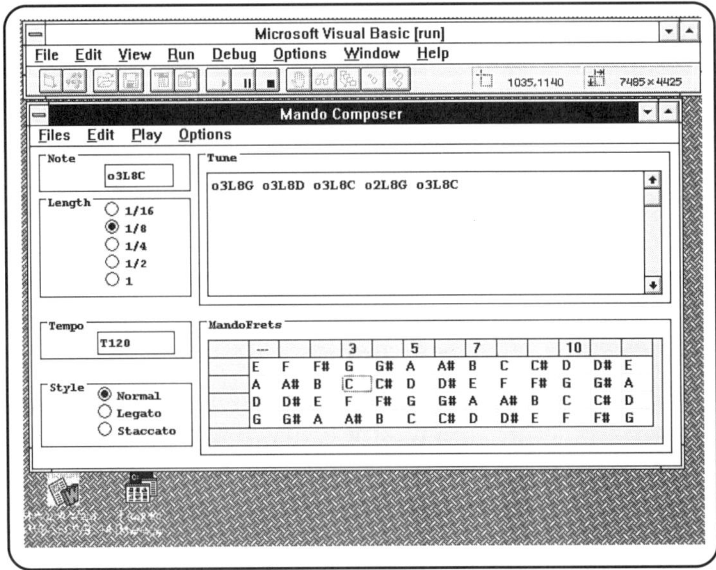

Figure 14.7. The Compose2 application during runtime after a few notes have been selected from the grid.

Figure 14.8 shows the File Open dialog during runtime.

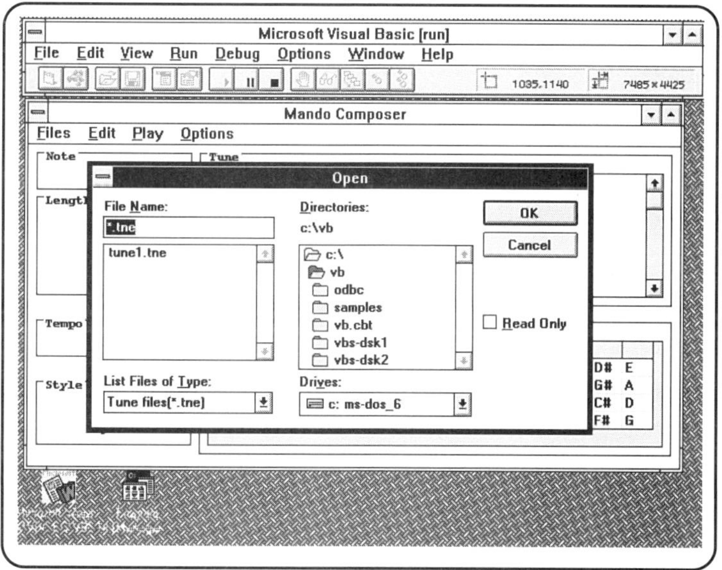

Figure 14.8. The File Open dialog during runtime.

Figure 14.9 shows the File Save As dialog during runtime.

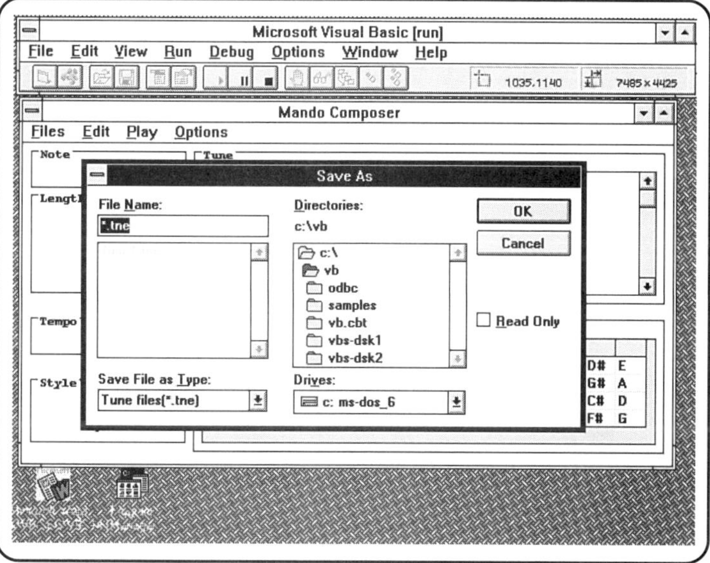

Figure 14.9. The File Save As dialog during runtime.

The complete listing for Compose2 is in Listing 14.2.

Listing 14.2. Compose2.

```
'Compose.Bas

DefInt A-Z

' SUB and FUNCTION declarations for prhall.vbx

    Declare Function Bload% Lib "prhall.vbx" (ByVal Lin$, X As Any,
    ➥ ByVal Length&)
    Declare Function Bsave% Lib "prhall.vbx" (ByVal Lin$, X As Any,
    ➥ ByVal Length&)
    Declare Function MhDefaultDrive% Lib "prhall.vbx" ()
    Declare Function MhDirectoryExists% Lib "prhall.vbx" (A$)
    Declare Function MhEcode% Lib "prhall.vbx" ()
    Declare Function MhExeName$ Lib "prhall.vbx" (ByVal Hwnd As Integer)
    Declare Function MhExePath$ Lib "prhall.vbx" (ByVal Hwnd As Integer)
    Declare Function MhFileExists% Lib "prhall.vbx" (A$)
    Declare Function MhFileDateCompare% Lib "prhall.vbx" (ByVal F1$, ByVal F2$)
    Declare Function MhKillFiles% Lib "prhall.vbx" (ByVal Attr%, A$)
    Declare Function MhSetDefaultDrive% Lib "prhall.vbx" (ByVal A%)
    Declare Function PLAY% Lib "prhall.vbx" (ByVal Lin$)
    Declare Sub PlayStop Lib "prhall.vbx" ()

'Compose2.frm

Sub FindNote (ColNum As Integer, RowNum As Integer, Note As String)
    Dim Length As String
    Dim Octave As String
    If Option1.Value = True Then Length = "L16"
    If Option2.Value = True Then Length = "L8"
    If Option3.Value = True Then Length = "L4"
    If Option4.Value = True Then Length = "L2"
    If Option5.Value = True Then Length = "L1"
    Select Case RowNum
        Case 4
            If ColNum >= 1 And ColNum <= 5 Then
                Octave = "o1"
            Else
                Octave = "o2"
            End If
        Case 3
            If ColNum >= 1 And ColNum <= 10 Then
                Octave = "o2"
            Else
                Octave = "o3"
            End If
        Case 2
            If ColNum >= 1 And ColNum <= 3 Then
```

```
                Octave = "o2"
            Else
                Octave = "o3"
            End If
        Case 1
            If ColNum >= 1 And ColNum <= 8 Then
                Octave = "o3"
            Else
                Octave = "o4"
            End If
        End Select
    Text2.Text = Text2.Text & Octave & Length & Note
    Text1.Text = ""
    Text1.Text = Octave & Length & Note
End Sub

Sub Form_Load ()
    Dim Count As Integer
    Dim Note As String * 2
    NumCols% = MandoFrets.Cols - 1
    For Count = 1 To NumCols%
        MandoFrets.ColWidth(Count) = MandoFrets.Width / NumCols% - 70
    Next Count
    Option2.Value = True
    mnuPlayNotes(0).Checked = True
    mnuPlayNotes(1).Checked = False

    MandoFrets.Col = 1
    MandoFrets.Row = 0
    MandoFrets.Text = " — "
    MandoFrets.Col = 4
    MandoFrets.Text = " 3 "
    MandoFrets.Col = 6
    MandoFrets.Text = " 5 "
    MandoFrets.Col = 8
    MandoFrets.Text = " 7 "
    MandoFrets.Col = 11
    MandoFrets.Text = " 10 "

    Open "Notes.txt" For Input As #1
    On Error GoTo FileError
    For r = 1 To 4
         For c = 1 To 13
            MandoFrets.Col = c
            MandoFrets.Row = r
            Note = Input$(2, #1)
            MandoFrets.Text = Note
         Next c
    Next r
    Close
    Exit Sub
```

continues

LISTING 14.2. CONTINUED

```
FileError:
    MsgBox Error(Err)
    Close
    Exit Sub
End Sub

Function GetStyle ()
    If Option6.Value = True Then
        GetStyle = "MN"
    End If
    If Option7.Value = True Then
        GetStyle = "ML"
    End If
    If Option8.Value = True Then
        GetStyle = "MS"
    End If
End Function

Sub MandoFrets_Click ()
    Dim Index As Integer
    Dim Txt As String
    Dim ColNum As Integer
    Dim RowNum As Integer
    ColNum = MandoFrets.SelStartCol
    RowNum = MandoFrets.SelStartRow
    Txt = MandoFrets.Text
    FindNote ColNum, RowNum, Txt
End Sub

Sub MandoFrets_KeyPress (KeyAscii As Integer)
    If KeyAscii = 10 Then
    Text1.Text = ""
    Text1.SetFocus
    End If
End Sub

Sub mnuClearNote_Click ()
    Text1.Text = ""
End Sub

Sub mnuClearTune_Click ()
    Text2.Text = ""
End Sub

Sub mnuEditTune_Click ()
    Text2.SetFocus
End Sub

Sub mnuExit_Click ()
    End
End Sub
```

```
Sub mnuNote_Click ()
       Temp$ = Text1.Text
       Result = PLAY(Temp$)
End Sub

Sub mnuOpen_Click ()
    On Error GoTo OpenError
    CMDialog1.Filter = "Tune files(*.tne)¦*.tne"
    CMDialog1.FilterIndex = 1
    CMDialog1.Action = 1
    OpenFile (CMDialog1.Filename)
OpenError:
    Exit Sub
End Sub

Sub mnuPlay_Click ()
    Dim c As Integer
    Dim r As Integer
    Dim Txt As String
    Txt = ""
    For r = 1 To 3
        For c = 1 To 4
            MandoFrets.Row = r
            MandoFrets.Col = c
            Txt = Txt + MandoFrets.Text
        Next c
    Next r
End Sub

Sub mnuPlaynotes_Click (Index As Integer)
    Select Case Index
        Case 0
            mnuPlayNotes(0).Checked = True
            mnuPlayNotes(1).Checked = False
        Case 1
            mnuPlayNotes(1).Checked = True
            mnuPlayNotes(0).Checked = False
        End Select
End Sub

Sub mnuSave_Click ()
    On Error GoTo SaveError
    CMDialog1.Filter = "Tune files(*.tne)¦*.tne"
    CMDialog1.FilterIndex = 1
    CMDialog1.Action = 2
    SaveFile (CMDialog1.Filename)
SaveError:
    Exit Sub
End Sub
```

continues

LISTING 14.2. CONTINUED

```
Sub mnuStop_Click ()
    PlayStop
End Sub

Sub mnuTune_Click ()
       Style$ = GetStyle()
       Temp$ = Style$ & Text3.Text & Text2.Text
       Result = PLAY(Temp$)
End Sub

Sub OpenFile (Filename As String)
    FileNum = FreeFile
    Open Filename For Input As FileNum
    Lines$ = Input$(LOF(FileNum), FileNum)
    Text2.Text = Lines$
    Close FileNum
End Sub

Sub SaveFile (Filename As String)
    FileNum = FreeFile
    Open Filename For Output As FileNum
    Print #FileNum, Text2.Text
    Close FileNum
End Sub

Sub Text1_Change ()
       If mnuPlayNotes(0).Checked = True Then
       Temp$ = Text1.Text
       Result = PLAY(Temp$)
       End If
       MandoFrets.SetFocus
End Sub

Sub Text2_Change ()
       If mnuPlayNotes(1).Checked = True Then
          Style$ = GetStyle()
          Temp$ = Style$ & Text3.Text & Text2.Text
        Result = PLAY(Temp$)
        MandoFrets.SetFocus
       End If
End Sub
```

Summary

That wraps up this chapter's study of the grid control and two important features contained within prhall.vbx (a bonus .vbx file donated by MicroHelp for this book).

As you can see from this chapter, these two .vbx files can be used in interesting ways.

Data Awareness and Data Management

Using the Visual Basic 3.0 Data Manager

Creating External Databases in Non-Microsoft Access Formats

Data Access from Visual Basic

An Introduction to Database Objects

Creating Data Access Applications

If your applications need to create databases or use data stored in external databases such as Microsoft Access, dBASE, or Paradox, data-aware controls are an excellent reason to upgrade to Visual Basic 3.0.

Data-aware controls can connect directly to the data contained in specific fields within database tables. You use these data-aware controls to view and manipulate database tables directly. You use these data-aware controls on forms to create "windows" onto databases. This allows you to create custom applications for manipulating data that's maintained in some database-standard format, such as Microsoft Access 1.0 and 1.1 or dBASE III or IV.

Data-aware controls in the Standard edition of Visual Basic 3.0 include text boxes, labels, check boxes, images, and picture boxes. The Professional edition adds three more controls (masked edit, 3-D panel, and 3-D check boxes)to the Standard edition's controls. Various third party vendors, such as MicroHelp and Crescent Software sell other data-aware controls.

You use the Visual Basic data-aware controls or third-party data-aware controls with the Visual Basic data control to display and manipulate fields from external databases. Table 15.1 shows the databases supported by the Visual Basic 3.0 data control.

TABLE 15.1. DATABASES SUPPORTED BY THE VISUAL BASIC 3.0 DATA CONTROL.

Microsoft Access 1.0 and 1.1
FoxPro 2.0 and 2.5
dBASE III and IV
Paradox
Btrieve
ODBC (in the Visual Basic 3.0 Professional edition only)

The data control is the connection between data-aware controls on a form and the tables maintained in external databases. You typically begin a connection between your application (form) and an external database by using the Toolbox to add a data control to a form. You then add other data-aware controls to the form to receive specific fields of data in the external database format. Figure 15.1 illustrates this scenario.

In this chapter you'll learn how to create databases using the Visual Basic 3.0 Data Manager and how to use databases created with the Data Manager or created within databases external to Visual Basic. Two of the applications in this chapter, Data1 and Data2, show how to create forms that display and use Microsoft Access tables. Data2 shows how to display information from two Microsoft Access tables on one form simultaneously. The methods used in this chapter to make connections to Microsoft Access work similarly with other databases, such as Paradox, FoxPro, and dBASE.

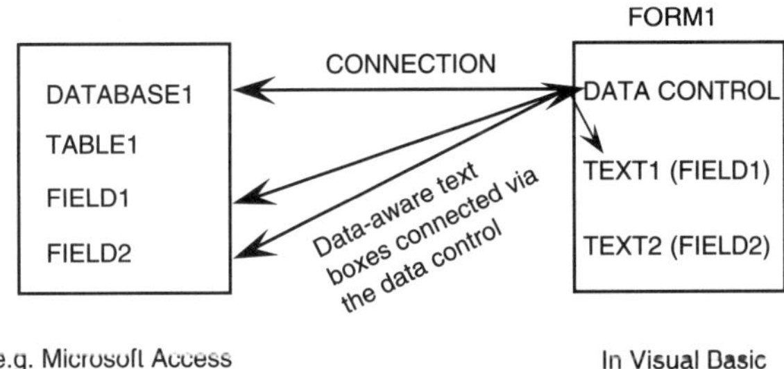

Figure 15.1. The data control is the connection between data-aware controls on a form and the tables maintained in external databases. Other data-aware controls on the form receive specific fields of data in the external database format.

The final application in this chapter, Data3, shows how to create databases from Visual Basic code. Note that you can only create databases from Visual Basic code if you have the Professional edition. However, you can easily manage and manipulate databases without code (as you'll see in this chapter) with the Visual Basic 3.0 Standard edition.

THE VISUAL BASIC 3.0 DATA MANAGER

You can use the Visual Basic Data Manager to create new databases (in the Microsoft Access .MDB format). You can also use the Data Manager to explore and modify the structure of existing databases in any of the several formats Visual Basic supports. Formats you can create or modify with the Data Manager are shown in Table 15.2. Note that these formats correspond to the formats supported by the data control.

The Data Manager in Visual Basic 3.0 can only create databases in Microsoft Access 1.0 or 1.1 formats.

TABLE 15.2. FORMATS YOU CAN CREATE OR MODIFY WITH THE DATA MANAGER.

Database Format	*Create*	*Modify*
Microsoft Access 1.0	Yes	Yes
Microsoft Access 1.1	Yes	Yes
Paradox 3.0 and 3.5	No	Yes
dBASE III and IV	No	Yes
FoxPro 2.0 and 2.5	No	Yes
Btrieve	No	Yes

Note that you cannot create Paradox, dBASE, FoxPro, or Btrieve database directly, but you can create them indirectly by creating a directory (the equivalent of a database for some database systems) for the database. After you've created the directory, you can add and modify tables to the database. See the section "Creating External Databases In Non-Microsoft Access Formats" later in this chapter for details.

HOW TO OPEN A DATABASE FROM THE DATA MANAGER

If you (or someone else) has used Microsoft Access, Paradox, dBase, FoxPro, or Btrieve to create a database, you can open (and manipulate) that database from the Data Manager.

To open an existing database from the Data Manager:

1. Select File/Open Database from the main Data Manager menu.
2. Select the type of database you want to open (Microsoft Access, FoxPro, dBASE III, dBASE IV, Paradox, BTRIEVE) from the submenu.
3. The Open Database Dialog opens. Enter the name of the database you want to open in the Open Database Dialog (see Figure 15.2).
4. Select OK to open the database.

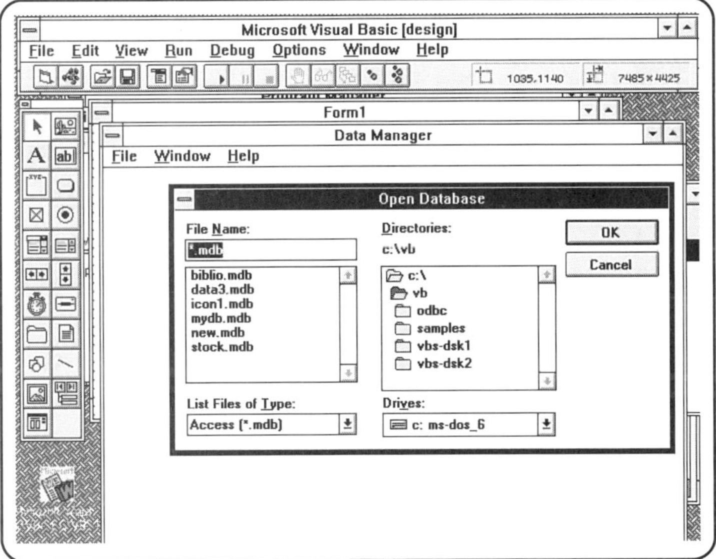

Figure 15.2. Enter the name of the database you want to open in the Open Database Dialog.

How To Create a Database with the Data Manager

To create a Microsoft Access-compatible database with the Data Manager:

1. Select File/New Database command from the main Data Manager menu.
2. Select the type of database you want to create (Microsoft Access 1.0 or 1.1) from the submenu.
3. The New Database dialog opens. Enter the name of the database you want to create in the New Database dialog (see Figure 15.3).
4. Select OK to accept the new database name.

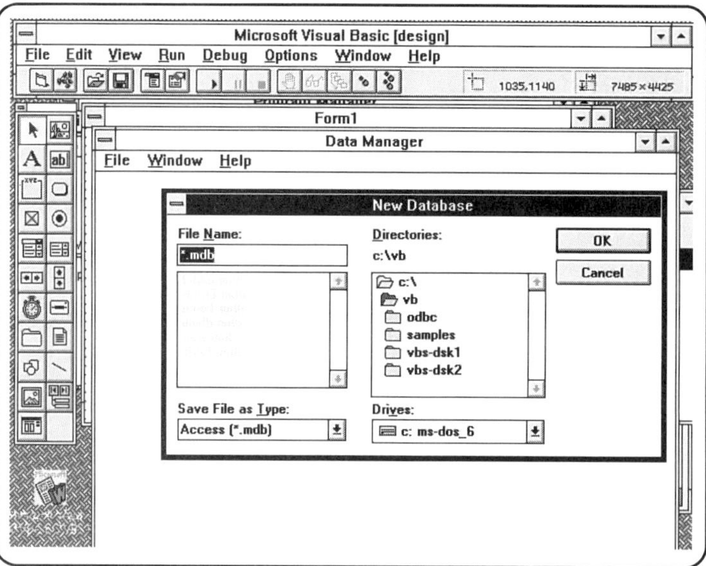

Figure 15.3. Enter the name of the database you want to create in the New Database dialog.

After you create the database file, you can use the Data Manager to add new tables and indexes to store the data.

Creating External Databases in Non-Microsoft Access Formats

Creating an external database in dBASE III, dBASE IV, FoxPro, and Paradox is indirect. Many external databases are simply directories. After you create the database directory, you can use the Data Manager to add tables and indexes to the directory. These tables and indexes become files in the directory. Note that Microsoft Access maintains all the components of a database (tables, indexes, etc.) in a single .MDB file.

To create one of these external databases:

1. Use the File Manager (or another application) to create a directory.
2. From the main menu of the Data Manager, use File/Open to open the database. The Open Database dialog opens asking you to pick the directory for the database (see Figure 15.4).

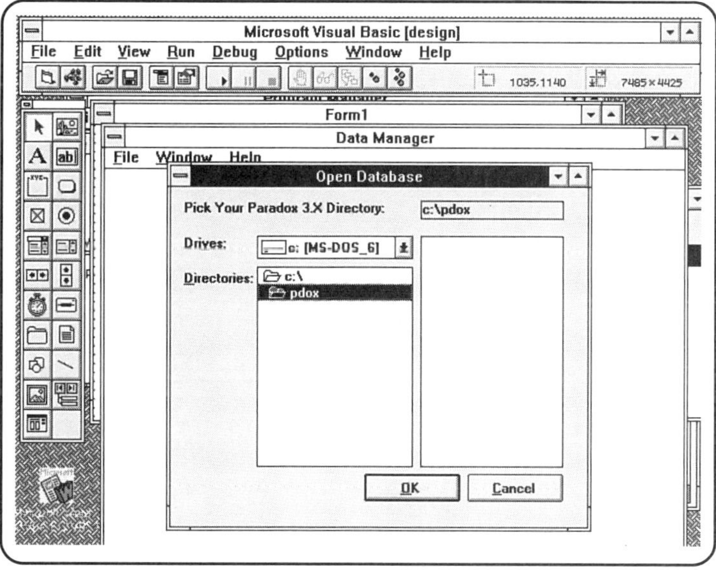

Figure 15.4. The Open Database dialog requesting the Paradox directory.

3. After the database (Paradox, in this case) is open, you can add and modify tables (see Figure 15.5).

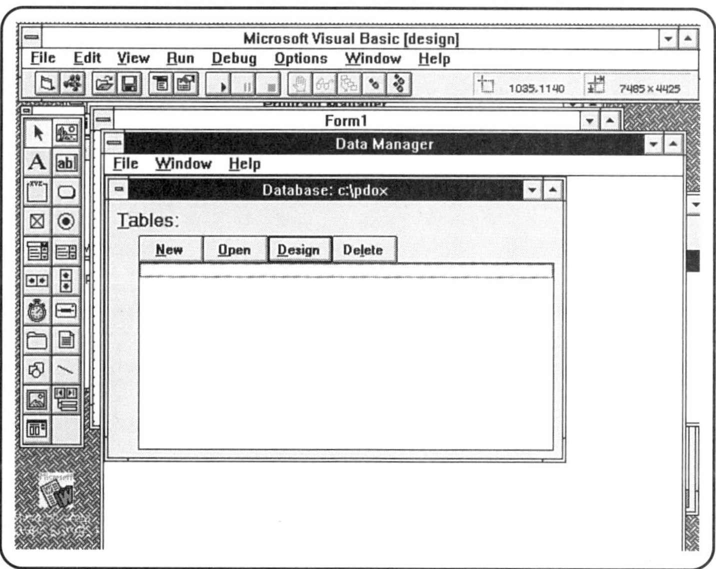

Figure 15.5. The Tables Dialog allows you to Design and Modify Tables in External Formats.

MODIFYING TABLE DATA

After you create or open a database (in any supported format), you can use the Data Manager to add records to a table, delete records from a table, or modify the data in a table. To add, delete, or modify data:

1. To open a table, first open an existing database. The Data Manger displays the Tables window.
2. Select the table you want to modify; then select the Open button. The Data Manager displays a Table Edit window (see Figure 15.6).

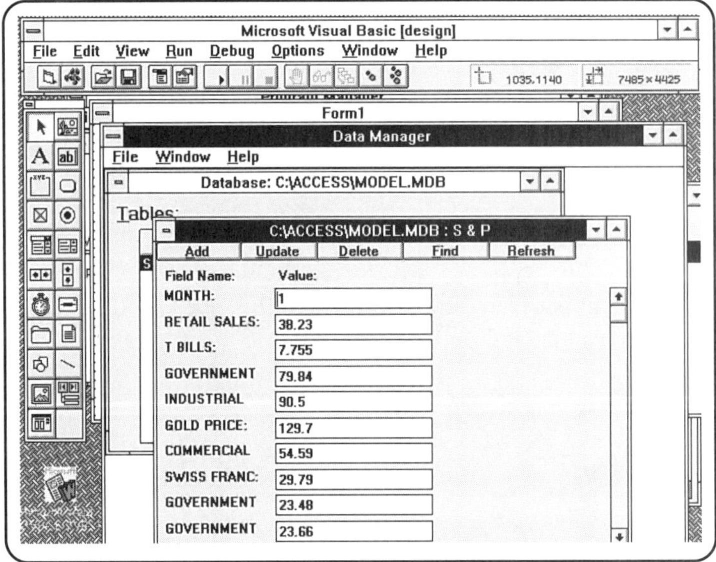

Figure 15.6. Select the table you want to modify; then select the Open button. The Data Manager displays a Table Edit window.

This window displays each of the table's fields and the data for a single record. You can use the scroll bar to scroll through the records in the table.

You can use the Table Edit window to handle the following tasks:

- Add a new record to a table
- Delete a record from a table
- Modify data in a record
- Find a particular record in a table

To add a new record to a table (from the Table Edit window):

1. Select the Add button.
2. Enter data for the table's fields.
3. Save the new record by selecting the Update button, or by moving to another record. (When you move to another record, the table is automatically updated.) To return the table to its previous state (without saving changes), select the Refresh button.

To delete a record from a table:

1. Select the record to delete.

To find a record in the Table Edit window, either:

A. Use the data control at the bottom of the Table Edit window to view the first, previous, next, or last record in the table.

   or

B. Use the Find button to find a specific record based on a search expression. (The Find button is particularly useful in large databases.)

The syntax for the search expression generally follows the syntax for Structured Query Language (SQL) `WHERE` clauses. For example, in the Authors table (in the BIBLIO.MDB example that ships with Visual Basic 3.0), you can locate the fifth record by entering `AU_ID > 4` as the search expression. `AU_ID` is the name of the author ID field.

To modify the data in a record:

1. Select the record you want to modify.
2. Enter new data for the record.
3. Save the new record by selecting the Update button, or by moving to another record. (Note agin that moving to another record automatically updates the table.) To return the table to its previous state, without saving changes, select the Refresh button.

Note that if you try to add or modify a record by entering a value for a field that violates the requirements for the data type, or violates a restriction established by the index, an error occurs. For example, again using the `AU_ID` field in the BIBLIO.MDB example, if you enter an ID that's larger than a long integer (the data type for the `AU_ID` field), an overflow error occurs, and the record isn't updated (see Figure 15.7).

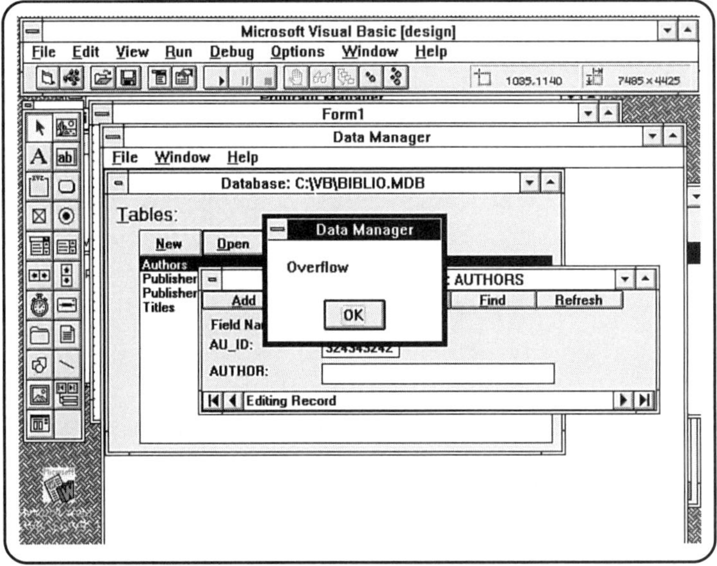

Figure 15.7. Overflow error occurs if numerical value exceeds data type restriction.

How To Create an Index

Indexes prevent the existence of duplicate records in tables and can improve performance.

To create an index with the Data Manager:

1. Create a new database (or open an existing database).
2. From the database window, select the New button to create a new table, or select the Design button to modify an existing table. The Table Design window opens (see Figure 15.8).
3. Select the Add button in the Indexes part of the Table Design window. The Add Index dialog opens (see Figure 15.9).

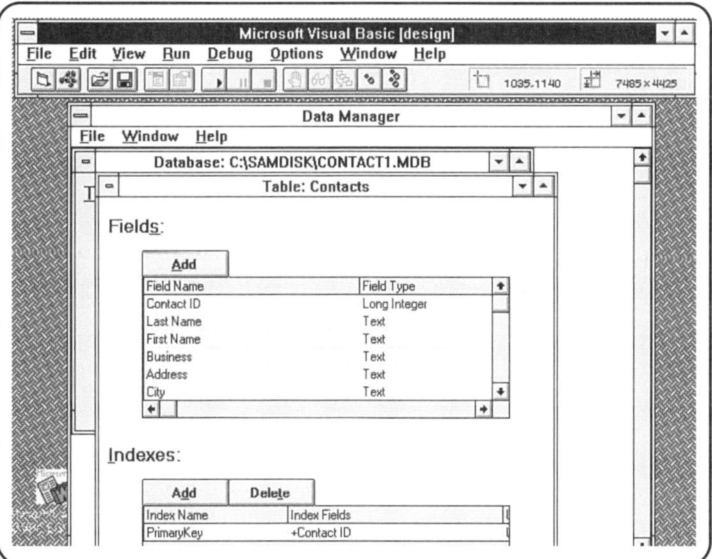

Figure 15.8. From the database window, select the New button to create a new table, or select the Design button to modify an existing table. The Table Design window opens.

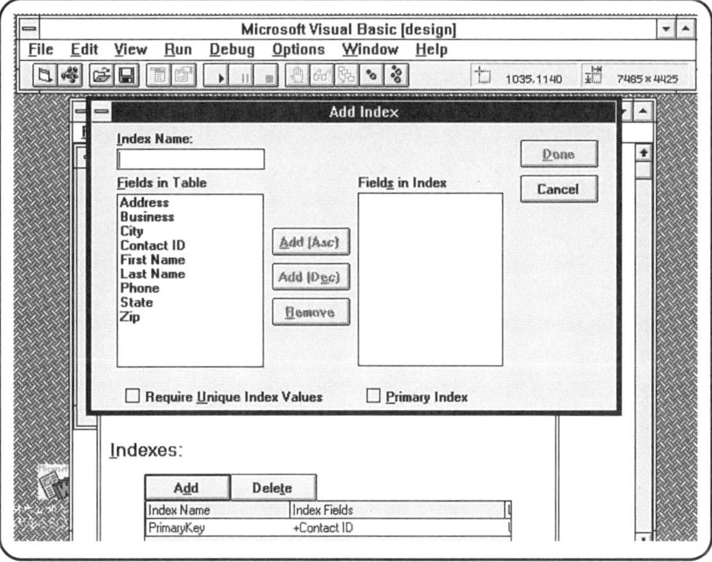

Figure 15.9. Select the Add button in the Indexes part of the Table Design window. The Add Index dialog opens.

4. Enter a name for the index in the Index Name text box.
5. Select a field name from the Fields in Table list. Select Add (Asc) to create an ascending index, or Add (Dec) to create a descending index.
6. If you want to create a Primary Index or want to require unique indexing, check the corresponding box at the bottom of the dialog (Primary Index or Require Unique Index).
7. Select Done to create the index.

Select the Primary Index check box to make an index the *primary* field for sorting the table. Checking this box also indicates that the index is to be unique. If a table already contains a primary index, Visual Basic generates an error message (see Figure 15.10).

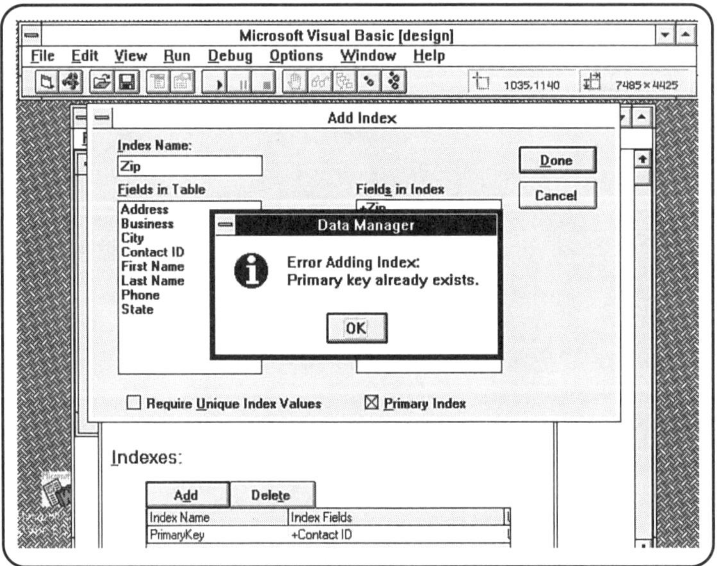

Figure 15.10. If a table already contains a primary index, Visual Basic generates an error message.

Select the Require Unique Index Values check box to prevent duplicate records in the table. If a database contains duplicate records or Null values in an index, and you select either the Require Unique Index Values or Primary Index check boxes, the Data Manager will not create a new index.

Some fields can't be used as an index, for example, MEMO or binary object fields.

How To Compact a Database

When the Data Manager compacts a database, it copies all the data from one database to another database and simultaneously organizes the data in the resulting database contiguously. This usually frees disk space.

Use the File/Compact Database command from the main Data Manager menu to compact a database. The Database to Compact From dialog opens (see Figure 15.11).

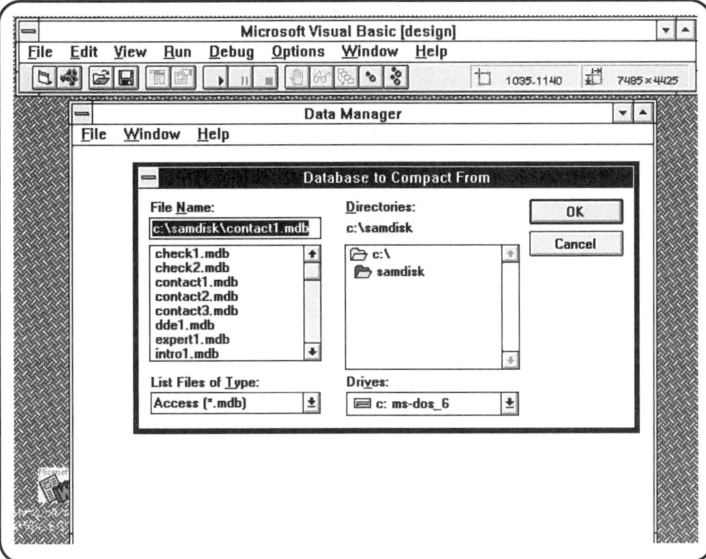

Figure 15.11. The Database to Compact From dialog opens.

Select a database to compact from.

Next, the Database to Compact To dialog opens (see Figure 15.12).

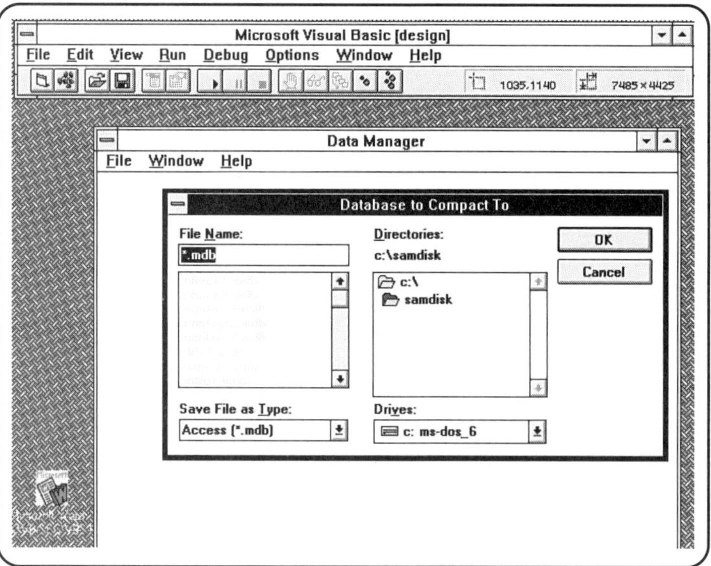

Figure 15.12. The Database to Compact To dialog opens.

Select the database to compact to.

You can compact only Visual Basic (.MDB) and Microsoft Access (.MDB) databases. Other databases (Paradox, dBASE, etc.) must be compacted using the compacting tools shipped with that database.

Make sure *not* to specify the same name for both the original database (Database to Compact From) and compacted database (Database to Compact To) files. If you do, and the Compact Database operation is disrupted or corrupted, your original database will be deleted.

HOW TO REPAIR A DATABASE

If Visual Basic (or one of your Visual Basic applications) terminates unexpectedly (due to a power outage, other hardware or software problem), you might need to repair a database that was in use when Visual Basic (or the application) terminated. You can use the Data Manager to attempt to repair a database.

To repair a database:

1. Select File/Repair Database from the main Data Manager menu.

   The Repair Database dialog is displayed (see Figure 15.13). Use the Repair Database dialog to specify the name of the database you want to repair.

2. Select OK to attempt a repair.

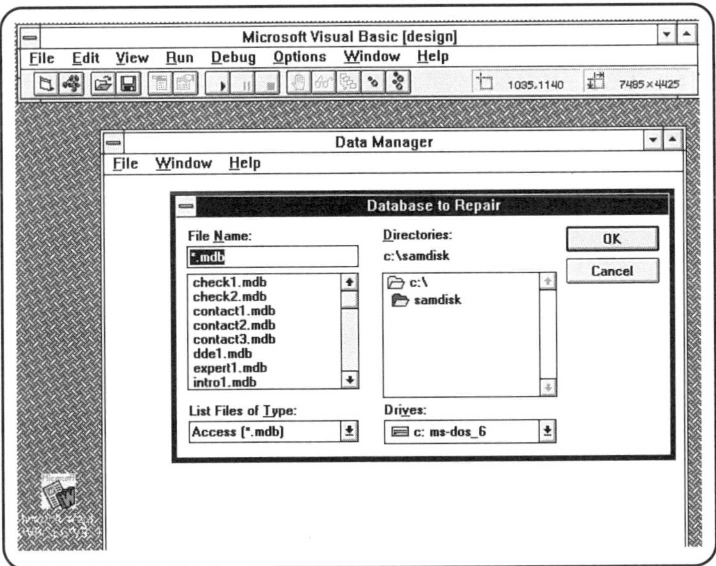

Figure 15.13. The Repair Database dialog is displayed.

When the Data Manager attempts to repair a database it checks all pages in the database for correct linkage, validates all system tables, and validates all indexes. If a page in the database can't be repaired, the Data Manager discards it.

A successfully repaired database may be larger than the previous (pre-repaired) database. Compacting a repaired database will usually decrease its size by removing unused database pages.

Data Access from Visual Basic

Regardless of how you create a database (using the Data Manager, Microsoft Access, another database, or even if the database is on a network), you can manipulate the data in the database from Visual Basic code.

The easiest way to create Visual Basic applications that let users access data in a database is to add a Visual Basic data control on a form. If you add a data control to a form, you can perform most data access tasks with little (or no) code.

After you add a data control to a form, you use the Visual Basic data-aware controls or third-party data-aware controls with the Visual Basic data control to display and manipulate fields from external databases.

If you bind a control to a data control, the bound control automatically displays data from a specific field (the field the control is bound to) for the current record. If the data control changes to a different record, all bound controls automatically change to display data from the current record. If a user changes or enters new data, the data control automatically saves the changes in the database when the data control moves to a new record.

An Introduction to Database Objects

Each database is a collection of data. A database can contain tables, indexes, and queries. The data control, just discussed, is the easiest way to connect your Visual Basic forms to databases. Most of the rest of this chapter will demonstrate this ease of using the data control. However, keep in mind that you can use the Visual Basic database object to work with databases, as well.

You use a variable of the database object type to access databases this way:

```
Dim Database1 As Database
Set Database1 = OpenDatabase("Somedb.mdb")
```

The previous two lines of code dimension (declare) a database variable; then open the database. After you've opened a database, you can use the database objects properties and methods and other objects (such as TableDef, Dynaset, Field, QueryDef, Snapshot, and Table) to manipulate the database.

The database properties include:

```
Collating Order
Connect
Exclusive
Name
QueryTimeOut
TableDefs Collection
Transactions
Updatable
```

The database object methods are:

```
BeginTrans
Close
CommitTrans
CreateDynaset
CreateQueryDef
CreateSnapshot
DeleteQueryDef
Execute
ExecuteSQL
ListFields
ListTables
OpenQueryDef
OpenTable
Rollback
```

For example, you can use a Database and its underlying TableDefs object to modify the structure of a database by adding a field to an existing table. The following code creates a New Field object variable for a Field, sets the data type, size, and attributes; then adds it to a `TableDef` (a `TableDef` represents a table in the database) with the `Append` method. Because a `TableDef` is (or maintaintains) the definition of a table, the table will have a new field named `NewField` after running this code:

```
Sub Form_Load ()
    Dim Database1 As Database    ' Declare database and
    Dim Field1 As New Field      ' field objects
    Const DB_TEXT = 10           ' Set type constant
    Const DB_UPDATABLEFIELD = 32
    Set Database1 = OpenDatabase("CONTACT2.MDB")
```

```
                                  'Open database
    Field1.Name = "NewField"      ' Set Field property.
    Field1.Type = DB_TEXT         ' Const = 10
    Field1.Size = 20              'Field size
    Field1.Attributes = DB_UPDATABLEFIELD  ' Const = 32
    Database1.TableDefs("Contacts").Fields.Append Field1
                                  'Append to TableDef.
End Sub
```

Figure 15.14 shows the new structure of this table, viewed from within the Data Manager, after running this code (saved in project DataA.MAK on the disk).

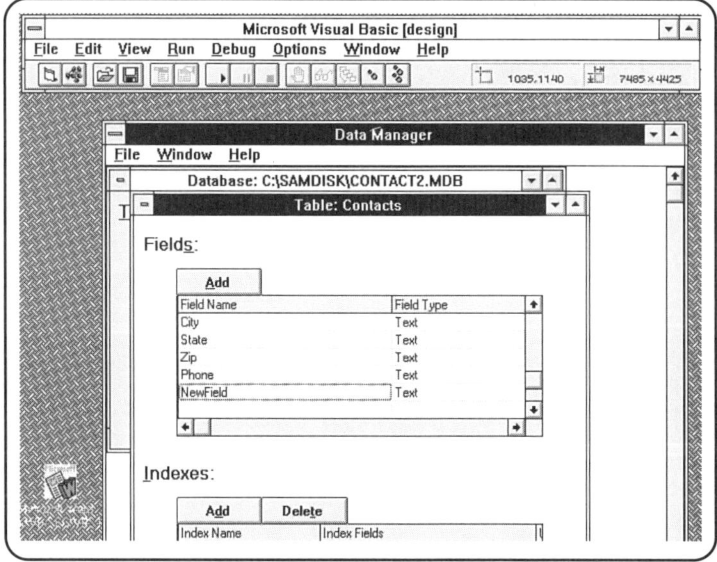

Figure 15.14. The new structure of this table, viewed from within the Data Manager, after running this code in DataA.

Similarly, you can use other Visual Basic data-aware objects to manipulate databases from code.

Binding a Data-Aware Control to a Data Control

For many (perhaps, most) of your data-aware applications, using the data control with bound data-aware controls will be easier and will reduce the code in your applications.

When a data control opens a database, it creates a `Dynaset` object containing data from the database. To view or manipulate this data on a form, you must *bind* one or more controls to a data control on the form.

You bind a control to a specific field in the `Dynaset` represented by the `Recordset` property of a data control. At design time only, you can bind controls to the data control with the `DataSource` property. At runtime, you can bind a field to the data control with the `DataField` property.

For example, to bind a text box (in Visual Basic 3.0, a data-aware control) to a data control at design time:

1. Open a new project (it has a default form).
2. Add a data control to the form (Visual Basic automatically names it, Data1).
3. In the Properties window for the data control, go to the `DatabaseName` property and click the (...) button next to the Settings list box to see a list of the databases available (see Figure 15.15).

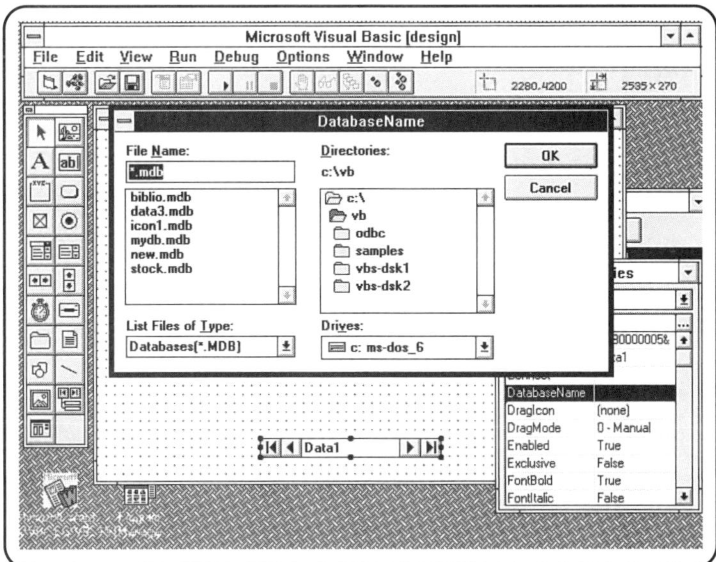

Figure 15.15. In the Properties window for the data control, go to the DatabaseName property and click the (...) button next to the Settings list box to see a list of the databases available.

4. Next, go to the `RecordSource` property and click the (...) button next to the Settings list box to see a list of the tables available.
5. Add a text box to the form (Text1).
6. In the Properties window for the text box, select the `DataSource` property and click the (...) button next to the Settings list box to see a list of the data controls on the form. Select the Data1 data control (see Figure 15.16).

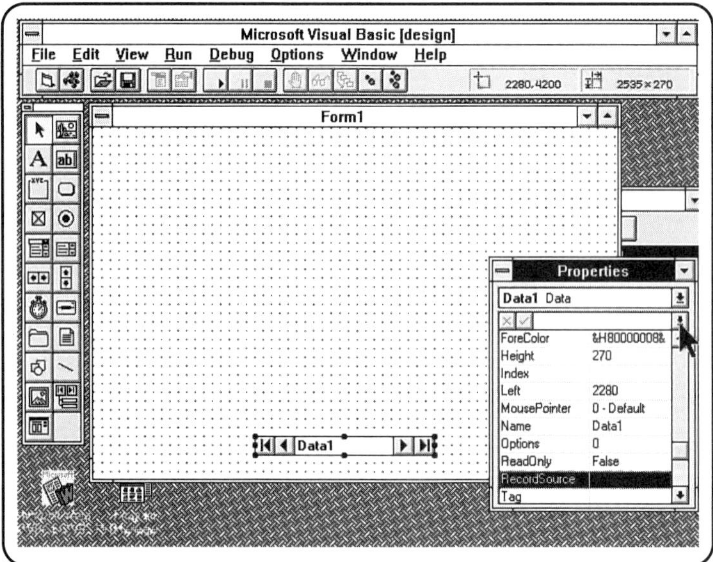

Figure 15.16. In the Properties window for the text box, go to the DataSource property and click the (...) button next to the Settings list box to see a list of the data controls on the form.

7. Next, select the `DataField` property (for the textbox), and click the (...) button next to the Settings list box to see a list of the available fields in the `Recordset` property of the data control. (If you haven't yet set the

`DatabaseName` and `RecordSource` properties of the data control, this list will be empty.) Select a field.

Data Access Application 1

Creating applications that use the data control is relatively simple. Let's begin by first using the Data Manager to create a database. This database, called Contact1, will consist of the following fields:

- Contact ID
- Last Name
- First Name
- Business
- Address
- City
- State
- ZIP
- Phone

To create this database, open the Data Manager using the Visual Basic Windows/Data Manager menu command. The Data Manager opens. Figure 15.17 shows the Data Manager. (Note: If you don't want to recreate the Contact1 database, you can simply use the one on the disk in the back of this book.)

Select File/New and Access 1.1 from the Data Manager menu to create a Microsoft Access 1.1 database.

The New database dialog opens (see Figure 15.18).

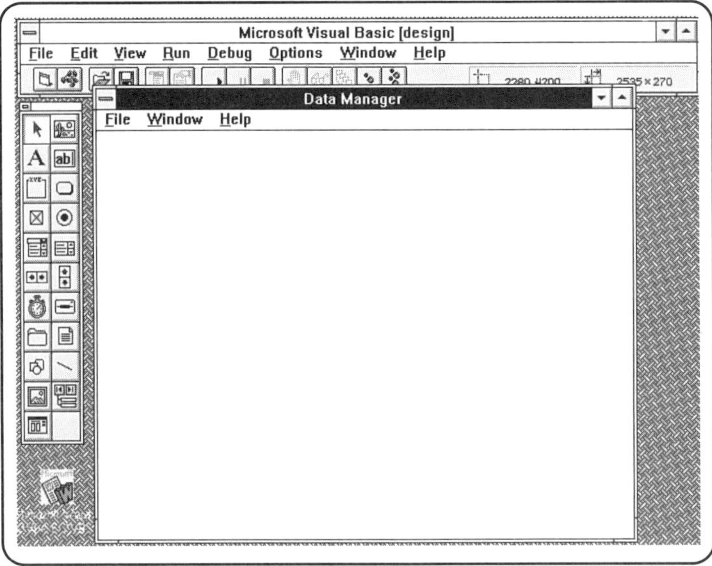

Figure 15.17. The Data Manager.

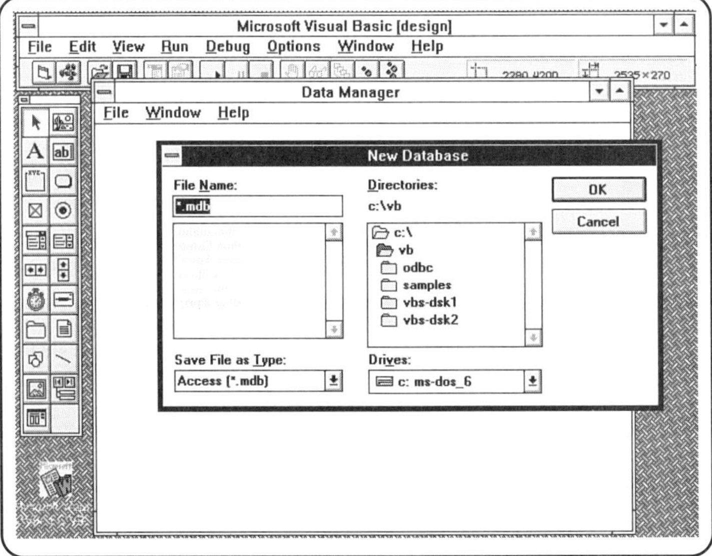

Figure 15.18. The New database dialog opens.

Indicate a name (contact1) for the database. The Tables dialog opens (see Figure 15.19).

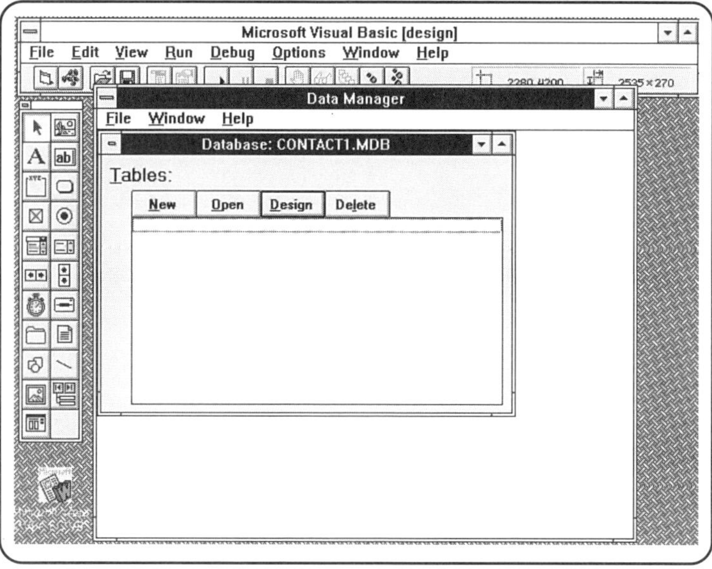

Figure 15.19. The Tables dialog opens.

Select New. The Create New Table dialog opens (see Figure 15.20).

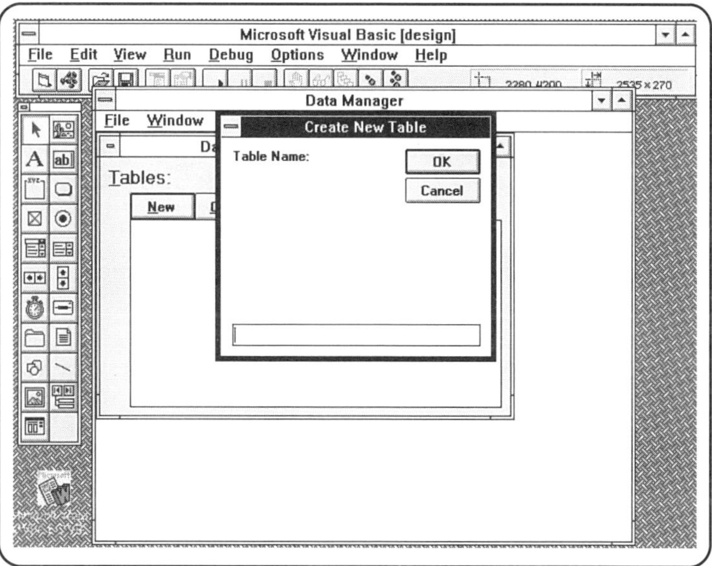

Figure 15.20. The Create New Table dialog opens.

Enter the table name, contacts.

The Table Fields and Indexes dialog opens (see Figure 15.21).

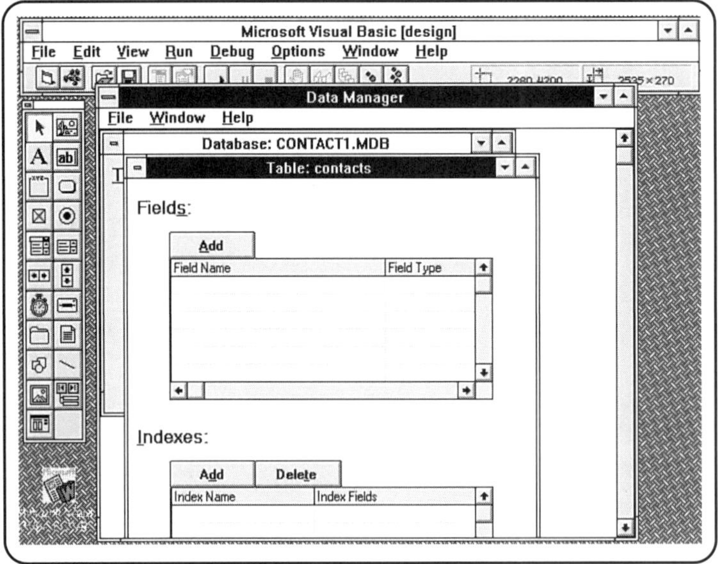

Figure 15.21. The Table Fields and Indexes dialog opens.

Select Add Fields. The Add Fields dialog box opens (see Figure 15.22).

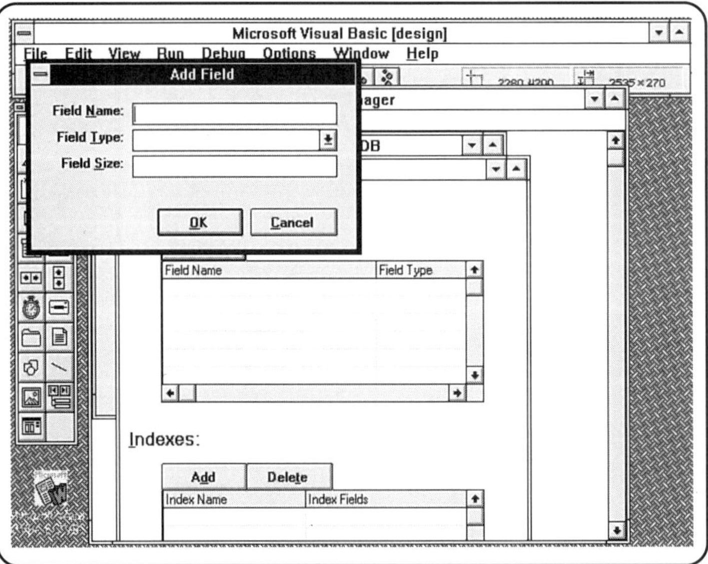

Figure 15.22. The Add Fields dialog box opens.

Enter the fields, one at a time in this dialog. Figure 15.23 shows the table after all fields have been added in design view.

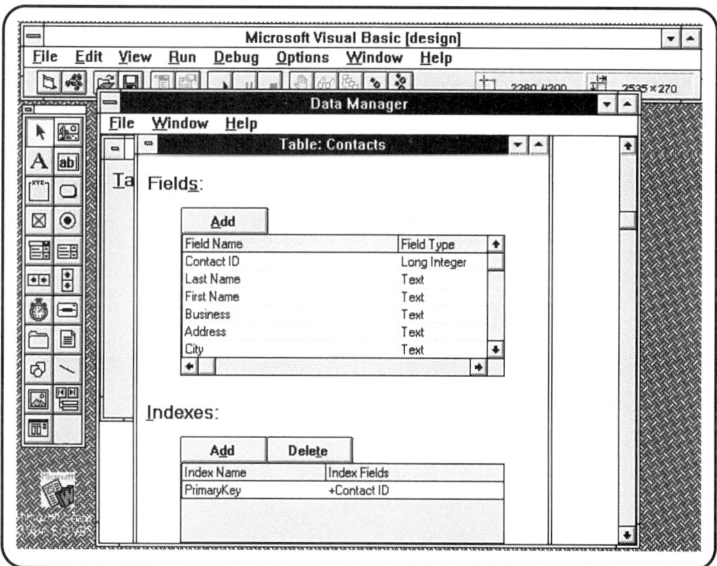

Figure 15.23. The table after all fields have been added in design view.

Save the table design and close the Data Manager.

Create a Form To View/Edit the Contacts Table

Next, back in Visual Basic design view, create a new project (saved on the disk as Data1).

1. Use the Toolbox to add a frame to the default form (save this form as Data1).
2. Within the frame, add four (or more) textboxes and a data control. Figure 15.24 shows this form in design view.

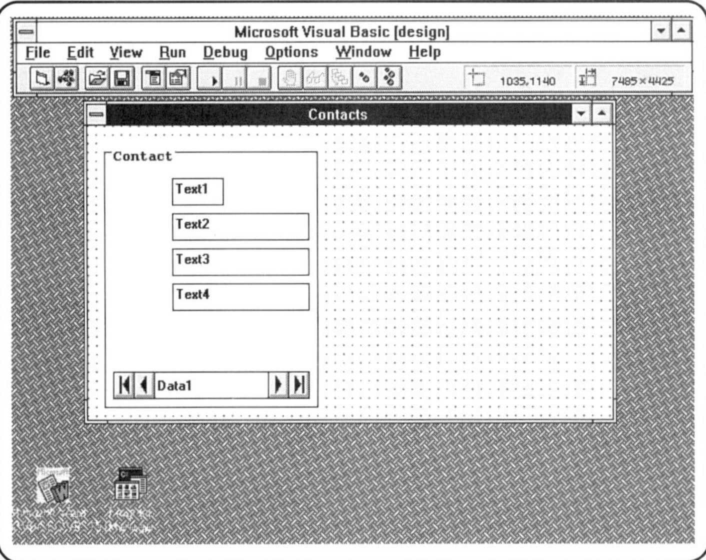

Figure 15.24. Within the frame, add four (or more) textboxes and a data control. This form in design view.

3. Use the Properties window to set the `Databasename` and `RecordSource` properties for the data control. The `Databasename` is *contact1.mdb*. The `RecordSource` is *contacts*.

4. In the Properties window for each of the text boxes, select the `DataSource` property and click the (...) button next to the Settings list box to see a list of the data controls on the form. Select the Data1 data control.

5. Next, select the `DataField` property (for the textboxes), and click the (...) button next to the Settings list box to see a list of the available fields in the `Recordset` property of the data control. (If you haven't yet set the `DatabaseName` and `RecordSource` properties of the data control, this list will be empty.) Select, in turn, one field for each textbox: ContactID, LastName, FirstName, and Business.

That'll do it. You don't need any code to edit these four fields of the database. When you run this form (the application), the data control handles the connection to the database, and the four bound text boxes "get" the field data for their corresponding fields. Figure 15.25 shows this application (no code needed) at runtime.

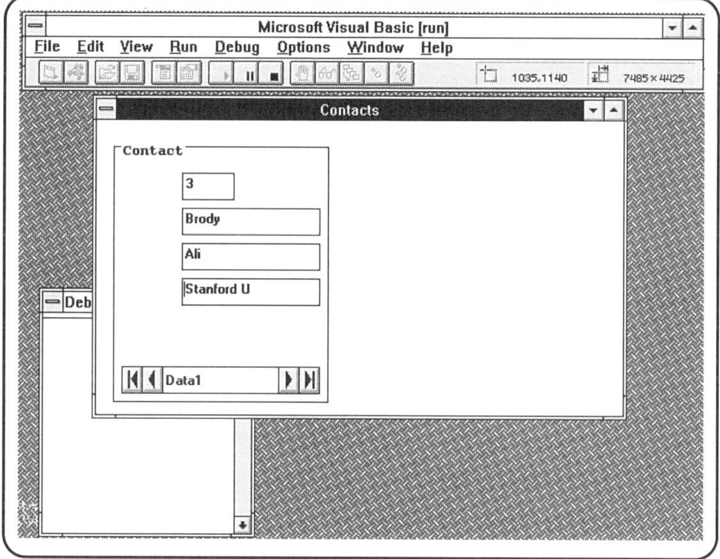

Figure 15.25. Data1 application (no code needed) at runtime.

DATA ACCESS APPLICATION 2

Let's complicate matters somewhat by letting one form display two tables simultaneously. To make matters even more interesting, let's relate these tables to each other.

Typically, in database applications, several tables are related to each other. For example, suppose that a second table in the contacts database, called *contacts notes*, refers to memos (or notes) about each business contact. Suppose also that a business contact can have more than one corresponding note.

Create this application by first borrowing the structure of the previous Contacts form. The easiest way to do this is to use the File/Save As Visual Basic menu command to save the Data1 form as Data2.

Next, add a second frame to the data2 form; then within the frame add a second data control and four more text boxes (one as a multi-line text box). Figure 15.26 shows this form in design view.

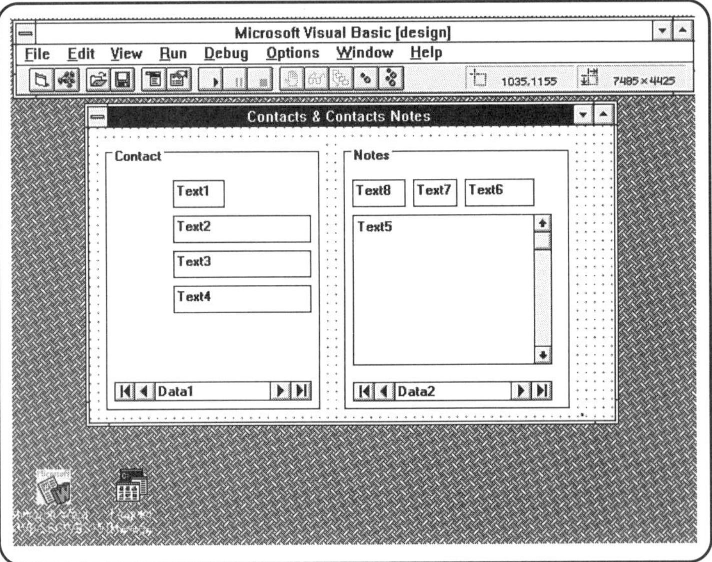

Figure 15.26. Data2 form at designtime.

Next, use the Data Manager to open the contacts database and to create the contacts notes table. It consists of four fields: MemoID, ContactID, Data, and Memo. Figure 15.27 shows this table in design view (within the Data Manager).

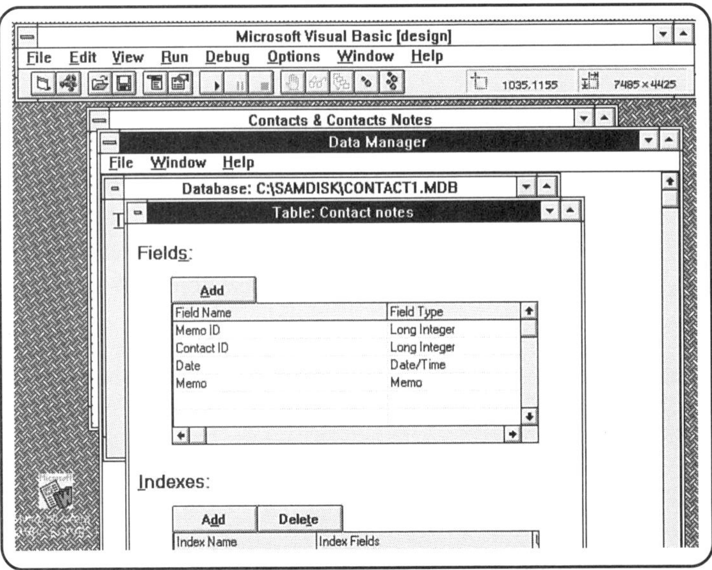

Figure 15.27. The contacts notes table in design view (within the Data Manager).

> Note that you can open more than one table within a database at a time in the Data Manager.

You'll use the ContactId to relate the contacts and contacts notes tables.

Save the contacts notes table and close the Data Manager.

Return to Visual Basic and use the Properties window to set the `Databasename` and `RecordSource` properties for the second data control. The Database name is *contacts.mdb*. The RecordSource is *contacts notes*.

In the Properties window for each of the text boxes, select the `DataSource` property and click the (...) button next to the Settings list box to see a list of the data controls on the form. Select the Data2 data control.

Next, select the `DataField` property (for the textboxes), and click the (...) button next to the Settings list box to see a list of the available fields in the `Recordset` property of the data control. (If you haven't yet set the `DatabaseName` and `RecordSource` properties of the data control, this list will be empty.) Select, in turn, one field for each textbox: ContactID, LastName, FirstName, and Business.

This application requires two little code modifications to coordinate or relate the two tables. Each time a user uses the data control on the contacts frame (Data1) to move to another record in the contacts database, you want the contacts notes database (controlled by Data2) to move to the first corresponding contact notes. You don't want contacts notes shown unless they correspond to a contact, right?

You can handle this easily by re-implementing the `Text1_Change` event procedure. Text1 contains the ContactID field. Each time the user moves to a new record, move to the first record in the Data2 (contacts notes) `Recordset`. (The `Recordset` is a reference to the underlying database object of a data control; in this example, the `RecordSet` for Data2 consists of all the records in contact notes, since that table is referenced by the Data2 control. The Data1 control Recordset consists of all the records in the contacts table.)

Then move through the `Recordset` (all the records of contacts notes) one at a time until the current record's ContactID matches the ContactID referred to by the Data1 control (contacts). If the ContactID fields match, the contact note record is a corresponding note for the contact. Here's the code:

```
Sub Text1_Change ()
    ID% = Data1.Recordset.Fields("Contact ID")
    Data2.Recordset.MoveFirst
    Do While Not Data2.Recordset.EOF
    If Data2.Recordset.Fields("Contact Id") = ID% Then
        Exit Sub
    Else
        Data2.Recordset.MoveNext
    End If
    Loop
    Exit Sub
End Sub
```

One additional consideration: what if a user uses the Data2 control scroll bar independently of the Data1 control to move through records of the contact notes table? You can prevent the user from selecting a contact note record that doesn't correspond to the current contact by re-implementing the Data2 control's Reposition event procedure.

The Reposition event procedure is called each time a user clicks a data control's scroll bar. So you can use this procedure to examine the next record and move past it, if the ContactID of contact notes (text9) doesn't correspond to the ContactID of contacts (text1):

```
Sub Data2_Reposition ()
    Do While Not Data2.Recordset.EOF
        If Text8.Text <> Text1.Text Then
            Data2.Recordset.MoveNext
        Else
            Exit Sub
        End If
    Loop
End Sub
```

Figure 15.28 shows the Data2 application at runtime.

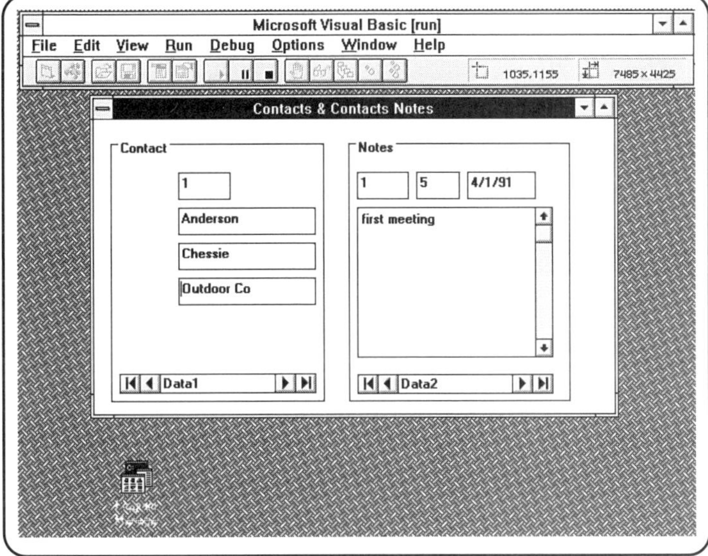

Figure 15.28. The Data2 application at runtime.

CREATING A DATABASE IN CODE

Although I won't go into too many details, you can create a database from code as well as from the Data Manager, Microsoft Access, or another database, if you have the Visual Basic 3.0 Professional Edition.

The final example in this chapter (Data3) creates another version of the contacts database, consisting of two tables: one for contacts and one for addresses. Each table contains three fields and the address table has two indexes.

The code in Listing 15.1 contains the complete code for this example. It consists of three procedures (`CreateNewDb`, `CreateContactTable`, and `CreateAddressTable`). These procedures are automatically run when the (default) form loads. Note also that the form does not use a data control or any bound data-aware controls.

Notice the error checking in the `CreateNewDb()` procedure. This is important because the `CreateDatabase` function generates an error if it tries to create a database that already exists.

Note also the use of the built-in Visual Basic `Choose` function in the `CreateContactTable` and `CreateAddressTable` procedures. The `Choose` Function returns (or selects) a specified value from a group of arguments.

LISTING 15.1. DATA3.

```
Sub CreateNewDB ()
    Dim Db1 As Database, Dbname As String
    Dbname = "data3.MDB"
    On Error GoTo DBCreateErr
    Set Db1 = CreateDatabase(Dbname, DB_LANG_GENERAL)
    CreateContactTable Db1
    CreateAddressTable Db1
    MsgBox "The database, " & UCase(Dbname) & ", is ready."
    Exit Sub
DBCreateErr:
    Resume Next
End Sub


Sub CreateContactTable (D As Database)
    Dim Td As New TableDef, Fld() As New Field
    Dim Idx() As New Index, I As Integer

    ReDim Fld(1 To 5), Idx(1 To 2)

    Td.Name = "Contact2"  ' Set the table name.
    ' Create Fields.
    For I = 1 To 4  ' Set properties for fields.
        Fld(I).Name = Choose(I, "PNum", "LName", "FName", "Phone")
        Fld(I).Type = Choose(I, DB_LONG, DB_TEXT, DB_TEXT, DB_TEXT)
        Fld(I).Size = Choose(I, 4, 30, 30, 15)
    Next I
    Fld(1).Attributes = DB_AUTOINCRFIELD    ' Counter field.
    For I = 1 To 4
        Td.Fields.Append Fld(I)
    Next I
```

```
    ' Create Table.
    D.TableDefs.Append Td
End Sub


Sub CreateAddressTable (D As Database)
    Dim Td As New TableDef, Fld() As New Field
    Dim Idx() As New Index, I As Integer

    ReDim Fld(1 To 5), Idx(1 To 2)

    Td.Name = "Addresses"   ' Set the table name.
    ' Create Fields.
    Fld(1).Attributes = DB_AUTOINCRFIELD    ' Counter field.
    For I = 1 To 5  ' Set properties for fields.
        Fld(I).Name = Choose(I, "ANum", "Addr1", "Addr2", "CityState", "ZIP")
        Fld(I).Type = Choose(I, DB_LONG, DB_TEXT, DB_TEXT, DB_TEXT, DB_TEXT)
        Fld(I).Size = Choose(I, 4, 30, 30, 30, 10)
        Td.Fields.Append Fld(I)
    Next I

    ' Create Indexes.
    Idx(1).Name = "PrimaryKey"
    Idx(1).Fields = "ANum"
    Idx(1).Primary = True
    Idx(1).Unique = True
    Idx(2).Name = "City"
    Idx(2).Fields = "CityState"
    For I = 1 To 2
        Td.Indexes.Append Idx(I)
    Next I

    ' Create Table.
    D.TableDefs.Append Td
End Sub

Sub Form_Load ()
    CreateNewDB
End Sub
```

SUMMARY

And that does it for this chapter's discussion of data awareness and data management Visual Basic-style. Visual Basic's data management tools are powerful, indeed, and will enable you to handle many database programming tasks, often without code. If you need to have additional control over database management, I suggest you consider using Microsoft Access with Visual Basic.

Third-Party Support and Custom Controls

Several companies mentioned in this book support Visual Basic through assembly language routine DLLs, custom application DLLs, and custom controls. You can contact these helpful people at the following addresses and numbers. When you call, tell them I sent you.

QuickPak Professional For Windows

This is an advanced programming library that includes more than 400 subroutines for highperformance file and disk I/Os, array sorting, and so on.

PDQComm

This is a serial communications package for Visual Basic.

Crescent Software, Inc.
32 Seventy Acres
West Redding, CT 06896
(203) 438-5300

Custom Control Factory

This is similar to the Animate button in Microsoft's Professional Toolkit, but it has additional animation cycles, animated option buttons, toolbar support, and so on.

CCF-Cursors

This has everything you need to create and use unlimited cursors—that is, mouse pointers. It enables you to detect mouse events in any standard Visual Basic control and in most, if not all, custom controls.

Desaware
5 Town & Country Village, #790
San Jose, CA 95128
(408) 377-4770
Fax (408) 371-3530

MicroHelp Muscle, VBTools Communication Library, Network Library, HighEdit, and VBXRef, a cross reference for Visual Basic applications

These packages include many useful assembly language tools and custom controls.

MicroHelp, Inc.
4836 Huntridge Drive
Roswell, GA 30075
(800) 922-3383
(404) 594-1185 in Georgia

Professional Toolkit for Visual Basic

Microsoft Corporation
One Microsoft Way
Redmond, WA 98052
(206) 882-8080

ButtonTool, EditTool, vBaseTool

This one features 3-D buttons, toolbars, 3-D panels, formatted input, data fields, and other 3-D effects.

OutRider Systems
P.O. Box 271669
Houston, TX 77277-1669
(713) 726-0386

3D Widgets /1, /2, /3

This features lots of 3-D tools: list boxes, combo boxes, menus, file boxes, frames, panels, and so on.

Sheridan Software Systems, Inc.
65 Maxess Road
Melville, NY 11747
(516) 753-0985

NeuroWindows DLL

For a good look at NeuroWindows, check out the demonstration examples on the disk in the back of the book.

Ward Systems Group, Inc.
245 West Patrick Street
Frederick, MD 21701
(301) 662-7950

Bonus Applications

Bonus Application 1: BlackJack

Two additional examples that didn't conform to the main body of text are included in this appendix. I had fun with these applications while I wrote this book. The first application is a blackjack game written in Visual Basic that utilizes several direct function calls to the Windows API. MicroHelp, Inc. contributed this example (and the next) to this book's disk.

Neither application is discussed here, but you can see what they look like when they're running and the complete code (thanks again to MicroHelp). You can study and modify them to your heart's content. Figure B.1 shows the Project window for the BlackJack application. Figures B.2, B.3, and B.4 show the application running during a game. Listing B.1. shows the complete code, which is also on the disk (called BlackJack).

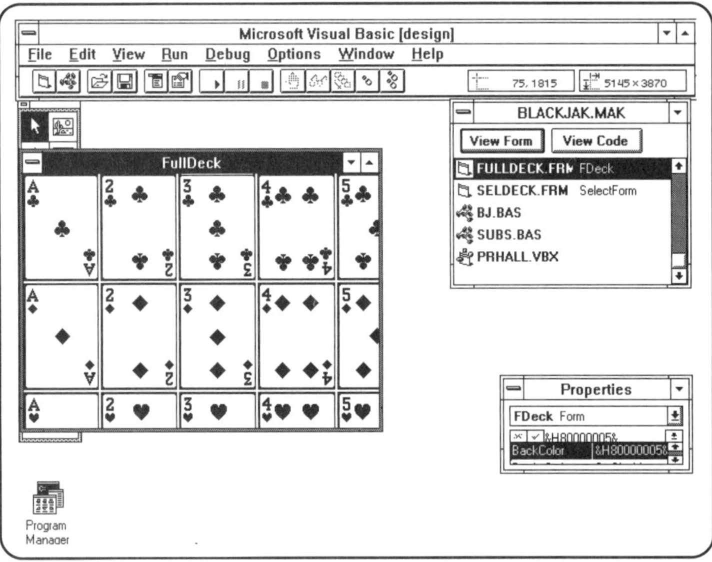

Figure B.1. The BlackJack Project window.

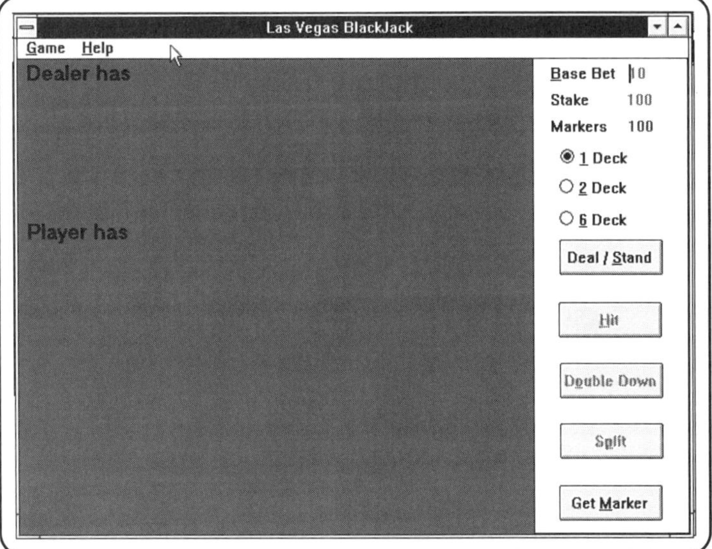

Figure B.2. BlackJack: beginning a game.

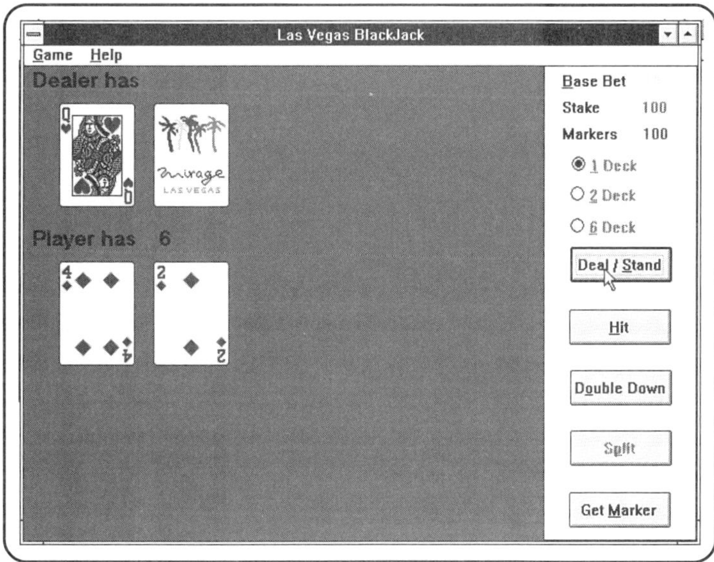

Figure B.3. BlackJack: playing a game.

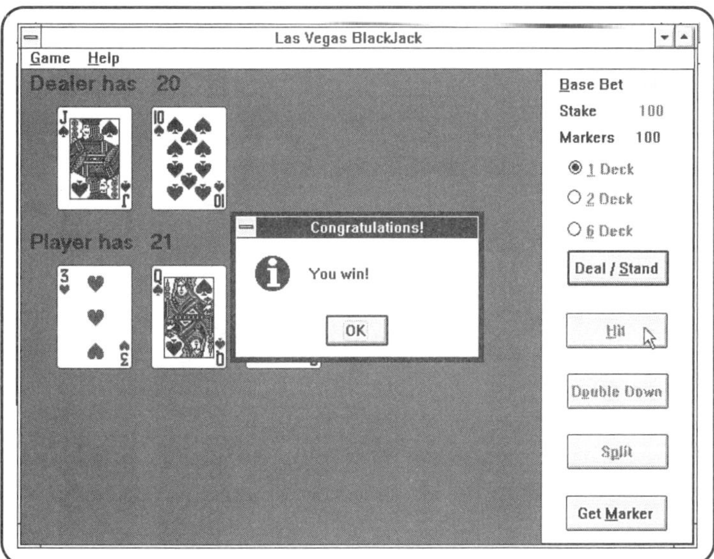

Figure B.4. BlackJack: winning a game.

Listing B.1. BlackJack game.

```
' About Form

Sub Command1_Click ()
    Unload AboutForm
End Sub

Sub Form_Resize ()
    Command1.SetFocus
End Sub


' BJ Form


' Sub StandButton_Click ()

     ' Deal or stand - if deal, disable bet box
    If HandInPlay Then   ' Then player wants to stand
       PlayerDone(ActivePlayer) = 1
       ShowValue ActivePlayer
       If ActivePlayer = PLAYERB Then
          AnalyzeHand
       ElseIf Split Then
          ActivePlayer = PLAYERB
          ShowHandIndicator
          If PlayerDone(PLAYERB) Then
             AnalyzeHand
          Else
             If DoubleButton.Enabled = False Then
                DoubleButton.Enabled = True
             End If
             If HitButton.Enabled = False Then
                HitButton.Enabled = True
             End If
             ' If the player has only two cards, and the stake
             ' is greater than or equal to two bets
             If HowManyCards(ActivePlayer) = 2 And
                    Stake& >= (Bet(PLAYER) + Bet(PLAYERB)) Then
                If DoubleButton.Enabled = False Then
                   DoubleButton.Enabled = True
                End If
             End If
          End If
       Else
          AnalyzeHand
       End If
    Else
      ' He wants a deal - check bet amount
      If Bet(PLAYER) <= 0 Then
```

```
        MsgBox "You must bet something or I can't deal!", 64, "Bad Bet"
    ElseIf Bet(PLAYER) > Stake& Then
        MsgBox "You can't bet what you don't have!" + CRLF$ +
        ➥   "Hint - Get a marker.", 64, "Dealer Cannot Extend Credit!"
    ElseIf Stake& <= 0 Then
        MsgBox "You don't have a stake." + CRLF$ +
        ➥   "Please get a marker at the cage.", 64, "You Are Broke"
    Else ' Bet amount is OK. Go ahead and deal
      Deal
      Split = False
      ActivePlayer = PLAYER
      BaseBetAmount.Enabled = False
      For I = SINGLEDECKBUTTON To SIXDECKBUTTON
          DeckButton(I).Enabled = False
      Next

      If HitButton.Enabled = False Then
         HitButton.Enabled = True
      End If
      For I = DEALER To PLAYERB
          Busted(I) = False
          PlayerDone(I) = False
          PlayerHasBj(I) = False
      Next

      Insurance = False
      ' Calculate dealer's hand
      Total(DEALER) = HandValue(DEALER)
      ShowValue PLAYER
      ' If dealer has ace up, ask if player wants insurance
      If CardValue(DEALER, 1) = 1 Then
         If MsgBox("Do you want insurance?", 4 + 32,
         ➥        "Dealer has an Ace Showing!") = MSGBOXYES Then
            Insurance = True
            ' If he said yes to insurance, and the dealer
            ' has Blackjack, the hand is over
            If PlayerHasBj(DEALER) = 0 Then
               YouLoseInsurance
               Exit Sub
            End If
         End If
      End If

      ' If either the dealer or the player has BJ,
      ' show the dealer's hidden card.
   If PlayerHasBj(DEALER) Or PlayerHasBj(PLAYER) Then
          DrawCard DEALER, 2, FACE
          ShowValue DEALER
      End If

      ' If both have BJ
```

continues

LISTING B.1. CONTINUED

```
If PlayerHasBj(DEALER) And PlayerHasBj(PLAYER) Then
   If Insurance Then
      YouWin
   Else
      YouPush
   End If
   SetUpForDeal
   Exit Sub
ElseIf PlayerHasBj(DEALER) Then
   ' If only dealer has BJ
   If Insurance Then
      YouPush
   Else
      YouLose
   End If
   SetUpForDeal
   Exit Sub
ElseIf PlayerHasBj(PLAYER) Then
   ' If Player has BJ, but not dealer
   If Insurance Then
      YouWin
   Else
      YouWinBJ
   End If
   SetUpForDeal
   Exit Sub
End If
' If the player has only two cards, and the stake
' is greater than or equal to two bets
If HowManyCards(ActivePlayer) = 2 And
        Stake& >= (Bet(PLAYER) + Bet(PLAYERB)) Then
   DoubleButton.Enabled = True
Else
   DoubleButton.Enabled = False
End If
' Check if it's OK to split the cards
EqualTest = False
If CardValue(PLAYER, 1) = CardValue(PLAYER, 2) Then
    EqualTest = True
End If
If CardValue(PLAYER, 1) >= 10 And CardValue(PLAYER, 2) >= 10 Then
    EqualTest = True
End If
If (Split = 0 And Bet(PLAYER) <= Stake& / 2) And
       (ActivePlayer = PLAYER) And (HowManyCards(PLAYER) = 2) And
       (EqualTest <> 0) Then
    If SplitButton.Enabled = False Then
       SplitButton.Enabled = True
    End If
```

```
        Else
            If SplitButton.Enabled Then
               SplitButton.Enabled = False
            End If
        End If
        ShowHandIndicator
        StandButton.SetFocus
      End If
    End If
End Sub


Sub HitButton_Click ()

  StandButton.SetFocus
  ' If it's OK to hit
  If HitButton.Enabled Then
     ' If you're not done playing the hand
     If PlayerDone(ActivePlayer) = False Then
        Hit ActivePlayer
        If SplitButton.Enabled Then
           SplitButton.Enabled = False
        End If
        If DoubleButton.Enabled Then
           DoubleButton.Enabled = False
        End If
        ShowValue ActivePlayer
        ' If you're busted, or have 21
        If Busted(ActivePlayer) Or PlayerDone(ActivePlayer) Then
            ' If it's a split hand
            If Split Then
                ' If you were playing the second hand
                If ActivePlayer = PLAYERB Then
                    ' You're done
                    AnalyzeHand
                Else
                    ' Play the second hand
                    ActivePlayer = PLAYERB
                    If PlayerDone(PLAYERB) Then
                       AnalyzeHand
                    End If
                End If
            Else
                AnalyzeHand
            End If
        End If
     End If
  End If
  ShowHandIndicator
End Sub
```

continues

LISTING B.1. CONTINUED

```
Sub DoubleButton_Click ()

    StandButton.SetFocus
    If DoubleButton.Enabled Then
       Bet(ActivePlayer) = Bet(ActivePlayer) * 2
       ' See if two bets are more than stake
       Temp = Stake& - Bet(PLAYER)
       If ActivePlayer = PLAYERB Then
          Temp = Temp - Bet(ActivePlayer)
       End If
       ' If doubling bet would end up betting more than
       ' stake, adjust the bet
       If Temp < 0 Then
          Bet(ActivePlayer) = Bet(ActivePlayer) + Temp
       End If
       DoubleButton.Enabled = False
       If SplitButton.Enabled Then
          SplitButton.Enabled = False
       End If
       PlayerDone(ActivePlayer) = True
       Hit ActivePlayer
       ShowValue ActivePlayer
       If Split Then
          If ActivePlayer = PLAYER Then
             ActivePlayer = PLAYERB
             ' If the player has only two cards, and the stake
             ' is greater than or equal to two bets
             If PlayerHasBj(ActivePlayer) = 0 Then
                If HitButton.Enabled = False Then
                   HitButton.Enabled = True
                End If
                If HowManyCards(ActivePlayer) = 2 And
                       Stake& >= (Bet(PLAYER) + Bet(PLAYERB)) Then
                   If DoubleButton.Enabled = False Then
                      DoubleButton.Enabled = True
                   End If
                End If
             End If
          End If
       Else
          If HitButton.Enabled Then
             HitButton.Enabled = False
          End If
       End If
       If PlayerDone(ActivePlayer) Then
          AnalyzeHand
       End If
       ShowHandIndicator
```

```
    End If
End Sub


Sub SplitButton_Click ()

    If SplitButton.Enabled Then
       SplitButton.Enabled = False
       PlayerBTextBox.Caption = "Player has"
       Split = 1
       Bet(PLAYERB) = Bet(PLAYER)
       Hands(PLAYERB, 1) = Hands(PLAYER, 2)
       DrawCard PLAYERB, 1, FACE
       For ActivePlayer = PLAYER To PLAYERB
           PlayerDone(ActivePlayer) = False
           HowManyCards(ActivePlayer) = 1
           Hit ActivePlayer
           ShowValue ActivePlayer
       Next
       ActivePlayer = PLAYER
       ' If split aces, then you're done
       If CardValue(ActivePlayer, 1) = 1 Then
          PlayerDone(PLAYER) = 1
          PlayerDone(PLAYERB) = 1
       End If
       If PlayerDone(ActivePlayer) Then
          ActivePlayer = PLAYERB
          If PlayerDone(PLAYERB) Then
             AnalyzeHand
          End If
       End If
       StandButton.SetFocus
       If PlayerDone(ActivePlayer) = False Then
          If DoubleButton.Enabled = False Then
             DoubleButton.Enabled = True
          End If
       Else
          If DoubleButton.Enabled Then
             DoubleButton.Enabled = False
          End If
       End If
       HandIndicator(PLAYER).Visible = True
       HandIndicator(PLAYERB).Visible = True
       ShowHandIndicator
    End If
End Sub


Sub AdvanceButton_Click ()
```

continues

LISTING B.1. CONTINUED

```
     StandButton.SetFocus
     Advance& = Advance& + 100
     Stake& = Stake& + 100
     ShowAdvanceAmount
     ShowStakeAmount
End Sub


Sub MenuInstructions_Click (Index As Integer)
    KeyDown HELPKEYCODE, 0
End Sub


Sub DeckButton_Click (Index As Integer)

  If DeckButton(Index).Enabled Then
     NewDecks = 0
     Select Case Index
       Case SINGLEDECKBUTTON
            NewDecks = 1
       Case DOUBLEDECKBUTTON
            NewDecks = 2
       Case SIXDECKBUTTON
            NewDecks = 6
     End Select
     If NewDecks <> Decks Then
        Decks = NewDecks
        Shuffle
        MsgBox "The cards have been shuffled!", 64, "New Dealer!"
        StandButton.SetFocus
     End If
  End If
End Sub


Sub BaseBetAmount_KeyPress (KeyAscii As Integer)

    If KeyAscii = 13 Then
       StandButton.SetFocus
    Else ' Restrict input to numbers
       If KeyAscii < 48 Or KeyAscii > 57 Then
          KeyAscii = 0
          Beep
       End If
    End If
End Sub


Sub MenuExit_Click (Index As Integer)
```

```
        If Len(HelpFileName$) Then
            WinHelp BjForm.hWnd, HelpFileName$, HELP_QUIT, 0&
        End If
        End
End Sub


Sub MenuNew_Click (Index As Integer)

    Bet(DEALER) = 10
    Bet(PLAYER) = 10
    Bet(PLAYERB) = 10
    Stake& = 100
    Advance& = 100
    Decks = 1
    WhichDeck = 0
    ShowBetAmount
    ShowAdvanceAmount
    Shuffle
    SetUpForDeal
    StandButton.SetFocus
End Sub


Sub MenuSelect_Click (Index As Integer)

     SelectForm.Show 1
End Sub


Sub MenuAbout_Click (Index As Integer)

    AboutForm.Show 1
    StandButton.SetFocus
End Sub


Sub AdvanceButton_KeyDown (KeyCode As Integer, Shift As Integer)

     KeyDown KeyCode, Shift  ' Process in SUBS.BAS KeyDown
End Sub


Sub DeckButton_KeyDown (Index As Integer, KeyCode As Integer, Shift As Integer)

     KeyDown KeyCode, Shift  ' Process in SUBS.BAS KeyDown
End Sub
```

continues

LISTING B.1. CONTINUED

```
Sub DividerBar_KeyDown (KeyCode As Integer, Shift As Integer)

     KeyDown KeyCode, Shift  ' Process in SUBS.BAS KeyDown
End Sub


Sub DoubleButton_KeyDown (KeyCode As Integer, Shift As Integer)

     KeyDown KeyCode, Shift  ' Process in SUBS.BAS KeyDown
End Sub


Sub HandIndicator_KeyDown (Index As Integer, KeyCode As Integer,
➥                             Shift As Integer)

     KeyDown KeyCode, Shift  ' Process in SUBS.BAS KeyDown
End Sub


Sub HitButton_KeyDown (KeyCode As Integer, Shift As Integer)

     KeyDown KeyCode, Shift  ' Process in SUBS.BAS KeyDown
End Sub


Sub SplitButton_KeyDown (KeyCode As Integer, Shift As Integer)

     KeyDown KeyCode, Shift  ' Process in SUBS.BAS KeyDown
End Sub


Sub StandButton_KeyDown (KeyCode As Integer, Shift As Integer)

     KeyDown KeyCode, Shift  ' Process in SUBS.BAS KeyDown
End Sub


Sub Form_Load ()

    ' Save original values for form in case it's resized
    BJWidth = Width
    BJHeight = Height
    DBWidth = DividerBar.Width
    DBHeight = DividerBar.Height
    DBLeft = DividerBar.Left
    DBTop = DividerBar.Top
    HTemp$ = MhExeName$(hWnd)
    If InStr(HTemp$, "VB.EXE") = 0 Then
```

```
   HelpFileName$ = MhExePath$(hWnd) + "\bj.hlp"
End If

Randomize Timer
Load FDeck
Load SelectForm
HitButton.Enabled = False
DoubleButton.Enabled = False
SplitButton.Enabled = False
CRLF$ = Chr$(13) + Chr$(10)
' Start-up values
For I = DEALER To PLAYERB
    Bet(I) = 10
Next
Advance& = 100
Stake& = 100

' Set properties for cardboxes greater than 5 for each hand.

' Difference is x coordinate, or width of card + spacer
Difference = CardBox(1).Left - CardBox(0).Left
' If you have more than 5 cards for a hand, first you overlap
' the first 5 cards, then you start overlapping with 6
For Who = DEALER To PLAYERB
    FirstX = (Difference \ 2) * 5   ' Where card 6 goes
    For WhichCard = 6 To 9
        WhichBox = Who * 10 + WhichCard - 1
        CardBox(WhichBox).Top = CardBox(WhichBox - 1).Top
        CardBox(WhichBox).Left = FirstX
        R% = DoEvents()
        FirstX = FirstX + Difference \ 2
        CardBox(WhichBox).Height = CardBox(WhichBox - 1).Height
        R% = DoEvents()
    Next
Next

' Assign CardColumn array and
' keep track of original .LEFT properties for later restoration,
' in case a player has more than 5 cards.
For Who = DEALER To PLAYERB
    For WhichCard = 1 To 9
        CardColumn(Who, WhichCard) = CardBox(Who * 10 + WhichCard - 1).Left
        MasterCardColumn(Who, WhichCard) = CardColumn(Who, WhichCard)
        ' Make unused cardboxes visible
        If WhichCard > 2 Then
           CardBox(Who * 10 + WhichCard - 1).Visible = False
        End If
    Next
Next

' Make hand indicator arrow boxes invisible
```

continues

LISTING B.1. CONTINUED

```
    HandIndicator(1).Visible = False
    HandIndicator(2).Visible = False

    PlayerBTextBox.Caption = ""    ' Don't show split hand "Player"
    Decks = 1
    Shuffle
End Sub


Sub Form_Resize ()

    DividerBar.Left = ScaleWidth - DBWidth
    DividerBar.Top = ScaleHeight - DBHeight
End Sub


Sub BaseBetAmount_LostFocus ()

    ' Convert to string first to ensure you don't get an
    ' overflow.
    A$ = LTrim$(RTrim$(BaseBetAmount.Text))
    If Len(A$) < 5 Then
       Temp = Val(A$)
    Else
       Temp = 0
    End If
    ' If not valid bet
    If Temp <= 0 Or Temp > 9999 Or Temp > Stake& Then
      MsgBox "You must bet from $1 to $9999, but not more than your stake",
      ➥       64, "BadBet!"
      BaseBetAmount.Text = Str$(Bet(DEALER))
    Else
      Bet(DEALER) = Temp
      Bet(PLAYER) = Temp
      Bet(PLAYERB) = Temp
      BaseBetAmount.Text = Str$(Bet(DEALER))
      If AboutForm.Visible = False Then
         StandButton.SetFocus
      End If
    End If
End Sub


' Seldeck Form

Sub BaseBetAmount_KeyDown (KeyCode As Integer, Shift As Integer)

    KeyDown KeyCode, Shift
End Sub
```

```
Sub Picture3_Click ()

End Sub


Sub Picture1_Click ()

End Sub


Sub Form_Load ()
      DeckNum(WhichDeck).Value = True
End Sub


Sub Option1_Click ()

End Sub


Sub SelectOk_Click ()
    For I = 0 To 4
        If DeckNum(I).Value Then
           NewDeck = I
           SelectForm.Hide
           Exit For
        End If
    Next
    If NewDeck <> WhichDeck Then ' If you changed decks
       WhichDeck = NewDeck
       If HandInPlay Then         ' And you're playing game
          If DealerVisible = False Then ' And card face down
             DrawCard DEALER, 2, BACK  ' Redraw card using new back
          End If
       End If
    End If
End Sub


Sub SelectCancel_Click ()
     SelectForm.Hide
End Sub


Sub Form_LostFocus ()
     SelectForm.Hide
End Sub
```

continues

LISTING B.1. CONTINUED

```
Sub MirageDeck_Click ()
    DeckNum(0).Value = True
End Sub


Sub RedDi_Click ()
    DeckNum(3).Value = True
End Sub


Sub RedSq_Click ()
    DeckNum(2).Value = True
End Sub


Sub BlueSq_Click ()
    DeckNum(1).Value = True
End Sub


Sub BlueDi_Click ()
    DeckNum(4).Value = True
End Sub


' Subs.BAS


DefInt A-Z

Sub ShowHandIndicator ()
    ' If the player has split hands, then show the arrow indicator for
    ' the active hand.
    If Split Then
       BjForm.HandIndicator(ActivePlayer).Picture =
       ➥       BjForm.HandIndicator(0).Picture
       BjForm.HandIndicator(3 - ActivePlayer).Picture = LoadPicture()
    End If
End Sub


Sub Shuffle ()

      ' Shuffle the cards
      Static Check(53)
      ' Set check array to all 1s
      For Count = 1 To 52
         Check(Count) = 1
      Next
```

```
      ' Stack the deck(s)
      For Count = 1 To CARDSINDECK * Decks
         RandomNumber = Rnd(1) * CARDSINDECK
         'If you haven't assigned this card yet for each deck
         If Check(RandomNumber) <= Decks And RandomNumber <> 0 Then
             Check(RandomNumber) = Check(RandomNumber) + 1' Mark it as assigned
             Cards(Count) = RandomNumber
         Else
             Count = Count - 1     ' Continue through loop
         End If
      Next
      CardsLeft = CARDSINDECK * Decks
      NextCard = 1
End Sub


Sub ShowBetAmount ()
      BjForm.BaseBetAmount.text = Str$(Bet(PLAYER))
End Sub


Sub ShowStakeAmount ()
       ' Show the stake in the text box
       BjForm.Amount(0).Caption = Str$(Stake&)
End Sub


Function CardValue (Who%, WhichCard%)
       Temp% = Hands(Who%, WhichCard) Mod 13
       If Temp% = 0 Then
             Temp = 13        ' Isolate to 1-13 (A-K)
       End If
       CardValue = Temp
End Function


Function HandValue (Who%)       ' Calculate the value of a hand

       Aces = 0                 ' Start with no aces
       Tot = 0                  ' and zero total
       ' For each card
       For WhichCard = 1 To HowManyCards(Who)
          Cvalue = CardValue(Who, WhichCard)
          ' If it's 10, J, Q, or K
          If Cvalue >= 10 Then
                 Cvalue = 10
          ElseIf Cvalue = 1 Then ' If it's an ace
              Aces = Aces + 1
          End If

          ' Accumulate the total
```

continues

LISTING B.1. CONTINUED

```
        Tot = Tot + Cvalue

        ' If hand totals eleven, and there's one ace, and only
        ' two cards in the hand, then it must be blackjack!
        If Tot = 11 And Aces = 1 And HowManyCards(Who) = 2 Then
              PlayerHasBJ(Who) = 1
              Tot = 21
              Exit For
        End If
      Next
      HandValue = Tot
End Function


Sub ShowFirst ()
    ' This sub adds text to the message if it's a split hand
    If Split Then
       If ActivePlayer = PLAYERB Then
           Message$ = Message$ + " (2nd hand)"
       Else
           Message$ = Message$ + " (1st hand)"
       End If
    End If
End Sub


Sub YouLose ()
    Stake& = Stake& - Bet(ActivePlayer)
    ShowStakeAmount
    Message$ = "You lose your bet!"
    ShowFirst
    MsgBox Message$, 64, "Too Bad!"
End Sub


Sub YouPush ()
    Message$ = "This hand is a push. At least you didn't lose!"
    ShowFirst
    MsgBox Message$, 64, "Nobody Wins!"
End Sub


Sub YouWin ()
    Stake& = Stake& + Bet(ActivePlayer)
    ShowStakeAmount
    Message$ = "You win!"
    ShowFirst
    MsgBox Message$, 64, "Congratulations!"
End Sub
```

```
Sub YouWinBJ ()
    Stake& = Stake& + Bet(ActivePlayer) + Bet(ActivePlayer) / 2
    ShowStakeAmount
    Message$ = "You win 1.5 times your bet!"
    ShowFirst
    MsgBox Message$, 64, "LOSE DEALER!"
End Sub


Sub YouLoseInsurance ()
    Stake& = Stake& - Bet(ActivePlayer) / 2
    ShowStakeAmount
    Message$ = "You lose your insurance bet!"
    ShowFirst
    MsgBox Message$, 64, "Oops!"
End Sub


Sub ShowValue (Who%)

      ' Calculates the hand value and displays it in a label
      Total(Who) = HandValue(Who)
      If Who = DEALER Then
         DealerVisible = True
      End If

      If PlayerHasBJ(Who) Then
         BjForm.ScoreBox(Who%).ForeColor = RGB(128, 0, 0)    ' Red
         BjForm.ScoreBox(Who%).Caption = "BLACKJACK!"
         PlayerDone(Who) = 1
         Exit Sub
      End If

      BjForm.ScoreBox(Who%).ForeColor = RGB(0, 0, 0) ' Assume black
      Temp = Total(Who)                  ' Secondary hand value counter
      Message$ = Str$(Total(Who))        ' Start with raw score

      ' If you're calculating dealer's score, adjust temp to account
      ' for all possible values
      Do While Who = DEALER And Temp <= 11 And Aces <> 0
         Temp = Temp + 10
         Aces = Aces - 1
         ' If the dealer has 17 or more, he must stand
         If Temp >= 17 Then
             Total(Who) = Temp
             Message$ = Str$(Temp)
             PlayerDone(DEALER) = 1
         End If
      Loop
```

continues

LISTING B.1. CONTINUED

```
      ' Whenever a player has 21, you no longer offer a hit
      If Total(Who) = 21 Then
         PlayerDone(Who) = 1
      End If

      ' If the player is done, then calculate final hand value
      If PlayerDone(Who) Then
             While Temp <= 11 And Aces <> 0
              Temp = Temp + 10
              Aces = Aces - 1
             Wend
             Total(Who) = Temp
             Message$ = Str$(Temp)
      Else
        ' Calculate all possible values
        While Temp <= 11 And Aces <> 0
         Temp = Temp + 10
         Message$ = Message$ + " or" + Str$(Temp)
         Aces = Aces - 1
        Wend
      End If
       If Temp = 21 Then
          Total(Who) = 21
          PlayerDone(Who) = 1
          Message$ = "21"
       ElseIf Total(Who) >= 22 Then
          Busted(Who) = 1
          PlayerDone(Who) = 1
          BjForm.ScoreBox(Who%).ForeColor = RGB(128, 0, 0) ' Red
          Message$ = Message$ + " and is busted"
       End If
     BjForm.ScoreBox(Who).Caption = Message$
End Sub


Sub DrawCard (Who%, WhichCard%, BackOrFace%)

      ' Draws a card

      WhichBox = Who * 10 + WhichCard - 1
      BjForm.CardBox(WhichBox).Visible = True

      If BackOrFace = FACE Then
         ' Copy previously loaded bitmap
         Ind = Hands(Who, WhichCard)  ' Relative to one
         Card = CardValue(Who, WhichCard) - 1   ' 0-12
         Suit = Ind \ 13 + ((Ind Mod 13) = 0) ' 0-3
         W% = 74: H% = 99 ' Bitmap spacing in big BMP
```

```
         X% = Card * W%
         Y% = Suit * H%
         W% = 72: H% = 97 ' Actual bitmap dimensions
         R% = BitBlt(BjForm.CardBox(WhichBox).Hdc, 0, 0, W%, H%,
     FDeck.FullDeck.Hdc, X%, Y%, SRCCOPY)
         BjForm.CardBox(WhichBox).Refresh
       Else
         ' Set up correct bitmap file to draw
         Select Case WhichDeck
          Case 0
           BjForm.CardBox(WhichBox).Picture = SelectForm.MirageDeck.Picture
          Case 1
           BjForm.CardBox(WhichBox).Picture = SelectForm.BlueSq.Picture
          Case 2
           BjForm.CardBox(WhichBox).Picture = SelectForm.RedSq.Picture
          Case 3
           BjForm.CardBox(WhichBox).Picture = SelectForm.RedDi.Picture
          Case 4
           BjForm.CardBox(WhichBox).Picture = SelectForm.BlueDi.Picture
        End Select
      End If
End Sub


Sub Hit (Who%)

      If BjForm.DoubleButton.Enabled Then
      BjForm.DoubleButton.Enabled = False
      End If
      If HowManyCards(Who) = 5 Then
         ' Move all the cards over for this hand (overlap them)
         ' and adjust the CardColumn array for this hand.
         ' Get difference (x) between first two cards
         Difference = BjForm.CardBox(1).Left - BjForm.CardBox(0).Left
         For I = 2 To 9
            WhichBox = Who * 10 + I - 1
            CardColumn(Who, I) = CardColumn(Who, I - 1) + Difference / 2
            BjForm.CardBox(WhichBox).Left = CardColumn(Who, I)
         Next
         R% = DoEvents()    ' Update the screen
      End If
      HowManyCards(Who) = HowManyCards(Who) + 1
      Hands(Who, HowManyCards(Who)) = Cards(NextCard)
      NextCard = NextCard + 1
      CardsLeft = CardsLeft - 1
      DrawCard Who, HowManyCards(Who), FACE
End Sub


Sub SetUpForDeal ()
```

continues

LISTING B.1. CONTINUED

```
    BjForm.HandIndicator(PLAYER).Picture = LoadPicture()
    BjForm.HandIndicator(PLAYERB).Picture = LoadPicture()
    BjForm.BaseBetAmount.Enabled = True
    If BjForm.HitButton.Enabled Then
       BjForm.HitButton.Enabled = False
    End If
    If BjForm.DoubleButton.Enabled Then
       BjForm.DoubleButton.Enabled = False
    End If
    For I = 0 To 2
       BjForm.DeckButton(I).Enabled = True
    Next
    HandInPlay = False
    ActivePlayer = PLAYER
End Sub


Sub AnalyzeHand ()

   ' Show the dealer's hidden card
   DrawCard DEALER, 2, FACE
   ' and his hand value
   ShowValue DEALER
   If BjForm.HitButton.Enabled Then
      BjForm.HitButton.Enabled = False
   End If
   ' if neither hand is busted
   If (Busted(PLAYER) = 0 And Split = 0) Or
         (Split <> 0 And Busted(PLAYER) = 0) Or
         (Busted(PLAYERB) = 0 And Split <> 0) Then
      ' if only one hand and he doesn't have BJ or
      ' two hands and one or other doesn't have BJ
      If (PlayerHasBJ(PLAYER) = 0 And Split = 0) Or (Split <> 0 And
              PlayerHasBJ(PLAYER) = 0 Or PlayerHasBJ(PLAYERB) = 0) Then
         ' play for the dealer until >=17 or busts
         While Total(DEALER) <= 16
           Hit (DEALER)
           ShowValue (DEALER)
         Wend
      End If
    End If
    PlayerDone(DEALER) = 1
    For ActivePlayer = PLAYER To PLAYER + Split
        If Busted(ActivePlayer) Then
           Outcome(ActivePlayer) = LOSE
        ElseIf PlayerHasBJ(ActivePlayer) Then
           Outcome(ActivePlayer) = WINBJ
        ElseIf Busted(DEALER) Then
           Outcome(ActivePlayer) = WIN
```

```
        ElseIf Total(DEALER) > Total(ActivePlayer) Then
           Outcome(ActivePlayer) = LOSE
        ElseIf Total(DEALER) < Total(ActivePlayer) Then
           Outcome(ActivcPlaycr) = WIN
        Else
           Outcome(ActivePlayer) = PUSH
        End If
        ShowHandIndicator
        Select Case Outcome(ActivePlayer)
           Case WIN
                 YouWin
           Case LOSE
                 YouLose
           Case WINBJ
                 YouWinBJ
           Case PUSH
                 YouPush
       End Select
    Next

    SetUpForDeal
    If CardsLeft < CARDSINDECK / 4 Then
         MsgBox "The cards have been shuffled!", 64,
                "The house doesn't like counters!"
         Shuffle
    End If
    BjForm.StandButton.SetFocus
End Sub


Sub Deal ()

      ' Hide cards not in use
      For Who = DEALER To PLAYERB
        For WhichCard = 1 To HowManyCards(Who)
            WhichBox = Who * 10 + WhichCard - 1
            BjForm.CardBox(WhichBox).Picture = LoadPicture()
            BjForm.CardBox(WhichBox).Visible = False
        Next
      Next

      ' Make unused boxes invisible
      BjForm.ScoreBox(PLAYERB).Caption = ""
      BjForm.ScoreBox(DEALER).Caption = ""
      BjForm.PlayerBTextBox.Caption = ""

      ' Reset CardBox().Left in case a player had more than five cards
      For I = DEALER To PLAYERB
        For J = 2 To 5
            If CardColumn(I, J) <> MasterCardColumn(I, J) Then
               CardColumn(I, J) = MasterCardColumn(I, J)
```

continues

Listing B.1. continued

```
            BjForm.CardBox(I * 10 + J - 1).Left = CardColumn(I, J)
         End If
      Next
    Next

    ' Here's the actual deal
    Hands(PLAYER, 1) = Cards(NextCard)
    Hands(DEALER, 1) = Cards(NextCard + 1)
    Hands(PLAYER, 2) = Cards(NextCard + 2)
    Hands(DEALER, 2) = Cards(NextCard + 3)
    NextCard = NextCard + 4
    HowManyCards(DEALER) = 2
    HowManyCards(PLAYER) = 2
    DrawCard PLAYER, 1, FACE
    DrawCard PLAYER, 2, FACE
    DrawCard DEALER, 1, FACE
    DrawCard DEALER, 2, BACK

    CardsLeft = CardsLeft - 4
    HandInPlay = True
    DealerVisible = False
    Bet(PLAYER) = Bet(DEALER)
    Bet(PLAYERB) = Bet(DEALER)
End Sub


Sub ShowAdvanceAmount ()
    ' Place the advance amount in the text box
    BjForm.Amount(1).Caption = Str$(Advance&)
End Sub


Sub KeyDown (KeyCode As Integer, Shift As Integer)

   If KeyCode = HELPKEYCODE Then
      If Len(HelpFileName$) Then
         WinHelp BjForm.hWnd, HelpFileName$, HELP_INDEX, 0&
      Else
         MsgBox "Online help is not available inside the Visual Basic" +
         ➥   " environment.", 64, "VB Bug!"
      End If
      Exit Sub
   End If
   If Shift = 4 Then
      ' This proc processes the Ctrl-keystrokes that
      ' are shortcut keys for menu items
      Select Case KeyCode
         Case 9'23  ' Ctrl-I
           BjForm.MenuInstructions.Value = True
```

```
        Case 1'30  ' Ctrl-A
          BjForm.MenuAbout.Value = True
        Case 14'49 ' Ctrl-N
          BjForm.MenuNew.Value = True
        Case 3'46  ' Ctrl-C
          BjForm.MenuSelect.Value = True
      End Select
      KeyCode = 0 ' So you don't act on keystroke below
   End If
   ' This procedure acts on "quick keys" keystrokes.
   ' If the appropriate field is enabled, then
   ' this proc simulates a mouse click on the field.
   Select Case KeyCode
     Case 66, 98'48  'B
       If BjForm.BaseBetAmount.Enabled Then
          BjForm.BaseBetAmount.SetFocus
       End If
     Case 49'2, 79  '1
       If BjForm.DeckButton(0).Enabled Then
          BjForm.DeckButton(0).Value = True
       End If
     Case 50'3, 80  ' 2
       If BjForm.DeckButton(0).Enabled Then
          BjForm.DeckButton(1).Value = True
       End If
     Case 54'7, 77 ' 6
       If BjForm.DeckButton(0).Enabled Then
          BjForm.DeckButton(2).Value = True
       End If
     Case 68, 100, 83, 115'31    'D/S
       If BjForm.StandButton.Enabled Then
          BjForm.StandButton.Value = True
       End If
     Case 72, 104'35    'H
       If BjForm.HitButton.Enabled Then
          BjForm.HitButton.Value = True
       End If
     Case 79, 111'11, 82'O
       If BjForm.DoubleButton.Enabled Then
          BjForm.DoubleButton.Value = True
       End If
     Case 80, 112'25    'P
       If BjForm.SplitButton.Enabled Then
          BjForm.SplitButton.Value = True
       End If
     Case 77, 109'50    'M
       If BjForm.AdvanceButton.Enabled Then
          BjForm.AdvanceButton.Value = True
       End If
   End Select
End Sub
```

BONUS APPLICATION 2: MUSIC

The second application contributed by MicroHelp, Inc. demonstrates Visual Basic's musical capability through the use of two assembly language routines, `Play` and `PlayStop`, in the VBTools library.

The complete application, including the VBTools subroutines needed to run it and the code for several tunes, is included on the *Secrets* disks. You can "play" and modify this example. Keep in mind, though, that this application uses only a fraction of the power in the MicroHelp toolboxes. These toolboxes contain hundreds of fast, innovative routines. Contact MicroHelp for a complete list of toolbox routines. Listing B.2 shows the complete code for the music application (called MUSIC on this book's disk). Figure B.5 shows the Project window for the music application. Figure B.6 shows the application running. To hear it, load the project from the disk.

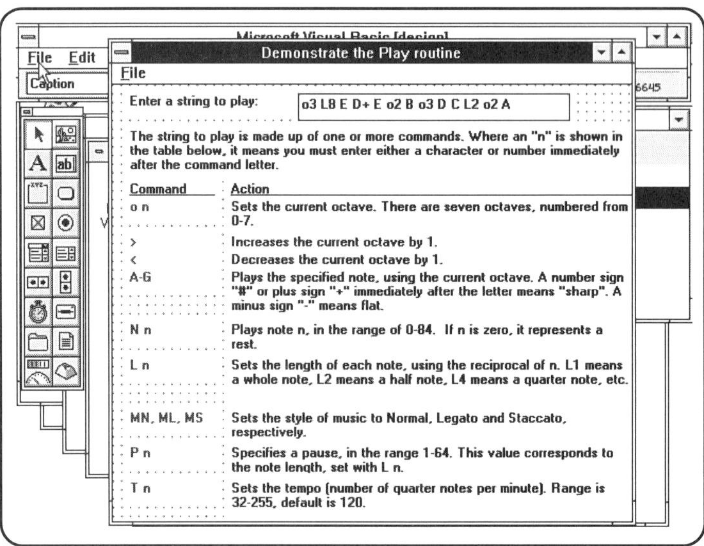

Figure B.5. The MUSIC application: a default tune.

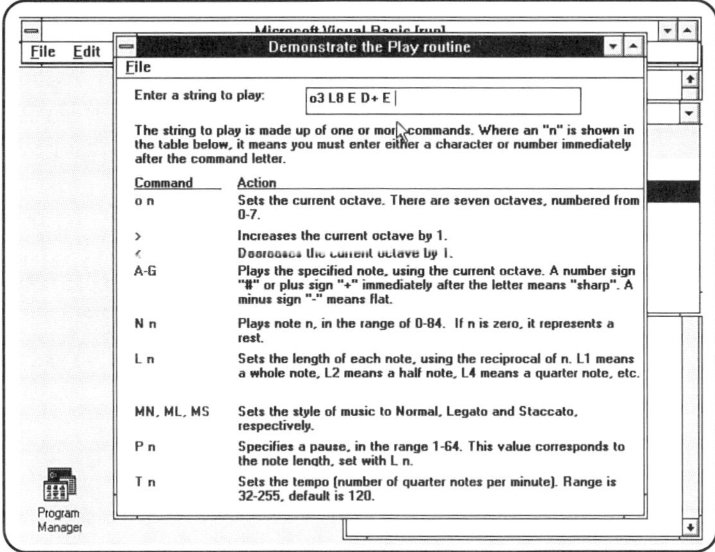

Figure B.6. The MUSIC application: editing a tune.

Listing B.2. MUSIC.

```
Global declarations


   Declare Function Play% Lib "vbtools.vbx" (ByVal Lin$)
   Declare Sub PlayStop Lib "vbtools.vbx" ()


' Play form events


Sub Text1_KeyPress (KeyAscii As Integer)
   If KeyAscii = 13 Then
      PlayStop
      KeyAscii = 0
      Temp$ = Text1.Text
      Result = PLAY(Temp$)
      ' Select all text for next time
      Text1.SelStart = 0
      Text1.SelLength = Len(Text1.Text)
   End If
```

continues

LISTING B.2. CONTINUED

```
End Sub


Sub MenuX_Click ()
    PlayStop
    Unload PlayForm
End Sub


Sub MenuB_Click ()
    PlayStop
    BeethovensFifth
End Sub


Sub MenuS_Click ()
    PlayStop
    SweetGeorgiaBrown
End Sub


Sub MenuW_Click ()
    PlayStop
    WilliamTell
End Sub


Sub Menu9_Click ()
    PlayStop
    NineTo5
End Sub


Sub MenuStop_Click ()
    PlayStop
End Sub


Sub Form_Load ()
    PlayStop
End Sub


Sub Form_Unload (Cancel As Integer)
    PlayStop
End Sub
```

```
' Music form


DefInt A-Z

Sub NineTo5 ()

    Result = Play("T255L401")
    Result = Play("GGGGGGGGGGGGGEFF+")
    For I = 1 To 2
        If I = 1 Then
            Result = Play("04G01GGGGGGGGGGGGEFF+")
        Else
            Result = Play("01GGGGGGGGGGGGGEFF+")
        End If
        For J = 1 To 2
            Result = Play("02G8G8G8G8BB8B803D8D8D8D8EG")
            Result = Play("CCEEG8E8G8AG8G")
            If J = 1 Then
                Result = Play("GEGEGGGGED01DDDDDD")
            Else
                Result = Play("BAGD8D8AAAGG01GGGL2006GD05BGD04BGD03BGL4EG")
            End If
        Next
        For J = 1 To 2
            For K = 1 To 3
                If K = 2 Then
                    Result = Play("01G403")
                Else
                    Result = Play("01C403")
                End If
                Result = Play("B-2A4G2EGGEGE8G.B-EG")
            Next
            Result = Play("01A03AAAA201D203BABA8B.04")
            If J = 1 Then
                Result = Play("D03EG")
            Else
                If K = 1 Then
                    Result = Play("D1")
                Else
                    Result = Play("D101G1")
                End If
            End If
        Next
    Next

End Sub
```

continues

LISTING B.2. CONTINUED

```
Sub BeethovensFifth ()

    Result = Play(" T225 O3 L8G L8G L8G L2E- P8 L8F L8F L8F ML L2D L2D MN P8")
    Result = Play(" T225 O3 L8G L8G L8G L8E- L8A- L8A- L8A-L8G O4 L8E- L8E-" +
        " L8E- ML L2C L8C MN O3 L8G L8G L8G L8D L8A- L8A- L8A- L8G O4 L8F " +
        " L8F L8F ML L2D L2D MN")
    Result = Play("T225 O4L8G L8G L8F L8E- O3L8E- L8E- L8F L8G O4 L8G L8G" +
        " L8F L8E- O3L8E- L8E- L8F L8G O4 L8G L8G L8F L8E- P4 L8C P4 L1G")
    Result = Play("T225 O3 L8A- L8A- L8A-ML L2F L2F MN")
    Result = Play("T225 P8 O3 L8A- L8A- L8A- L8F L8D L8D L8D O2 L8B L8A-" +
        " L8A- L8A-L8G O1 L8G L8G L8G L8C O3 L8A- L8A- L8A- L8F L8D L8D L8D")
    Result = Play(" T225 O2 L8B- L8A- L8A- L8A- L8G O1 L8G L8G L8G L8C O3" +
        "L8G O4 L8C L8C L2CO3 L8B L8B L8B O4 L8D L2D L8D L8D L8D L8E- L8E-" +
        "L8D L8D L8F L8F L8E L8E- L8G")
    Result = Play("T50  O4 L8G L8F L8F L8A- L8A- L8G L8G L8B- L8B- L8A- L8A-" +
        "L8C L8C L8B L8B-L8D L8C L8E-L8E-L8E-L8C L8G L8G L8G L8E-L8C O3 " +
        "L8G L8G L8E- L8C L8C L8C")
    Result = Play("O2 L8B-O4 L8F L8E- L8E-L8B L8G L8F L8F L8D O3 L8B L8G L8F" +
        "L8D O2 L8B O3 L8C L8C L8C O4 L8E-L8E-")
End Sub


Sub SweetGeorgiaBrown ()

Result = Play("t255msl10o4")
    Result = Play("o4d2.c+4c2.o3b4a4g4f+4e4d2")
    For C = 1 To 10
        Result = Play("t230l50o3do4dt255")
    Next
    GoSub 12310
    For X = 1 To 2
        For C = 1 To 3
            Result = Play("mlt235l64o3bo4d")
        Next
        Result = Play("p16")
        For C = 1 To 8
            Result = Play("o3bo4d")
        Next
        Result = Play("p32")
        For C = 1 To 4
            Result = Play("o3b-o4d-")
        Next
        Result = Play("p32")
        For C = 1 To 6
            Result = Play("o3ao4c")
        Next
        Result = Play("p32")
        For C = 1 To 14
            Result = Play("o3gb")
```

```
        Next
        Result = Play("p32p2")
    Next
    Result = Play("t25514mso3")
    Result = Play("o3bt230l64f+af+af+af+af+af+af+af+a")
    Result = Play("t25514mso3p2")
    GoSub 12310
    For X = 1 To 2
        Result = Play("t25514mso3p8l32")
        For C = 1 To 2
            Result = Play("o3f+b-")
        Next
        Result = Play("p32")
        For C = 1 To 4
            Result = Play("o3gb")
        Next
        Result = Play("p32")
        For C = 1 To 4
            Result = Play("o3gb")
        Next
        Result = Play("p32")
        For C = 1 To 4
            Result = Play("o3gb")
        Next
        Result = Play("p32")
        For C = 1 To 4
            Result = Play("o3f+a")
        Next
        Result = Play("p32")
        Result = Play("f+8p32")
        For C = 1 To 12
            Result = Play("o3ab")
        Next
        Result = Play("p16")
        If X = 1 Then
            Result = Play("l4o2msbe")
        Else
            Result = Play("l4o2msb")
        End If
    Next
    Result = Play("t25514mso3degbo4dd+eo3ba2o4do3b8g.p4o4d4d+4")
    A$ = "mll32o3g+o4e"
    AA$ = A$ + A$
    B$ = "mll32o3f+o4d+"
    BB$ = B$ + B$
    Z$ = A$ + "p16" + B$
    For C = 1 To 8
        Result = Play(Z$)
        Result = Play("p16")
```

continues

LISTING B.2. CONTINUED

```
Next
Result = Play("msl4o4p8e4.o3bg+e1")
A$ = "ml132o3go4e"
AA$ = A$ + A$
B$ = "ml132o3f+o4d+"
BB$ = B$ + B$
Z$ = A$ + "p16" + B$
For C = 1 To 8
    Result = Play(Z$)
    Result = Play("p16")
Next
Result = Play("msl4o4p8e4.c+o3ba1")
A$ = "ml132o3f+o4d"
AA$ = A$ + A$
B$ = "ml132o3fo4c+"
BB$ = B$ + B$
Z$ = A$ + "p16" + B$
For C = 1 To 8
    Result = Play(Z$)
    Result = Play("p16")
Next
Result = Play("msl4o4p8d4.o3af+dd8e4d8e4")
For C = 1 To 8
    Result = Play("l52o3dgb")
Next
Result = Play("d8e4d8e4")
For C = 1 To 6
    Result = Play("l52o3dgb")
Next
Result = Play("p4")
For C = 1 To 4
    Result = Play("l52o3dgb")
Next
Result = Play("p16")
For C = 1 To 8
    Result = Play("l52o3d+f+a")
Next
Result = Play("p8")
Result = Play("t255l4mso2ef+g+ebg+o3c+o2bo3e2o2bg+8mle8mse4")
For C = 1 To 2
    Result = Play("o3g+52o4d52e52")
Next
Result = Play("p16")
For C = 1 To 4
    Result = Play("o3g+52o4d52e52")
Next
Result = Play("p16")
For C = 1 To 4
    Result = Play("o3g+52o4d52e52")
```

```
    Next
    Result = Play("p16")
    For C = 1 To 4
        Result = Play("o3g+52o4d52e52")
    Next
    Result = Play("p16")
    Result = Play("t255l4mso2ef+gebgo3c+o2ao3e2c+o2b8mla8msa2b4")
    Result = Play("o2l8ef+gabgb4b-g-b-4afa4ef+gabgb4b-g-b-4a4o1b4g8")
    Result = Play("o3l4d8egbo4dd+8eo3b.")
    For C = 1 To 8
        Result = Play("l52o3bo4e")
    Next
    Result = Play("p16")
    For C = 1 To 8
        Result = Play("l52o3bo4e")
    Next
    Result = Play("p16")
    For C = 1 To 8
        Result = Play("l52o4cf+")
    Next
    Result = Play("p16")
    For C = 1 To 8
        Result = Play("l52o4cf+")
    Next
    Result = Play("p16")
    For C = 1 To 3
        Result = Play("l52o3bo4f+a")
    Next
    For C = 1 To 18
        Result = Play("l52o3bo4eg")
    Next
    Result = Play("l4mso1f+16g8")

    Exit Sub
12310
    Result = Play("t255l4mso3")
    Result = Play("ef+g+.e8bg+o4c+.o3b8o4e2o3b8g+4.e4o2d16d+16ee-d")
    Result = Play("o3ef+g.e8bgo4c+.o3a8o4e2c+8o3b.ao2g16g+16aa-g")
    Result = Play("o3def+.d8af+b.a8o4d2o3a8f+.d")
    Return
End Sub


Sub WilliamTell ()

    Result = Play("T255MNL16")
    Result = Play("o2mnb4p8msbbmnb4p8msbbb8g#8")
    Result = Play("e8g#8b8g#8b8o3e8o2b8g#8e8g#8")
    Result = Play("b8g#8b8o3e8o2mnb4p8msbbmnb4")
```

continues

LISTING B.2. CONTINUED

```
Result = Play("p8msbbmnb4p8msbbmnb4p8msbb")
Result = Play("b8bbb8b8b8bbb8b8b8bb")
Result = Play("b8b8b8bbb8b8mlb2")
Result = Play("b2b8p8p4p4")
Result = Play("p8mso1bbb8bbb8bbo2e8f#8g#8o1bb")
Result = Play("b8bbo2e8g#g#f#8d#8o1b8bbb8bb")
Result = Play("b8bbo2e8f#8g#8eg#mlb4bmsag#f#")
Result = Play("e8g#8e8o3bbb8bbb8bbo4e8f#8")
Result = Play("g#8o3bbb8bbo4e8g#g#f#8d#8o3b8bb")
Result = Play("b8bbb8bbo4e8f#8g#8mleg#b4")
Result = Play("bag#f#mse8g#8e8o3g#g#g#8g#g#g#8g#g#")
Result = Play("g#8o4c#8o3g#8o4c#8o3g#8o4c#8o3g#8f#8e8d#8")
Result = Play("c#8g#g#g#8g#g#g#8g#g#g#8o4c#8o3g#8o4c#8")
Result = Play("o3g#8o4c#8o3b8a#8b8a#8b8g#g#g#8g#g#")
Result = Play("g#8g#g#g#8o4c#8o3g#8o4c#8o3g#8o4c#8o3g#8f#8")
Result = Play("e8d#8c#8g#g#g#8g#g#g#8g#g#g#8o4c#8")
Result = Play("o3g#8o4c#8o3g#8o4c#8o3b8a#8b8o2bbb8f#f#")
Result = Play("f#8f#f#f#8g#8a8f#4mna8msg#8mne4")
Result = Play("msg#8f#8f#8f#8o3f#f#f#8f#f#f#8g#8")
Result = Play("a8mnf#4msa8g#8mne4msg#8f#8o2bb")
Result = Play("b8o1bbb8bbb8bbo2mne8f#8g#8o1bb")
Result = Play("b8bbo2e8g#g#f#8d#8o1b8bbb8bb")
Result = Play("b8bbo2e8f#8g#8eg#mlb4mnbag#f#")
Result = Play("e8g#8e8o3bbb8bbb8bbo4e8f#8")
Result = Play("g#8o3bbb8bbo4e8g#g#f#8d#8o3b8bb")
Result = Play("b8bbb8bbo4e8f#8g#8mleg#mlb4")
Result =
          ➥Play("mnbag#f#mne8g#8e8o3mle56f56g56a56b56o4c56d56mne8eee8e8g#4.")
Result = Play("f#8e8d#8e8c#8mso3bo4c#o3bo4c#o3b")
Result = Play("o4c#d#eo3abababo4c#d#o3g#ag#ag#abo4c#o3f#")
Result = Play("g#f#g#f#g#f#g#f#g#f#d#o2bo3mlbo4c#d#e8d#8e8")
Result = Play("c#8o3msbo4c#o3bo4c#o3bo4c#d#eo3abababo4c#d#o3g#")
Result = Play("ag#ag#abo4c#o3f#g#f#g#f#af#emne8p8mlc#4")
Result = Play("mnc#o2cmso3c#o2co3d#c#o2baag#ec#c#c#c#e")
Result = Play("d#o1cg#g#g#g#g#g#o2c#eg#o3c#c#c#c#o2co3c#o2co3d#")
Result = Play("c#o2baag#ec#c#c#c#ed#o1cg#g#g#g#g#mng#")
Result = Play("o2c#eg#o3msc#ed#c#d#o2cg#g#g#o3g#ec#d#o2cg#g#g#")
Result = Play("o3g#ec#d#o2bg#g#a#gd#d#g#gg#gg#ag#f#e")
Result = Play("o1ba#bo2eo1bo2f#o1bo2g#ed#eg#eaf#bo3g#f#ed#")
Result = Play("f#ec#o2bo3c#o2bo3c#d#ef#g#o2ababo3c#d#ef#o2g#")
Result = Play("ag#aco3c#d#eo2f#g#f#g#f#g#f#g#f#g#f#d#o1b")
Result = Play("co2c#d#eo1ba#bo2eo1bo2f#o1bo2g#ed#eg#eaf#b")
Result = Play("o3g#f#ed#f#ec#o2bo3c#o2bo3c#d#ef#g#o2ababo3c#")
Result = Play("d#ef#o2g#ag#abo3c#d#eo2f#o3c#o2co3c#d#c#o2af#mne")
Result = Play("o3mlef#g#abo4c#d#mne8mseee8e8g#4.")
Result = Play("msf8mse8d#8e8c#8o3bo4c#o3bo4c#o3bo4c#d#eo3a")
Result = Play("bababo4c#d#o3g#ag#ag#abo4c#o3f#g#f#g#f#")
Result = Play("g#f#g#f#g#f#d#o2bo3mlbo4c#d#mne8eee8e8g#4.")
Result = Play("msf#8e8d#8e8c#8o3bo4c#o3bo4c#o3b")
```

```
Result = Play("o4c#d#eo3abababo4c#d#o3g#ag#ag#abo4c#o3f#")
Result = Play("g#f#g#f#ag#f#e8o2b8o3e8g#g#g#8mng#g#g#8")
Result = Play("g#g#g#8o4c#8o3g#8o4c#8o3g#8o4c#8o3g#8f#8e8")
Result = Play("d#8c#8g#g#g#8g#g#g#8g#g#g#8o4c#8o3g#8")
Result = Play("o4c#8o3g#8o4c#8o3b8a#8b8a#8b8g#g#g#8")
Result = Play("g#g#g#8g#g#g#8o4c#8o3g#8o4c#8o3g#8o4c#8o3g#8")
Result = Play("f#8e8d#8c#8g#g#g#8g#g#g#8g#g#g#8")
Result = Play("o4c#8o3g#8o4c#8o3g#8o4c#8o3b8a#8b8a#8b8")
Result = Play("o2f#f#f#8f#f#f#8g#8a8f#4a8g#8")
Result = Play("e4g#8f#8o0b8o1b8o2f#f#f#8f#f#f#8")
Result = Play("g#8a8f#4a8g#8e4g#8f#8")
Result = Play("bbb8o1bbb8bbb8bbo2e8f#8g#8")
Result = Play("o1bbb8bbo2e8g#g#f#8d#8o1b8bbb8")
Result = Play("bbb8bbo2e8f#8g#8eg#mlb4mnb")
Result = Play("ag#f#e8o1b8o2e8o3bbb8bbb8bbo4e8")
Result = Play("f#8g#8o3bbb8bbo4e8g#g#f#8d#8o3b8")
Result = Play("bbb8bbb8bbo4e8f#8g#8o3eg#mlb4")
Result = Play("mnbag#f#mlef#g#mnamlg#abo4mnc#mlo3bo4c#d#mnemld#")
Result =
        ➥Play("ef#mng#ao3bo4ao3bo4ao3bo4ao3bo4ao3bo4ao3bo4ao3bo4ao3bmle")
Result = Play("f#g#mnamlg#abmno4c#mlo3bo4c#d#mnemld#ef#mng#ao3bo4ao3bo4a")
Result = Play("o3bo4ao3bo4ao3bo4ao3bo4ao3bo4ao3bp16mlg#o4g#o3mng#p16mld
        ➥#o4d#o3mnd#p16")
Result = Play("mleo4eo3mnep16mlao4ao3mnap16mlg#o4g#o3mng#p16mld#o4d
        ➥#o3mnd#p16mleo4eo3mnep16")
Result = Play("mlao4ao3mnao4go3go4go3go4go3go4go3go4msg8e8c8e8o4mng#")
Result = Play("o3g#o4g#o3g#o4g#o3g#o4g#o3g#o4msg#8e8o3b8o4e8mng
        ➥#o3g#o4g#o3g#o4g#")
Result = Play("o3g#o4g#o3g#o4msg#8f8c#8f8mna#o3a#o4a#o3a#o4a#o3a#o4a
        ➥#o3a#o4msa#8")
Result = Play("g8e8g8b8p16mna#p16ap16g#p16f#p16ep16")
Result = Play("d#p16c#p16o3bp16a#p16ap16g#p16f#p16ep16d#p16f#mle")
Result = Play("f#g#mnamlg#abmno4c#o3mlbo4c#d#mnemld#ef#mng
        ➥#ao3bo4ao3bo4a")
Result = Play("o3bo4ao3bo4ao3bo4ao3bo4ao3bo4ao3bmlef#g#mnamlg#abmno4c#o3mlb")
Result = Play("o4c#d#mnemld#ef#mng#ao3bo4ao3bo4ao3bo4ao3bo4a
        ➥o3bo4ao3bo4a")
Result = Play("o3bo4ao3bp16mlg#o4g#o3mng#p16mld#o4d#o3mnd#
        ➥p16mleo4eo3mnep16mlao4ao3mnap16")
Result = Play("mlg#o4g#o3mng#p16mld#o4d#o3mnd#p16mleo4eo3mnep
        ➥16mlao4ao3mnao4go3go4go3go4g")
Result = Play("o3go4go3go4g8e8c8e8g#o3g#o4g#o3g#o4g#o3g#o4g#o3g#o4g#8")
Result = Play("e8o3b8o4e8g#o3g#o4g#o3g#o4g#o3g#o4g#o3g#o4msg#8mnf8c#8")
Result = Play("f8a#o3a#o4a#o3a#o4a#o3a#o4a#o3a#o4a#8g8e8g8b8")
Result = Play("p16a#p16ap16g#p16f#p16ep16d#p16c#p16o3bp16a#p16")
Result = Play("ap16g#p16f#p16ep16d#p16fmled#ed#mne8bbb8")
Result = Play("bbb8bbo4e8f#8g#8o3bbb8bbb8")
Result = Play("bbo4g#8a8b8p8e8f#8g#8p8o3g#8")
Result = Play("a8b8p8p2o2bco3c#dd#")
Result = Play("eff#gg#aa#bco4c#d#ed#f#d#ed#f#d#e")
```

continues

LISTING B.2. CONTINUED

```
    Result = Play("d#f#d#ed#f#d#ed#f#d#ed#f#d#ed#f#d#e")
    Result = Play("d#f#d#e8eo3eo4eo3eo4eo3eo4e8o3bo2bo3bo2bo3bo2bo3b8")
    Result = Play("g#o2g#o3g#o2g#o3g#o2g#o3g8eo2eo3eo2eo3eo2eo3e8eee8")
    Result = Play("e8e8o2bbb8b8b8g#g#g#8g#8g#8")
    Result = Play("eee8e8e8o1b8o2e8o1b8o2g#8e8b8")
    Result = Play("g#8o3e8o2b8o3e8o2b8o3g#8e8b8g#8o4e4")
    Result = Play("p8eee8e8e8e8e4p8.")
    Result = Play("ee4p8.o2ee2")

End Sub
```

SOME THIRD-PARTY DONATIONS

After I finished writing the main body of this book, several companies kindly offered to contribute custom controls and assembly language routines to the book. These custom controls and assembly language routines are completely functional and can be incorporated into your own Visual Basic applications simply by adding the appropriate VBX file to your project. The VBX files are included on the disk in the back of this book.

In addition, short examples illustrate how you might use these VBX files in your applications. These examples (and brief descriptions of the VBX file contents) are included in this section. The addresses and phone numbers for these companies are listed in Appendix A, "Third-Party Support and Custom Controls."

Remember that these VBX files are completely functional and that they are only a sample of the custom controls and assembly language routines available from these companies. For complete information about the other (somewhat extended) support available from these companies, contact them directly and tell them I sent you.

The following three companies contributed to this section:

- Crescent Software
- Outrider Systems
- Sheridan Software

MicroHelp and Ward Systems contributed custom controls and demos to the main body of the text and Appendix A. The MicroHelp VBX and Ward Systems demo applications also are included on the disk.

Outrider Systems, Inc. (Spin Button)

The spin button is a spinner control you use in conjunction with another control to increment and decrement numbers. You can use it to scroll back and forth through a range of values or a list of items. The spin button is contained in the VBX file called SPIN.VBX.

To use a spin button in a project, simply add the SPIN.VBX file to the project.

Use the spin button to increment or decrement numbers displayed in a text box or other control. At runtime, when the user clicks on the up (or right) arrow of the spin button, `SpinUp` events are generated repeatedly until the user releases the mouse. Similarly, when the user clicks on the down (or left) arrow, `SpinDown` events are generated until the user releases the mouse.

When you use this control, write code for the `SpinUp` and `SpinDown` events that increments or decrements values. Use the `Delay` property to determine how often the `SpinUp` and `SpinDown` events are generated.

The spin button supports additional color properties that you set using the Visual Basic color palette.

All of the properties, events, and methods for this control are shown in the following list:

Properties

BackColor
BorderColor
BorderThickness
CtlName
Delay
DragIcon
DragMode
Enabled
ForeColor
Height
Index
Left
LightColor
MousePointer
ShadowBackColor

ShadeColor
ShadowForeColor
ShadowThickness
SpinOrientation
TabIndex
TdThickness
Tag
Top
Visible
Width

Events

DragDrop
DragOver
SpinDown
SpinUp

Methods

Drag
Move
Refresh

The following example (called SPIN on Disk 2) uses the spin button:

```
Sub Spin1_SpinUp ()
    ' Increment the value in the text box on every SpinUp event
    Text1.text = Str$(Val(Text1.text) + 1)
    ' Display the current value in the text box
    Text1.Refresh
End Sub


Sub Spin1_SpinDown ()

    'Decrement the value in the text box on every SpinDown event
    Text1.text = Str$(Val(Text1.text) - 1)
    ' Display the current value in the text box
    Text1.Refresh
End Sub



Sub Spin2_SpinDown ()
    'Decrement the value in the text box on every SpinDown event
    Text2.text = Str$(Val(Text2.text) - 1)
    ' Display the current value in the text box
    Text2.Refresh
```

```
End Sub


Sub Spin2_SpinUp ()
    ' Increment the value in the text box on every SpinUp event
    Text2.text = Str$(Val(Text2.text) + 1)
    ' Display the current value in the text box
    Text2.Refresh
End Sub
```

When you create and distribute applications that use the spin button control, install the file SPIN.VBX in your client's Microsoft Windows \SYSTEM subdirectory.

Crescent Software (Instant Change Scroll Bars & Custom Routines)

Crescent Software donated two VBX files to the *Secrets* project:

- INSTSCRL.VBX
- CRESCENT.VBX

Instant Change Scroll bars (in INSTSCRL.VBX) are similar to Visual Basic's standard scroll bars, but also include an event procedure that is invoked whenever the user moves a scroll indicator. This extra procedure lets you give the user constant feedback as a scroll bar is moved.

Instant Change Scroll bars can be either horizontal or vertical scroll bar controls.

When you distribute applications that use the Instant Change Scroll Bar controls, install the file INSTSCRL.VBX in your client's Microsoft Windows \SYSTEM subdirectory.

All of the properties, events, and methods for this control are shown in the following list:

Properties
CtlName DragIcon DragMode Enabled Height Index LargeChange Left Max Min MousePointer Parent SmallChange TabIndex TabStop Tag Top Value Visible Width

Events
Change Changing DragDrop DragOver GotFocus KeyDown KeyPress KeyUp LostFocus

Methods
Drag Move Refresh SetFocus

The following example (INSTANT on the disk) uses the Instant Scroll bars:

```
Sub InstHScroll1_Changing ()
    'Save the current value of the Red scroll bar.
    RedVal = InstHScroll1.Value
    'Update the background color of the sample pallet.
    Picture1.BackColor = RGB(RedVal, 0, 0)
End Sub


Sub InstVScroll1_Change ()
    'Save the current value of the Red scroll bar.
    RedVal = InstVScroll1.Value
    'Update the background color of the sample pallet.
    Text1.BackColor = RGB(RedVal, 0, 0)
End Sub
```

The CRESCENT.VBX contains several low-level support routines written in assembly language. These include: `WinVer`, `SysDir`, `GetSystemsResources`, `Modeinfo`, `In and Out`, `Peek and Poke`, and `ReadSectors` routines. A project showing how to declare and use these routines is included on the disk and described in Chapter 9.

Sheridan Software (3-D Command Button Control and 3-D Panel)

The 3-D command button is similar to the standard Visual Basic Command Button control, which carries out a task when the user either clicks the button or presses a key. In addition, the 3-D Command Button can display a 3-D caption, a bit map, or an icon. A variable bevel width makes the button appear to be raised off the screen.

The 3-D command button has several custom properties that enable you to adjust the 3-D appearance of the control. When you draw a 3-D command button on a form, the custom properties for the control are remembered and used as a template for the next 3-D command button you create. Because the 3-D gray-scale look requires a background color of light gray, the `BackColor` property isn't available with this control. This control should be used on Visual Basic forms that have the `BackColor` property set to light gray (`&H00C0C0C0&`).

> Sheridan Software takes a slightly different approach to custom control files. When you create an application using the 3-D command button, use the DESIGN.VBX file on Disk 2. When you distribute applications that use the 3-D Command Button control, you should rename the file RUN.VBX (on Disk 2) to DESIGN.VBX and install it in your client's Microsoft Windows \SYSTEM subdirectory. These are DESIGN and RUNTIME versions of the same .VBX. They have different names

(DESIGN and RUN) so that you can distinguish them from each other, but the RUNTIME version of your application is still looking for the .VBX name DESIGN. You must rename RUN to DESIGN, therefore, when you distribute your applications. As you might expect, DESIGN can be used only in DESIGN mode. RUN can be used only with EXE files. You need both of them if you intend to distribute applications using the 3-D command button or 3-D panel.

All of the properties, events, and methods for this control are shown in the following list:

Properties
AutoSize
BevelWidth
Caption
CtlName
DragIcon
DragMode
Enabled
FontBold
FontItalic
FontName
FontSize
FontStrikethru
FontUnderline
Font3D
ForeColor
Height
Index
Left
MousePointer
Outline
Picture
RoundedCorners
TabIndex
TabStop
Tag

Top
Visible
Width

Events

Click
DragDrop
DragOver
GotFocus
KeyDown
KeyPress
KeyUp
LostFocus

Methods

Drag
Move
Refresh
SetFocus

The following example (3-D on the disk) shows you how to use the 3-D command button:

```
Sub Form_Click ()
    Const CF_BITMAP = 2
    SSCommand1.Picture = Clipboard.GetData(CF_BITMAP)
End Sub
```

3-D Panel Control

The 3-D panel can be used to display plain or three-dimensional text on a 3-D background, to group other controls on a 3-D background as an alternative to the Frame control, or to give a 3-D appearance to standard controls such as list boxes, combo boxes, scroll bars, and so on.

The 3-D panel is a 3-D rectangular area of variable size that can be as large as the form itself or just large enough to display a single line of text. It can present status information in a dynamically colored circle or bar with or without showing percentage.

Although you can create some dramatic effects with the 3-D panel, the control has only four basic visual properties: `BevelOuter`, `BevelInner`, `BevelWidth` and

`BorderWidth`. By combining these properties in different ways, you can generate interesting backgrounds for text and controls.

Unlike most 3-D controls, the 3-D panel has a `BackColor` property. It defaults to light gray but can be changed to any color you choose. Used sparingly, the `BackColor` property can give presentation panels additional impact without getting in the way of the form's usefulness. Similar to Frames, 3-D panels can have other controls placed on them.

The 3-D panel has several custom properties that enable you to adjust the 3-D appearance of the control. When you draw a 3-D panel on a form, the custom properties for the control are remembered and used as a template for the next 3-D panel you create.

Sheridan Software takes a slightly different approach to custom control files. When you create an application using the 3-D panel, use the DESIGN.VBX file on Disk 2. When you distribute applications that use the 3-D panel control, you should rename the RUN.VBX file (on Disk 2) to DESIGN.VBX and install it in your client's Microsoft Windows \SYSTEM subdirectory. These are DESIGN and RUNTIME versions of the same .VBX. They have different names (DESIGN and RUN) so that you can distinguish them from each other, but the RUNTIME version of your application still looks for the .VBX name DESIGN. You must rename RUN to DESIGN, therefore, when you distribute your applications. As you might expect, DESIGN can be used only in DESIGN mode. RUN can be used only with EXE files. Don't get these files confused. You need both of them if you intend to distribute applications using the 3-D command button or the 3-D panel.

All of the properties, events, and methods for this control are shown in the following list:

Properties

Alignment
AutoSize
BackColor
BevelInner
BevelOuter
BevelWidth

BorderWidth
Caption
CtlName
DragIcon
DragMode
Enabled
FloodColor
FloodPercent
FloodShowPct
FloodType
FontBold
FontItalic
FontName
FontSize
FontStrikethru
FontUnderline
Font3D
ForeColor
Height
Index
Left
MousePointer
Outline
Parent
RoundedCorners
ShadowColor
TabIndex
Tag
Top
Visible
Width

Events

DragDrop
DragOver

Methods

Drag
Move
Refresh

API Edit Control Example

This last, short example shows you how to use the Windows API to manipulate a text box. This example, called API on the disk, shows you how to undo, set the text box length, count lines, set and go to a bookmark, count characters, and so on. It's menu driven and the complete code is in listing API. Note that it requires a text box and a label.

LISTING B.3. API CALLS.

```
' Declare the API functions

Declare Function GetFocus% Lib "user" ()
Declare Function SendMessage& Lib "user" (ByVal hWnd%, ByVal wMsg%,
                                          ByVal wParam%, lp As Any)



' EM (edit control) constants (not all of these are used in this example,
' but are included for reference).


Const WM_USER = &H400
Const EM_LIMITTEXT = WM_USER + 21
Const EM_UNDO = WM_USER + 23
Const EM_GETLINECOUNT = WM_USER + 10
Const EM_GETSEL = WM_USER + 0
Const EM_GETLINE = WM_USER + 20
Const EM_LINEFROMCHAR = WM_USER + 25
Const EM_LINEINDEX = WM_USER + 11
Const EM_LINELENGTH = WM_USER + 27
Const EM_SETSEL = WM_USER + 1
Const EM_REPLACESEL = WM_USER + 18


' Form level variable for cursor position

Dim Ending%


' events

Sub UndoCom_Click ()
    'Make sure the text box has the focus.
    Text1.SetFocus
    'Get the text box handle.
    hWd% = GetFocus()
    RetVal = SendMessage(hWd%, EM_UNDO, 0, 0)
```

```
    If RetVal <> 0 Then
      Label1.Caption = "Undo successful."
    Else
      Label1.Caption = "Undo unsuccessful."
    End If
End Sub

Sub SetTextCom_Click ()
    If SetBox% = 0 Then
      'Make sure the text box has the focus.
      Text1.SetFocus
      'Get the text box handle.
      hWd% = GetFocus()

      Text1.text = ""
      TextLimit% = &HFAAA

      RetVal = SendMessage(hWd%, EM_LIMITTEXT, TextLimit%, 0)
      If RetVal <> 0 Then
          Label1.Caption = "Text limit set to " + Str$(TextLimit%) +
          ➥    " characters."
          SetBox% = -1
      Else
          Label1.Caption = "Text set unsuccessful."
      End If
    Else
      Label1.Caption = "Text limit set to " + Str$(TextLimit%) +
      ➥    " characters."
    End If
End Sub


Sub NumLines_Click ()
    'Make sure the text box has the focus.
    Text1.SetFocus
    'Get the text box handle.
    hWd% = GetFocus()
    Msg$ = "Number of lines = "

    Label1.Caption = Msg$ + Str$(SendMessage(hWd%, EM_GETLINECOUNT, 0, 0))
End Sub



Sub Form_Load ()
    Show
End Sub



Sub LineindexCom_Click ()
```

continues

LISTING B.3. CONTINUED

```
    'This procedure gets the number of bytes that precede a line.
    'The returned number indicates the CR/LF after each line. The
    'third argument to SendMessage() specifies the line number, where
    'the first line number is zero. If the third argument to SendMessage()
    'is -1, then the current linenumber is used as the default.

    LineNumber = -1
    Text1.SetFocus
    Pos% = SendMessage(GetFocus(), EM_LINEINDEX, LineNumber, 0&)
    Label1.Caption = "#Char's before line = " + Str$(Pos%)
End Sub



Sub SetCom_Click ()

'This procedure gets the ending position of the current selected text
'for setting a bookmark.

    Text1.SetFocus
    location& = SendMessage(GetFocus(), EM_GETSEL, 0&, 0&)
    Ending% = location& \ 2 ^ 16          ' High-order byte.
    Label1.Caption = "Bookmark set at location = " + Str$(Ending%)
End Sub



Sub GotoCom_Click ()

    ' This procedure goes to the bookmark.

    Text1.SelStart = Ending%
    Label1.Caption = "Bookmark at position :" + Str$(Ending%)
End Sub
```

Glossary

Access key A keystroke combination that provides quick keyboard access to a menu, command, or control. Unlike shortcut keys, access keys do not execute commands when you press them. At design time, you designate a letter in the caption as the access key. At runtime, this letter is underlined, and the user can access the menu or command by pressing Alt and the letter.

Application A Visual Basic program.

Argument A constant, variable, or expression passed to a Visual Basic Sub procedure or Function.

Array A one-dimensional type that can hold more than one element.

ASCII American Standard Code for Information Interchange; a sequence of 128 standard characters.

Attached tables Tables stored outside a Microsoft Access database that can be manipulated from within the database. The tables can be stored in another Microsoft Access database or in a different database system, such as Paradox or dBASE.

Axes The horizontal and vertical lines that define the range of values plotted on a graph. The x-axis is the horizontal line. The y-axis is the vertical line.

Base type Defines a common interface to a group of descendant types. It generalizes the intended uses for a hierarchy of types. In other words, it describes the range of messages that an object of a type can handle. A base type may also be called an *ancestor*.

Behavior An object-oriented or object-based term that is broadly synonomous with "method," indicating the way an object operates or functions. Each set of methods is specific to an object (although objects can have methods that share names). Thus, an object's behavior consists of its set of methods.

Binding (early) Resolving a method call at compile time. See *binding (late)*.

Binding (late) Resolving a method call at runtime. When you resolve a method call, you insert the code to determine the address (or another reference) of the method definition at the point where the method has sent a message.

Bit map A picture or, more specifically, the data representing a picture.

Break mode One of three Visual Basic modes. In break mode, the application is halted and the Visual Basic debugging tools become available to trace through the application a step at a time.

Breakpoint A place in a program where normal execution is interrupted to allow manual intervention. You can set breakpoints to halt execution at specific statements in a procedure (for example, where you suspect that problems may exist).

Built-in type A type (such as double, char, and so on) included in (or built into) a language. The compiler can handle it and doesn't have to learn about it every time it encounters one.

Caption Property setting that determines the text displayed on a control or form.

Channel In DDE conversations, represents the path or link between the client and server applications.

Chaos Stochastic (or random) behavior occurring in a deterministic system.

Characteristic Another name for data declared within a type.

Checkbox A control you may use to enable a user to specify an option (On/Off, Yes/No, for example). An X in a checkbox indicates that the option is selected.

Clipboard The storage area in the Windows system for exchanging text and picture data.

Clipboard object A Visual Basic object used to manipulate text and graphics within the Windows Clipboard.

Code window A window or form you use to enter the code for your Visual Basic applications.

Collection An ordered set of similarly typed objects.

Column In a grid or database, the vertical display of a field of data.

Combo box A Visual Basic control, which you can create with the Toolbox, that enables a user to select items from a list.

Constant A specific, unchangable value used in calculations.

Control A graphics object you can place on a form. Controls are visually displayed in the toolbox. (You can add custom controls to the Toolbox, using the Load Custom Control menu command.)

Control array A group of controls sharing a common name, type, and event procedures, as well as general (but not specific) functionality.

Controls User interface devices. Visual Basic (through the Visual Basic Toolbox) supports the following controls:

Check boxes	Images
Combo boxes	Labels
Command buttons	Lines
Common Dialogs	List boxes
Data Control	OLE
Directory list boxes	Option buttons
Drive list boxes	Picture boxes
File list boxes	Shapes
Frames	Text boxes
Grids	Timers
Horizontal scroll bars	Vertical scroll bars

Control variable A variable that represents a control. Use a control variable to access and manipulate the control.

Cursor The shape on the screen that represents the position for the next input. In text-based applications, a cursor is either a block, a line, or something in between. In Windows applications, however, because a cursor is a 32-by-32 pixel bit map, a Windows cursor may be many different shapes and is itself a bit map.

Data The contents of individual fields and records in a table.

Database An organized collection of information stored in tables, forms, queries, reports, macros, and modules.

Database application A database + any links to other applications necessary to manipulate the database. (Often used synonomously with database.)

Database variable A variable that enables you to manipulate databases. Use it in conjunction with other design object variables (table, form, etc.) to maintain databases from Visual Basic.

Data-centered computing Building applications around the data maintained in Microsoft Access (or other database) tables. Data are managed and maintained in one place but are accessible to potentially many applications. These applications can access the data via Access engines (such as the one in Visual Basic Professional), DDE, and OLE links.

Datasheet The display of data in a row and column format.

Data type The kind of data a field contains.

Debug object A Visual Basic object used to send output to the Immediate window in 1.0 or the Debug window in 2.0 or 3.0.

Design objects Objects you create with Visual Basic tools and place on forms in design mode.

Design time The mode (or time) during which you develop your Visual Basic applications.

Directory list box A Visual Basic control that displays a hierarchical listing of directories. Users can use this box to select and browse directories at runtime.

DoEvents A Visual Basic statement that causes Visual Basic to yield control to the Windows operating environment, which, in turn, can allow other applications to temporarily perform tasks.

Drive list box A Visual Basic control that displays the valid drives in a system.

Dynamic array An array you dimension within a procedure. Visual Basic allocates memory for the array at runtime. Visual Basic allocates memory for non-dynamic arrays at compiletime.

Dynamic binding Another name for late binding. See *binding (late)*.

Dynamic data exchange (DDE) A Microsoft Windows protocol that lets applications share data.

Dynamic link libraries (DLL) A library of indexed functions and procedures. A DLL is an executable module of code linked into an application at runtime. DLLs enable application developers to develop and maintain independent program components. DLLs are similar to modules, but are more powerful because they can be linked into an application at runtime, shared by many concurrently executing programs, and written in a variety of languages, regardless of the language used to access the DLL.

Dynamic variable allocation Creating and destroying variables at runtime rather than at compile time. See *binding (late)*.

Dynaset A set of records produced by running a query or a filter. A subset of the records maintained in one or more tables.

Encapsulation An object-oriented term for combining data (characteristics) with the methods (behaviors) for manipulating it and organizing code into user-defined types.

Error trap The result of enabling an error handler using the On Error statement. You set error traps within procedures to enable them to recover from some runtime errors.

Event An occurrence that affects an application from the outside world. Some examples are keystrokes, mouse clicks, a character from a serial port, and occurrences triggered by the system software (DOS, BIOS), such as a "timer tick."

Event procedures Procedures in Visual Basic that are predefined for objects to respond to user- and system-generated events.

Expression A combination of constants, operators, Functions (but *not Sub procedures*), fields, controls, and properties that together evaluate to a single value.

Field In a Microsoft Access (or other database) table, a column of information that contains one kind of information. A set of related fields composes one record.

Field type Specifies the kind of data a field can contain.

File Information stored as a unit under one name on a disk.

File list box A Visual Basic control that displays a listing of files on a user's system.

Form A window (or dialog box) that holds controls. Forms are the fundamental component of any Visual Basic application.

Form-level variable A variable recognized by all the procedures attached to a form.

Frame A Visual Basic control that appears as a rectangle and is used to group other controls for simultaneous display.

Function procedure A procedure that always returns a value.

GDI See *Windows GDI*.

General procedures Procedures that are not executed unless they are called by another procedure. These can be declared and defined at the form level or in separate modules.

Global module A module automatically specified for every Visual Basic 1.0 application. Use it to declare global variables and constants. Each Visual Basic 1.0 application has exactly one global module. (Not applicable in Version 2.0 or 3.0.)

Global variable A variable that is accessible from any module (and any procedure) within a project. Declare a global variable using the `Global` keyword at module-level. For example, `Global Num As Long`.

Graphical user interface (GUI) The Windows name for a painting surface. A GUI treats everything—text, dots, fills, and pictures—not as DOS-style, ASCII characters but as pixels turned on and off in a display context. Windows is an example of a graphical user interface (a GUI).

Handle A name used to identify and access a form or control.

Hot link A DDE link between two applications in which the data passed from the server to the client application is updated automatically.

Icon The graphical screen element that represents your application program's state. You select an icon from the Program Manager's window to run programs, for example. An icon is a bit map too.

Idle loop An important loop in Visual Basic, it's executed only when nothing else in the user's environment requires attention. Used in conjunction with DoEvents(). (See DoEvents() in the index for references to more information.)

Index In a Microsoft Access table, a way to order fields to speed up data access.

Initialization Setting a variable or instance of a type to a specific value.

Instance A variable of a type.

Keyword A word reserved for internal Visual Basic use. You cannot use keywords in your own code.

Link A DDE conversation.

Local variable A variable that can be accessed only by the method or procedure in which it's declared.

Lock (locking) On a network (or other multi-user system), a way to prevent more than one user from modifying a table at a time.

Logical operator In Visual Basic, any of five operators (And, Or, Xor, Imp, Eqv, and Not) that can be used with expressions.

Logical value A value assigned to an expression when it's evaluated. The value can be True or False.

MDI (Multiple-Document interface) Lets you create applications in which one parent form (an MDI form) holds (or maintains) multiple child forms (i.e. a form is a child form if its `MDIChild` property = True).

Menu A menu displays application options and enables the user to make selections. The menu's resource identifies the order and number of these options.

Message The name of a method passed to an instance of an object type. When you send a message to an instance of an object, you call one of its methods. To send a message to an instance of an object, you specify the object and the method you want to invoke. For example, if `SomeType` is an instance of an object and Init is a method, the following line of code sends an `Init` message to the object:

```
SomeType.Init;
```

Method In Visual Basic, a procedure or function declared within an object that is used to access the data within the object. You cannot declare your own methods in Visual Basic, but you can use its built-in methods to manipulate objects.

Model A mathematical representation of some aspect of the world.

Object In Visual Basic, a general term for forms, controls, and the special Visual Basic objects: Clipboard, Debug, Printer, and Screen.

Object linking and embedding (OLE) A technique for creating document-centered applications. OLE differs from DDE in that it enables you to edit a linked object in the application that created it.

Object variable A variable that represents one of the Visual Basic object types.

OLE (Object linking and Embedding) A technique for creating document-centered applications. Differs from DDE in that OLE allows you to actually edit a linked object in the application that created it.

Operator Defines an operation to be performed on a value or values, such as addition or subtraction.

Picture box A Visual Basic control for displaying and manipulating pictures.

Pixel A dot that represents the smallest graphics element of measurement on a screen.

Polymorphism A single interface with many implementations. Specifically, calling a method for a variable whose precise type isn't known at compile time. The behavior is established at runtime by way of *late binding*. In Visual Basic, polymorphism is best expressed with control arrays and event procedures.

Project The files that make up a Visual Basic application.

Project window A window within the Visual Basic system that lists all the files currently belonging to a project.

Property A characteristic (or attribute) of a Visual Basic form or control. Visual Basic controls and forms have enumerated property settings. Change these settings at design time or in code to manipulate the controls or forms.

Record-locking Preventing other users from accessing a record while a record is in use.

Record number A unique number that identifies each record in a table.

Recordset A set of records you treat as objects.

Reserved word Names of commands, keywords, functions, system variables and operators that you cannot use as variable or array names.

Row In a grid or table, a horizontally displayed record of data.

Runtime This refers to any time an application is running (whether within the Visual Basic system or in a separate EXE file).

Scope This is the lifetime and accessibility of a variable. Scope defines which parts of a program can access specific variables. For example, a variable declared within a function is (by default) local and can be accessed only by code within the function.

Screen object A Visual Basic object used to activate a form or control at runtime.

SQL Structured Query Language. A query definition language supported by Microsoft Access.

Static variable A locally declared variable that maintains its value after the procedure finishes. Any subsequent calls to the procedure containing the static variable reflect the maintained value.

Stop statement Use a Stop statement (see Stop) to create permanent breakpoints.

Strange attractor In phase space, an attractor is a point or limit cycle in a dynamic system, which draws or attracts a system. In other words, as the system changes state, it can reach equilibrium (settle down) to a point or a cycle. A strange attractor is an attractor that's "broken up" or fragmented in phase space. It represents a system whose order, when plotted in a timeseries, isn't obvious, but shows itself in a shape (an order) in phase space.

String An alphanumeric value, or an expression consisting of alphanumeric characters.

Structured programming This combines two ideas: 1) structured program flow; that is, the flow of control of a program is determined by the syntax of the program code; and 2) invariants, assertions that hold every time control reaches them.

Subprocedure A procedure (or routine) that doesn't return a value.

Syntax error An error that occurs because of an incorrectly expressed statement.

Table A structure, consisting of rows (records) and columns (fields), that contains information.

Text box A Visual Basic control for manipulating text. A text box can handle single- or multiline text. If its multiline property is set, the text box acts like a mini-editor.

Timer A Visual Basic control that can respond to the passage of time as determined by the system clock. The timer control is the only Visual Basic control that has no graphical properties.

Toolbox The Visual Basic "box" on the left side of the screen used to create controls for a form during design time.

Type The part of a variable that indicates the range of values (or states) it can assume and the operators you can apply to it. *Type* is everything you can know about a class of objects that a variable or instance can represent.

User-defined type A variable declared in the global module in Visual Basic 1.0 or any module in Visual Basic 2.0 or 3.0 that can include one or more built-in types:

```
Type  AType
 AnInt As Integer
 AString As String
  .
  .
  .
End Type
```

Variable A storage area in memory for holding data that can change while an application is running.

Variant data type The default return value for variables that aren't explicitly declared.

Wildcard characters Any of the characters: `*`, `?`, `#`, `!`, `-`, `[]` that you can use to include or restrict items in pattern-matching expressions.

Windows graphics device interface (GDI) The Windows GDI enables you to write applications that display and manipulate graphics independent of a specific display device. For example, you can write applications that use the same code, yet can be displayed in EGA, VGA, or Hercules modes. Windows achieves device independence by using various device drivers that translate GDI function calls into commands that make sense to the specific output device used. Therefore, you write code as though the output device doesn't matter, which is generally how it is.

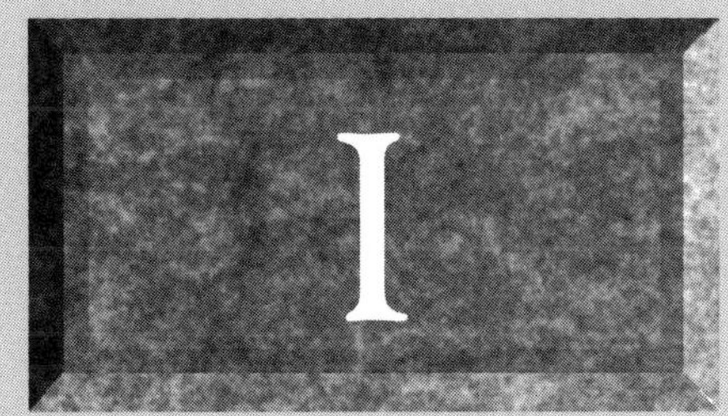

INDEX

Symbols

A

D

F

H

M

N

P

Q-R

S

T

W-Z

Add to Your Sams Library Today with the Best Books for Programming, Operating Systems, and New Technologies

The easiest way to order is to pick up the phone and call

1-800-428-5331

between 9:00 a.m. and 5:00 p.m. EST.

For faster service please have your credit card available.

ISBN	Quantity	Description of Item	Unit Cost	Total Cost
0-672-30178-4		Access 1.1 Developer's Guide	$39.95	
0-672-30440-6		Database Developer's Guide with Visual Basic 3.0	$39.95	
0-672-30362-0		Navigating the Internet	$24.95	
0-672-30363-9		Your Borland C++ Consultant	$29.95	
0-672-30338-8		Windows File Formats	$29.95	
0-672-30370-1		Visual C++ Developer's Guide	$49.95	
0-672-30284-5		Secrets of the Visual C++ Masters	$34.95	
0-672-30030-3		Windows Programmer's Guide to Serial Communications	$39.95	
0-672-30286-1		C Programmer's Guide to Serial Communications	$39.95	
0-672-30391-4		Virtual Reality Madness	$39.95	
0-672-30372-8		Teach Yourself Visual C++ in 21 Days	$24.95	
0-672-30292-6		Programming Windows Games with Borland C++	$34.95	
		Shipping and Handling: See information below.		
		TOTAL		

❑ 3 ½" Disk

❑ 5 ¼" Disk

Shipping and Handling: $4.00 for the first book, and $1.75 for each additional book. Floppy disk: add $1.75 for shipping and handling. If you need to have it NOW, we can ship product to you in 24 hours for an additional charge of approximately $18.00, and you will receive your item overnight or in two days. Overseas shipping and handling adds $2.00 per book and $8.00 for up to three disks. Prices subject to change. Call for availability and pricing information on latest editions.

201 W. 103rd Street, Indianapolis, Indiana 46290

1-800-428-5331 — Orders 1-800-835-3202 — FAX 1-800-858-7674 — Customer Service

Book ISBN 0-672-30437-6

What's on the Disk

The companion disk for *Secrets of the Visual Basic 3 Masters*, Second Edition contains the following software:

- Complete source code and files for the book's sample applications
- VBX custom controls from MicroHelp and Crescent Software
- Bonus sample applications

Installing the Disk

The software included with this book is stored in a compressed format. You need to run the installation program on the floppy disk to install the software. You'll need at least 2.7 megabytes of free space on your hard drive.

1. From Windows File Manager or Program Manager, choose File + Run from the menu.
2. Type *<drive>*INSTALL and press Enter, where *<drive>* is the letter of the drive that contains the installation disk. For example, if the disk is in drive B:, type B:INSTALL and press Enter.

Follow the on-screen instructions in the installation program. The files will be installed to a directory named \VBMASTER, unless you change this name during installation.

When the installation is complete, the file VBMASTER.TXT will be displayed for you to read. This file contains information on the files and programs that were installed.